KV-669-230

"BY MY ABSOLUTE ROYAL AUTHORITY"

Changing Perspectives on Early Modern Europe

James B. Collins, Professor of History, Georgetown University
Mack P. Holt, Professor of History, George Mason University

(ISSN 1542-3905)

Changing Perspectives on Early Modern Europe, the newest series from the University of Rochester Press, brings forward the latest research on Europe during the transformation from the medieval to the modern world. The series publishes innovative scholarship on the full range of topical and geographic fields and includes works on cultural, economic, intellectual, political, religious, and social history.

Private Ambition and Political Alliances:
The Phélypeaux de Pontchartrain Family
and Louis XIV's Government, 1650–1715
Sara E. Chapman

The Politics of Piety: Franciscan Preachers
During the Wars of Religion, 1560–1600
Megan C. Armstrong

"By My Absolute Royal Authority":
Justice and the Castilian Commonwealth
at the Beginning of the First Global Age
J. B. Owens

Magdalen College Library
Class No. 347.46
OWE

Ex dono Dr. Christopher McNeill
2007

3060 8892

"BY MY ABSOLUTE ROYAL AUTHORITY"

Justice and the Castilian Commonwealth at the Beginning of the First Global Age

J. B. Owens

MAGDALEN COLLEGE LIBRARY

 University of Rochester Press

Copyright © 2005   J. B. Owens

All Rights Reserved. Except as permitted under current legislation,
no part of this work may be photocopied, stored in a retrieval system,
published, performed in public, adapted, broadcast, transmitted,
recorded, or reproduced in any form or by any means, without the
prior permission of the copyright owner.

First published 2005

University of Rochester Press
668 Mt. Hope Avenue, Rochester, NY 14620, USA
www.urpress.com
and of Boydell & Brewer Limited
PO Box 9, Woodbridge, Suffolk IP12 3DF, UK
www.boydellandbrewer.com

071052   ISBN: 1-58046-201-4

Library of Congress Cataloging-in-Publication Data

Owens, J. B. (John B.), 1944–
   "By my absolute royal authority": justice and the Castilian common-
wealth at the beginning of the first global age / J.B. Owens.
      p. cm. – (Changing perspectives in early modern Europe, ISSN 1542-3905)
   Includes bibliographical references and index.
   ISBN 1-58046-201-4 (hardcover : alk. paper)
   1. Justice, Administration of–Spain–History–16th century. 2. Prerogative,
Royal–Spain–History–16th century. I. Title. II. Series.
KKT250.O96 2005
347.46'009'031–dc22
                                                        2005014425

A catalogue record for this title is available from the British Library.

This publication is printed on acid-free paper.
Printed in the United States of America.

CONTENTS

Acknowledgments   vii

List of Abbreviations   x

Glossary   xi

Note on the Maps   xvii
    Map 1: The Iberian Peninsula   xviii
    Map 2: The Area of Contention   xix

Chapter 1
    Rethinking the Hispanic Monarchy in the First Global Age   1

Chapter 2
    John II's Controversial Reward   17

Chapter 3
    The Catholic Monarchs and the Legacy of John II   45

Chapter 4
    Rebellion against Crown Administration as a Defense of
    Absolute Royal Authority   79

Chapter 5
    Pursuing Justice: Due Process, Procedure, and the Adjudication
    of a Major Lawsuit in the Absence of Coercive Muscle   115

Chapter 6
    Making Judgments: Letrado Theories and Interpretive Schemes   143

Chapter 7
    Philip II, the Great Fear, and the New Authoritarianism   175

Chapter 8
    The Paradox of Absolute Royal Authority   213

Notes 245

Works Cited 299

Index 351

ACKNOWLEDGMENTS

Since the late 1960s, I have so enjoyed my research on the nature of Castilian monarchical government between 1400 and 1700 that it was hard to stop and write this book. By the time I finished planning the project, it had become so long and complex that I had to break it into three parts, of which this is the first.

Without writing another long manuscript, I find it impossible to list all of the individuals, particularly those associated with archives and libraries, who have assisted me. However, this book deals in part with the significance of institutions, and I must acknowledge the contributions of several. Even though my work was greatly slowed for well over a decade by serious family and personal medical problems, the leaders of two exemplary scholarly organizations, the Sixteenth Century Studies Conference and the Society for Spanish and Portuguese Historical Studies, repeatedly extended their encouragement and support so that I could remain connected with my project even when I felt overwhelmed by other responsibilities. For more than a quarter century at Idaho State University (ISU), my colleagues have provided an environment in which scholarship mattered despite frequent struggles with inadequate resources. My former dean, Victor Hjelm, has been a pillar of support, and Edwin House, former chief research officer, stepped in with a vital grant from his office that gave me time to complete this book. In my beautiful but isolated mountain valley, it would not have been possible to continue work on Spanish history had it not been for the efforts of Nancy Anthony and her interlibrary loan staff at ISU's Oboler Library. Finally, it has become customary for historians of Spain on this side of the Atlantic to acknowledge the help of the staff of the Madrid bookseller Marcial Pons, and I join in expressing my gratitude to this Spanish treasure because without their assistance I would be unable to keep up with the specialized publications in my areas of interest.

I am grateful to several scholars who read all or part of some version of this book and made useful comments: James Collins, Daniel Crews, the late Andre Gunder Frank, Robert Kingdon, Helmut Koenigsberger, Helen Nader, Sara Nalle, Stanley Payne, David Ringrose, the late John Salmon, Domenico Sella, and several anonymous readers. Francisco Miguel García Gómez helped me prepare the two maps. I have not been able to incorporate all of their suggestions, and none of them bears any responsibility for my errors.

A number of sources financed research for this book. I began the work with a Ford Foundation fellowship provided through the University of Wisconsin, a Fulbright dissertation fellowship, and a grant from the Spanish Ministry of Culture. Although they were sometimes given for other but related purposes, I have also benefited from a grant from the U.S.-Spanish Joint Committee for Educational and Cultural Affairs, a fellowship from the National Endowment for the Humanities, two ISU sabbatical leaves, maintenance grants from the Comunidad Autónoma de la Región de Murcia and the Dirección General de Relaciones Culturales y Científicas of the Spanish Ministry of Foreign Affairs, travel grants from the American Council of Learned Societies and the American Philosophical Society, five small grants from ISU's Faculty Research Committee, and one from the Research Council of my former employer, New York University.

To borrow a phrase from Joseph Levenson, my children, Amy, Christopher, Mark, and my "sometimes daughter" Lupine Bybee Miller, added years to my research and joy to those years. They enjoyed their years in Spain and, in the end, became more Spanish than they perhaps realize.

My parents, Alice and Willard Owens, planted the seeds of my interest in political and judicial institutions through their involvement in civic affairs. My mother, now deceased, formed part of a generation of young women who, influenced by Eleanor Roosevelt and inspired by the United Nations' Universal Declaration of Human Rights, became political activists. My father dedicated his considerable talent as a constitutional and labor lawyer to the defense of the interests and rights of North American workers, especially of the coal miners among whom he was born and raised. Although my parents might not agree, their activities exposed confusion about the political direction that organized labor should take, confusion that stemmed from a fundamental lack of connection between the theoretical tools and conceptual vocabulary of received political and social thought and the actual experiences of politically active workers.

Rather than attempt to understand U.S. struggles in a new way, I was drawn to the history of another country. I fell in love with a young woman who was passionately interested in Spain, and by my senior year at Oberlin College, my research interests increasingly focused on Spanish history. It was then that I encountered the political thought of Juan de Mariana and began to formulate the questions that have driven my subsequent research.

I dedicate this book to my wife, Grace W. Owens, who has remained passionately interested in Spain and has provided a context for my professional and personal life for almost four decades. However, the dedication is due to much more than this. As a leader in the cause of human rights, Grace has demonstrated that through the repeated, eloquent articulation of the highest civic principles, an individual can shape the way others understand their world and formulate judgments as a basis for their actions. She constantly inspires her students, associates, and me to comprehend that, ultimately, it is individual human action, our action, that creates world history. Without Grace's example, this book might literally have remained unwritten.

J. B. O.
April 2005

ABBREVIATIONS

AC	Actas Capitulares
ACG	Archivo de la Chancillería de Granada
AGS	Archivo General de Simancas
AHMT	Archivo Histórico Municipal de Toledo
AHN	Archivo Histórico Nacional, Madrid
AMC	Archivo Municipal de Córdoba
AMTal	Archivo Municipal de Talavera de la Reina
BN	Biblioteca Nacional, Madrid
Br.	Bachiller
Caj.	Cajón
C.	Codex Justiniani (Code)
Col. Bel.	Colección Belalcázar, AHMT
CR	Cartas Reales
D.	Digesta Justiniani (Digest)
Exp.	Expediente
Inst.	Institutiones Justiniani (Institutes)
Ldo.	Licenciado
Leg.	Legajo
NR	*Nueva Recopilación* (issued 1567)
Osuna	Colección Osuna, AHN

GLOSSARY

ad perpetuam rei memoriam	To the enduring memory of it (for example, of a judicial proceeding, lawsuit).
adelantado	Royal representative, with appellate jurisdiction, in an area originally on a Muslim frontier; also *adelantado mayor.* Title became hereditary in certain aristocratic houses.
alcaide	Governor or warden of a castle or fortress.
alcalde	Magistrate; also criminal justice of an *audiencia.*
alcalde mayor	Appellate magistrate, of a municipal council, a lord, or the monarch; often in the service of a royal *corregidor.*
alfoz	Territory over which a municipality had jurisdiction; also *términos.*
alguacil mayor	Chief constable.
almirante	Literally "admiral"; honorary high Court official who in theory would be the supreme commander of the royal fleet. Became hereditary in the main branch of the aristocratic Enríquez family.
arbitristas	Essayists who offered practical reforms (*arbitrios*) to enhance the kingdom's prosperity, increase royal revenue, or improve military preparedness.
audiencia	Royal appellate tribunal, often with extensive administrative authority, in Castile and the Crown's overseas domains. Those of the *chancillerías* of Granada and Valladolid were the most important peninsular ones.
bachiller	First university degree. Used as a title by *letrados.* Abbreviation: Br.
bando	Clique, camp, faction, network. Used to describe rival groupings.
Cámara de Castilla	Committee of the Council of Castile that distributed royal patronage.
carta ejecutoria	Sealed royal writ; official document announcing a judicial verdict.
Chancillería	One of the regional royal judicial institutions, including *audiencias,* in Granada and Valladolid, which were supervised by the Council of Castile.

cierta ciencia	Literally "accurate knowledge"; translated as "reasoned consideration" because the phrase was a lawyer's definition of an action based on adequate information and the exercise of reason.
comedia	Dramatic work; play.
comendador	Commander of a military order; holder of an *encomienda* of an order.
común	Non-elite Castilians; also *menudo*.
comunero	Participant in the Castilian rebellion of 1520–1521.
comunidad	Corporation of a municipality's *vecinos*.
Comunidades	Common name for the Castilian rebellion of 1520–1521.
condestable	Literally "constable"; honorary high Court official who in theory would be the supreme commander of the royal army. Became hereditary in the main branch of the aristocratic Velasco family.
consulta	Position paper; especially one prepared by a royal council for the monarch.
converso	"New Christian"; Christian convert from Judaism or descendant of such a convert.
corregidor	Royal high commissioner posted to important municipalities to correct and prevent abuses of justice and government and breakdowns of civic peace and harmony. Presided at municipal council meetings and oversaw judicial administration and military affairs. If he lacked legal training to exercise his appellate jurisdiction, he was often assisted by an *alcalde mayor*.
corregimiento	Institution of a *corregidor* and his assistants.
Cortes	Representative assembly summoned by the monarch. After the conquest of Granada, eighteen cities and towns sent representatives.
doblas de oro	Gold coins minted at the weight and fineness of two ("doubles") of the *maravedí de oro* as defined in 1497 by the Catholic Monarchs.
ducado	Ducat; monetary unit equal to 375 *maravedís*.
encomienda	Territory under the jurisdiction of a military order, which included at least one town.
escrito de razones	A written statement of rights or arguments in a lawsuit.
fiscal	Prosecutor.
heredamiento	Landed estate.
hermandad	Literally "brotherhood." League of municipalities to deal with criminal activities across their mutual boundaries and with grazing disputes. The Santa Hermandad, "Holy Brotherhood," was established by

	the Catholic Monarchs as a Crown institution and used to prosecute the war against Muslim Granada.
hidalgo	Member of a privileged lay group exempt from certain taxes.
hoz	Ravine or narrow pass.
infante	Prince; younger sibling of a monarch or heir to a throne.
juez de . . .	Special commissioner or magistrate, judicial commissioner, special justice, special investigative judge.
juez de residencia	Magistrate sent to investigate the conduct of a departing official, especially a *corregidor,* whose authority the *juez* exercised during his tenure.
junta	An assembly or meeting of advisers without a legally defined status.
jurado	Municipal councillor in theory representing the *vecinos* of a parish.
legajo	Bound or unbound bundle of documents.
letrado	Someone with *letras* ("letters"), meaning a mastery of Latin. Increasingly used to refer to someone with a university degree in law.
Libro Becerro	Bound register of jurisdictional privileges.
licenciado	Second university degree. Used as a title by *letrados.* Abbreviation: Ldo.
lugar	Unincorporated community; village.
maravedí	Monetary unit of account; 375 *maravedís* or *maravedíes* (mrs) = 1 *ducado.*
mariscal	Marshal.
mayorazgo	Entailed estate or trust removed from the partible inheritance required in Castilian law.
mayordomo	Steward; overseer; treasurer; majordomo.
mediano	Poorly defined social stratum between commoners and territorial aristocrats.
menudo	Commoner; see *común.*
Mesta	Royally chartered, privileged organization of stock owners.
montes	Usually unimproved hilly, mountainous, brushland, or woodland area used for forest resources and pasture, although the Montes de Toledo included a number of small villages.
Morisco	Baptized Christian of Muslim, "Moorish" ancestry.
Nueva Recopilación	Codification of Castilian law issued in 1567.
oidor	Justice of an *audiencia.*
poderío real absoluto	Absolute royal authority.

portero	Doorman.
privado	Royal favorite.
privanza	Position of the royal favorite.
procurador	A person with the legal power to represent a corporate entity or another person. Municipal representative at court or to a royal assembly. Also, the representative of a party to a lawsuit. If authorized to present cases before a judge or judges, the *procurador* was similar to an English barrister. If preparing a case for a party without authorization to present the case in court, the *procurador* was similar to an English attorney or solicitor.
Procurador síndico	Official responsible for administering a municipality's lawsuits and perhaps for presenting cases before local magistrates as a barrister.
propio motu	By one's own initiative, motivation. Castilian version of the Latin *proprio motu*.
receptor	Receiver or transcriber of evidence for a law court.
regidor	Municipal councillor, in theory and sometimes in fact by royal appointment. Increasingly with lifetime tenure and the ability to pass the office to a specific successor.
regimiento	Collective of a municipality's *regidores* or the position of a *regidor*.
relator	Reporter of a judicial institution who organized and summarized the evidence presented by the parties to a dispute.
república	Commonwealth (Castilian).
res publica	Commonwealth (Latin).
sala	One of the constituent tribunals into which an *audiencia* was divided; literally, the chamber in which a meeting would be held.
Santa Hermandad	Holy Brotherhood. See *hermandad*.
señorío	Lordship.
servicio	Tribute granted to the monarch by vote of the Cortes for a fixed period and under specific terms.
Siete Partidas	Law code compiled in the 1260s by command of king Alfonso X.
sobrecarta	Second decree or warrant repeating an earlier order.
términos	Territory over which a municipality had jurisdiction or the boundary of such jurisdiction; also *alfoz*.
vecino	Householder or "citizen" enjoying the privileges and performing the duties of a member of a municipal community.

veinticuatro	Municipal councillor. Used rather than *regidor* in some Andalusian cities, which in theory each had only 24 such councillors.
villa	Town. Municipality with juridical independence from any other town, although subject to the lordship of the monarch, a city, or an individual.
visita	On-site investigation of an institution.

NOTE ON THE MAPS

The maps were prepared under my direction by Francisco Miguel García Gómez of the University of Valladolid's Department of Geography while he was a visiting faculty member at the Geographic Information Systems Training and Research Center of Idaho State University. He utilized the cartographic function of ArcGIS 9®, ESRI's GIS software (www.esri.com).

The ellipsoid datum is the World Geodetic System 1984 (WGS 84), and the projection is Aitoff. Although each map has a scale bar, readers should be aware that the Aitoff Projection is an "equal area" one, which means that the maps cannot be used for an accurate comparison of distance. The datum for the data about rivers was not available, and therefore, readers will note places where the point location does not correspond accurately to the actual location in relation to a nearby river.

With one exception, necessary latitude and longitude coordinates for the point locations were obtained from the Alexandria Digital Library Gazetteer Server (www.alexandria.ucsb.edu/gazetteer/). Because the village of El Hornillo disappeared in the seventeenth century, we estimated the coordinates from the Instituto Geográfico y Catastral 1/50,000 projection "Villarta de los Montes" (#734) of 1954 and the Servicio Geográfico del Ejército's Cartografía Militar de España 1/50,000 projection of 1959 of the same quadrangle (#734). These maps show the few buildings that were then located at the place bearing the name of El Hornillo. These paper maps are part of my personal cartography collection.

The two maps included in this book are not survey-grade quality and are provided only to help readers orient themselves to places mentioned in the text. The authors of the maps and the University of Rochester Press accept no responsibility for any errors that might occur as a result of other uses.

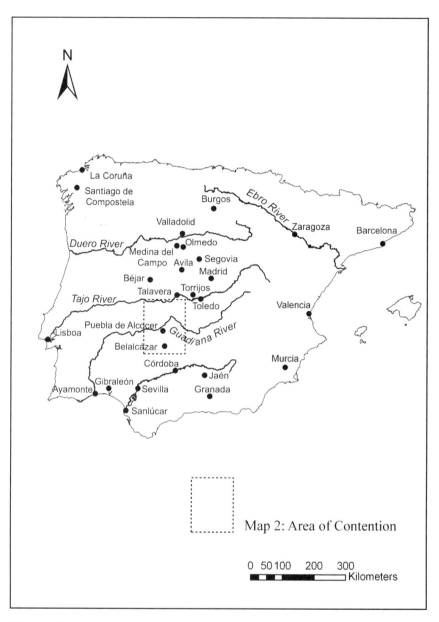

N

La Coruña

Santiago de
Compostela

Burgos

Ebro River

Valladolid

Zaragoza

Barcelona

Duero River

Olmedo

Medina del
Campo

Avila

Segovia

Madrid

Béjar

Talavera

Torrijos

Tajo River

Toledo

Valencia

Lisboa

Puebla de Alcocer

Guadiana River

Belalcázar

Córdoba

Murcia

Gibraleón

Jaén

Ayamonte

Sevilla

Granada

Sanlúcar

Map 2: Area of Contention

0 50 100   200   300
                              Kilometers

Map 1: The Iberian Peninsula

Map 2: The Area of Contention

Chapter 1

Rethinking the Hispanic Monarchy in the First Global Age

The Topic and Its Importance

This book focuses on judicial administration. During its "Golden Age" from the fifteenth century to the seventeenth, the kingdom of Castile experienced a remarkable proliferation of judicial institutions, which historians have generally seen as part of a metanarrative of "state-building." Yet Castile's frontiers were extremely porous, and a Crown government that could not control the kingdom's borders exhibited neither the ability to obtain information and shape affairs nor the centrality of Court politics that many historians claim in an effort to craft a tidy narrative of this period. It was not the "power" of the institutions of a developing "state" that kept Castilians loyal to the monarchy. Contemporaries expected that rule by a monarch who possessed "absolute royal authority," which is what I mean by "absolute monarchy," would provide the best means of obtaining good government, which they defined as the ability to provide for the commonwealth (*res publica, república*) justice, domestic tranquility, and peace. Castilians remained loyal because they shared an identity as citizens of a commonwealth in which a high value was given to justice as an ultimate purpose of the political community and they believed that the sovereign possessed "absolute royal authority" to see that justice was done. This expectation of royal justice served as a foundation for the political identity and loyalty that held together for several centuries the disparate and globally dispersed domains of the Hispanic Monarchy.[1] Due to this core conviction, perceptions of how well Crown judicial institutions worked were a fundamental determinant of the degree of support a monarch could attract to meet fiscal and military goals. Remarkably, despite the importance for the ruler's creditworthiness within the commonwealth of the perceived quality of judicial administration, no one has given serious attention to how well royal justices were able to handle difficult lawsuits that raised politically troubling questions and involved major litigants.

This study maps part of this unfamiliar terrain through a focus on an extended, high-profile lawsuit, which was watched carefully by generations of Castilian leaders. Throughout its history, it was the only dispute of its kind that was repeatedly brought to the monarch's attention in the general petitions of the Cortes, the kingdom's representative assembly.[2] Moreover, both parties saw fit to circulate printed versions of briefs in an effort to influence opinion among the commonwealth's leaders, and both reminded monarchs about the "quality" of the matter in written and oral contacts. Justices from the late fifteenth century to the reign of Philip II (reigned 1556–1598) had difficulty resolving the conflict because the proper exercise of "absolute royal authority" was itself the central legal issue, and because the dispute pitted against each other members of important groups who demonstrated a tendency to give prominence to different interpretive schemes as they tried to comprehend their world. From this perspective, the account brings together political ideas and political action.

This book explores the interactions of those employing the varied conceptions in Castilian political and legal thought about the proper exercise of absolute royal authority, on the one hand, and institutional attempts to resolve conflicts between important groups within the context of the kingdom's judicial administration, on the other. The meaning of "absolute royal authority" did not inhere in the words themselves, always signifying the same thing. Meaning was governed as well by the implied or expressed question to which those using the phrase responded and the available alternatives they denied.[3] Political action was shaped in part by a cultural environment of interpretive schemes that was neither hierarchically arranged nor static. To recognize patterns in the world around them as a basis for making judgments that in part shaped and constrained their actions, politically active Castilians developed and employed interpretive schemes involving both ideas of good government and justice and understandings of the responsibilities and rewards associated with personal service to one's lord. The actual interpretive scheme used by an actor in a particular situation would be cued by experience and by the immediately preceding scheme. In developing judicial administration within this cultural environment, rulers and their officials did not erect political institutions as rational, efficient, coercive means to achieve "absolutism" and build "state power."[4]

The problem of how political thought and institutions shaped action demands attention. Ideas shaped the actions of the monarch's officials and subjects as significantly as did the institutionally defined relationships among individuals and groups. These actors, including natives and residents of the ever-changing Hispanic Monarchy's non-European domains, did much to establish and maintain the regular routes of economic, political, and cultural interactions that formed the basis of the first global age in world history, 1400–1800. To better understand this crucial period, we should reshape writing about the politics and political thought of European monarchies so that historians do not reduce the era, as the use of the teleological term "early modern" clearly does, to the antechamber of nineteenth-century constitutionalism, "nation state"-building, imperialist "capitalism," and "Western" global dominance.

Our Analytical Vocabulary Forms a Barrier to Understanding Monarchy in the First Global Age

Theorists of state development usually argue that a state's "strength" is defined in terms of the simultaneous increase in its autonomy and its capacity. However, attempts by Castilian monarchs, their regents, and their principal servants to achieve autonomy tended to undermine capacity while a willingness to surrender autonomy in certain spheres enhanced the capacity to achieve goals defined in conjunction with a broad spectrum of the commonwealth's political actors. To explain why such collaboration did not express state "weakness," I found this account on an alternative perspective. However, a common analytical vocabulary impedes the development of any new approach to the political life and ideas of the first global age by reinforcing the concept of state-building as a narrative focus in historical research and writing. I have made a conscious effort to interpret the evidence without recourse to some of this vocabulary's most familiar components.

We inherited the mechanical metaphors and models that started to become common in political texts only during the era of Thomas Hobbes. Because for us "power" carries an almost automatic suggestion of effective "force," I generally restrict the use of the word "power," in the translation of words like *poder,* to those occasions when coercive force is clearly intended. Otherwise, I have chosen "authority," so that I translate a phrase such as *poderío real absoluto* as "absolute royal authority."[5] I have also avoided the "centralization versus decentralization" scheme because behind it lurks the assumption that a concentration of coercive "power" makes government more effective than it otherwise would be. Moreover, for many writers, "centralization" points toward "modernity," thereby making any process of "decentralization" somehow regressive or, at best, a manifestation of "nonlinearity." The use of "center" also implies a "periphery," and social scientists sometimes take this polarity to express something about where significant action is initiated, about the source of "control," or about the process of "discipline." Modern works on the first global age often identify centralization with the monarch, bestowing on the ruler the historical task of disciplining peripheral privileged individuals, groups, and communities to conform to organizational patterns, especially in the fiscal and military spheres, dictated by the Crown.[6]

Historians and social scientists frequently employ the terms "feudalism" and "capitalism" as labels for stages between which a transition takes place, but they serve more as components of ideological stances than useful categories of scientific analysis. In any of its forms, the idea of a transition from feudalism to capitalism is so closely tied in social theory to the state-development one that it is difficult to disentangle them, and like the latter, it is teleological in that it privileges what is supposed to have been originally an English development, using this as a model against which all other "national" developments are measured. The resulting essentially Eurocentric social theories distort world history by explaining, perhaps justifying, the superiority of certain countries (such as England) or regions (such as northwestern Europe) on the basis of supposed "internal" characteristics unrelated to their place within larger global interactions.[7] Real world history involves a concentration on regular interaction networks of varying density connecting loci over an often global space. Networks of interactions evolve, often almost stochastically, and transform the contexts and nature of human action, not individual societies, states, or civilizations, which indeed cannot exist as the stable historical actors often "peopling," through an unacceptable process of reification, historical writing.[8] Because they continuously acted to shape their own lives in the midst of such a complex process, individuals inventively deployed the resources of Castile's rich cultural environment in their quest for understanding and identity as members of a commonwealth.

The Argument Summarized

"By my absolute royal authority": most readers probably show no surprise when they encounter Castilian royal decrees asserting a monarch's absolute, preeminent position as the kingdom's sovereign. Some historians organize their general treatments of "early modern" Europe around the idea that this was a period of initial state-building, a process to which the "absolutism" of Philip II's "Spain" and Louis XIV's France contributed a great deal. I began the research on which this book is based because I was puzzled by the prominence just after the end of Philip II's reign of a treatise whose ideological position apparently ran counter to this modern historiographic trend. I discuss this work, Juan de Mariana's *The King and the Education of the King* (1599), in some detail in chapter 8.[9] As it turned out, governments were neither capable of nor interested in imposing administrative uniformity or obedience on a subject population through a monopoly of coercive force, and monarchs did not have the sort of impact on historical developments that some historians have attributed to them, because rulers depended so much for effective action on the collaboration of local notables and territorial aristocrats.

The dynamism of Castile's monarchy stemmed from the presence within the commonwealth's cultural environment of potentially contradictory interpretive schemes about the nature of monarchical government. People recognized contradictions, however, only when they had to make difficult choices. I examine this situation on a scale greater than that of the individual actor. Although influenced by a common cultural environment, because of their respective roles in the social environment, local notables, who dominated Castile's municipal institutions, and territorial aristocrats, who exercised seignioral jurisdiction over often vast areas, tended on balance to make judgments on the basis of different interpretive schemes. Local notables more frequently evaluated political life on the basis of the institutional provision of justice by the Crown; territorial aristocrats reacted more to the opportunities and recognition they received for personal service to the monarch. Because group definition really involves fluid, overlapping designations, those outlined here, rather than entities constantly present in history, constitute only a heuristic device used to recognize some fundamental, dynamic patterns within a kingdom whose ruler, in theory, possessed absolute royal authority.

Monarchs, their great councils, and other royal advisers actually reacted most often to the actions of others, often by mediating conflict between differentiated groups or their representatives. The Crown found it difficult to gain sufficiently broad cooperation in any situation in which there appeared to be a conflict between justice according to standards of written law and the royal need to reward great vassals. Paradoxically, Castile's monarchs, despite their absolute royal authority, generally ruled more effectively when they acted collaboratively with local notables and had trouble when they claimed the authority to act autonomously as they wished. In part, apparently autonomous action damaged rulers because so many contemporaries felt this type of royal action was largely the result of undue aristocratic influence at Court. Even when their goals were different, monarchs and their elite subjects often did a better job of advancing their competing interests through collaboration. However, the terms of such collaboration could vary, and this variation frequently shaped the ability of the Crown to realize the objectives of its leaders for the Hispanic Monarchy. At one pole, the level of collaboration would shape an environment characterized by corruption, crippled public finance, disinvestment, and weak support for the global goals of the Crown. At the other, elite members of the Castilian commonwealth would exhibit high levels of civic responsibility, a commitment to effective public finance, sustained capital investment, and support for overall government initiatives on a global scale. Therefore, the major municipal corporation governed by local notables often constituted the dynamic core of political life.

Yet, if these local notables were dissatisfied with Crown administration, they were reluctant to challenge the institution of monarchy frontally because they thought it was the only form of government capable of maintaining justice, prosperity, domestic tranquility, and the realm's defense. They remained conscious that unrestrained factional conflict among Castilian elites, especially if it became violent, jeopardized the highly disproportionate share of Castile's wealth that this tiny minority received. As a consequence, local notables tried to maintain respect for an "absolute" royal authority needed to resolve such disputes peacefully even while they engaged in a variety of stratagems to resist, deflect, reshape, and frustrate Crown policies and orders that they felt were arbitrary and improper. To protect themselves in the face of arbitrary royal action in violation of the law, local notables would enhance their personal ties to territorial aristocrats perceived to have influence at Court, thereby further reducing the opportunities for autonomous royal action or the appearance of such action. Thus, rather than an entity with a firm and settled identity, the monarchy, with rulers who could theoretically employ their absolute royal authority, served as a shifting, flexible paradigm by which contemporary situations were evaluated, particularly those related to the exercise of royal authority within the regime. Within this interpretive framework, urban patricians, aristocrats, and monarchs usually worked out the compromises necessary to maintain their privileged positions within the commonwealth.[10] This process of compromise produced the elaboration of better defined royal judicial institutions. Within both the Castilian Crown's peninsular and huge overseas domains, the administrative organs were, therefore, much more complex by the reign of Philip II, at the end of the lawsuit on which I focus, than in that of John II (1406–1454), at the dispute's beginning.

Monarchs or their regents and favorites sought to achieve their goals by working to identify and respond to the expectations and needs of other actors. Careful attention to the use of certain political languages provides a useful way to understand how monarchs and their immediate servants fit into networks of interactive relationships.[11] One such group of languages involved the concepts of service to one's lord, frequently expressed through the idiom of vassalage. Monarchs and their representatives often employed this language when they demanded that others act in a certain way or justified grants of jurisdictions, property, revenue shares, and offices. And in this language, too, vassals sometimes refused to comply on the grounds that the action would really be a disservice to the lord or would so undermine vassals' honor and estates that they could not serve adequately. A second group of such political languages focused on the monarch's responsibility to maintain the Christian commonwealth in peace, harmony, and justice through good government. Again, while these concepts offered a basis for royal commands, they also provided standards for judging the rulers' conduct and for justifying resistance of all sorts. For elite, usually male, political actors, these political languages enabled discussions of royal policies and behavior that were considered essential to the maintenance by this small percentage of Castilians of their disproportionate enjoyment of the kingdom's resources. The repeated use of such concepts served to give royal authority an important place within the cultural environment, and, therefore, to give royal action an important place within the social environment. Thus, to reject the metanarrative of "early modern state-building" in no way means that the choices and actions of monarchs and their principal advisers are not suitable subjects for political history; it simply means that they are not the only subjects or even always the most important ones. Both thought and institutions provide the necessary context for explaining the actions of political actors, including those involved in the great Comunidades rebellion of 1520–1521 and its aftermath, which were pivotal events in the long dispute on which I focus in this book (see chapter 4).

I differentiate my conclusions from two prominent historiographical tendencies. I reject, in dealing with judicial administration, the idea that rulers and their officials established these institutions to construct a "state." An organizing focus on a grand narrative of state-building or on the actions of monarchs and their close advisers seriously distorts the history of the huge Hispanic Catholic Monarchy in the first global age. There was no "absolutism," no "state," no "bureaucracy." Hierarchical, rigid, authoritarian, seemingly "bureaucratic" forms of Crown administration proliferated because they did not work, and their elaboration was checked only by the lack of supporting resources. Habsburg kings pulled institutional decisions geographically close to themselves, "centralized" them, when they sensed that dissatisfaction within the commonwealth had undermined their capacity to get necessary support. However important the sovereign's leadership was for shaping the course of events, no monarch, no Crown administration, no royal Court had the coercive power to structure the kingdom's political life.

In this book I emphasize the use of the phrase "by my absolute royal authority" when such rhetorical action was intended to justify rewards for service to a lord by someone who might be construed as a "client." Faced with evidence of "bureaucratic" weakness, some recent historical writing has attempted to place the royal Court in the role of the state, arguing that "clientage," highly personal relationships between patron and client, permitted the monarch to control and direct the kingdom's political destiny. This is the second historiographical tendency I reject. The story told here demonstrates that clientage was an ineffective tool of administration, a sign of "weakness" not "strength," and that reliance on a favorite to organize government was particularly damaging to the monarch's political influence when there was widespread dissatisfaction with the quality of royal justice. Finally, the clientage model has been used to argue that political ideas played no important role in political action, and this book shows that, understood as expressions of interpretive schemes that permitted actors to recognize patterns in the world around them on which to formulate judgments, such ideas shaped action just as decisively as those factors associated with the actors' roles in the economy, political institutions, and membership in solidarity groups.

An Extended Trouble Case: The "Belalcázar Lawsuit"[12]

Out there, beyond the books historians write, existed, and exists, a real world we try to understand by uniting voices and themes that we piece together from what survives when a reality has passed. We produce abstractions, hoping that these provide a partial understanding of what no longer lives. I offer an abstraction of a part of Castilian history at the beginning of the first global age, which I have developed using a specific approach.

We can apprehend the centrality to common political identity within the Castilian commonwealth of a complex of interpretive schemes employed by members of groups with different roles in the social environment only through the investigation of a long period of time. We cannot understand "absolute" monarchy without examining over an extended period, exceeding even particularly long reigns such as those of Philip II or Louis XIV, the dynamic group interactions for which royal administration provided a context. I explore these interactions through a detailed examination of an "extended trouble case." The "extended case" method involves the study over a long period of time of some particularly important series of relationships with special attention to interaction with other parts of the social and cultural environments. Time serves as an important variable exposing the degree to which the meaning of political vocabulary was contingent on the interpretations and aspirations of individuals and groups. This approach avoids the rush to establish definitions of institutions and political ideas, which would arbitrarily bound, and thereby distort, an interpretation of the period's political life. The "trouble case" method involves the study of disputes between individuals or groups with different interests and roles that cannot be resolved by any clear, previously elaborated rule. The solution of the conflict can be used as an indication of the predominant interpretive schemes as well as of the authority and effective influence of the economic, institutional, and solidarity groups affected by the norm the decision establishes.[13] A legal dispute constitutes an appropriate vehicle for an examination of human action within its social and cultural environments because judicial administration and law mattered very much to Golden Age Castilians. I assume throughout this book that legal institutions, the way they operate, and the norms they seek to embody make a fundamental difference to people's lives within any political regime.[14]

The book takes as the extended trouble case at its narrative center a dispute, prolonged for well over a century, between a major municipal corporation, that of the city of Toledo, and an important aristocratic family, ultimately represented by the House of Béjar. Contemporaries often called it the Belalcázar lawsuit because it initially involved one of the House of Béjar's aggregated titles, that of count of Belalcázar. During one of the many civil wars characteristic of his reign, king John II precipitated the dispute in

1445 when he granted to a powerful, mid fifteenth-century warrior an aristocratic lordship, which was carved from Toledo's jurisdiction without due
process even though the city had purchased the property from an earlier
ruler.[15] The quarrel centered on control of the so-called viscounty of Puebla
de Alcocer, a relatively large territory in northeastern Extremadura, south of
the Guadiana River at the western edge of the Montes de Toledo (see maps
1 and 2). Major cities often held lordship over large domains, and Toledo
had claimed the viscounty by right of purchase since the mid thirteenth century. Territorial aristocrats derived their wealth and influence not only from
private resources but also through seignioral jurisdiction over towns and villages and their surrounding rural areas.

Because the conflict was formulated as a lawsuit, I provide a detailed
study of the attempts of various royal judicial institutions, particularly the
attempts of a "supreme" court, the Chancillería of Granada, to provide the
justice that constituted their central purpose and underpinned the evaluation
by members of the Castilian commonwealth of the exercise of absolute
royal authority. Ultimately, these evaluations would shape in important
ways the actions of those within the commonwealth on whose support the
royal capacity to reach the monarch's goals depended. Adjustments in the
law and in the organization and procedures of law courts constituted a central aspect of royal government. Litigation over matters so closely related to
the positions of important individuals and groups within the economy and
political institutions obviously strained the resources of Castilian judicial
administration. As one of its major goals, this book provides, through the
first detailed study of the procedures used during attempts to resolve an
explosive dispute, insight into the process through which such adjustments
were made. This book makes a major contribution to an understanding, by
those interested in European and Latin American legal history, of the work
of investigating justices and royal tribunals, since virtually nothing exists that
exposes how these institutions functioned, as a number of works, especially
some microhistories, have done for Inquisition tribunals.[16]

The centrality of a single dispute makes this a type of microhistory. As
with many other microhistories, the concentration on a single, spectacular
narrative is justified because concerns jump to attention that are otherwise
lost in the welter of judicial business routinely handled by Castile's judges
and law courts. Microhistories have often been written on the basis of judicial records. However, their authors frequently fail to give adequate attention to the ways in which the procedures and legal constraints within which
the actors worked often shaped their contributions.[17] Although it is difficult
to narrate, I have exposed, especially in chapters 3, 5, and 6, the impact of
judicial procedure on the creation of the documentary collection on which
I have founded my microhistory of the Belalcázar dispute, in order to provide a necessary clarification of the nature and limitations of the sources.

Moreover, I have constructed my microhistory from a much more extensive, crowded, and seemingly disordered documentary record than is often
the case. The Belalcázar collection in Toledo's municipal historical archive
alone consists of some 32,000 pages of material in 45 *legajos* (bundles).[18]

However, judicial procedures do not just provide a frame for the story. In
an important respect, they *are* the story. From the thirteenth to the fifteenth
century, legal theorists had developed understandings of absolute royal
authority, particularly in regard to contractual relationships and property,
which laid a heavy emphasis on due process, a theme that shines a bright
light on matters of procedure. Moreover, by the period of the Belalcázar dispute, many among the political leadership of the Castilian commonwealth
had become familiar with ideas developed by jurists about the relationship
of rights based in natural law to the proper exercise of monarchical authority. These ideas, therefore, played a significant role in political arenas
beyond the courtroom.[19] Readers require a precise understanding of the
professional behavior of the jurists and other Crown officials involved to
grasp the meaning of the story I tell.

Disputes in institutions such as law courts do not reflect conflict elsewhere.
Instead, the dynamic locus of political life was often situated away from the
monarch and his or her immediate advisers. As an arena of interaction
among municipal corporations, territorial aristocrats, *letrados* (holders of law
degrees) as a corporate group, and royal officials, the course of the Belalcázar
dispute itself involved an ongoing formulation and perpetuation of its terms
and therefore was continuously constituted as one of the fashioners of subsequent interaction. In other words, although this narrative of an extended
trouble case provides only a partial account of Castilian political life because
it focuses on a particular range of significant issues, the dispute was nonetheless a form of political activity on the same level as other, perhaps more
familiar types of political behavior. Because the ruler's theoretical authority
was so tied to a recognition of the need for the resolution of conflict, the commonwealth's leaders regularly evaluated royal judicial administration to formulate their judgments. Adjudication remained, therefore, an important
factor of public life, either directly as in the dispute examined here or indi-
rectly as was often the case with fiscal and military administration.

The interpretive schemes of Castilian political and legal thought were
not independent of the institutionalized forms of human interaction, just as
the latter are not autonomous from interpretation. However, for purposes
of analysis, I separate out these factors rather than lump them together into
an entity called "culture" or "civilization," which then too often becomes
reified by some historians into a perpetual cause of human action. I consider these factors metaphorically as aspects of social and cultural environments that constrained and enabled human action.[20] The various economic
relationships, institutions of government and justice, and solidarity groups I

discuss constituted the social environment. On the other hand, the cultural environment was composed of interpretive schemes that actors developed through a process of socialization by participation in the life of human collectivities. The ability to understand and function within these environments in much the same way as other Castilians did, including the ability to innovate or strategize to transform individual roles, formed a "network of mutual expectations" that defined a "sociological citizenship" distinguishing them from outsiders.[21]

I view the interpretive schemes of the cultural environment as cognitive, mental models or habits-of-mind. Guided by these models to recognition of significant patterns in the world around them, people seek an interpretive understanding of that world, which permits them to make judgments and act coherently, either to conform to prevailing norms or to seek change. Recent research on the brain and cognitive psychology suggests that these habits-of-mind, rather than constituting rigid structures that always impose the same interpretation, consist of interlinked schemes, the recognition of which is cued, in a dialectical manner, both by events in the social environment and by the immediately antecedent pattern recognition. Thus, shared habits-of-mind, expressed but not created in the common discourse, ease communication and interaction among those socialized in the same way, thereby creating a sense of group identity. There may, however, be disagreements depending on which of the linked interpretive schemes are cued for particular individuals and groups by experience and earlier pattern recognition. Actors identify apparent contradictions among the available interpretive schemes when disturbances occur in the social environment to be understood.[22]

Therefore, the very meaning of monarchy was contingent on the interpretive and strategic actions of individuals within social and cultural environments that were subject to continuous if veiled innovation during an age of increasing global integration. I use my extended trouble case as a narrative thread from the perspective of which I show how sovereigns such as Philip II often undermined their creditworthiness and the capacity of royal government when they acted according to their own will contrary to norms widely accepted within the commonwealth.

After 1580 and the passage of the Crown of Portugal to the Habsburg dynasty, the Hispanic Monarchy consisted of domains spread around the globe, including half of modern Italy, significant areas of modern France, the Low Countries, all of the Iberian Peninsula, all of the European-governed Americas, important commercial centers in Africa and Asia, the Philippines, and islands in the Atlantic and Pacific Oceans. Many people throughout these domains shared with Castilians the same legal and religious sources for their interpretive schemes. Therefore, rulers whose actions would be negatively evaluated by their Castilian subjects also ran the risk of undermining their capacity to govern in other territories. One seventeenth-century Habsburg monarch, Philip IV (reigned 1621–1665), suffered, due to the alienation of his subjects, the permanent loss of the Crown of Portugal and most of its extensive overseas domains in the Atlantic, Asia, Africa, and America, the loss of the Aragonese domains in southern France, a temporarily successful independence movement in Catalonia, and massive revolts in the kingdoms of Naples and Sicily. Obstruction also took other forms. Castilian Crown officials increasingly faced difficult negotiations with suspicious urban representatives in the Cortes over most royal administrative and fiscal initiatives, municipal leaders found numerous means to frustrate government demands for revenue and troops, and many people engaged in smuggling and other forms of fiscal fraud.

What general support the Crown could obtain was based largely on another aspect of Castilian identity. Political identity was largely local, and its central values were expressed in various communal practices. Among these practices, religious devotions that centered on local images and shrines played a predominant role, and these sustained interpretive schemes hostile to Islam and Protestant Christianity, both of which explicitly denigrated such devotions. Therefore, faced with a religiously divided Europe and the threat of Ottoman expansion, Habsburg rulers could find some assistance within the commonwealth for war against Muslim and Protestant countries, particularly when these directly threatened European Castile or its non-European domains. The Crown could even generate support for so remarkable a measure as the expulsion of all Moriscos (Christians of Muslim origin) between 1609 and 1614. But it was not enough. By the mid seventeenth century, the Hispanic Monarchy faced a genuine crisis characterized by bankruptcy and military defeat, with important consequences for European and world history.

In the chapters that follow, I pay attention only to major Castilian political events to which the sources connect the lawsuit and to those that served to sustain and enhance contemporary interest in the issues around which the determination of the various judicial decisions revolved. Because the Belalcázar narrative does not permit an adequate consideration of all of the groups and institutions that played roles in the government of the Golden Age Castilian commonwealth, this book forms the first volume of a trilogy. From the mid fifteenth century to the mid seventeenth, over the course of their interactions with Crown institutions, with territorial aristocrats, and with ecclesiastical bodies, the local notables, both male and female, formed increasingly cohesive municipal oligarchies as the major basis for asserting themselves within the political kingdom. The second volume of the trilogy will examine this long process of oligarchic formation. Because so many of Toledo's crucial documentary sources have disappeared, the second volume will focus on the major families based in the southeastern city of Murcia, a municipality closely tied to Toledo, with similar institutions, and possessing an abundant surviving collection of relevant documents.[23]

Over the whole context of the interactions of monarchs and their officials, territorial aristocrats, churchmen, and local notables hangs the question of how such a small percentage of Castile's population managed to enjoy a hugely disproportionate share of the available resources without the physical means to coerce the acceptance of this situation by the majority. The third volume will deal with this broad topic, and the research for the presentation of a Castilian "moral economy" is well advanced.[24]

Chapter Summaries

Royal secretaries ever more frequently inserted the phrase "by my absolute royal authority" into a whole series of documents in the period after king John II was declared of age in 1419. By the 1440s, it had become a familiar formula. In chapter 2, I introduce the dispute that gave rise to the long, highly visible lawsuit on which the book focuses, as a "clue" to understanding political life in a major European monarchy. I identify the various groups and institutions that shaped the idea and exercise of royal authority, and I offer a short synopsis of the context within which the long Toledo-Belalcázar conflict began.

Chapter 3 challenges the familiar contention that Ferdinand and Isabella controlled the power of the territorial aristocracy by establishing effective authoritarian rule on the basis of institutions and legal norms founded but unsuccessfully utilized by their Trastámara dynastic predecessors.[25] It focuses on the first sustained attempt, in this reign, to resolve the Toledo-Belalcázar dispute by judicial means. The Catholic Monarchs failed because they were unable or unwilling in the pursuit of their military and fiscal goals to dispense sufficiently with the use of rewards for the personal service of their aristocratic vassals in order to consolidate political support by administering the commonwealth according to prevailing norms of good government and justice. After Isabella's death, aristocratic factional conflict again disabled effective monarchical rule.

In writing about the Comunidades, the great uprising of 1520–1521, historians have sometimes described the rebel leadership's aims as either a final attempt to defend "medieval constitutionalism" or as a revolutionary effort to destroy "absolute monarchy" in favor of some more progressive political entity foreshadowing eighteenth-century revolutions. Chapter 4 argues, through a concentration on Toledo's efforts to obtain a proper judicial review of its claims by the new government of Charles of Habsburg, that the conflict in part involved an attempt to establish, through the familiar use of rebellion to force negotiation, a monarchy whose exercise of "absolute royal authority" would sustain good government and justice. Although the *comuneros* were defeated, the rebellion forced a transformation of the practical exercise of "absolute royal authority" in the area of judicial administration.

Although Charles V and his advisers won the Comunidades war, the emperor emerged from the conflict determined to attract broad Castilian collaboration for the effective exercise of royal authority. As part of his program, he increasingly empowered Crown judicial institutions to resolve conflicts on the basis of accepted norms of law and justice. The narrative in chapter 5 constitutes the core of the book because it shows how the officials of a Crown judicial institution sought to resolve, without sufficient royal coercive muscle, a dispute made serious by its ties to groups–territorial aristocrats and local notables who governed major municipalities–that tended to employ different interpretive understandings of justice and absolute royal authority. I examine in detail the process by which the justices of a major royal tribunal, the *audiencia* of the Chancillería (regional royal judicial institution) of Granada, sought for three decades to adjudicate the Toledo-Belalcázar dispute, eventually ruling in favor of Toledo's claims. The Chancillería played a pivotal role in Charles V's effort to build effective collaborative relationships with leaders of the Castilian commonwealth, because of widespread dissatisfaction, among those who governed the kingdom's municipalities, with the Council of Castile as a judicial body.

During the trial in Granada, the lawyers for Toledo and the count of Belalcázar, a title by then belonging to the House of Béjar, increasingly refined their expressions of the interpretive schemes by which they felt the justices should decide the dispute. Chapter 6 shows how, in a manner that was not possible during earlier stages of the lawsuit, they clarified the content of those schemes of interpretation of the cultural environment that pertained both to good government and justice and to personal service to one's lord. Their positions, perhaps directly in some cases, would shape many of the Castilian political debates throughout the century from the time of Philip II's accession to the throne in 1556.

Chapter 7 challenges the view that Philip II enjoyed sufficient information and the capacity to implement policies and argues instead that in the midst of a series of major political, military, and religious crises early in his reign, the king and his advisers, with a combination of anxiety and arrogance, often managed affairs in ways that appeared arbitrary and sapped support for royal policies. I tease out of the inadequate evidence an explanation of why the Council of Castile reversed the verdict of the Granadan tribunal, and I show how this result and its context occasioned negative evaluations of Philip II's administration by the interpretive standards of good government and justice.

Philip II and the Council of Castile resolved the major lawsuit on which this book focuses in favor of the principle that "absolute royal authority" gave rulers the right to act according to their own will, contrary to widely supported legal principles, but the Crown failed to develop on this basis the broad collaboration within the commonwealth that was necessary for meeting royal goals. Influenced, as John II had been, by domineering personal favorites, the Habsburg kings of the seventeenth-century Hispanic Monarchy were unable to marshal from their domains, and especially from Castile, the elite support necessary to defend their European position or their global composite monarchy well. With a particular focus on the political thought of Juan de Mariana, chapter 8 demonstrates that the interpretation of the proper exercise of absolute royal authority advocated by Toledo's representatives in its dispute with the House of Béjar remained an influential current in Castilian political and legal thought despite its dramatic rejection by Philip II and his closest advisers. Castilians used legal principles to articulate schemes by which judgments could be made and on which action could be based, and they constructed the resulting ideologies in ways that were always contingent on the institutional context and formative role of legal rules and procedures. In conclusion, I offer a summary of the paradoxical nature of absolute royal authority in the first global age. Monarchs who were perceived as exercising their authority in the interests of good government and justice were more likely to attract the broad collaboration necessary for meeting their goals than were rulers who felt that such authority gave them the latitude to act according to their own will, in defiance of established norms of law and justice.

Chapter 2

JOHN II'S CONTROVERSIAL REWARD

Introduction

Among members of the Royal Council dissatisfied with John II's incapacity in the 1440s was one of the reign's principal chroniclers, bishop Lope Barrientos. As a model of proper royal conduct, he offered a description of king Henry III, John II's father and predecessor, which established a standard by which the reign of his son could only be considered a disaster at every point. The latter mismanaged his estates, had too many unreliable, venal officials and counselors, was undervalued by aristocrats and little regarded by humbler peoples, and maintained so little justice that none felt secure.

> He [king Henry III] always focused on regulating his finances, increasing his revenues, and providing justice to his kingdoms, and when any man pays lots of attention to some goal, he will necessarily reach it. This is even more the case for the king when he enjoys the services of good ministers and officials. This king met to review his actions with some notable men, monks and nobles, prelates and jurists, and with their counsel he organized his kingdoms and judicial administration. No one can deny that he exhibited fine judgment in evaluating and selecting good people for the Royal Council, which is no small virtue in a prince, and kept the kingdom peaceful and well governed; and in a short time, he had a great treasure, because he wasn't a free spender, and when the king is parsimonious, keeps track of expenditures, and receives great revenues, he will necessarily be rich. This king, don Enrique, was greatly feared by the grandees of his kingdom and much loved and respected by the common people because he always maintained peace and harmony and each person was secure proprietor of what he had.[1]

As the first reign during which the phrase "my absolute royal authority" was employed regularly in Crown documents, the conflict-ridden era of king John II of Castile (1406–1454) revealed the strange paradox, to which Barrientos alluded, of the kingdom's monarchs who exercised this theoretically absolute authority. Usually John claimed that he was using this special application of royal grace in order to reward vassals for services that

MAGDALEN COLLEGE LIBRARY

enhanced the monarch's ability to govern. However, arbitrary action by the king according to his own will rather than the dictates of the law did not provide greater capacity for political leadership but rather reduced the support for the Crown on which effective royal government was based. Tyrannical rule loosened the sovereign's ties to the lesser nobility and urban elites, whose active collaboration he needed for his authority to be respected. A ruler acting arbitrarily in violation of the law did not enhance but actually sapped his ability to govern, because without the security that legal guarantees of their persons and property provided, the less influential leaders of the commonwealth would become the clients of powerful aristocrats who would then be in a position to shape royal actions. Adherence to the rule of law made the monarch respected and more capable of guiding political affairs; "tyranny" led to ineffectual royal government.[2] As a rule, prominent men of the Trastámara era could only see institutional constraints on a king's authority as aiding the political aspirations of aristocratic Court cliques rather than justice. In order to best protect persons and property, prevent factional conflict, and defend the commonwealth from its external enemies, local notables advocated as an ideal an "independent" monarch, free of such constraints and combining in his or her person the roles of supreme legislator, executive, and judge. They then evaluated the ruler on the basis of how that authority was exercised, and they acted accordingly. In general, this Trastámara-era conception of the monarch as someone who could, when necessary, exercise preeminent, "absolute" authority established interpretations of the political community and patterns of relationships within the social environment. These would play major parts in shaping the way politically active Castilians interpreted and strategized for several centuries to come, although these interpretive schemes were continuously reformulated as the Crown added domains on an almost global scale.

In this context, a prolonged conflict well into the era of Philip II (reigned 1556–1598) over the Puebla de Alcocer lordship (see map 1), a dispute increasingly known as the Belalcázar lawsuit, would provide many with occasions to formulate judgments that would in part shape their political actions. The city of Toledo and the aristocratic House of Sotomayor quarreled about jurisdiction over a group of rural communities south of the Guadiana River in what is now the province of Badajoz. The dispute quickly gained prominence among contemporaries, who watched and evaluated the actions of those involved. For example, in a move indicating how important the Puebla de Alcocer issue was becoming as a symbol of the misuse of absolute royal authority in the aggrandizement of aristocrats, the other major municipalities took the unprecedented step of including a demand for the town's return to Toledo's jurisdiction in the general petitions of the Cortes (representative assembly) of Valladolid of 1447, just two years after the grant. Such general public attention would continue until Philip II imposed silence about the matter.[3] In addition to its role for over a century as a focus of litigation and political judgments, the conflict also illustrates the nature of monarchy as a process elaborated within the kingdom's social and cultural environments.

In this chapter, I cover three things. First, I explain the details of John II's grant of the Puebla de Alcocer lordship to Gutierre de Sotomayor, for these events constituted the evidence during subsequent judicial scrutiny of the resulting dispute.[4] Moreover, prevailing standards for the proper exercise of absolute royal authority demanded that the monarch adhere strictly to due process in matters related to contracts and property rights. Second, I examine the circumstances leading the monarch to take an action so extraordinary that he felt compelled to assert his absolute royal authority as its basis. This context was fundamental to the arguments the parties would later present in court. Moreover, the fifteenth-century Castilian civil wars provided an important framework for Golden Age authors of histories, political treatises, and works of imaginative literature, as we see in the final chapter where I examine the cases of Juan de Mariana and Lope de Vega. Where possible, I use Gutierre de Sotomayor's career to illustrate grandee actions and motivations. Third, in my account of these events, I pay special attention to aspects crucial to an adequate understanding of the king and his relationship to the Castilian political community or commonwealth: lordship and the municipality as the fundamental institutions of economic and political life; the competing views of the territorial aristocracy and local notables about the exercise of royal prerogatives; government by a royal favorite; and the role of rebellion. The Puebla de Alcocer conflict makes an interesting focus for an extended journey through several generations. It retained a periodically important place in the commonwealth's leadership discourse for such a long time precisely because its resolution demanded a consideration of these potentially conflictive matters in contexts in which they were of pressing concern.

John II's long reign was much more complex and conflictive than the following discussion indicates, but space does not permit a fuller account. Castile possessed multiple military frontiers, with Portugal, France, Navarra, the domains of the Crown of Aragón, and Muslim Granada. Therefore, the monarch, his principal advisers, and the elite leaders of the commonwealth were frequently preoccupied with matters of war finance and troop mobilization. The administrations of many major municipalities endured periodic turmoil, and leading nobles exploited the kingdom's various internal conflicts to advance the economic and political positions of their houses. The expansion of aristocratic control of territorial jurisdictions and royal revenues meant that various powerful warriors, including the king's own cousins, possessed resources they could use to challenge the king's authority. The vast lands of Castile's military monastic orders of Alcántara, Calatrava,

Santiago, and St. John provided another platform for troublesome political and military intervention into Castilian affairs. Since the late fourteenth century, Castilians had witnessed, in certain areas (for example, Córdoba and Toledo), violent assaults on non-Christians and their converted relatives, especially on the *conversos* (Christian converts from Judaism and their descendants).[5] Many Christians were agitated by growing movements within the ecclesiastical sphere for the reform of Church institutions and a renewal of devotional life and religious fervor. These currents were especially strong within the major mendicant orders of the Dominicans and Franciscans, who often attempted to spread their variegated visions of a purified Christian commonwealth by popular preaching, and Castilian churchmen, both lay and regular, played significant roles in the contemporary struggle over the leadership rights of the papacy and a general council of the Church. Not surprisingly, these developments overlapped in multiple ways, which ultimately made it difficult for any of the members of the political kingdom to pursue a consistent course for very long, as a history of the Puebla de Alcocer dispute often shows.

The Reward for Services

In order to arrange a proper marriage for his son Alonso, Gutierre de Sotomayor (ca. 1400–1453) first had to build an adequate entailed estate for him, and received as the most important lordships places separated from municipal jurisdictions. The foundation of this Sotomayor entail saddled Gutierre's heirs with lawsuits for well over a century and plagued the Crown with conflicts. These raised such troubling "constitutional" issues that monarchs and their principal advisers often feared that a resolution of the cases would, as a matter of practical politics, undermine the capacity of royal government.

   In the process of consolidating military support against his cousins, the *infantes* (princes) of Aragón,[6] on 6 November 1444, king John II of Castile granted lordship over the towns of Gahete (later called Belalcázar) and Hinojosa, which had been part of the municipal territory of Córdoba, to Gutierre de Sotomayor.[7] The following year, Gutierre received a donation that created the most serious problems for his heirs: Toledo's town of Puebla de Alcocer with its castle, jurisdiction, and lordship as an entailed estate, in combination with Gahete and Hinojosa, for his son Alonso. The grant was in recognition of Gutierre's military services and in remuneration for them, despite the possession of the territory by Toledo. By his "own initiative and reasoned consideration and absolute royal authority" (*propio motu e cierta ciencia e poderío real absoluto*), John abrogated all laws that might prevent such an act, even those that specifically stated that they could be abrogated only by the Cortes.[8]

Toledo's governing council considered Puebla de Alcocer and the surrounding territory as part of the city's *Montes* (its underdeveloped, hilly area), purchased from king Ferdinand III in Jaén on 4 January 1246. Although Toledo had found it difficult to retain, in the turbulent reign of Alfonso XI, a place so distant from the city itself, the recently crowned Henry II affirmed Toledo's title in 1369, and the city had been firmly in control of Puebla de Alcocer at least since 1377.[9]

Toledo's hold on Puebla de Alcocer began to weaken after the warlords who then controlled the city refused entrance in early January 1441 to John II and his retinue. The king ordered the officials "of the towns of Puebla de Alcocer and Herrera and the other settlements of the montes and lands of the city of Toledo" to ignore any commands from Toledo's council. Instead, they were to accept Gutierre de Sotomayor, grandmaster of the military order of Alcántara, which had nearby jurisdictions, as the Crown's agent in charge of appointing new local authorities.[10] On 22 April, John II announced to Puebla de Alcocer's council that he was removing the town from the full jurisdiction and lordship that Toledo had possessed until then and incorporating it into the Crown domain, from which it could never be separated. Puebla's officials were to have no connection with Toledo's council and from now on derived their authority directly from the king.[11]

During the changing political circumstances of the next few years, Toledo apparently regained administrative control over Puebla de Alcocer, which Gutierre had invaded in the meantime.[12] In documents that would later be used by Toledo's lawyers to frame their arguments about the king's intentions, John II assured several concerned parties that Toledo maintained jurisdiction over the western Montes. In response to its council's petition, the king wrote from Burgos to Puebla de Alcocer on 16 October 1444 that contrary to rumors reaching the town, it would not be separated from Toledo's jurisdiction or granted to any knight. Indeed, if someone else claimed the town, its residents had the right to resist. In February 1445, John II wrote to Toledo's *alcalde mayor* (appellate magistrate) that he had not given and did not intend to give Puebla de Alcocer to anyone, and on 4 March, the king informed Toledo's leaders that his will in the matter remained, as he had said before, that it would not be granted to anyone else.[13] Yet, just a month later, on 7 April, the sovereign granted the town and its jurisdiction to Gutierre de Sotomayor.

After fighting elsewhere in Extremadura, grandmaster Gutierre and his Alcántara troops reinvaded Puebla de Alcocer on 12 January 1446. While Gutierre de Sotomayor was gobbling up their city's territory, some members of Toledo's governing council who were at the royal Court wrote to the city to tell their fellow councilors about the grant.[14] In securing Toledo's claim to the territory despite the passage of time, the fact that the city immediately protested became important at a later date.

On Sunday, 13 February 1446, when John II was residing temporarily in Toledo's royal fortress, the city council presented a formal protest against the Puebla de Alcocer grant with the support of both the patricians resident in the city and those at Court in the king's service. Toledo used a delegation of twenty-one city officials instead of the usual one or two representatives to reinforce in John's mind the council's concern over the loss of the western part of the Montes. To make an even more powerful impression, the petition was read by Toledo's *regidor* (councilman) Dr. Fernando Díaz de Toledo, a man in whom John apparently had every confidence because he was the royal secretary and authenticator of royal documents, was *oidor* (justice) of the *audiencia* (high royal appellate tribunal), had been one of the king's chief legal advisers on the secret Royal Council for several decades, and had been one of those sent into Toledo in 1441 to negotiate on the king's behalf with the warlords who controlled the city at that time.[15]

On this occasion, Toledo's patricians offered no general declaration of political principles. They simply petitioned for a royal judicial forum that would permit the city to prove its allegations by the kingdom's laws and recover the same jurisdiction over Puebla de Alcocer that it had enjoyed prior to Gutierre de Sotomayor's invasion. The master of Alcántara had on his own authority taken Puebla de Alcocer, and this town was the property of Toledo, which had been purchased with its own money and had traditionally followed its orders. All three estates had contributed money for its purchase. Toledo maintained its own forts, bridges, and towers with the rents from Puebla, and without this revenue, the city would be unable to do what was necessary for the king's service or uphold its own honor. John II provided an official transcript of the session in order to protect the city's rights, and he ordered the presentation of the evidence needed to begin the requested hearing.[16]

Because the king did not intend to grant the promised judicial review, he and some of his advisers became concerned about the reaction of Toledo's leaders and a week later granted Gutierre de Sotomayor permission to build a castle on the hill above Puebla de Alcocer. During the following year, Gutierre carved out a sizable territory in the region. Although the letter was never delivered, on 7 March, John wrote to Toledo commanding its officials and any others connected with the affair not to move against Puebla de Alcocer until he ordered an investigation of his "loyal knight" Gutierre de Sotomayor's possession of the town.[17]

The king never provided Toledo with the promised judicial review. Instead, he summarily confirmed Gutierre de Sotomayor's grant the following year (30 May 1447), just three months after the Cortes had demanded the devolution of Puebla de Alcocer to Toledo. Instead of a paper document like the 1445 grant, the confirmation was a parchment on which many of the kingdom's great men were listed as present. In addition to repeating the original grant, the king added a huge fine for anyone who opposed the provision and licensed Gutierre to crush any resistance. Along with the standard assertion of absolute royal authority in the original, John II proclaimed that he could act in this way because he recognized no superior in the temporal realm.[18]

Unsure whether this confirmation would be sufficient, the master of Alcántara sought further royal support while at Court for the king's wedding. In Soria the following 30 September, John II gave a commission to Br. Diego de Piedrahita to survey the area and fix the boundaries between the domains of Gutierre de Sotomayor and the surrounding jurisdictions. This was obviously not the hearing Toledo had requested because Gutierre's jurisdiction was assumed, only boundary issues fell within Piedrahita's commission, and there were to be no appeals. Sotomayor had already been able to get the king to approve, on 5 and 28 August, Piedrahita's similar survey of the Gahete and Hinojosa areas, which had been removed from the jurisdiction of Córdoba and given to Sotomayor.[19]

Kings commonly used royally appointed magistrates in cases of disputed jurisdictional rights and boundaries. Perhaps one of the most famous of such investigations is that undertaken early in the reign of the Catholic Monarchs Ferdinand and Isabella by Esteban Pérez de Cabitos of the lordship of Lanzarote in the Canary Islands.[20] Piedrahita had already been given, on 27 September 1446, a royal commission to survey Gahete and Hinojosa, but suspecting him to be Gutierre's client rather than an impartial judge, Córdoba's officials jailed him so that he could not really begin his work until 27 May 1447 after obtaining in the previous March an extension of his commission.[21]

After his experience in Córdoba, Piedrahita chose on 20 April 1448 to send a summons to Toledo rather than go there in person. On 4 May, the city council protested against the summons, Piedrahita's commission, and the grant itself. Among other things, the councilors alleged that the judge was Gutierre's servant and the location of the hearing in Guadalupe was inconvenient and much closer to the other party. Questioning the authenticity of the grant, they quoted a 1442 "law of Valladolid" (discussed below) against such alienation of jurisdiction and John II's 1444–1445 assurances to Puebla de Alcocer, Toledo, and the alcalde mayor that the town would not be separated from the city's jurisdiction. The protest concluded with a list of the places claimed by Toledo in the area and a statement that all of the places not mentioned in Piedrahita's commission (that is, all but Puebla itself) were outside the boundaries of Puebla de Alcocer. As Toledo's lawyers would later stress, Piedrahita subsequently refused to consider these allegations on the ground that a determination of the grant's validity exceeded his commission. On 25 June, a royal guard refused to let Toledo's representative present the allegations directly to the king at his residence in Burgos.[22]

On 1 July, Piedrahita declared that all parties except the master of Alcántara had forfeited through absence their right to a hearing, and during the following two weeks, Piedrahita or someone he had commissioned hiked around the region marking the boundary of Gutierre de Sotomayor's conquests. His carelessness was to cost Gutierre's sixteenth-century heirs the village of El Hornillo on the north side of the Guadiana River. Of more immediate concern, Piedrahita included within Gutierre's boundaries the town of Siruela, which Gutierre eventually had to return to its lord,[23] and several places in the jurisdiction of Talavera, whose lord was the archbishop of Toledo. After Gutierre's death, the archbishop excommunicated Gutierre's heir, Alonso de Sotomayor, and Talavera's governor attacked the region. Under such pressure, Alonso had to surrender in the 1450s all parts of Piedrahita's survey that were claimed by Talavera.[24] Piedrahita finalized the bulk of his boundary-marking work in the town of Alcántara on 15 July 1448 under the watchful eyes of Gutierre and his chief official in the Puebla region.[25]

In the midst of growing insecurity after the king's marriage, Gutierre de Sotomayor appeared unsure of the constancy of John II's favor. After he learned in March 1448 from Córdoba's representatives that Diego de Orellana, Gutierre's nephew and seignioral alcalde mayor for Gahete and Hinojosa, had taken Fuenteovejuna and some pasture land from the city of Córdoba, claiming that they belonged to Gahete and Hinojosa, the king wrote to Córdoba's council from Valladolid. John said he was shocked by the actions of the master of Alcántara because he had made him no grant of the municipality, and he gave the city permission to resist the aggression and maintain its possession of the area involved. The following fall, Toledo also sought to undermine royal support for the House of Sotomayor.

In order to protect the Puebla de Alcocer region from an attack by Toledo, Gutierre de Sotomayor had fortifications built with labor coerced from the citizens of Puebla de Alcocer and other places included in its jurisdiction by Piedrahita, as well as from Siruela and the Talavera villages that would later be lost. Although Toledo tried to stir up a rising in Puebla de Alcocer against the new lord, the city was handicapped in its ability to respond with force because the western edge of its Montes was so far away and perhaps because of divisions among the city councilors over how to proceed.[26]

Aristocratic Factional Wars

The competition among noble lineages that became prominent in support of the Trastámara dynasty had already produced factional struggles under Henry III (reigned 1390–1406), and matters became worse under his son John II, for what was perceived as the excessive aggrandizement of certain individuals or families by the Crown would set off hostile reactions from those aristocrats who felt that their position was threatened by their relative exclusion from merited rewards. In and out of his role as favorite and the flash point of aristocratic struggles until his execution in 1453, Alvaro de Luna was the dominant figure of his age. His attempts to use royal patronage to build his own influence brought instability to John's reign, ultimately undermining rather than enhancing royal authority. In the end, no amount of wealth and military power was sufficient by itself to overcome any warrior's sense of insecurity.[27]

During the long regency for the young king, the major lordships and the grandmasterships of the military orders of Alcántara and Santiago fell under the control of the increasingly powerful infantes of Aragón, and this heightened magnates' insecurity in the absence of a dynamic king and effective judicial administration. When John II came of age in 1419, a major segment of Castile's grandees wanted the king to choose a political course that would be more independent of the infantes, and to this end, they used the influence over the monarch of his older companion, Alvaro de Luna, and Luna's desire to exploit that relationship to achieve his own rise. Although after several years of conflict, the territorial aristocracy felt some measure of security from the Aragonese Trastámaras, some of them had become concerned about Luna's growing influence and joined the infantes' party to secure the favorite's exile from Court in 1427. By this time, the infantes' own insecurity was heightened to the point where they more vigorously pursued the economic and political roles they hoped would make their position unassailable. However, this assertiveness only served to build grandee support for Luna's return the following year, and the infantes' campaign for hegemony collapsed by 1432.

There was no way that Alvaro de Luna, who had received the prestigious title of royal *condestable* ("constable"; honorary aristocratic Court official), could gain a permanent advantage because his aggressive efforts to build the wealth and political position of his House had raised the territorial aristocracy's suspicions about his intentions. Aware that his accumulation of lordships and revenues was upsetting some grandees, Luna rashly arrested one of them, the *adelantado* (royal representative in a frontier region) of León, in August 1437, and even before the adelantado's escape a year later, it was apparent that, rather than promoting submission through fear, the condestable had greatly increased the threat to all he had gained.

Turmoil dominated the following years as Luna and the infantes alternated in control of the Court on an almost annual basis. Their attempt to seize control of John II at Rámaga in 1443 revealed the infantes' intention to use the Crown's authority for their own ends, and even prince Henry, who had been concerned about Luna's influence over his father, saw that the infantes only desired to place "all the kingdom under their control . . . and even now, they and their adherents and followers took all the kingdom's revenues and taxes in such a way that little came to the king for his maintenance."[28] Strengthened as a result, the condestable was able to put together a strong enough aristocratic band to defeat the cadet Trastámaras at the battle of Olmedo in the spring of 1445. Moreover, the infante Enrique's death from wounds received there undercut the infantes' influence in Castile because many of his lordships were distributed to others and Luna took his grandmastership of the order of Santiago.

The further magnification of Luna's wealth and political primacy in the aftermath of Olmedo quickly produced grandee discontent, and those aristocrats opposed to the royal favorite found a new leader to replace the fallen infante Enrique in the person of prince Henry, John II's son and heir to the Castilian throne. The prince and his close advisers, Juan Pacheco and Pedro Girón, were concerned that Luna's vast control over so many lay and ecclesiastical jurisdictions would compromise Henry's own future independence of action. Having forfeited the trust of most of the great nobles through his selfishness and duplicity when in charge, Luna progressively lost the confidence of the king, who increasingly resented Luna's dictatorial control over Court affairs and the monarch's personal life. Although Luna's accumulated power was so great that it was difficult to remove him, he was eventually seized by chief royal justice Alvaro de Zúñiga, son and heir of the count of Plasencia and one of the kingdom's most politically active magnates, and executed by royal order in 1453.[29]

The Nimble Magnate Gutierre de Sotomayor

In an environment so characterized by mutual suspicion and violent conflict that no amount of wealth and military power provided security even to the greatest warriors, Gutierre de Sotomayor emerged from the shadows in 1426 as a *comendador* (commander) of the military order of Alcántara. Over the next three decades, he adeptly advanced his interests through personal service, and his career illustrates well how the leaders of aristocratic families utilized the era's civil wars to build their houses' economic and political prominence. Gutierre did not obtain his initial post because of any special military ability or vocation as a monk or warrior for Christ; he obtained it because his uncle Juan de Sotomayor was Alcántara's grandmaster. Because of the number of towns over which they had jurisdiction and the number of fighting men the military orders of Santiago, Calatrava, and Alcántara could muster, anyone intending to increase his wealth and military power would want to control these orders.[30]

Juan de Sotomayor often played a dangerous game in the turbulent environment of the 1420s, as the infantes sought to maintain the predominance in Castile of the Aragonese branch of the Trastámaras. By 1429, he swore loyalty to the king and was sufficiently in the good graces of Alvaro de Luna and John II that he was ordered to assist Luna in an attack on the infantes Enrique and Pedro in Extremadura. He received the town of Alconchel, south of Badajoz, as a lordship for his nephew Fernando de Soto. Despite such rewards and his agreement to a mutual security pact with Luna's supporters, Juan de Sotomayor betrayed the king, facilitated the infantes' control of the fortress town of Alburquerque, and gave them the support of the order of Alcántara. For this treachery, the king later used the authority of a papal bull to depose the master in March 1432.[31]

A royal ambassador returning to Portugal tried to convince the master to restore northern Extremadura to royal authority, but this emissary was seized and confined in the town of Alcántara with Gutierre de Sotomayor as his guard. Before the infante Enrique and Juan de Sotomayor moved him to the more secure Alburquerque, the ambassador managed to convince his jailer that the future was with Luna's faction and that he should betray his uncle. Although the chronicles do not agree on all the details, Gutierre de Sotomayor was told that he would be the new master of Alcántara, a post he finally obtained in August 1432, and his uncle would be pardoned. On 1 July, Gutierre announced that his uncle was a prisoner of the infante Enrique, and he arrested the infante Pedro whom the king then used as a bargaining chip to end the crisis. The new master's continued loyalty paid off, for when the infantes were pardoned and returned to Castile in the fall of 1436, Juan de Sotomayor, Gutierre's potential rival, was one of only two men excluded from the general pardon.

In the ups and downs for Luna during the subsequent decade, Gutierre de Sotomayor often appeared as his most loyal supporter along with Luna's brother Juan de Cerezuela, the archbishop of Toledo (d. 4 February 1442). In 1438, the aristocrats who opposed Luna's growing predominance named Gutierre as one of the few people considered fully attached to the condestable, and he and Luna were directly challenged by the rebels in May 1439. When Alvaro de Luna was able to return to Court, it was Gutierre in the fall of 1440 who helped the governing patricians of the Extremaduran towns of Cáceres and Trujillo remain independent of the infante Enrique's authority. Therefore, the powerful grandmaster, whose Alcántara holdings were nearby, was the ideal person to name in January 1441 as royal agent for the takeover of Puebla de Alcocer and other places. The following month, the king ordered the *alcaide* (warden) of the Trujillo fortress to turn it over to the master of Alcántara. Two months later, Gutierre's force defeated some of Luna's enemies at Arroyomolinos. Then, in June, he entered the major commercial town of Medina del Campo with the army of Luna and Cerezuela and subsequently fled with them when the infantes and their aristocratic supporters conquered the town and gained physical control of the king.

Because the infantes' party threatened his mastership of Alcántara, Gutierre de Sotomayor retained his connection to the condestable and organized the army that forced the infante Enrique out of Córdoba in the summer of 1444, denying him predominance in Andalucía. As a reward for this service, on the following 6 November, John II granted Gutierre the towns of Gahete and Hinojosa from Córdoba's jurisdiction, and despite his promises during the preceding months, the king gave Puebla de Alcocer to Gutierre on 7 April 1445. This may have been timed to pay other dividends. When those in John II's war council doubted whether they should fight the infantes at Olmedo, it was the arrival in early May of the master of Alcántara with between 500 and 600 knights of his order and its jurisdictions that turned opinions toward battle. In the conflict itself, Gutierre decisively led his unit in support of that of prince Henry against the flank of the infante Enrique's warriors. After the victory, with Luna as the new master of Santiago, prince Henry and his current chief advisers, the brothers Juan Pacheco and Pedro Girón, suddenly left Court for Segovia, and Gutierre was ordered to chase and stop them so that Henry would not replace the infantes as a rallying point for opposition to Luna's regime. He caught only Girón and then joined Luna in negotiating a mutual security agreement with prince Henry and Pacheco. On 30 August, the king confirmed the grants to Gutierre of Córdoba's towns of Gahete and Hinojosa. In the fall of 1445, John II called Gutierre to help recover the fortress town of Alburquerque for the Crown, and as a reward the master received the town of Alconchel, which had been given earlier to his uncle.[32]

Because his gains were potentially endangered by Alvaro de Luna's opponents, Gutierre de Sotomayor readily agreed to serve when the condestable led the Royal Council. Therefore, Gutierre brought troops to Arévalo in the spring of 1447 in preparation for a possible conflict with prince Henry, at which time the king confirmed his earlier grants, and because Luna had arranged the event, Gutierre appeared prominently the following August at John II's wedding to his second wife, princess Isabel de Portugal, mother of the future Castilian queen. However, because he recognized John's growing antipathy to Luna, who ever more frequently controlled the king's life, Sotomayor became less visible at Luna's side. He was not in the list of those swearing in the summer of 1448 to uphold the king's service, and although he was summoned in the spring of the following year during Luna's unsuccessful effort to end the Sarmiento revolt in Toledo (discussed below), the chronicles are mute on his whereabouts when Luna's opponents generated conspiracies to eliminate the favorite.[33] To avoid falling with the condestable-master of Santiago, the master of Alcántara somehow managed in 1450 to arrange for his son Alonso, lord of Puebla de Alcocer, a marriage to Elvira de Zúñiga, the daughter of Alvaro de Zúñiga, who as chief royal justice, was the man responsible for the arrest and execution three years

later of Alvaro de Luna. In the anti-Luna confederations signed among individual grandees, Gutierre de Sotomayor was listed among the protected
friends along with members of the Zúñiga family.[34]

In an era during which it was hard to recognize alliances that would not
lead to personal and family disaster, Gutierre de Sotomayor had twice, with
regard to both his uncle and Alvaro de Luna, shown that he knew when to
abandon service to an influential patron and change sides. By protecting
most of the royal grants on which he established the House of Sotomayor as
an aristocratic dynasty, the master of Alcántara left the resolution of the bitter, divisive dispute over Puebla de Alcocer to John II's children, all of
whom failed over the next half century to end a quarrel that remained as a
focus of political judgment and action.

Seignorial Jurisdiction and Municipality as Framing Institutions

Institutions are important. They are the product of constantly changing
human interactions and continuously create a context within which other
interactions occur. Moreover, the actions of individuals are in part shaped
by their institutional roles. Because of the origins of the Belalcázar dispute,
two fundamental Castilian political institutions, seignorial jurisdiction
(lordship) and the municipality, framed the long wrangle between the governing council of the city of Toledo and the House of Sotomayor. Except in
regard to those few seignorial jurisdictions over land that contained no
municipality, the two institutions were intimately linked because lordship
involved jurisdiction over municipalities and municipalities were often
lords.[35] Conflicts among jurisdictional lordships and municipalities provided perhaps the most frequent opportunities for Crown intervention in
Castilian political life.

No work meets the obvious need in the literature for an exhaustive treatment of seignorial jurisdiction, and I will not attempt in a few paragraphs to
fill that role. In the past twenty-five years, historians have published an
impressive number of monographs and articles on particular aristocratic
lineages, lordships, and communities subject to lordships, and a review of
these works indicates that seignorial jurisdictions fit into no easily delineated categories.

Between the civil wars of 1368 and 1474, a potent Castilian aristocracy
developed through a drastic replacement of elites.[36] Many of these prominent families were elevated in rank by rewards received as followers of the
newly victorious Henry II (reigned 1369–1379). His grants often involved
seignorial jurisdiction over towns, their municipal territory, and the villages
within their territorial boundaries. Depending on the nature of a particular
grant, the jurisdictional lord possessed the right and responsibility to appoint

officials and provide judicial administration for the vassals within his lordship and to collect certain fees and taxes. In theory, the conduct of seignioral
authority was subject to Crown supervision because the monarch had the
ultimate responsibility to provide justice. Although there were important
variations from one lordship to another in terms of the lord's authority,
these lay lordships possessed jurisdiction similar to that exercised by various
types of ecclesiastical lords, including the commanders of the military
orders, and by towns and cities over the villages within their often extensive
municipal limits. Given the importance of such jurisdictional lordships for
the governance of the kingdom's population and resources, individual magnates enhanced their political roles by controlling more and larger ones.[37]
The concentration of offices and lordships brought about through marriages
among magnate families helped reinforce the increasingly closed nature of
the developing territorial aristocracy, and gains were generally preserved for
future generations through the continuing formation of entailed estates.
Grandees frequently used the income derived from the exercise of their
royal Court and territorial offices to purchase productive agricultural land to
diversify their houses' economic bases, and they sought subsequent grants of
seignioral jurisdiction over those areas where they already owned farms and
pastures. An even more important source of wealth for the acquisition of
property and lordships was the Crown's assignment to a noble of a portion
of the royal revenues.[38]

The throughout the period, municipalities constituted the building blocks of
lordships. For a lordship to exist, there would have to be jurisdictional
authority over at least one town. Like an aristocratic lordship, the city exercised jurisdiction over a territory, its *términos* or *alfoz,* which would contain
towns and villages as well as arable land, pastures, and unimproved areas,
often called *montes,* used as a source of wood and stone and for fishing and
hunting. Ecclesiastical institutions, including the military orders, also held
jurisdictional lordships over towns. Although the exact authority conceded
to a lord varied, in general, seignioral jurisdiction delegated to its holder
some of the monarch's ordinary jurisdiction under the Crown's supervision.
The institutional interaction between municipalities and their lords exhibited throughout the kingdom a bewildering variety, and the only constant
was that the seignior was expected, through oversight of judicial administration, to maintain peace, harmony, and the common good. The lord generally intervened in municipal affairs by naming officials directly responsible
to the seignior, often with the same titles, such as alcalde mayor, as similar
officials named by the monarch.[39]

The municipality was the most comprehensive type of Castilian political organization, for as a corporate entity it exercised the most complex
set of competencies of any institution or official in the kingdom.[40] Virtually all aspects of human interaction were subject in some way to municipal

administration through the application by its officials of ordinances established by its governing council. Because each municipality included términos over which it exercised jurisdiction beyond the walls or perimeter of its
administrative center, its government both organized much of the life
within the town itself and dictated, at least in theory, much about the use of
woodlands and water resources, grazing, farming, and rural manufacturing.
Although some municipalities such as Córdoba and Toledo had large urban
populations and large and more diversified términos, no municipal government was autonomous in its conduct of public affairs because its social and
cultural environments were larger than urban boundaries.[41]

Contrasting Understandings of Monarchy

As in the case of John II's grant of Puebla de Alcocer to Gutierre de
Sotomayor, virtually all of the benefits obtained from the king's hands during these troubled times by Luna, the master of Alcántara, and the territorial
aristocracy involved the declared exercise of the sovereign's "own initiative
and reasoned consideration and absolute royal authority." The repetition in
these circumstances of the necessary legal clauses reinforced among
Castile's magnates an understanding of absolute royal authority in a context
of valued noble service to the monarch justly compensated by the king's
gifts of jurisdictions, revenues, and offices. Constant reiteration meant that
interpretive schemes derived from this perspective were those most likely
cued as grandees sought to understand the events swirling around them and
formulate judgments that shaped their actions, and their assessment of what
would be most in the ruler's service did not always correspond to that of the
king, as John II sometimes complained. Conditions were often closer to
anarchy than to the peace, harmony, and justice so frequently articulated in
the period's documents as the proper aims of government.

Among the less prominent ranks of the commonwealth, men with smaller
estates, who by this time held most of the important leadership posts in the
vast majority of the major municipalities, sometimes expressed concern over
the effects of the rapid growth of large aristocratic and ecclesiastical seignioral jurisdictions, for they felt that the increase in such lordships cost the
Crown the appointments and revenues necessary for the effective exercise of
royal authority. To implant their ultimate jurisdiction over municipal affairs,
fourteenth-century monarchs helped small groups of wealthy and influential
men to control municipal governance in the cities and major towns through
royal appointments as councilors, usually known as regidores or *veinticuatros*
(in some Andalusian cities), with lifetime tenure and increasing means to pass
their posts their heirs. These local notables increasingly built up their corporate authority and freed themselves from the burden of taxes and other fees

paid by municipal *vecinos* (citizens). They constituted a patriciate that remained quite open to other citizens who prospered during Castile's fifteenth-century economic growth and to wealthy newcomers from elsewhere. Patricians also valued military leadership and the educational accomplishments of letrados, as university law graduates were increasingly known.

They shaped their political activity to increase, not decrease, respect for royal government. Although major municipalities were not isolated polities and their interactions were intensifying, royal authority was important in a large, institutionally fragmented kingdom that faced serious military threats along all of its frontiers. Effective Crown government was also necessary to contain the nonpatrician groups, often called the *común* or *menudos*. These plebeians were not always content with their limited political roles and might turn any disorder into an occasion for revolution directed against those arrangements of the kingdom's social environment that gave a relative handful of Castilians, including locally notable patricians, disproportionate control over economic resources.[42] Because factional conflicts among notables often provided occasions for commoner attacks on these notables' economic and political positions, urban notables encouraged respect for the monarch as the ultimate source of justice who could legitimately resolve their divisive disputes. In some urban centers, the best examples being Salamanca and Valladolid, events led to a formal binary organization of patrician political life around lineage-groupings. Although in particularly violent periods these and similar groupings (*bandos*) were granted a constitutional role in the distribution of municipal offices, they were never as comprehensive a vehicle of patrician action nor as durable as vital entities as is often claimed. Patrician families in other urban centers, such as Burgos and Zamora, interacted in quite different ways.[43] The frequent aristocratic civil wars for control of Crown government were also reflected within municipalities as local notables sought to protect their interests by becoming clients of grandees, as the examples of Murcia and Seville clearly demonstrate.[44]

At any time in this period when private force and influence were interpreted to be the arbiters of public affairs, men lacking such resources tended to follow the banner of the great, who were expected to guard the interests of their supporters. Clients lent support to their patrons in the hope that the authority their leader gained would be used for their protection and advancement. Thus, local notables were always an important component of the camps contending for the principal roles in the commonwealth's political institutions, and relationships between the Crown and major municipal corporations often turned on these patricians' actions.

For example, the infante Enrique was able to use the city of Toledo as a base of operations in the early 1440s. Under the spring 1439 compromise agreement that exiled Alvaro de Luna from Court, all of Castile's urban centers returned to loyalty to the king. Toledo, however, was not to be occupied by the forces of any major seignior as a guarantee for the compact. Yet late in the year, Luna's friends arrived back in the Royal Council, and it appeared certain that he would soon return to John II's side.

Because Luna's lucrative Escalona lordship was so close to Toledo, the infante Enrique was reluctant to leave such an important prize open to surprise attack or to a possible agreement with the favorite. Therefore, in March 1440 with the permission of Pedro López de Ayala, Toledo's alcalde mayor and alcaide of the royal fortress, Enrique stationed a military unit in the city. Ayala did not surrender Toledo's fortifications to the infante but kept them under his personal authority. The alcalde mayor's actions did not represent the wishes of all Toledo's patricians because Ayala had expelled some of them from the city. When the king tried to negotiate with his cousin and Ayala, he sent as his representatives a group of Toledan regidores, including one of his own prominent officials, Dr. Fernando Díaz de Toledo, all of whom were taken prisoner. When Ayala admitted the infante and his warriors, he sought support for his clique in the event of an attack similar to one two weeks earlier on the city of Avila, which was organized by magnates opposed to the infantes of Aragón, including the count of Alba with jurisdictional bases near Toledo.

John II put on a show of anger at the infante Enrique's apparent violation of the earlier agreement and on 4 January 1441 left his residence in Arévalo, where he had been surrounded by vigilant great lords. The king was reunited with all of his old counselors and their armed retainers in Avila, and this force then marched on Toledo, to which the monarch was refused entrance on 8 January. While the infante Enrique sent a circular letter to the "kingdom," meaning the governing councils of major municipalities, stating that he refused the king's request for entrance only because he feared Luna's men who were around the king, John II took the refusal as a declaration of war. The subservience of at least one group of Toledo's governing notables to the interests of the infante Enrique set off the series of events that cost Toledo its lordship over Puebla de Alcocer and led to the battle of Olmedo in 1445, where the infantes were beaten and Enrique killed.[45]

Local notables could not, however, be a willing component of aristocratic networks. Although this sort of subservience was offensive to the meek, it galled even more those individuals who saw themselves as legitimate holders of significant roles and positions within the social environment. In any kingdom with a small number of wealthy men and a vast number of farmers, herdsmen, day laborers, and artisans individually receiving a much smaller share of Castile's production, any man of substance, even if his estate did not approach the spectacular holdings of a few territorial aristocrats, felt himself demeaned by his feelings of insecurity in periods of anarchy, civil war, or arbitrary government. Moreover, such men would often react when a patron somehow damaged his clients' honor. For example, in

1429 on a visit to Toledo, the infante Enrique mistreated a group of knights and regidores who subsequently returned to the city and as a group renounced their oaths to him and the associated maintenance payments on the ground that their honor had been damaged.[46] Lesser nobles and local notables were too easily commanded, exploited, and abandoned by the great to suit their sense of dignity or to allow them to feel secure in their position. They sought their security in legal guarantees of their rights and holdings, enforced by the administration of a monarch free of institutional checks, who acted in accordance with divinely inspired principles of justice and equity. Thus, members of this group frequently articulated the concept of absolute royal authority as the guarantor of justice that those influenced by liberal constitutionalist principles now find so strange.

The different outlooks discussed should not be taken as positions constantly articulated in the surviving documents, because that would suggest that the factors determining political action were solely those relating to economic organization or political institutions. It would be false to suggest that the grandees were not interested in having their economic status and institutional positions secured by legal documents or that local notables lacked concern for individual honor or disdained the use of personal influence and faction when the actions of individual aristocrats and patricians so often demonstrated the contrary. The dichotomy was not a stark confrontation continuously present in the period's history, but is rather a heuristic device to explain that history.[47] The cultural environment of the Castilian political kingdom contained a complex set of interpretive schemes related to the exercise of "absolute royal authority." Those employed by any individual in a particular situation to understand his or her world and formulate judgments contributed to shaping the action taken by that individual. But that individual's action was also shaped by his or her roles within economic and political institutions built around seigniorial jurisdiction and municipal corporations and within solidarity groups held together by lineage, clientage, or "ethnic" background. Given the turbulent nature of John II's reign, individual actions within such complex social and cultural environments frequently appear contradictory because no one element or factor provided consistent motivation. Monarchy formed an institutional context for sometimes conflicting assessments of the exercise of royal authority and, therefore, never constituted an entity subject to a fixed definition.

Castile's representative assembly, the Cortes, could serve as a forum for those opposed to the exercise of absolute royal authority to abrogate laws in order to reward magnates with additional lordships and Crown revenues. Historians have difficulty using Cortes documents because monarchs, Crown officials, and the commonwealth's other leaders drew on a number of available interpretive schemes to understand these assemblies and what went on there, and they inconsistently employed the terms for the meetings and their procedures. The Cortes never had the institutional status of, for example, the Royal Council or the Chancillería, and there was, therefore, no impetus to draft the types of ordinances or other documents that would fix with greater precision who sat in the Cortes or what they might do while there. At times monarchs would legislate in direct interaction with those assembled in a Cortes, or they would promulgate in the Cortes legislation issued by the Royal Council. A meeting might mostly involve the *procu-radores* (delegates) of cities and major towns, or it might also include important groups of aristocrats and ecclesiastics. Patrician representatives often played important roles because it was through them that monarchs arranged the approval and collection of many of the kingdom's most important taxes, including the extraordinary *servicios* (tributes), paid by municipal corporations. Furthermore, the petitions to the Cortes and related correspondence between the Crown and major towns and cities are hard to evaluate without knowing something about how particular urban positions were generated within the municipal councils involved. However, despite variations, the general context remained the same: monarchs required extensive support from the commonwealth's leaders, and meetings of the Cortes provided an important forum in which to seek such support.[48]

Patricians had no effective way to coerce a monarch to exercise authority in accordance with their interpretive schemes without damaging the very royal authority they felt was necessary for good government, but the ruler was also dependent on local notables' active support, which was more likely to materialize for a royal administration acting to implement the general policies regularly recommended by Cortes procuradores. These representatives repeatedly petitioned the king to take personal charge of the government and reform judicial administration. Indeed, from the thirteenth century onward, Cortes declarations reveal that Castile's patricians were remarkably consistent in condemning ever more frequent royal provisions that were contrary to law, Crown grants made at the expense of the royal domain, and failure to respect royal confirmations of municipal privileges and uphold laws. The freedom of action of Cortes procuradores was not reduced in the period after the Cortes of Ocaña of 1422 when the Crown took over the payment of municipal delegates, and they continued to play such an active role that those such as Alvaro de Luna, who sought to monopolize royal government through their personal relationships with the monarch, sometimes did not want to hold Cortes meetings.[49]

Therefore, John II did nothing unusual when he promulgated the "Law of Valladolid," which Toledo's representatives would frequently cite in their attacks on Gutierre de Sotomayor's assumption of jurisdiction over Puebla de Alcocer. The legislation responded to a petition at the Cortes of Valladolid in 1442 in which the municipal representatives made clear their pessimistic assessment of the political climate:

> Your High Lordship sees how because of the immense donations Your
> Highness has made, your royal Household, Kingdoms and their inhabi-
> tants, universally and individually, and especially the capacity and author-
> ity of your royal Crown, suffer misery and damage. Experience has made
> this harm notorious.

The procuradores asked that such grants not be made or if made that they
might be resisted by force or otherwise despite any derogatory clauses.

> And that Your Lordship declare this by royal law and by a pact and con-
> tract that with us and all your Kingdoms you establish. In exchange, your
> Kingdoms, and we in their name, will serve you with great quantities of
> money for your necessities.[50]

To regain the support of patrician leaders of rebellious urban centers and
establish some independence from the infantes' hegemonic influence at
Court, John II promulgated an order on 5 May, "with the force and vigor of
Law, pact, and firm and stable contract," which overturned many earlier
grants through the use of his absolute royal authority and prohibited the
alienation of Crown patrimony, except under extraordinary circumstances
and even then using restrictive procedures involving municipal representatives. Any other grants or alienations could be resisted without penalty, and
the king explicitly overturned any action contrary to this law "by [his] own
initiative and reasoned consideration and absolute royal authority." The
patrician procuradores at the assembly at which this order was promulgated held a substantially different view of the proper exercise of absolute
royal authority from that prevalent among aristocrats struggling to dominate the monarchy.[51]

Even though John II's use of the conventional language of absolute
authority responded mostly to the personal interests of grandees, growing
support for the underlying concept came from those who wanted the
monarch to have the capacity to restrain in the public interest the rapacious-
ness of the great warriors and direct Castile's military power against Muslim
Granada. Because the increasing interaction of prominent patrician political
actors with a broadening geographic sphere allowed them more and more
to see the connections between their personal interests and the well-being of
the expanding community or commonwealth of which they sensed they
were a part, monarchical government headed by a sovereign exercising concentrated, supreme legislative, executive, and judicial authority really represented the aspirations of these political actors. In particular, the roles in
municipal political institutions played by patrician regidores depended con-
stitutionally on a legal order established by royal authority, often in the face
of local opposition movements that demanded broader citizen participation
in urban government.[52] However, writers of fifteenth-century political treatises who stressed the sovereign's supreme authority also emphasized that

the essence of monarchical government was justice, because if justice and the laws were not supported by the Crown, the monarch would be converted into a tyrant.[53] Therefore, a series of interpretive schemes associated with monarchy, tyranny, justice, and royal freedom from influence by particular interests provided the conventional understanding of politics by which many members of the commonwealth understood and formulated judgments about actions and utterances.[54]

To avoid being merely figureheads for some powerful aristocratic faction, monarchs had to convince the commonwealth's non-magnate leaders that theirs would be a just rule. Only the assurance of such a regime could draw widespread support from local notables and undercut the influence great lords derived from their wealth, influence with lesser knights, and jurisdiction over municipal militias. It was in hope of achieving the sort of reign described by bishop Lope Barrientos, quoted earlier in this chapter, that patrician Cortes deputies in 1445 accepted, just prior to the decisive battle of Olmedo that eliminated the divisive political manipulations of John II's Aragonese cousins, a declaration of absolute royal authority that should not be checked or formally judged by its subjects.[55]

Government by a Royal Favorite

Monarchs, however, had to exercise authority themselves because they had to avoid the impression that their responsibility for administering justice was at all influenced by personal or political considerations, that is, by any consideration but the dictates of the law itself. Because monarchs had to govern the kingdom personally, rule through a favorite, a powerful figure whose position and influence were primarily personal rather than institutional, such as Alvaro de Luna, also damaged rulers' reputations with municipal councilors and made urban patricians dependent on aristocratic factions. Small wonder that John II enjoyed a tremendous surge of support when he had Luna arrested in 1453, and even the local notables who had risen in royal service through Luna's patronage supported the monarch's efforts to rid himself of his favorite.[56] Because relatively small numbers of warriors were involved in most battles, broad support from cities and major municipalities could bring the monarch victory in crucial clashes, as may have been the case at the battle of Olmedo in 1445.

Although Alvaro de Luna played an important role in amassing the fortified towns, armed vassals from military orders and lordships, and income from royal revenues sufficient to confront opponents,[57] Castilian monarchs enjoyed a special authority that allowed them to gather sufficient military power to guarantee royal autonomy from grandee pressure more effectively than men such as Luna, and in doing so, the rulers would not be perceived as rivals of the aristocracy as the great royal favorites were.[58] The king's unique standing was clearly underlined when the town of Medina del Campo was conquered in June 1441. Plausibly fearing for their lives, Luna, his brother the archbishop of Toledo, and Gutierre de Sotomayor escaped with their men when defeat was foreseen. However, during the town's subsequent sack, John II stood near the Plazuela of San Juan, in the midst of complete calm, receiving the formal salutations of his invading vassals as each came to kneel before him and kiss his hands. That scene of tranquility in the midst of disorganized violence was so striking that it inspired the poet Juan de Mena to compare it to Christ in the Garden of Gethsemane.[59] Therefore, fifteenth-century commentators such as Alvar García de Santa María were substantially correct when they claimed that the inability of the monarch to govern personally "was the cause of the factionalism and hatreds among the kingdom's grandees, each one against others, each one of them trying to become more intimate with the king so that they can become more powerful and build up their houses and estates."[60]

As bishop Barrientos indicated, it was thought proper for the monarch to seek the advice and aid of good men, including trained legists, in the administration of justice and other essential aspects of the kingdom's government.[61] The king obviously needed help in such a large and important task, and he required expert advice and assistance if for no other reason than to keep him from delegating responsibility to territorial aristocrats. Because they often emerged from families similar to those of the royal officials, the local notables could have some confidence that the trained legists and many of the other royal officers had been socialized into a similar cultural environment and shared the notables' political assumptions and aspirations. This attitude toward decisions by letrados explains the preference by Cortes procuradores for a greater role in royal judicial administration of the law court known as the audiencia, because this body was dominated by those with formal legal training.[62]

However, despite repeated royal ordinances issued in the Cortes denying validity to any Crown action that was contrary to law, John II continued to grant usurped municipal jurisdictions to great lay and ecclesiastical lords. As a result, local notables disengaged from the Crown, many municipal councils remained suspicious and resistant to the extension of royal authority, and instability and incapacity characterized monarchical government. Beginning with the Cortes of Tordesillas-Valladolid (late 1446–early 1447) and leading directly to Alvaro de Luna's execution in 1453, Cortes procuradores expressed continuous hostility to Luna's predominance at Court. In the end, the great defect of the favorite's attempts to enhance royal authority was that much of the commonwealth's leadership would not enthusiastically support any option they felt was intended only to build up the position of some aristocrat.[63]

Rebellion

Local notables expressed dissatisfaction with arbitrary rule in violation of natural and divine law and aristocratic manipulation of royal authority for private ends rather than the commonwealth's good, and they sought ways to get the sovereign to exercise his absolute authority without tyranny. The expression of dissidence was a real problem in polities governed by a ruler unwilling to resolve conflict in cooperation with parliamentary and munici- pal institutions. Understandably, writers carefully framed their statements of the matter. For example, law 25 of the second *Partida,* title 13, on which the declaration of absolute royal authority at the 1445 Cortes of Olmedo was a gloss, argued that when the monarch endangered his soul and the dynasty's honor and damaged the kingdom through actions against reason and law, the people had a responsibility, if they wished to avoid "recognized trea- son," to counsel him and act in ways that would make him turn away from improper conduct. The latter path was poorly mapped out, and where the ruler depended more on broad-based collaboration than coercive force to get his way, rebellion provided the one sure means for any significant group to attract his attention. If the grievances prompting an uprising or a refusal to respond to official commands were common, the king would ignore the rebels' demands only at the risk of seeing the revolt spread. Rebellion did not necessarily have to involve armed insurrection led by local notables. Because the emerging patrician families, through their dominance of munic- ipal institutions, controlled so much of Castile's fiscal and military adminis- tration, inefficiency and delay in carrying out royal orders were also tactics undermining Crown initiatives that were widely interpreted as arbitrary infringements of fundamental constitutional norms.[64]

The political literature of the time recognized that such rebellious expres- sions resulted from the sovereign's misgovernment. Although there was no formal procedure to check monarchs other than the right to counsel them and recommend reforms, it was widely felt that rulers and their advisers who acted arbitrarily and in violation of the laws were tyrants; the only true mon- archs were those who governed rightly, honestly, and justly. The prevailing idea was that a bad king destroyed the kingdom. Many of the monarchs' notable subjects would not obey their orders if these orders were considered tyrannical. They felt God would not aid such rule, and the kingdom would collapse into disorder with cries of "Long live the king! Death to the bad gov- ernment!" This distinction between the royal institution and the decisions of administration members tended to preserve faith in monarchy as a form of government even in the face of violent attacks on Crown officials.[65]

Local notables could stimulate a rebellious response to arbitrary royal government simply by abstaining from their role of carrying out royal com- mands and suppressing local disturbances caused by administrative activities such as taxation. They thereby ensured that grievances would be expressed through riots or other violent resistance to tax farmers. Or they could attach the communities that they led to the cause of an aristocratic league. Or they could themselves give leadership to the turmoil, often claiming that commoners had coerced them into playing such a role. An interpretive scheme placing high value on just rule was something employed as well by men and women whose roles and positions within the social environment increasingly left them outside of the commonwealth's active political life.[66]

Although there were numerous ways local notables could pressure the Crown, they preferred compromise to open disobedience, which not only grated against common schemes of interpretation of the cultural environment but also threatened the order of the social environment from which they benefited. Patrician regidores would not, as a rule, be quick to stir up a rebellion that might become an occasion for popular assault on the economic organization and political institutions that made it possible for a relatively small number of municipal citizens to enjoy a disproportionate share of wealth and influence. I show in chapter 4 that the danger of real revolution put a limit on how far normal politics could go toward violent conflict.

Sensible kings allowed the possibility of rebellion to influence their decisions and bargained with their subjects. Because fifteenth-century Castilian rebellions were thought to be motivated by inadequacies in Crown government, monarchs negotiated with rebels. Because royal promises were often broken, there were frequent changes in urban loyalties, and leaders of municipal revolts were seldom punished, in an otherwise puzzling lack of judicial rigor. Although urban instability can be attributed to the influence of opposing noble cliques within the major municipalities, patrician leaders worked together too often for factional conflict to provide a wholly satisfactory explanation.[67]

I examine below an example of this process that was directly relevant to the Belalcázar lawsuit because the rebellion complicated Toledo's efforts to obtain the return of Puebla de Alcocer and generated an ambiguous pardon. An attempt by Alvaro de Luna's government to collect what local authorities in Toledo felt was an illegal tax led to an insurrection in January 1449. Curiously, the man who took the leadership of the rebellion was Pedro Sarmiento, a formerly loyal royal official whom John II had placed in charge of Toledo's fortifications when its alcalde mayor, Pedro López de Ayala, was removed from the effective exercise of his offices due to his alliance with the infante Enrique. Made heady by his sweeping victory over the infantes' league at the battle of Olmedo in 1445, but also needing to stabilize his position with the warrior aristocracy, Luna resorted to yet another round of concessions, confiscations, personal pacts, and even illegal imprisonments. Sarmiento and those Toledan patricians who had opposed Ayala's attempts to build up his own estate through the exploitation of municipal corporate resources when he was alcalde mayor were especially upset by royal demands throughout 1446 and 1447 that Ayala be given secure lordship of the villages of Cedillo, Humanes, Huecas, Peromoro, and Guadamur, which the majority of Toledo's councilors felt had been granted to him illegally.[68]

All the procuradores attending the Cortes of 1448 (Valladolid, Tordesillas, Madrigal) openly attacked Luna's leadership as royal favorite, and the Crown was not able to get complete support for new revenues.[69] Heedless of the storm he was creating, Luna attempted a forced collection of 20,000 *doblas de oro* from Toledo, which led to a rebellion against his "tyranny" and violation of the city's privileges. The king's advisers worried that the refusal to obey would spread to other major municipalities. In an effort to strengthen his own insecure position, Sarmiento championed anti-Jewish and anti-converso violence that seriously divided the city's citizens and sufficiently alarmed all important patrician factions that they called on prince Henry to enter Toledo, expel Sarmiento, and end the potentially revolutionary popular violence. The prince's ability to unite fractious local notables, including Ayala and his opponents, made Toledo one of the bases for his opposition to Luna's influence over his father.

When prince and king were reconciled, Henry utilized his influence to negotiate a generous pardon for Toledo and its patrician leaders. In recognition of its past services, John II agreed to pardon Toledo for any rebellious acts during the rising of 1449 and any earlier disturbances of the public order, which presumably included Ayala's refusal to admit the king within Toledo's walls in 1441 when the alcalde mayor was allied with the infante Enrique. Any part of the municipality's property or territory under its jurisdiction confiscated by the Crown because of such rebellions was to be returned, and no judge was to hear any lawsuit relating to these matters. Anyone who had received a royal grant of places within Toledo's jurisdiction had no further right to them, and all judicial decisions and sentences against any of the groups to whom the pardon was addressed were revoked by the king's absolute royal authority.[70] Although it was not the only factor in Luna's fall from royal favor, Toledo's great rebellion contributed to John II's reassessment of the political situation in his kingdom. John II's own explanation of Luna's arrest employed the language commonly used to justify, in support of royal service and the kingdom's good, resistance by subjects to the tyranny of royal servants.[71]

The Frustration of Justice in a Violent Age

With John II's death in 1454, Toledo's leaders could entertain hopes of recovering city jurisdiction over what came to be known as the viscounty of

Puebla de Alcocer. In the aftermath of the Sarmiento rebellion of 1449, the future king Henry IV had become a patron of the city, helping to secure its pardon from John II. Moreover, when Henry IV inherited the throne, he brought with him a program of administrative and judicial reform that promised the sort of monarchy desired by urban patricians. With all of the emphasis early in Henry IV's reign on the improvement of judicial administration, Toledo might have expected an opportunity for a court challenge to John II's grant of the Puebla de Alcocer region to Gutierre de Sotomayor. However, because Alvaro de Zúñiga, the father-in-law of Gutierre's son and heir Alonso de Sotomayor, was part of the group, with Juan Pacheco, marquis of Villena, and the latter's brother Pedro Girón, master of Calatrava, that dominated the Royal Council between 1457 and 1463, the city's leaders may have been reluctant to demand a hearing on their claims.[72]

Henry IV did order the documents necessary for a consideration of Toledo's claims to the viscounty of Puebla de Alcocer to be brought to the Council of Castile in 1464. Perhaps he was influenced by the demand of the Cortes of Toledo of 1462 that he act to maintain his father's oath, at the Cortes of Valladolid twenty years earlier, not to grant lordships over the towns and villages of the royal domain. On 22 March 1464, the Council sent to Toledo from Madrid an order to send a procurador with full powers to conduct business relating to the dispute. The procurador was to bring with him the records of the investigations made in relation to the jurisdictions taken from Toledo as well as depositions and documents from those city officials who knew about revenues and other financial matters related to these areas. Two days later, the Council requested Toledo's *Libro Becerro* (bound register of jurisdictional privileges) recording the limits of the city's territorial jurisdiction so that the Council could see what had been lost.[73]

The disputed territory was restored to Toledo in Salamanca on 20 May 1465 in response to a petition from the city's representatives, regidores Perafán de Rivera and Juan de Guzmán. The regidores had alleged that Puebla de Alcocer and the entire region near the Guadiana River, which had been purchased by Toledo, had been seized by Gutierre de Sotomayor against all the laws of God and man. Although justice had repeatedly been sought, king John II had ordered the return of the region only in his will. Toledo's petition pointed out that the revenues and other financial advantages derived from the region were important for maintaining churches, monasteries, and programs for widows, orphans, the poor, and general spending for the common good, peace, and tranquility of the kingdom. Thus, Gutierre's illegal seizure in violation of the city's good title prejudiced the welfare of the king's subjects as well as the legal order of the realm. Because in the face of this wrong, no title that Gutierre received could be worth anything, they argued that the return of all these lands should be ordered along with 800,000 *maravedís* compensation for each year the area had been held. If the jurisdiction were not surrendered, the municipal council wanted royal permission to take it by force.

In response to this petition, the order of restoration quoted the law promulgated at the Cortes of Valladolid on 5 May 1442, which Henry IV had confirmed. Because it was clear to king and Council that Toledo had purchased the lands, rather than receiving jurisdiction over them by royal grant, whatever Gutierre de Sotomayor and his heirs presented to support their claims was of no value. Nor could any laws overturn the decision, even the pope's, because the document stipulated that the case not be presented to Rome.[74]

Much the same sort of bargaining for royal favor seems to have taken place regarding Córdoba's disputes with the House of Sotomayor. Five members of Córdoba's council had asked Henry IV to order Alonso de Sotomayor to return certain of the city's pasture lands that he held without valid title. In Jaén on 5 March 1464, over king Henry's signature, the Crown ordered the restitution of the pastures, and Córdoba seized the land. Then in Salamanca on 11 June 1465, the Royal Council issued an order of restitution similar to that granted to Toledo on 20 May. It revoked the seizures by both Gutierre de Sotomayor and Pedro Girón, master of Calatrava, and ordered the return of Gahete, Hinojosa, Fuenteovejuna, Bélmez, and their lands to Córdoba. Henry backed off a bit from his commitment, however, in an effort to maintain his support from the important Zúñiga family. In a letter of 18 July from Madrid, the king ordered Córdoba to do nothing against the lands of Alonso de Sotomayor despite any royal provisions. The monarch wanted everything returned to its former state and no further disturbances of the peace in that region, and although the city's protest had been sympathetically received, the order stood. In April 1464, Alonso de Sotomayor had been murdered by a disgruntled vassal, and his widow, Elvira de Zúñiga (d. 1483), was guardian of the new count, Gutierre I de Sotomayor. She had requested the royal order to do nothing against Alonso de Sotomayor's lands,, which seems actually to have referred only to the pasture land.[75]

Because of such vacillation, I suspect that the final result of the Royal Council hearings was an attempt to line up support for the approaching conflict with the king's half-brother Alfonso rather than a considered judicial decision. Henry IV was declared deposed in Avila by partisans of Alfonso on 5 June, and just five days later, those among Toledo's leaders favorable to the latter expelled Henry's representative and placed the city in Alfonso's service. Both Henry and Alfonso greatly elevated the number of royal grants during the crucial years of 1465 and 1466. On 10 May 1465 in Alba de Tormes, only ten days before the Council's verdict, Henry IV had issued to Toledo over just his own signature a revocation of Gutierre de Sotomayor's grants, restoring Puebla de Alcocer and other areas to the city. The previous April he had confirmed all of Toledo's privileges and revoked all grants made against the city's interests. Along with other benefits, when he was near Valladolid on 29 June, Alfonso granted the same restoration of Puebla de Alcocer to Toledo as a reward for coming over to his side. Although Henry revoked his letter sent from Jaén to Córdoba, there was no recorded attempt to abrogate the Royal Council decisions involving that city or Toledo. Maybe these judgments represented more serious judicial consideration than circumstances would seem to have allowed. However, all of these documents betrayed Henry IV's incapacity by authorizing Córdoba and Toledo to take the lands by force if they were not surrendered.[76]

Because 150 kilometers of rough terrain separated Puebla de Alcocer from the city, it is surprising that Toledo attempted a reconquest of the area. The attack took place in the context of the antiseignorial resistance by Castilian cities in the last decade of Henry's reign. According to Martín Sánchez de Cerro, a resident of Fontanarejo and witness at the 1495 hearing discussed in chapter 3, militia leaders from the city had assembled a group of men from the Montes de Toledo in Arroba. From there this force overran Villarta, Fuenlabrada, and the rest of the northern part of the viscounty of Puebla de Alcocer. The count's officers were removed from these towns and officers of Toledo put in their place. The effort floundered on the fortresses with which Gutierre de Sotomayor had thoughtfully provided his heirs. Herrera would not fall, and its officials would not surrender after seeing the treatment of their colleagues in the conquered municipalities. Toledo's army received no additional help from the city and had to fall back in the face of reinforcements that came to strengthen the Herrera garrison. The House of Sotomayor's men regained all of the lost territory and even seized some livestock from Arroba, southeast of Navalpino.[77]

The political life of the kingdom and of Toledo itself was torn apart by violent factional conflict. In the aftermath of prince Alfonso's death, the municipal representatives to the Cortes of Ocaña in 1469, in a clear expression of the monarch's absolute royal authority as understood by local notables, tried to get king Henry to reform the Royal Council, revitalize a paralyzed audiencia, and in general recognize that, as their supreme lord, he was "obliged by silent contract to maintain his subjects in justice." Henry IV had pardoned Toledo for its opposition in the civil war, but royal authority was so endangered that the city's patricians apparently saw no opportunity to demand before royal justices the restoration of Puebla de Alcocer.[78] Despite the continued significant economic and political roles of territorial aristocrats, in order to restore the Crown's capacity to govern, Henry's successors, the Catholic Monarchs Ferdinand and Isabella, would have not only to respond to the Cortes petitions of major municipal corporations but also to allow Toledo's council a judicial review of its claim to Puebla de Alcocer.

Chapter 3

THE CATHOLIC MONARCHS
AND THE LEGACY OF JOHN II

Royal Leadership as a Balancing Act

John II left his heirs, Henry IV and the Catholic Monarchs, Isabella and Ferdinand, a bitter, dangerous, and widely followed quarrel between the city of Toledo and the heads of the House of Sotomayor, now counts of Belalcázar. Although John also bequeathed royal institutions and laws to resolve such conflicts, Crown officials lacked the capacity to do so. The history of the Belalcázar case, as the litigation was increasingly known, reveals that John had further bequeathed an influential group of magnates who were capable of pressuring rulers to observe more personal relationships with their great vassals, which could be used to block the continuation of the trial to a final verdict.

The Catholic Monarchs understood the special importance of royal justice in Castile. Both were members of the Castilian House of Trastámara, which had been established as the ruling dynasty when Henry II overthrew and murdered Peter I in 1369. Henry justified this act on the basis of king Peter's alleged failure to maintain justice in the kingdom. In 1465, Isabella's older half brother Henry IV had been symbolically removed from the throne and replaced by her younger brother Alfonso on exactly the same grounds. Although Ferdinand would become the male head of the House of Trastámara when his father, John II of Aragón, died in 1479, Isabella insisted in the marriage agreement of 1469 and afterwards that Ferdinand was no more than her co-administrator of justice in Castile and was equally bound "to guard justice and all the good usages, laws and customs of these kingdoms and domains." Isabella took the crown herself when Henry IV died while Ferdinand was in Aragón, but in January 1475, they worked out a complex division of responsibility. The document included a provision that, in consultation with the Royal Council, they would administer justice together, although when apart, each could do so.[1]

The part of the story of the Belalcázar-Toledo conflict related in this chapter illustrates some important aspects of the political dynamics of the

Trastámara era of Castilian history. Successful monarchical government depended to a large extent on a constant and difficult balancing of royal actions and declarations so that the interpretive schemes cued for the commonwealth's leaders would be those that helped shape elite collaboration. On the one hand, Isabella and Ferdinand would have to assure the magnates through ample personal contact, at Court and through correspondence, that they were adequately honored and their preponderant economic and jurisdictional roles were secure from degradation by any specially favored clique. In the aftermath of a five-year civil war for the throne, it was not easy to calm grandee worries given Isabella's factional ties and Ferdinand's family origins and connections. Moreover, the Crown vigorously asserted that letrados would be judging the legality of aristocratic claims to jurisdictions, offices, and revenues, which raised aristocratic suspicions that this would really be just a tool to despoil those who were out of favor with the Catholic Monarchs or their favorites. On the other hand, because of all the personal attention given to the territorial aristocracy, many would interpret as due to informal grandee influence any royal conduct, whatever its actual motivation, that appeared to be an arbitrary violation of procedures established by law and the ordinances of judicial institutions. This perspective might well shape the action of patricians and letrado officials with regard to resistance to royal leadership and any strengthening of the magnates' clientage networks, which would undermine the Crown's capacity for action. Hence, the successful governance of Castile depended heavily on the personalities and judgment of its monarchs.

Political instability marked the kingdom over most of the fifteenth century. Even the fabled reign of Ferdinand and Isabella, in which so many have wished to see the beginnings of the modern state and Spanish nation, did not create conditions for the trial and verdict, according to Castilian law, on the competing claims to the viscounty of Puebla de Alcocer. However, the Catholic Monarchs realized that their close ties to key territorial aristocrats and their failure to permit what their own laws demanded would cost the dynasty the degree of cooperation from local notables necessary to secure royal authority, prevent serious grandee factionalism, and avoid the disruption of municipal government. Eventually, the Crown permitted the initiation of judicial proceedings.

Institutional Reform and the Ideology of Just Rule

In his preface to the 1491 edition of the *Siete Partidas,* Dr. Alonso Díaz de Montalvo, veteran jurist of the final turbulent years of John II, asserted that "in order to mitigate and obviate the great evils, injuries, misfortunes, contentions, and inimical wars that there had been in these kingdoms," the

Catholic Monarchs, Ferdinand and Isabella, "by divine disposition wanted justly and rightly to reign and govern their kingdoms not only with arms but even more with laws and royal institutions."[2] The authors of written sources of law clarified many of the interpretive schemes by which leaders of the Castilian commonwealth identified patterns in the events around them. Because many wanted the Crown to resolve conflicts on the basis of these laws, monarchs who did so could potentially tap a major source of support. This creative process involved the use of letrados, specially educated experts in these written sources, and the organization of these experts into particular institutions with effective procedural rules. Of course, those using such institutions, willingly or unwillingly, had to employ such experts as well.[3]

The concept that the best guarantor of justice would be a monarch serving as supreme legislator, executive, and judge and exercising, when necessary, absolute royal authority was an important part of Castile's cultural environment, and a large section of the commonwealth's leaders would likely support any sovereign who sought to achieve tranquility and prosperity on the basis of just rule. The Crown needed to exhibit capable and consistent government in providing effective institutions for the realization of these desires. To avoid being simply figureheads manipulated by a powerful grandee faction on whose support they depended, Ferdinand and Isabella had to recover from the territorial aristocracy the capacity for political leadership. Through the program of effective judicial administration Díaz de Montalvo described, the Catholic Monarchs strove to rally the discontented local notables to their cause and away from aristocratic power brokers.

Political institutions are not secondary aspects of community life, simply reflecting more fundamental social or cultural organization. Political institutions themselves shape human action. Because they provide a context within which human interactions occur, they may sustain, or appear to sustain, parts of both the social and cultural environments. Of course, in the approach used in this book, political institutions are themselves part of the social environment, but because they are founded and gain continued support at least in part to achieve some valued purpose, many people with roles in them may "socialize" others to particular interpretive schemes of the cultural environment, thereby transforming the patterns of human action.

Ever-more-clearly drafted ordinances increasingly defined the roles of judicial officials, and the preparation of these men, through formal education and prior experience, exposed them to sophisticated expressions of interpretive schemes associated with law and justice. Moreover, those who availed themselves of judicial administration, even if only through interaction with their representatives before its officials, learned something of the content and use of such schemes, which might then become more prevalent as factors shaping action. Within this context, the elaboration of judicial institutions in the Trastámara era played a major role in the processes of political interaction among Castilians.[4]

Although still in the midst of a military conflict to secure Isabella's Castilian crown, the Catholic Monarchs proclaimed their reform program in the spring of 1476 to representatives at the Cortes of Madrigal. The aristocracy would serve the Crown only in areas where their standing and experience were of value–military affairs, diplomacy, and important governorships. Such offices would reinforce the magnates' sense of their special place in the commonwealth, but their holders could expect preferment only as loyal defenders of royal authority. Other aspects of royal governance would involve considerable participation of officials drawn from among local notables, especially those letrados with a sophisticated legal education that steeped them in prevailing scholarly conceptions of just rule. Moreover, the rulers acted on patrician petitions similar to those submitted since late in John II's reign and established the "Santa Hermandad"("Holy Brotherhood"; municipal league) as a royal judicial and military organization to help restore peace to the kingdom.[5]

With the war's end, the Crown summoned another Cortes in Toledo in 1480. Many decisions taken there merely ratified Henry IV's similar reforms, but even so, the scope of the program is startling. As had been the pattern during John II's reign and later, most of the initiative was left to the municipal delegates and their petitions for the correction of past abuses, such as the misappropriation of extraordinary taxes approved by municipalities for war against Muslim Granada. One of the main initiatives with clear fiscal implications was the so-called "Act of Resumption" or "Law of Toledo," which was to provide the legal basis for attacks on questionable grants of jurisdictions and royal revenues.[6]

Rather than innovate in their reform of the Council of Castile, the Catholic Monarchs pulled together the ordinances of John II and especially Henry IV (the ordinances of 1459), which these earlier kings had been unable to implement fully, to convert that institution from a preserve of the Crown's great vassals to a more advisory, judicial, and administrative body whose members were primarily highly educated letrados.[7] Next to getting their son recognized as heir, Ferdinand and Isabella placed their highest priority on the reorganization of the Council. Although excluding magnates from Council positions could not eliminate the jurisdictional bases of their political authority, the drafters of the 1480 ordinances sought to open for the ruler an administrative space separated from their interactions with great men in order to get the support of local notables necessary to enhance royal authority in the face of the territorial aristocrats' political demands. As time went on, the Council deliberated with greater independence, culminating in 1489 with the appointment of a Council president who clearly functioned as something more than an assistant to the monarchs or their viceroy.[8]

With so many trained jurists as members, the Council of Castile served as a judicial tribunal, but over the course of the fifteenth century, an increasing percentage of important disputes, especially those cases brought on appeal from local or royally commissioned justices, were in theory reserved for the Chancillería's high tribunal known as the audiencia. The Catholic Monarchs were determined to make the Chancillería of Valladolid the most widely respected institution of royal justice. Although it apparently developed from public royal judicial hearings by the monarch acting as supreme judge, the audiencia took shape as an entity with its own regulations as a consequence of the Trastámara takeover and king Henry II's reforms at the Cortes of Toro of 1371. At the Cortes of Briviesca in 1387, king John I established a more significant role for this tribunal in relation to the monarch and Royal Council. Yet the troubles of the next three reigns had kept this audiencia from achieving quite the envisioned role as rulers felt it was necessary to keep major conflicts involving civil litigation more under their direct supervision and that of the Council. For example, John II ordered in 1428 that the Council send all lawsuits "between parties" (that is, civil disputes) to the Chancillería, but although he repeated this command when he issued the so-called Ordinances of Guadalajara in 1436, the Council continued to adjudicate such matters directly or arrange hearings before specially commissioned judges, opening the process, from the perspective of the patrician leaders of Castile's cities and major towns, to frequent aristocratic manipulation.[9]

The 1480 legislation called for an audiencia with a churchman as president and four justices called oidores, an increase of one over past practice. In addition, there were to be three *alcaldes* (magistrates) to handle criminal cases, a Crown *fiscal* (prosecutor) to look after the royal interests, and two lawyers to defend the poor. The Chancillería was given more and more important cases to handle, and this enhanced role increased both its influence and its range of action. Eventually there would be sixteen oidores divided into four tribunals, and a second Chancillería was established in 1494 in Ciudad Real (later it was moved to Granada). The staffing of a corporate entity with permanently assigned magistrates rather than those with only special commissions to hear specific cases would increase collegiality and potentially fortify the audiencia officials' sense of their role in maintaining quality judicial administration.[10]

As leaders, the Catholic Monarchs, like their Trastámara predecessors, placed a great deal of emphasis on their responsibility to provide judicial administration of high quality as the cornerstone of peace, harmony, and good government within the commonwealth. Then as now, leadership is judged, and how it is judged affects the continuous changes in the pattern of human interactions. Therefore, support for the monarchs and their principal advisers hinged to a great extent on the way in which, from 1480 onward, the commonwealth's prominent members perceived that royal officials and institutions were meeting their announced goal of providing justice. Because it was so contentious and difficult to resolve, the course of the well-known Belalcázar lawsuit over possession of the viscounty of Puebla de Alcocer would shed continuous light on the quality of royal leadership and the monarchs' ability to meet their primary responsibilities.

Toledo Seeks Justice in the Face of Aristocratic Influence

Because at the Cortes of 1480, held in Toledo, the Catholic Monarchs appeared firmly established on the Castilian throne and had placed great emphasis on judicial reform, the city's leaders presented a formal petition for judicial review of the rival claims to the Puebla de Alcocer region. On Monday, 31 July, letrado Br. Francisco Ortiz, one of Toledo's jurados, appeared with three other municipal councillors before Ferdinand and Isabella, their secretary Alfonso de Avila, and Dr. Fernando Sánchez Calderón of the Council of Castile. This document provides an excellent illustration of the way in which, by the late fifteenth century, *mediano* (social stratum between commoners and aristocrats) and letrado discourses about the monarch had joined to form a common element within the kingdom's cultural environment.

Ortiz reminded the royal couple of the grievous damage that the count of Belalcázar and his ancestors had inflicted on Toledo by seizing and occupying Puebla de Alcocer and the other settlements and lands of the city's jurisdiction. He argued that these acts were against the dictates of both God and justice because Toledo had purchased the territory and possessed it "from time immemorial." Although the count claimed he held these lands by virtue of a grant from Isabella's father, the city had disputed this claim before John II himself and before Henry IV because the occupation, even if it were by such a grant, was against right and the laws of the kingdom as well as against John's express promise made at the Cortes of Valladolid in 1442, which each subsequent monarch had ratified. The Catholic Monarchs had earlier pledged to remedy, at some convenient time, the great damage that had been done. Toledo, Ortiz said, knew how the difficulties through which the kingdom had passed had kept Ferdinand and Isabella from acting; indeed the troubles had kept the city from seeking redress until now. When Ortiz had asked the Council to start proceedings, its members had told him the opening of this case would cause a scandal because the other grandees would think they too might be forced to return the territories of other cities and towns that they held through grants from past rulers. But Ferdinand and Isabella had finally come to Toledo free of impediments or necessities and could, therefore, order a hearing of the case so that justice could finally be done. In conclusion, Ortiz urged the monarchs to see that a continued refusal to hear the case was disrupting justice and, as such, went against their own policy of not denying justice to loyal vassals who had performed many services. Moreover, they had allowed others a judicial review of their claims, and because Toledo had a special place in the kingdom, it certainly deserved attention. Without sufficient territory for its sustenance, Toledo's council was too poor to meet its responsibilities, and the city's many riots and scandals were rooted in this poverty. Yet now, Ortiz went on to say, the Catholic Monarchs had the opportunity to remedy all the economic problems and public disorder, do justice, and relieve the burdened consciences of father and brother, John II and Henry IV, because with peace and harmony in the kingdom, a resolution of the dispute could be undertaken, as both God and reason obliged, even though the count was powerful. However, if the decision did not go in Toledo's favor, he would protest, and he asked for an official, notarized record of his presentation to avoid prejudicing his party's right to the property and jurisdictions in question.[11]

Ortiz's full presentation, merely summarized here, was impressive, at least in its written form. With his explicit assertion that fear of the territorial aristocracy's reaction was preventing the implementation of justice, Ortiz exposed two things that constantly shaped the shifting royal judgments about the issues raised by the dispute and vacillation in the efforts to resolve it. Aristocratic civil wars were so fresh in the minds of all of the commonwealth's leaders that they were confused about the magnates' roles in relation to royal government. Moreover, the cultural environment contained conflicting interpretive schemes about how royal authority should be employed to maintain legal rights to property and to reward vassals for their services. There is no recorded answer to the city's request; indeed, there may not have been a formal one. However, Toledo's leaders were likely given to understand that the monarchs were unable to act at that time, especially in view of the approaching war with Nasrid Granada. Such an answer would have reflected the Crown's actual situation, but because the city was losing considerable revenues from the disputed territory, the Crown's refusal to settle the issue raised questions about Ferdinand and Isabella's new program of judicial reform and endangered the long-term prospects for the effective exercise of royal authority.

Toledo waited with patience. The next recorded attempt to obtain a hearing for the city's claims came on 7 December 1490 in Seville. Regidor Diego García de Cisneros and jurado Lope de Villa Real reminded the Catholic Monarchs that the count of Belalcázar was illegally holding some of the city's lands. Although the Crown's pressing needs had dictated the monarchs' earlier decision to suspend all proceedings, Cisneros and Villa Real argued that the reasons for such a suspension no longer obtained, and they asked that Toledo's jurisdiction be restored or at least that a license to begin judicial proceedings be issued. In response, Ferdinand and Isabella ordered the suspension of any consideration of the case and ruled that no further petition be submitted except with the Crown's previous permission, although they insisted that it was not their intention to prejudice Toledo's case in any way.[12]

They gave no reason for this blunt rejection, but the war in the south had entered its final phase. Moreover, during the struggle to conquer Granada, an event occurred which made the monarchs particularly sensitive about any potential damage to the House of Sotomayor. While fighting on the Granadan front in the summer of 1484, under the command of the king, count Gutierre II de Sotomayor, whose wife was Ferdinand's cousin, had died in combat, an event that greatly upset Ferdinand. His heir and the current count, Alonso de Sotomayor, was still only eight or nine years old in 1490, and his mother and guardian, Teresa de Enríquez, had died at age twenty-eight only a year earlier. Other relatives besides king Ferdinand provided the young count with influence at Court.[13] The powerful condestable Pedro Fernández de Velasco (1414–1492) perhaps played a more important role than any of these other relatives in blocking all attempts to bring lawsuits involving the count of Belalcázar before a judge. He served repeatedly as the Catholic Monarchs' Castilian viceroy, and therefore as supervisor of the activities of the Royal Council, when the rulers were at the southern front or absent in Aragón. Velasco was Alonso de Sotomayor's great-uncle, and the condestable's sister, the boy's grandmother María de Velasco, became his legal guardian in 1491. As an indication of the monarchs' close emotional ties to the House of Sotomayor, in 1497, the queen arranged young Alonso's marriage, with important consequences for Toledo's efforts to recover the Puebla de Alcocer region.[14]

Of course, just this sort of royal responsiveness to personal relations between monarch and magnates, usually framed in the context of recompense for valued services, partially molded aristocratic conceptions of the proper exercise of absolute royal authority. Frequent repetition meant that such interpretive schemes were more likely to be cued for grandees as they sought to understand the world around them as a basis for action. Monarchs employed the resulting discourse to attract assistance from territorial aristocrats who desired grants of jurisdictions, revenues, and offices, but personal favoritism involved danger because such compensation built up the influence of major vassals to the point where denying their desires could lead to formidable opposition to the Crown.

No full-scale study explores the Catholic Monarchs' interactions with their great vassals. However, despite the magnates' exclusion from many royal administrative posts, the magnates' significant economic and territorial roles, frequently coupled with their dissatisfaction over exclusion from much direct Crown governance, prevented Ferdinand and Isabella from feeling fully secure in the exercise of their prerogatives. In fact, the members of the territorial aristocracy exerted considerable personal influence, not only in the regions where they had extensive estates but also at Court.[15]

Despite recent reforms, late fifteenth-century Castilian Crown administration remained too rudimentary and the number of its officials too small to prevent aristocratic influence. The territorial aristocracy did lose the right and ability to dominate the actions of the legitimate monarch. However, magnates' attempts at such domination, in earlier reigns, had been to secure against hostile parties and royal favorites, such as Alvaro de Luna, the vast domains they had assembled for their houses. Because Ferdinand and Isabella were willing to sustain these domains, great nobles did not feel the same need to control the ruler. Under the Catholic Monarchs a consensus emerged among the commonwealth's aristocrats and local notables that the maintenance of status and privileges was a component of just rule.[16] Within this framework, demands on the government that were formulated narrowly enough to arouse little general controversy would stand a good chance of satisfaction if they were presented by the wealthy and well connected. In the face of limited institutional continuity and the weak articulation of the responsibilities of royal officials, it was hard to formulate major policy decisions and operate under their guidelines. Therefore, momentary political and personal decisions dominated government to the benefit of members of the territorial aristocracy who were in the best position to compromise the autonomy of Crown administration, for the grandees were often necessary to ensure the capacity of the Catholic Monarchs to achieve their goals. Until rulers were willing to support the relative autonomy of royal institutions, the judicial process, like other administrative processes, could only with difficulty achieve the capacity to render decisions corresponding to the written norms that Crown officials were supposed to uphold. As long as justice was vacillating and at the mercy of special interests, there could be no just rule. Yet the Catholic Monarchs first had to bring order out of the anarchy left by repeated civil wars.

The war they launched against Muslim Granada provided repeated opportunities for Ferdinand and Isabella to stimulate favorable interpretations of their rule by both territorial aristocrats and local notables. The former were provided with precisely the sorts of personal contact with monarchs and significant responsibilities that fed their concept of honor. Delegates to the Cortes had demonstrated throughout the fifteenth century that patricians were most willing to grant extraordinary revenues to the Crown for warfare on the southern front, and the emergence of the Santa Hermandad as the Crown's vehicle for mobilizing municipal militias and generating funds gave the monarchs a frequent forum in which to solicit the active cooperation of local notables in the cities and major towns.[17]

Sustaining Memory

Despite eloquent pleas, such as that of jurado Francisco Ortiz in 1480, for judicial redress, Toledo's patricians had to wait until the end of the Granada crusade. With the war finally over, the city council made a fresh attempt to begin consideration of the Belalcázar conflict. In Barcelona on 16 October 1493, regidor Martín Vázquez de Rojas appeared before the Council of Castile and its president don Alvaro de Portugal with a petition about Toledo's claims. He outlined the illegal seizure of the towns by Gutierre de Sotomayor, and then claimed that both John II and Henry IV had ordered the towns' restitution but had been unable to act. Toledo's loyalty to the Catholic Monarchs and the city's patience in not pressing for a hearing to avoid causing trouble for the Crown were duly stressed. However, Vázquez de Rojas concluded, in the interests of tranquility and justice and because Toledo was the chief city of the realm, the restoration of Puebla de Alcocer and the other places listed in the petition should be ordered in conformity with law, the testament of John II, and the executive order of Henry IV. Although the Council again ordered the case suspended, Vázquez de Rojas's presentation did elicit a more promising response than the earlier ones. On 2 November 1493, Ferdinand and Isabella sent a letter from Barcelona to Toledo in which they said the city could make a formal request on the matter of Puebla de Alcocer and Herrera when the monarchs returned to Castile. They would then order "that which we feel will be of service to us," a vague phrase indicating that circumstances would continue to dictate their actions.[18]

Some break in the suspension of the case had to occur because the Catholic Monarchs could not indefinitely put off Toledo's council without permanently harming its case, for judgments relating to regional jurisdiction and land tenure depended a great deal on the testimony of witnesses who were familiar with local conditions. Specially commissioned royal boundary judges were arranging the transfer of many rural towns and villages and small parcels of land on just this basis.[19] Finally, in 1495 and 1496 the Crown allowed hearings on seignorial rights over Puebla de Alcocer, Herrera, and the surrounding territory before Ldo. Bela Núñez, the specially commissioned investigating boundary judge for the Toledo region. To permit a better understanding of the exercise of royal authority, I show how this judicial process involved interaction among a number of municipalities, Crown institutions (the Council of Castile in this instance), and the Catholic Monarchs' roving Court.

Ferdinand and Isabella first allowed a 1495 hearing over Toledo's claim to territory seized beyond Gutierre de Sotomayor's grant in violation of the 1480 Law of Toledo: Villarta, El Hornillo, Helechosa, the bridge over the Guadiana River, and the surrounding pasture land. It is not really clear from their commission to Núñez whether or not, when they issued it in Madrid on 2 April 1495, the Catholic Monarchs were aware of the case Toledo's leaders wanted to present. However, the commission stated that the judge could restore everything Toledo claimed by right of purchase that had been taken in violation of the Law of Toledo. Apparently, Núñez was primarily to act on claims presented earlier by Toledo to two other investigating judges whose hearings had been blocked by the Crown at the request of the assembly of Toledo's cathedral canons.[20]

When the new commission was presented to him in Toledo's city hall on 25 May, Núñez agreed to hear the city's claims and appropriate testimony to substantiate them. At the end of June, city barrister Juan de Toledo accredited himself, although he waited until 8 August to present the claim against the count of Belalcázar. He charged that Toledo had lawful title to all the villages and other property named in the claim, that against the city's wishes the area had been unjustly and forcibly occupied in defiance of legislation enacted at the Cortes of Toledo, that the count and his grandmother María de Velasco, as his guardian, should be ordered to return the area, and that the judge was obliged to effect this restitution. Núñez answered that he would decide the case in accordance with the city's titles and the Law of Toledo.[21]

Núñez held a second and more important hearing in 1496, dealing with jurisdiction over the entire area. While they were in Tortosa on 29 February of that year, the Catholic Monarchs had sent a royal instruction to Núñez, ordering him to take depositions and to file them as a perpetual memorial about the lands Toledo claimed had been illegally taken from the city. There were to be no restrictions on the judge's authority to conduct the hearing, but the Toledan regidor who represented the city at Court, comendador Diego Ramírez de Lucena, wanted to make sure of this and requested that the monarchs be more specific about their intention that Núñez hear matters relating to territory in the possession of the count of Belalcázar. Lucena argued that this clarification was necessary because the judge was aware of the earlier suspensions of the case and any further delay in the matter would greatly harm the city. Ferdinand and Isabella obliged in a letter of 12 March to Toledo's council, in which they emphatically reiterated that evidence was to be taken *ad perpetuam rei memoriam* (that is, as a permanent record of the judicial proceedings) about the territory that the city claimed from the count.[22]

Because the minutes of their meetings have not survived, the excitement among city council members can only be suggested by their choice of a prominent regidor, Diego García de Cisneros, to organize the presentation of Toledo's case. The details of the legal proceedings that followed are important for several reasons. First, they involved one type of judicial institution, the specially commissioned boundary judge, which the Crown employed to resolve the disputes over jurisdictions and property that were at the root of so many conflicts during the fifteenth-century civil wars. Second, although the reader will be spared most of the names, a number of

Toledo's patricians, most of them regidores and jurados who sat on the municipal council, became involved in preparing documents and delivering them to various places and authorities. Moreover, these assigned duties emerged from the deliberations of the full council, as the surviving minutes of the councils of other cities, such as Murcia, make clear. In the process of pursuing the city's case against the House of Sotomayor, Toledo's leaders conceptualized their council's corporate rights and needs, and their repeated elaboration of the resulting interpretations made it more likely that these would be cued when the patricians and other city officials were caught up in some disruptive situation and needed to understand the world around them in order to formulate judgments as a basis for action. The conflict would continue for over seventy more years, providing a focus of political activity for Toledan patricians, and the perpetual memorial that Ldo. Núñez established of the events surrounding the transfer of Puebla de Alcocer's jurisdiction would serve as a constant reminder of city concerns about the proper exercise of absolute royal authority. Moreover, as the Cortes procuradores had demonstrated in 1447 when they included the Puebla de Alcocer issue in the kingdom's general petitions, the dispute was one in which patrician leaders of other cities and major towns were also interested.

After the Catholic Monarchs clarified their intentions, regidor García de Cisneros presented the necessary documents to Bela Núñez, who agreed to obey the royal order and receive evidence *ad perpetuam rei memoriam.* Instead of presenting a formal claim, on 26 April Cisneros submitted a statement of rights or arguments (*escrito de razones*) because the judge was really only given the authority to gather evidence and not to render a verdict. For this reason Cisneros made no request for restoration of the territory, but asked Núñez to take the testimony of certain old men, who knew the situation, as a perpetual memorial so that the city's rights would not be damaged by their death. The document listed among other places Puebla de Alcocer, Herrera, Talarrubias, Casas de Don Pedro, Peloche, Fuenlabrada, Villarta, Helechosa, Los Bodonales (now Bohonal), El Hornillo, Acijara,[23] the bridge over the Guadiana River at Villarta, and all the pasture and arable land around these places. Cisneros repeated assertions made in earlier city petitions, emphasizing Toledo's purchase of the territory with its own money and the seizure of the territory by Gutierre de Sotomayor, whose heir, the current count of Belalcázar, still controlled the contested area. Although Toledo had asked the various monarchs and their councils for justice many times in the past, justice had always been impeded, and Cisneros appealed to the judge to do what was proper in order to preserve Toledo's rights. Hearing of these earlier royal suspensions, Núñez demanded to see the relevant documents, and his notary entered transcriptions of these into the official record.[24] Apparently the judge found nothing in these documents that would interfere with his current commission.

As Toledo had done during Br. Piedrahita's earlier hearing in the late 1440s, the count of Belalcázar refused to recognize or participate in either of the hearings before Ldo. Bela Núñez, and they were held in his absence. In the 1495 hearing, in August, a Toledan jurado delivered to Belalcázar castle a summons for the count and his grandmother, as his guardian, to appear within thirty days with whatever titles and witnesses they had to defend their jurisdiction over the region claimed by the city. The summons was read to María de Velasco, the guardian, but the defendant failed to appear. Although in September and October, the city's barrister requested that the count and his grandmother be declared in default, Núñez took no action for reasons discussed below.[25]

In the 1496 hearing, on 27 April, count Alonso de Sotomayor and María de Velasco were summoned by Núñez to appear in the town of Siruela, near Puebla de Alcocer. The judge made it clear that if they or their procurador did not come, only Toledo's witnesses would be heard. This summons was delivered on 6 May at Belalcázar castle, where the messenger discovered that both the count and his grandmother were in the northern town of Simancas. Because he had no further instructions from Núñez, the messenger delivered the summons to the castle's warden, who disclaimed any responsibility to disclose his masters' whereabouts or send anyone to Siruela. When no representative of the House of Sotomayor answered the summons, Diego García de Cisneros requested that the count and his grandmother be declared in default. Because Cisneros introduced three witnesses to testify that Belalcázar was the principal residence of the count and his grandmother, thereby demonstrating that the summons had properly been delivered, Núñez declared he would proceed and begin hearing witnesses.[26]

In both hearings, Toledo presented witnesses to make the points necessary for a successful argument of its case: the nature of the city's prior ownership and control of the region, the manner in which the land had been taken (important because the 1480 laws on land exchange outlawed violent seizure), the unjust way Piedrahita's survey had been conducted, and Toledo's subsequent attempts to recover the area. As competent witnesses, the city introduced for the most part elders from rural settlements who were often illiterate but had a broad experience with the areas in question, both before and after Gutierre de Sotomayor's occupation. In general the witnesses seem to have been well chosen, their testimony spontaneous and knowledgeable. They were mostly residents of towns around the disputed area (for example, Siruela and Castilblanco). They readily pleaded ignorance when unable to answer a question, and in general, they confined their testimony to as narrow a focus as possible.

Núñez took testimony in response to a written list of questions. The list used in 1495 contained only eight questions for witnesses deposed in late August. The questions dealt with the witnesses' acquaintance with Toledo and its officials, their knowledge about the count of Belalcázar and the wardship that had been set up for him, and their familiarity with the territories claimed by Toledo. Then the witnesses were asked if they knew the city of Toledo had possessed the places at issue and used them as though it had lordship over them. A further question asked if the witnesses knew that the city maintained title and *vel quasi* possession (that is, maintained proprietorship although it was not in actual possession of the territory) to the region in question, if the land was in fact presently occupied against Toledo's will by the count and his grandmother, and if these had the authority to return the territory. The seventh question asked if witnesses had information about Toledo's attempts to obtain justice and if they knew that the passage of time had not prejudiced the city's claims. Finally, it was asked if all this information was in fact common knowledge and frequently discussed.[27]

On 16 May 1496, Toledo presented for the second hearing a considerably longer questionnaire, containing thirty-three questions. By virtue of a longer royal commission, Núñez had more time to take depositions, and he journeyed to municipalities on the edge of the disputed area so that there would be no problem about the elderly witnesses' ability to travel, as there had been in 1495 when they had often had to make a long and arduous journey to Toledo. He took depositions in May and June in Siruela, Castilblanco, and Horcajo, and then in Toledo. The 1496 interrogatory began much like that of 1495, but the witnesses were required to provide greater detail about their association with Toledo, about the count, his guardianship, and his genealogy, and about their familiarity with the disputed area. As before, they were asked about the city's prior and continuing jurisdiction. Detailed information on the actual occupation of the lands was to be given. Toledo's lawyers posed questions about the boundaries of Toledo's Montes, whether the disputed area lay within those boundaries, what the former and present income from the claimed lands was, and what rights of lordship had formerly been exercised by the city. One question asked about the origin and maintenance of the Villarta bridge over the Guadiana River. The witnesses were asked about the length of time the city had possessed the area and about the purchase of the land. Then a notary read to witnesses a copy of the thirteenth-century letter of sale from king Ferdinand III, and they were asked if the Montes corresponded to the limits outlined therein and if these limits contained the disputed area. To demonstrate the damage done to the city by the occupation, two questions dealt with the effect of the loss of revenues on public works in the city and the consequences of the loss of pasture land for the livestock industry.

At this point in the questionnaire, the lawyers included four technical questions (#22–#25) designed to deal with a troublesome point: the existence of boundary markers within the region. First, it was asked where those markers were and how in three separate occupations Gutierre de Sotomayor had moved well beyond them, even to the point of seizing lands that belonged to others besides Toledo. The questions mentioned that the markers divided an area, which was perhaps known as the viscounty, from the rest of the territory seized by Gutierre, but the line indicated would exclude Herrera, Fuenlabrada, and all of the area to the north. Second, it was asked if anyone had tampered with these internal markers. More importantly, Toledo asked if there was, in fact, any tradition of two lordships in the area as divided by these markers and if those towns beyond them had ever owed jurisdiction or services to those within (that is, to Puebla de Alcocer).

To clarify John II's true intent in the matter, the questionnaire requested information about the turbulence of the time and how the king was forced by the necessities of war to make many grants. The witnesses were asked if these troubles had made the city unable to defend itself when a boundary judge had come to set up the markers between the lands of Toledo and those of Gutierre de Sotomayor. A further question probed the relationship between that earlier judge and Gutierre and the fraudulent manner in which the investigation had been conducted to justify the occupation. The concluding questions bore on the theme of the unsettled conditions in the realm that had allegedly prevented the Crown from doing justice to the city's cause and, after justice had been done, from enforcing the verdict. The final question was whether all this information was, in fact, public knowledge.[28]

The resulting testimony gave firm support to Toledo's claims. Because the witnesses were afforded considerable latitude in their answers, these have a concreteness that makes them sound credible. Moreover, from the little stories many of the more talkative ones chose to tell, one obtains a real feeling for the tragic circumstances in which these rural residents had found themselves during the anarchic reigns of John II and Henry IV. The responses vividly portray the fear created by the invasion of the master of Alcántara and his warriors. Witnesses extensively discussed the unusual forced labor that Gutierre de Sotomayor had exacted, even from the citizens in Siruela, Valdecaballeros, Castilblanco, and Alía, for construction in Puebla de Alcocer, Herrera, Fuenlabrada, and faraway Belalcázar, although no question specifically requested such information. They recalled the livestock that was stolen from them and the tributes that were exacted by force by men such as Gutierre's overseer.

Although their narration was often vague, the witnesses conveyed their pain clearly enough. For instance, witness number eighteen in the 1495 hearing, an illiterate weaver named Pedro Martínez who lived in Arroba, recalled a confrontation between Gutierre de Sotomayor and Pascual Gómez, one of the residents of Villarta. The master of Alcántara had asked Gómez who was the better lord of the town, and Gómez said the city had been preferable. Although he had not been present at the incident, Martínez reported that there was a big argument in Arroba over whether the master had hanged the overly candid Gómez. He added, however, that those who said Sotomayor had not hanged Gómez also stressed that if the master had ordered an execution, everyone in Villarta would have been much too terrified to speak against him. Sotomayor had laughed at their helplessness.

Witnesses stressed Toledo's complete lordship over the entire territory and confirmed that the city had sent revenue collectors to all parts of it. Several witnesses irritatedly pointed out that some of their local autonomy had been taken away after Gutierre's occupation. The local judicial officials had all been changed, and criminal cases could not be heard by the local alcalde but had to be sent to Belalcázar. All the witnesses who felt they could answer the question confirmed that Toledo had had the free use of the disputed region's pasture lands, and they sometimes mentioned the herds of specific Toledan patricians and institutions.

Toledo obtained excellent testimony about the internal markers. Virtually all of the witnesses asserted that they had never heard anything about two separate lordships under the city, although there were several toll gates within the area. Some witnesses thought these might date from Gutierre de Sotomayor's time. Several witnesses said they had heard that the area had been a viscounty under a Bernaldín de Cabrera, but they all seemed unsure about when this was or how Toledo managed to get the territory back before its occupation by the master of Alcántara. Most of the witnesses, often those from Fuenlabrada or Herrera, indicated that they had only heard of this earlier viscount after the occupation and after Gutierre's claim that the jurisdiction should be a viscounty under the lordship of his heirs.[29]

Although these answers about the internal markers perhaps did not fully clarify the jurisdictional history of Puebla de Alcocer and its relation to the other towns and pastures, Toledo used them as the foundation for the witnesses' discussion of the ruthless way in which the troops of the order of Alcántara occupied whatever they chose. The occupation, according to the witnesses, proceeded in three steps and took at least a year. The first step was the taking of Puebla de Alcocer in September 1445 by the master of Alcántara and comendador Jorge of that order. Eight months later, when it was realized how weak the region's defenses were, the comendador of the nearby *encomienda* (jurisdiction of a military order) of Lares, Gonzalo de Raudona, who was Gutierre de Sotomayor's cousin,[30] had led his troops in the conquest of Herrera and Fuenlabrada. Finally, the comendador of Lares swept up the rest of Toledo's lands and kept right on going to seize those of the lord of Siruela, just north of the encomienda of Lares, and those of the town of Talavera, and thus of the jurisdiction of the archbishop of Toledo. One of the witnesses from Siruela, Martín Fernández, pointed out how unjust the taking of Siruela had been because its lord, Hernando de Velasco, had been a supporter of John II at the battle of Olmedo where Fernández had been one of his soldiers. Two residents of Arroba who were witnesses in

1495 claimed that Gutierre's forces went all the way to "La Retuerta" (now Retuerta de Bullaque) with the intention of taking all of that region. There Gutierre met with Alvaro de Luna, but they left because the land in that part of the Montes de Toledo seemed of low quality.

To compound this picture of ruthless, violent, and illegal conquest, the witnesses supplied details of the fraudulent way in which Br. Piedrahita had conducted his survey, and they freely offered their opinion, as "experts" on the region, that the survey had been a sheer fabrication. It seemed to be a generally known story that the testimony taken by Piedrahita was extracted by intimidation by the master of Alcántara and his proprietary alcalde in Herrera, Pedro Sánchez. The details varied slightly depending on whom the 1496 witnesses knew or had heard about. The alcalde, in Piedrahita's presence, would ask each witness if he knew that the boundaries of Puebla de Alcocer's jurisdiction went to that point. If the witness then answered that he knew they did not, or that he just did not know, or even if he hesitated, he was verbally abused by both Gutierre de Sotomayor and Sánchez with Gutierre finally saying that the boundary did go as far as that particular point and then asking if the witness had not heard about it from him. All the witnesses were afraid to contradict the powerful master of Alcántara and thus testified that they had indeed heard that the boundaries of Puebla de Alcocer ran to whatever point was then in question. This story, which was told by many of the 1496 witnesses, often relatives of those intimidated, made the city's case about the irregularity of the occupation a convincing one.

The fates of the two hearings of 1495–1496 were different. I cannot determine the importance of the earlier one in the later trials to determine jurisdiction over the village of El Hornillo, north of the Guadiana River, because neither the transcripts of the proceedings nor the arguments before the Council of Castile or the Chancillería of Granada have survived. It is possible that the hearing was never properly concluded. On 1 September 1495, a certain Luis de Chávez appeared before Núñez as barrister for María de Velasco, the count of Belalcázar's guardian. He informed Núñez that the judge had no jurisdiction over the dispute because his party had title to all of the territory in question and that the towns had been taken according to the procedures ratified in 1480 by the Law of Toledo. Therefore, because Núñez's commission was to adjudicate violations of the Law of Toledo, and, moreover, because the dispute had already been decided by a commissioned boundary judge, Br. Piedrahita (this had not been mentioned in the 1495 hearing), no further action could be taken at that level. The next day, Núñez responded that the monarchs had sent a message asking him to consult with them about these cases before ruling. They had acted on information supplied, significantly, by Council president don Alvaro de Portugal. Despite many protests from Toledo, the judge refused further action beyond providing an official transcript of the proceedings. Because of this indeterminate ending and because the 1495 claim was substantially different from the claim eventually made in the El Hornillo lawsuit, Toledo's lawyers may have found little use for this testimony, but it was later mentioned as part of the proceedings in the El Hornillo case when the final verdict was given in 1540.[31]

The 1496 hearing, however, played a major role in the dispute's development because it was one of the foundations of Toledo's evidence against which, with the passage of time, the counts of Belalcázar were never able to argue successfully. In 1497, the city, forgetting temporarily about the El Hornillo dispute, had its Court representative, regidor Martín Vázquez de Rojas, present a claim for all of the viscounty, accompanied by the 1496 evidence taken *ad perpetuam rei memoriam,* to the Royal Council as the first move toward opening a full-scale trial before that body. With the count and his barrister properly notified, seven members of the Council, with president don Alvaro de Portugal presiding, agreed on 15 March to provide justice and ordered a notary to transcribe for the count Toledo's petition, its claim, and the testimony taken by Bela Núñez. However, five days later, Ferdinand, acting without Isabella although in consultation with the Council, temporarily suspended any hearing on the dispute.

When he heard of this action, apparently without any formal notification, Vázquez de Rojas protested on 3 April. He made four points: the earlier permission for a hearing could not and should not be negated; it was against all human and divine law not to resolve the conflict justly; a further delay was prejudicial to the city's residents because of the large amount of revenue lost every year; and the denial of justice was a violation of royal custom. Vázquez de Rojas asked for a continuation of the trial or, barring that, some assurance that the suspension was not permanently prejudicial to Toledo's rights and that the 1496 transcript would remain a perpetual memorial. The Council agreed to certify all Vázquez de Rojas had presented, but felt obliged by the suspension order to issue no further statements, even after an additional request by Vázquez de Rojas a week later. It did formally assure him that nothing would be done to validate for the count the documents Toledo had to send to the Council for another case involving the count of Belalcázar and the Mesta, the royally chartered organization of stock owners. These parties were litigating over fees collected for sheep crossing the Villarta bridge, and the Council of Castile had forced Toledo to submit its old royal grants about the bridge so that the count could support his claims about customary practices. Toledo had been afraid that the Council would reissue the documents in the count's name, thereby jeopardizing the city's claim to the bridge.[32]

The Crown had assured itself that Toledo's rights could not be damaged by delay, the recovery of lost revenues being always possible. All further requests for a hearing were denied until almost the end of Isabella's reign when the city disputed its boundary with the viscounty before another boundary judge, Ldo. Zomeño. Toledo submitted valuable documentary evidence, but this hearing was also quickly suspended. The local notables were allowed to observe the Crown's sincere desire to act but also to see that its capacity for action was too circumscribed to permit the unfettered provision of royal justice. Because the assistance of patricians was the backbone of any increase in effective royal leadership, only continued patrician collaboration with the Catholic Monarchs could ever alleviate this situation, but the chances of local notables' support for the Crown would be greatly reduced if they suspected continued aristocratic manipulation of judicial administration.

Aristocratic Influence and the Suspension of Justice

Because Ferdinand and Isabella's authority was so compromised, they had to risk bringing their whole judicial reform program into disrepute through their handling of this and similar cases. When boundary judges throughout the kingdom were returning illegally seized jurisdictions to their rightful lords, the rulers could not provide Toledo, one of Castile's greatest cities, with even the chance to recover what its patrician councillors felt was municipal property. The Crown feared that it would seriously endanger its relationship to a large and important segment of its aristocratic support if it did not heed demands that no hearing be held. Although justice had been shoved down grandees' throats to the extent that they returned small towns and common lands they had seized, these exchanges never seemed substantially to threaten an individual's economic or political role. Toledo's dispute with the count of Belalcázar was another matter.

At this time the holdings of the counts of Belalcázar consisted of two parts. One was the viscounty of Puebla de Alcocer; the other was a slightly smaller territory containing the towns of Hinojosa (now "del Duque") and Belalcázar, the latter containing the counts' beautiful residence, which gives the town its name. Although its roof and interior are now gone, the tower and walls are still a splendid sight. The castle-palace is situated in a pleasant park on the town's northern edge.[33] It would have been a tremendous blow to lose the viscounty, but the situation was worse than that. Gutierre de Sotomayor had obtained Hinojosa and Belalcázar (then Gahete) from Córdoba under circumstances similar to those under which he had been granted Puebla de Alcocer. Although Córdoba may not have purchased Hinojosa and Gahete as Toledo had purchased its Montes, Córdoba's council had owned major areas of pasture and arable land in the territory. To allow a hearing on Toledo's claims would surely bring similar demands from Córdoba and put the House of Sotomayor's entire estate in jeopardy.

Yet the counts in this period were hardly the great warriors that the master of Alcántara and his son had been. Gutierre II de Sotomayor, grandson of the master of Alcántara and count when Br. Ortiz had requested a trial in 1480, had been an unproven young man who had received the title only because his older brother, perhaps in reaction to the lives of his father and grandfather, had chosen to become one of the fifteenth century's leading Castilian holy men, friar Juan de la Puebla.[34] Gutierre II had shown some martial interests but died in 1483 fighting in the Granada war. Alonso II de Sotomayor, the count in the 1490s, was an orphan and legal minor whose affairs were ultimately in the hands of the Crown. Surely this weak dynasty was in no position to influence Ferdinand and Isabella.

Its relatives were, however. Gutierre II had married Teresa de Enríquez, daughter of the almirante ("admiral") of Castile, Alonso Enríquez (d. 1485). Until her death in the fall of 1489, Teresa served as administrator of the estates of her young son and efficiently sent military units to aid the Catholic Monarchs in the conquest of Granada. Her mother was a Velasco, sister of the kingdom's former condestable, Pedro Fernández de Velasco (d. 1492), and aunt of the current one, Bernardino (died 1512), who was married to an illegitimate daughter of king Ferdinand. The almirante and condestable were two of the most important aristocrats in Castile, and on their support hung the fate of the reign during its early years. The Catholic Monarchs had such faith in the condestables, father and son, that these magnates were given full authority as viceroys when the rulers were attending to business in Aragón or were with the army on the Granada frontier. Indeed, Toledo's council may have timed the presentation of its petitions of 1490 (in Seville) and 1493 (in Barcelona) to coincide with Ferdinand and Isabella's separation from their condestable-viceroys and the majority of members of the Council of Castile. Gutierre II de Sotomayor's son Alonso, with his Enríquez blood, was a first cousin once removed of king Ferdinand, whose mother was Teresa de Enríquez's aunt. Alonso's Velasco grandmother was his guardian. This grandmother, María de Velasco, and her son the almirante Fadrique had been given the special honor in April 1497 of serving as godparents of the newly married prince Juan and his wife. The event took place only one month before king Ferdinand refused to allow the Royal Council to hear Toledo's lawsuit on the basis of the evidence gathered by Bela Núñez. Close connections also existed with the family of Alonso's grandmother, Elvira de Zúñiga, because Fadrique de Zúñiga, Elvira's brother, was the boy's guardian until his death in June 1491.[35] This assemblage of grandees was not going to allow one of their helpless relatives to be despoiled of his entire inheritance, and the Catholic Monarchs could not ignore their demands, for they depended on the goodwill of this group.

In addition, in 1497 Alonso de Sotomayor was probably already betrothed to his future wife, Isabel de Castro, the great-great-granddaughter of John I of Portugal. This betrothal came at the time when one of John's great-grandchildren, king Manuel I, married princess Isabella of Castile and Aragón. The child of this latter union, born in 1498, was expected to unite the entire peninsula but died two years later. Alonso's father-in-law was don Alvaro de Portugal (d. 1503), president of the Council of Castile and, after the monarchs themselves, perhaps the most influential figure in the governance of the realm, and this connection was more important than royal dynastic and diplomatic maneuvers.[36] Alvaro, lord of Tentugal, had been Portuguese chancellor under kings Alfonso V (d. 1481) and John II (d. 1495) of Portugal. As the youngest of the brothers of Fernando de Portugal, third duke of Bragança, Alvaro was deeply implicated in the aristocratic plot to depose king John II with the support of the Catholic Monarchs. The latter were concerned about the intentions toward them of an able, dynamic ruler leading a kingdom against which they had had to fight to secure the Castilian crown for Isabella against the claims of her niece. When the duke of Bragança, brother-in-law of the king's wife, was arrested, tried, and executed in 1483, Alvaro was banished from court and made a prudent escape to Castile. He served as a messenger who connected the Catholic Monarchs to yet another plot led by king John's young first cousin and brother-in-law, Diogo de Portugal, duke of Viseu, who planned to murder the king but lost his life at the king's own hand in the summer of 1484. Needless to say, in the course of these turbulent events, Alvaro de Portugal lost all his estates, but apparently it was not his extraordinary sacrifices in the interest of the Catholic Monarchs nor the fact that he was Isabella's second cousin that secured Alvaro's administrative influence in Castile. His older brother, the marquis of Montemor, had done the same but received no significant Castilian post because the rulers found his judgment to be untrustworthy. They placed Alvaro on the Royal Council, and he rose to become its president both because his background and circumstances made him a fairly reliable aristocratic servant of the Crown and because his administrative ability was valued.

Nonetheless, he was fully capable of using his exalted position to advance his own interests. In his chronicle of the reign, Alvaro's fellow royal counselor, Dr. Lorenzo Galíndez de Carvajal, told how when Alvaro was president of the Council, he attempted to use his position to gain his revenge against the royal governor of Asturias for a wound received years before in a fight, an abuse of his office that forced the monarchs to intervene and reprimand him. Alvaro's value to the regime climbed when, on the death of John II of Portugal in 1495 without a legitimate heir, his young brother-in-law and first cousin Manuel, younger brother of the murdered duke of Viseu, ascended the Portuguese throne and married princess Isabella of Castile, whose mother, queen Isabella, was Manuel's first cousin. Although Manuel restored much of the holdings of his surviving Bragança relatives (of the four sons of the second duke of Bragança, only Alvaro was still alive), Alvaro elected to remain in Castile in Ferdinand and Isabella's service, providing a valuable link to the affairs of their western neighbor. He solidified his Portuguese link by marrying another of his daughters to Jorge de Portugal, illegitimate son of John II and master since 1492 of the Portuguese military orders of Aviz and Santiago. In these circumstances, it is not surprising that only five days after Toledo sought in 1497, on the basis of the testimony gathered by Bela Núñez, to carry its lawsuit to the Council of Castile, with Alvaro de Portugal presiding, king Ferdinand suspended deliberation on the matter.[37]

Toledo's patrician council would have to understand the delicate state of the monarchs' affairs and wait patiently. Two problems caused royal vacillation. The Crown was still quite dependent on the goodwill of its major vassals. At the same time, the network of royal officials was too inadequately developed to permit the formulation and consistent observance of policies, and there was no royal archive where the records of earlier grants, orders, decrees, and letters could be stored for consultation. Although monarchs were accustomed to reacting to their officials' reports and their subjects' petitions rather than to taking the initiative, the lack of adequate institutional memory increased the possibilities for political influence by the economically and politically prominent.

The printing of legal codes and the ordinances of royal institutions established widely available standards for evaluating the quality of royal justice that had been unknown in earlier reigns. Therefore, when monarchs and regents acted in violation of laws and procedures in virtue of a claimed autonomous, absolute royal authority, as they frequently did in the period after Isabella's death in 1504, "corruption" among the royal officials directly responsible for providing justice would drain support from the Crown and build up support for territorial aristocrats whose activities would make royal government incapable of effective action. Such "autonomy" did not enhance royal capacity but undermined it.

Leagues, Clients, and the Trastámara Twilight

The local notables' confidence in the monarchy dropped upon Isabella's death on 26 November 1504.[38] In her will the queen had acknowledged the problems the territorial aristocracy had caused in her efforts to be a just ruler. She expressed dissatisfaction both with the way grants had been distributed to magnates and with the failure to extend judicial reforms far enough. The events of the next few years were to show the continuing importance of the great titled nobles. Eventually, local notables would become so frustrated with what they viewed as the increasingly arbitrary and corrupt nature of royal administration that the Crown would face a widespread Castilian rebellion.[39] Because even the Catholic Monarchs had to struggle to establish a capable government and win elite support, it is not surprising that after queen Isabella's death, the resulting dynastic problems hamstrung royal administration at Court and in institutions elsewhere.

Because a high valuation of just rule informed local notables' view of and support for the Crown, the ways in which the royal judicial administration handled major conflicts played a fundamental role in stimulating the growing patrician hostility that eventually occasioned revolt. A weak, divided Crown government resulted in inefficient, inconsistent, and sometimes corrupt behavior by the royal officials most responsible for dispensing justice. Isabella's daughter, Joanna, inherited Castile, which she would rule with her husband, archduke Philip of Habsburg. The arrangement, however, left Ferdinand, who had been joint ruler of the kingdom for thirty years, excluded from its government. He lost the title of king of Castile and received in his wife's will permission only to act as an administrator until his daughter should come to the kingdom. At the time, Ferdinand acutely felt the need for Castilian military might to pursue his foreign policy in the Mediterranean. Because reports about Joanna's emotional instability had heightened the concern of local notables about the effectiveness of royal administration, Ferdinand received firm backing from the patricians' representatives at the Cortes of Toro in 1505 to continue as Castile's governor, and procedural rules elaborated at that assembly, known as the Laws of Toro, clarified and enhanced the Crown's judicial authority. Philip had policy ideas of his own, however, and they did not include allowing his father-in-law to govern Castile. To bolster himself against Ferdinand, Philip began to assemble an aristocratic party, which included the Zúñiga duke of Béjar, whose lands and title would shortly pass to the count of Belalcázar. The grandees still felt that they were automatically entitled to influence and were quite willing to step into an active political role. However, as Philip did not understand Castilian well, he relied heavily on a favorite, don Juan Manuel, on whom he began to lavish grants, and the elevation of this special confidant produced discontent among the territorial aristocracy much like that during the reign of Henry IV.[40] In this atmosphere, rival political cliques, held together by the patronage and influence of the magnates, began to coalesce.

As part of this move toward firming up political connections, Alonso de Sotomayor, count of Belalcázar, formed a league for mutual aid with Pedro de Puertocarrero (sometimes given as Portocarrero), lord of Moguer and Villanueva de Fresno, on 2 March 1506. The pact was not valid for action against the monarch, and each party listed friends: among those of the count were the Enríquez almirante, the Zúñiga duke of Béjar, and the count of Cabra, Francisco Fernández de Córdoba, nephew of the age's most renowned military leader, the "Great Captain"; among those of Portocarrero were the marquis of Villena, the count of Benavente, and the marquis of Priego. The agreement spoke specifically about possible action by the city of Córdoba against the count of Belalcázar because the marquis of Priego was one of its councillors and its alcalde mayor.[41]

Philip's death on 25 September 1506, just five months after his arrival in Castile, and Joanna's growing instability allowed Ferdinand, after a short but crowded period of administrative uncertainty, to reassume his position in Castile as his daughter's regent in 1508. He finally took the official oath as regent at the Cortes of Madrid in October 1510.

The changing personnel of the Council of Castile reflected the administrative disorder suggested by these leadership shifts. When Philip of Habsburg came to Castile, he dropped three of Ferdinand's close collaborators: Dr. Martín Fernández de Angulo (d. 1516), Ldo. Francisco de Vargas (d. 1524), and Ldo. Luis de Zapata (d. 1522). The Council was not entirely stripped of those in whom Ferdinand had shown confidence, because Dr. Juan López de Palacios Rubios (d. 1524) and Ldo. Luis González de Polanco (d. 1542) retained their posts. Philip left in place another prominent existing councillor, Dr. Lorenzo Galíndez de Carvajal (d. 1527), probably because of his ability and as an acknowledgment that archbishop Cisneros needed some influence. However, Philip flooded the Council with new faces: Ldo. Fortún Ibáñez de Aguirre (d. 1547), Dr. don Pedro López de Ayala (d. 1513), who was dean and canon of the cathedral of Toledo, don Alonso de Castilla (d. 1541), Ldo. Miguel Guerrero, Ldo. Francisco de Sosa (d. 1508), and don Alonso Suárez Valtodano as president. After Philip's death, Cisneros expelled all of these from the Council, presumably with Ferdinand's knowledge, although Aguirre and Sosa were brought back within two years. Ayala had been Ferdinand's choice in the 1490s as ambassador to Scotland, but as he appeared to have jumped to Philip's service, Cisneros and Ferdinand apparently chose to dispense with his services. Instead, another Toledan and close supporter of Ferdinand, don Juan de Silva (d. 1512), third count of Cifuentes, was made president of the Council. Don Garcilaso de la Vega (d. 1512), father of both the poet and the comunero leader don Pedro Laso de la Vega, was another who had been close to Ferdinand but then switched his loyalty to Philip, and although not expelled from the Council on Philip's death, don Garcilaso remained out of favor. Don Alonso de Castilla was returned to a Council seat when Philip's son Charles became co-ruler with his mother.[42]

Because so much depended on the personal characteristics of rulers, regencies have always been difficult times for monarchies, and the period after Isabella's death offered territorial aristocrats both an opportunity to increase their lordships and influence and a threat of personal damage to any magnate who did not participate in the resulting struggle. In this situation Ferdinand had to rely on the manipulation of noble cliques to achieve his ends. To control municipal resources or convert urban lands into individual seignioral jurisdictions, grandee factions tried to extend their authority into the administration of important cities, thereby often dividing local patricians to the point of violence. For example, the duke of Béjar sought to recuperate a greater political role for the Zúñiga family in Avila, and Plasencia's population feared that the Zúñiga would recover the lordship over the city that the family had lost under the Catholic Monarchs.[43]

The factions in Toledo have often been taken as illustrations of the new trend because factional struggles there loomed large in the sixteenth-century chronicles of Alonso de Santa Cruz and Pedro de Alcocer.[44] Although the relationship between the rhetoric of friction between patrician bands and the reality of urban life in Castile can be overrated, the dangers of armed conflict were real in periods when royal authority was weak. Given the broad authority of municipal government under both local ordinances and royal legislation, patrician families had to possess the major city offices to defend their interests. Fourteenth- and fifteenth-century monarchs had guaranteed city council positions to the most important local notables, in large part to mitigate fighting for municipal leadership. Patrician dependence on the Crown for the maintenance of the domination of perpetual regidores and for the reduction of violence among locally prominent families provided a useful source of royal influence in the government of major municipalities.

One complicating factor in Toledo was that several of the early sixteenth-century regidores had clearly entered the territorial aristocracy. The most prominent of these were don Juan de Silva, the count of Cifuentes, and don Pedro López de Ayala, the count of Fuensalida. Because urban resources could be important in any aristocratic struggle such as that which emerged after queen Isabella's death, these nobles attempted to revitalize the factional ties of the previous generation within the Toledan patriciate to increase their influence. The open fighting produced by this aristocratic intervention established an important context for the major Comunidades rebellion, discussed in chapter 4, because many patricians would be forced to decide, when faced with the threatening atmosphere in 1520 surrounding Charles's departure and the creation of a poorly supported regency government, whether their long-term interests were better served by their administrative role in a city that continued to exercise jurisdiction over significant resources or by maintaining ties to territorial aristocrats with obvious desires to add further municipal lands to their seignorial jurisdictions.[45] The counts of Cifuentes and Fuensalida quickly supported the regency administration and remained untouched by any temptation to rebel. Those patricians who chose to strengthen their role as city leaders would have to recognize that to some degree they would have to lead in the interest of the community or face a dangerous level of popular hostility. Although a great deal remains to be discovered about the interests behind personal conflicts and shifting alliances, patricians were clearly not all divided into solidified, personalist bands, and confrontations between kinship-based cliques were not all that divided them. Even though the Comunidades followed a period of intense factional struggle, many Toledan patricians maintained solidarity based on principles enunciated in rebel discourse despite severe divisions based on particular interests. Whatever the Comunidades was, it was not a continuation of the conflicts between existing urban, lineage-based cliques.[46] Elite fear of the consequences of these municipal struggles were a source both of potential support for the Crown as a mediator and of potential frustration that could lead to rebellion if the royal government appeared unable to dampen patrician divisions and maintain patrician families' dominance. As even the clashes in the period after Isabella's death showed, patrician leaders were smart enough to see that their freedom of action could be enhanced through their mutual solution of local conflicts without the intervention of the monarchy.

To secure Toledo for the aristocratic band of Philip of Habsburg in an effort to exclude Ferdinand of Aragón from any role in Castilian affairs, the second marquis of Villena, don Diego López Pacheco (1443–1529), had attempted to impose a new *corregidor* (royal high commissioner) in place of don Pedro de Castilla who had served since 1491. Taking advantage of the confusion over the corregidor's authority in the aftermath of king Philip's death on 25 September 1506, the leader of Toledo's important Ayala family, don Pedro López de Ayala, third count of Fuensalida, tried to reassert his direct control over the city's fortress. Although don Pedro de Ayala maintained the right to be called Toledo's chief constable (*alguacil mayor*), his grandfather had been forced in the late 1470s to surrender the fortress to queen Isabella's corregidor. Another Toledo figure much honored by the Catholic Monarchs, don Juan de Silva, third count of Cifuentes, had remained loyal to Ferdinand, and in the fighting to repel Fuensalida's armed attack on Castilla's house, Cifuentes's followers had become involved. Don Juan would shortly become Ferdinand's president of the Council of Castile, a post he would hold until his death in 1512.[47]

A potential Ayala-Silva conflict frightened Toledo's patricians because it carried with it the possibility of municipal disorders like those in the reigns of John II and Henry IV and possible revolutionary movements against patrician domination of city government. Such divisions tended to promote popular cognitive development leading commoners to think independently and question deference and obedience to established authorities.[48] As was often the case, the factionalism of 1506 internally split major patrician families, on this occasion the Carrillo, Guzmán, and Suárez lineages, who could then serve as bridges to arrange a settlement. Actually, the counts of Cifuentes and Fuensalida were themselves closely related.[49] On 12 December 1506, Vasco Suárez, on behalf of the Ayala faction, and the regidor Juan Carrillo, on behalf of Silva's group, served as go-betweens to accept mutual oaths in a concord arranged under the auspices of the cathedral canons and the city's council (some of the jurados were deeply involved in the settlement process).

Vasco Suárez also received the oath of don Pedro de Castilla who was a party to the concord, but for some reason the marquis of Villena was not included. The agreement explicitly stated that the parties wanted to avoid any situation in which the death of some principal factional chief would lead to the sorts of long-standing hatreds that divided the patricians of other cities. In language much like that of the earlier agreements of hermandades, all swore to unite in the capture and punishment of anyone who disturbed the peace by forming armed groups and creating public scandals. All the individual oaths and signatures had been obtained by the following day, and the settlement was officially proclaimed by municipal criers at all major points of public congregation. Unfortunately, spirits were sufficiently elevated that more fights followed despite a further agreement between the counts and their followers on 2 January 1507, and this time, among the wounded were several principal gentlemen. To prevent such clashes from getting worse, the counts agreed on 5 January to leave Toledo with their immediate followers for two months, and when some of the populace appeared nervous about the return of these nobles, the two swore to a peace pact arranged by the duke of Infantado on the following 28 February.[50]

Apparently in the long run, the pact did little to calm the fears of those anxious to maintain communal stability. Some time after the death of don Juan de Silva in 1512, the majority of Toledo's regidores petitioned the regency government to exclude the two counts (don Fernando de Silva was now the count of Cifuentes) from the city council. In an undated order, Ferdinand rejected the council's action and ordered that body to allow the counts to assume their seats. Some time after Ferdinand's death in 1516, cardinal-archbishop Cisneros as regent also refused a request from Toledo's regidores to exclude the two counts, and he even ordered the corregidor to favor the count of Fuensalida, a close relative of Cisneros's vicar general and personal representative in Brussels. Apparently, the divisiveness threatened by the counts' leadership produced greater cohesiveness among many of Toledo's patrician families, and growing opposition to the influence within Toledo of the marquis of Villena further advanced this movement toward cohesion.[51]

Despite a dispute over the *corregimiento* (the institution of a corregidor and his assistants) of Jerez de la Frontera involving the same families, Toledo's patricians maintained sufficient cohesion to present a solid front to the royal government during the months leading up to the comunero rebellion, and families from both the Ayala and the Silva supporters were represented both among comunero leaders and within the royalist camp.[52] Indeed, even serious disputes among regidores, which emerged from the conflicts of 1506 and later, could be buried to promote the perceived interests of the urban corporation, on the prerogatives of which patricians so depended for the advancement and defense of their roles within Castile's social environment. Motivated by the open fighting of the period, regidor Juan Gaitán, whose brother regidor Gonzalo Gaitán signed the 1506 concord among the Silva group, completed a fortified house in the *heredamiento* (landed estate) of Buzarabajo, within Toledo's jurisdiction. Regidor *mariscal* (marshal) Hernán Díaz de Rivadeneira and don Pedro de Ayala, both of whom signed the 1506 concord on the Ayala side, denounced this construction to the Royal Council as dangerous, and the dispute dragged on until 1516. However, both Ayala and Gaitán were major comunero leaders, and Juan Gaitán's brother Gonzalo served with Ayala as Toledo's delegates to the rebel Junta.[53]

In contrast, Córdoba's patrician cliques with ties to territorial aristocrats did not join the rebellion, in part because they were far too divided to be willing or able to act decisively. Murcia's patricians were not politically mature enough to inspire confidence in cohesive administration and lost all leadership of their rebellious city. Perhaps the varying experiences of major municipalities during the factional conflicts of Henry IV's reign help explain the fates of their respective patrician administrations during the comunero rebellion.[54]

The striking, long-time feature of Toledo's government was not factional discord but rather the slow and wavering development of a stable oligarchy through intermarriage and conscious attempts to avoid fighting. This tendency underlay the various pacts between December 1506 and February 1507, which were designed to prevent patrician divisions in the face of disputes with a corregidor whose local authority must have been undermined by the unstable Crown administration. Perhaps, as the 12–13 December pact suggested, the possibility for conciliation among the patricians existed because no important person had been killed in the various altercations. The relative solidarity accounts for the city council's ability to formulate and carry out consistent policy, but its officials must have known, on the basis of the experiences of fifteenth-century Castilians, that such recent cohesion was too fragile to survive a prolonged period of poorly supported royal government. The frequent cooperation by members of families with a long record of mutual hostility suggests that political principles, as opposed to personal aspirations, may have played an important role that could be obscured if we were to concentrate on family alignments as the chief cause of local conflict.[55] The frequency of Cortes sessions between 1497 and 1516 also indicates an attempt by Crown authorities to attract general, as opposed to factional, collaboration on the basis of principle.

The Frustrating Search for Justice

During the time between Isabella's death in 1504 and the beginning of the Comunidades rebellion in 1520, Toledo petitioned for a hearing on the disputed title to lands held by the count of Belalcázar, but the city received only excuses and postponements. Isabella's illness and death immediately affected the progress of Toledo's dispute with the count, because another hearing had been granted. In October 1503, the Catholic Monarchs sent another boundary judge, Ldo. Zomeño, to Toledo. He was supposed to clear up all of the matters relating to territorial jurisdiction left unfinished by the earlier judges, including Ldo. Bela Núñez. This order appears to have emerged as part of the same interest in legal matters that led to the unusual clauses in Isabella's will and to the commission given at the Cortes of Toledo in 1502 for a further elaboration of Castilian law, which eventually became the *Leyes de Toro* of 1505 in which the supremacy of royal law and judicial administration was established.[56]

The Crown monitored Toledo's initial claims with care. In January 1504, the city presented a demand for the pasture lands called Estena and Ríos Fríos. Because the count of Belalcázar complained to the Catholic Monarchs that he had a royal grant for the territory, they ordered Zomeño in February to send them a report about the case without holding further hearings. Toledo accompanied the report with a deputation sent to inform the Crown that the city council was asking only for what had been violently taken beyond the limits of the Puebla de Alcocer grant. After hearing these assurances, Ferdinand and Isabella in April permitted Zomeño to hear the Estena-Ríos Fríos case. City representatives again presented their initial arguments, and this time Luis de Chávez represented the count. On 4 May, however, the Council of Castile suddenly reversed the royal permission and ordered the case and a further report about it sent to that body. Apparently, the hearing was supposed to continue without a verdict being given, because jurado Pedro de Ortega, later comunero Cortes procurador and financial administrator, presented Toledo's evidence on 31 May. As part of the hearing, Br. Piedrahita's survey was placed in evidence by Chávez, and the Catholic Monarchs wrote to Zomeño again on 15 July to say that if the count of Belalcázar presented a survey, the judge should use it to arrange Toledo's boundaries. The ultimate resolution of the Estena-Ríos Fríos case remains a mystery.[57]

The failure to get a decision in the Estena-Ríos Fríos case may have discouraged but did not stop Toledo. By virtue of the 15 July letter, the city presented, on 10 January 1505, a demand for the return of El Hornillo and its lands. This was directed not only against the count but also against the officials and residents of Villarta, Helechosa, Los Bodonales, and El Hornillo. Although the claim mentioned that all of the Puebla de Alcocer region had been seized from Toledo, it specifically said that more than the territory in John II's grant was taken, including Herrera, Fuenlabrada, Helechosa, Villarta, and the pasture lands of Cijara and Estena. Piedrahita's survey was impugned, in part by explaining how he had included within the boundaries of Puebla de Alcocer important towns that were actually under the jurisdiction of Talavera. But El Hornillo, the claim stated, was outside even this fraudulent survey. On these grounds, Toledo requested the restoration of this property in accordance with the law.

The other parties were notified, and the count of Belalcázar petitioned Zomeño to stop the hearing on the grounds that he was exceeding his jurisdiction in a case involving Puebla de Alcocer and Herrera, that he needed a commission specifically to hear the El Hornillo case, that King John II had given a grant for the entire area, and that the commission Zomeño did have was issued when Toledo warped the truth and after the Chancillería of Ciudad Real had declined to hear the case because no survey had been presented. Even if Piedrahita's decision had been presented, it had not been done in such a way as to allow Zomeño to decide the case under his commission. Besides, the petition also emphasized, the lands had been held by the House of Sotomayor for a long time. All the points of Toledo's claim were then refuted, and Zomeño was asked to declare the case beyond his commission.

Toledo replied that all of these points were untrue. For the first time, Toledo offered an explanation of the idea that the region was a viscounty. In the reign of the fourteenth-century king Alfonso XI, a certain don Bernaldín, viscount of Cabrera, had arranged an exchange of towns with the king, involving Puebla de Alcocer, Herrera, and Casas de Don Pedro. After some confusion, Toledo got the settlements back, but even though their temporary lord had been a viscount, the area had never been made a viscounty. An investigation of Piedrahita's survey presented no problem because it had been properly submitted in evidence before Zomeño in the Estena-Ríos Fríos case, which was perhaps initiated only to obtain a transcription of this crucial document. In addition to the count's grant and the survey, Toledo also provided, in February 1505, Ferdinand III's letter of sale for the Montes, Henry IV's revocation of the Puebla de Alcocer grant, and the 1495 testimony taken by Bela Núñez. Although Toledo secured, presumably from the Council of Castile, an extension of the judge's commission, the count's barrister delivered to Zomeño a letter of 28 February from Ferdinand, acting alone after Isabella's death the previous November. Without saying from whom, Ferdinand said he had heard about the case and wanted it concluded without a ruling and sent to the Royal Council where a final determination would be made.[58]

This interlude, which allowed Toledo to get so much profitable evidence on the record, was due to the death in Segovia in September 1503 of Alvaro de Portugal, the count of Belalcázar's father-in-law, whose influence at Court had caused so many problems for Toledo's attempts to obtain a judicial review by Ldo. Bela Núñez of its claims in the Puebla de Alcocer area. Don Alvaro may have been president of the Royal Council only until 1499, but the Catholic Monarchs allowed him to protect his son-in-law.[59] In the confusion after Isabella's death, Ferdinand did not feel he could alienate the count

of Belalcázar as an ally and close relative of the Enríquez and Zúñiga families by allowing Zomeño's hearing to continue.

Now that Toledo had all the important evidence on record, its council
showed a new determination to get some kind of restitution. On 28 November 1509, the corregidor promulgated a municipal ordinance, which after
summarizing Toledo's case, stated that this great city had a responsibility to
those who had suffered as a result of the injustice done them throughout the
course of the dispute. It was decreed that on 1 March, at the beginning of
every business year, the city council would make the case its first order of
business, to see that Toledo's interests were properly pursued. One assumes
that the *procurador síndico,* as the official who oversaw Toledo's legal affairs,
presented an annual report on his efforts to seek redress through royal justice and that there was then an expression of regidor opinions on the
proper course to pursue. The jurados perhaps took the opportunity for a
related discussion in their own meeting. Unfortunately, the minutes of these
sessions have not survived. In any event, this extraordinary ordinance,
which was observed for decades, dramatically indicates how important the
dispute was to Toledo's council and therefore how consequential the
Crown's handling of the matter would be in shaping patrician political attitudes and actions. Córdoba's council established a similar annual observance, which was maintained at least into the late seventeenth century. And
given the influence of Toledo's leadership with the governing councils of
other important Castilian cities and towns, royal vacillation and arbitrari-
ness in the handling of the Belalcázar conflict likely cost the monarch significant support among local notables.[60]

As part of this program, regidores Martín Vázquez de Rojas and treasurer
Alonso Gutiérrez de Madrid with jurado Br. Alonso Ortiz went to Granada
with Toledo's power of attorney to obtain the services of Alonso Alvarez de
Villareal, who was accredited by the audiencia as a barrister (*procurador de
causas*). In their name, Villareal presented an order from the Catholic Monarchs given in Medina del Campo on 15 July 1504, the same day that the
city received the order for Zomeño to use Piedrahita's survey if it were submitted to his court. The monarchs told the oidores to hear pleas from Toledo
about its lands held by the count of Belalcázar beyond the grant made to
Gutierre de Sotomayor. Although Piedrahita's verdict was mentioned, the
audiencia was to render judgment on the basis of the grant itself. Perhaps the
Royal Council's termination of Zomeño's hearing of the El Hornillo lawsuit
made Toledo's leaders reluctant to present the Chancillería with a royal
order during the period of uncertainty after Isabella's death. However, once
it decided to act, unshackled by the royal order's broad language, on 21
May 1511, the city presented a claim to all the territory from the boundaries
of Puebla de Alcocer to the lands of Toledo, including Herrera and Fuenlabrada. The count received a formal summons in Belalcázar on 6 June, and

when he failed to send a representative by 25 June, Toledo asked that he be declared in default so that the trial could continue. Apparently, the audiencia responded that Ferdinand had ordered the court not to proceed. Although Toledo protested on the ground that it had not received such an order, the court reaffirmed on 11 July that until king Ferdinand as regent specifically ordered a trial, it could not hear the case.[61]

The city of Córdoba fared no better in its attempts to get a hearing on lands taken by Gutierre de Sotomayor, because the Chancillería justices received the same sort of conflicting instructions. In Medina del Campo, on 30 September 1504, Ferdinand issued a letter to the Chancillería (still in Ciudad Real) to hear the city's plea about lands held by the count of Belalcázar outside of the master of Alcántara's original grants, despite any earlier suspensions of such hearings issued by him or by the queen. After returning to assume the administration of Castile for his daughter, Ferdinand on 5 July 1508 notified the court that the count of Belalcázar had informed him that Córdoba was attacking an old survey in order to take some pasture land. The king asked the court to see if this land was located inside or outside the boundaries of the survey and to ascertain the document's date. A memorandum containing all this information was then to be sent to him, without a judgment.

In January 1511, Córdoba's barrister, the same Alonso Alvarez de Villareal who represented Toledo, presented to the Chancillería a letter of the previous October from Ferdinand. Córdoba had told him it had many cases before the audiencia involving the count of Belalcázar and also other parties. Because Córdoba claimed that the court was delaying on the ground that the oidores had to decide older cases first, Ferdinand was asked to order Córdoba's case to be heard despite the court's ordinances. Ferdinand commanded that within thirty days the Chancillería send him a report on all the cases that Córdoba had pending, so that he could make a decision. Because this same barrister was employed by Toledo for its Belalcázar case, there was obviously some coordination by the two great cities of their similar judicial business, and this pattern of collaboration would continue in later decades, showing how institutions could serve as points of interaction among groups of local notables.

Despite such coordinated pressure, the idea of a hearing on Córdoba's claims did not advance very far. At the request of the count of Belalcázar, in January 1515, Ferdinand again wrote to the Chancillería of Granada about the pasture land Córdoba claimed. Although it does not appear that the court had submitted the memorandum ordered in 1508, Ferdinand had decided without a hearing that the lands were inside the boundaries of Piedrahita's survey, ordered Córdoba to perpetual silence in the matter, and told the court to send him the case's transcript.[62]

For almost two decades after the death of queen Isabella in 1504, Castile lacked a ruler with the authority and leadership characteristics necessary for effective, stable monarchical government, and the commonwealth's leaders were increasingly divided into hostile bands. The result was a deterioration of the Crown's administrative capacity, growing disorder, and ultimately a great rebellion that provided an opportunity for some to challenge elite control of a disproportionate share of the kingdom's resources. Out of the turbulence of the Comunidades rebellion, an opportunity emerged for the city of Toledo at last to receive a full judicial hearing of its claims to the so-called viscounty of Puebla de Alcocer.

Chapter 4

REBELLION AGAINST CROWN ADMINISTRATION AS A DEFENSE OF ABSOLUTE ROYAL AUTHORITY

Introduction

This chapter argues that the Comunidades, the great uprising of 1520–1521, involved an attempt to establish, through the familiar use of rebellion to force negotiation, a monarchy whose exercise of "absolute royal authority" would sustain good government and justice. Historians have justifiably given more attention to the Comunidades rebellion than to any other violent confrontation in Castilian history prior to the Napoleonic wars of the early nineteenth century. I stress the rebellion's importance because the conflict and its development reveal the nature of this monarchy as a regime in which the character and ability of the sovereign were crucial elements in the effectiveness of the Crown administration and in the degree of support that the royal government enjoyed among the commonwealth's leaders. The early rebel leaders were motivated by the Crown's failure to deliver the benefits of a monarchy that combined in its ruler the roles of supreme legislator, executive, and judge, rather than by a desire to replace it with another form of government. Because it is crucial for an understanding of this type of government, I also want to underline the major limitations on local notables' use of rebellion as a political tool. However, despite such limitations and the defeat of the insurrection, many of the rebel municipal councils' demands shaped Crown policy through the early decades of Charles V's reign as Castilian king.[1]

To guide the reader through the complex argument that follows, I offer a brief abstract. After providing an overview of the Comunidades, I show how the frustration of Toledo's council over royal vacillation in the handling of the Belalcázar lawsuit contributed to the failure of the Cortes of 1520 and the beginning of a rebellion to force the Crown to negotiate reforms in royal administration. Because attempts at negotiation between the leaders of the comuneros (as the rebels were known) and Crown representatives were fragmented and inconclusive, I use a local negotiation during the rebellion

between the town of Talavera and its lord to illustrate what the representatives of Cortes cities and towns initially had in mind. With the failure to
conclude negotiations between the rebels and the Crown promptly, antiseignioral violence increased, and plebeian rioters began to reconstitute
municipal government to reduce considerably or eliminate entirely the
influence of patrician oligarchies in cities and major towns. Moreover,
some rebels began to articulate ideas that redefined the nature and roles of
Castile's representative assembly and monarchy. These more extreme
actions suggested a fundamental potential for a transformation of government, which would have shattered the central focus of political identity
within the commonwealth on a monarch who would sustain justice through
the exercise of "absolute royal authority" and would have jeopardized disproportionate elite control of economic and political resources. The fear
generated among territorial aristocrats, urban patricians, and Crown officials was sufficient to form a basis for collaboration around a program to
enhance royal leadership, which gave Charles V an opportunity to improve
judicial administration in order to restore the common identity that held
Castile together.

The Comunidades of Castile: A Brief Overview

The Crown lacked consistency in its approach to the legal disputes between
cities and territorial aristocrats over alienated and usurped jurisdictions, and
such capricious royal action left patricians frustrated and suspicious. In the
midst of growing administrative chaos during the second regency of
cardinal-archbishop Cisneros after the death of king Ferdinand, the city
council of Burgos sought in 1517 to organize a reforming assembly of patrician representatives of the Cortes municipalities, but this initiative died
when it became apparent that Charles would shortly arrive in the kingdom
to take over as co-ruler with his erratically behaving mother, Joanna, who
was confined in Tordesillas under the care of the marquis of Denia and his
wife. However, the self-interested corruption of Charles's Flemish advisers
and the failure of the Crown to respond in 1518 to the Cortes deputies'
demands for reform with significant improvements in royal administration
fed the dissatisfaction of the urban leadership even further. When, after only
five months in Castile, Charles left to meet with his Aragonese subjects,
Toledo in 1519 circulated a call for another assembly of Cortes members, but
this initiative died with the announcement that the king was returning and
would again meet with a Cortes. Charles's advisors called this Cortes to
meet in the spring of 1520, both to undercut this initiative and to obtain
funds for their young monarch's trip to the Holy Roman Empire to receive
the imperial crown in Aachen after he had been elected emperor. In order

for the king to be able to abandon the kingdom as quickly as possible after extracting additional revenue from municipal representatives, the assembly was convoked in the far northwestern region of Galicia (it met in Santiago and La Coruña) rather than in one of the customary core Castilian cities. Because the king's impending departure from the peninsula threatened an even further deterioration of royal administration and dashed hopes that had been raised so high, Toledo refused to participate in the meeting.

Although Crown officials obtained a favorable vote from a majority of the urban delegates who did attend, they foolishly provoked the commonwealth in a situation in which no one felt the special subsidy could actually be collected. As Charles was leaving, the population rioted in some Cortes municipalities, sometimes murdering returning procuradores who had voted for the subsidy, and local insurrections developed against the officials of the king's foreign regent, cardinal Adrian of Utrecht (a future pope). In this inflamed environment, Toledo called on 6 June for yet another assembly of Cortes cities and towns acting under their own authority, as a *santa junta* ("holy assembly"), to petition the Crown for immediate redress of their grievances to remedy the "seven sins of Spain" caused by the "tyrants." Basically the rebel municipal councils wanted the monarch to reside in the kingdom, to use the revenues from his Castilian subjects within the kingdom and in its interest, to observe the requirement that royal and ecclesiastical positions be held only by Castilians, to expel corrupt officials from the Council of Castile and from the royal administration in general, and to provide justice to his subjects through effective institutions of judicial administration. Only four other municipalities sent representatives when the Junta began meeting in Avila at the beginning of August, but when on 21 August, the regent's forces attacked and burned the major commercial center of Medina del Campo, center of the kingdom's most important trade fairs, the membership grew to fourteen (without the Andalusian cities of Córdoba, Granada, Jaén, and Seville) and other municipalities supported the cause. Emboldened by this increased support, the Junta reassembled in Tordesillas to govern in conjunction with queen Joanna. On 26 September, the Junta, which had by then proclaimed itself the "Cortes and General Junta of the Kingdom," decreed the suspension of the Council of Castile and took to itself the administrative authority for all aspects of Crown government. It also called on all cities and towns to swear an oath of brotherhood and union in support of the Junta's government.

With the failure to negotiate a prompt end to the rebellion, popular parish assemblies increasingly pushed the comunero movement toward more radical attacks on political and economic privilege. Rising antiseignioral violence in the countryside drove increasing numbers of territorial aristocrats, who had been largely cool toward Charles's essentially Flemish administration, into support for the regency government to which the two major aristocratic Court officials, the almirante and the condestable, were added in the fall of 1520. Meanwhile, antipatrician activities within many towns and cities reduced support for the rebellion among urban elites. One event that would be of particular importance in the military conflict that followed was the city of Burgos's withdrawal from the Junta in November; the great aristocrat of that area, the condestable Velasco, worked with nervous patricians to effect this without the city council being overthrown by plebeian comuneros. A strengthened royal army was able to seize Tordesillas, along with the queen and some of the Junta's procuradores, on 5 December. With opposition to the rebellion continuing to grow, the comuneros suffered a series of military defeats, which eventually led to the collapse of the movement. The worst of these defeats came at Villalar (about 40 kilometers southwest of Valladolid) on 23 April 1521, when a comunero army led by the Toledan Juan de Padilla (1490–1521) was crushed. Padilla and several other leaders were executed the next day. This disaster isolated active comunero support in Murcia and Toledo.[2]

Although increasing extremism eventually led to the defeat of the Comunidades, the events of 1520–1522 did a great deal to clarify the nature and purposes of monarchy for leaders of the commonwealth. Upon his return to the kingdom in July 1522, Charles showed that he understood the role of rebellion within the design of a monarchy endowed ideologically with absolute authority. He acted on 1 November to confirm the general pardons issued by his viceroys, few rebels were executed, and even many of the few hundred who were initially excluded from early royal pardons were rehabilitated within a few years.[3] More importantly, Charles undertook reforms that responded to many of the concerns expressed by the rebel patricians.

Royal Vacillation in Providing Justice and Patrician Frustration in Toledo

The administrative disorder and resulting factionalism had gradually increased after Ferdinand's death on 23 January 1516. Joanna's son Charles, who was in the Low Countries, was proclaimed ruler with the not particularly popular archbishop Cisneros as regent. In the face of growing hostility toward Crown policy, noble quarreling in preparation for a possible disputed succession, and urban riots, Cisneros tried to hold Castile together while begging Charles to come to the peninsula. Agents and favor-seekers traveled to Charles's Court and fanned peninsular discord from the Netherlands. Without firm royal control, the magnates were creating chaos. Some aristocrats plotted against Cisneros, using as their focus Charles's brother Ferdinand, who unlike Charles had been brought up in Castile. The major municipalities resisted taxes, militia organization, and the Inquisition, there were riots in Madrid, Toledo, and even in Valladolid where Cisneros had his government, and the archbishop had to prevent an independent meeting of the Cortes in March 1517.

Severe irregularities and great corruption characterized Royal Council business, and a lack of supervision by that body encouraged abuses by other royal officials, who attempted to protect themselves by cutting deals with the territorial aristocracy. In many cases, administrators simply became slack in the dispatch of their duties. For example, Ferdinand wrote to the Chancillería of Granada scolding the justices for not sending the necessary brief explanation of their verdicts when required.[4] The high level of administrative drift and the resulting importance of factionalism and clientage were undermining the effectiveness and reliability of judicial administration in ways that cost the Crown the local notables' collaboration. This period of confusion particularly harmed municipal corporations trying to use the law courts to recover lands, towns, and other jurisdictions they felt had been obtained illegally by the territorial aristocracy.

After Ferdinand's death, the count of Belalcázar took no chances. He obtained a royal order from Charles in Brussels on 28 November 1516, instructing the Council of Castile to refuse any hearing to either Toledo or Córdoba on matters relating to the count's jurisdictions. Charles wanted reports on the earlier suspensions and told the Royal Council to postpone hearings until he arrived in the kingdom. The count may never have delivered this order, which appears to have been a typical product of the lack of coordination between the Royal Council in Castile and the Council resident with Charles in Flanders. With more serious consequences at the time, the count of Urena and his son, the future comunero leader don Pedro Girón, convinced the Council in Flanders to overturn an unfavorable decision by the Chancillería of Valladolid in their attempt to obtain the duchy of Medina Sidonia, a judgment already approved on appeal by the Council of Castile and sent back to Valladolid for final execution of the verdict.[5]

Charles's arrival in Castile destroyed whatever efficiency and justice remained in the royal administration. Within this context, patricians developed their interpretation of and growing opposition to the regime, and Charles's failure to win the support of local notables created the conditions for rebellion. In language strikingly similar to the scolding lectures delivered to fifteenth-century Castilian sovereigns, patrician leaders underlined, in the introduction to their petitions to Charles at his first Cortes in Valladolid in 1518, the fundamental role of the rule of law as the framework for their conception of monarchy. Heaven ordained the king to reign well, they stressed, and reigning well meant administering justice. Of his many qualities, only the administration of justice made him a king. In return for the king's provision of justice to his vassals, they gave him part of their earnings and estates and served him personally when called, observing a tacit contract that obliged the monarch to defend justice. In doing so, the king would be known as a "just judge." However, because the task of judging was great, the monarch needed to select officials to carry part of the load, although the ruler would be left with the supreme authority. Like Moses, the king needed to select men who were wise, experienced, God-fearing, enemies of avarice and of other passions that would blind and pervert judgment. As Dr. Zumel, the Burgos procurador who provided so much of the 1518 Cortes's intellectual and rhetorical leadership, pointed out to Charles and his favorite, Guillaume de Croy, lord of Chièvres, monarchs did not gain the goodwill of their subjects by violating the kingdom's laws, and they were not well served by officials who did so in their name. Such a course could lead only to a bad end. Patricians used these terms to evaluate Charles's administration and express their fears about an ineffective monarch.[6]

The new monarch came to a kingdom suffering from fourteen years of neglect, and he had to deal with the problems caused by the resulting deterioration, with his right to the throne far from universally recognized. His mother, queen Joanna, was after all still alive. Governing under such conditions would have been a difficult job even for a mature, experienced ruler with some conception of the existing patterns of elite and municipal interaction, but the new king was an awkward boy, not yet eighteen on his arrival, who spoke no Castilian and was firmly in the grasp of advisers from the Low Countries. Magnates and local notables alike perceived the Netherlanders as incapable of concern for the common good of Castile and motivated only by personal interests. Unlike his father, Charles had not sought to build up an aristocratic faction to support his position in the kingdom. His Flemish advisers gobbled up important offices, and the Crown distributed favors in what seems an almost random fashion. In violation of Isabella's edicts, the king gave three bishoprics to foreigners, including the primatial see of Toledo, which went to Guillaume de Croy, the adolescent nephew and namesake of Charles's chief confidant, Chièvres. A great deal of money probably changed hands. Charles twice tried to get large sums from the Mesta. Chièvres was made one of the two chief royal accountants, an office that proved a valuable revenue source when he almost immediately sold it to the duke of Béjar for 30,000 ducats.[7]

Under the leadership of the Council of Castile, this banquet of corruption rapidly drew in the judicial administration. When the Cortes of 1518 opened in Valladolid, Córdoba's representatives presented a strongly worded petition to Charles. They told the king that the city had possessed Gahete and Hinojosa since the days of the Reconquest, having received title in compensation for its aid to the Crown. Despite royal pledges at the Cortes of 1442 and in Córdoba in 1444 that the towns would not be taken, John II granted them two years later to Gutierre de Sotomayor, who took the area before Córdoba's council was even informed about the transfer of jurisdiction.

King John made some insufficient provisions to the city, and Henry IV finally revoked John's grant of the towns. Córdoba retook one but could not hold it during the period of civil war and was unable to get it back. The Catholic Monarchs gave their word that they would restore the territory, and Córdoba waited. The rulers' action was checked, however, by "the favor shown the count, don Alonso de Sotomayor, by grandees and relatives, especially by don Alvaro de Portugal, president of the Council of their majesties, his father-in-law." The Crown could not confirm Henry IV's restitution of Gahete and Hinojosa without the agreement of don Alvaro, and the city did not want to exercise its right to retake the lands until Charles arrived in Castile. The petition asked the king not to receive the supplication of the count of Belalcázar, his relatives, or any other magnates contrary to this request for confirmation, suggesting that Charles grant what Córdoba petitioned so that the cities of Andalucía could provide him with the help he had requested. The representatives awaited his decision.[8] Presumably their votes in the Cortes would wait too.

The Royal Council acted quickly to confirm Henry IV's revocation, given in Salamanca on 11 May 1465, of the grants of Gahete and Hinojosa to the master of Alcántara and of Fuenteovejuna and Bélmez to the master of Calatrava. Córdoba's procuradores had brought the original document to the Cortes, and the Council reaffirmed its validity. On 27 March 1518, in Valladolid, five royal councillors, in the name of Joanna and Charles, ordered the chancillerías and other judicial officials to recognize Henry's edict in their decisions.[9] The action was of questionable legality but was not challenged by Gutierre de Sotomayor's heirs because they were not informed about it for twenty years.

Toledo opted for the more established administrative path by getting its case reopened at last before the Chancillería of Granada. This procedure corresponded closely with the city's actions during Cisneros's second regency. When other Cortes cities were following Burgos's lead to establish an assembly of urban procuradores, Toledo instead sent a memorial to Brussels to request that Charles come to Castile. Impressed by Toledo's respectful attitude, Cisneros had written to his representative in Brussels, the Toledan don Diego López de Ayala, supporting the petition and asking him to say whatever else he would like as a native of the city.[10] In Granada, the judges would seek to demonstrate, through their careful adherence to proper procedures, that they were providing a forum in which law rather than personal influence would be the guiding principle and where justice would be done. In Valladolid on 15 March 1518, curiously the day Burgos procurador Dr. Zumel, Charles's great opponent in the Cortes, was bribed, the king issued a letter to the judges of the Chancillería of Granada instructing them to hear Toledo's claim to Puebla de Alcocer, Herrera, Fuenlabrada, and all related towns and lands, any previous suspension of hearings notwithstanding. Under the leadership of Luis Puertocarrero, count of Palma and corregidor, on 7 July Toledo's council commissioned as its representatives regidor Hernán Pérez de Guzmán, one of the activists in the period prior to the comunero rebellion, and jurado Juan Ramírez de Vargas. On 17 September, Pérez de Guzmán and Ramírez de Vargas presented Charles's letter, their commissions, and a second claim before the Chancillería to reinforce Toledo's original claim of 1511. Toledo's council attached such importance to the case that its preparation was assigned to many more lawyers than was normal, and the count of Belalcázar would later do the same. The audiencia issued a summons naming both count Francisco de Sotomayor and a comendador Rol, his guardian, but when a court official presented the summons in Lora, a village in the jurisdiction of the order of the prior of San Juan, Rol claimed he was not the boy's guardian but only cared for the children of the former count now that their father was a friar. Because Rol was a comendador of the order of Alcántara, he would need permission from his superiors in order to take the position as guardian, and he contended that the Crown should provide a guardian for the purposes of legal business.[11]

There was some difficulty in the count's affairs at the moment when he was summoned to court. After making his will in Belalcázar on 21 July 1518, Alonso de Sotomayor had entered the monastery of Santa María near Herrera as Friar Alonso de la Cruz. He had founded this monastery the year before as part of the Provincia de los Angeles, which his uncle, Gutierre I de Sotomayor, as Friar Juan de la Puebla, had founded. Because don Alonso's wife had died on 7 July 1516, Friar Martín Rol, the comendador of the order of Alcántara referred to above, had been entrusted with the responsibility of preparing for the marriage of Francisco de Sotomayor, don Alonso's son. After his novitiate, don Alonso made his final vows on 23 June 1519.[12]

On 9 October 1518, Antón Pérez, who, along with Alonso Alvarez de Villareal, had been retained as barrister by Toledo's officials, asked the court to hold the count of Belalcázar and Friar Rol in default and to notify them again if necessary. A notary of the town of Belalcázar then stepped forward as the count's representative by virtue of a guardianship and commission to litigate all cases with Toledo and Córdoba, and he selected Juan de Medrano as the count's barrister before the court. Toledo felt that the commission was legally insufficient and demanded and got, on 19 October, another summons that involved a stiff fine. When Toledo's barristers finally overcame a series of delays and got a properly empowered Medrano to respond in early December to the city's charges, in essence, the count of Belalcázar claimed that the king had ordered a hearing only on cases Ferdinand had suspended, and the dispute under discussion was not one of those. Moreover, John II had ordered that no more be said about Puebla de Alcocer after Piedrahita's survey, and the president and justices of the

Chancillería of Granada, therefore, should not handle the case and should reject everything in Toledo's petition. Medrano's presentation made similar claims about Córdoba's suit. The court, however, ruled on 10 December that it could handle the case and ordered the presentation of evidence.[13]

Medrano boycotted all of the sessions after the 10 December ruling until 22 December when he presented a royal order issued in Zaragoza on 5 December by the Council of Castile. The count's representative had informed Charles that the cases with Toledo and Córdoba dealt with jurisdictions granted by king John II. To defend his possessions, the count obtained a suspension of the case, and the Chancillería was ordered to send an account of everything presented by the two cities and to do no more until notified. On the same day, the monarch had written to the Council of Castile to suspend the hearing in Toledo's attempt to recover El Hornillo, and commanded the Council to order the suspension of those cases being heard in Granada that involved Toledo and Córdoba in disputes with the count of Belalcázar while he looked into the matter, as the count had asked. These suspensions were to take effect despite any provisions made in the Cortes of Valladolid or any other.[14]

While Pérez and Villareal worked to arrange for the rapid preparation of the material required by the king, Pérez de Guzmán and Ramírez de Vargas went to present Charles with a protest prepared by one of Toledo's letrados. The document listed a number of points designed to show that the suspension was unjust: the trial was underway, the original seizure was illegal, and Toledo had already suffered severe damage through the long series of suspensions.[15] The protest was of no avail. In a petition about particular concerns that was drafted for Toledo's procuradores to present to the king at the Cortes of 1520, the suspension of the hearing headed the list. The priority given to the Belalcázar dispute demonstrates the importance of Toledo's frustration with inconsistent royal judicial administration in shaping its council's opposition to Charles's plans.[16] One suspects that among the radicals,[17] regidor Hernán Pérez de Guzmán, who had overseen the Belalcázar case in Granada, was particularly influential in the crucial city council debates of October and December 1519 when Toledo decided to organize a formal pressure group of Cortes municipalities. In the end, by the time the Cortes met, exasperation with Charles's arbitrary style of government had reached such a point that Toledo's procuradores neither attended the sessions nor presented their petitions.

It is hard to know exactly why Charles gave an ear to the count of Belalcázar's demands for another suspension. The count had, however, just acquired some influential relatives through his marriage to Teresa de Zúñiga y Guzmán, daughter and heir of the marquis of Ayamonte and his wife, Leonor Manrique. Doña Teresa was also the only heir of her uncle, the second duke of Béjar, Alvaro de Zúñiga. Despite some early distress at not being consulted before the marriage contract involving such important vassals was signed in October 1518, the king and duke both consented to the marriage before the end of the year. The count agreed to perpetuate the names of his wife's family and become Francisco de Zúñiga, Guzmán y Sotomayor. At just this time while he was in Zaragoza, Charles had to arrange a difficult compromise in a long dispute between Antonio de Zúñiga, the duke of Béjar's brother, and Diego de Toledo, son of the duke of Alba, over the priory of San Juan of the order of Hospitallers. The priory had been given to Zúñiga by cardinal Cisneros, but to avoid a conflict between two of the kingdom's great aristocrats, Charles had to listen to Alba's protest and achieve a compromise in the matter. It seems likely that because one of his kin was being asked to surrender some of his rights, the duke of Béjar would feel it proper that his heir be granted his petition, the suspension of Toledo's and Córdoba's cases against him.[18]

Events from Isabella's death to the Cortes of 1520 had repeatedly cued for Toledo's patricians in general, and for key activists among the city's councillors and officials in particular, interpretive schemes that led them to recognize patterns in Crown administration and Castilian politics. On the basis of their understanding of these patterns, they formulated consistently negative judgments about royal government. Toledo was not the only major municipality whose leaders were similarly affected.[19] In part at least, this negative evaluation shaped elite political action in ways that would seriously endanger the future in Castile of the new Habsburg dynasty.

The Failure of the Cortes of 1520 and Rebellion as a Means to Force Negotiations to Improve Royal Administration

While manipulation of the kingdom's laws and judicial administration was taking place, the urban notables, in the Cortes, implored their new ruler to restore good government to the kingdom. They presented a large number of petitions urging improvements in judicial processes, including those of the Inquisition, and a brake on Flemish exploitation of the kingdom. Yet Charles and his advisers failed to create even the appearance of interest in these pleas. Matters deteriorated further when, in the summer of 1519, Charles received the imperial crown. Since the meeting of the Cortes in 1518, the clergy had been suggesting in sermons that Charles was a prisoner of his Court, the members of which were uninterested in Castile's welfare. In order to exercise his authority effectively, the monarch depended on the collaboration of the patrician leaders of major cities and towns, and repeated failures to respond to their representatives could lead not only to a withdrawal of support but to open rebellion by the Crown's opponents among local notables.

Toledo led further petitioning by Cortes municipalities to get the Crown to respect Castile's laws. Diego Hernández Ortiz, a jurado who was an honorary royal guard with Charles's Court in Barcelona where the king was meeting with the Catalan Cortes, and regidor Gonzalo Gaitán, one of those who signed the commission to open Toledo's case in Granada, remained at Court after the failure of an earlier mission and increased their pressure to get the Crown to permit a trial in the Belalcázar dispute. Failing again, they began writing to the Cortes cities and towns in exasperated tones, especially after a stern rebuff on 4 November. Córdoba sent its assent for common action on 18 November, and others joined the two cities. Within some urban centers, leaders perceived a lack of firm Crown action in matters related to the commonwealth's good, and this fed frustration over the unwillingness of the royal administration to allow justice to be done when major municipalities attempted to recover jurisdictions they felt had been illegally alienated to territorial aristocrats.[20]

On 2 December, the count of Palma, Toledo's corregidor, informed the city's council that Charles had written on 4 November to request an end to all petitions because the Cortes would soon be summoned. Despite efforts by Palma to calm the councillors, they followed the lead of their former legal representative in Granada for the Belalcázar dispute, Hernán Pérez de Guzmán. He suggested, on 5 December, that the king did not understand their motives and a new mission should be sent "to ask [for a] hearing and justice." As representatives, the councillors selected the regidores don Pedro Laso de la Vega, don Alonso Suárez de Toledo, and Gonzalo Gaitán and the jurados Br. Alonso Ortiz, who in 1511 had helped organize Toledo's attempt to open the Belalcázar case in Granada, and Miguel de Hita. The council sent them off as messengers and blocked the granting of credentials to Cortes representatives. When the count of Palma informed Charles of the mission, the king tried to keep it from even reaching him. The Crown removed Palma, who was also regidor don Pedro Laso de la Vega's brother-in-law, and replaced him with don Antonio de Córdoba who, while equally unable to control the council meetings, kept Charles and his courtiers better informed.[21]

Valladolid also refused to send Cortes representatives empowered to vote for a new tax, even though Charles was in that city to influence its leaders. Toledo's petitioners arrived there just as the king was preparing to leave, and they were supported by the representatives of Salamanca. Charles told Laso de la Vega and Suárez that he would receive them in Tordesillas and then fled from Valladolid with a mob's chant of "Long live Don Carlos the king and death to evil counsellors!" in his ears. Subsequently, the messengers of Salamanca and Toledo got nothing but a scolding from the Council of Castile and the king and were then roughly handled in Santiago. In reply to a Cortes petition asking Charles not to grant suspensions of lawsuits and to quash those already issued, the king said he would do as the municipalities requested, but it is doubtful if he was believed. By questionable means, the Crown pried out of only eight cities the votes granting the king an extraordinary tax. The monarch made Adrian of Utrecht, an alien, regent in spite of promises to appoint a native regent and gave only cursory attention to the urgent petitions of the urban notables. When Charles left La Coruña on 20 May 1520, Toledo's population had already rioted in response to rumors from Galicia. Because not even the king believed the new tax was legal or collectable, the Crown had imprudently taunted an angry commonwealth.[22]

These events exposed the Cortes as a body incapable of expressing the discontent of the municipal notables strongly enough to influence the monarch. Even though the commonwealth's leaders were reluctant to so disturb public order that their own positions could be called into question, revolt offered the only means to attract the attention of a monarch who had forgotten the collaborative nature of his rule, and royal officials heard the rumblings of rebellion as Charles left the peninsula. The king had not even defended himself by creating a domestic faction to act in his, and their, interests. Because he had so firmly rebuffed the Castilian aristocracy by appointing his Flemish tutor as regent instead of more customary candidates, such as the almirante or condestable, many grandees stood aside and allowed the young monarch to be chastised.[23] However, with a few exceptions, the great nobles would not join a popular revolt, because it was unseemly and because their massive territorial jurisdictions and wealth could hardly be damaged by Charles's misrule. Eventually the flare-up of antiseignioral violence would drive most territorial aristocrats into active opposition to the rebellion, and their defense of Charles would help push some rebel leaders to more extreme positions.[24]

Worry about the foreigners who surrounded the young monarch and provided many of his advisors, including his favorite Chièvres, grew not out of some particularly Castilian xenophobia, as the thesis associated with Angel Ganivet and the "Generation of 1898" asserts,[25] but from the conviction that these individuals were likely to place their personal interests above the commonwealth's general good. For example, many notables opposed sending Castilian royal revenues outside of the kingdom and advocated retaining the peninsula's famed wool in sufficient quantity to meet the needs of major production centers, such as Cuenca, Segovia, and Toledo.[26] Part of the population, especially that of certain important municipalities, was losing its means of economic support to the benefit of a few individuals, mostly foreigners or members of the territorial aristocracy, especially those who maintained large herds of sheep and were members of the Mesta.[27] In the eyes of patrician leaders, the Royal Council was refusing to remind Charles of his responsibilities and, therefore, abetting the "corruption." The rebel municipalities would later willingly pay more to support their government and armies; at this time, therefore, they rejected additional royal taxes not because of any inability to pay, but due to worries about who would benefit from the funds they provided. They opposed Charles's departure in the face of the deterioration of royal administration and the lack of control over the territorial aristocracy so evident since the death of queen Isabella. Patricians increasingly perceived that all Castile's difficulties stemmed from the corruption of Crown government by the assertion of personal interest against the maintenance of the rule of law.[28]

To be employed successfully as a political tool, rebellion required prompt negotiations before the serious divisions within the commonwealth provided an opportunity for genuine revolution to alter the nature of economic life and political institutions. However, for at least four months after the beginning of urban riots in late May, the patrician municipal councils had no respected Crown authority with which to deal, due to Charles's departure as the insurrection was beginning and viceroy Adrian of Utrecht's position as a poorly supported foreigner. When, on 9 September 1520, in an effort to gain support from the territorial aristocracy, a desperate Charles appointed the almirante and condestable as viceroys along with Adrian, almirante Fadrique Enríquez attempted the customary form of negotiation with the rebels, many of whose initial fiscal demands had already been met, but by then it was too late to obtain agreements from some of the cities and major towns whose current leadership now expected more concessions from the Crown. Moreover, advocates of repression dominated the Council of Castile, no doubt in part because many of the royal councillors had been accused by comunero propagandists of contributing to the abusive, arbitrary, and self-serving practices that were the focus of early rebel demands.

Talavera: An Example of Negotiation in the Midst of Rebellion

Because today we find it difficult to conceive of widespread rebellious violence as part of a political system rather than a sign of its breakdown, the argument of this chapter requires an example of the process. In the face of the failure of any sustained negotiations between the rebel assembly and the Crown, real negotiations in the midst of the Comunidades were more localized. The example given here possesses special relevance because some of the essential information about these events survives only in the trial record of the Belalcázar lawsuit. The town of Talavera (modern Talavera de la Reina) used the rebellion to undertake successful negotiations with Crown authorities, in this case with the administrator of its seignorial lord, the Archbishopric of Toledo, about a central aspect of Talavera's administration of its subordinate villages.[29] Because of royal patronage over Castilian episcopal appointments, the details of these events clearly reveal the way rebellion could be used in negotiations between patricians and authorities more closely tied to the Crown.

In a letter from Worms dated 17 May 1521, Charles thanked Talavera's council for not joining the rebels and for remaining loyal to his regency government. He cited as the sources of his information, among others, his viceroys and don Francisco de Mendoza, governor of the archbishopric of Toledo, and specifically noted Talavera's loyalty after the death of cardinal-archbishop de Croy, who had died in Worms on 10 January 1521 after a fall from his horse. The letter concludes with the monarch's thanks and the hope that the town's leaders would continue to help Mendoza maintain peace during the king's brief absence.[30] If it is true that Talavera remained loyal until May 1521, the town would not have changed sides afterwards because the defeat of the rebel army at Villalar on 23 April clearly indicated that the movement was near its end, even though Toledo would not be brought completely under royal control until the following winter.

With one of the most populous and powerful centers of the rebellion, Toledo, just 85 kilometers away, up the Tajo River, it was with difficulty that Talavera's council avoided the incorporation of its militia into the rebel army. Because the town formed part of the seignioral jurisdiction of the archbishopric of Toledo, Talavera had to act decisively when on 27 January it received notice from governor Mendoza of the archbishop's death. Two days later, the town council sent its official condolences to the emperor and expressed its hope that a new archbishop would be named promptly.[31]

Despite the fact that on 18 January Talavera's council had assented to Toledo's program for maintaining peace in Castile, the councillors concentrated on the preparation of the town's militia for the defense of its walls and fortifications. As would have been done in municipalities within the royal jurisdiction, after receiving Mendoza's news of de Croy's death, the council required the corregidor to surrender his official staff of justice, and the regidores then named their own alcaldes and alguacil mayor as provided by the town's privileges when officials of an archbishop had lost their authority through the death of the man who had appointed them. At the same time, Toledo was pressuring Talavera to abide by the terms of the traditional hermandad between them and send troops until the monarch provided for the pacification of the kingdom and the good of his subjects as "those gentlemen of Valladolid," referring to the rebel Junta, had petitioned him to do. Although there was some division within Talavera, both the council and the parish assemblies, which were a common citizen response to the rebellion in comunero municipalities, agreed to a vague reply emphasizing that no men could be sent from the town or its lands because all were necessary for guard duty. The town's gates were closed and guards posted.[32]

As one would expect of a town within the jurisdiction of the archbishopric, Talavera's leaders were alarmed when rebel military chief don Antonio de

Acuña, bishop of Zamora, claimed the title of archbishop.[33] On 4 March, the council wrote to Toledo to get more details about Acuña's intentions and to learn what that city's council thought about his claims. During the debate, several regidores made it clear that because Acuña lacked papal permission to assume the see, he should not be received by Talavera as lord nor given possession of the jurisdiction. In meetings with the parish assemblies, Talavera's alcaldes were able to get an agreement that if the bishop of Zamora came to Talavera without the proper documents, he should not be accepted. On the same day, the council had received a letter from another archiepiscopal town, Puente del Arzobispo, about 35 kilometers to the west down the Tajo River from Talavera, asking that Talavera order the rural parishes within its jurisdiction, particularly those of the Jara de Talavera south of the river, to aid Puente del Arzobispo in the defense of the area. The following day, the council replied favorably to Puente del Arzobispo's petition and requested news of the arrival of any major military unit. In the following weeks, Talavera strengthened its fortifications and increased its gunpowder supply.

The crisis came to a head on 31 March 1521 when news arrived that Acuña was in Toledo and had taken the archbishopric. Talavera's council responded by ordering all gates shut and guarded and establishing night patrols to maintain order. The town would not receive any soldiers, grandees, knights, or others and would intercept all correspondence. Talavera's householders swore an oath to uphold these provisions, and the town remained loyal to the Crown. When Acuña ordered that Talavera and Puente del Arzobispo send him their seignorial rents and that Talavera prepare to participate in the war or be condemned as an enemy of the commonwealth, the council held an emergency meeting with the canons of the collegial church and the abbots of the town's monasteries. Although various opinions were expressed, all eventually agreed to prepare the town's defense and refuse to accept any archbishop who was not canonically elected and received by the cathedral canons of Toledo. Bishop Acuña had sought only popular acclamation, and the mob had forced the cathedral canons, who were cooling toward the comunero movement, merely to make him administrator of the archbishopric's jurisdiction. Talavera's dean announced that all the secular and monastic clergy would leave town if Acuña arrived, and the population unanimously accepted this. Although the bishop of Zamora continued to pressure Talavera to accept him as archbishop of Toledo, its council retained the support of parish leaders, religious authorities, and local letrados and refused to reduce its guard or send troops or money for Acuña's army. Moreover, Talavera tightened its defensive pact with Puente del Arzobispo. Through all of its preparations, Talavera's council received the support of the parish representatives and the citizens in general, and it sent messengers to the communities in its jurisdiction with orders that they should not obey any authority not sent directly by the town's council.[34]

Although it provides the background to Charles's letter, this narrative does not explain why Talavera remained loyal to the king instead of becoming, in the summer of 1520, an enthusiastic proponent of rebellion. The town felt intense pressure to join the rebellion because one of its major centers, Toledo, was so close. Moreover, archbishop Guillaume de Croy, Talavera's lord, the nephew of one of Charles's most hated Flemish advisers, was an absentee and a foreigner, whose nomination in violation of Castilian law on royal episcopal patronage was one of the rebels' chief grievances. There is ample evidence of a great deal of communal discontent in Talavera in the late spring of 1520. The various religious confraternities often sent representatives to Talavera's council, to demand action in the name of the people on a number of issues. If they had not already done so, these confraternal delegations would eventually have led to the open meetings in parish churches and the election of *diputados* (parish representatives) who carried the opinions of the assemblies to the town council, as they did in comunero cities and towns.[35] Clearly this type of movement was a threat to the existing municipal patriciate, and with the monarchy weakened, the regidores would either have to show themselves to be governing in the citizens' interest or face being overthrown.

The confraternities of Talavera exhibited one major interest in the summer of 1520, and if the councillors could satisfy the town population on this point, they stood a good chance of keeping Talavera out of the general rebellion and themselves in office. Wine-making constituted a significant part of Talavera's economic life, and because producers were having trouble marketing the local vintage, the confraternities' delegates came to the town council to demand action. From the petitions and other documents recorded in the minutes of council meetings, we know that during the reign of Ferdinand and Isabella, archbishop of Toledo Alfonso Carrillo (d. 1482) had given Talavera the privilege of controlling vine planting by the villages within Talavera's jurisdiction, but some years before his death in 1517, cardinal Cisneros used his authority as archbishop of Toledo and Talavera's lord to allow the expansion of village vine cultivation. This overruled Talavera's prohibition of new plantings and violated, unjustly in the town's view, its time-honored privilege. The archepiscopal permission ran only for a certain period of time, but the planting had continued after the stated terminal date.[36] Because Talavera's subject villages were a major market for its wine, their unrestricted vine cultivation and wine-making in the wake of Cisneros's action were disastrous for the always fragile economy of this small town.[37]

On Friday, 21 June 1520, the parish delegates petitioned the regidores in the name of the people for the restoration of the right to tear up illegally planted vines. When they spoke of illegal vines, they meant only those planted after the expiration of Cisneros's permission, but the councillors answered that they were trying to get the archbishop to restore the original privilege and Talavera's right to destroy all the vineyards it had not approved.[38] Talavera's patricians employed royalist fears that the town would pass into the comunero camp to restore their council's control over an area of the economy important to their town and no doubt to the personal interests of several among them. Therefore, the council decided on Wednesday, 27 June to send to Mendoza, as archbishop de Croy's governor, a request that the town be allowed to use its right to tear up illegal plantings if the archbishop himself would not order their destruction.

The following day, Juan Díez, Mendoza's secretary, came from Toledo with a message from his master dated 25 June. As June had been the "Month of Mobs"[39] in many Castilian municipalities, the archbishop's governor wanted to investigate conditions in Talavera. Unfortunately for posterity, Díez delivered most of the message orally, but there was enough in writing to indicate that there had been trouble in Talavera and that Mendoza wanted the council to keep things under control.

After a reading of Mendoza's letter, the councillors approved their petition asking for restitution of the town's right to tear up illegally planted vines within its jurisdiction, a right granted by an earlier archbishop and confirmed by Ferdinand and Isabella. Although the regidores deliberately failed to make it clear whether they were asking merely for permission to destroy vines planted since the expiration of Cisneros's grant or whether they wanted their privilege entirely restored, they stressed that restitution of the right was a principal demand of the people, emphasizing the danger to patrician authorities if Mendoza did not respond positively.

The business of the petition having been completed, the council went on to consider its reply to Mendoza's message. On Saturday, 30 June, it drafted its response and appointed two of its members, Diego Giro and Francisco Vázquez, to carry the response to the governor. In its message, the council informed Mendoza that everything was under control in Talavera but hinted that it would be a great aid in keeping the public peace if the governor would accede to various demands of the people and above all, that with regard to the vines. Giro and Vázquez were to explain to him the background of the problem and inform him that the town's complaint against Cisneros's action was even then being heard in the Chancillería of Valladolid. But the law courts were slow and expensive, and an order from the governor in favor of Talavera would obviously do much to calm public unrest.

The delegations from the confraternities came with their demands again on Wednesday, 4 July. Not only was unlicensed wine-making hurting the town economy, they claimed, but the rural communities were buying wine from outsiders. To stop these illegal purchases, they wanted both an increase in the number of the boundary guards protecting the town's lands and an investigation, and they again asked specifically for controls on vine cultivation and wine-making.

Although the absence of detailed municipal documentation until September makes it hard to know what happened during the rest of the summer, on some authority Talavera sent its towns an order to tear up their vineyards. At least one distant place, Castilblanco, decided to resist and rebelled against Talavera. Talavera sent an armed force to retake the municipality, and in the conflict that followed, Castilblanco fell to Talavera's superior strength and many of the rebels were arrested. The exact sequence of events is not clear from the surviving documents. Yet Talavera's order to destroy the vines met with stubborn resistance in Castilblanco, and this called for the use of a large amount of force in an area that was a considerable distance from the town (certainly more than 80 kilometers over the roads of the period). Because Castilblanco sits on a high hill above a relatively open plain, the attacking force must have been large, for entering the village in the face of resistance would have been difficult.[40]

In fact, Mendoza had yielded to Talavera's arguments. In an uncatalogued letter from Mendoza to Talavera regidor Juan de Ayala, dated 20 July 1520,[41] the governor reported how at the request of Talavera, formal permission had been granted to Alonso Yáñez, accountant and lawyer of the town, to go to all the parishes of Talavera's lands to see that these communities conformed to the privilege of archbishop Carrillo, which had been presented in the archbishop's council. Mendoza gave permission to tear up all vines planted since Cisneros's death. Yáñez was to go in person to all the places involved to execute the privilege, and Ayala was to accompany him to find out which vines had been planted after Cisneros's death. Those he found were to be torn up in conformance with the privilege of Carrillo and the grant of Mendoza (in archbishop de Croy's name).

Talavera would have found this grant conveniently vague. As Carrillo had given the town total control over vine cultivation within the limits of its jurisdiction, the section about destroying vines planted since Cisneros's death could be ignored in favor of a more general destruction of unlicensed plantings. Mendoza probably knew that his attempt to limit the destruction to vines planted during the preceding two years would be disregarded and put in this clause only to avoid prejudicing the case over the privilege should proceedings ever be resumed in the Chancillería of Valladolid.

Although I have discovered no supplementary documentation to fix with precision the sequence of events, it appears likely that Mendoza's permission for Talavera to control vine cultivation preceded the town's order to Castilblanco and the village's revolt. Therefore, Mendoza's action allowed Talavera to achieve its goals under its council's leadership before the question of communal aims to reorganize political institutions led to an open breach with patrician rule. After this initial victory under the leadership of local notables, rural revolution against the collective seignorial interests that the municipal citizens and patriciate now held in common would further reduce divisions between them and lead to the perpetuation of the existing institutions, although some accommodation was made with regard to the development of parish assemblies. Their geographic location close to Toledo made the councillors and population of Talavera cautious, but fear of rural insurrection helped keep the town out of the camp of the Junta and its more prominent military leaders, such as the bishop of Zamora. Yet, as their earlier negotiations with governor Mendoza made clear, municipal leaders understood how to use the threat of rebellion to gain important concessions from higher authorities, using the same tactics as the patricians of Badajoz, Jaén, and Mérida.[42] Thus, the Talavera case fits well within the pattern of urban rebellion characteristic of the previous century, when municipal patricians made use of the threat of disorder to get a hearing for their demands while trying to avoid a slide into revolutionary violence that would ultimately undermine their political, and therefore economic, primacy at the local level.

Talavera's council members may have been willing leaders rather than coerced supporters of citizen demands. After all, the councillors represented interests, both agrarian and mercantile, that would have benefited from a restoration to them of vine cultivation control. In their petitions to Mendoza, they always made it appear that the town council had been forced against its will by the threat of communal violence into making requests about the matter. Talavera's patriciate claimed it was only trying to maintain peace and the town's loyalty to the archbishop and Crown. If only Mendoza would grant a few concessions, the councillors were certain that they could keep Talavera in the royalist camp. Yet if the councillors were going to be major beneficiaries of the concessions, it is likely that their claim of inability to calm the turbulence without action from Mendoza was insincere and that they had in fact encouraged the agitation while remaining available for negotiation with Mendoza and free from the taint of disloyalty.

An intelligent episcopal and royal administrator would realize that only serious problems would lead municipal leaders to incur the risks involved in manipulating popular movements in such a dangerous environment and would negotiate necessary changes before the situation deteriorated to the level of open violence. As everyone in the period assumed the poor were always subjects of their passions,[43] such violence was thought to represent a disservice to God, the monarch, and the common good for which the commonwealth's leaders, including the lord, would be more responsible than plebeian rioters. The major comunero municipalities tried similar negotiation tactics, and both Adrian of Utrecht and almirante Enríquez, as viceroys, showed a willingness to accommodate rebel demands. However, delayed responses by Crown authorities, the hard-line attitude of many of the more compromised members of the Council of Castile, against whom the rebellion was in part directed, and the viceroys' lack of credibility with many rebel leaders, especially after condestable Velasco's cynical negotiations to draw Burgos away from the Junta, meant that battles were fought.[44]

Potential for Revolution Created the
Context for a Post-Rebellion Transformation

Without prompt negotiations of the type that developed between Talavera's council and archepiscopal governor Mendoza, the rebellion began to move toward more extreme positions, although attempts to reach a negotiated settlement satisfactory to both Crown and rebels were continuously made by the viceroys and at least some comunero procuradores. The extremism came in three forms initially: attacks on the seignioral regime, the reconstitution of municipal government, and the presentation of new ideas about the relationship of monarch and representative assembly. The three would in certain circumstances be pulled together into a genuinely revolutionary vision, sometimes perhaps united with an apocalyptical element. The issue is significant for this microhistory because the manifest potential for revolution frightened such a wide spectrum of the political kingdom that it provided a basis for broad post-rebellion collaboration between the Crown, the territorial aristocracy, and the major cities and towns that would enable the monarch and his principal advisers to undertake a reform program that provided a context for a full judicial hearing of the Belalcázar conflict.

First, a combination of increased direct seignioral attempts to extract rural resources and greater royal fiscal pressure, often to raise funds to pay Crown debts to the territorial aristocracy, had produced a growing atmosphere of conflict in Castilian rural communities since the late fifteenth century, and the administrative confusion and divisions of the period since Isabella's death had already occasioned demonstrations of hostility against the seignioral regime. With the outbreak of the Comunidades rebellion, antiseignioral violence became widespread.[45] Despite the desire of many comunero cities to recover places they felt had been illegally alienated from their jurisdictions, assaults on the estates of the territorial aristocracy had not been a goal of the rebel Junta, but the open attacks on the institution of lordship had several effects. Most obviously, they drove many prominent territorial aristocrats into support of a regency government to which they had been cool because they felt that Charles had ignored them. However, cities and towns also had seignioral jurisdiction over a large number of places, and potential uprisings there might be sufficient to keep threatened municipalities from supporting the Comunidades rebellion or to encourage municipal councils that had earlier supported the rebellion to profess loyalty to the viceregal administration. The matter has been insufficiently explored, but concern for the stability of their seignioral jurisdictions may have influenced major Andalusian cities to refuse to send procuradores to the rebel Cortes and then to take the openly hostile step on 20 January 1521 of forming the League of La Rambla. These municipalities formed the League not only to support the royal administration but to fight the spread of rebellion within their jurisdictions. Antiseignioral uprisings in the Tierra del Campos region beginning in September 1520 partly motivated Burgos's patricians to withdraw their procuradores from the rebel conclave, and Jaén's leaders turned away from their early supportive attitude toward the rebel leadership due to similar concerns.[46]

Corregidor don Diego Osorio may have influenced Córdoba's patricians to distance their city from the Junta. Even though he was the brother of comunero leader don Antonio de Acuña, bishop of Zamora, and father-in-law of one of Burgos's procuradores to the Junta, Osorio had earlier been corregidor in Burgos and had witnessed the growth of dangerous communal violence there.[47] In the two decades prior to the Comunidades, Córdoba's populace had often indicated a high level of general discontent and potential for violence.[48]

The use of popular unrest to force changes from the royal administration was not an atypical tactic in an age when there was little opportunity to present demands in such a way as to compel attention and achieve redress of grievances. Local notables had no reason, however, to undermine irrevocably the concept of obedience to superiors, which was an important foundation of the seignioral institutions from which they benefited, and, thus, they had no desire to overthrow monarchical government. Through timely compromise, the Crown's representatives retained Talavera's loyalty and that of certain other major municipalities, but, it would seem, such disputes were handled poorly in much of Castile. Time ran out and the plebeian voice replaced that of the patricians as the one expressing more revolutionary goals.

Historical relations between collective urban lordships and their subordinate villages constituted only one of the variables that influenced support for the Comunidades and made it hard for patricians to walk the narrow line of rebellion while retaining ammunition for negotiation. The institutionalization of rebellion within the cities and major towns often took the form of organizations formed by voluntary oath-taking to defend the common good and oppose abuses of authority, injustice, and tyranny.[49] Within the important municipalities, citizens challenged the *regimiento* (collective of regidores) government and attempted to restore what they thought were older patterns of greater direct citizen participation in the election of urban councillors and in the formulation of policy. Such a challenge obviously existed in Talavera. In many places, ordinances about the election and responsibilities of the jurados still reflected a period of greater intervention by the populace. The comunidad of Burgos and its diputados had intervened directly in municipal administration during the final crisis decade of the reign of king Henry IV (d. 1474).[50] Small wonder that Burgos's popular representatives assumed authority so quickly in the summer of 1520 or that the city's patricians were so sensitive to the drift toward a revolutionary attack on their position. Earlier frustrating experiences with attempts to establish representation for the interests of the comunidad apparently contributed to a lack of general citizen enthusiasm for the comunero movement in the city of Chinchilla.[51] Moreover, although the matter remains largely unstudied, diputados representing householders with regard to various aspects of local administration, such as control of the irrigation system in Murcia, were a normal part of municipal government in some if not all places both before and after the rebellion.

The variations among rebel cities and towns were notable. Some patricians compromised in redesigning municipal political life, often retaining a prominent role in the rebellion that would later cost them their lives, as in the case of the famed militia leader Juan de Padilla, or extended exile, as in the case of don Juan Fajardo, Murcia's procurador to the rebel assembly. After the rebellion, many local notables who had played a prominent role in the comunero administration claimed that they had only been faking support in an effort to retain influence and minimize popular excesses, an excuse offered by Humanist Juan Maldonado on behalf of his friends in Burgos. Often, however, rebel commoners would expel the proprietary regidores, and some of these were killed by mobs. The Murcian comunidad exiled all of the regidores and jurados and their closest relatives although these men had been among the most radical supporters of Toledo's opposition initiatives since 1519. Clearly the movement toward an urban council made up entirely of elected representatives, many of them commoners rather than *hidalgos* (privileged, tax exempt), was an aspect of considerable revolutionary potential.[52] However, one wonders how long such institutions would have been retained in the absence of some substantial transformation of the prevailing seignorial regime of which the municipal corporations were so much a part. The representation allowed within the urban comunidad was not particularly radical because it was limited to the municipal parishes, preserving the seignorial jurisdiction of the city or town itself. Increasing hostility to patrician rule certainly accounted for defections to the royalist camp, and the fears of local notables for their own positions significantly weakened potential support for the rebellion in places such as Burgos, Cuenca, Guadalajara, and the cities of Andalucía. Murcian patricians would have gladly joined these others in the loyalist camp had they not been so quickly overcome by the popular rebellion against their government. More populist municipal administrations were bound to have an effect on the Junta, especially after 5 December 1520 when a royalist assault on Tordesillas, where the assembly met, resulted in the capture of thirteen of the original procuradores whose replacement was then in the hands of more radical local leaders. Indeed, a number of the procuradores felt uncomfortable when forced to move to Valladolid, dominated since November by extremist parish diputados.[53]

The use of supposedly earlier types of municipal political institutions also explains in part the nature of the rebel assembly that attempted to govern the kingdom. In their use of the term *junta,* the procuradores were clearly suggesting theoretical ties to the brotherhoods or confederations (hermandades) formed by a number of municipal councils at various times during the preceding centuries to protect the Crown and the kingdom from the abuses of greedy aristocrats and corrupt officials, as well as from the general lawlessness caused by incapacitated royal administration.[54] Henry IV had had some success in mobilizing these organizations against the aristocratic leagues formed against him, and the Catholic Monarchs had organized the brotherhoods to provide militia troops and money for the long war against Muslim Granada. The Santa Junta of the comuneros clearly echoed the early hermandades and the Santa Hermandad of Ferdinand and Isabella. Indeed, in some parts of Castile, the formation of the rebel Junta was preceded by the establishment among cities and towns of formal leagues for mutual defense.[55]

Yet the comunero procuradores declared themselves not only a Junta but also a Cortes, and they thereby tied to their program another source of extremism: arguments for a greater political role for an assembly representing the kingdom. I will devote more space to this matter because these ideas have not received adequate scholarly attention and they directly threatened the central focus of the political identity that sustained the Castilian commonwealth.[56] According to their prevailing political vision, Castilians felt that there was a correspondence between the common good and rulers' true interests, which monarchs would recognize if properly informed. Usually rebels directed their insurrection against the abusive, arbitrary, and corrupt administrators of monarchs who, when made aware of their kingdom's troubles, would act to provide remedies. The problem the comuneros repeatedly faced in their efforts to justify rebellion in this manner was that the royal authority with which they had to negotiate was always defective. When the city of Burgos tried to convene a Cortes in 1517, royal administration was hamstrung by the existence of two governments, that of Cisneros in Castile and that of Charles in Flanders.[57] Charles was young and inexperienced when he arrived in Castile. His handlers were anxious to have him receive the imperial crown as soon as possible after his election, and although Toledo tried in the fall of 1519 to organize major municipalities for a joint presentation of grievances, the king departed before this initiative could produce results. Adrian of Utrecht's status as a foreigner identified with Charles's Flemish advisers made him part of the problem and undermined his authority as viceroy and his negotiating ability. He failed in

August 1520 to entice the assembly slowly forming in Avila to meet in Valladolid where matters could be discussed with him as royal governor of Castile, and this failure exposed both his vulnerability and the rebel leaders' uncertainty about how to proceed. The rebel assembly picked up significant support in the aftermath of the Medina del Campo fire, which had been provoked as a result of the Royal Council's decision to suppress the rebellion by military force. But even before this disaster raised the level of hostility against the regency, the comunero leaders had clearly decided to petition queen Joanna for redress. Many continued to believe those who had been denying the seriousness of her illness at least since the Cortes of 1506. In late August 1520 after the Medina fire, the procuradores of the fourteen Cortes municipalities supporting the rebel Junta began to assemble in Tordesillas to be near the queen who lived there. It was at this point that the Junta procuradores defined themselves as a Cortes[58] Slowly the magnitude of her illness and her incapacity to act manifested themselves. Moreover, the royalist attack on the town on 5 December cost the comuneros control of the queen and left them without any royal representative with whom to negotiate on the basis of their now more extreme demands, although attempts to negotiate with Charles and his viceroys continued.

The political ideal was monarchy in which the ruler would use his or her authority to establish justice and good government, but defective royal authority would make it difficult to achieve these goals. Already during the minority of king Henry III in the early 1390s, the Castilian Cortes had acted on behalf of the kingdom to establish a regency council chosen from its own ranks, and after the death of the king-consort Philip the Handsome, the Council of Castile called a Cortes in 1507 without authorization from queen Joanna.[59] However, these Cortes responses to the existence of a weak regency of uncertain legitimacy did not produce a theoretical justification founded on universal political principles. As they sought, during the fall of 1520, to maintain the authority they had gained after the Medina del Campo fire, the Junta's leaders enunciated such principles in dialogues with, among others, the increasingly dissident city of Burgos and one of the recently appointed viceroys, almirante Fadrique Enríquez de Cabrera. Although the matter has not yet received adequate attention from scholars, comunero debates about the authority of their Junta distinctly echoed ecclesiastical conflicts over a Church council, and the appeal of a body of thought on the proper role of a representative council is not surprising given the need of an increasingly ambitious Junta to justify its claim to supreme administrative authority. In the midst of the Comunidades rebellion, any claim of supreme authority for the representative assembly could have revolutionary implications.[60]

Within the fourteenth-century Church, while the papacy was in Avignon, critics charged that papal administration was defective. These charges became especially strident during the period of the Great Schism of the West (1378–1418), when there were two and finally three popes, and major heretical movements emerged in England and Bohemia. There developed an increasingly broad conciliar movement, whose intellectual leaders argued that, in the absence of papal leadership able to achieve a necessary reform of ecclesiastical discipline and a renewal of faith and morals, a general council became the supreme authority within the Church. Using ideas derived in part from such diverse sources as Marsilius of Padua, William of Ockham, and experts on canon law, some conciliarists formulated theoretical positions claiming that when papal authority was defective, authority devolved to the community from which it had originally come as God had provided. After a shaky start at the Council of Pisa, these conciliarists achieved their greatest practical impact at the Council of Constance (1414–1418), which managed to end the schism, struck at heresy with the trial and execution of the Bohemian religious leader John Hus, and launched a reform program. By the decree *Haec sancta* of 1415, the body declared the superiority of the general council on Church reform, matters of faith, and the settlement of schism. The decree *Frequens,* in 1417, made the council a periodic fixture in Church government. However, a subsequent council at Basel (1431–1449) undermined the support for many conciliarist claims when, during a prolonged dispute with pope Eugenius IV (1431–1447), the delegates created a new schism with the election of pope Felix V (1439–1449). Although pope Pius II, himself a former secretary of the schismatic pope Felix V, in 1460 forbade further appeals for general councils to be called, such appeals arose at various times right through the first half of the sixteenth century because there was such a strong link for many people between the conciliar idea and Church reform. Perhaps the most important of these appeals occurred in 1511 when dissident cardinals attempted to assemble a council in Pisa, which stimulated much conciliarist publishing and writing in the years just prior to the Comunidades.[61]

Because of the long history of the conciliar movement and the heavy involvement of major European intellectuals, various arguments were available on the role and responsibilities of the general council in the governance of the Church. Conciliar ideas continued to be reiterated in ecclesiastical and university circles into the early sixteenth century, and such positions became more generalized in political thought. In these conceptually expanded versions of conciliarism, the institutional expression of the community, to which authority devolved when its papal or royal exercise was defective, was its representative assembly, which would meet to remove the abuses that existed as a result of the unusual situation and restore proper "monarchical" authority. Although scholars have worked out the impact of conciliarism on political writers in other European kingdoms, most notably in England and France, I am not aware of any similar study on the broad impact of conciliarism on Castilian thought. However, post-rebellion, sixteenth-century Iberian works on the proper role of the representative assembly, many of them by canonists and theologians, were sufficiently rich and numerous to be cited and discussed by some defenders of the English "Glorious Revolution" of 1688–1689.[62]

Although the city council of Burgos adhered to the Junta after the Medina del Campo fire, it quickly voiced suspicion and criticism of the assembly's motives and claims of reforming authority. While just as convinced as their colleagues that Castile faced a serious emergency, Burgos's leaders understood the Junta to be an advisory body serving the monarch, whose authority was paramount. They repeatedly claimed that the government of the kingdom should be left to those named by Charles and that the procuradores should limit themselves to drafting a list of remedies, which would be submitted to the king so that he would command what was just and good. Until Charles had heard this petition and responded, the assembly should do nothing, according to Burgos, to implement the reform program, nor should the Junta continue to control the town of Tordesillas and the person of the sick queen, Joanna. Burgos tried at the beginning of September to get other cities to support its cautious policy, and although it officially subscribed to the Junta's oath of brotherhood, Burgos continued to harp on the theme of caution in letters to Salamanca and Valladolid, to cardinal Adrian, and to the Junta itself. Its council refused to unshackle its procuradores, who had only limited representational authority and were required to consult with the city government before they voted on any Junta initiative. Burgos's attitude irritated the Junta, which by then had proclaimed itself a legitimate Cortes. By the third week in September, the Junta had decreed the suspension of the hated Royal Council, and Burgos's procuradores wrote to their city to report that they had voted against the measure as instructed. They further informed Burgos that the Junta was no longer even considering, as its principal activity, making a plea to Charles to enact its recommended reforms. Rather, its central purpose had become that of remedying by its own actions the damage done "by the bad government, and they will not consider the difficulties that the means to achieve this effect can bring."[63] In its plea to Salamanca to order its Junta procuradores to cease their involvement in governmental affairs, Burgos enunciated clearly its own vision of the cities' role in the monarchy:

> To avoid the evils of the kingdom and to remedy the wrongs and in order to conserve and augment the liberties and exemptions, it was agreed that there would be formed a general junta of the procuradores of the cities in order that together they could consider what should be done, and that which was found to be just and good they would request the Royal Majesty to command be done in a way that would be in the service of God

and the good of the commonwealth, so that it would be ruled and governed in peace and justice and with benevolence and love, and not with rigorous subjection because the soft yoke lightens the burden, and that which one does with love lasts while that with violence is not perpetual.[64]

When it broke with the assembly, Burgos offered, on 11 November, a final eloquent defense of its actions and independent position, as well as a warning to the Junta's procuradores of the consequences of their lack of respect for their monarch and their deviation from the true wishes of their cities. These procuradores, Burgos claimed, had been sent only to petition their majesties, not to use the insignia of royal authority, seize the sick queen, dissolve the government and Royal Council, and take over all the judicial and fiscal offices. These actions lacked all legitimacy. In doing so much wrong, Junta representatives were damaging their own reputations and the reputation of the kingdom by usurping royal authority. Because the Junta had not produced the appeal to the person of the monarch for which it had been convoked, Burgos's leaders explained that, since their city was the kingdom's traditional head, they had done so, through the good offices of the condestable, for Charles was expected to return soon. For Burgos's leaders, the kingdom was clearly a "body" subject to the "royal lordship."[65]

In its own response to Burgos's complaints, the Junta put a theoretical capstone on its leadership claims enunciated at the time it decided to stay (*sobreseer*) the authority of the Council of Castile and asked all cities and towns to swear an oath of brotherhood and union in support of the rebel assembly. It argued that Castile was an organic association, a mystical body, which possessed the sovereign attributes necessary to make decisions to which even the monarch was subject.[66] Using this organic metaphor, the Junta on 30 October declared that Burgos was an inadequate member of the body, was changeable and disloyal, and was selling out to the condestable, the territorial aristocrat with his residence in Burgos who was one of the king's new governors, for the satisfaction of the narrowly defined interests of Burgos and its leaders.[67] However, Junta members appeared uncertain about their ideological stance in the carefully crafted epistle they sent to Charles on 20 October 1520. They explained the sequence of events that made necessary their assembly and the subsequent removal of the Royal Council. Until Charles could name new councillors dedicated to good government and make a decision about the proposed reforms, the Junta wanted the king to authorize the cities and towns with Cortes representation to oversee the judicial system and the kingdom's general administration. This position appears to have developed from a vision of the Cortes as the body that would step in and temporarily take supreme authority during a serious emergency that had compromised the effectiveness of royal government. However, a number of the "chapters" in the list of recommended reforms sent along with the letter reveal a much more generous conception of the Cortes's political role and a number of significant restrictions on the authority of the prince. The document advocated limitations by the assembly, as representative of the kingdom, on the monarch's control of appointments, the form of his administration, the nature of fiscal and monetary policy, and even his grants to individuals, and also advocated that papal bulls should be preached in Castile only after review by the Cortes. Further, the Junta procuradores wanted the Cortes to meet at least every three years. Clearly these provisions were drafted by men confident that the Cortes justifiably had a major, continuing role in the commonwealth's government. And one item in the petition revealed an even more radical cast to some comunero thinking: the Junta wanted the king to recognize a right of resistance if reform statutes were violated. This recognition constituted part of the text of a sworn declaration, drafted by the Junta for the monarch, in which he established the proposed reform by his absolute royal authority through a contract with his kingdom, its procuradores, and the comunidades and their residents. The resulting provisions were to have the status of perpetual laws ratified in the Cortes.[68]

Although this October letter and petition contained demands and a theoretical conception of the relationship between monarch and representative assembly that was sufficient to upset Burgos's leaders, these leaders may already have been fearful of the Junta's ultimate intentions toward Charles because of the tenor of some of the initial reform proposals. While neither its dating nor its authorship is certain, it is possible that the document known as "Capítulos de lo que ordenaban de pedir los de la Junta" was a working draft under discussion while the Junta was still in Avila in late August, when we know that the procuradores were already trying to put together their petition to the Crown.[69] Some of the proposed "chapters" of the "Capítulos" were similar to the often strident demands that Burgos itself would submit to the Crown in late October,[70] but the draft included other sections that would have removed Charles from the succession, drastically limited royal war-making powers and rights of appointment, even of royal councillors, and established a much more representative Cortes with its membership drawn from the royal municipalities, secular clergy, nobles, and observant friars from each of Castile's bishoprics. Burgos would have been especially sensitive to any expansion of Cortes representation because that would seriously dilute the city's traditional influence as *cabeza del reino* ("head of the kingdom") of only eighteen represented municipalities, a "head" that addressed the assembly first in any debate.[71] This document was authored by some group convinced of the ultimate primacy of Cortes authority in Castilian political life, and I discuss below the reasons why I suspect that friars were among the draft's authors.

The Junta revealed its clearest debt to conciliar thought when it proclaimed itself the representative of the organic, mystical body of the kingdom, for it was on this basis that the fathers at Constance, and later at Basel, based the supremacy of a general council.[72] Burgos's leaders were not the only ones to recognize that this claim was the crucial foundation of the Junta's assumption of the Castilian government. When the Junta reiterated this stance in a letter to the almirante, he replied on 22 November 1520 that the procuradores were nothing more than individuals named to represent their individual cities. They, therefore, lacked any authority over the monarch, and their claims produced only division, violence, and the breakdown of justice. "Therefore gentlemen," he concluded, "considering these things one could better . . . name your junta wicked to destroy the kingdom rather than holy to reform it."[73] In the 20 October 1520 reform program that the Junta sent to Charles V, the assembly asked the monarch to recognize that their body was the proper one to take over the kingdom's judicial and other administrative functions during the current crisis. The circular letters of Burgos and Toledo in 1517 and 1519, respectively, had expressed the same vision of the Cortes as an institution that could temporarily take supreme authority during an emergency, and it is in the context of other ideological positions that this idea appears related to the arguments of some of the earliest conciliar thinkers. More striking is the confidence the Junta expressed that the Cortes had a major, continuing role in the kingdom's government, when it included in its program the demand that the representative assembly meet at least every three years. The fathers at Constance had attempted to secure such regular meetings for a general council with their 1417 decree, *Frequens*. Even though the draft proposal to expand Cortes representation to include all royal cities and towns in the royal domain, as well as nobles, secular clergy, and friars, was not adopted, the suggestion is very reminiscent of decisions taken at Basel, where the breadth of participation and equality of votes made that council unique in conciliar history.[74] At the conclusion of their proposals, the procuradores appended a draft proclamation for Charles to issue in his name and by his absolute royal authority, and in this statement, he was to recognize that the proposed reforms constituted a contract with his kingdom in which he guaranteed that these items would be perpetual laws. Although a reform program submitted to Henry IV at the Cortes of Ocaña in 1469 had also spoken of a "silent contract" between kingdom and monarch,[75] and might have served as a precedent in the context of other aspects of the comunero Junta's ideological program and the detailed, written provisions of the 1520 "contract," it is worth pointing out that this sort of contractualist view of the relationship between ruler and community constituted the basis of some of the most radical aspects of conciliar thought during the Council of Basel.[76]

Although the limited survival of comunero documents after the defeat of the Comunidades rebellion will perhaps not permit a detailed study of rebel ideology, these conciliar echoes were neither accidental nor due only to some earlier generalization of conciliar thought within broader currents of Castilian political discourse. Rather, they represent a direct application of the more universalized conciliarist principles to an intense controversy over the nature of the kingdom and the role of its representative assembly. The explicit use of conciliarist treatises was important because conciliar theorists not only facilitated the articulation of a particular perspective but also drew out implications that might have been neglected by comunero ideologues if they had not been familiar with these earlier works. And among the principal rebel ideologues were letrados, clergyman, and friars whose professional and institutional backgrounds could well have given them an opportunity to read the conciliar fathers.

Canons of Castile's major episcopal churches voiced harsh attacks on arbitrary royal government on the eve of the rebellion, and some of them became active leaders in the comunero movement itself. Although municipal council consultations with local jurists and religious leaders were not unusual, Augustinian, Dominican, and Franciscan friars, especially those based in the famed university center of Salamanca, played a prominent role in the formulation of the comunero political program from the early development of urban opposition to arbitrary royal government. The initial justification for municipal limits on the representational power of the procuradores given to the Cortes of Santiago-La Coruña in the spring of 1520, contrary to royal demands, was provided by learned members of the major religious orders in Salamanca. As often happened in Castilian municipalities, Salamanca's city council had sought the advice of these teachers and scholars and then asked that these friars convey their opinion to other cities so that all would send procuradores to Charles bound by similar strict instructions. Not only did this document already contain many of the chapters of the Santa Junta's later petition to Charles V, but it already spoke about *las Comunidades destos Reynos*.[77] Among the rebel leaders excluded from the royal pardon of 1522 were several of the more important rebel ideologues: the Dominican Alonso de Medina, the Franciscan Juan de Bilbao, guardian of his order's Salamanca house, and the Dominican Pablo de León, one of León's procuradores to the Junta and part of the small group that consistently insisted on the right of the assembly to govern.[78] Opponents of claims of Junta supremacy recognized the ideological leadership of such men. On 11 November, in their final attempt to justify their actions and convert the Junta to their own view of the Cortes's role, Burgos's leaders lashed out in a letter at the sinister influence of the rebels' ecclesiastic ideologues. They argued that the Junta's supposed lack of respect for the king was due to the fact that: "by counsel of your apostles, you have taken from the King our Lord his title."[79] In the letter's dramatic concluding sentences, the Burgaleses heaped all the responsibility for the Junta's deviation from its original purpose and proper role on the shoulders of these clerical advisers.

> These religious cats you should, gentlemen, eject from among you. They are the cause that there has been sown among us this corrupting vice and these tumults, and they shamelessly, and without fear, preach false things. Such scandalous murderers should not be permitted to exist. We wish that they would arrive in our area so that the theme of their sermons would be the justification for their punishment. You, gentlemen, we believe, at the beginning of this business, were clean without malice, and were of saintly intention, but these types, like animals made wicked by contagious evil, have infected you. We fully believe that they will be investigated and that quickly will be extirpated these false apostles, shadow of those that must serve the Antichrist. It is necessary to investigate if they are human, understanding the nature of each one, because it must be presumed that they are really demons walking around in the forms of men.[80]

Several other bits of evidence suggest that this attack on the rebels' clerical ideologues was more than simply a rhetorical conclusion. One of the two versions of this letter that Danvila included in his collection has appended to it a royal prosecutor's criminal accusation, in the monarch's name, against the rebels before the Royal Council. One of the charges was "that in order to justify the said crimes, many of you and your collaborators at the beginning of your uprising and sedition sent through all the cities, towns, and villages of these our kingdoms friars and other ecclesiastical and secular persons who falsely by pamphlet and speech persuaded artisans, farmers, and other common people of the said municipalities."[81] Moreover, in responding to the Junta's communication of late November, the almirante also seconded Burgos's warning to the rebel procuradores about the bad influence of their preachers.[82]

I am unaware of any detailed study of relationships from the mid fifteenth century onward between Castilian universities and the conciliar movement and its writings, which would be necessary if we are to gain some sense of the conceptual options available to comunero intellectual leaders.[83] However, men with university connections were extensively involved in the conciliar movement, which suggests the availability of relevant manuscript and later printed treatises in university libraries. Moreover, several of the most important intellectual leaders of the papalist and conciliarist groups during the period of the Council of Basel were Castilian representatives. Juan de Torquemada (often called Johannes de Turrecremata) felt that the Council of Constance, which he had attended, was the proper institutional vehicle for dealing with a serious emergency such as the Great Schism. However, at Basel he was an early advocate of papal supremacy and then wrote what remained for a long time that doctrine's most systematic defense. Torquemada was a Castilian Dominican who initially attended the Basel Council in the 1430s as the personal representative of king John II. Alfonso de Santa María arrived in Basel in 1434 as dean of the cathedral of Santiago de Compostela, but by the summer of 1436, he had become bishop of his native Burgos. He emerged as one of the more articulate defenders of the Constance decrees *Haec sancta* and *Frequens,* but he abandoned the Basel assembly when it deposed pope Eugenius IV and initiated another schism. Perhaps the most tenacious and influential defender of the sovereign supremacy of the council in Church affairs was Juan de Segovia (Juan Alfonso González de Segovia), the theologian who was sent as the sole representative of the University of Salamanca. Best known for a history of the Council of Basel, which included all its major decrees and statements, this radical conciliarist, who stuck with the Council until its close in 1449, donated his library and personal papers to the University of Salamanca, where they may have remained as a repository of conciliar thought for any scholar who wished to appropriate arguments from such material to articulate particular interpretive schemes.[84]

Conciliar thought developed on the same bases in canon and civil law as the theoretical understanding, so favored by local notables, of the proper exercise of the monarch's authority (discussed in chapter 6). The comuneros' central concern for these issues indicates the degree to which dissatisfaction with the quality of royal judicial administration and frustration with the arbitrary handling of legal disputes fundamental to the municipal governments of major cities, such as Córdoba, Cuenca, Segovia, and Toledo, played a role in defining the rebellious attitudes of Castilian patricians. Because conciliar thought was used to clarify and justify Junta members' ideological positions founded on those interpretive schemes cued for them by frequent employment and political experience, it is not surprising that, while the Junta gave a much greater role to the Cortes, it showed no tendency to innovate in the organization of judicial administration.[85]

Sometimes, historians have been too indifferent to the conceptual schemes and discourses employed by actors in periods of conflict, introducing anachronistic categories to describe the meaning of important documents. Standard works have often paid little attention to what the ideas meant to those who formulated and used them; such works employ terms such as "nation" and "citizen" when discussing comunero documents that spoke of "kingdom" and "subject" or "vassal." These distinctions are of importance because the way all participants in the events of the Comunidades era used their familiar political interpretive schemes to recognize patterns in the world and to formulate judgments about their often changing situations affected their physical and linguistic actions. To force on their documents the rhetoric of the French Revolution in an effort to define the modernity of the Comunidades or to give Castile pride of place as an innovator in Europe's revolutionary history invites distortion both of the comuneros and of the major ideological developments of the Enlightenment and the French Revolution.[86]

Although we lack an adequate monograph on the subject, it appears that the comunero Cortes moved progressively toward ever more extreme versions of conciliar thought as its leaders faced ever more serious problems in defining a Crown administration with which they could deal. Combined with a more anti-magnate focus and with attempts to apply models of more open governing councils and urban brotherhoods to achieve justice, the use by the rebel Cortes of more extreme forms of conciliar thought perhaps permitted some comunero leaders to produce a truly revolutionary program by the winter of 1521. I point to the possible impact of conciliar perspectives on the emergence of competing understandings of their movement and its governing representative assembly among rebel political and intellectual leaders, in order to suggest another way in which the Comunidades manifested a revolutionary potential. From this orientation there might have emerged a troubling transformation of the political institutions that many local notables viewed as sustaining their disproportionate share of resources. Most of them continued to feel that for this purpose they needed government by a monarch with widely respected authority. The failure of the rebel Cortes to open representation to municipalities other than the usual eighteen cities and major towns that customarily assembled suggests that the majority of the procuradores who led that body did not draw any particularly dramatic revolutionary conclusions from their theoretical attempts to deal with formal defects in royal authority. Yet even the vague suggestion of such a broad program for the transformation of the patterns of Castilian political and economic life frightened some people, the movement became increasingly isolated from the groups who constituted the usual leadership of the commonwealth, and the viceregal government won.

Rebellion or Revolution

Every human collectivity exhibits conflict among groups. When those involved are part of the dominant elite, they tend to conceptualize these conflicts in terms of interpretive schemes that support their dominance in the social environment. For early rebel urban leaders, the territorial aristocrats were bad not because of their wealth but because they asserted the priority of their personal interests over the common good and damaged justice. Monarchy was not bad; royal administration was temporarily defective because of the individuals involved and the effects of evil counselors. The prevailing discourse during the revolt did not open to the future but to the past and to ideological streams such as the conciliar movement. Yet the rise of anti-seignioral and antiprivileged agitation and any proposal to substitute the sovereignty of a representative assembly for that of the monarch were potentially revolutionary. These aspects of the Comunidades were not part of the initial rebel vision. Their manifestation scared some patricians into opposition to the movement, and where these local elites were not overthrown or isolated, they often led their towns and cities into the royalist camp.

Although the four major accounts of the Comunidades have all defined the comunero movement as revolutionary,[87] the essentially conservative, nonrevolutionary nature of even the most extreme patrician leadership is far more striking.[88] The famed "Draft Perpetual Statute" of the rebel assembly, which some have seen as an innovative, revolutionary constitution, took the form of a petition from the procuradores of municipalities represented in the Cortes to monarchs (Joanna and Charles) who were expected to establish its provisions as law through the exercise of their "absolute royal authority."[89] The notable element in Castilian history had been the strengthening of the seignioral regime in the Trastámara period as a fundamental part of a monarchical government, which showed itself well able to adapt to the opportunities of more extensive overseas commerce and Castile's expanding global domains. For the most part, members of the urban patriciate appeared to understand clearly their place in such a regime and the fact that that advantageous location was dependent on a broadly supported, capable royal leadership. From this perspective, both the antiseignioral movements of Castilian peasants and the antipatrician parish assemblies and representation in urban areas were conservative returns to supposedly older patterns of life undermined by the rising importance of the powerful Trastámara territorial aristocracy and the development of urban patrician regimientos. In the absence of any new interpretive scheme by which participants in the rebellion could define their positions within the polity's institutional design, reliance on long-available ideas by peasants, artisans, and even university-trained intellectuals is understandable. A rebellion whose leaders spoke in terms of a "kingdom" and "vassals/subjects" did not look toward a French Revolution that used an ideological vocabulary dominated by the concepts of "nation" and "citizen."

Although the antiseignioral and antipatrician violence certainly had revolutionary potential, no effective revolutionary perspective emerged, because the commonwealth's leaders continued to feel dependent on monarchical authority to maintain the organization of economic and institutional roles from which all the elite groups benefited. The particularistic concerns of peasants and artisans would remain a menace to these leaders,[90] but in the Golden Age the popular potential for violence posed no fundamental threat to the pattern of relations that privileged aristocrats, patricians, and officials. Indeed, the kingdom's legal organization provided increasing opportunities for the humbler proprietors and heads of households to be inserted into the prevailing institutional design through the establishment of new municipal corporations with broad administrative powers within their jurisdictions and with the ability to challenge royal officials and territorial lords of all kinds in courts of law, thereby undercutting popular recourse to violence.[91] Perhaps utopian millenarianism surfaced among some comuneros because of their inability to conceive of a practical polity without popular dependence on leadership by elite groups.[92] Counterfactual arguments about what would have happened if the popular forces had not been so soundly defeated lead us nowhere. The Comunidades was meaningful in Castilian history as a rebellion to pressure the Crown, which eventually frightened the commonwealth's leaders. Although no similar insurrection would occur in Castile during the remainder of the Habsburg era, the historical memory of the comunero revolt (and the contemporary Germanía in Valencia), coupled with bouts of more localized Castilian violence and major uprisings in other royal domains such as Aragón, Catalonia, Portugal, Naples, and Sicily were sufficient to keep the potential for rebellion a significant factor in the calculations of the political kingdom about how to arrange a degree of collaboration among elite groups and institutions to achieve at least some of the goals of all. To avoid turbulence and preserve domestic peace, necessary goals in a dangerous but economically attractive global environment, the monarch had to act to meet the desires of the territorial aristocracy for personal recognition and contact, and of the local notables for just rule. Balancing these demands was somewhat easier in the 1520s for a determined, more mature, and better advised Charles V, because popular hostility and threats to the fundamental interests of territorial aristocrats and urban patricians meant greater potential backing for a royal government willing to act to attract such collaboration.

Even though the rebellion was defeated, the fact that the Comunidades occurred had a profound effect on the interpretive political perspective of the small elite that had long benefited so disproportionately from the monarchy and from the seignioral regime on which monarchical government had been erected in Castile. The violent assault on this government and regime lent increased urgency to the solution of matters that divided and made vulnerable those who claimed to be the commonwealth's natural leaders.[93] Moreover, many people witnessed serious fractures in their common identity with a monarchy based on the exercise of absolute royal authority to provide justice, on which the cohesion and perpetuation of the Castilian commonwealth was based. Although they had repeatedly missed chances during the rebellion to negotiate and develop support for capable royal government, afterwards Charles and his advisers would seize their opportunity, and this change in orientation would provide the opportunity for a full trial of the Belalcázar lawsuit.

Chapter 5

PURSUING JUSTICE:
DUE PROCESS, PROCEDURE, AND THE ADJUDICATION OF A MAJOR LAWSUIT IN THE ABSENCE OF COERCIVE MUSCLE

A New Beginning for the Exercise of
Royal Justice and for the Belalcázar Lawsuit

The officials of a Crown judicial institution would now try to resolve, without sufficient royal coercive muscle, a dispute made serious by its ties to groups–territorial aristocrats and local notables who governed major municipalities–that tended to employ different interpretive understandings of justice and absolute royal authority. I avoid any tendency to consider these officials as the bureaucrats of the emerging "Spanish" state or the royal law courts known as audiencias, with their letrado justices and other personnel, as important components of any bureaucratic hierarchy. During his long reign, Charles V gave these audiencias an extraordinary role in the administration of his Castilian domains on three continents. However, when one turns one's attention from superficial organizational charts of Castilian government to the important details and periodic dramas of administrative processes exposed in the present chapter, a picture emerges of institutions that had to function with considerable autonomy, even from direct royal intervention, if the monarch's authority were to be enhanced and the Crown were to receive the kind of broad collaboration from the commonwealth necessary for the government of a global polity during a major transformation of world history. Of course, the existence of these institutions would make it more difficult for the Crown to act arbitrarily. As we have seen, the meaning of absolute royal authority was unstable and depended on human interactions for which political institutions frequently provided a context. In the aftermath of a major Castilian rebellion, Charles V would do what none of his predecessors had dared to do for seventy years: he would assign adjudication of the Belalcázar case to one of his great audiencias, that of Granada, knowing that the Crown's future capacity for action depended on how well that institution's justices responded to their responsibilities.[1]

When the now crowned emperor Charles V returned from the Empire to his newly pacified kingdom of Castile in July 1522, he established a new course. He sought the advice of new men and showed an increasing awareness of the responsibility of ruling a number of polities spread over a large area. After an evaluation of the appalling results of the early years of his rule, the monarch responded to some of the complaints that had fed rebellion and openly sought the support of local notables shaken by the specter of revolution. Moreover, although the French army that had invaded Navarra in the spring of 1521 and the accompanying rebellion in that kingdom had been defeated by the autumn of that year, Charles knew that he would need to build support within the Castilian commonwealth to meet any further French adventures along the Pyrenean front, especially since the comunero rebellion had left the royal treasury in a shambles.

Because several of his close advisers had died since 1520, Charles relied heavily on the advice of his new grand chancellor, Mercurino Arborio di Gattinara (d. 1530). Gattinara was a member of the Savoyard lesser nobility and a former adviser to both the duke of Savoy and the archduchess Margaret, Charles's aunt. An eminent lawyer, Gattinara had served as president of the royal tribunal of Dôle, during which time he had assumed responsibility for judicial administration in the Franche-Comté. His education of Charles had begun at least as early as 1519 when he had suggested care in selecting advisers and officials, warned against any preference for favorites from the Netherlands, stressed the importance of observing a kingdom's laws and customs, and recommended that well-staffed law courts be allowed to act with total freedom from royal interference. Later on Gattinara extended his admonitions to matters of style: express genuine concern for the complaints of subjects, avoid excessive new laws, keep grandees from positions of authority at Court, and continue the reform of the administration, including the Inquisition, in the interests of better government.[2] To make sure that his reforming initiatives bore fruit, Charles remained in the peninsula until the end of the decade, and he increasingly relied on two other men with a good understanding of Castilian domestic affairs, secretary Francisco de los Cobos and archbishop Juan Pardo de Tavera, president of the Council of Castile.[3]

Although the story of the creation of any sort of aristocratic corporate group is probably a myth developed by seventeenth-century authors of family histories, Charles acted even during the revolt to increase symbolically the territorial aristocracy's sense of security and recognition by permitting the great titled magnates to enjoy some special, exclusive prerogatives. Building on precedents dating back at least to 1451, in recognition of their *grandeza* (status as grandees), some magnates were allowed in 1520 to keep

their heads covered in the royal presence and given the intimate consideration due to *primos* or cousins as they were called by the monarch.[4] However,
because the revolt had exposed the way governmental vacillation and subservience to great lords' interests had diminished royal authority, Charles
intended to sustain the grandees' public prominence while reducing private
aristocratic manipulation of Crown institutions.

The monarch quickly expressed his new administrative disposition by
rejecting requests for special royal intervention in the Puebla de Alcocer dispute. When the count of Belalcázar and his wealthy and prominent relatives,
including the almirante, requested that the emperor secure the count in his
title to the viscounty of Puebla de Alcocer, their petitions were refused even
though the count had made an important contribution to the defeat of the
rebellion while Toledo had been its leader. This refusal to compensate a
magnate whose close kin had made major contributions to the forces that
crushed the revolt formed part of a pattern of rejection by Charles of grants
as favors for aristocrats' service. As his broad-based pardon of the rebels
demonstrated, the monarch understood the initial intention of the revolt and
was not going to risk continued difficulties by refusing to listen to the local
notables' demands.[5]

The king was also in a better position to avoid undue influence from the
territorial aristocracy. On the one hand, the latter stages of the revolt, when
the radical Junta had called for a war of "fire, sack, and blood" against the
grandees, had weakened the great nobles' feelings of economic and territorial security and conversely increased their sense of dependence on the
monarchy, even if they were denied all the authority they wished to have
over Crown administration. On the other hand, the vast new opportunities
for diplomatic and military plums provided by Charles's expanding
domains made them more amenable to the monarch's wishes. Moreover,
the development of seignorial indebtedness and the close personal relationship between the king and the aristocratic lords allowed the ruler to intervene in the magnates' affairs and secure their support for the stability of the
monarchy without resorting to the wild expansion of noble jurisdictions
that had created such instability during much of the fifteenth century and
during the period after 1504. Charles, unlike Henry IV, was able to encourage grandees' dreams by constantly surrounding himself with the great,
showering them with genuine affection, and sending them on all sorts of
prestige-filled missions. Unless he could keep this close comradeship from
raising the distrust of the rest of the political kingdom, however, the
emperor would find himself under the influence of men who had subtly
gained significant authority.[6]

Much more systematically than his grandparents, Charles used the
Cortes to win the support of local notables for the Crown.[7] Indeed, to a
large extent he established the sort of role in Castile's governance that the

Cortes was to enjoy until its final meeting (1660–1664) at the end of the reign of Philip IV.[8] The Cortes met fifteen times during Charles's reign, and after each session, the body elected a standing committee of procuradores, which was left in place to oversee revenue collection and to keep Charles informed about the kingdom's general condition and remind him of his resolutions. The activities of this committee perhaps compensated to some extent for Charles's earlier refusal to consider mandatory Cortes sessions every three years. At the Cortes of Valladolid in July 1523, the emperor launched a reform program whose various steps were proclaimed at Cortes assemblies throughout the 1520s. A great many of the reforms were those that had been requested by the rebel Junta in the winter of 1521. Rather than suppress the political role of the urban patrician lineages who had caused him so much grief, Charles left them in charge of the great municipal councils and made an appeal for their loyalty and help. Admitting his earlier mistakes, Charles proposed that the Cortes help him set up an administration that would be run, as Gattinara had proposed, by letrados who would make decisions based on those formal legal principles considered to be the hallmark of just rule. Complaints about the quality and activities of the corregidores and other local royal officials dominated the early sessions but diminished later, suggesting that improvement was achieved in this area. The Council of Castile was reformed, special councils for Finance and the Indies were created, Navarra's government was reorganized, and an attempt was made to reduce the inquisitors' sphere of action. The Cortes procuradores were given great freedom to express their views. Because these representatives saw the monarch not as tyrannical master but as just lord, they did not hesitate to counsel him on his personal conduct, family matters, and household management. To show his interest in all of these patrician concerns, in 1525 Charles decreed that the petitions should receive responses before each session closed.[9]

Much government work would now be handled through institutions far more autonomous from Court supervision than in the past, and opening audiencia courts to appeals about the status and operation of aristocratic lordships both reduced the magnates' independent position for attacks on Crown authority and popular violence against seignioral "tyranny."[10] In the area of judicial administration, Charles went well beyond the reforms of the Catholic Monarchs and reduced the Council of Castile's role in actual judicial proceedings in order to avoid the appearance of or opportunity for undue influence from territorial aristocrats surrounding the monarch and his Court.[11] Despite a deterioration of compliance with proper procedures and required behavior by some Chancillería officials in both Granada and Valladolid during the turbulent period after Isabella's death, the comunero rebels showed respect for the Chancillería audiencias while attacking the corruption and abuses of the Royal Council.[12] To increase support from local notables, the Crown further improved the ordinances of these law courts and took measures to heighten their prestige. In the spring of 1523, Ldo. Francisco de Herrera, head chaplain of the royal chapel of Toledo, who in 1524 became archbishop of Granada and audiencia president, reformed Granada's ordinances after a comprehensive investigation. The new regulations were concerned with honest and efficient official action and with the fees for various services. For example, judicial officials were neither to gamble nor to take anything in excess of fees, including food, so that no taint of corruption would be attached to their duties. After this elaborate effort to remove those problems that might undermine public confidence in the Chancillería, the Crown acted to enhance the institution's prestige. While in Toledo, on 2 June 1525, the emperor ordered that the Chancillería of Granada's building be made more impressive and that the structures across the street be torn down to make room for a beautiful square. Both building and square still exist.[13]

Charles, however, not only promised justice to the commonwealth's leaders, but he also showed he was both willing and able to keep his promise in specific instances. At the Cortes of Valladolid in 1523, Toledo's procuradores, regidor don Gutierre de Guevara and jurado Alonso de Sosa,[14] made a special point of requesting a reopening of the Belalcázar trial. In its final attempts to negotiate a favorable surrender in the fall of 1521, well after the defeat at Villalar and the execution of its military leader, Juan de Padilla, Toledo indicated that the fundamental motivations of its rebellion were not just abstract concerns about the quality of justice in the face of defective and corrupt Crown administration. Toledo's patrician leaders used the handling of the Belalcázar dispute as a concrete basis for measuring the kingdom's problems. When a settlement was worked out in October 1521 with don Antonio de Zúñiga, prior of the military order of St. John and since January the head of the royal army in the Toledo region, the only point that Toledo raised that was not related to the events of the rebellion itself was the demand for a definitive solution of the Belalcázar matter.[15]

On 24 August 1523, Charles ordered both sides to present all of their information about the case within six months so that he could decide how it could be handled with justice. When the summons was delivered to the count of Belalcázar by Toledo's regidor, Francisco de Marañón, count Francisco de Sotomayor said he would obey and, because he was on his way to Court to serve the emperor, he would inform Charles of his rights. The king was unmoved by Sotomayor's subsequent protest that the Catholic Monarchs had not allowed a challenge to his House's control of the estates, which had been obtained for services similar to those rendered by other aristocrats. At the Cortes of 1525, the city told Charles that the count, marquis of Ayamonte since 26 March 1525, had failed to comply with Charles's orders and had induced the Council of Castile to suspend further proceedings. But the situation was changing. The Council of Castile had already reactivated the trial with regard to possession of the village of El Hornillo, north of the Guadiana River, and Charles responded decisively to Toledo's petition at the Cortes, ordering the Chancillería of Granada to hear the case. Jurado Diego de Rojas delivered this order to the oidores in Granada on 26 January 1526, and in succession they followed the usual procedure of acknowledging royal authority by placing the royal order in their hands, putting it on their heads, and saying they would obey. After eighty years of waiting, the city was at last going to receive a judicial review of its claims.[16]

Córdoba benefited from the new royal disposition too, because in March 1526, Charles ordered the Granadan justices to hear Córdoba's suspended lawsuit involving Belalcázar, Hinojosa, and their lands, mentioning that he had previously ordered the same in Toledo's case against the marquis. While in Granada the following July, the emperor, at Córdoba's request, ordered that some lawsuits between the marquis and Córdoba that were ready for adjudication be concluded quickly to avoid damage to the parties.[17]

Charles was probably brought under great pressure to postpone these trials once again. The group of nobles whose interests the cases attacked were not outcasts but highly favored courtiers. The marquis, whose Ayamonte lands bordered Portugal, was given the honor in 1524 of escorting Charles's sister Catherine to marry John III of Portugal and in 1526 of bringing to Castile its future queen, Isabella. The duke of Béjar, to whom the marquis was heir, was given the special privilege at this time, along with the duke of Alba, of being one of the few great nobles asked to sit on the Council of State. But after showing such favor to the group of magnates involved, no further suspension of lawsuits was possible if Charles wanted his pronouncements to be credible. He had promised at the Cortes of 1523 to revoke all suspensions of lawsuits and to suspend no others. However, it was aristocratic preferment at Court that gave the emperor the leverage to refuse magnates' requests for suspensions without causing himself any severe political damage. The nobles had not been given the impression that the Crown was hostile to their interests, and they certainly must have felt in the aftermath of the Comunidades era that a broadly supported Castilian royal government was an essential bulwark against further frightening assaults on their seignioral jurisdictions.[18]

Charles was convinced that he should not intervene in judicial matters, and he even tried to limit the judicial role of the Council of Castile, the majority of whose members were always men with extensive legal training and experience. The emperor wished to be free to deal with issues of war and diplomacy. Moving other administrative matters away from his Court and personal Household was both necessary and desirable, and this physical separation often typified much of his diversified conciliar administration.

Many aspects of the peninsular pattern were replicated throughout Castile's expanding non-European domains.[19] Monarchs increased their capacity for successful action by doing what the commonwealth's patrician leaders wanted, and by 1525 the Venetian ambassador reported that no other Castilian ruler had ever had as much authority as Charles within his kingdom.[20]

In the first global age, government became more effective in those countries in which "sovereignty" was diffused throughout many institutions rather than being concentrated in the monarch's person and Household administration. Much of the effectiveness of English, and then British, government relative to that of France in the period from the mid seventeenth to the late eighteenth century resulted from English notables' perception of authority's diffusion and their action on the basis of the patterns thus recognized.[21] The same could be said of the Dutch United Provinces and in particular of Holland's regents. Members of the Dutch and English political commonwealths built a broad policy consensus about public credit and war, which permitted the development of public financial institutions and a revenue increase sufficient for long-term military success in a highly competitive European and global environment.[22]

No contemporary would have seen Charles V's insistence that the Chancillería of Granada decide the lawsuit over the Puebla de Alcocer grant as a diffusion of authority that might provide a broader consensus for Castile's political direction, but that was what was at stake. Because the locus of the commonwealth's political life was the municipality, it was necessary for the Crown to encourage, where possible, institutions as contexts within which urban leaders would interact. Such interactions would become a basis for the development of more common elite social and cultural environments within which patterns would be recognized in similar enough ways for a consensus to emerge about policy direction and action. Without such a broad basis of elite collaboration within the commonwealth in Castile's European and global initiatives, it would be difficult for the Habsburg dynasty to retain its predominance. The choice of interpretive schemes employed to recognize patterns in the world as a basis for action depends on experience and the immediately preceding pattern recognition. Therefore, the nature of such institutions was crucial for privileging certain interpretive schemes, even for those who participated in a particular institution primarily through representatives, as was the case in a lawsuit. To enhance their authority and effectiveness, monarchs and their immediate advisers had to act in ways that made more prominent those institutions that promoted aspects of the cultural environment conducive to cohesion and consensus while diminishing the frequency of pattern recognition productive of factionalism and disdain for the commonwealth's welfare. This often meant that the Crown had to permit important decisions to be made away from the royal Court.

Watched by the Commonwealth: The Chancillería of Granada
as a Forum for Resolving the Troubling Belalcázar Conflict

The justices of the Chancillería of Granada must have been aware that they
had not undertaken an easy task when they agreed to hear the Belalcázar
case. The dispute they were expected to resolve was one that for eighty years
the Crown had felt was too delicate to place before royal judges, except
under special circumstances on three or four brief occasions. Despite the passage of time, the conflict had neither disappeared nor even died down.
Toledo's council still looked upon the Belalcázar lawsuit as its most important
continuing business and, as provided in the ordinance of 1509, councillors
opened each year's meetings with a formal consideration of the state of the
matter and a discussion of their strategy for furthering the city's cause.[23]
Because the bulk of most Castilian municipalities' income was derived from
the revenues of their jurisdiction, it is easy to understand why Toledo's leaders gave so much attention to regaining the Puebla de Alcocer region.

Meanwhile, don Francisco de Zúñiga, Guzmány Sotomayor, the count of
Belalcázar, had risen through marriage from the status of a lesser titled noble
to that of a seignioral lord of high rank, becoming the marquis of Ayamonte.
On the death in 1531 of his wife's uncle, don Alvaro de Zúñiga, he would
inherit the vast holdings of the duke of Béjar, marquis of Gibraleón, and
would thus become one of the greatest territorial aristocrats in Castile. Like
the great royal dynasts of the period, both corporate bodies and individual
nobles felt that their most important function was to preserve their inheritance for their descendants, and the marquis of Ayamonte had a particularly
good reputation for careful economic management.[24] His threatened jurisdictions were of considerable value in this period. With the Mesta and stock-
raising at their peak, the county of Belalcázar and the viscounty of Puebla de
Alcocer sat right in the middle of the great pasture lands at the end of the
transhumant migration routes, and all four of the Mesta's winter meeting
places, Siruela, Guadalupe, Talavera, and Montalbán, were nearby. Moreover, the Guadiana Montes no doubt continued to provide leased pasture to
non-transhumant herds as they had in the early fifteenth century for some
Toledan patricians and monasteries. It is no wonder that the duke of Béjar
was, with the duke of Infantado, one of the leading sheep owners.[25] Perhaps
the county and viscounty had even greater value for the marquis because,
while his other lands and titles came to him through his wife, the Belalcázar
and Puebla de Alcocer holdings were the original foundation of his
Sotomayor family dynasty.

There was an additional set of difficulties, of course. Although the
Chancillería was the body before which the city preferred to present its case,
from a great noble the tribunal could expect only hostility and lack of
respect. Back in the age of the Reconquest, cases involving magnates could

only be judged by the monarch and his Curia (council of vassals). Fifteenth-century territorial aristocrats felt that the king should personally handle all their problems and that disputes involving grandees would be considered by the Council of Castile, then dominated by aristocrats. Hostility to magistrates as a group seems to have been part of aristocratic self-perception. This hostility manifested itself prominently when after returning to Castile, Hernán Cortés, conqueror of the Aztecs and marquis del Valle, who was related by marriage to the marquis of Ayamonte, left Salamanca saying that he could not stand the company of letrados. In 1485, however, as part of their general program of judicial reorganization, the Catholic Monarchs ordered a great number of such cases to be sent to the law courts where they would normally be heard, and much of the resulting pressure would fall on the Granadan audiencia, for much of the litigation involving grandees was in the south.[26]

Despite all royal efforts to build up the prestige of the Chancillería and its claim to judge in the monarch's name, a great noble would still feel that its letrado justices should not try a case involving someone of his rank if the conflict involved, as the Belalcázar case did, his rights as a loyal vassal of the king. If justice for an individual litigant is the feeling "that internalized expectations have been met," an aristocrat would see none in a Chancillería hearing and would feel that he had been treated unjustly. He would also feel that the legal issues by which the case would be decided were improper ones. Perhaps he suspected as well that the paramount importance given to these legal issues reflected a bias against the magnates on the part of the judges, who would be mostly drawn from the university-trained members of the kingdom's urban elite.[27] This aristocratic attitude would be reflected at times in the way the case was handled in the marquis' name.

A great deal was at stake for the audiencia itself. The Crown had granted the Granadan oidores significantly increased responsibility and prestige which, if handled well, would result in the continuous growth of the institution's importance in the affairs of the kingdom. This growth carried weight for all members of the Chancillería because they derived their place and personal dignity in the commonwealth from the prestigious role of the tribunal. Indeed, the great attraction of a judicial post was not the profit but the dignity that went with such office holding. Other administrative officials, especially the royal secretaries, held much more lucrative positions. Group interest, then, gave both justices and, one senses, other court officers a tremendous *esprit de corps,* which would be directed toward the proper disposition of important cases.[28]

Personally, success might mean a great deal to the individual justices, for from their ranks important positions in the royal councils and the Church were often filled. The careers of two of the best known royal councillors demonstrate the point. Juan López de Palacios Rubios, who was so important in the development of royal administration, especially in America, was, after his graduation from Salamanca, oidor first of the Chancillería of Valladolid in 1491 and then of the Chancillería of Ciudad Real in 1494. After 1497 he moved to the Council of Castile where he played a major role and also held the important position of president of the Council of the Mesta. Even more spectacular was the rise of the noted jurist and political thinker Diego de Covarrubias de Leyva. After his graduation from Salamanca, he tutored at the prestigious Colegio de Oviedo. He then became a justice of the Chancillería of Granada. From this beginning he went on to become bishop of Ciudad Real, archbishop of Santo Domingo in the Indies, and delegate to the Council of Trent. During the last five years of his life, he capped his career by becoming president of the Council of Castile and bishop of Cuenca.[29]

Procedure, Due Process, and the Sense of Justice

Yet, despite the justices' willingness to handle such an important case, a dilemma remained: how to get two rich and prestigious parties, one of whom looked upon the tribunal as essentially illegitimate, to accept a negative decision at least to the extent that the outcome would not endanger the delicate balancing that was necessary for the monarch to be a popular and hence effective ruler. Perhaps because a consideration of procedural details does not make for snappy reading, I have not found scholarly works that reveal much about the administrative life of the peninsular audiencias. I want to discuss some of the procedures used to handle the Belalcázar lawsuit for several reasons. First, especially in cases, such as the Belalcázar lawsuit, that centered on contractual relationships and property rights, prevailing legal and political opinions placed a heavy emphasis on due process, which means that we need to examine the procedures followed by the tribunal in order to evaluate what its justices had to do to build respect for their institution. After all, the Castilian commonwealth's political identity centered on the image of a monarch maintaining justice, and the audiencia provided a forum within which the image became a reality. Furthermore, because the documents produced by the trial provide the foundation for this microhistory, readers need to understand the motives and procedures for establishing the archival record. This information also makes a contribution to our understanding of a major but poorly understood royal institution, the activities of whose justices and officials had as significant an impact on Castilian history as those of the monarch, royal family members, aristocrats, and bishops about whom historians often provide detailed studies. Moreover, the following account reveals that there were several elements of a successful solution to the dilemma the justices faced, all of which were diligently utilized by the court.

Although there were aspects of civil procedure that extended the length of trials, the justices willingly provided the time needed for a complete hearing in order to make the verdict seem as just as possible. They also realized that the acceptance and enforcement of the verdict would depend a great deal on the court's prestige as a body authorized to issue documents in the monarch's name. To a large extent, the Chancillería's reputation grew when it appeared that it was not dependent on other institutions for the exercise of its responsibilities. In particular, its officials had to avoid all appearance of intervention in its affairs by the Council of Castile or the ruler. In other words, rather than serving as some intermediate level of a hierarchy, this law court had to maintain judicial independence in order to increase its dignity and the regard with which it was held within the commonwealth. Finally, the justices had to remove any stain of corruption or bias from the court's verdicts.

Leisurely Consideration and the Provision of Justice

The first element of a successful verdict in the Belalcázar lawsuit was time. Historians have sometimes assumed, when they mention a particularly long trial of some important case during this period, that the duration was due to inefficient procedure and lazy justices. Yet sixteenth-century Castilian judges seem to have been at least as hard working as their modern counterparts in the United States. By the Medina del Campo ordinances of 1489, they met for three hours every day, except holidays, to go over evidence presented and then at least one additional hour to reach verdicts. Public sessions were held on Tuesday and Friday of every week, or the next day in the event of a holiday, to receive petitions and announce decisions.[30] There were not many complaints about deviations from this rule.

Court procedure was, however, time-consuming, and despite repeated Cortes protests[31] and Charles's diligence, no real improvements were made in this regard. Essentially, both parties exchanged their evidence, first in support of their initial claims and then in reply to material presented by the other side. These written exchanges were for the benefit of the parties, with the judges merely overseeing the rules for gathering and submitting evidence. The judges would not examine the material until the oral and written arguments were presented. Even then they would wait for a court reporter (*relator*) to organize and summarize the material. Oral evidence, in the form of depositions, was given weight equal to that of documentary evidence, but no attempt was made by the court to evaluate the significance of the testimony to be taken. This lack of argument over the relevance of the oral testimony opened the possibility of unnecessary depositions, and gathering such testimony was a lengthy process. No real attack was made on this problem.[32]

Other difficulties received more attention without really speeding up deliberation. The lack of a standardized and coherent body of laws and customs caused some delays. Through the Cortes, urban leaders demanded in every decade of Charles's reign that a compilation of laws be produced. The king tried to do something about the matter, beginning with a commission in 1532 to Pedro López de Alcocer of the Chancillería of Valladolid to compile the kingdom's laws. The work, however, passed through a number of hands before it was finished in 1567, and even then the resulting code was still ambiguous because it failed to abrogate all earlier works.[33] Another difficulty was the lack of sufficient personnel to handle the steadily increasing volume of litigation. Attempts to increase the number of officers and chambers were made in 1532, 1537, and 1542, but the effort was inadequate. Charles's absence after 1543 probably kept him from acting on one promising suggestion made by the Cortes, a new Chancillería in Toledo. A lesser audiencia, similar to the one founded at Santiago in 1505, was started in Seville by a decree of January 1556. The effort to cut the number of trials before the Council of Castile, where proceedings moved extremely slowly, must have helped reduce their length.[34]

Thus, there is some truth to the belief that procedures caused delays. However, lawsuits involving less politically influential parties were dealt with in much briefer hearings. The essential aspect of the long trial was the court's awareness of the difficulty or danger that plagued the era's judicial administration—that of enforcing the eventual decision. A lengthy trial had the advantage of postponing the problem, perhaps until a time when enforcement would be less difficult. More importantly, however, the extended hearing allowed both sides to present as complete a case as they were able, thereby lending as much of a coloring of justice to the verdict as possible. The greater the recognized justice of the enforcer's (the Crown's) position, the less the likelihood of serious consequences. The fact that the Chancillería wanted its decision to reflect such a complete hearing is revealed by the success of the marquis of Ayamonte's lawyers in arguing for more time on the ground that an affair of this quality deserved leisurely consideration.[35]

The count of Belalcázar showed, however, that he was not as interested in having a great deal of time to prepare his case as he was in delaying any final decision as long as possible in the hope that the monarch would follow earlier practice and quash any hearing of Toledo's claim to the viscounty of Puebla de Alcocer. A determined and wealthy litigant bent on delaying the proceedings as much as possible could use the leniency of the court as well as aspects of its procedures to good effect.

The greatest problem was the way in which oral evidence was taken. A court official called a *receptor* (receiver of evidence) would transcribe testimony given in response to written interrogatories prepared by the party on whose behalf the evidence was to be collected.[36] There were rules governing the number of questions that could be asked and the number of witnesses whose responses could be taken on any given question. Regulations prescribed time limits for taking these depositions, but the tribunal could allow extensions in the case of delays resulting from factors beyond the control of the party seeking the evidence. Because the court would not examine, until the final stage of the trial, the significance of the testimony to be taken or the value of the witnesses to be questioned, there was ample opportunity for taking unnecessary depositions under circumstances that were certain to cause delays.

Such problems were frequently created in a number of ways, and the lawyers for the marquis tried them all. One successful tactic was to attempt the interrogation of witnesses who would be certain not to reply: priests and monks who needed permission from their superiors. This method worked especially well when the clerics involved were serving in isolated areas so that permission could neither be requested nor be granted quickly. Another successful means to the same end was to send the receptores to places under quarantine due to plague; of course, they would refuse to go. Litigants bent on delays would try to send receptores out to isolated areas during bad winter weather, or time the request so that the receptor would have to leave just before a major holiday, thereby encouraging his cooperation in arranging a delay of up to a month. The Belalcázar lawyers could set off a dispute over a receptor's salary, to be paid by the party requesting his services and not by the court, some time in the middle of his work, and the receptor would often stop working until he was paid, thus leaving the job incomplete at the end of the official time period.[37]

The most spectacular opportunities for delay were created by the tremendous expansion of the territory under the jurisdiction of the Castilian monarch. In November 1526, just after the commencement of the first of the two hearings the Belalcázar lawsuit would receive before the high court, the marquis' lawyers requested depositions from witnesses living in Yucatán and the Caribbean and serving with the royal army in Italy. Although one usually does not concede a point in a lawsuit, there was nothing in the questions to be asked that would have elicited answers detrimental to Toledo's claims, and had there been any opportunity to argue the point, the city would surely have yielded on the points in the interest of a speedier trial. But the tribunal would hear no arguments about the value of the questions. When the receptor's departure for America was delayed for almost six months, the justices ruled that the official limit for questioning witnesses would begin only when the receptor departed. At the end of January 1528, the marquis of Ayamonte's barrister asked for more time because the receptor had returned without interviewing all the witnesses or even going from Santo Domingo to Yucatán. There had been a salary dispute when the marquis' American representative had gotten two months behind in the receptor's pay, and the latter was reluctant to risk a possible delay due to bad weather in returning to Castile because he would certainly get no extra money. Although the time limit was declared to have expired, the justices were reasonably generous because they allowed a long period, one year, for the transcription of this evidence and permitted the presentation of other witnesses. By actually trying to send additional receptores to America, the marquis' lawyers consumed about three years of the trial.[38]

Nor did the marquis' lawyers stop here, even during the first of the two hearings. In February 1530, barrister Juan de Medrano asked for sufficient time to take testimony from witnesses who were with the king in Italy. The tribunal denied this request, but after Medrano protested, the justices amended their decision, declaring that the marquis could take the depositions without time limit and that this testimony would be examined by the court, presumably if submitted in time to be considered.[39] Following the difficulties with the earlier overseas witnesses, this decision seems fair. The law allowed the marquis no more time for such depositions, but the tribunal wanted to show that he was receiving every opportunity to prove his case. Because much time was necessary to assemble and review the evidence before a verdict could be given, there was probably ample time to get the testimony of these witnesses in Italy into the record. That no attempt was made to do so indicates that the marquis' intention in making the request was merely to delay the verdict.

In 1536, a decision favorable to Toledo was made in the case. This, however, opened up the possibility of a hearing on appeal, in which the whole process could be repeated. The count of Belalcázar, marquis of Ayamonte, had become duke of Béjar and marquis of Gibraleón, and his new barrister, Gastón de Cayzedo, made a request to send a receptor to America in his petition protesting the verdict. Peru was added to the list of locations chosen to take advantage of the expanding frontiers of Castile's domains. Because the witnesses and questions were much like those of ten years earlier, one can only assume that this request was just another attempt to delay the proceedings. This time, the House of Béjar benefited from delays engineered by the appointed receptor, Francisco de Cárdenas, so that he could evade the rules about replacing retiring officials and arrange for his son García de Cárdenas to act as his substitute. After the usual delays over arrangements, bad weather, and even the threat of pirate raids and war, the son finally sailed for America in June 1537, only to die months later, along with the duke's representative, from disease in the Mexican jungle. The court did not learn of this tragedy until April 1538.

Although Toledo protested that some sort of time limit had to be adhered to, as the law required, so that the case would not become "ynmortal," a replacement was sent whose departure was delayed for five months by salary disputes and bad weather. However, the justices did act, in March

1539, to avoid any repetition of the Cárdenas affair when they ruled that, if anything happened to the new receptor, another one, who was in New Spain taking depositions in a case between the duke and the city of Córdoba, could finish the new receptor's work. In part because Toledo showed that the receptor deliberately delayed his work because his slow progress apparently satisfied the duke, who was paying his salary, the tribunal denied, in March 1540, any new calculation of the base date for the overseas time limit, and this decision apparently concluded the possibilities for delay through attempts to get depositions from witnesses at the far ends of Castile's American domains.[40] However, the damage had been done. A part of the proceedings that was supposed to take only eighteen months had been drawn out for more than four years. Thus, by using the possibilities of Castile's enormous new overseas domains, almost five years had been added to the trial, and the delay actually represented over seven years more than the time allowed for collecting oral evidence in Castile itself.

The justices frequently showed that they would try to cut short obvious attempts to delay the proceedings. Indeed, the court initiated a number of interesting reforms to reduce delays. But as long as the judges would examine evidence only in its final written form, and particularly as long as no attempt was made to evaluate the relevance of oral testimony to be taken beyond the Chancillería's walls, much time would be unnecessarily consumed by procedures. Thus, the vastness of the overseas domains could prove an impediment to peninsular judicial administration even when a lawsuit dealt with business that concerned only Castile.

The duke's procuradores were not the only ones who tried delaying tactics. In the course of a 1536 dispute where it was supposed to return some money to the duke, Toledo tried to use the excuse of bad weather to obtain more time to put a case together, but the tribunal showed no leniency to Toledo at all. Because the duke felt that the monarch rather than letrados should be deciding his affairs, the court was much more concerned about denying him any cause for complaint than about similar protests from Toledo's leaders, who supported the Granadan audiencia as the proper agency to handle such cases.[41] The duke was certainly not concerned about the delays caused by his lawyers because he was, after all, enjoying the revenues from the disputed territory and probably hoping for a change in the monarch's attitude.

The court itself was far from indifferent to the delays caused by inefficient procedures. The judges were under constant pressure from Toledo, which naturally wanted a quick settlement. Moreover, the case dominated the negotiations between Toledo's representatives and the Crown at every session of the Cortes, and the city's official correspondence registers reveal that its council appealed to the Crown to act in the interest of a speedy trial even when the Cortes was not in session. All these efforts resulted in a series of letters to the Chancillería from Charles or his regents ordering that the case be resolved with justice as briefly as possible.[42]

Under this pressure and because they were no doubt eager to make their institution more effective and therefore more important, the justices made procedural reforms that would decrease delay without, however, giving the duke's representatives grounds to charge that they were not given sufficient time to present their case. Rather than extend time limits and thereby delay the case, the tribunal allowed the duke to use more receptores and to gather evidence that could be submitted any time before the case was concluded for final determination. To avoid further delay resulting from sending receptores to America, the judges empowered the receptor in Córdoba's litigation with the duke to finish the work in Toledo's case if anything happened to Cárdenas's replacement. The court showed a growing tendency to make the duke's procuradores more specific about the documents they wanted transcribed and why certain witnesses could not come to Granada to testify. After Toledo complained that Cayzedo kept holding onto parts of the original trial transcript to delay the proceedings, the tribunal ordered that a copy be made at Toledo's expense and that original documents should no longer be used by the parties.[43]

One of the most important reforms with relevance to the conclusion of the trial came in 1552 when the case was about to be heard by the second of three required tribunals (*salas*). Toledo's solicitor, jurado Gregorio Tello, asked that a time limit be set for the challenging of justices, and after taking note of the large number of such challenges, the court complied. Not only did it speed the final consideration of the case, but when the marquis of Gibraleón, who did not officially take the title of duke of Béjar until his mother's death in 1565, and the town council of Puebla de Alcocer, now a party to the case, tried to hold off the final verdict by last-minute challenges to the president (the bishop of Avila), Ldo. Gaspar de Jarava, and R. Ruiz, the court (Ldo. Girón, Ldo. Juan de Araña, Ldo. Hernando de Salas, Ldo. Diego Bezerra, Ldo. Alonso de Castilla, and Ldo. Montalvo) ruled that by law the challenges had been submitted too late to prejudice a final decision. The royal edicts on the limits and timing of challenges were issued in 1554, 1556, and 1559, and scholars often point to such Crown commands as evidence for the creation of a rationalized royal bureaucracy. However, as so often happened, royal orders specifying changes in procedure, in this case the procedure regarding challenges to delay a trial, came only after the successful use of the procedure in one of the two Chancillería audiencias, which enjoyed sufficient autonomy to undertake procedural experimentation in a continuing effort by officials of judicial institutions to remove unnecessary sources of delay.[44]

There is also evidence that the court became tougher after about 1543 with the duke's representatives when they tried to delay the proceedings.

Time limits were denied and new evidence, of little importance and presented well beyond the time allowed for such presentation, was not admitted into the transcript. When the younger brother of the marquis of Gibraleón, don Francisco de Guzmán y Sotomayor, marquis of Ayamonte, tried to enter and recommence the case in 1550 on grounds that because his brother don Alonso had no heirs, he could inherit the viscounty of Puebla de Alcocer, he was allowed to enter the case, but without returning the trial to an earlier procedural stage. Oidor Ldo. Girón even ordered the court's constable and the chief doorman (*portero*) to force the marquis of Gibraleón's procuradores to return part of the original transcript that they had been given for a short time, and this threat against the marquis' representatives showed a new determination to enforce procedural rules and put an end to delay.[45]

All of this reform and determination certainly had its effect. But the real block to greater efficiency was, no doubt, having to deal with the growing volume of business produced in a litigious age without clearly defined laws or sufficient facilities and personnel.[46]

Prestige and the Image of Capacity for Action

After the element of time, the second element necessary for a successful result was to maintain the prestige of the court by never rendering a minor decision that would expose, through a reliance on other agencies to enforce judicial decisions, the judges' essential incapacity for action outside of the Chancillería surroundings. The Granadan oidores often took great care to define a sphere for their orders within which they could act effectively to gain compliance. A dispute over the expenses necessary to send representatives to America emerged as one of the most drawn out and confused examples of the difficulties that enforcement of verdicts caused.

Because Toledo would have to spend a great deal to see that the receptor got to America and did his job properly, the other party had to pay something toward these expenses. A provision for this payment was made in the first instance, but after the 1536 verdict, the duke's procuradores asked that their party be refunded the 40,000 maravedís paid to Toledo on the ground that neither party had been condemned to pay costs. When Toledo failed to show promptly how it had spent the money, the tribunal ordered the city to return it within nine days. Bad weather in the fall of 1536 and the court's refusal to extend the time limit for the presentation of evidence forced Toledo to produce only a summary of its expenses and finally to decline on the ground of insufficient time any opportunity to prove its claims. An order to return the money to the duke of Béjar was issued on 5 December 1536.

For some reason the duke waited until the spring of 1538 to press for collection. It was always a problem to get court decisions enforced because one relied upon local officials who, with the confusion of jurisdictions among the era's political institutions and multiple sources of law, often entertained various kinds of appeals. In this case, the royal *juez de residencia* (judge of official conduct), conducting the standard judicial review of Toledo's previous corregidor, chose to hear the city's arguments that the Chancillería judges had already ruled out of order. Although the juez had ordered the execution of the royal order in March, when faced with Toledo's refusal to pay, he held a hearing. In July, the juez deducted the 20,230 maravedís Toledo claimed as expenses and ordered the city to pay the remainder to the duke if he secured bond for its return in the event of a reversal. Finally, in April 1539, the Chancillería of Granada affirmed its earlier decision that the duke should receive the entire 40,000 maravedís, but fearing trouble, the duke's barrister, Gastón de Cayzedo, asked that an oidor be sent to Toledo to execute the sentence. This request put the court in a difficult position. It seemed clear that only by sending a Chancillería justice would the money be collected, but the court risked having one of its chief magistrates rebuffed by the city. He would be incapable of acting without the help of some other agency. There was a real chance that the prestige of the Chancillería of Granada would be undercut.

Circumstances provided a solution that would avoid open defiance of an oidor. Toledo had requested 50,000 maravedís in additional expenses because the original allowance had been spent on Cárdenas's fatal expedition and another receptor sent in his place. After several months of hearings, the tribunal ruled that the duke should pay this money to the city, and Cayzedo asked that the amount Toledo owed his party be deducted from the new assessment or that the city be compelled to pay. Hearings on this claim became the responsibility of oidor Dr. Peñas, who had been handling the issue of Toledo's expenses. Although it was not strictly correct under the form of the duke's and the city's separate royal orders to pay, Dr. Peñas avoided any further embarrassment to the Chancillería by making the 20,230 maravedís Toledo had not paid the duke part of the expense money that he owed the city. To Dr. Peñas it seemed better that the law should be bent than that the Chancillería's prestige should be put in jeopardy. The duke would not need an oidor to collect his money and there could be no embarrassment from a further refusal to pay. The whole issue was quashed two days later, on 12 March 1540, when the tribunal denied both the duke's petition for a new overseas time limit and Toledo's request for additional expense money.[47]

As in the Luis Pérez Caro affair discussed below, the court was loath to investigate or try those not directly associated with the audiencia because it might have to depend on other institutions or officials and expose its incapacity for effective action. The inability to handle problems away from the Chancillería might result, however, in injustices being done. This kind of problem occurred in March 1530 when Ldo. Coronel, representing the marquis of Ayamonte, and receptor Hernando del Gadillo were in Toledo to search for evidence in the municipal archive. In May, the marquis' barrister, Juan de Medrano, claimed that Toledo's officials were deliberately delaying, that they were hiding evidence, and that Gadillo was not doing a good job. Toledo replied that it was showing the marquis' representatives all the evidence included in the court order and was complying with it "to the letter without deviation." In July, Medrano asked for permission to examine documents beyond the chronological limits of the original order; he also asked for more time due to Gadillo's poor work and the difficulties that Toledo had created. The tribunal had no way of knowing whether Toledo was actually withholding evidence in violation of the court's search order, whether the marquis' representatives were just fishing for evidence without any real idea of what they wanted, or whether they were annoyed because they were not finding anything and were just trying to delay the case, as Toledo claimed. Therefore, in September, the tribunal handed down a decision that avoided the necessity of further investigation or charges of wrongdoing. It denied Medrano's request for more time but extended the chronological limits of the documents to be examined to the period 1463–1466 as he had asked. Also, the justices allowed the marquis' representatives to continue their search for evidence and ruled that any evidence submitted before the case was concluded for decision would be examined. This decision solved the dilemma because if the city was in fact impeding the marquis' representatives, they would have ample time to finish. On the other hand, if there was no substance to Medrano's charges and further delay was his only desire, the trial would not be extended. It seemed likely that justice would be done without the court risking its prestige.[48]

Autonomy and the Reputation as an Effective Instrument of Royal Justice

Closely related to the concern with the implementation of minor procedural decisions was a third element thought necessary for getting the parties to accept a verdict in the lawsuit. The Chancillería had to avoid any appearance of intervention in its affairs by the Council of Castile or the monarch. Judicial independence would increase the dignity of and respect for the law court, thereby making the Crown more willing to enforce the Chancillería's decisions while at the same time making those decisions more widely accepted and thus easier to enforce.

In this respect, Charles played his role well. There is a story showing that his attitude remained in line with Gattinara's precept about not interfering in judicial administration. When the emperor was visiting the estate of the prince of Bisigniano near Naples, probably in 1536, the princess asked Charles to pardon a convicted friend, but he refused on the ground that he could not intervene in matters of justice. It may be held against him that he uncharacteristically granted her request after she argued that mercy was the privilege of rulers, but his customary attitude was clear. Consistency is a rare virtue and the lady was a famous beauty. Although the religious divisions of the Holy Roman Empire made the task of building a generally accepted source of judicial decisions impossible, Charles's attempts to set up an imperial high court, independent of political manipulation and deciding cases according to codified laws such as the *Carolina,* the preparation of which he subsidized, can be seen in the same light. The Estates of the Empire had an interest in keeping important cases from the Reichshofrat, a judicial body staffed by imperial councillors whose decisions were felt to be motivated by nonjudicial considerations, and in 1547 Charles tried instead to secure the position of the Reichskammergericht, the standing imperial court of justice. The advice that Charles gave to his son Philip when he left the boy as his regent in 1543 reveals the same orientation. He cautioned the boy to avoid any suggestion, especially in the administration of justice, that his actions and decisions resulted from "passion, prejudice or anger." Philip was to avoid getting involved in private matters or making promises. All factional quarrels were to be avoided, he should never appear to be under the influence of one man, however good, and all grandees were to be excluded from government, except in military affairs.[49] This style of rule was what the local notables desired, and it would increase the prestige of institutions such as the Chancillería of Granada.

Nonintervention, however, also depended on fair and honest proceedings in the Chancillería, because the Council of Castile maintained a watchdog role. The duke of Béjar realized the court's sensitivity on this point, and his lawyers used the threat of Council intervention to win the reversal of at least one procedural decision. This problem occurred as a result of Cayzedo's attempt in October 1540 to initiate the substantiation of his claim that Toledo's letter of sale from king Ferdinand III was false. Because the petition was submitted on the same day that the tribunal confirmed the conclusion of evidence submission, there were grounds for suspecting another attempt to delay a decision. Despite Cayzedo's customary claim that "in a matter so arduous, of such quality, and so ancient" there was no reason not to give more time for consideration and his argument that it was a new matter that had just come to the lawyers' attention, on Tuesday 15 March 1541, the justices ruled that Cayzedo's request was indeed out of order.

The following Friday, Cayzedo entered a detailed and complex appeal prepared by a committee of the duke's best lawyers. The appeal's many arguments might not have swayed the court from its determination to permit no further delays in a case that had already gone on so long and that the monarch had ordered to be expedited on several occasions, but the concluding argument was a clear threat. It reminded the court what had happened when the duke tried to argue the falsity of king Henry IV's revocation of king John II's grants of Belalcázar and Hinojosa, which Córdoba had presented in its case. This document was more important to Córdoba's claim than Toledo's similar one was to its case, because Córdoba held the domain concerned by a grant from king Ferdinand III rather than by purchase, and the legal rights involved with the two kinds of title were substantially different. The Chancillería gave rulings prejudicial to the duke, but the Council of Castile proceeded to infringe upon the Chancillería's independence by ordering that the revocation be summarily removed from consideration and given no weight.[50]

These proceedings in the Council of Castile had upset Toledo's patricians. Toledo's municipal council had its representatives meet with those of Córdoba to discuss the matter even if Toledo decided to do nothing official, for it was feared that indirect damage would be done to Toledo's case in Granada. After hearing the duke's threat and recalling the infringement of its independence by the Council of Castile in the Córdoba trial, the court reversed itself on 2 August 1541 and agreed to receive evidence on the falsity of king Ferdinand III's letter of sale to Toledo. The president of the Chancillería took the unusual step of attending the session in which the decision was made.[51]

Judgment Unstained by Corruption or Bias

As the third element, the avoidance of outside intervention, suggests, the success of all the others depended on a fourth: the ability of the Chancillería to avoid all taint of bias or corruption in the final judgment. During the course of the trial, the judges went to great lengths to keep the proceedings clear of charges of foul play. At one time (February–March 1547), the court allowed challenges to eight of the sixteen oidores then on the bench.[52] Because it had been the practice of the Chancillería since some time before 1542 to have the alcaldes rather than the oidores hear such challenges, the reasons for them do not form part of the trial transcript and the relevant documents have apparently not survived in the Chancillería's archive. Many of the challenges, however, probably involved matters of kinship to one or both of the parties. Kinship was clearly the case with the court's president in the late 1530s and early 1540s, the archbishop of Granada. He was Hernando Niño, a member of an important Toledo patrician family. When he became president in 1539, at least one relative, his brother Juan, was a regidor. In 1544 at least three relatives held this office. Having so many oidores unable to hear the case created numerous problems when petitions were taken to public audiences only to find that, due to the challenges, there were too few justices to give a ruling. By 1547 all three members of the original chamber Dr. Gálvez, Ldo. Melchor de León, and Ldo. don Juan Sarmiento, who had handled all of the procedural motions for the appeal stage of the trial, had been removed from the case, but instead of trying to replace them individually as they were challenged, the court merely impaneled a new tribunal consisting of Ldo. Alarcón, Ldo. Frías, and Ldo. Salas.[53]

The oidores were not the only ones affected by this care in avoiding partiality. In response to its own ordinance passed while it was still in Ciudad Real in 1503, the court also acted to remove lower officials. In 1536, Diego López de Portillo was removed as receptor because he and Toledo's barrister, Alonso Alvarez de Villareal, were married to sisters. Receptor Luis de Santestevan was dismissed in 1543 because he, his brothers, and his father had worked for a certain Juan Alvarez who was from Toledo. Alvarez's sons, who had been born there, were friends of regidor don Juan de Ayala, Toledo's solicitor in Granada for the case, and been guests in his house. Toledo successfully challenged receptor Fernando del Gadillo in 1541 solely on the ground that he had been dropped from the Córdoba case after that city's barristers, who were the same as Toledo's, had objected to him.[54]

The office of *relator* (reporter of evidence) was considerably more important than that of receptor, and a long hearing ensued when, on 9 October 1542, Toledo challenged Ldo. Juan Rodríguez de Baeza, who had been named relator in the Puebla de Alcocer case. The city claimed that he had been selected because of his connections to oidor Dr. Peñaranda, whom Toledo had challenged and who was in charge of replacing the earlier relator who had retired. Worse yet, Baeza had been barrister and guardian at court for the duke of Sessa and his sisters, one of whom was about to marry the marquis of Gibraleón, son of the duke of Béjar. The marquis had, as viscount of Puebla de Alcocer, opposed the execution of the Council of Castile's verdict in the El Hornillo case. Baeza was handling the legal preparations for the wedding and was a good friend of Ciprián de León who represented the duke of Béjar in the case. Moreover, Baeza's son-in-law, Gonzalo Rodríguez, worked for the other side. The future marquise of Gibraleón, doña Francisca de Córdoba, would control the viscounty of Puebla de Alcocer's tributes as part of the marriage settlement, and the marquis, as the eldest son of the duke of Béjar, was likely to become a party in the case.

Baeza tried to challenge Dr. Gálvez, who handled the investigation, on the ground that Gálvez had "ill will" toward him, but there was nothing concrete in this charge. In fact, it looks as if Gálvez may have disliked Baeza as a manipulator who had little respect for the proprieties of his office and seemed genuinely unable to see why his background disqualified him for so sensitive a position in an important case. Because he had held office for a quarter century, he was the product of an earlier, and perhaps more corrupt, era in the Chancillería's history. The court took the case away from Baeza despite his vigorous protests.[55]

At times, even though a challenge was not sufficiently substantiated to warrant the removal of the official involved, the court might act to placate the challenging party. In such circumstances the court would appoint a companion to do the work with the official being challenged but at the expense of the party that brought the challenge. This solution was employed when Cayzedo challenged Br. Guedeja, Baeza's replacement, on grounds that really indicated displeasure at Guedeja's unwillingness to manipulate the order in which cases were considered. Baeza had tried to put the El Hornillo case, now involving only the adjustment of the boundary since the Council had awarded the village to Toledo, before the Belalcázar case in order of consideration, which would have further delayed a verdict in the latter. The court refused to remove Guedeja but ordered that Ldo. Alonso Hernández act as Guedeja's companion.[56]

When corruption did strike, however, the court acted swiftly to deal with it. In July 1536, Cayzedo accused *mariscal* (marshal) don Pedro de Navarra, corregidor of Toledo, of intimidating the elderly witnesses whose depositions Luis Pérez Caro was ordered to take. Cayzedo claimed that Pérez Caro and Ldo. Coronel, the duke of Béjar's representative, were questioning a chronicler, Juan Hidalgo, when three constables, sent by the corregidor, arrested Hidalgo and carried him through the streets as a warning to other witnesses not to testify. At the same time, unjust claims were made about Ldo. Coronel in order to further intimidate witnesses. The court asked for more information about the incident and ordered the corregidor and all other officials to desist under threat of a hefty 200,000 maravedís fine.

Thus, the court acted immediately to prevent any infringement of the duke's ability to prepare a defense, but there was more to the story than Cayzedo had indicated. Toledo had already issued a commission to its representative at the Chancillería, jurado Alonso Martínez de Mora, to present evidence about the bribing of witnesses to obtain false testimony and the suborning of Pérez Caro to permit this practice. The city had sent out three investigators, regidor Francisco de Marañón, jurado Ldo. Antonio Alvarez, and Ldo. Francisco Gutiérrez, to gather testimony in Talavera, Puebla de Montalbán, and Toledo itself about how Pérez Caro was doing his work. The commission's composition indicated its importance. The investigation revealed that the receptor was eating and staying with the duke's procuradores, Ldo. Coronel and Juan de Porras, and it was suggested that the witnesses were poor men who were being bribed to lie about their age and testimony.

Pérez Caro sent in his version of what happened. He reported that in Talavera on 17 July, Gutiérrez told him that Toledo found him "odious and suspicious" and charged him with allowing the suborning of witnesses and having an illegal relationship with the duke's procuradores, but Pérez Caro had refused to stop work unless bond were posted. At that moment, Porras came to complain about the city's harassment of potential witnesses and told the Hidalgo story. The duke's procurador also expressed indignation that the corregidor had made unjust charges against his master, including the charge that the towns had been stolen from Toledo. Porras told the receptor he had argued that this was untrue because they had been lost during a rebellion, but the corregidor replied only that bribing witnesses would not be allowed. The public outcry against the duke's representatives was, according to Porras, so great that they did not dare stay in the town.

Martínez de Mora made his formal complaint on 4 August, and after examining the evidence, the court removed Pérez Caro but gave the duke time to send out additional receptores. In the meantime, Toledo had asked the Council of Castile to investigate the matter, and after the duke's representative before that body, Melchor de la Peña, tried to withhold the transcriptions in his possession, the Council, on 30 August, ordered the Chancillería of Granada to appoint an oidor or some other respectable person to receive further evidence. At Toledo's request, the Chancillería stopped the work of another of the duke's receptores and ordered Pérez Caro put in irons so that the royal prosecutor could file criminal charges against him for being too friendly with Ldo. Coronel and Juan de Porras. Apparently the evidence that Pérez Caro knew about the bribes was shaky, but the prosecutor asked that the penalty be the stiffest possible as a warning to others who might break the ordinances against such illegal fraternization.

The receptor's defense was that, because the municipalities he worked in were small, he had to stay with the duke's representatives. Toledo's evidence had shown this claim to be untrue, and Pérez Caro practically admitted this when he said that he went to the inn in Talavera because it was the best. He told the prosecutor that he felt he could not take testimony about the suborning of witnesses because of his limited commission, and he denied being present when the duke's men sought witnesses. What is more, he argued, others did the same, and he had thirty years of court service without a blemish. Despite these claims, the court convicted him and sentenced him to a prison term to be imposed later, a six-month suspension from office, and a 30-ducat fine. One suspects the justices felt Pérez Caro was guilty of more than a lack of discretion.

However, Toledo had brought Juan Hidalgo to Granada and deposited him in the audiencia's jail, where the justices interrogated him and found that a velour cloak had been given him as a bribe. They also determined that Pérez Caro probably did not know what had happened, and after a subsequent intensive review of his record as a court official, the tribunal, on 4 November, upheld the conviction but reduced the suspension to three months, withdrew the fine, and imposed no additional jail time.[57]

Although *cartas ejecutorias* (sealed royal writs announcing a verdict), as we shall see, are not particularly good evidence for the actual course of a judicial proceeding, there is some indication that the audiencia was willing to act decisively to condemn questionable actions by commissioned judges. In September 1538, the Council of Castile commissioned Br. Martín de Azebedo to hear a claim by the city of Trujillo against the duke of Béjar and the councils of Puebla de Alcocer and Casas de Don Pedro over some land near the latter town. Azebedo gave a verdict in favor of Trujillo in December. The duke appealed in January 1539, and the appeal went by commission of the Council of Castile to the audiencia of Granada, an action apparently designed to further the Crown's desire to limit the number of cases before the Council. After receiving evidence from both sides about the proceedings before Br. Azebedo, the court, on 26 June 1540, overturned the boundary judge's ruling. Although, as always, the carta ejecutoria is vague about the matter, the reversal of Br. Azebedo's verdict resulted from some wrongdoing associated with his companion, Pedro Ramírez, in which, one assumes, Trujillo was involved. Not only did the judicial system act decisively to undo the damage caused by corrupt practices, but it also, as was earlier suggested as possible in cases of small importance to the commonwealth, acted rather quickly, the whole matter being dealt with in less than two years by the time the court confirmed, on 6 August 1540, the June verdict.[58]

The Chancillería judges seem to have gotten good results from their efforts to keep proceedings clear of the taint of corruption, especially considering the prohibition against using the resources of other institutions and officials and the somewhat loose general standards on conflict of interest. Indeed, a careful reading of the *visitas* (investigations) of the Chancillería of Granada for 1536, 1542, 1549, 1563, and 1567 reveals that things went pretty well, not perhaps by some ideal standard but certainly by the standard of courts in many areas of the United States. If the Chancillería did at least as well as a modern judicial system with its advantages of better communications, larger numbers of officials, better procedures, and clear law, one would have to say that it did well. If criticism is needed, it is of the contemporary U.S. judicial system because that of sixteenth-century Castile compares with it so favorably.[59]

Charles V Rejects Aristocratic Pressure

There is some evidence that the court was succeeding in paving the way for acceptance of its final verdict, and to ensure this result, the emperor had to resist persuasive requests from the House of Béjar and its supporters for royal intervention. Charles suffered from severe financial difficulties in the late 1530s and called upon his territorial aristocracy, at the Cortes of Toledo of 1538–1539, to approve a tax on foodstuffs that would directly affect their interests. In general, the magnates expressed special dissatisfaction with the way the post-Comunidades reforms of judicial institutions had placed the fate of their lawsuits in the hands of justices such as the oidores of the Chancillerías. They wanted Charles to name some aristocrats to the Council of Castile, which would then have final review of all such cases. In the losing fight for approval of the tax in the noble assembly, the duke of Béjar was a leader of the emperor's supporters against an opposition headed by the condestable of Castile. Nor was this the duke's first great service to the emperor. In 1532, he had equipped an army and joined Charles in Austria on his crusade against the Turks. Also, at about this time and during the next few years, the duke had valuable Court connections. In 1541, Francisco de los Cobos's daughter married the duke of Sessa, whose sister was, a year later, to become the wife of the duke of Béjar's eldest son and heir. As marquise of Gibraleón, she would be given the rents of Puebla de Alcocer.[60]

The duke of Béjar was himself in financial trouble. Despite careful management and a reasonable style of living for a territorial aristocrat, he had financial problems. To solve them he made his wife consent to the sale of some of the lands she had inherited from her mother. Financial pressure had so upset the duke that, as the duchess later testified before a notary, he locked her up in isolation to force her consent. Poor doña Teresa de Zúñiga claimed she had actually feared she would be killed if she protested her treatment before or during the sale.[61]

Faced with problems so serious that his actions seem somewhat unbalanced, and having rendered great services to the Crown, the duke approached Charles, some time in 1538 or 1539, with a petition about the Belalcázar lawsuit.[62] Although the document was prepared in consultation with his House's letrados, it shows how the duke and his advisers wanted to argue their side of the dispute when they were at Court rather than dealing with stuffy oidores in Granada. The first verdict of the Chancillería in the case (1536) had been in favor of Toledo, and the matter was then being heard on appeal. The duke told Charles that the 1536 decision, if the justices were allowed to uphold it, would weaken the Crown's right to castigate traitors and reward loyal servants, and royal authority would be limited by what the sovereign's judges chose to allow. Two inferences would be made from such a verdict. First, all past confiscations would be called in doubt, and the monarchy had "the largest and best part" of them. Second, the verdict would nullify a proper use of absolute royal authority and give the domains to those who wanted to be disloyal. The duke asserted that the justices felt that none of Toledo's past actions, which evidence had shown to be damaging to the monarch, had made any difference in their deliberations and suggested that the verdict, if upheld, might encourage disloyalty now. This challenge to Charles's authority was going on in his own audiencia, something his grandfather had not allowed to happen, referring apparently to Ferdinand's action of 1511. The duke asked that two or three members of the Council of Castile examine the affair and that the emperor uphold royal capacity and authority and restore to the duke what had been a fair reward for his services. The petition was a powerful statement of the view that the monarch had the authority to reward services by loyal vassals without judicial review when such grants were challenged by another party, and it was presented by one of the emperor's most loyal and influential territorial aristocrats. Charles, however, in keeping with his determination not to interfere with justice, denied the petition, and the duke's lawyers and other advisers despaired of ever getting any help from this quarter.

Obviously fearing that he would lose his contested domains in court, the duke sought to salvage something by way of a compromise. On 8 January 1539, the condestable of Castile began an attempt to settle the dispute out of court. To demonstrate its interest in such a settlement, Toledo's council agreed to allow the duke to keep his beautiful palace above Puebla de Alcocer as well as his houses in the town when the case was finished. Ldo. Puebla, Toledo's chief attorney in the case, notified the monarch about the agreement, and Charles was doubtless relieved that some of the sting would be removed from any decision that was unfavorable to a loyal, wealthy, well-connected, and dependable vassal.[63]

The rest of the effort to settle the case did not go well. In a letter of 10 January to jurado Martínez de Mora in Granada, Toledo indicated that the condestable's approach to the city, which also involved the almirante, was going to be part of a deal relating to the El Hornillo lawsuit before the Council of Castile. Indeed, a decision favorable to the city in the El Hornillo case was handed down the following March, perhaps because the duke gave up trying to delay those proceedings. An offer to settle the Belalcázar lawsuit was made, and Martínez de Mora, as an expert on the dispute, was asked for his opinion (now lost). Letters were sent out, on 20 December 1540, to the regidores not in Toledo to ask them to return for a discussion of the matter because it was so important. Martínez de Mora was subsequently told, however, that there were problems and he should work aggressively on the Belalcázar lawsuit even though negotiations were continuing. Toledo's council was trying to get the execution of the verdict involving El Hornillo completed because the duke was delaying it at some cost to the city, and there is an indication of some despair over ever getting the village and its lands back from so tenacious an opponent. In a letter a week later to the jurado, the city council showed a definite fear that the duke was now only using the negotiations as a means to delay legal proceedings even further. Martínez de Mora was to continue the prosecution of the Belalcázar case and explain the situation to the Chancillería justices.

Finally, on 17 January 1541, perhaps irritated by the duke of Béjar's delaying tactics over El Hornillo as well as in Granada, the city's jurados ordered that no further attempt be made to negotiate a settlement of the Belalcázar case.[64] One party was to win the entire viscounty of Puebla de Alcocer, and the courts would decide the victor.

A narrative focus on the development of the "early modern state" privileges limited types of interaction: those involving the monarch and the royal Household and Court. In the events narrated in this chapter, the monarch and at least one Court institution, the Council of Castile, play roles, but the interactions are so complex that no entity appears that could be labeled as "the state" and reified into an actor. The investigation of such interactions is the more accurate and scientifically cautious way to explore historical processes, because this method exposes better than statist analyses or purely local studies the complex interplay of factors from the social and cultural environments that shape human action. Although it might be objected that these events are not really important and therefore are not capable of displaying the coercive power of the state, they were obviously important to participants, as the survival of the parties' documentary collections suggests. Moreover, because change is continuous, it is difficult to determine when some sequence of events is "important" in any transcendent sense, for something that appears insignificant by the usual historiographical standards might in fact be a fundamental aspect of a major transformation. Decisions made by actors involved in the Belalcázar case have that quality. In chapter 6, we will see that the verdict would turn on legal issues that were sophisticated constitutional principles on which, from the perspective of interpretive schemes common within Castile's political kingdom, the commonwealth's future depended.

Chapter 6

MAKING JUDGMENTS: LETRADO THEORIES AND INTERPRETIVE SCHEMES

Introduction

A trial provides a forum in which the significant issues are frozen in a way that makes them resonate with the parties, and in high profile contests, among those with similar concerns. The trial sorted the fluid mix of different interpretive schemes available within the Castilian cultural environment into starkly contrasting positions. When they realized that the only chance to keep Toledo from regaining the viscounty of Puebla de Alcocer probably lay in the outcome of the judicial proceedings, the duke of Béjar's lawyers increased their efforts to improve their case. By the time of the Granadan audiencia's second decision in 1555, both sides had presented the evidence and arguments clearly showing that the root problem of the lawsuit was the nature of the monarch's authority.

Of course, the complex interactions among the parties to the dispute and the royal officials involved yielded subtle alterations in the meaning of absolute royal authority as it had been perceived by protagonists in the fifteenth century or during the Comunidades rebellion. Moreover, these interactions took place during a period in which territorial aristocrats became estranged from the political life of the Cortes as an institution and the interpretive schemes cued for participants there. Because of the increasing financial difficulties of many aristocratic houses, grandees became more dependent on royal service and intervention in their affairs by a monarchy approaching the bankruptcy of 1557. The commonwealth's political leaders, therefore, viewed a final settlement of the conflict as the ratification of a sophisticated articulation, couched in the discourse of letrados, of some interpretive perspective used to evaluate royal leadership. Whatever the motives of those who rendered it, interested observers perceived the audiencia's verdict to be a public affirmation of a classification scheme giving priority either to the assertion that good government is based on rewards in recognition of service, a view defended in this instance by a member of the territorial aristocracy, or to a view that stressed the importance of the provision of justice based on written law applied by a judiciary composed of trained, professional jurists, advocated here by the patrician leaders of one of Castile's major cities. Although these interpretive schemes were components of a cultural environment common to magnates and local notables alike, in relation to interactions with the Crown, the expectation of reward for service tended to be a shaping characteristic of grandee action while those who were not great seigniors more often valued monarchy as an institution protecting legally established rights.

Because effective royal rule in Castile depended on balancing the aspirations conceived and expressed in these terms by political actors, the foundation of such rule was the general absence of a stark confrontation of opposed interpretive schemes between which the Crown would have to choose. Any decision in such a prominent case could potentially endanger the monarch's capacity to govern because the justices would support the valuation and classification more characteristic of one group, thereby potentially antagonizing the other, and such harm would be more likely if the verdict were somehow perceived to be consonant with a contemporary pattern of royal action. The question of the monarch's relationship to the law intellectually embodied these conflicting understandings of the style of rule: was the king bound by the law's dictates in reference to his subjects' property rights or could he violate the law as he willed, to reward his vassals' services?

I examine the evidence presented during the trial over Puebla de Alcocer and its associated towns and lands in detail because it reveals important aspects of interpretive schemes of the cultural environment. For those letrados and other members of the commonwealth's leadership for whom the proper exercise of absolute royal authority demanded the extension by Crown judicial institutions of due process to disputing parties, especially where matters of contract and property were concerned, the major events described here, and in chapter 5, helped shape evaluations of the monarch's government. Moreover, the evidence presented during the trial constitutes a significant part of the documentary base of this microhistory and must, therefore, be evaluated to support the veracity of my account.[1] Of course, in a lawsuit, lawyers often develop a theoretical position solely to shape the interpretation of evidence by judges in ways favorable to their clients. Often, this work results in an artificial framework, which distorts the reality of relationships and events when it does not disguise them completely. That is not what happened in the Belalcázar case. Despite the procedural struggles and the attempts to raise as many issues as possible, in the end the crucial perspectives on which the parties wanted the final decision to turn, although perhaps expressed in a more sophisticated discourse of legal thought than was common within the Castilian commonwealth, were exactly those that were often the most important in shaping political action, as the Comunidades crisis had highlighted.

The parties provided two types of evidence: oral testimony, much of it given before Chancillería receptores in different domains of the Castilian Crown, and documents, either originals or official transcriptions made from the originals by the receptores. The quantity of material presented, and fortunately most of it still exists, was substantial.[2]

Toledo's Evidence

Perhaps because Toledo's council and lawyers had waited so long to make their presentation, their case was well developed right from the early years of the trial. They submitted evidence to show that Puebla de Alcocer and the other settlements were part of the territory that Toledo had purchased in the thirteenth century and that the city's jurisdiction had been confirmed by subsequent monarchs. They intended to demonstrate that Toledo had held the territory, with full jurisdiction, until it was lost to the master of Alcántara. Although Toledo's representatives would not concede that the document containing John II's grant of Puebla de Alcocer to Gutierre de Sotomayor was genuine, they still wanted to show that it was given in violation of the law, that because of the pressure the king was under as a result of civil wars and invasions, John made the grant against his intent,[3] and that he later revoked the dismemberment of Toledo's territory. The city's lawyers also argued that don Gutierre seized the area by violence and that Br. Piedrahita's 1448 survey was fraudulent. In particular, they emphasized that the other places in the viscounty had never been under the jurisdiction of Puebla de Alcocer. Despite what occurred during John II's reign, Toledo claimed that Henry IV revoked his father's grant in 1465 on the grounds that it was against the law and contrary to his father's testament. To satisfy the law's requirements about claims against lands held for a long time, Toledo's lawyers had to show that the municipal council had continually requested justice but that the Crown's difficulties and dependence on the grandees had prevented the city from receiving a hearing and judgment.

To support these claims, the city presented Ferdinand III's letter of sale for the Montes, issued in Jaén, 4 January 1246.[4] Its letrados also submitted a series of later documents to bolster Toledo's claim of continuous possession under the terms of Ferdinand's letter. These included three boundary decisions by Alfonso X: between Toledo and the master of Alcántara (12 July 1262); between Toledo and neighboring Talavera (11 September 1262); and between Toledo and Córdoba (6 May 1264). Toledo presented the charter it had granted to Puebla de Alcocer in 1288 in an effort to populate the area (2 February 1288; confirmed 19 March 1290). Its representatives also added documents from the reign of Alfonso XI, who awarded Puebla de Alcocer and some nearby fortifications to Toledo in settlement of a dispute with

Diego García de Toledo, chief constable of the city, and others, which dealt with a complicated exchange of lands between Toledo and the king involving a grant to Bernaldín, viscount of Cabrera in Catalonia. They introduced as well two confirmations of Toledo's holdings, including Puebla and Herrera, by Henry II (1369 and 1371) and a series of confirmations involving Alfonso XI (1347), Henry II (1371), and John II (1417). In 1530, Toledo added to this collection another division of lands by Alfonso X, this one between the city and the order of Calatrava (28 August 1269).[5] All of these documents mentioned at least part of the disputed region and often indicated that the land had been held by purchase from Ferdinand III.

On the basis of these documents, Toledo demonstrated the type of jurisdiction the city had exercised over the towns. The city submitted a book of council minutes for the year 1425; a copy was made of all of the business transacted with the area in question. These notarial records specifically mentioned Puebla de Alcocer (sometimes just as Alcocer), Herrera, Fuenlabrada, Helechosa, Villarta, and the bridge over the Guadiana River, Casas de Don Pedro, and the pasture lands of Cijara and Estena. The documents indicated that Toledo exercised jurisdiction as lord of the towns and lands involved. Among the matters dealt with were the collection of taxes and rents on both produce and livestock migrations, the appointment and conduct of town officials, the repair of the Villarta bridge, disputes with the Mesta, and matters involving both civil and criminal justice. In addition, all of the towns conducted their affairs with Toledo directly, without any deference to or intervention by Puebla de Alcocer's council. Toledo's letrados also added some miscellaneous supporting documents from about the same time dealing with payments to officials, tax receipts, and other transactions and communications not usually included in the council minutes.

The capstone of the documents relating to prior ownership did not become part of the record until the second hearing when, in May 1536, Toledo presented a transcript of a 1496–1497 case between the Mesta and the count of Belalcázar. In these proceedings the count admitted Toledo's prior ownership in order to obtain a royal order commanding the city's officials to hand over certain documents about passage rights to the Villarta bridge that had been kept in the municipal archive.

Toledo's representatives also included in their documentary collection items that raised doubts about John II's intentions and supported the authenticity of his and Henry IV's revocations of the grant, and they presented documents showing the city's attempts to obtain justice. The major item here was Henry IV's revocation of the grant, based in part on the 1442 law of Valladolid, which was quoted in the text and reveals one prevailing interpretation of the meaning and intent of that statute, and in part on John II's final testament, which was not quoted. They submitted Br. Francisco Ortiz's 1480 petition to Ferdinand and Isabella, but the 1490 and 1493 petitions to the

Catholic Monarchs were presented to Ldo. Bela Núñez and thus were included in the evidence that the Crown had accepted *ad perpetuam rei memoriam* in 1497. In 1530, the city placed in evidence the 1446 petition to John II and the general pardon of 1451, which had restored all of Toledo's lands seized or granted to others by the Crown. Just after the first verdict in 1536, Toledo presented the evidence that had been given in 1504 before Ldo. Zomeño, including the protests about Br. Piedrahita's survey both to the judge and to the king, as well as John II's 1444–1445 assurances to Puebla de Alcocer, Toledo, and Pedro López de Ayala that the status of the town of Puebla de Alcocer would not be changed.[6]

The *ad perpetuam rei memoriam* depositions of 1496 served as the foundation of Toledo's oral evidence because they provided eyewitness accounts of Toledo's prior jurisdiction over the region and knowledgeable statements about the nature and source of this jurisdiction. The testimony also contained information about the area's seizure by Gutierre de Sotomayor, the conduct of Piedrahita's survey, general conditions during the reigns of John II and his children, and Toledo's attempts to obtain justice (see chapter 3). Receptores took depositions in 1526 that were added to this 1496 material and carried the course of the dispute up to date. Except for material discussing whether the towns claimed by Toledo were within the boundaries indicated in Ferdinand III's letter of sale, most of the 1526 responses were of little value because no eyewitnesses were involved. However, two questions dealt with the wars of the Catholic Monarchs, with their dependence on the kingdom's territorial aristocrats and the favors the Crown had bestowed on these aristocrats, and with the way this favoritism toward the magnates interfered with Toledo's attempts to get justice and led to the repeated suspension of the case. A final question asked about the financial damage done to Toledo by the loss of its jurisdiction. Additionally, Toledo wanted to verify the identities, age, and suitability of the 1496 witnesses.[7]

My review of this evidence indicates that the plaintiff had put together a particularly strong case. At the moment when the audiencia's judges were due to render their first decision in the lawsuit, the duke of Béjar found himself in a difficult position because the passage of time had made oral evidence of dubious value. However, although most of his evidence fell short of refuting Toledo's points, the duke's lawyers did make a good enough case to focus the court's final decision on an interpretation of royal authority.

The House of Béjar's Evidence

Perhaps because they still hoped to encourage the Crown's intervention and, more probably, in order to gain time, the marquis of Ayamonte's lawyers (don Francisco would not become duke of Béjar until 1532) first presented witnesses, from both sides of the Atlantic, to show that the Sotomayor family had maintained peaceful and complete jurisdiction over the territory in question for sixty years or the memory of man. They specifically asked if the marquis maintained guards to keep residents of Toledo's lands from using those of the viscounty. If one concedes anything in a lawsuit, Toledo would certainly have conceded this much, while claiming it was all illegal.[8]

The marquis unsuccessfully attacked, first, Toledo's claim that the viscounty was part of the territory sold to the city by Ferdinand III and then, during the second hearing, the authenticity of the letter of sale. The first attack was three-pronged, with the initial thrust aimed at whether the Herrera mentioned in the letter of sale was the one held by the marquis. His most important document was a grant to Puebla de Alcocer (4 December 1362) from Diego García de Toledo, whose title to the area was later revoked by Alfonso XI. García de Toledo acknowledged that Herreruela was mistakenly taken from Puebla, and the village was returned to Puebla's jurisdiction. The witnesses whose depositions were taken in 1529 were asked two questions relating to Herrera: (1) had it been an underpopulated place called Herreruela until it grew under the count's protection and was renamed Herrera? and (2) was there a village called Herrera near Los Yébenes that had been depopulated for a long time and that Toledo now confused with the Herreruela of the viscounty? Much later, in 1548, the House's lawyers presented a revenue declaration drafted by Toledo's chief notary in May 1535. The document delineated Toledo's revenue district of the so-called Cuadrilla de Herrera, which contained Navahermosa, Navalmoral, Navalucillos, and the area around these places.[9]

The second thrust was an attack on the idea that the Alcocer in the letter of sale was the Puebla de Alcocer held by the duke of Béjar. In October 1543, his barrister obtained transcriptions of a 1245 grant to Córdoba presented in another case and of parts of certain chronicles. All of these sources mentioned a village called Alcocer.[10]

The final thrust was the most complicated. The aristocrat's lawyers argued in January 1545 that Puebla de Alcocer was not included in Ferdinand's letter of sale because the town was not part of the exchange between archbishop of Toledo Rodrigo and Ferdinand III, which gave the Montes to the king in the first place (20 April 1243). In support of this claim, they placed in evidence on 9 June the archbishop's exchange of lands with Ferdinand III, Ferdinand's subsequent letter of sale to Toledo, and all of the material from the dispute with Toledo involving jurisdiction over the village of El Hornillo. Along with the other documents submitted in October 1546, they included a chapter from a hunting guide written in the reign of Alfonso XI.[11] Finally, on 17 August 1547, the marquis of Gibraleón's barrister (on his father's death in 1544, don Alonso did not become duke of Béjar because his mother retained her title) was permitted to place in evidence the survey made by Dr. Gálvez for the El Hornillo case.[12]

The aristocrat's letrados argued at this point not only that the count of Belalcázar's Puebla de Alcocer and Herrera were not the Alcocer and Herrera mentioned in Ferdinand's letter of sale, but also that they could not have been because the boundary of that sale clearly fell to the east of the viscounty. Because there were no boundaries mentioned in the letter of sale and the places named were mentioned without any clear order based on spacial relationships, the territorial limits of the Montes had to be determined by looking at the exchange with archbishop Rodrigo on which the sale was alleged to have been based. In the document detailing that exchange, they considered this statement most important: "from Marches until Estena, and that Estena with its jurisdiction also as it is, goes in a straight line until the *hoz* of the Guadiana." All of the other place names in this part of this boundary description had apparently gone out of use by the sixteenth century, but Estena was a pasture north and west of Horcajo. When Dr. Gálvez did his survey designed to divide the viscounty of Puebla de Alcocer from Toledo's lands, he ran the boundary from Estena to the west of El Hornillo and then to an *hoz* (ravine or narrow pass) on the Guadiana River somewhere south of El Hornillo and west of Arroba. This, the marquis of Gibraleón's lawyers claimed, was the western boundary of archbishop Rodrigo's exchange with the king and therefore of the Montes of Toledo as sold to Toledo by Ferdinand III. Ldo. Manjárrez (or Manjares), long a principal legal adviser of the Béjar House and executor of don Francisco's will in 1544, even provided a hand-drawn map of the region to show the location of the boundary. In addition, the Council of Castile had set the boundary between the viscounty and Toledo in its 1539 decision in the El Hornillo case. It was argued that the fourteenth-century hunting guide supported this claim by mentioning no boundary between the Peloche-Fuenlabrada area and the lands of Capilla further to the south.[13]

The evidence submitted by the defense was far from irrefutable. The oral evidence in support of the claim that Herrera had been Herreruela and that Toledo had possessed another Herrera near Los Yébenes was thin. Only two witnesses affirmed this, as eyewitnesses, in the depositions taken by one receptor and none of those interrogated by the other receptor affirmed it. The two eyewitnesses claimed to be 103 and 112 years old, respectively. Two people had mentioned another Herrera when Pérez Caro took testimony on the letter of sale in 1536: one was Toledo's chief notary, who discussed the Cuadrilla de Herrera, and the other was so confused that his testimony could hardly be considered reliable, especially as it was entirely hearsay. Ldo. Manjárrez tried to be as vague as possible about the substance of this testimony in his brief. The argument about other places named Alcocer could just as easily be used to claim that the name was common so there was no reason to believe that the place in the letter of sale was any other than the one that eventually became Puebla de Alcocer. Because he was not writing a legal document or an accurate survey but a description, the hunting guide's author would not necessarily have included boundaries.

Two serious problems arise as soon as the claims about the exchange with archbishop Rodrigo are carefully examined. First, the hoz on the Guadiana was probably not a place name; instead, it was probably, as it is now, a term that means something different in each village of the region. A hoz does exist where Dr. Gálvez mentioned it, but it is certainly not the only one on the Guadiana as the river flows in and around the viscounty of Puebla de Alcocer. Modern dams make it hard to locate the others, but there are at least two major narrow ravines on the river after it again turns southwest. One is on a line between Herrera and Casas de Don Pedro while the other is south of the latter town and northwest of Puebla de Alcocer. Because the other places to which the exchange referred cannot be located, the hoz could just as easily be one of these, or some other.[14] To obscure this possibility from the judges, Manjárrez truncated his map so that it showed only the stretch of the river where it flows northwest, in other words, only the part where the House of Béjar wanted the boundary between the viscounty and Toledo drawn.

A second problem was just as serious. Although Ferdinand III mentioned in the letter of sale that the Montes had belonged to the archbishop, he did not specifically mention the exchange. In fact, in discussing the multiple sources of the archbishop's holdings, Ferdinand left the impression that the archbishop could have obtained the area being sold at different times and in different ways. The governing factor in determining the boundaries of the property was not the letter of exchange but rather the charters of the archbishop indicating his purchases and grants received from earlier monarchs.

Thus, the internal logic of the House of Béjar's presentation was weak. It collapsed completely, however, when the documents and arguments presented by Toledo were taken into account. As the Diego García de Toledo letter was written by a man later held, by Alfonso XI, to have taken Puebla de Alcocer illegally, any subsequent disposition of the village's property would be *ipso facto* void. Toledo exposed one of the elderly witness who claimed Herrera was called Herreruela as a liar who was not 103 years of age, and showed that the testimony of the other was so contradictory and confused as to be worthless. Because his corruption trial threw anything done by receptor Pérez Caro in 1536 into doubt, the testimony he recorded would have been of little value.[15]

The continuity of possession shown in the city's documentary collection struck the real blow to the whole idea that the viscounty villages were not part of the purchased Montes. The document dealing with the division of lands with the order of Alcántara specifically places Toledo's Alcocer just north of the Zújar River and north and west of the Sierra de Lares. If this was not the site of the fifteenth-century town of Puebla de Alcocer, then it could only be the site of the castle above it. The same document described a boundary line along the Guadalemar River which, flowing east and then south of Fuenlabrada, remained the boundary of the viscounty. And the letter of sale specifically mentioned the lands of the order of Alcántara as lying along one of the Montes's boundaries. The boundary between Córdoba and Toledo was drawn along the Siruela River which, again, was roughly that of the viscounty. Especially devastating were the documents relating to the abortive exchange involving the count of Cabrera. These not only gave a quite accurate description of the region, placing Herrera, not Herreruela, in its present location, but clearly indicated that Puebla and Herrera were separate entities. What is more, the boundary drawn for the land to be exchanged excluded Fuenlabrada, Cijara, Helechosa, Villarta, and all the land to the north. Casas de Don Pedro was mentioned as being within the area to be exchanged. This evidence would damage the House of Béjar's claim that the viscounty had always been a unit under the jurisdiction of Puebla de Alcocer. The fifteenth-century documents and oral testimony strengthened a picture that was already clear from the documentary record of the thirteenth and fourteenth centuries. Even if the viscounty were not part of the exchange between the archbishop and Ferdinand III, long and unchallenged custom had placed it firmly within the Montes purchased by Toledo, and the case presented by the Béjar lawyers was too weak to shake that tradition, as Toledo pointed out.[16]

The duke of Béjar's representatives had even more difficulty supporting the assertion that the letter of sale itself was fraudulent. After the duke's barrister, Gastón de Cayzedo, threatened to involve the Council of Castile, the audiencia, in August 1540, allowed the duke to present evidence supporting his claim that Ferdinand III and his mother, queen Berenguela, who is mentioned in the letter, were both dead by the date of the sale and that none of the family members were in Jaén, the place of the sale, on that date. Again the duke's lawyers asked for depositions from a long list of witnesses, most of whom were notaries or jurists with various academic degrees. Some of the witnesses came to the Chancillería; because a document's authenticity was questioned, an oidor had to oversee the procedure. In part, the oral testimony may have been merely a device to gain time in which to find other material, because Cayzedo listed a large number of witnesses who were impeded from coming by illness, age, or distance so that oidor Ldo. Frías had to go and get this testimony *in loco*. The depositions from these witnesses no longer exist, but apparently their testimony was fruitless because Ldo. Manjárrez did not even mention it in the section of his brief where he attacked the letter of sale.[17]

Later, in 1546, the Béjar lawyers were able to submit some documentary evidence. It included the *Rótulos,* a kind of chronicle made up of short inscriptions, of the chapel of San Luis of Jaén's Franciscan monastery. One inscription mentioned the capture of Jaén on 25 November 1233, and Manjárrez argued that because Toledo had not shown that Ferdinand III had to take Jaén twice, the king could not have been there on 4 January 1246.[18] The problem here was that the letter of sale said nothing about the conquest of Jaén, only that Ferdinand was with the army near the city. Because Jaén was a frontier municipality until the reign of the Catholic Monarchs, there was nothing unusual about the royal army being nearby, particularly in Ferdinand III's reign.

The other relevant documents submitted in 1546 were some prologues from old manuscript copies of the *Siete Partidas* owned by various oidores of the Chancillería. These all contained information indicating that the reign of Alfonso X, Ferdinand III's son, had begun in 1241 (*era de* 1279) and thus five years before the alleged letter of sale. Ferdinand III, of course, died in 1252. The problem was the existence of a multitude of *Partidas* copies, many of which contained numerous mistakes. Indeed, it was impossible to reconstruct one that would faithfully represent Alfonso X's original work.[19] What the Béjar lawyers had found were copies with significant mistakes in the prologue, the part of least importance to the judges who owned them, which changed the dating of Alfonso's reign.

Toledo's lawyers put together a careful and devastating attack on the impugning of the letter of sale. Beginning in February 1542, they presented a large variety of documents. These included chapters about Ferdinand's death and other events of his reign from numerous chronicles in libraries in Granada and Toledo, the prologues from prestigious copies of the *Partidas* in Granada and Valladolid, and numerous grants made by Ferdinand III and Alfonso X. These grants were mostly from the years 1246 to 1254 and came from Seville, Toledo (from both the cathedral and the monastery of San Clemente), and the convent of Los Vélez of the order of Santiago.[20] This mountain of documents and chronicles was more than enough to defend the dating of the letter of sale.

During the first trial, the lawyers of don Francisco de Sotomayor, then still just marquis of Ayamonte, also attacked the grant revocation made by Henry IV as fraudulent. Cayzedo began his attack in October 1530, just after he had received power of attorney from the marquis, whose majority the court had recently declared. Cayzedo alleged that the form of the revocation was wrong, that many of its statements were false, and that it violated Henry's intentions because he was under pressure. At the Cortes of Niebla in 1473, he had revoked all provisions from 1464 until 15 September 1473 that prejudiced the interests of third parties. And Toledo had even been on the side of prince Alfonso at the time of the revocation. Cayzedo asked that Toledo be ordered to produce the originals of some of its documents, including the revocation. Toledo complied on 13 December, but Cayzedo had to petition the audiencia to force the city to include an edict of prince Alfonso, which had been part of its earlier presentation. This royal order was a revocation of Gutierre de Sotomayor's grant given on 29 June 1465 when Toledo had joined Alfonso's revolt; realizing too late that it was damaging to its own case, the city had tried to withhold the edict.[21]

Once his lawyers had seen the original revocation by king Henry IV, in January 1531 Cayzedo again challenged its validity. The city had not told Henry of its crimes against John II that caused the places to be seized, nor of the master of Alcántara's service to the king. Cayzedo charged that many false claims were included, such as a revocation of the grant in king John's will. He alleged that the revocation was of especially little value because Toledo was part of the party of the infante Alfonso and the document itself was marred.[22]

The following July, Cayzedo asked that fourteen other edicts of Henry IV from about the same time that belonged to the duke of Arcos be brought in for a comparison with that of Toledo. The secretaries who had signed these other edicts were Alfonso de Badajoz or Alvar Gómez, while the secretary in Toledo's document was Hernando de Badajoz. Six witnesses testified as experts: three Chancillería receptores and three of its notaries. The witnesses were asked if they could see that the alleged revocation document was effaced and blotted in three places and whether such marks were usual. Then they were asked if "Yl Rey" was Henry's usual signature instead of "Yo el Rey" as in Toledo's document, and the revocation was compared with the duke of Arcos's fourteen documents. The experts were further asked if the seal was the proper one. The last five questions dealt with the secretary who signed Henry's grants. The witnesses were asked whether Alfonso de Badajoz signed most of Henry's provisions and never, except in Toledo's document, Hernando de Badajoz. Then a comparison was made between the fourteen documents signed by Alfonso de Badajoz and Alvar Gómez and Toledo's revocation signed by Hernando de Badajoz. A final question asked whether the secretary had to sign royal provisions to validate them.

The witnesses showed that their expertise extended beyond a familiarity with documents to a knowledge of the ways of litigation. As the oldest witness, receptor Pedro Jiménez de Ariel, even acknowledged, the questionnaire was set up to introduce the fourteen provisions early on, in an effort to lead the witnesses into broad generalizations. All of them were, however, extremely careful in their answers. Their professional outlook led them to protest that no notary of worth would ever allow erasures in a document without having them properly indicated, especially in an important document. No one who has worked with documents from the period, and certainly not the audiencia justices, would attach much importance to this claim, particularly as the three blotches involved nothing crucial. On the questions about the royal signature, the seal, and the secretary, none of the experts could be induced to generalize beyond saying that in these respects Toledo's document was different from those of the duke of Arcos. Certainly none of the witnesses showed any tendency to say after this comparison that Toledo's revocation was false because of these differences, and the duke of Arcos's provisions had not themselves been validated for the purpose of the comparison. The marquis of Ayamonte's lawyers could not even get a statement that the secretary's signature was necessary.[23]

Their efforts did not save the duke of Béjar from an unfavorable verdict in 1536. The judges must have been a little suspicious, however, because they refused Toledo's repeated requests that the original version of Henry IV's revocation be returned and instead had it locked away in the Chancillería's safe deposit chest. In the second trial, when Toledo sought to validate the revocation, the city was unable to recover the document. Its validity was probably brought into even greater question by the Council of Castile's 1539 action against Córdoba's similar document, even though this involved not the original grant but a reversal of its ratification by the Council in 1518.[24] This exchange of inconclusive evidence probably left the Granadan tribunal unsure of the genuineness of Henry IV's revocation but perhaps the document was assumed to be in Toledo's favor because no expert had declared it false. However, it would not carry much weight as evidence with the justices, and the final decision over the Puebla de Alcocer grant would depend on which party better sustained its arguments on the other elements of the case.

Each Party's Problems

Each side had a chance to challenge the witnesses presented by the other side. The way they proceeded with their challenges reveals something about the problems each party faced.

The House of Béjar's lawyers issued blanket challenges to all of Toledo's witnesses from 1496, 1526, and 1536. For the most part, the charges were the typical ones used in the period's law courts: witnesses were accused of being poor, base, low born, without conscience, libidinous and unchaste, beggars, crazy, drunkards, of bad life and reputation, liars, blasphemers, thieves, animals, residents or vassals of Toledo, enemies of the count of Belalcázar, and in 1540, friends of regidor Marañón of Toledo. The evidence substantiated little that was specific enough to impugn the testimony given by Toledo's witnesses, especially in regard to that given in 1496, which was the most damaging.[25]

Toledo's strategy was quite different and far more effective. The city's lawyers challenged only one among the hundreds of witnesses presented by the House of Béjar because they obviously felt that he was the only one whose testimony was at all damaging. Even then, they waited until 1536 to do this, although the original deposition was taken in 1531. The witness was García Rodríguez, a stonecutter who lived in the village of Brozas near the Portuguese border. Toledo took depositions from six witnesses who exposed Rodríguez as a poor beggar in 1531 and indicated that there was real doubt as to whether he was anywhere near the 103 years of age he had claimed.[26] Unsupported by other evidence, Rodríguez's testimony would not bear much weight.

The main thrust of the Béjar case was toward the circumstances of the grant itself. Gutierre de Sotomayor's descendants' lawyers presented him as a loyal vassal of John II whose services were indispensable in sustaining the king against his enemies. They tried to bolster their claim with depositions, this time taken from over 100 witnesses in 1529. These witnesses were asked about the general nature and seriousness of the infantes' revolt from 1430 to 1445; the infantes' attack on the king, Alvaro de Luna, the archbishop of Toledo, and the master of Alcántara when they were in Medina del Campo; don Gutierre's successful efforts to keep Córdoba and Seville out of the infantes' hands while the king was under his cousins' control and prince Henry was organizing the opposition; the master's services at the battle of Olmedo; and his capture of the infante Pedro in Alcántara. In all of these questions the witnesses were asked to stress the indispensable nature of Gutierre de Sotomayor's services and the great personal expenses he incurred in the royal service.[27]

After so much time had passed, not much of value came out of this testimony even though some of the witnesses, such as the *mayordomo* (steward) of Seville's cathedral and the secretary of the duke of Arcos, were more prominent than the marquis' usual choices. On these points, however, don Francisco's lawyers supported his claims with documentary evidence from the archives of Seville and from chapters of the chronicle of John II submitted in part by Toledo and later added to by the marquis.[28] The Seville documents were chapters from that city's *Libro del Cabildo* for 1444; the citations were from the period February through June. It is clear from these that Gutierre de Sotomayor, under the authority of prince Henry and with the aid of the count of Niebla, the master of Calatrava, and Perafán de Ribera, chief governor of the frontier, had secured Seville against the infante Enrique, recaptured the area around that city, and organized an army for the reconquest of Córdoba to which the infante had fled. The marquis' lawyers claimed that despite the author's pro-Toledo bias, the chronicle also supported the other points although these were better explained in other chronicles.[29]

Thus, Francisco de Zúñiga y Sotomayor's lawyers presented an effective body of evidence to show that his illustrious ancestor Gutierre de Sotomayor had been a loyal and important vassal of king John II in a number of critical situations. Toledo tried to argue from the chronicle chapters it submitted that don Gutierre had acted as a servant of Alvaro de Luna and not of the king. Its representatives even presented a grant from John II to a certain Francisco de Zorita, or Zocorita, in which the latter's relationship with Luna was stressed.[30] But the entire argument was weak and did nothing to impugn the master of Alcántara's superior record of royal service. Certainly it was never shown that he was ever in opposition to John II.

On the other hand, the House of Béjar's lawyers tarred Toledo with the brush of rebellion against the Crown, both as a historical tendency and in this particular instance. The city's history gave them a lot of material with which to work. Starting with the famous *Crónica general de España* from the time of Alfonso X, don Francisco's lawyers showed how, because Toledo had been built on a treacherous dragon's cave, it was from the first disposed to divisions and rebellions as the shelter for an arrogant and cunning population. This early orientation manifested itself in revolts against both Muslim and later Christian rulers, including rebellion in favor of Sancho against Alfonso X, against Peter I, then in favor of Peter against Henry II. In several places in the evidence and arguments, the aristocrat's representatives also mentioned the revolts against Henry IV and Charles V.[31]

All of this was just a warm-up for a discussion of the revolts that were important to the case: those of the 1440s. The House's barristers attempted in 1529 and again in 1531, when more specific questions were asked, to obtain testimony about these revolts. The interrogatory dealt with the infante Enrique's entrance into Toledo against John II's orders in 1440, the capture of the royal ambassadors and the refusal to admit the king, and the terrible events during the revolt of 1449 under the leadership of Pedro Sarmiento. In the 1531 questioning, don Francisco tried to show that the city was in continuous revolt from 1440 until 1446, thus until after the battle of Olmedo, when Pedro López de Ayala was replaced in his offices, as well as from 1449 until John's death in 1454, the 1451 pardon having been given under pressure and against John's will. None of the witnesses' replies proved helpful, except for those which were easily challenged by Toledo. Receptor Pérez Caro took more testimony on the subject in 1536, but all of this evidence remained under a cloud after his corruption trial.[32]

The weakness of the oral evidence, however, made little difference on this point because the documentary evidence was overwhelming. In the first place, the chronicle of John II's reign presented the 1441 and 1449 revolts, especially the latter, as among the most important events of the era. The duke of Béjar also submitted other documents to confirm Toledo's rebellions on both occasions. In December 1541, his lawyers introduced as evidence two letters from John II to Seville (from Torrijos, 10 January 1441; and from Avila, 18 January 1441). In the first, the king reported to Seville that certain influential people were trying to encourage a rebellion against him and that when he went to Toledo, the city rejected his authority. The second letter named the infantes Juan, king of Navarra, and Enrique as the instigators of the revolt along with certain knights.[33]

In May 1548, the marquis of Gibraleón's barrister presented a letter from John II to Puebla de Alcocer (Avila, 22 April 1441) removing jurisdiction over the town from Toledo and integrating it into the Crown lands, never to be separated from these. Puebla was to appoint local officials to serve the king. There are two obvious reasons why the House of Béjar's lawyers waited so long to place this letter in evidence. First, it clearly indicated Toledo's complete and prior lordship, an implication that Ldo. Manjárrez was unable to dispute effectively. It was also in the form of a royal reward to Puebla de Alcocer and stated that the town would forever remain under the Crown's jurisdiction, a promise violated by the later grant to Gutierre de Sotomayor. Another letter from king John to Seville (24 September 1450) was submitted in 1546; it explained that because Toledo was in revolt, the monarch found it difficult to provide troops to defend the frontier against Muslim Granada.[34]

Josepe de Quirós, barrister of Puebla de Alcocer, which added itself as party to the case in a last-minute effort to delay the final decision, was allowed to insert a letter (from Torrijos, 2 [*sic*] January 1441) into the transcript even though the proceedings had ended. It was from John II to Puebla de Alcocer and Herrera specifically and to the other places of Toledo's Montes in general. He told them that Toledo had refused entrance to the king and that orders from the city should, therefore, not be obeyed. The customary rents were to be collected by the master of Alcántara who would also appoint new officials, and no other powerful person was to be received in the towns without royal permission.[35] Although not submitted in time to affect the verdict, it is hard to see how this letter could have made the case for Toledo's rebellion any stronger, and the letter of 22 April established a much more definitive separation of Puebla de Alcocer from Toledo's jurisdiction. Thus, earlier presentation would not have altered the justices' final decision.

The Issue of Rebellion

In response to the claim that the city had lost Puebla de Alcocer as punishment for rebellion, Toledo put up a well-reasoned defense, prepared by Ldo. Ortiz, which blamed individuals while exonerating the community to which the disputed territory belonged. Because there was such general interest in this lawsuit, Toledo arranged to have this brief and several others printed and distributed as a contribution to debate among the commonwealth's leaders in general and among letrado intellectuals in particular on the merits of Toledo's claims about the proper exercise of royal authority.[36] Rightly seeing that it was the rebellion of 1441 that was the most important in terms of the case, Ortiz concentrated his efforts on that event. First, it was impossible for the corporate body (*la universidad*) of the community to commit any crime because the city was "a dead body without feeling," and both logic and propriety would be violated by claiming action on the part of such a body. Even if it were possible, however, to speak of a city in revolt, Ortiz argued that it could not be done in this case because the action was taken only by particular individuals who did not constitute Toledo's corporate body.

In one of his arguments for the nonparticipation of the municipal corporate body in the rebellion, Ortiz's logic appears strained and unconvincing, but it dealt with an important legal point: a corporate group could not be held responsible for the crimes or mistakes of individuals unless they could be shown somehow to represent the whole body. For the universidad legally to be involved in an action, two-thirds of the body would have to participate. But, according to Ortiz, when the infante Enrique was taken in, it was not by the action of two-thirds or even half of the body. The community was made up of two parts, the plebeians and the gentlemen (*caballeros*), and the latter had all been expelled, according to the chronicle. This expulsion left only half of the community in the city. Moreover, because Pedro López de Ayala had expelled part of the former group, there were really fewer than half of the community's members present, and because no one would want to argue that ecclesiastics were involved in a rebellion, even some who remained did not participate. The rebellion, therefore, was not carried out by the universidad nor by the *pueblo* (people): "the *pueblo* is something different from the *plebe,* and it is not reasonable that the *pueblo* should pay for the *plebe* [that is, for the *plebe*'s crimes]."

Ortiz was on firmer ground when he argued that no general decision to rebel was made, and, therefore, the community should not be held responsible for the actions of individuals. If the individuals leading the rebellion were powerful tyrants, such as Ayala, who expelled or executed opponents, then the corporate body was especially without responsibility. The other residents would have kept silent due to "justified fear" for which the community could not be legally held responsible because it received nothing in return for the rebellion. In fact, "the comfort and profit that Toledo received was to be robbed of its properties and citizens by Pero [*sic*] López de Ayala" as the reign's chronicle showed. Furthermore, the opposition to Ayala and the infante Enrique was demonstrated when king John sent as his ambassadors to Toledo two of its citizens and regidores, adelantado Perafán de Ribera and Dr. Fernando Díaz de Toledo.

The infante Enrique, according to the chronicle, had authorization from the king, given in 1439, which allowed him to be received in any city of the realm. Because only Ayala, who was after all a royal appointee, would have known about any order not to receive the infante, Ortiz argued that his reception could not be held as prejudicial to Toledo's reputation. Ayala was the royal magistrate and his men occupied all of the fortifications. The community possessed no legal or physical means to oppose his will. Despite the claims in the hearsay evidence of the House of Béjar's witnesses, the chronicle spoke of no actual fighting which would have alerted the residents to the king's presence or the tyrants' opposition to him. Against Ortiz's arguments, Ldo. Manjárrez was unable to provide any evidence from the chronicle accounts of the 1441 revolt that would indicate anything but that Ayala used his entrenched position to manipulate Toledo's actions.[37]

The 1449 revolt received a briefer treatment because Ortiz felt that the same arguments applied. Rather than a crime committed by the community, it was a rebellion by a group led by king John's own official, Pedro Sarmiento. Moreover, the rebellion was in response to the crimes of the "tyrant" Alvaro de Luna, crimes for which he was later castigated by the king, and John II also pardoned Toledo while punishing Sarmiento.

Despite such arguments, it was clear that Toledo, for whatever reason, had several times been disloyal to the king. On the other hand, Gutierre de Sotomayor was a faithful, consistent vassal of John II. The chronology was the problem. The Sotomayors' case would have been much stronger if Gutierre's grant had been a reward for some particular service, had come at a time when Toledo was in revolt, and had involved a jurisdiction clearly in the king's authority to give. In fact, all of these circumstances were absent. John made the grant prior to the battle of Olmedo, and, although the grant of Córdoba's former domains acknowledged Gutierre's efforts in 1444, the Puebla de Alcocer grant made only vague mention of these services. It looked too much as if the master of Alcántara's services were being purchased in advance. There was no evidence that Toledo was then in revolt, and, indeed, the chronicle provided reasons to believe that the city was not a supporter of the infantes at the battle of Olmedo in 1445. King John's letters to Puebla de Alcocer, Toledo, and Ayala and the transactions between Puebla and Toledo clearly indicated that Puebla was under the jurisdiction of the city and not that of the Crown in 1445.

The defendant's letrados made no real attempt in their evidence to develop a firm chronology such as that on which Toledo founded its points. The clearest example of chronological organization was the interrogatory of 1529 where the questions were asked in an order that left the impression that both revolts were related to the infantes' 1445 activities and that both occurred just before the grant. As can be seen from Ldo. Manjárrez's later use of the oral testimony, this was a deliberate attempt by the House of Béjar's lawyers to cover up the weaknesses in their presentation. Manjárrez offered a vague summary rather than a detailed discussion in order to obscure not only the sequence of events but also the paucity of substantive replies to the questions.[38]

Toledo's lawyers sorted out the course of events for the court. They submitted chronicle chapters for 1439–1446 and 1449–1452, which gave a sense of the chronology of events.[39] Nonetheless, in the face of clear evidence of Gutierre de Sotomayor's service and the city's revolts, their claim that the grant was against king John's wishes had been weakened by the other party's discussion of the context of the grant.

King John II's 1451 pardon of the city was far from specific about his intentions relating to the revolt of ten years earlier, and the particular events mentioned were those of the 1449 revolt. There was, however, no limit on the king's restoration to Toledo of its goods or possessions that had been granted to others, and all such grants were to have no value. The House of Béjar's lawyers were quick to point out that because the troubles of 1441, and, they added, those occurring until 1445, were never mentioned, it was probable that the pardon referred only to the consequences of the 1449 revolt.[40]

The Legal Expropriation of Property

If king John II's pardon of the city, which was far from specific, and Henry IV's revocation, whose validity was questioned, were disregarded, and if Toledo's defense of its prior lordship over the territory was accepted, and if John II's grant to Gutierre de Sotomayor was acknowledged as deserved and as having been made, and Toledo made only the weakest attempts to dispute the last-mentioned point, the case would turn on the issue of whether John II had a right to make the grant.[41] Under the laws of Castile, he did not. At least from the meeting of the Cortes of Madrid in 1329, the foundation of Castilian property law was that the Crown could not make grants of municipally held domains. In fact, municipal councils themselves could not alienate such territory because it belonged not to the council but to the residents. Even John II acted on several occasions to affirm the royal incompetence to dispose of municipal property. The Cortes constantly denied such authority to the monarch.[42]

To take the town of Puebla de Alcocer as punishment for revolt, there would have to have been a trial.[43] The House of Béjar's lawyers tried but failed to prove that there was one; the only evidence they could muster was the testimony of García Rodríguez, who claimed that a hearing was held in Torrijos after king John left the outskirts of Toledo. Toledo not only effectively attacked this witness, but chided the other side's procuradores for delaying the trial so long that their oral evidence was now of so little value. They told the Béjar representatives that a perpetual memorial of such testimony could have been made, as Toledo had done. Toledo's letrados clearly implied that such a record was not assembled because no trial was ever held.

Moreover, the chronicle revealed that on 9 January 1441, John II sent an ultimatum to the infante Enrique to release the royal ambassadors within four days, and by the time it expired, the king was in Avila. Without additional proof there seemed no reason to believe that a trial had been held before the expiration of the ultimatum. The king also wrote to the infante from Torrijos that he intended to be lenient with those responsible for refusing him entry. Surely, the city's lawyers argued, if he wanted to be lenient with the infante Enrique, who had started the entire affair, he had no intention of proceeding against Toledo, and the contrary had not been proven. There was no declaration of the crime, and to the claim that the property was lost *ipso jure* (that is, by the operation of the law without other action) in response to such a notorious rebellion, Toledo replied that the 22 April 1441 document showed that the city still had jurisdiction more than three months after the alleged revolt. Moreover, in the donation to Gutierre de Sotomayor, king John said he was granting the lordship even if the town belonged to Toledo or someone else; this showed that he did not know the domain's status, and he mentioned no crime. Even if the idea that rebellion *ipso jure* deprived one of possession, which was not the law, the property would have to have been confiscated formally, and Toledo's lawyers pointed to both oral and documentary evidence to show that no such legal action was ever taken. Of course, they argued, there was no crime anyway, and a trial would have been necessary to prove one.[44]

The House of Béjar's lawyers countered that the 1447 confirmation of Gutierre de Sotomayor's grant, coming as it did after the 1446 protest by Toledo, showed that some hearing had been held. Or if there had been none, Piedrahita provided the required hearing when the survey was done in 1448. There was nothing, however, in the confirmation of the grant to indicate any sort of hearing, and Piedrahita, as the Béjar lawyers admitted, correctly declined to hear arguments about Toledo's ownership of the territory on the ground that such a hearing exceeded his instructions from the king. Moreover, Toledo had raised serious questions about the propriety of Piedrahita's conduct.[45]

To take the jurisdiction for the Crown without cause, presumably in the public interest, the king would have had to give equal value in exchange. He had given none. Ldo. Manjárrez indicated his helplessness before this provision of the law by suggesting that it involved the substitution of incorrect wording in the *Partidas*. Another of the Béjar lawyers, in a brief discussed below that dealt specifically with the king's right to take lands belonging to Toledo, indicated the clear legal prescription against expropriation without indemnification. Toledo allowed that the monarch could take over the administration of or dominion over property in time of difficulty, but pointed out that such administration did not involve possession. The law provided that the Crown had lordship or *señorío* over all property in the kingdom, but only for its protection and not to dispose of it arbitrarily as though it were the monarch's personal possession.[46]

Of course, the monarch had to have the final say on what course of action would lead in difficult matters to the realization of the public good. His authority was absolute within the constraints of reason and justice, concepts that had to be evaluated in reference to natural and divine law. In formal jurisprudence, the legal theorists known as the Postglossators had developed the most respected views of what this later medieval conception of monarchical authority really meant. The impact of these legal theories in Castile can be seen quite clearly in the late fifteenth-century glosses on the *Siete Partidas* and other sources of law by Alonso Díaz de Montalvo, and the Postglossators' ideas dominated most of sixteenth-century legal thought.[47] It should come as no surprise, given the stress on law as the embodiment of justice in the common conception of monarchy, that legal scholars were driven to produce the most precise discussions of that institution. Among intellectuals, the letrados were the ones who handled disputes over the proper exercise of monarchical authority as part of their professional duties.

Because the legal education of that time stressed the study of the *Corpus Iuris Civilis* (the medieval name for the Code of the Emperor Justinian)[48] and the *Corpus Iuris Canonici* (canon law), the Postglossators expressed most of their ideas in commentaries on various parts of these collections, especially the first. In general, they granted to monarchs any powers that were thought to have been held by Roman emperors.

All theorists began with the idea expressed in the the the part of Justinian's Code called the Digest that *princeps legibus solutus est,* the prince is free of the binding ties of the law (D., 1, 3, 31). Moreover, by the provisions of the so-called *lex regia,* what pleased the prince had the force of law *(quod principi placuit, legis habet vigorem;* D., 1, 4, 1, 1; also C., 1, 17, 1, 7 and Inst., 1, 2, 5). But such great authority was not meant to imply the possibility of arbitrary action, because the monarch's role was the public one of ensuring justice for his subjects, and in the common view of the Middle Ages, law was the realization of justice. Thus, to these harsh-sounding maxims on absolute royal authority, the Postglossators attached the idea that the prince was bound by law because his authority rested on it. This citation was known as the *lex digna;* the maxim developed was *princeps legibus alligatus,* which embodied the idea that the prince was bound by or tied to the law (C., 1, 14, 4). Justice was the only principle of government, and the ruler should be the living example of this, thus holding his subjects' trust.[49] Through the use of the paradox that the monarch was free of the law's ties yet must submit to the law as part of his role as guarantor of justice, legal theorists sought to explain the ruler's relationship to justice. Yet they had to show how a monarch could adapt to changed conditions in his pursuit of the public good if he were constrained by existing laws.

According to most of the Postglossators, if the public good, that is, his subjects' security, were somehow threatened, the monarch could, with just cause, set aside what was usually referred to as "ordinary justice" and violate the kingdom's positive laws. He might do so because by divine and natural law he must maintain his kingdom in peace and order, and these sources of law are higher than any realm's statutes. In violating positive law, he was seen as exercising a special absolute authority, a *plenitudo potestatis* ("fullness of power"), superior to that of ordinary authority and possessed only by the monarch. If such *plenitudo potestatis* were invoked, a court or other government body lost the right to refuse compliance with a royal order or reverse a royal action on the grounds that it was illegal or contrary to the public interest. The prince had to act *ex proprio motu,* that is, as he desired rather than in response to the request of some individual petitioner. Any decision to violate positive law could be made only *ex certa scientia,* after careful consideration to achieve an accurate understanding. For legists, such reflection implied that proper advice had been sought. Most importantly, the monarch had to include a *clausula non obstante,* a specific declaration that his command should be obeyed despite any existing legislation or other royal declarations in the matter. If the monarch were aware of some particular law or laws that his declaration violated, he could make his intentions clearer by specifying what laws he wanted suspended. In actual fact, most important courts were reluctant to stand behind such royal orders that were not clearly motivated by a desire to serve the public interest, unless they involved little damage to any innocent party.[50]

Obviously, the question of expropriation of property was likely to be an important category when laws were being abrogated.[51] The Postglossators generally felt that, although a monarch could certainly seize an individual's property, such an action should be taken only with good cause and in the public interest. Thus, the harshness of the phrase *omnia principis esse* ("all is the prince's") in Justinian's Code (C., 7, 37, 3) was considerably softened by late medieval jurists, although they in fact expanded the ruler's authority in this area over what had been allowed by their immediate predecessors. Earlier legists, the Glossators, denied any royal authority to expropriate property. Because, however, personal property was held not only by virtue of positive law but as a natural right, the general opinion of the Postglossators was that the ruler must compensate the owner for his loss, giving him as much or greater value in exchange. The monarch was lord of the property of his subjects only in order to protect such property. To defend the property of all, he could take the goods of an individual, but he had to mitigate the damage done through compensation.[52] God established monarchical government in order that basic human rights and liberties, including the security of property, would be defended. Rule contrary to this responsibility was tyranny, although there was considerable dispute over what could be done about the tyrant-prince.[53] Thus, as the ruler's authority to act in violation of positive law derived from divine and natural law, he had to act in accordance with such higher legal sources. Moreover, correspondence to these sources in the exercise of authority was what was meant by reason.

Under a law that the king had proclaimed at the Cortes of Valladolid on 5 May 1442, no monarch could make a grant such as the one to Gutierre de Sotomayor, not even using his absolute authority. This law specifically referred to grants of Crown lands, prior law having determined that those distributions were the only ones the king could ever make. Although Toledo's lawyers repeatedly cited this "Law of Valladolid," the legislation was not clearly binding in Toledo's Belalcázar case because the Catholic Monarchs in 1480 had recognized all alienations of the royal patrimony before 1464, but its promulgation would give added weight to the view that John II was acting unlawfully or under duress in making the grant in 1445. Because Ferdinand and Isabella had given no indication that they meant to allow illegal grants made at the expense of cities or persons, the House of Béjar, unless its lawyers could prove, as they did not, that the territory was king John's to give, derived no benefit from the 1480 provision.[54]

"By My Absolute Royal Authority"

Left with a grant that was invalid because it was illegal, the Béjar lawyers had to fall back on the principle of royal action by virtue of the Crown's absolute authority. They would have to pronounce the words so hated by the Cortes procuradores and the patricians they represented: the king was acting, they argued, by virtue of his *cierta sciencia e propio motu e poderío real absoluto* ("reasoned consideration and own initiative and absolute royal authority") as the grant clearly stated. Such an action was above the prescription of any law.[55] Although personally suspicious of royal actions in violation of the law, the author of the crucial brief, Dr. Pedro Núñez de Avendaño, was forced in his defense of the Sotomayor title to the viscounty of Puebla de Alcocer to support the king's absolute authority above the law. He could really defend king John's grant to Gutierre de Sotomayor only by arguing for an authority that was "supreme and absolute" because Toledo had not been given the "fair exchange" required by law. Avendaño said it was clear that John II was using this authority, because the phrase *cierta sciencia e propio motu e poderío real absoluto* was in the grant. Thus, the king could have granted Gutierre the territory "despite any contrary laws and customs that there were or are."[56]

Avendaño went beyond the long-standing views of jurists in order to postulate the prince's ability to act unfettered by any restraints. Some sixteenth-century French theorists moved conceptually in the same direction, but there the change was clearly in response to the political situation in the aftermath of the St. Bartholomew's Day Massacre of 1572.[57] Castile experienced nothing like the French Wars of Religion. Moreover, as the peninsular theoretical changes were the product of the 1540s and early 1550s, they were independent of developments in French theory. Thus, the work of Avendaño, the proponent of one of the period's most extreme theories of unrestrained royal authority, reveals the nature of the new views and the historical events that brought about the change. Without knowing this background, it is impossible to place the work of Castile's great political theorists, such as Francisco Suárez or Juan de Mariana, much less that of its renowned legal scholars, in the proper context. It is ironic that in order to defend some of their domains, members of Castile's territorial aristocracy would be driven to advocate principles of royal authority inimical to their own power.

Avendaño sought to overturn traditional views by changing the definitions of the monarch's ordinary and absolute powers. His major work, *De exequendis mandatis regum hispaniae* (1543) is far too complex for discussion here.[58] However, the basis of the changes he made in the legal theory of expropriation in his larger work can be seen easily in the Belalcázar brief he prepared between 1545 and 1548 in defense of the interests of Alonso de Zúñiga y Sotomayor, count of Belalcázar and marquis of Gibraleón, who had become the House of Béjar's principal party in the lawsuit on the death of his father, don Francisco, in 1544.

Avendaño was chief counsel for the Mendoza duke of Infantado. His aristocratic master's daughter had recently wed Francisco de Guzmán y Zúñiga (later Zúñiga y Sotomayor), marquis of Ayamonte and younger brother of the marquis of Gibraleón. Because it seemed that the marquis of Gibraleón would have no children, the marquis of Ayamonte knew that he or one of his children would likely inherit the duchy of Béjar and any rights to the viscounty of Puebla de Alcocer that went with it. On this basis, in 1550 the marquis of Ayamonte was admitted by the Chancillería of Granada as an active party in the trial. Apparently, he prevailed on his new father-in-law to lend him the services of the lawyer whose recent book made him one of the kingdom's leading experts on the proper exercise of monarchical authority. Actually, Avendaño was probably part of the Belalcázar legal team prior to 1550 because the briefs would have been prepared before then; all the others from the same archival bundle are from the second hearing and would have been written only after the termination in 1546 of the legal period for the addition of any new evidence.[59]

Because it was ever more apparent that the audiencia's final decision would turn on the legality of John II's expropriation of Toledo's land, Avendaño directed his comments to this issue. He was asked to prepare a response, favorable to the House of Béjar, to the following question as he posed it in his brief: "If the property that is the subject of this litigation belonged to Toledo and was purchased with its own money as it claims, could the king make of the property a reward to master Gutierre de Sotomayor by reason of the services that he had rendered to the king even if Toledo had not committed against the king the crimes of rebellion and lese majesty?"[60] The corrected draft manuscript of this brief is probably all that ever existed as this type of opinion was generally not submitted directly to the court but was rather incorporated into the final written arguments.

In this brief and in his work generally, Avendaño leaned toward the traditional "Bartolist" method of legal argument rather than to the new "Humanist" jurisprudence. It was not that he was unaware of contemporary developments in legal scholarship. His citations in this brief indicate a familiarity with sixteenth-century jurists, such as Andreas Alciatus (d. 1550), Philippus Decius (d. ca. 1537), and Andreas Tiraquellus (d. 1558), while the citations in his printed works show he was aware of the latest publications in his field. Rather, as a doctor of both civil and canon law, he felt the methods of logical argument he had learned in the course of his studies were best suited to developing an argument in response to the question he posed. Thus, most of his writing relied heavily on the commentaries of the great Postglossators of the fourteenth and fifteenth centuries, and much of his logic will likely sound strange to modern readers, although lawyers of Avendaño's time raised rather different questions than we might about the relevance of his citations and general understanding of Castilian and natural property law.[61]

In the view of the Postglossators, the first requirement for the proper expropriation of property was that there be a "just cause," that is, that the action be taken in the public interest. Avendaño, therefore, began with a consideration of this point. Although the date of the grant, just prior to the first battle of Olmedo, raised questions about the circumstances that motivated it, Avendaño was able to build a case for the idea that John II was properly remunerating Sotomayor for services that enabled the monarch to protect Castile from an invasion by the king of Navarra and the other infantes of Aragón. Because the realm was in danger, such remuneration was sufficient *justa causa*.

Avendaño tried to leave the impression that no further requirements were necessary to make legal a grant so important to the public interest and that the following points in no way depended on whether there was proper cause for royal action. His organization, however, indicates that he knew such logic was not an acceptable definition of law for the audiencia's oidores. Thus, while implying no necessary connection between the question of royal authority and that of just cause in an attempt to strengthen the Béjar case, he nevertheless moved directly to a discussion of the relation between monarchical actions and the law, as one would have expected him to do in light of prevailing theories on the matter. Moreover, he stated that the king had two types of authority: the one ordinary and subject to the disposition of the law that the king wished to sustain; the other supreme, absolute, and not subject to the law, which could be used in cases where the king thought it necessary.

Avendaño offered, however, the surprising declaration that there was no doubt the king, using his ordinary authority and with just cause, could take the property from Toledo and give it to the master of Alcántara as long as he gave the city "fair exchange," proper compensation for its loss. He buttressed this remarkable extension of absolute royal authority to the ordinary sphere not only by citations to all the commentaries on C., 7, 37, 3 of the *Corpus Iuris Civilis* but also to those laws of the *Siete Partidas* that embodied some of the same principles.[62] Indeed, he discussed the major texts on the question of a monarch's *plenitudo potestatis* as though this type of authority were his as a matter of course. Avendaño offered quite common arguments about exercising the royal will, soliciting advice, and employing the *non obstante* clause, except that he treated everything as part of the ordinary authority of the prince. In his claim that a king, like the pope, could by nature act *supra jus et contra jus et extra jus* ("above the law and against the law and outside the law") without anyone having the right to protest, he used virtually the same words as one of the most extreme theorists of absolute royal authority writing in France during the religious wars, the Scotsman William Barclay, professor of civil law at Angers, who published his views in 1600.[63] This claim, moreover, was followed in the brief by a list of the most extreme maxims in defense of royal authority that could be culled from the authoritative civil law commentators. These included not only the concept of the king as *lex animata,* with all of its connotations of a divine being serving justice and the public good,[64] but also that of the monarch as *legibus solutus,* whose very will indicated the presumption of a just cause and itself constituted law.

However, in the midst of this breathtaking assertion of royal authority, Avendaño still had to deal with the requirement of compensation. No proper "fair exchange" had ever been offered. And, he asked, if such compensation was necessary for the king to take the property legally, did the Béjar House have title to it, leaving the monarch still responsible for Toledo's claim, or did title never pass originally to the master of Alcántara? Avendaño argued for the former on the grounds that fair exchange was not required by common or Castilian law before the property was seized and that title could still pass to the person who received a grant of the property. His common law citations were the familiar ones involving C., 7, 37, 2 and 3 of the *Corpus Iuris Civilis,* while he used *Partida* 5, title 5, law 53 to prove that Castilian law required no prior fair exchange. This last mentioned citation dealt with the sale or gift of private property by the king, and it clearly stated that property title passed to the grantee while the original owner had four years in which to seek damages. Confidently, he concluded that such a law was more than sufficient defense for the claim that title passed to the master of Alcántara while compensation remained a royal responsibility. To this conclusion he appended proofs that the title would become that of the grantee while the monarch retained responsibility for some sort of compensation even if the property's original owner was a minor, which was the city's legal status.

Avendaño surely knew that *Partida* 5, title 5, law 53 was a statute whose actual status as law in the sixteenth century was subject to question, especially given the formally subordinate role of the *Siete Partidas* in Castilian legislation. It was not included, for example, in the *Nueva Recopilación,* and even such an extreme defender of absolute royal authority as Gregorio López doubted in his gloss on this law that any grant made under its provisions without prior fair exchange would be valid.[65] Avendaño acknowledged in the brief that both *Partida* 2, title 1, law 2 and *Partida* 3, title 18, law 31 (laws that demanded prior fair exchange for royal expropriation) raised doubts about whether title passed to another by royal grant if no prior fair exchange were given. However, he argued that *Partida* 5, title 5, law 53 was put in the code to remove such doubts and to bring Castilian property law into conformity with common law, by which he meant the Roman law of the *Corpus Iuris Civilis.* Thus, by this law the grant made to Gutierre de Sotomayor was valid even if the king had not given Toledo the prior satisfaction required by other laws.

Avendaño was no fool, however, and he knew that this use of a questionable law to overturn two other frequently cited ones in the same code would impress none of the oidores who would hear the case. Although claiming that his arguments up to that point removed any doubt as to the legality of John II's grant or the House of Béjar's title to the property, he went on to say that in this case the question was even more without doubt (*más sin duda*) because the king wished to use not only his ordinary authority but also that which was "supreme and absolute" and not subject to the disposition of the law. The king, Avendaño pointed out, said just this in the grant that was made "by my own initiative and reasoned consideration and absolute royal authority that I want to use and here use." A monarch acting in this manner could strike down laws that forbade actions he desired, and Avendaño explicitly included in the laws abrogated by these words those laws in the *Partidas* that presented the Roman lawyers' conceptions of imperial authority and the idea that royal actions contrary to natural law were invalid. By making such natural law ideas only a matter of positive, statute law, Avendaño in fact removed any restraint but divine judgment from a ruler's actions. In defense of this kind of rescript against law (*rescriptum contra ius*), he offered only the citations he had earlier used in his discussion of expropriating property under the king's ordinary authority.[66] Here he was setting aside only the requirement of fair exchange, but the Postglossators discussed such exchange only when absolute authority was used, because for them no expropriation was possible under ordinary authority. Thus, in this sixteenth-century brief, the Postglossators' complete discussion of expropriation as an attribute of absolute authority was pushed back into the area of ordinary *authoridad*,[67] and only the justifications for action contrary to law by a monarch using his absolute authority were carried into Avendaño's discussion of this type of authority. The requirement of prior fair exchange in *Partida* 2, title 1, law 2 on imperial powers dealt only with ordinary power. This point was obvious, claimed Avendaño, because were it not so the king would have no greater authority and free disposition than that of an ordinary judge who could, in the public interest, take away property by paying its price to the person who owned it.

This drastic extension of royal authority was the high point of the brief. It solved, if the justices would accept the idea of so unrestrained a monarch (they did not), the problem Avendaño posed for himself at the outset. The rest of the manuscript contains interesting material, a discussion of when property became the monarch's during expropriation and even a just war argument to justify Gutierre de Sotomayor's violent seizure of the land, but none of this material was central to the matters on which an eventual judicial decision would turn.[68]

Thus, Avendaño formulated his theory in defense of aristocratic domain and property obtained through royal grants in the turbulent fifteenth century. The theory had to be a new one because under the terms of any earlier understanding of the royal authority to expropriate property, the Puebla de Alcocer grant was illegal. Toledo's was not the only claim of this kind against the House of Béjar, because Córdoba had demanded the return to its jurisdiction of Belalcázar and Hinojosa, a dispute that was also being adjudicated by the Chancillería of Granada, and the duke of Infantado, Avendaño's regular employer, may himself have had similarly vulnerable territory within his holdings.

Ironically, the most extreme of the Postglossators' statements in the late fourteenth and fifteenth centuries throughout Europe in defense of monarchical authority were intended to bolster royal capacity in the face of opposition from rebellious territorial aristocrats. Yet in sixteenth-century Castile, the lawyers of these magnates' heirs were advancing even more extreme theories of absolute royal authority in defense of the very grants that had been extorted from vulnerable fifteenth-century kings. It should come as no surprise that the other great theorist of the time to posit such an extreme thesis of absolute royal authority was Gregorio López, a man better known now than Avendaño because so many scholars have used his edition of the *Siete Partidas*. He was even more closely connected to the trial over the viscounty of Puebla de Alcocer than Avendaño. As the chief solicitor for the House of

Béjar, López had the major responsibility for guiding the Belalcázar–Toledo lawsuit during part of its trial before the Chancillería of Granada.[69] One should not wonder then, given the new awareness of their kingdom's history, that later sixteenth-century Castilian political writers, such as Juan de Mariana, reacted so violently to arguments for unrestrained royal authority because such arguments were developed to defend aristocratic holdings obtained in the fifteenth century at the expense of justice, public order, and individual security.[70] In the view of these later sixteenth-century writers, the consequences of such arbitrary royal action showed it did nothing to further the public good.

Judging the Exercise of Royal Authority

Thus, the justices of the Chancillería of Granada would have to resolve the ambiguous theoretical relationship between claims for the monarch's supreme authority and his mandate to rule justly within the law. As a related matter, they would have to decide if the king, as the source of justice, could rule justly through a personal, informal relationship with his great vassals. Although the argument would be over the paradoxical nature of royal authority, the manner in which the House of Béjar's case over Puebla de Alcocer was developed, with its stress on personal service and royal reward, would keep this problem of style—the relationship between monarch and territorial aristocrats—before the justices.

The formal logic of the Béjar case was that the ruler had an absolute authority above the law, which he could use whenever he saw fit. Toledo prudently never really replied to this proposition; it did not have to, for its whole presentation embodied the counterargument. Only once in their surviving pleadings did any of Toledo's lawyers approach comment on the monarch's supreme authority: in the argument supporting the second, 1555, verdict. Although this document was filed about five weeks after the ruling was given, it naturally summarized the arguments that had been presented during the deliberations. At the point where Br. Piedrahita's 1447 commission was being discussed, Toledo's lawyers suggested that the wording showed that Gutierre de Sotomayor's holdings were a grant not of Crown lands but of those taken under the supreme lordship (*supremo señorío*). They had earlier questioned in a general way the king's right to take the land, but here where it was a specific problem, they did not discuss the matter but said the grant was invalid by *defecto de voluntad* (a defect of will or intention).[71]

Spanish political theorists of the period also avoided attacking royal supremacy. Yet neither the great political theorists, nor Toledo's lawyers, nor the city's governing patricians, nor, more importantly, the justices of the Chancillería really believed in absolute royal authority as defined by the lawyers of the House of Béjar or felt that its exercise was in the kingdom's interest. The medieval basis for this attitude, as we have seen, was a paradoxical theory according to which the monarch had absolute authority, but at the same time, in his role as supreme magistrate responsible for maintaining justice, he should obey the laws, act in a moral manner, rule in the interest of the commonwealth rather than his personal good, and in general proceed "as a good king toward good vassals." Such conduct was never subject to precise definition or categorization. The law could be set aside in limited, infrequent instances; for example, the monarch had the right to pardon offenders.[72]

The patrician leaders of Castile's major cities kept a watchful eye on the monarch's activities, protesting actions contrary to laws and the abrogation of laws outside of the Cortes sessions. In response to such protests made in the fourteenth century, the king decreed, in the Law of Briviesca (Cortes of Briviesca, 1387), that no actions contrary to law would have any value. When the municipal procuradores were trying to convince John II to govern in a manner that they felt they could support, he specifically reaffirmed this law at the Cortes of Valladolid in 1442.[73] Although there was no formal institutional check on the monarch other than the right to counsel him and recommend reforms, the commonwealth's intellectual and political leaders clearly felt that a ruler who acted arbitrarily and in violation of the laws was a tyrant; the true king would only be one who governed "with rectitude." The tyrant's orders would not be obeyed, God would not aid his rule, and the kingdom would collapse into disorder with cries of "Long live the king! Death to the bad government!" The prevailing idea was that a bad king destroyed the kingdom.[74]

These precepts retain their interest for the modern scholar, despite their seeming lack of logical consistency, because they are a reasonably accurate reflection of the dynamic interrelationship of prevailing interpretive schemes and the conditions of monarchical rule in the Trastámara era. Moreover, these ideas about just rule remained part of the common baggage of political thought in the Habsburg period.[75] After the horror of the fifteenth-century upheavals and with those of the sixteenth and seventeenth century constantly before the eyes of intellectuals and political figures, I do not find strange the continued presence of this perspective within Castile's cultural environment. Those interested in the systematic codification of the law were local notables who had suffered the most from ambiguous laws and arbitrary enforcement and thus wanted a means of checking up on judicial administration,[76] but in the sixteenth century, important institutional developments and the huge geographical extent of the Habsburg domains would subtly shift the meaning of these precepts of royal government even when they were expressed in identical terms.

All four of the great Castilian political theorists of the sixteenth century, Francisco de Vitoria, Domingo de Soto, Francisco Suárez, and Luis Molina, believed that a true monarch ruled in a manner shaped by certain moral and legal precepts, and they were suspicious of those whose style of rule was too independent of these constraints. For them, "the true dignity and pre-eminence of the king was that of the just ruler obeying his own laws."[77] With some deviation on the part of Vitoria, all of the great theologians (Alfonso de Castro, Soto, Molina, Suárez), all of the great jurists (Francisco de Vázquez Menchaca, Martín de Azpilcueta, Diego de Covarrubias), and even writers of political tracts such as Juan Márquez continued to think in terms of a compact between the community and the ruler with authority being derived from the former and exercised by the latter in the commonwealth's interest rather than in his own. Soto outlined the extension of this idea to matters of property: the monarch had rights of dominion and jurisdiction but not of possession and, therefore, could not make use of the property of his subjects except when it was necessary for him to administer it in the community's interest. This administration presumably did not affect posses-sion. Failure to obey the laws and the promulgation of unjust laws by the monarch were the acts of a tyrant and not that of a just ruler, according to the theorists of the sixteenth century. Diego de Covarrubias held such a doc-trine of the nature of tyranny as early as 1545, and he was an oidor of the Chancillería of Granada at the time the Toledo-Belalcázar dispute was receiving final consideration and was later the president of the Council of Castile. He felt that a distinction could not be made between the ordinary and absolute authority of human kings and that one should abhor any men-tion of the latter. All royal authority had to be exercised according to divine, natural, and human law; to go beyond this was tyranny.[78]

All of the works of these authors were printed, freely circulated, and widely read. As the Covarrubias example shows, university legal education inculcated the spirit of "just rule" in letrados who went into public service, and such ideas were certainly common among lawyers in private practice. The customary attitude of the Cortes was well known, especially after the events of 1518–1520, and the procuradores' position would have been gen-eral among the educated groups of the cities whose "heart and soul" was the law according to Suárez de Figueroa in 1617.[79] Moreover, these ideas about "just rule" retained an important place in political thought throughout the Habsburg era. They were such a common element of the Castilian cultural environment that Calderón de la Barca could write in act 2 of *La vida es sueño:*

> En lo que no es justa ley
> No ha de obedecer al Rey.
> [In that which is not just law,
> One does not have to obey the King.][80]

For judges, as for other educated men, these precepts of monarchical rule formed the cornerstone of the kingdom's largely unwritten constitution. Moreover, as more and more legislation was passed by the monarch, those who interpreted and applied the law had a tendency in their search for legal wisdom to disregard such royal acts in favor of other sources of law, such as the scholarly work of those jurists of earlier centuries whose treatises embodied the familiar attitudes with all of their political, ethical, and theological connotations. It was in this cultural environment that the audiencia's justices gave their final verdict in the case in favor of Toledo's demand for a restitution of the towns of the so-called viscounty of Puebla de Alcocer.

Chapter 7

PHILIP II, THE GREAT FEAR, AND THE NEW AUTHORITARIANISM

Reversing Course: Trial by the Council of Castile

This chapter challenges the view that Philip II enjoyed sufficient information and the capacity to implement policies. This challenge undermines the contention that his "centralization" constitutes a chapter in European "state-building" characteristic of an "early modern" era of European history. Instead, in the midst of a series of major political, military, and religious crises early in his reign, the king and his advisers, with a combination of anxiety and arrogance, often managed affairs in ways that appeared arbitrary and sapped support for royal policies. Sensing opposition within the commonwealth, the king appeared reluctant to grant too much authority to the officials of institutions over which he could not exercise direct supervision. In this context, it was the Council of Castile, rather than the audiencia of Granada, that would render the final verdict in the trial of the city of Toledo and the House of Béjar over control of the viscounty of Puebla de Alcocer.

In his early years as Castile's king, the multiple crises of the Hispanic Monarchy, discussed below, often overwhelmed Philip II. Out of the climate of fear gripping the royal Household and Court in their new permanent seat in Madrid emerged an authoritarian exercise of monarchical authority, which appeared quite different from the administrative leadership of Philip's father. Although Philip and his principal advisers may have felt that the resulting autonomy gained by the Crown would enhance the king's capacity to rule, the king found himself increasingly opposed within his domains even by the leaders of the Castilian commonwealth who were otherwise disposed to support him so that he would remain among them. Instead of goodwill, he bequeathed to his seventeenth-century heirs a legacy of elite suspicion, resistance, and corruption that would help undermine the Hispanic Monarchy's European and global position.

Until royal action eliminated all but private, oral expressions of their perspectives, local notables recorded views indicating the degree to which they perceived the Crown's decision in the Béjar-Toledo dispute as an arbitrary, unjust exercise of royal authority motivated by the personal influence of a territorial aristocrat. This perception would help undermine Philip's capacity to respond effectively to the many challenges to his domains. Although other factors were involved, Philip alienated local notables through his arbitrary style of rule and conduct of judicial administration, and in doing so, he undermined his ability to shape personally the course of Castilian developments as he desired. In this chapter, I sort through the surviving evidence to show why members of the political kingdom might arrive at such an evaluation of the Council of Castile's final ruling in the Béjar-Toledo case.

On 28 June 1555, the audiencia of Granada ruled for the second time against the count of Belalcázar, marquis of Gibraleón. We have no way of knowing how or why the judges voted as they did or how sharp the division was among the twelve who decided the case. Both the book where votes were recorded and the president's secret record of the reasons for the votes have disappeared; the comments in the visitas of the period indicate that they were not well kept anyway. There is some evidence that the vote was not close. Toledo tried unsuccessfully to withdraw its challenge to one of the justices, Ldo. Botello, because he had voted in the city's favor, and if a potentially hostile judge was willing to support Toledo's claim, it seems probable that most if not all of the others were also willing to support it.[1]

There was a long delay, from at least 1549 until 1555, before the justices reached their decision on the appeal. Given the mountain of evidence in the case as well as the volume of other business, the final review was bound to take time. To some extent, the extended reflection may have been part of the effort to make the final verdict appear as just and well considered as possible. Another reason it took so long to announce a final verdict was probably the unsettled Castilian political situation created by shifting regency governments after Charles V left the peninsula in 1543. Because it had taken an order from the regent, princess Juana, in May 1555 to get the verdict announced,[2] the political situation may have made some of the judges reluctant to act on their own. The nature of the Chancillería of Granada as a royal institution and as a space for interaction among royal officials, territorial aristocrats, and local notables was shaped in part by interactions beyond the judicial process itself, and without the firm support Charles had given the Chancillería during its earlier deliberations on the Belalcázar case, the oidores were likely hesitant to go forward.[3] However, the justices also extended their consideration due to procedural requirements stemming from the Crown's desire that one of the kingdom's most important lawsuits be decided by an unusually high number of judges and due to the numerous challenges to the justices.[4]

The 1555 verdict was not the end of the extended, troubling Belalcázar dispute. On 16 January 1556, Charles V abdicated in favor of his son Philip, who thus became the new ultimate source of Castilian justice. Because Philip II of Castile has often been listed among Europe's archetypical "absolute" monarchs, the fate of Toledo's lawsuit with the House of Béjar over the Puebla de Alcocer region during Philip's reign permits a critical evaluation of the nature of monarchy in the face of claims for the theoretical utility of concepts such as "absolutism" and the "absolutist state."

A "Second Supplication" Prolongs the Trouble Case

By the time Philip became Castile's king, Alonso de Zúñiga y Sotomayor, count of Belalcázar, marquis of Gibraleón, and male head of the House of Béjar since his father's death in 1544, had been granted yet another trial under the fourteenth-century right of second supplication. The original 1390 law of second supplication, called the Law of Segovia for the Cortes at which it was promulgated, granted a hearing before the king on the exhaustion of all other appeals with the payment of a bond of 1500 *doblas de oro* to be forfeited if the earlier verdict were sustained. Through a convenient legal fiction, both the audiencia and the Council of Castile could act for the monarch. Part of the major administrative reforms of the late fourteenth century, the Law of Segovia was intended to reduce appeals designed simply to prolong litigation and to keep the Royal Council from dealing with lesser cases so that its members could direct their attention to matters significant for the kingdom. In the context of that period, however, it was probably more importantly a way of maintaining the monarch's personal role in judicial administration, at least where the interests of major vassals were concerned. However, both the Catholic Monarchs and Charles V tried through legislation to limit the number of appeals in second supplication because they tied up too much of the Council of Castile's deliberation time. Because of the way the Council was organized as a judicial body by the "Ordinances of Medina del Campo" (1489) and the Catholic Monarchs' practice of sending second supplications regarding the audiencia's review verdicts to the Council, scholars have assumed that this hearing would be before the Royal Council acting in the king's name. It appears, however, that before the legislation of 1565, the chancillerías could also hold trials on second supplications.[5] It was such a hearing that was being arranged in the Chancillería when an order arrived to transfer all documents in the case to the Council of Castile. Toledo transmitted the order but under circumstances that indicate the city was not acting in a manner contrary to the usual municipal aversion to placing such litigation before the Council.

Although the marquis of Gibraleón had been arranging a second supplication before the Chancillería of Granada, Melchor de la Peña, his representative at the regent's Court, was also arranging for a similar hearing before the Council of Castile. On 10 August 1555, the regent, princess Juana, along with Ldo. Otálora and Dr. Velasco, the two letrados prince Philip had ordered her to consult about such matters, issued a commission to the Royal Council to hear the case at the second supplication stage. The Council wrote to Francisco de Escobedo, notary for the case in Granada, on 27 August, ordering him to send the original transcript to them in Valladolid at the marquis of Gibraleón's expense, but the marquis chose not to deliver the order to the Chancillería, which continued its own hearings.[6] Because a panel of five judges was provided for in the legislation of 1532 on this type of appeal, Royal Council members Ldo. Galarza, Dr. Anaya, Dr. Ribera, Dr. Diego de la Gasca, and Dr. Cano issued a summons to Toledo on 26 August, and the city discovered that the marquis had an order to take the proceedings before the Council. Toledo secured a Council order for Escobedo to transfer the trial transcript because its patrician leaders saw that the marquis' maneuvering was just another attempt by the House of Béjar to delay a final verdict and that don Alonso would have the case removed to the Council of Castile only after the hearing before the Chancillería of Granada had been extended for as long as possible. Royal secretary Domingo de Zavala finally received the material at the regent's Court in Valladolid on 28 December.[7]

The Council of Castile accepted the case at this point as part of what, in comparison with the 1530s and 1540s, looks like a flood of grants of second supplication by princess Juana's government.[8] The intent of the sixteenth-century legislation on this type of appeal was to limit its use as much as possible. A law proclaimed in 1499 in Madrid and reaffirmed in 1502 implied that such an appeal should be denied if there were two conforming decisions in the case, and this reading of the law was confirmed in 1539. In 1501 the 1499 law was changed again, deleting a portion saying that cases being heard on appeal in second supplications regarding a decision in one Chancillería would be heard in the other. From then on such appeals would be sent to the monarch so that the decision about whether the case should be heard and by whom would be made by the ruler. Presumably, this change was intended to restrict the automatic nature of such an appeal. The 1539 decree doubled the value any property involved in litigation had to have before a party to a lawsuit would qualify for this type of appeal, and it put great stress on the fact that the importance and difficulty of the litigation should also be taken into account even if the value was sufficient. By legislation of 1541 and 1543, the Council of Castile determined whether second supplication cases should be heard. The law of 1539 in particular seemed a response to the Cortes's continuing requests that cases be kept, as far as possible, from going before the Council of Castile. There was still some confusion about whether such an appeal should be permitted in a case with two conforming verdicts. In 1539, it could not. The *Nueva Recopilación* of 1567, however, seems to have returned to the law of 1502, which implied that there could be an appeal in such circumstances, but not if the appealing party was in possession. Obviously, this provision was designed to make it

easier to enforce a verdict because presumably most decisions with two conforming rulings would be upheld on appeal, at which time the execution of
the verdict would be a formality if the appealing party had already surrendered possession of any disputed property.[9] Because all rules regarding two
conforming verdicts were overlooked when the marquis of Gibraleón's
appeal was allowed, it is probable that purely judicial considerations were
not the deciding factor. In such a troubled political climate, Toledo's chances
of recovering the viscounty of Puebla de Alcocer were endangered when the
marquis retained possession and thereby the ability to thwart efforts to
enforce an unfavorable final decision.

The Crown's growing lack of control over Castilian affairs, many of its
own officials, and Castilian political life in general apparently motivated this
flood of grants of second supplication. Regencies were never easy times for
monarchies, but the period between 1529 and 1543 had been punctuated by
the emperor's regular return to the realm. Although there were clear signs of
growing unease and factionalism in Castilian cities and major towns by the
late 1530s, the empress Isabella (d. 1539) and her Council had done a generally effective job of maintaining broad support within the political kingdom
for her regency government. After that period, however, Castilians would
not see a monarch again for almost seventeen years. Charles V tried to compensate for his absence, as he had done earlier and continued to do in other
domains when possible, by having a member of his family act as regent. Yet
the success of this policy depended in part on the experience and leadership
qualities of the individual involved, and nowhere, certainly not in Castile,
was a regency considered a satisfactory substitute for a resident ruler. The
one point of continuity was queen Joanna of Trastámara, the emperor's
mother, who did not die until 11 April 1555, but her reported instability and
long isolation from public affairs clearly disqualified her for any role.

Charles V had been out of the kingdom of Castile since the end of 1542.
When he left Barcelona in May 1543, he made a teenage boy, the future
Philip II, his regent, but whatever order there was in Castilian administra-
tion before 1548 was probably due much more to the experienced advisers
Charles had provided for the prince: cardinal-archbishop of Toledo Tavera,
who had so effectively aided the empress as president of the Council of
Castile and then briefly served as regent himself until prince Philip was
appointed; cardinal-archbishop of Seville García de Loaisa y Mendoza,
president of the Council of the Indies and Charles's confessor; don Juan de
Zúñiga, Philip's tutor and personal adviser; and chief secretary and financial
expert Francisco de los Cobos. These men were all dead before the next
regency government: Tavera died in 1545, García de Loaisa and Zúñiga in
1546, and Los Cobos in 1547. Dr. Hernando de Guevara, the last of the
councillors Ferdinand had left to his grandson, died in 1546. Thus, the core
of royal servants who had been responsible for over two decades of relative

Castilian tranquility died within a period of two years, and this was to have a detrimental effect on the regency governments that followed.

The Crown suffered a severe, progressive deterioration of its influence during the following decade. Philip journeyed to the Empire in October 1548, and the new regents were his sister María and her husband and first cousin Maximilian. Without effective assistance their regency was probably a disaster. Maximilian was displeased because his presence in the peninsula was clearly designed to give his cousin Philip an opportunity to follow Charles to the imperial throne, and the two reluctant regents sat in Valladolid or nearby Cigales and did little to oversee the royal councillors' work. Yet there were severe internal problems in the peninsula that needed royal attention, attention that was not forthcoming from caretaker rulers whose interests lay elsewhere. In 1550, Maximilian went to Augsburg, and Philip did not return to Castile until 1551. In July, 1554, he left the kingdom again to marry the English ruler Mary Tudor, and his other sister, Juana, the nineteen-year-old widow of the recently deceased prince of Portugal, left her infant son to return to Castile as regent, a post she would hold until Philip returned as king in September 1559.[10]

Thus, by the time the Council of Castile agreed to hear the marquis of Gibraleón's appeal from the Chancillería of Granada, years of inattention to serious internal difficulties had undermined the royal government's authority. The factionalism so characteristic of the early decades of Philip's reign in Castile had already emerged around the inquisitor-general and archbishop of Seville, Fernando de Valdés, and the duke of Alba, Fernando Alvarez de Toledo. Several interacting developments contributed to the growing fragmentation of Crown action. The existence of multiple Habsburg courts working at cross purposes, especially those of Charles, Philip, and Juana, increasingly reduced policy considerations to a narrowly defined focus on short-term plans for amassing enough money to fight the next battle. At the Castilian Court in Valladolid, serious divisions in the regency government resulted from both personal animosities and competing religious understandings. On the one hand, inquisitor-general Valdés was an intensely competitive courtier trying to secure his own primacy by putting loyal clients on crucial royal councils and tribunals. Because doña Juana represented a more Portuguese and Jesuit orientation toward mystical, individual spiritual experiences, Valdés's existing preference for a faith based only on unquestioning adherence to Church doctrine and public devotions was reinforced in opposition to Juana's views, and he and the Inquisition he led were ever more watchful for heresy in high places. Philip's shrewd Portuguese friend Ruy Gómez de Silva gained significant influence over the younger Philip's decisions, and Ruy Gómez's growing importance was greeted with hostility by the important royal advisers who would become his adversaries, most notably the duke of Alba.[11]

Concerned about their own influence and advancement, Castilian royal officials at all levels had no idea either whom to please or what standards might be used to evaluate their performance. In an often desperate search for security, they sought the favor of those at Court who appeared able and willing to protect them. They took whatever actions and made whatever decisions their patron wanted. Even in these personal connections there was often no stability because some would shift loyalties when another potential patron appeared better placed. Without solid support from the Habsburg dynasty's leaders, their officials had an understandable tendency to avoid potentially dangerous conflicts by accommodating the demands of the great. Work had so slowed that futile orders to speed up official business, such as those mentioned above on the provision of justice, became common. Corruption increased in the sense that institutional regulations were openly violated. Perhaps the most spectacular example of official collusion with the prominent was the disappearance of privately owned silver deposited in Seville's House of Trade before it could be seized as a forced loan to finance the Habsburg military enterprise in northern Europe.[12]

The monarchy was experiencing serious financial difficulties, which ultimately led to the suspension of interest payments in 1557. These problems had begun in the 1540s, and even the efforts of Los Cobos had not reversed the trend. Worse yet, in the late 1540s and 1550s, the grandees, perhaps both offended and given confidence by the absence of the monarch and even his heir, began to form cabals and gave every appearance of becoming troublesome. In 1559, a certain Ldo. Palomares informed the king that some prominent magnates had met in Valladolid to ratify a position established in the late 1540s. As if to echo the House of Béjar's earlier request that Charles V take control of the Belalcázar trial, they claimed that only the monarch in person could serve as their judge, thereby denying the jurisdiction of royal officials, audiencias, and chancillerías. These aristocrats were certainly not helpful when approached by Los Cobos in the 1540s for loans; the duke of Alba and others declined to provide anything and the duke of Béjar gave less than he was asked for. Patrician confidence was perhaps sapped by mid-century reverses in economic sectors from which the urban-based notables derived much of their wealth, in conjunction with the increasingly greater urban role played by the grandees, which heightened many territorial aristocrats' sense of authority. In general, there existed a growing condition of administrative chaos and corruption accompanied by general insubordination, which benefited aristocratic attempts to gain influence.[13]

In this unsettled and crisis-punctuated atmosphere, it does not seem odd that the regency would grant any petitions that were neither obviously illegal nor immediately dangerous to the Crown's interests. The lack of adequate continuity of institutional action allowed narrowly defined requests which did not seem to affect enough of the kingdom to provoke divisive debate, to be granted, because no coherent policy was being followed and such requests could slip through the cracks. And a Crown government willing to sell *hidalgo* status, public offices, ecclesiastical jurisdictions of all sorts, and almost anything to meet the financial demands constantly arriving from the courts of Charles and Philip in the north might even have viewed the bond necessary for an appeal of second supplication as a welcome source of revenue.[14] All this vending activity disrupted established administrative interactions and alienated important groups within the commonwealth from active collaboration with the Crown. After his return to Castile in 1559, Philip II would have to deal with the consequences of years of government drift and the serious disaffection of political leaders. It was in this context that the Council of Castile would hear the appeal of the well-known and much-watched Belalcázar case and render what turned out to be the final verdict.

Toward a Personalist, Authoritarian Regime

Although the trial transcript was available to the Council of Castile at the end of 1555, no hearing was held at that time. Nor apparently was Philip II anxious to have the trial begin after he returned to the kingdom, because Toledo received no response to several attempts to start the hearing on the second supplication granted to the House of Béjar. Philip was in Toledo in February 1561 when the city's representative at Court asked him to order the Council to commence proceedings. There seems to have been some action on this petition, for at their usual 1 March discussion of the case, Toledo's municipal councillors spoke of the lawsuit's records as though they were in the hands of a relator (court reporter).[15] Before he allowed the Council to hear the case, however, Philip undertook a series of judicial reforms of at least the magnitude of those of Charles V in the 1520s and as little noticed by historians.

This reform effort responded in part to Cortes petitions, especially those of 1563, which complained about the confusion and delays in the administration of justice.[16] Many of the changes were directed toward greater speed, efficiency, and dignity in judicial procedures and were thus in line with the efforts of Philip's predecessors.[17] As we saw in the case of royal orders about the handling of challenges to judges, many of these merely ratified procedural norms previously established by rulings in the various councils and audiencias.

Many of Philip's other changes, however, moved in the opposite direction from those of his father and great-grandparents. Culminating in 1565, perhaps spurred on by his new and zealous Council president, Ldo. Diego de Espinosa, Philip promulgated procedural alterations, generally from his retreat in the Segovia Woods and without Cortes consultation, designed not only to diminish the prestige of the chancillerías but also to control and perhaps even coerce the justices. For example, the audiencia's authority depended in part on the importance of the cases heard there, and Philip ordered Granada's justices not to hear cases involving certain elite groups. Philip launched a potentially more serious attack on both the prestige and the independence of the chancillerías when he ordered in December 1565 that the royal prosecutors were to sit on the bench with the justices. Since 1561, the king had compelled these prosecutors to make annual reports to him about all cases relating to royal finances or taxable property, and although other objections were raised, the oidores resisted the new procedure mainly because the prosecutor would hear the reasons for the votes and would therefore violate the secrecy of the court. Of course, the prosecutor could also report on the attitudes of individual judges. Philip knew what he wanted, and he demanded in February 1566 that his original order be followed.[18]

At the same time that the chancillerías were being undercut, the king was increasing the judicial role of the Council of Castile, making it clearly the highest court, from whose verdicts there could be no appeal even in its own chambers. One such act, of 9 February 1565, ordered that there be no procedural claims of nullity after verdicts of second supplication in an attempt to overturn them. Years later, in 1609, members of the Council of Castile indicated to Toledo's representative, jurado Juan Belluga de Moncada, that they knew about the Toledo-Belalcázar case and that it was precisely in order to close the door to any continuation of that lawsuit by Toledo that this 1565 law was enacted. It seems unlikely that this information was new to city leaders. As a result of the new royal attitude, the Council of Castile received more and more judicial business, thereby reversing Charles V's effort to give greater responsibility for judicial administration to the audiencias as institutions more removed from the political concerns of the royal Court, at which local notables felt the territorial aristocrats' influence might be decisive.[19]

Historians who see the reign of Philip II as another chapter in the continuing development of "absolutism" with its more centralized, coercive reshaping of all aspects of government will find nothing unusual in the tone of this legislation. This type of interpretation of the era's monarchies provides, however, limited explanatory aid. Philip took these measures, and did so in this particular manner outside of Cortes sessions, not because he confidently felt himself to be in a position from which he was capable of effective intervention in the kingdom's affairs but because he sensed he was in trouble. Weakness gave birth to a new royal authoritarianism. At age thirty-two, Philip had returned to an unsettled polity,[20] and to defend himself he wanted matters affecting his Court, and in particular his great nobles, to be under his personal supervision and control. The king felt threatened by the territorial aristocracy and did not want minor royal officials or those far from Court antagonizing them, and because these letrado officials might be preoccupied by the potential impact on their careers of grandee influence at Court, which appeared to be enhanced during the long and fragmented regency, Philip also feared decisions would favor magnates' claims to the detriment of the Crown.

To achieve this consolidation of control, during the first fifteen years of Philip's reign, especially during the period of Ldo. Diego de Espinosa's leadership, 1565–1572, the king's letrado advisers organized a regime with an authoritarian and confessional cast. This heavily letrado and ecclesiastical government alienated many members of the territorial aristocracy, and their complaints to Philip apparently played a role in changing Philip's coordination of political activity at Court.[21] Philip even began emulating the common aristocratic disdain of letrado royal servants and tried to temper the hostility of his officials toward the aristocracy.[22] After the death in 1572 of Ldo. Espinosa, the Council of Castile's president, Philip increasingly centered policy discussions in juntas in which nobles rather than letrados predominated, leaving the various royal councils to administer policies made elsewhere. Whatever the reality of Philip's pattern of consultation with close advisers, the apparent intervention in government of noble Court politicians must have reinforced a general impression within the commonwealth of undue grandee influence, thereby enhancing the magnates' ability to attract clients and further isolating the Court from collaboration with local notables.

Philip might have organized his Court differently, however, had he merely feared the influence of the territorial aristocracy on his rule. The king also felt he needed the grandees in order to confront successfully his massing enemies, both internal and external. A man contemplating such difficulties in such a state of mind would be careful not to antagonize the wealthy and powerful around him. Protestant heretics continued to expand their territorial control in Europe, including in some of Philip's northern domains, and in the late 1550s, "Protestant" groups were exposed in Seville and Valladolid. Some Inquisition tribunals became more active, and the archbishop of Toledo was arrested and tried for heresy. On another front, the Ottoman Empire and its allies were attempting to extend their influence in the Mediterranean by conquest, corsair raids had intensified against the peninsula's southern coasts, and finally on Christmas Eve of 1568, Granadan *Moriscos* (baptized Christians of Muslim ancestry) rebelled.[23]

Developments in his Netherlands domains weighed most heavily on Philip's mind, and at least as early as the fall of 1566, the Council of State intensely debated what Philip should do. In the north, he vigorously attempted to defend his Church through an anti-heresy campaign and the creation of new bishoprics. Beginning in November 1565, magnates in the Netherlands organized the League of Compromise, and in April 1566, some two hundred of the League's noble leaders forced their way into the presence of Margaret of Parma, Philip's half-sister and regent there, to present their petition against the Inquisition. The repeated demonstration of royal incapacity provided an opportunity for militant, public Protestant activities in the Netherlands, such as the hedge-preaching and iconoclastic movements that extended into 1567. Although magnates horrified by widespread disorder rallied to Margaret and produced several important rebel defeats in March 1567, many noble and urban leaders escaped into exile and continued to plot. The duke of Alba had arrived in the Netherlands in August 1567 with an army to crush subversion, but the situation could not have looked permanently secure, even after Alba's great victory at Jemminghen in July 1568 appeared to reverse the rebel success the previous May at the Battle of Heiligerlee. Rebel polemicists emphasized that their conception of "freedom" included municipal and provincial privileges, and echoes of rebel "constitutionalist" principles could be heard in objections to the fiscal exactions Alba demanded when he summoned the Low Countries' States General in March 1569. Not only did the established Church continue to appear endangered, but Netherlandish leaders persevered in denying Philip the authority he felt was rightfully and necessarily his as monarch.[24]

The crisis atmosphere intensified in the years 1568 to 1570. A number of historians have commented on the irresolute quality of Philip's actions during this period and on his tendency to panic and see some problems as much greater threats than they actually were. To maintain authority and avoid limitations on the information he received, Philip allowed a high level of factional intrigue at his Court in Castile but sought to balance the cliques so that none could monopolize the advice he received. In part for this reason, Philip was notorious for undercutting, without notice, subordinates who proved to be successful administrators, and courtiers felt his favor was highly unstable. With corruption and intrigue rampant, much of it caused by his own actions, Philip had to take on more and more direct responsibility for the outlines of policy, and this meant that he had to spend enormous amounts of time reading every important dispatch, letter, and council policy statement, often responding with detailed instructions even for distant viceroys.[25] He tried to keep close watch on his councils and chancillerías, and his surveillance networks supposedly extended even into university classrooms to monitor what was taught.

Increasingly the king felt more comfortable shielding himself from personal contact with anyone but those whose position was entirely dependent on royal favor. Unlike Charles V, who was constantly surrounded by his subjects and especially by his great vassals, Philip tried to insulate himself as much as possible, and this was expressed in the elaboration of solemn, cold Court ritual and in the lack of effort to travel and visit his subjects. The ultimate expression of this desire for privacy was, of course, the Escorial, however little time Philip may have actually spent there. Perhaps because of what he saw while king of England or the influence of his wife's comments about French practice, Philip established Madrid as the site of the royal Court with a series of residences in the vicinity at which he spent a good amount of time. The most famous of these residences in Philip II's time were El Pardo, in the Segovia Woods, and El Escorial. This system enabled Philip to interact directly and frequently with his councillors, although often in writing, while reducing the need to be hosted by aristocrats and munici- palities. His biographers are not in complete agreement about the degree to which the establishment of a fixed capital and Philip II's residential prefer- ences corresponded to his personality. Certainly, his genetic inheritance from his grandmother queen Joanna "the Mad" offered the potential for a personality development that tended to make him reclusive. Moreover, Philip had moved geographically a great deal since 1543, and he may not have liked the experience. Yet in the face of so many other possible explana- tions, which together would adequately account for the designation of a cap- ital, I rate the personality factor as much less important than others. Whatever the reasons, although he considered other residential patterns until the early 1580s, his innovation in Castilian royal practice does rein- force the image of a withdrawn, suspicious, insecure monarch so widespread in historical writing on his reign.[26]

Discomfort with direct, personal interaction may account for his treat- ment of the Cortes. Even before he received the Castilian crown, he decreed from England in 1555 that he would legislate when the Cortes was not in session, whether or not such legislation abrogated earlier laws given in con- junction with a session of that body. Throughout his reign, he refused to meet with its representatives or to reply quickly to its petitions, and he tried unsuccessfully to get the procuradores to attend without limitations on their commissions and to keep them from consulting with their home councils during the actual meetings.[27] Although the Cortes met frequently during his reign, consultation, and all that it meant for an effective monarchy, played no role in Philip's style of rule, as his prolonged difficulties with his final assembly showed.

In addition to establishing patterns of consultation with local notables through the use of representative institutions such the Cortes and the Assem- bly or Congregation of the Clergy,[28] Charles V had also strengthened royal conciliar and judicial institutions as points of convergence for political inter- actions emanating from the various localities of his expanding Castilian domains. Apparently convinced that he and his close advisers could provide adequate guidance through policy directives and procedural ordinances, the emperor had delegated a good deal of authority to trusted subordinates. Philip II, however, neither delegated authority nor remained open to gen- uine consultation that would have mended the damaged relations with the commonwealth's suspicious political leaders, and, therefore, he encountered only limited possibilities for drawing local notables into active collaboration of the type really necessary to sustain the Crown's long-term military and religious commitments.

The Council of Castile Renders Its Verdict

Because of the development of such a highly personalist, authoritarian regime, 1566 was not the best time for Toledo to have the Council of Castile finally consider the Belalcázar case. Yet on 8 July 1566, in part because Philip had made the legal reforms he wanted and in part to prepare for the Cortes battle that was certain to occur the following December, he wrote to Toledo, in response to yet another of its municipal council's petitions, to tell its patrician councillors that, in recognition of the city's services and fidelity to the Crown, he was ordering the case to be determined with all the brevity that considerations of justice would allow. Apparently this order did not greatly speed the proceedings because the councillors were, in December, still obviously annoyed at the way the case was dragging on and again wanted to approach Philip.[29]

Because the Cortes was meeting, regidor don Francisco de Rojas and jurado Baltasar de Toledo, Toledo's delegates there, requested in January 1567 that the kingdom send gentlemen to beg his majesty that a decision be rendered in the Belalcázar lawsuit. Although acknowledging the extraordinary nature of such a request, the Cortes in 1563 had petitioned the monarch in the kingdom's name that the case be decided promptly, a clear indication that the Belalcázar dispute had lost none of its importance among local notables as a means by which to measure the monarch's exercise of authority. Some procuradores were uncertain whether the Cortes should again pressure Philip about the matter, and don Antonio del Castillo Portocarrero of Salamanca, perhaps because of Portocarrero ties to the House of Béjar, led a small group opposed to Cortes assistance for Toledo. Although the majority wanted to offer Toledo some aid in securing a prompt verdict, they could not agree on how it should be done. Moreover, the debate in March revealed the influence of the duke of Béjar's position: both of Seville's procuradores noted that one of the parties to the suit should not be supported because the duke had asserted that the original grant was justified "by services done in the pacification of the kingdom," and Juan de Henao of Avila proclaimed it certain that "the duke possessed this estate by very just titles and for outstanding services in support of the Royal Crown and benefit of these kingdoms." Perhaps it was significant that the duke of Béjar was part of the royal entourage at the opening of the Cortes.[30]

Indeed, more ominous than the mere temper of the times was Philip's permission in 1564 for Francisco de Zúñiga y Sotomayor, then still just marquis of Gibraleón as his mother, the hereditary duchess of Béjar, was still alive, to float a large loan so that he could reside personally at Court to over-see his appeal of the Granadan audiencia's decisions awarding Puebla de Alcocer to Toledo. He could use any seignioral rents for collateral, except those of the disputed viscounty. There were signs of nervousness in Toledo in February 1567 when regidor don Diego de Silva reported to its council that he had heard that don Francisco, by then duke of Béjar, had come to Court a few days earlier and was actively at work on the case.[31]

The transcripts of the hearing before the Council of Castile have disap-peared with all of the originals from Granada, but this loss is not serious. In the first place, the rules of the second supplication were that only the earlier proceedings would be examined and no new evidence presented, and regi-dor don Martín de Ayala reported that the Council intended to follow these rules. Both sides seem to have retained their final arguments before the audi-encia, and Toledo made it clear that rather than seek some special judgment, the city wanted all cases in the realm decided on the same issues as this one.[32] In the second place, a transcript of the proceedings would not clarify the doubtful aspects of the eventual Council decision because neither the for-mal nor the actual reasons for the judges' votes would have been recorded.

On Monday, 15 March 1568, the Royal Council in Madrid gave its ver-dict; it reversed the audiencia's decision and found for the House of Béjar. The judges (Council president Ldo. Diego de Espinosa, Dr. Diego de la Gasca, Ldo. Bartolomé Atienza, Dr. Gaspar Durango, and Ldo. Pedro Gasco) imposed on Toledo's officials perpetual silence about the matter, leaving the city absolutely no recourse to request or claim anything that per-tained to the viscounty of Puebla de Alcocer.[33]

Toledo's patricians were outraged, and the city council showed no incli-nation to be silent despite the Council of Castile's order. A note in the diary of Sebastián de Horozco provides a good indication of the city's shock. After pointing out that the earlier Chancillería decisions had been given by six-teen to twenty of the most famous legal scholars and judges of the time, he declared that the Council verdict was "something never thought possible nor even now believable." The only consolation was that "God who is the true judge knows the truth" and would express it on the day of final judg-ment. Toledo, he went on, had spent an infinite sum of money as a result of "its certain and clear justice" and remained in debt from its efforts. More-over, the city had lost the 200,000 ducats the duke of Béjar had been willing to pay to settle the conflict if Toledo would surrender its rights in the matter. Horozco's tone was one of bitterness and perhaps suspicion.[34]

A man with his connections and interest in the case was likely expressing opinions that were widespread in Toledo about the outcome of the Council hearing. Sebastián de Horozco was a famous jurist and author who, although he never published anything in his own lifetime, enjoyed great popularity with his fellow citizens. His family connections with Toledo's elite and letrado circles were important. Marcos de Covarrubias, his father-in-law, was the brother of Alfonso Covarrubias. Alfonso's wife María was a member of the Gutiérrez Egas family. Alfonso and María's sons, Diego and Antonio de Covarrubias y Leyva, were distinguished churchmen and lawyers who represented their kingdom at the Council of Trent, and Diego became president of the Council of Castile on Ldo. Espinosa's death in 1572. Diego and Antonio were first cousins to Horozco's wife, María Valero y Covarrubias. The fact that their sons, both well-known Toledan intellectuals in their own right, were living with their mother's distinguished cousin during part of the time he was president of the Council indicates that Horozco and his wife were close to Dr. Diego de Covarrubias.[35] Although he did not participate in the Belalcázar decision there, Covarrubias was an oidor of the Granadan Chancillería at the time and would, therefore, have been familiar with a lawsuit so closely related to his Toledan roots. Not only was Horozco intimate with Toledo's ruling families but he also had an interest in such an important case. He wrote a book, now unfortunately lost, expressing his legal views on the matter, and presumably it circulated among the city's intellectual elite.

Horozco's bitterness and suspicion were certainly carried over into the legal consultations, city council sessions, and public debates held to discuss ways to recover jurisdiction over the towns.[36] The city council came together on Tuesday, 23 March to deal with the matter. The corregidor, interestingly, wanted all of the lawyers brought together as soon as possible. That the Crown's own local representative took such an initiative to violate the Royal Council's gag order suggests the degree to which the final Belalcázar decision was seen as a perversion of justice by those familiar with the case. The municipal councillors named a team to review Toledo's options (regidores don Alonso de Rojas and Juan Gómez de Silva and jurados Alonso de Cisneros and Gregorio [or Gonzalo] Pérez de Ubeda) and sent a letter to don Gutierre de Guevara and Alonso Dávalos at Court, ordering them to assemble all of Toledo's lawyers there. In accepting the position given him, don Alonso de Rojas expressed the great pain he felt that such a prominent tribunal of the kingdom's leading judges had passed such a verdict in such an important matter, and he dedicated himself to the struggle against the decision. He emphasized that his suspicions were directed only toward the Council of Castile.[37] The results of the city's efforts would only increase don Alonso's pain.

The Appearance of Aristocratic Influence

Ldo. Espinosa and his colleagues may have reversed the earlier verdicts issued by the Chancillería of Granada because they defended a different vision of the relationship between royal authority and the law. Many of them served as agents of royal authoritarianism employed to eradicate Muslim practices among Granada's Moriscos and to impose on the kingdom's clerical institutions the decrees of the recently concluded Council of Trent.[38] In the face of repeated municipal protests and despite explicit royal guarantees, over the previous twenty-five years, the Crown had pursued a series of expedients to raise revenue, which many local notables viewed as illicit and a politically foolish erosion of the tax base that cities and towns needed if their governments were to help sustain the monarchy. The Council of Finance was selling municipal offices and common lands. Villages within municipal jurisdictions were purchasing their status as autonomous towns, and prominent and wealthy citizens were buying hidalgo status and the resulting tax exemption. Income from important royal taxes paid by the unprivileged citizens passed directly to those who purchased this right, and groups of "vassals" passed from one jurisdiction to another, generally that of a noble house and entailed estate. The Crown presented some of these asset sales as rewards for monetary services. Royal officials also seized private bullion shipments from America and forced the renegotiation of Crown loan contracts, forcing those harmed by these actions to accept government bonds (*juros*) as compensation.[39] Moreover, to assist aristocrats in the management of their houses' finances, Philip II expanded on the claims and activities of his father's government to exempt grandees from the terms of legal agreements, particularly entails.[40]

However, even if Philip and the Council of Castile were asserting, in their defense of John II's grant to Gutierre de Sotomayor, what they felt to be a legitimate understanding of the exercise of absolute royal authority and the use of "grace," most local notables likely viewed the decision through a different lens. For them, the presence of territorial aristocrats and their influence around the king constituted a grave danger to the administration of justice. Rather than ratifying the ruler's perspective, for them the Council's decision and its context in such a high-profile case helped reinforce the prevailing view of local notables that monarchs had absolute authority to defend fundamental legal guarantees of property and proper judicial procedures. The Court connections of the House of Béjar lent strong color to feelings that the Belalcázar decision turned on these connections, rather than on some variant legal theory contending for support among urban patricians. Royal capacity to achieve the Crown's ambitious goals for the global Hispanic Monarchy would depend largely on the terms of collaboration provided by municipal leaders. As was seen during Cortes sessions and direct negotiations with the councils of major cities and towns, these notables increasingly lacked faith in the monarch's promises, for they might be broken arbitrarily. Their hostility to Philip's new authoritarianism reached the point where, by the 1590s, they were demanding written contracts in exchange for the approval of new tributes. Therefore, the claim for greater royal authority did not increase the monarch's capacity but actually undermined his leadership. However much local notables felt that loyalty to the monarch was necessary for them to maintain their disproportionate share of their region's resources, their suspicion about the intentions of kings and kings' ministers would continue to frustrate royal initiatives during the reigns of Philip II's successors, with significant consequences for the role of Castile and the Hispanic Monarchy in the first global age.[41]

Nonjudicial factors may have played a role in the decision, but barring the discovery of direct comments on the matter in the personal correspondence of the duke of Béjar or one of the judges, we can only join Toledo's leaders in speculating about what these factors were. Speculation was and remains necessary because so many of the important relationships were personal and the exchanges oral. Even when providing Philip with formal advice on appointments to vacant offices, cardinal Espinosa, the chief royal adviser of the late 1560s, did so orally.[42]

The commonwealth's leaders generally assumed that members of the territorial aristocracy would use their positions to help relatives and influence the outcome of lawsuits. For example, Philip II wrote to the Jesuit leader and future general Francisco de Borja to seek his recommendations for high positions in the administration. In his reply of 5 May 1559, referring to the presidency of the Council of Castile, Borja reported that if Philip wanted to name a grandee, the problems with the duke of Alburquerque included his "many relatives and lawsuits," and while he recommended the count of Oropesa, he did so despite recognizing that this candidate too had "some lawsuits and the inconvenience of the relatives."[43] Both the king and Borja recognized that the course and outcome of political processes at Court depended heavily on networks of personal relations because the monarch and his close advisers had to rely on the cumbersome vehicle of individual patronage to promote their policies. The Crown was more often reacting to changing interactions than initiating such changes. So much activity was beyond Court control, and even there it was hard to get things done in the midst of conflicting personal interests. The Court was not the only source of patronage in Castile, for important posts and sources of income were controlled by others. Nor was service at Court necessarily a goal for all members of the groups, such as letrados, for example, from among whom such servants were selected, and this would likely make such men much less reliable agents when posted elsewhere as Crown officials. Even those resident at Court might not be suitable for implementing the ruler's will because of conflicting ties. Perhaps concerns about the influence of such ties on the actions of officials explains why, when those employed were letrados, they were also often churchmen, who were supposed to have fewer family interests than other men. As a further limitation on the use of royal patronage, the number of posts whose holders could be appointed directly was rather small, and it was difficult to keep track of them.[44]

In discussing patronage relationships, both present-day and sixteenth-century commentators tend to present them as more stable than they were. Commentators often fail to recognize the degree to which such interactions were reciprocal: to count on a client's loyalty and effective service, the patron had to respond frequently to the client's needs and desires. In this regard, the patron was to a degree as dependent on the client as the client was on the patron, and because limitations on adequate sources of patronage might often make it difficult to respond to a client's requests, clientage connections were potentially unstable. It was for this reason that significant shifts in support occurred. Although it is easier to examine such transfers of personal loyalty where they involved men as prominent at Court as the royal secretary, Francisco de Eraso, and the royal confessor, friar Bernardo de Fresneda,[45] the potential for instability was present in all such relationships.[46] In his autobiography written in the mid-1570s, the Cordoban ecclesiastic and eventual bishop of Zamora, Dr. Diego de Simancas, reported a conversation he had had in the 1550s with the duke of Sessa. Simancas was under pressure to accept as a service to the monarch a position in Rome he did not really want, and the duke told him that "in order to serve the king one had to employ both one's person and estate, but neither one's soul nor honor" and Simancas remained as oidor in Valladolid.[47] Simancas also turned down the job of royal regent of Navarra because the salary was too low to maintain his honor. Clearly even if the patron was the ruler himself, the client's honor would have to be maintained, and this would require resources and continual responsiveness to the client's needs. As the global Hispanic Monarchy became more complex and geographically larger, the Crown required greater effort and resources to sustain effective royal authority throughout its domains, and increasingly the Habsburg rulers found the task beyond their capacity.

Friendly salutations in correspondence and patterns of visitation do not invariably prove close collaboration. Such formulaic activity was not necessarily motivated by frequent collaboration or even genuine friendship. In major urban centers, many such actions were attempts to paper over serious factional divisions in order to avoid group weakness and sometimes even the outbreak of violence. For a particular group to be able to promote its interests, however those were defined, its leading members had to be able to act in this way. As Ruy Gómez de Silva showed early in his career as royal favorite, such smooth interactions with others were necessary for the successful courtier,[48] and it appears that other influential courtiers depended throughout their careers on a similar ability to maintain civil relationships even with those they sometimes opposed when recommending actions on such hot topics as military or religious policy. This talent certainly appears as a significant element in the growing influence of other Court figures, such as Ldo. Diego de Espinosa and Dr. Martín de Velasco (discussed below). Further, when connections of patronage and friendship are alleged, it is often hard to see from the evidence presented how the resulting influence was actually used in concrete situations.

Whatever the motives and theoretical merits of Philip's claims to act in a manner contrary to law and to alter ordinances without consultation with the kingdom represented in the Cortes, local notables likely suspected that the influence of those well placed at Court stimulated many royal actions. Although it is no longer possible to argue that Philip's Court was neatly divided into "parties" supporting either the prince of Eboli, Ruy Gómez de Silva, or the duke of Alba, Fernando Alvarez de Toledo, constant bargaining over personal influence lay behind much that happened among those directly serving the monarch. Because the duke of Béjar had no legal training, the only reason he had come to Court to oversee the Belalcázar suit before the Council of Castile was to mobilize such influence, as Toledo's well-informed councillors understood, and among the most important of the House of Béjar's connections was the prince of Eboli.[49]

Philip had shown such personal favor to Ruy Gómez, at least since his second Castilian regency in the early 1550s, that the astute Portuguese courtier was increasingly able both to win politically useful loyalties among those in royal service at the various Courts among which Habsburg authority was divided from 1554 onward and to enhance his status through ever closer ties to the territorial aristocracy. These interrelated sets of connections were the basis of the so-called Eboli party that so struck the Venetian ambassadors and the papal nuncio in the early 1560s. These observers may well have overemphasized Ruy Gómez's influence in some areas, however. He and his friends supposedly supported a more open religious policy, but the *Ebolistas* did not prevent the inquisitor-general, Francisco de Valdés, the royal confessor, friar Bernardo de Fresneda, and their allies such as Dr. Simancas from exploiting fears of heresy in the aftermath of the trial and execution of "Lutherans" discovered in Valladolid and Seville, to arrest and try Bartolomé de Carranza, the archbishop of Toledo.[50]

Ruy Gómez founded his early aristocratic ties on the marriage Philip helped him arrange to Ana de Mendoza y de la Cerda, heir to the House of Mélito (named for the County of Mileto in Naples), one of the cadet *mayorazgos* (entailed estates) of the Mendoza family. Philip's formal and secret arrangements with doña Ana's father, Diego de Mendoza, second count of Mélito, were fundamental to securing this desirable match for his friend, and this favor shown by prince Philip may have benefited the count in litigation with his mother in the kingdom of Naples. Among other distinctions, Ruy Gómez's father-in-law went on to become duke of Francavila, regent of Aragón, first president of the new Council of Italy, and viceroy of Catalonia, all without demonstrating much administrative talent. The actual negotiations in 1553 were conducted by doña Ana's maternal uncle, Juan de Silva, fifth count of Cifuentes, fellow *sumiller de corps* (gentleman of the bedchamber) of Philip's household with Ruy Gómez, and the latter's lifelong friend.[51]

Although Philip's personal affection for Ruy Gómez remained strong, the prince of Eboli's political influence had declined by 1565. With the loss of the close political collaboration with the monarch that had made him so prominent at Court, Eboli had begun to secure his position by permanent means: a move into the territorial aristocracy. As in the past, Philip played a prominent role in helping his friend obtain the kind of acceptance among Castile's grandees that would validate Ruy Gómez's eventual ascension to grandee rank as duke of Pastrana.[52]

Although the building of an ample and stable entailed estate required Ruy Gómez to pull together considerable landed wealth and revenues, he had to generate more personal relationships with the territorial aristocracy in order to shed the inferior status that was the basis of Alba's antagonism to him. His own marriage to doña Ana had provided him with valuable family connections within the aristocracy, but the platform for his escape from the adverse political conjuncture of the mid-1560s to the security of high standing was the splendid marriage he arranged for his oldest daughter, Ana de Silva y Mendoza, who was born in 1561. In the summer of 1566, it was arranged that, when she had attained a suitable age, she would wed Alonso Pérez de Guzmán el Bueno, the duke of Medina Sidonia, future commander of the Armada, who had been born in 1549. The duke and his family were willing to consider the match because they felt a need for protection at Court where officials were trying to recover royal revenues earlier alienated to the House of Medina Sidonia. Given the special role of personal influence at Philip's Court, Ruy Gómez's position and experience as an important member of the Council of Finance recommended him strongly as a protector. The relationship would continue to develop in the coming years, culminating as the initial agreement specified in the formal betrothal of 1572 and the wedding in 1574, after Ruy Gómez's death.[53]

Whatever the eventual benefit of the marriage for the House of Medina Sidonia, the contract also served to establish direct ties between Ruy Gómez and the House of Béjar. During the negotiations, the young duke of Medina Sidonia was represented by three people. One was his mother, Leonor Manrique de Zúñiga y Sotomayor (d. 1582), countess of Niebla, the younger sister of the duke of Béjar. The second representative was the marquis of Ayamonte, Antonio de Guzmán y Zúñiga (d., as Milan's governor, 1580). If don Antonio's older brother, don Francisco, duke of Béjar, and his son, don Francisco, later count of Belalcázar, had preceded don Antonio in death (the first-mentioned lived until 1591; the second until 1601), don Antonio would have become duke of Béjar, marquis of Gibraleón, and count of Belalcázar. The third representative was the duke of Medina Sidonia's great-uncle, Pedro de Guzmán y Zúñiga, count of Olivares, grandfather of Philip IV's famous favorite. Moreover, it appears that whatever relationship was developing around the House of Medina Sidonia's dealings with the Council of Finance had even earlier origins, for among those who testified in April 1565 on behalf of secretary Francisco de Eraso in the investigation that would lead to his disgrace were, in addition to Ruy Gómez, the countess of Niebla, the marquis of Ayamonte, and the count of Olivares.[54] If the perception at Court was that a close family connection with Ruy Gómez would help the House of Medina Sidonia with its legal problems, it is likely that those at Court also felt the protection would be extended to the House of Béjar.

Francisco de Zúñiga y Sotomayor, duke of Béjar and count of Belalcázar, and the prince of Eboli had already engaged in personal negotiations of the same type the year before. Ruy Gómez had negotiated, on behalf of Ana Pimentel, an agreement for the duke to take as his second wife Brianda de la Cerda, her daughter with the late Diego Sarmiento y de la Cerda, the count of Salinas. Moreover, the following spring, Ruy Gómez used his influence at Court to obtain for the duke the necessary permissions from the Council of Castile for the special financial arrangements that were necessary to cover the required bride payment (*arras*) of 8,000 *ducados*.[55]

The House of Béjar's new ties with Ruy Gómez may have assisted the duke of Béjar in other ways. For example, during the final years of his push to become a Castilian grandee, Ruy Gómez made a number of purchases financed by Melchor de Herrera, who would eventually become marquis of Auñón.[56] It would be interesting to know who provided the loans that allowed the duke of Béjar to establish residence at Court in order to oversee the Belalcázar lawsuit. Apparently as a result of Ruy Gómez's primacy within the royal financial administration at the time, Herrera was put in charge of the General Treasury of Castile in September 1565, a position that also gave him a seat on the Council of Finance. After the disgrace of Francisco de Eraso, but without losing his connection to the prince of Eboli, Herrera became a close collaborator of Diego de Espinosa as the latter increasingly became Philip II's major adviser on Castilian affairs. Herrera was initially brought to Ruy Gómez's attention by the latter's friend, the duke of Sessa, Gonzalo Fernández de Córdoba (1524–1578), under whose command Herrera had fought in Milan in the late 1550s.[57] The duke of Sessa's sister, Francisca de Córdoba, was the wife of Alonso de Zúñiga y Sotomayor, count of Belalcázar and marquis of Gibraleón, the duke of Béjar's older brother whose death without heirs had opened the way for don Francisco to assume the major titles of his House.

Of course, the duke of Béjar was related in some way to a high percentage of the great houses of Castile's territorial aristocracy. As mentioned above, his younger sister, Leonor, was by marriage the countess of Niebla. At about the same time that a marriage was negotiated between her son and Ruy Gómez's daughter, another was arranged for her daughter, Andrea Coronel de Guzmán, and the duke of Béjar's son, count Francisco III (who received the Belalcázar title on his marriage, although his father did not die until 1591). Count Francisco III's mother was the duke of Béjar's first wife, Guiomar de Aragón y Mendoza, a daughter of the duke of Infantado. The duke and doña Guiomar also had a daughter, Teresa de Zúñiga, who in 1567 married Rodrigo Ponce de León, marquis of Zahara, eldest son of the duke of Arcos. The duke of Arcos's late wife (d. 1565) was María de Toledo y de Figueroa, daughter of the count of Feria, Lorenzo Suárez de Figueroa, and his wife Catalina Hernández de Córdoba, marquise of Priego; María de Toledo y de Figueroa was, therefore, the sister of Gómez Suárez de Figueroa, count of Feria (in 1567, first duke of Feria), who was one of Ruy Gómez's most widely recognized supporters at Court.[58] Because the House of Béjar's sixteenth-century family records are incomplete, there may well be marriages about which we know nothing, but the duke had close family connections with influential members of the Eboli faction, and a number of these alliances were made or reinforced on the eve of the final decision in the case.

Court Officials and Factions

Court cliques did not just include aristocratic dynasties; prominent Court officials were also involved. Important secretaries began to establish connections with the territorial aristocracy in Charles V's reign. The year before the duke of Béjar's son married a sister of the duke of Sessa (a marriage Los Cobos arranged), a daughter of Francisco de Los Cobos married the duke himself. One of Los Cobos's lieutenants, Sancho de Paz, married a daughter of the duke of Infantado; she was thus sister-in-law to the marquis of Ayamonte, don Francisco, later duke of Béjar.[59]

The parties to the Belalcázar dispute were more immediately concerned with those on the Council of Castile who might review it: the letrados who served as councillors. Licenciado and later cardinal Diego de Espinosa, president of the Council of Castile, played a crucial role in the final determination of the Belalcázar dispute. Not only did he serve on the tribunal that issued the verdict but by law he had the responsibility for selecting the other councillors involved. Espinosa was a hard worker who quickly captured Philip's favor and, therefore, won a great deal of influence with him. Espinosa dominated the Royal Council, packing it with his own men, which further increased his influence, and he rose rapidly, becoming bishop of Sigüenza, a member of the Councils of State and of Italy, inquisitor-general, and finally, in 1568, a cardinal. But his pursuit of wealth eventually undercut his usefulness as a royal servant, his arrogance increasingly irritated Philip, and he was eventually disgraced after a dispute with the duke of Medinaceli and died in 1572.[60]

Ldo. Espinosa was one of those figures at Court whose career clearly shows how erroneous it is to present factions as stable entities organized around some great patron. He placed himself at the service of whoever would have him until that person, finally, was the monarch himself. Once he was in a position to do so, Espinosa then sought out others who were equally flexible, regardless of their earlier associations, and used their talents to assist him in formulating and carrying out policies. These were generally other letrados, often clergymen like himself, who therefore had fewer family ties and responsibilities than other possible candidates for government posts. Those closest to Espinosa on the Council of Castile were men already there when Espinosa became its president in 1565. Among those he increasingly integrated into his own clique were councillors whose importance dated back to the early 1550s, Dr. Velasco and Ldo. Menchaca, both of whom had been identified as *Ebolistas* when Ruy Gómez appeared to be the dominant influence with Philip. Of course, such cautious and successful courtiers were willing to assist Ruy Gómez when doing so did not trouble their other projects. Along with Menchaca and Velasco as his aides, Espinosa separated himself, while on the Council of Finance between 1568 and 1572, from any slavish association with Eboli's positions. Menchaca and Velasco also served with Espinosa on the important committee that decided Morisco policy in 1565, and their positions on the Council of Castile and especially in the Cámara (the Council's patronage committee)[61] meant they could help Espinosa drum up through patronage the support he needed in the ongoing struggle to raise funds to fight the Hispanic Monarchy's wars.[62]

The decline of Ruy Gómez's influence with Philip II on policy matters appears to have coincided with the investigation by Ldo. Jarava of the general accounting office (Contaduría Mayor), which led in April 1566 to the condemnation of Eboli's close collaborator, royal secretary Francisco de Eraso. Philip originally intended to take the duke of Alba's advice and return to the Netherlands to lead personally the restoration of royal authority in the rebel provinces. The king apparently pushed to get Espinosa a cardinal's hat in order to give him more prestige and authority with the territorial aristocracy because Philip intended to leave this cleric-letrado as regent in his absence. The king's plan perhaps explains why Espinosa also developed friendly relations with the duke of Alba. Not surprisingly, in the midst of multiple crises, Philip often relied on those who could get things done, and it was much more likely that someone like Espinosa, who avoided antagonizing those whose assistance might be needed, would be able to handle the necessary organizational tasks. In the end, however, it appears that the territorial aristocracy worked to undermine Philip's confidence in the administrative primacy of a letrado whom they felt had usurped their rightful political role and failed to give adequate attention to their petitions and needs.[63]

A number of influential letrados at Court were familiar with the Belalcázar case before the appeal hearing began, and, if motivated by personal connections, might have spoken with some authority and influenced the outcome. One of the most experienced and prominent members of the Council of Castile was Dr. Martín de Velasco. Once Philip returned to Castile in 1551, Dr. Velasco's career developed rapidly. Although he was made a member of the Council of Castile only in 1552, just at the end of the presidency of Hernando Niño de Guevara, Velasco quickly attracted such favorable attention that he was one of the two letrados (the other was Ldo. Otálora) that princess Juana, as regent, was to consult about Castilian business. Therefore, he had co-signed with the princess and Otálora the order to transfer the Belalcázar documents to Valladolid so that the case could be heard by the Royal Council on a second supplication appeal. He also held posts in the Council of Finance and the Castilian Cámara, the latter position permitting him oversight of royal patronage. Described as someone who enjoyed Philip's confidence even before Philip became king and as a "fundamental pawn of the so-called 'Eboli party,'"[64] Velasco could clearly shape the views of many of his fellow Castilian councillors. Because he had been an oidor of the Chancillería of Granada in the early 1550s, he would probably have been ineligible to decide the Belalcázar lawsuit in the Council of Castile, but he was a close confidant of Council president Espinosa who chaired the tribunal. As such he was a member of the core group involved in coordinating the foreign and military policy of the Hispanic Monarchy and a firm supporter of religious orthodoxy along with Espinosa and the royal confessor, Fresneda. In 1567, Velasco was part of the royal commission established to discuss the reform of monastic orders; the other members were Espinosa, Fresneda, Ldo. Menchaca of the Council of Castile and the Cámara, friar Francisco Pacheco, the queen's Franciscan confessor, and Gabriel de Zayas as secretary.[65]

Ldo. Gaspar de Jarava signed the June 1555 decision in favor of Toledo. He was a member of the Council of Castile from 1562 to 1567. He had left Granada in 1556 to become an alcalde de Corte (magistrate of the royal Court), and from 1559 to 1562 had been a member of the Council of the Indies. Jarava had clear ties to Eboli's group.[66] Two of the other 1555 signatories, Ldo. Gómez de Montalvo and Ldo. Pedro de Pedrosa, had served on the Council of Castile while the Belalcázar appeal was under consideration (serving in 1563–1565 and 1554–1563, respectively). Although not directly involved in the Belalcázar lawsuit while in Granada, three other members of the Council of Castile at the time of the 1568 decision, all believed to favor *ebolista* positions, had served in the Chancillería in major posts during the later stages of deliberations there: Dr. Gaspar Durango (alcalde), Ldo. Cristóbal Morillas (alcalde *de crimen;* magistrate of the criminal tribunal), and Ldo. Francisco Hernández de Liévana (fiscal). Durango was one of the five letrados on the Council of Castile who rendered the final judgment. One of the other men on that tribunal was Dr. Diego de la Gasca. Although he never served in Granada, he was among those members of the Council of Castile who decided in 1555 to hear the Belalcázar lawsuit on appeal from Granada, and the tribunal's senior member then was Ldo. Beltrán de Galarza (d. 1557), who had been an oidor in Granada in the early 1540s.[67] Although he did not hear that appeal request, another member of the Council of Castile in 1555 was Ldo. Pedro López de Arrieta, who had become an oidor in Granada in 1535. Arrieta, who died in 1563, was sufficiently respected for his learning that he was working on the long-sought *Recopilación* of Castile's laws in 1555. Perhaps the councillor most identified with Ruy Gómez was Ldo. Francisco de Menchaca, who had served on the Council of Castile since 1551, and it is therefore worth noting that Menchaca had been an alcalde of the Chancillería of Granada before being transferred to Valladolid in 1535. Martín Ruiz de Agreda was another councillor (1560–1567) who had served the Chancillería of Granada, as a fiscal, at about the same time Menchaca was there. Although Ldo. don Juan Sarmiento was among those recused and unable to judge the Belalcázar lawsuit by the winter of 1547, he was another former Granadan oidor who was prominent at Court when the matter was under consideration. He became a member of the Council of the Indies in 1552 and served as that body's president from 1562 until his death in 1564, and he was sufficiently influential and well enough connected to Ruy Gómez to have been named president of the Council of Finance, although he apparently died before he could assume the post. Dr. Velasco, Dr. Gasca, and Ldo. Menchaca were all brought into the Council of Castile under the patronage of its president (1547–1552), Hernando Niño de Guevara, and all apparently became identified as Ebolistas during their long tenure as royal councillors. Another councillor in the period when the Belalcázar case was under consideration was Gracián Briviesca de Muñatones, who became associated with the Ebolistas when he was a member of the Council of the Indies and then served on the Council of Castile from 1560 until 1567.[68] Thus, while the Belalcázar appeal was before the Council of Castile, there was at Court a significant group of letrados who were both familiar with the dispute and associated with the faction with which the House of Béjar was aligned. Such associations would certainly color local notables' evaluation of the justice done by the Council's verdict in the case.

Domingo de Zavala was the royal secretary who handled the Belalcázar documents from the time of their arrival at Court in Valladolid in 1555. Zavala may have had some important connection to another royal secretary,

Antonio Pérez, who was a prominent member of the Eboli clique. On 17 July 1567, Philip II authorized Antonio Pérez to serve as royal secretary for life. The necessary appointment document was prepared by Pedro de Hoyo, Philip's secretary, and countersigned by the royal councillors Ldo. Menchaca and Dr. Velasco. Pedro de Hoyo was one of the secretaries whose rise had been due to the support of Francisco de Eraso, and he had been, therefore, closely associated with Eboli's influence. But in the formal ceremony of Pérez's presentation before the Council of Castile in Madrid on 17 November 1568, during which he swore the necessary oath, the secretary who bore witness to the event was Domingo de Zavala. It seems likely that for such an important event, the one chosen from among the Council's secretaries would have had a close relationship with Pérez. It has been claimed that it was Pérez, as secretary of Castile, who acted as link between king and Council, interpreting the wishes of the one to the other.[69]

When one examines the Council of Castile while the Belalcázar matter was before it, two things become obvious. First, the nature of the dispute would not have been unfamiliar even if the city of Toledo and the Cortes had not done so much to publicize it. Second, letrados who identified with the interests of those around Ruy Gómez were present in more than sufficient numbers to steer any conversation about the case's merits toward ideological positions favorable to the House of Béjar. Indeed, the other two members of the tribunal that rendered the 1568 decision, Bartolomé Atienza and Pedro Gasco, were both brought into the Council of Castile as Ebolistas.[70]

It is conceivable that the decision was merely the result of the influence of one of the prominent noble factions at Court to which the duke of Béjar was closely related. Apparently, there was a fair amount of influence peddling. For example, the Venetian ambassador in the mid-1560s, Giovanni Soranzo, felt that the royal confessor, friar Bernardo de Fresneda (1509–1577), was receiving money for helping those with business at Court, perhaps to maintain an expensive lifestyle for which the Franciscan and bishop of Cuenca was criticized by the Papacy. Moreover, Fresneda's influence was sufficient to subvert judicial administration within his own order.[71]

Although we have no direct evidence of it, with such vast possibilities for pressure and with the duke of Béjar at court using his influence, the Eboli faction likely played a role in the final decision. Because the duke of Alba left for the Netherlands in April 1567, his opponents were dominant at Court. Espinosa was one of the five judges on the panel that decided the case, and we know that Council members were often old men at the end of their careers who desired tranquility and were thus easy to manipulate on issues not clearly involving the well-being of the kingdom, whatever their private scruples. There are indications that the Ebolistas were successful in getting favorable Council decisions in other cases.[72] Factional politics was not, however, the sole possible reason for the Council's decision. Philip II may well have intervened personally to influence the final result, motivated perhaps by his assessment of the legal issues raised by the parties about the proper exercise of royal authority. So much has been made by the reign's historians of the Alba-Eboli differences that important ideological divisions have been overlooked or inadequately discussed.[73]

Was There Direct Royal Intervention in the Final Verdict?

There is a Castilian legend, begun in his own time and passed on by several recent historians, that Philip was a dutiful son who followed his father's great concern for justice, outlined in Charles's 1543 advice to the prince-regent. The legend is usually supported by various accounts of Philip's intervention to save the humble from injustice even at some cost to the Crown. Often quoted is the story, from royal chronicler Cabrera de Córdoba, that Philip told royal councillor Dr. Martín de Velasco, who did not hear the Belalcázar matter, that in case of doubt, verdicts must always go against the king. In this pursuit of just rule, Philip adhered to both popular and academic attitudes toward the monarch's moral obligations.[74]

At least some of these stories are probably true, but there are two things to note about Philip's ideas on justice. First, when he felt threatened or particularly pressed by enemies, he was perfectly willing to abandon justice, as he made clear in repeated orders to his sister Juana's regency government in the 1550s. On numerous occasions, Philip violated "perfectly valid laws" to get his way on tax proposals. These repeated violations of Philip's own exalted concepts of kingship resulted, at least in Sicily, from his anxiety to stem the Turkish advance in the Mediterranean. Moreover, if all of the stories can be believed, when he felt sufficiently threatened he could be ruthless. In October 1570, he ordered the secret murder of Baron de Montigny in Simancas castle, and he was a party to the murder of Juan de Escobedo on 31 March 1578. Later in the reign, two great Aragonese nobles died mysteriously in a Castilian prison. The most grisly event of the early years of Philip's reign was the illegal arrest on 18 January 1568 of his own son, an act impotently protested by his subjects, coupled with the prince's mysterious death on 24 July.[75]

Second, Philip's famous acts of clemency involved personal intervention at all levels of judicial administration. Philip II was the focus of some sophisticated legend building. Philip and his close advisers felt that familiar constitutionalist ideas about the monarch as the guarantor of justice contributed so significantly to shaping his vassals' judgment of his leadership that these characteristics should be emphasized. As we will see, not all Castilians were prepared to view Philip in this positive light. Although stories about personal intervention perhaps enhanced the king's public image, the effect of such actions on the conduct of his letrado officials could only have been to encourage resistance, demoralization, and corruption. Moreover, as some of the entries in royal secretary Antonio Gracián's diary indicate, Philip remained informed about grandee judicial business. One should not be surprised that when Philip wanted to replace Espinosa as president of the Council with the Toledan Dr. Diego de Covarrubias, who was called the "Spanish Bartolus," Covarrubias hesitated to accept, perhaps because in his writings he showed that he was opposed to the king's ideas about justice. The good bishop of Segovia feared that his views would clash with those of his sovereign to his detriment and that of his family.[76]

It is hard to know what Philip's personal attitude toward the duke of Béjar was. One would think that it was favorable, influenced by that House's long record of royal service and by its relationship to the party of his favorite, Eboli. In his will, Charles V had asked his son to return the duchy of Plasencia, taken from the Béjar House under the Catholic Monarchs, to the duke and to make him another grant on the grounds that the House had been so loyal and had rendered such great services. We know that Philip allowed the duke to go further into debt so that he could personally oversee the development of his case with Toledo, and the monarch also made the necessary arrangements, both financial and religious, for the marriage of count Francisco III to the count's first cousin. With the increasing Muslim threat to the Spanish coasts, Philip was probably especially interested in the affairs of the family that controlled the marquisates of Gibraleón and Ayamonte, which must have been important components of any defense of western Andalucía. And existing documents dealing with the multiple mortgages on the duke of Béjar's estates indicate that the duke's finances were not good, perhaps aggravated by the expensive legal proceedings with Toledo and Córdoba. If he were ordered to give up the viscounty of Puebla de Alcocer, and then perhaps the county of Belalcázar, in addition to returning all the revenues from the viscounty since its seizure (a provision of the 1555 decision), don Francisco could well have become desperate. Such desperation might have made the execution of a verdict unfavorable to him dangerous or at least extremely difficult.[77]

The duke's late brother had earlier shown how difficult his House could be about the execution of even minor rulings against its interests. When Toledo received its favorable verdict from the Council of Castile in the El Hornillo case, a Council member, Ldo. Quintana, was sent out to arrange for the transfer of the land by virtue of a writ to execute the decision, given in the monarchs' names on 6 February 1540 and presented to Quintana on 26 March. In response to this decision, Alonso de Zúñiga y Sotomayor, then titular count of Belalcázar and marquis of Gibraleón, orchestrated a series of delays involving the opposition of the towns of Puebla de Alcocer, Herrera, and Fuenlabrada on the ground that El Hornillo was really theirs. Judging from the letters of a frustrated Toledan council, the judge, who was present in the aristocrat's jurisdiction rather than safely with the Council, was somehow intimidated by the marquis into hearing these arguments in direct contravention of his commission. The city bombarded cardinal Tavera, who was Charles V's regent in Castile, Los Cobos, and the president of the Royal Council with letters demanding that something be done to correct *la mala obra* ("bad work") of Quintana. The Council of Castile, on 8 July, sent Ldo. Alderete, another of its members, to arrange the new boundary. To show it meant business, the Council allowed him to take a royal constable and exceed the time limit of his commission if necessary. Due to illness, Alderete was unable to finish the work until January 1541. Possession of the newly surveyed territory was taken by regidor Fernando (or Hernando) Niño and jurado Juan Bautista Oliverio on 8 February. Because Toledo protested the placement of some of the boundary markers (the marquis, in effect, protested them all), the El Hornillo case went to the Chancillería of Granada where it was accepted on 22 December 1542. This dispute was not finally concluded until 18 June 1574.[78] In the face of these difficulties surrounding a relatively minor readjustment of the boundary between Toledo's Montes and the lands of the House of Béjar, it is difficult to imagine the problems the Crown's judiciary would have faced if it had been necessary to transfer jurisdiction over the entire viscounty of Puebla de Alcocer.

Moreover, at the time the decision against Toledo was taken, Philip was very anxious about both the defense and the internal stability of his kingdom. He felt a need for the support of his grandees, and he showed signs of favoring the Béjar House, perhaps in response to his father's wishes or because it was attached to the Eboli clique. Yet although these were reasons enough to cue certain interpretive schemes for the king and to motivate his personal intervention, the relationship of the issues of the case to his problems would also have led Philip to favor the duke of Béjar's arguments. The king was a well-educated man, interested in intellectual affairs, particularly the study of law, and tried to keep "in close touch with its interpretation and administration."[79] We can thus presume that he would have been fully aware of what was involved in this case. Moreover, he would have been familiar with a minority movement in legal thought, begun perhaps by Gregorio López in the glosses of his 1555 edition of the *Siete Partidas,* to grant the monarch absolute authority to expropriate his subjects' property against the prescriptions of the law.[80] Suspecting that it would favor the duke's cause, Royal Council president Espinosa and perhaps royal secretary Antonio Pérez would have been certain to outline the case in his favor even if the review had not been requested.

A decision in favor of Toledo would strike down a grant made by an earlier king to a loyal vassal. John II made the grant at a time when the kingdom seemed to be crumbling around its ruler, who felt he needed as much support as possible. Moreover, the contending party, the city of Toledo, had been part of the rebellious forces and was now hinting, in its briefs before the Council of Castile, that the rebellion had somehow been legitimate. If Philip sensed that these were the implications of a ruling favorable to Toledo, he would surely have decided that he must not allow such a verdict. Philip felt that he did have authority unrestricted by the law, a right to act as he willed, even if his action were contrary to the law and even if the sole criterion for a decision were his personal relationship to his great vassals. This was the authority and the right he thought he most needed to save the kingdom and the faith, the authority and the right to subvert the law for the good of his subjects.[81]

How such views were conveyed to the judges hearing the case is something beyond the purview of historians dependent on the documents that have survived more than four centuries. We know that Philip's councillors tried to align their views with his, even when these were not clearly expressed.[82] It seems likely that once in chambers to render the final verdict, Espinosa let the judges know what the king thought about such issues, if indeed they needed to be told after the shuffling of personnel that had been going on during the few years just prior to the decision.

The House of Béjar's position had always been that Gutierre de Sotomayor had received the viscounty in return for loyal support of John II during a terrible rebellion in which Toledo had lost Puebla de Alcocer and the other towns as punishment for joining the cause of the infantes of Aragón. The late 1560s were a bad time to be associated in the minds of Philip and his principal advisers with rebellion. They were greatly preoccupied with the growing revolt in the Low Countries. As early as the fall of 1566, the Council of State intensely debated what Philip should do. On one side were ranged those including Fresneda, Ruy Gómez, and Espinosa who argued that the count of Feria should lead an army to the Netherlands while Philip remained in Castile. On the other was the duke of Alba who wanted Philip to lead the military campaign personally. But throughout 1567, as Philip was preparing for the royal crusade advocated by Alba, there was a worsening crisis in the king's relationship with prince Carlos, whom Philip finally had arrested in January 1568. Given the fact that his only male heir was jailed under troubling circumstances, that his daughters were infants born in 1566 and 1567, and that he had earlier experienced troubles with his sister Juana as regent, Philip did not feel that he could personally lead the Netherlands expedition.[83]

The issues of rebellion and royal power could hardly be discussed in the terrible year of 1568. Even before the final verdict, in January, Philip had imprisoned his son to keep the prince from being used for subversion, and the prince had died in July, perhaps at the king's order. The queen died the following October leaving no male children and none of sufficient age to face the crisis if Philip's recent illness overcame him. Worse yet, on Christmas Eve, the Moriscos in Granada began their expected revolt, and the specter of invasion of his kingdom by "infidels" confronted Philip. It was his great vassals who were leading the armies against the rebels. Among them would be relatives of the duke of Béjar and members of the Eboli faction: the marquis of Mondéjar, the duke of Arcos, the duke of Sessa, and the marquis of Los Vélez.[84]

Probably because there was no desire to have the legitimacy of rebellion discussed, the Council of Castile agreed to a petition presented in Madrid on 12 November 1568 by regidor don Martín de Ayala and jurado Ldo. Santamaría. They asked that all mention of any revolt by Toledo against the king be struck from the carta ejecutoria containing the final verdict (the duke had already received a copy) because it was not true and damaged the honor both of the city and of those now dead who had been particularly loyal to the Crown. The formal request to remove all of the allegations and arguments over Toledo's rebellions was actually made on 25 November by Melchor de la Peña, acting for the duke, who was probably anxious not to have trouble with Toledo. La Peña was able to get a separate copy of all the excluded material from Domingo de Zavala, notary for the case.[85]

Toledo Protests the Perceived Injustice of the Council of Castile's Verdict

Toledo's council needed to find some way to continue the lawsuit. It held various legal conferences on how to make further difficulties for the duke of Béjar. To this end, its representatives approached some of the great legal minds of Salamanca for help. Toledan Fernando Niño de Guevara wrote in August to regidor don Alonso de Rojas that he had assembled "all the flower of letters that are here" to discuss the case. To counter this effort the duke, whose House was traditionally influential in Salamanca, had sent one of his brothers to terrorize the university faculty. All of the lawyers and scholars dealing with the case showed signs of fear, were reluctant to sign their opinions, and manifested continuous concern about secrecy. Indeed, don Pedro de Guzmán, who was coordinating Toledo's efforts in Madrid, wrote to don Martín de Ayala and Juan Gómez de Silva on 24 March 1569 that the lawyers there were terrified, wanted to tone down the wording of the petitions about the injustice of the verdict, and felt the whole issue was just too hot to be dealt with at that time.[86]

Don Pedro de Guzmán also indicated that he expected to receive a response soon to the city's requests for additional deliberations, because Philip had returned to Madrid on 23 March. Toledo sent its commission of representation to its barrister at Court, Pedro Sánchez de la Torre, and to its

solicitors there, Guzmán and jurado Juan de Cisneros, on 20 April, and
Sánchez de la Torre presented the city's petitions on 3 May. The Council of
Castile gave these to Philip, and the king immediately ordered Sánchez de la
Torre's arrest. With a direct royal order of this kind, Philip presumably
strengthened any impression Toledo's patricians and officials may have had
that Philip had influenced the verdict. After further examination of the petitions and briefs that had been submitted, the Council of Castile ordered the
arrest on 28 May of a number of the lawyers who had signed them. Others
tried to delay responding to the Royal Council's summons by claims of illness, but one of these was arrested in June. On 4 July, the lawyers and
Sánchez de la Torre were all suspended from office at the king's pleasure
and given heavy fines, which twelve days later were reduced by half.[87]

When this action was discussed by Toledo's council on 13 July, there
were some, such as Francisco de Silva, perhaps partial to the Eboli Court
clique through his ties to the House of Cifuentes, who pointed out that the
Council of Castile had forbidden anyone to do what the city had tried to do.
The more typical reaction was outrage, which because of Philip's obvious
initiation of the order to arrest the lawyers, made it impossible to feel that
the monarch had merely been badly served by the original verdict.[88] Moreover, Philip did nothing to calm these passions. He wrote to the city on 24
July, using the scolding tone he adopted when he felt threatened by a subordinate's actions.

From the king to the municipal councillors of the City of Toledo:

> You are already aware that, in accordance with the Law of Segovia, we
> have in our Council given a final verdict in the stage of second supplica-
> tion in the dispute that your city had in litigation with the duke of Béjar
> and that he has been given the documents necessary for the execution of
> this ruling. Then, we were given by your honors a petition in which cer-
> tain causes and reasons were alleged that would allow the reopening of the
> above-mentioned case.

> However, after a review of your petition in our Council to which we sent it
> and *after further consultation with us,* it appears that this petition should not
> have been admitted nor received nor ought you to submit any other about
> the matter. In addition, in having endeavored and attempted to petition for
> the reopening of the aforementioned case, your actions have been excessive
> and heedless of propriety. Because of the bad example and consequences of
> this action, the barrister and lawyers who were principally involved ought to
> be, as they have been, castigated. As it was that you were moved to submit
> the petition as well as the opinion of the previously mentioned lawyers
> when it was so notorious that one could not [that is, the city was not empow-
> ered to do so] nor ought to do so, you are not excused from guilt. As well
> as being censured, you are hereby warned that in similar circumstances
> you will proceed in a different manner or else. You will send us a detailed

account of any costs incurred in the preparation and submission of this petition so that we can see that any further action which is necessary will be taken. Dated in Madrid the 24th of July 1569/ I the king/ by order of his majesty/ Antonio de Crasso (countersigned by Domingo de Zavala).[89]

Needless to say, after the receipt of this letter, the city council remained officially silent about the case, and with the final settlement in 1574 of the boundary between El Hornillo and the duke of Béjar's lands, the dispute's legal history ended.[90]

If Philip thought, however, that this harsh gag order would suppress comment about such a high-profile lawsuit until it slipped from memory, he was mistaken. In 1609, Toledo attempted to reopen the case, apparently feeling that because Court corruption was then so widespread, anything might happen. However, the duke of Béjar, Alonso Diego de Zúñiga y Sotomayor (d. 1619), whose wife was Juana de Mendoza, daughter of the duke of Infantado, still had more influence than the city.[91] Almost a century after Philip's letter, memory of the matter was strong enough that the result of the Belalcázar-Toledo lawsuit played a role in another trial. In a 1664 lawsuit before the Council of Castile in which the Mesta and the royal prosecutor were trying to limit Toledo's jurisdiction over its Montes, Mesta lawyers and the prosecutor attacked Ferdinand III's letter of sale as the basis of Toledo's lordship over the region. When all mention of rebellion was removed from the carta ejecutoria of the Belalcázar-Toledo verdict, the document left the impression that the Council of Castile had ruled that Toledo had not purchased the Montes from king Ferdinand III. The Mesta specifically claimed that the earlier verdict in the case with the duke of Béjar over the viscounty of Puebla de Alcocer had denied the document's validity and indicated the ill repute in which the letter should be held.[92]

Judicial procedure shaped the nature of the documentary record that we have, but these documents served to reiterate interpretive schemes and experiences that would cue recognition of patterns in events and judgment about their significance as a basis for action in other areas of life. By its very nature, a lawsuit produces a series of partial, contradictory, and biased accounts, which has made it hard to construct a narrative of anything but the trial itself. Because we currently lack necessary evidence about Philip II's role in the final verdict on jurisdiction over the viscounty of Puebla de Alcocer, I can only suggest possibilities perceived by contemporaries. Certainly, the circumstances of the decision, the issues involved, and certain aspects of the case's handling all pointed to some kind of royal intervention. It is legitimate to ask what difference this impression made among contemporaries.

Neither Toledo nor any of the other patrician-controlled Cortes municipalities rose in revolt as they had in 1520. What is more, the duke of Béjar and his relatives played a major role in the pacification of the Morisco rebellion in Granada. Even after the fighting ended, the duke aided Philip in the latter's Morisco control measures. And Philip continued to receive good value from his close relations with the duke. The duke went 100,000 ducats in debt in 1571 to see that the new queen was properly accompanied to Castile. In 1572, the duke was asked to help prepare the defense of Andalucía and set an example for others, and Philip hinted that when conditions improved he would again aid the duke as he had in the past. Another member of the House of Béjar, the marquis of Ayamonte, one of the duke's younger brothers, was governor of Milan from 1573 until his death in 1580, and another, the marquis of Villamanrique, served as viceroy of New Spain (from 1585 to his death in 1590). Because his family's Ayamonte lands were so near the border, the duke of Béjar was one of the great nobles of the south who, at their own cost, conquered Portugal in 1580 for Philip. Still later in the reign and near the end of his life, the duke took responsibility for the defense of the Algarve and performed other services. His son was equally helpful.[93] Not only did it appear that no great damage had been done to the Crown by the solution of the Belalcázar-Toledo conflict but also the pattern of monarchical-aristocratic collaboration it ratified apparently paid off at least in the short run, for the House of Béjar provided services that merited rewards.

Despite the apparent short-term advantages the king seemed to have gained from the final verdict in the Belalcázar-Toledo lawsuit over the viscounty of Puebla de Alcocer, this type of decision did make a difference in the relationship between the Crown and the political kingdom in a commonwealth where identity was founded on the idea that the monarch provided justice through the exercise of his absolute royal authority. Personal intervention by the monarch—influenced, as it appeared to contemporaries, by the wealthy and powerful—sapped the morale of the judicial system. The ability of the territorial aristocracy to exert increased personal influence over the actions of the royal government during the regency of the 1540s and 1550s and the temptation to official corruption that resulted from such magnate meddling perhaps allowed Philip to think he was lending credibility to the judicial system by playing a more active role in decisions at all levels. Such visible intervention would show that the monarch was acting to correct abuses of authority by his officials, and perhaps such activity did contribute to Philip's authority when the monarch's affairs appeared to go well. In the decade after 1580 when the reign's early troubles were over, Castilians had a king who was a major figure in European politics, and this prominence opened tremendous opportunities to the kingdom's elite, opportunities that were financed by the increased wealth from America.

Once Philip and his closest servants felt that patronage and intimidation had produced a pliant judiciary, however, the king seemed unable to avoid using such influence in ways that a majority of the commonwealth's leaders suspected were devious and unjust. The mere presence of important factions at Court, however well-balanced they were to maintain Philip's long-term independence from reliance on any one of them, would increase the tendency, which had persisted even in Charles's reign, of the less well-connected to seek out the great as spokesmen for their interests. The decision about the viscounty of Puebla de Alcocer had affirmed that favors were granted for personal service to the patron. In the long run the grandees' influence would increase because, while some writers would continue to articulate the interpretation that the sovereign was unrestrained by law and issued commands that must be carried out unquestioningly, such a type of government was unacceptable either to the territorial aristocracy or to the lesser nobility and local notables. Much to the frustration of later royal advisers such as the count-duke of Olivares, Philip IV's favorite, the monarch would fail to get the sort of collaboration that might have allowed the Hispanic Monarchy to retain the European position its American wealth and multiple domains should have permitted.

When, among the interpretive schemes available in the cultural environment, justice was so central to political identity within the Castilian commonwealth and judicial administration was so central to the provision of justice, substantial alterations in the form of judicial administration, especially a shift away from the role given by Charles V to the audiencias toward a larger role for the Council of Castile, which many municipal leaders opposed, played a major part in determining the assessment of Crown creditworthiness, broadly understood. Although these changes did not undermine faith in the ideal of a monarchy exercising absolute royal authority to maintain justice, many Castilian leaders increasingly distrusted the actions of Philip II's government, and this suspicion of the motives behind Crown policies, requests, and commands continued. Through the Cortes, municipal leaders attempted to rein in royal abuses through the imposition of specific contractual obligations on the Crown in their approval of the tribute known as the millones. Even the efforts of Olivares, early in the reign of Philip IV, to use royal favors to buy sufficient support to introduce major reforms, such as a funded debt, were not enough to overcome concerns within the commonwealth about the arbitrary, unjust exercise of royal authority, and no amount of complaining by the ministers of seventeenth-century Habsburg kings would stop the growth of smuggling and fiscal fraud. The resulting "centralization," as more authority was drawn to Madrid and the various juntas under the direct control of royal favorites, was not an aspect of effective "state-building" but a symptom of the failure to exercise royal authority in a way that would garner the support within the commonwealth necessary to confront the weakening position of the Hispanic Monarchy. The king and his advisers gained greater autonomy with which to formulate policy, but the Crown increasingly lost the capacity to implement royal commands that did not correspond to the wishes of some substantial group within the commonwealth.

Although they would do much to infuriate officials in Madrid with their ability to delay, deflect, and ignore royal commands, local notables would not use rebellion, at least in Castile, as a means to push the monarch to negotiate substantial changes in the way he governed because it had been exposed as a dangerous tool, especially in a religiously divided Europe and in the face of the Ottoman threat. The Habsburg dynasty was successful, therefore, at the level of maintaining much of a composite monarchy of domains spread over the globe, but the Crown was frustrated in its attempts to mobilize from these domains the human and material resources to retain many of the non-Castilian areas. The basic interpretive schemes about justice and royal authority common in Castile were shared with the domains of other Iberian monarchies, including those of the Crown of Portugal. In some of those, rebellion was a greater possibility, and in Portugal, the presence of an acceptable alternative dynasty as a focus of identity and loyalty would mean the permanent loss by the Habsburg Hispanic Monarchy of Portugal and most of its vast overseas domains.

The issue of a decline in Crown creditworthiness was much more complicated than simply a concern for the quality and direction of royal judicial administration. Recognition of the Belalcázar verdict's symbolic consequences showed up, however, even in the debates of Toledo's lawyers over how to extend the hearing beyond the 1568 decision. Some said the law was clear and no further effort was possible. Others suggested that certain parties—churches, monasteries, and welfare homes—that were damaged by the loss of revenue from the lands could ask that the trial be restored to the stage just before the verdict, as minors were able to do. Essentially, this theory and the idea that no second supplication should have been allowed after two conforming verdicts were the arguments used in the petitions that led to the arrest of some of Toledo's legal staff. But several of the letrados suggested that the city petition the king, rather than the Council of Castile, to allow some additional consideration of the matter. One, Br. Francisco Martínez Muñoz de Jarandilla, openly advised that the proper people be retained to present a prudent request at the proper time.[94]

Despite Philip II's cultivation of the image of a monarch who supported justice and the rule of law, the disruption of administrative procedures caused by influence peddling and intense factionalism was well advanced even before his death.[95] Although other factors were involved, Philip alienated local notables through his arbitrary style of rule and conduct of judicial administration, and in doing so, he undermined his personal ability to shape the course of Castilian developments as he desired. Politically active members of the commonwealth regularly judged Philip II's leadership, and given the great practical and ideological importance placed on the administration of justice within the framework of good government, the ways in which his actions in this area were evaluated affected a wide range of interactions among members of the political kingdom and ultimately the support and cooperation the Crown could expect for its enterprises. The monarch and his advisers at Court could not hope to achieve their military goals if they were not enthusiastically embraced by the Castilian commonwealth. In the first global age, the amount of continuous coercive force available to the Crown was much too limited to compel a large number of people spread geographically around the world to act as the Crown wanted or even to make the effort to do so.

However, unlike his father in 1520, contemporaries viewed Philip as an essentially Castilian ruler whose authority had to be enhanced by proper conduct in order to maintain the elite's exalted position and disproportionate control of resources. As long as Philip was present in the peninsula and thus available for negotiation, regional notables were unwilling to lead a violent rebellion. Castile's leaders at least did not grumble in unison with those of other polities within the Hispanic Monarchy's domains who were deprived of the royal presence, an endemic problem in this type of regime.[96] Moreover, the Crown's financial difficulties led to a significant expansion of the number of municipalities that enjoyed extensive control over local affairs.[97] Town leaders were not likely to be disloyal to a monarch who both permitted and defended such independence from those with greater resources and influence. The example of neighboring France, torn apart by repeated civil and religious conflict, gave sufficient warning of where violence could lead. Given the troubles of the era, local leaders provided a surprisingly high level of loyalty and collaboration.

Although there were a number of factors that might make the commonwealth's political leaders unwilling to rebel, among these, their continued enjoyment of a disproportionate share of resources or the lack of the time, energy, and knowledge to develop and pursue alternatives, civic passivity and the pursuit of narrowly defined elite interests would make it difficult to mobilize sufficient financial and human resources to confront the Habsburg dynasty's multiple military crises. Even given adequate sources, it would be difficult to observe, describe, and understand the continuous alterations of patterns of interaction among groups and individuals residing in so many municipalities in Castile, America, and Pacific Oceania, but scholars have discovered a number of overlapping networks where the lack of adequate support for the Crown manifested itself. Rather than enhancing royal authority, as historians of "absolutism" have long claimed, authoritarian and arbitrary government produced sharp limitations on the Crown's capacity and increasingly cued interpretive schemes, within the cultural environments of many places, that would help shape patrician and aristocratic actions that compromised royal authority, and prominent authors such as Juan de Mariana perpetuated and continuously reinforced such schemes.

Chapter 8

THE PARADOX OF ABSOLUTE ROYAL AUTHORITY

Introduction

Authoritarian and arbitrary conduct became increasingly common in the governments of the rulers of the Habsburg dynasty, and was a factor in the remarkable seventeenth-century decline of the Crown's capacity to obtain adequate support from the leaders of Castile's commonwealth. Frequent recourse to royal assertions of the monarch's authority to violate the law or more direct threats, such as the threat Philip II sent to Toledo's council, did not eliminate alternative interpretations of "absolute royal authority." These interpretive schemes retained a substantial place in Castilian political thought and continued to shape the actions of political leaders in ways that compromised the sovereign's policies and administration. In the face of historiographical emphases on "reason of state" theories or on treatises for courtiers and other royal servants, it must be stressed that many members of the political kingdom sustained an ideology of absolute royal authority within a framework of consultation and consensus. They viewed this interactive process as necessary to maintain the collaboration essential for competing parties to reach some of their goals and achieve the best possible result during a challenging era. Both of the interpretive schemes of Castile's cultural environment about absolute royal authority, which were brought into conflict over the course of the Belalcázar lawsuit, remained significant despite the ratification of one of them by Philip II's regime. The continued creation of institutions to exercise such authority throughout the global Hispanic Monarchy produced greater complexity, and this made it increasingly less likely that one particular view would predominate. No Castilian "absolutism" emerged in terms of the growth of ever more effective means for the "state" to shape "society," and other commonwealths where adequate elite collaboration emerged, such as those of the Dutch and English, asserted themselves against the troubled Iberian global monarchies.

Castilians identified themselves as citizens of a commonwealth on the basis of their shared use of interpretive schemes and conceptual language about the importance of justice in the community and the necessity for absolute royal authority to sustain this predominant value. As I mentioned in

chapter 1, a book by political theorist and historian Juan de Mariana introduced me to the way the issue of royal authority might have been discussed
by those with a formal literate education. I was later intrigued to discover in
the work of playwright Lope de Vega these same interpretive schemes about
justice and royal authority as the core of Castilians' political values, because
that suggested to me that such perspectives were shared with those denied
the opportunity for a formal education. Because these works neatly illustrate
the continued resonance among local notables of essentially conservative
interpretive perspectives on the exercise of royal authority, which were
already common in the fifteenth century, I want to discuss these authors now.

I do not offer this discussion as a history of political ideas from the late
sixteenth to the early seventeenth century, for even if limited to the issues
raised in this account, such a complex subject would demand a monograph.
Many authors of such histories have emphasized that, during this period, the
meaning of views reasserting "constitutional" perspectives about the purpose of absolute royal authority shifted subtly, even if expressed in the same
terms as before. Contemporary thinkers now rejected not only arbitrary
government of the personalist type associated with John II and Alvaro de
Luna but also that associated with violations of the law and contractual relationships justified by some "reason of state" writers as essential for effective
monarchical authority. I suspect that many experts have concentrated on
the latter writers to the neglect of more conventional views because "reason
of state" treatises appear attractive and in step with a metanarrative about
the rise of the modern state. Philip II's demonstrated sensitivity to any public discussion of the Belalcázar lawsuit suppressed specific written comments
to the point where almost nothing has survived. Therefore, to grasp the
impact of the final verdict in the lawsuit, one must keep in mind the older,
still significant interpretive schemes, expressed in different ways by Mariana
and Lope de Vega, that sustained Castilians' political identity with their
commonwealth. Many of the Castilian commonwealth's leaders must have
been profoundly disturbed by the way Philip II had dealt with the
Belalcázar-Toledo lawsuit. Such "autonomous" royal action likely undermined royal capacity, as the intense battle at the end of Philip's reign over
increased taxation highlighted. I have abstracted a history over a long
period to show how, in an attempt to understand the world as a basis for
action, the political kingdom evaluated the personal agency of the monarch,
his favorites, and his royal officials. Despite the introduction into Castilian
political writing of other means of discussing royal authority, the interpretive positions elaborated during the long Belalcázar conflict retained their
vitality and central importance for any grasp of the Hispanic Monarchy during the seventeenth-century crisis.

Because of its importance in Mariana's works, historians' assessments of the
late sixteenth-century Castilian Cortes have influenced their understanding of

his meaning. Recently, a "constitutionalist" perspective on Habsburg Castile has almost displaced the older, more familiar emphasis on "absolutism," and a number of fine works have demonstrated the continued viability of the kingdom's representative institution. Concerned about a Crown government whose policies undermined monarchical authority, the Cortes municipalities sought to make the assembly a forum for shaping royal administrative practice. The Crown faced a renewed fiscal crisis in the aftermath of the Armada's defeat in 1588 and Philip's decision to intervene directly in the French civil war after the assassination of Henry III in 1589. In this context, the cities and major towns were able to use their consent for new taxes, a role strengthened by the fiscal disputes of the 1570s, as leverage to obtain specific agreements from the king on a number of administrative matters. Debates over the Crown's attempts to increase the tax burden in Castile revealed a deep-seated suspicion of the king's intentions, and both popular and elite hostility manifested themselves even more dramatically through the circulation in different parts of Castile of satires about the king's tyrannical rule.[1] The negotiations in the 1590s over the terms by which the Cortes would be willing to grant the extraordinary tax known as the millones expose the degree to which Philip II was distrusted by the municipal representatives and the patrician councils of which they were members. To obtain the new level of taxation, the Crown had to negotiate with the notables represented in the Cortes, and this process of consultation and consensus-building maintained the assembly's importance in Castilian political life well into the seventeenth century.[2]

Yet taken within the discursive context of petition presentation in the Cortes and of the companion discussions in municipal council sessions, it is clear that the documents reflect multiple perspectives on a monarchy exercising "absolute royal authority" rather than a move toward some new model of parliamentary supremacy. Any apparent tendency to grant the Cortes too great a role was contested, and at the same time, some writers were publishing treatises stressing the value of personal service to the monarchy by royal "ministers" charged with providing good counsel and with *administering* the commonwealth according to the sovereign's wishes.[3] When applied to the roles of Gutierre de Sotomayor and Alvaro de Luna in sustaining John II in the face of disloyal relatives, grandees, and leaders of municipalities such as Toledo, such views had constituted the core defense presented by the House of Béjar's legal staff during the trial over the viscounty of Puebla de Alcocer (especially during its second consideration in Granada between 1536 and 1555), and they were central to the discursive self-representation of members of the House who served as viceroys of the crucial royal domains of Milan and New Spain.

Because some historians, particularly those of Castilian political thought who search for the first appearance of the "state" concept, have understandably been drawn to what was new, it is important to assert the significant continuity within the cultural environment of classificatory and valuative perspectives. With the increasing intensity of interaction between Castilian loci and other regions on a global scale, and within the context of European Christian religious conflict, the meanings of these perspectives and the language in which they were expressed altered between the reign of John II and the seventeenth century. However, far from being overcome by theoretical positions justifying the suzerain's actions according to nothing more than his own will, interpretive schemes that emphasized the monarch's fundamental role of providing justice to his vassals and sustaining his authority for this purpose by obeying the law himself continued to predominate, especially in areas such as contracts, property rights, and due process. Judgments by many of the commonwealth's leaders based on such norms continued throughout the Habsburg era to shape political action as interpretation and strategization, and the basic identity that held together the commonwealth was preserved.

Local notables appear genuinely to have believed that a monarch who observed these constitutional principles would be most likely to attract the collaboration necessary to provide for the commonwealth's defense and to adjudicate domestic disputes with justice. Because they wanted a monarch respected enough to be capable of achieving these goals, local notables were reluctant to accept as legitimate those royal actions that were contrary to the normative meaning established by constitutional principles. The Crown depended heavily on the governments of cities and major towns to obtain through negotiation and administrative interaction the revenue and troops required for the Hispanic Monarchy's various wars. Therefore, the perception of royal action by local notables from their classificatory and valuative perspectives would influence the degree of support or resistance the monarch would face. Notables actually wanted the Crown to depend heavily on Castile in order to ensure royal residence in the kingdom, but that did not mean their support was guaranteed, as the collapse of service even by territorial aristocrats during the minority of and regency for Charles II demonstrated.[4]

Despite some mid sixteenth-century attempts to reserve for the ruler certain prerogatives above the laws of the kingdom, the letrado theological-political interpretive schemes on the monarch as the guarantor of justice under the law were reflected in and sustained by the writings of the jurists and theologians of the intellectual movement known as the Second Scholasticism.[5] In some respects, Mariana's writings represented a "popular" expression of this current. Moreover, there are signs that the magistrates of audiencias and other royal judicial institutions often continued to employ such perspectives when they rendered decisions against Crown officials whose actions were viewed as arbitrary and contrary to law. In part, such tendencies may have represented a desire to replace the prestige the Crown had withdrawn from judicial institutions, particularly the chancillerías, in the 1560s. Patronage as a means to win and maintain the support of magistrates was inadequate because resources were insufficient to meet the expectations of so many oidores, especially given the size and complexity of the Castilian Crown domains.[6]

How people interpreted the world around them, how they felt about the kingdom's course and about the opportunities to realize personal dreams and projects also had an impact on whether Castilians were encouraged to show creativity and initiative, to participate in and comprehend public life, to acquire knowledge, and to make productive investments. Historians' concerns with the grand strategic and fiscal preoccupations of the Hispanic Monarchy have sometimes obscured the degree to which issues of law and justice remained important in contemporary evaluations of government. Among the issues that troubled the influential patrons of the young visionary of Madrid Lucrecia de León in the 1590s was a perceived decline in the quality of judicial administration. Despite the extended period of economic and military setbacks that extended well into the seventeenth century, the political and creative life of the kingdom's elite remained as lively as any in Europe, and royal justice was a frequent topic.[7]

Juan de Mariana and the Common Understanding of the Exercise of Royal Authority

Although not unique in his methods or conclusions,[8] Juan de Mariana (1535/1536–1624), a Jesuit writer and doctor of theology, was probably the most famous intellectual opponent of arbitrary rule. Mariana was born in the kingdom of Toledo and established residence in the city of Toledo in 1574 after an education at the University of Alcalá and travels to Rome, Sicily, and Paris, where he witnessed the St. Bartholomew's Day Massacre. In Toledo, he wrote his *History of Spanish Deeds,*[9] in which kings who maintained high standards of justice and good government were singled out for special praise. He used the views developed during his historical studies to illustrate the theoretical position advanced in his *The King and the Education of the King*[10] (hereafter, *De rege*), which had been commissioned by Philip III's teacher for the instruction of his royal pupil, still a prince at that time. The published version was clearly intended for a general audience of those who could read Latin and appreciate his grafting of a Humanist historical vision onto Scholastic political principles.[11]

Mariana's *De rege* has often been distorted by readings that claim it as part of the development of the theory of the state. Because Mariana wrote before the analytical popularity of the "state" concept and mechanical physics, I read *De rege* as a work with a more conservative than innovative cast. Although some have described Mariana's political thought as a revival of medieval views, the perspectives he defended had in fact been central to sixteenth-century debates, and many of the ideas he expressed would remain, without significant changes in form or language, part of the common political discourse of educated Castilians until the late eighteenth century.[12] Although publication delays would frustrate his intentions,[13] Mariana sought through influence over a future ruler to preserve the kingdom from arbitrary government. Mariana's program for the education of the future Philip III has to be understood within the twin frameworks of Jesuit pedagogy and the understanding of good government and monarchy of patrician municipal leaders, particularly those of Toledo where Mariana wrote and published the book.

Renaissance Humanists objected to medieval Scholastic authors because the deductive organization and lack of attention to rhetoric meant that Scholastic treatises were incapable of moving people toward a life of true virtue. Yet when Machiavelli used an ancient political ethics centered on the survival and well-being of the human community rather than on God's word, he exposed the danger of teaching Greek and Roman classics without shaping instruction through a Christian moral interpretation. Jesuit teachers employed the materials of the Renaissance Humanist curriculum within the context of a Scholastic deductive approach, and this instructional method underlies Mariana's recommendations.[14]

Although not as tightly structured as the Scholastic treatises on politics written by university-based scholars at Coimbra and Salamanca, including some fellow Jesuits, the overall organization of *De rege* is nonetheless deductive, despite the abundant use of historical examples for illustrative purposes. Reading Mariana's educational treatise within this complex Jesuit tradition, one can see that he develops in book I the curriculum's framing principles for evaluating monarchical government, discusses the course of studies in book II to show how a future ruler should be educated in order to carry out his role properly, and offers in book III specific examples and recommendations about the way the monarch should handle contemporary problems. The arguments in the second and third books were clearly to be read in the context of the principles of good government established in the first. In pulling out small sections and deducing their meaning without reference to other sections, especially those in book I, one is in grave danger of producing a highly distorted interpretation.

Some commentators have produced strange readings of *De rege* through their failure to recognize the deductive nature of Mariana's organization of the book and firm commitment to his principles of monarchical government. For clarity, I offer the following example. Richard Tuck has challenged Quentin Skinner's placement of Mariana within the anti-Machiavellian and anti-Tacitist group of Jesuit authors. Tuck bases his argument on three observations:

Mariana's "copious use of Tacitus," praise of the Roman author as a historian whose work should be part of the syllabus for the education of a future monarch, and discussion of the ruler's use of deception.[15] I do not know what Tuck considers "copious use" of an author, but I doubt that most readers would thus characterize Mariana's citations of Tacitus. Other than in the discussion of the royal reading list, Mariana included in his index only five citations, but he failed to include his references to Tacitus's observations about German nursing customs (Mariana 1611: book II, chapter 2: 113) and examples of nauseating flattery by courtiers (II,11: 177). As a careful reading of the passage in which Mariana includes Tacitus among the historians to be read by the prince (II, 6: 137) shows, Mariana based his recommendation heavily on the number of "evils and dangers" that Tacitus reveals.[16] Mariana used Tacitus to provide historical examples of the bad things that happen when a ruler does not act properly. Shortly after his praise of Tacitus, Mariana also praised Cicero as a source of "useful precepts for the government of the commonwealth" (II, 6: 138), and when Mariana borrowed phrases from the Latin classics, he most frequently drew them from Cicero's writings.[17] This praise and repeated citation of Cicero shows that Tuck is in error when he includes Mariana among the "new humanists."

Mariana placed his only significant discussion of dissimulation (he consistently condemned lying [III, 15: 336]) in the chapter on prudence (III, 15). The major case in his discussion of dissimulation reveals the "class" bias that Mariana shared with the other political writers of his age. When the lower orders are agitated and rebellious, Mariana recommended, "It is convenient to calm the agitation with some artifice and even to dissimulate, and, in my judgment, to accede sometimes to their petitions" (III, 15: 329–30). Afterwards, the ruler can punish the leading agitators individually to weaken the mob's will. However, the ruler should avoid such agitation by attempting to govern according to the opinion of his subjects (III, 15: 330–31). Mariana appears to have made a distinction between the elite vassals who were members of the political kingdom and the mass of a ruler's subjects who were not. He felt that rulers should not reveal their feelings or intentions in three other situations: when an adviser said something the ruler did not like, to avoid shutting off future advice (III, 15: 329); when a ruler was ordering military exercises without the intention of going to war, so that his soldiers would exert themselves and neighboring princes would weaken themselves with unnecessary preparatory expenses; and when a ruler was sending out ambassadors, because if they did not know the ruler's intimate secrets, they would be better able to comply with his orders (III, 15: 336). None of these recommendations received extended treatment, suggesting that Mariana, who customarily laced his text with historical examples, did not consider the matter of much importance. Moreover, he emphasized that even these recommendations had to be understood within the context of his general principles of royal government (prologue: 10; III, 15: 337). Given the popularity of Tacitus among writers on political themes at this time, these references are neither surprising nor decisive for an interpretation of Mariana's thought.[18]

The politically prominent members of Toledo's developing oligarchy continued to act within a cultural environment whose most frequently cued interpretive schemes underpinned political principles that gave to monarchs an absolute authority to establish and maintain justice, good government, and the common good. However, this authority did not permit a ruler to act in violation of the kingdom's "fundamental laws" nor grant to him or her the free disposition of any subject's property, for such actions were those of a tyrant rather than of a true king.[19] Mariana reflects this.

According to Mariana, the community established a mixture of municipal assemblies and monarchy as the form of government best able to maintain public tranquility and to preserve the lives and property of its members from violent oppression by the strongest (I, 1: 16).

> Therefore, since every man's life was threatened by injury from without, and even blood relatives and intimate friends did not restrain themselves from killing each other, those who were pressed by the more powerful began to draw themselves together with others in a mutual compact of society and to look for someone outstanding in justice and trustworthiness. By his aid they hoped to ward off domestic and foreign injuries, and by establishing justice to restrain and bind down all classes, high, middle and low, by a fair system of law. Thus it was that at this time there first arose town assemblies and the regal dignity. The latter was attained not by riches nor electioneering, but by temperance, probity and acknowledged manliness. In this manner, from the need of many things, from fear and the realization of frailty, the consideration for each other (which distinguish us as men) and civil society, by which we live well and happily, were born. (Mariana 1948: 113)

Because the ruler's authority was derived from the political community, the authority of the latter was ultimately greater than his, he was organically part of the commonwealth (I, 6: 61; I, 8), and fundamental laws could not be abrogated or altered without the approval of the political community's representatives (I, 8: 73).

> The protectors of the people have no fewer and lesser arguments. Assuredly the commonwealth, whence the regal authority has its source, can call a king into court, when circumstances require and, if he persists in senseless conduct, it can strip him of his principate. For the commonwealth did not transfer the rights to rule into the hands of a prince to such a degree that it has not reserved a greater authority to itself; for we see that in the matters of laying taxes and making permanent laws, the commonwealth has made the reservation that except with its consent no change

can be made. . . . only with the desire of the people are new imposts ordered and new laws made; and, what is more, the rights to rule, though hereditary, are settled by the agreement of the people on a successor. (Mariana 1948: 146 [translation slightly revised])

De rege fit comfortably within the political discourse of the millones debates of the 1590s and was, therefore, not a remnant of some archaic vision asserted in the face of a predominant "absolutism." Nor was Mariana's the dying gasp of this view of the proper exercise of royal authority. Because the ruler had no right to the property of his subjects (III, 8: 270), Mariana argued, the Cortes had to approve the collection of all taxes (I, 2: 23; I, 3: 36; I, 5: 45–46; I, 6: 57; I, 9: 81; III, 7: 267). He thus asserted without citation a long-standing legal requirement that was still acknowledged, with citations to the *Nueva Recopilación* issued by Philip II, as late as 1834 in the *Estatuto Real*.[20] Although Mariana rejected the application of conciliar thought to the pope's authority, accepting the position of his religious order, he echoed the comunero ideologues of the early 1520s in his use of this conceptual framework to explain the relationship between a monarch and his representative assembly (I, 6: 57; I, 8: 74–75).

In the midst of so much current scholarly attention to the struggles in the Cortes over fiscal matters, it is important to note that Mariana perhaps placed even greater emphasis on the sovereign's responsibility to provide an effective administration of justice according to the law, because in this regard, too, he employed an interpretive scheme by which the commonwealth's political leaders continued to evaluate royal government as those of the early sixteenth century had done. After Philip II's sharp reaction to Toledo's attempts to overturn the Council of Castile's verdict in the Puebla de Alcocer trial and the royal prohibition against further discussion, no writer would mention the dispute in a printed book. Yet such a spectacular and politically central case was remembered at least into the 1660s, and the perceived circumstances of its conclusion continued to shape the political thought and actions of many Castilian authors and leaders, especially those such as Mariana whose consideration of these matters took place in Toledo itself.[21]

Because, Mariana argued, suspicion arose about the ruler's fairness, written laws were established as guides to proper conduct (I, 2: 18).

A double reason for committing the laws to writing appeared. Since the fairness of the Prince came into question through there being no one so outstanding as to be equally devoted to all men and free from wrath and hatred, the laws were published, to apply always to all alike. Indeed, the law is a calm science, drawn from the divine mind, prescribing proper and salutary matters and prohibiting the contrary. (Mariana 1948: 115)

In an obvious defense of the famous *Lex digna* of the Emperor Justinian, Mariana emphasized that the true monarch accepts the limitations that the law places on him and realizes that to maintain the commonwealth and enhance his own dignity, he must uphold the law by his own conduct (I, 2: 23; I, 8: 69 and 74–75). In fact, book I, chapter 9, entitled "Princeps non est solutus legibus" ("The Prince Is Not Free from the Laws"), provides a commentary on the *Lex digna* in the tradition of John of Salisbury.[22] Indeed, those commonwealths cannot long endure in which justice is badly administered (III, 12: 307).

> No more onerous plague can be contrived than a king serving his own interests, or governing the public or private affairs of his subjects in accordance with only his own ideas or those of his courtiers. The wretched disasters of mighty countries declare this, as well as sad misfortunes within the memory of all. When, in truth, the King forsakes his benevolence, and tyranny makes its entrance, and the courtiers rule in his name, it is inevitable that the whole commonwealth be entirely overturned and the subjects who have trusted in his sense of justice be thrown headlong into the most grievous ruin. (Mariana 1948: 121)

Mariana emphatically insisted that it was wrong for the monarch to overturn a judicial decision on the basis of his own opinion or that of his courtiers (III, 15: 335).

> Then when once the judges agree in their opinions and votes, the Prince should consider it wrong to decide otherwise about a matter that has come up. Otherwise, I give warning of a sure plague, grave inconveniences, if he should follow his own judgment or that of his courtiers. (Mariana 1948: 348)

Needless to say, Mariana felt that great care should be taken to appoint magistrates who conform to the highest standards (III, 3: 235).[23] The monarch should seek the counsel of good and knowledgeable men (III, 15: 328–29), and he must reward those who distinguish themselves in the service of the commonwealth regardless of their background (III, 4).

Any ruler who felt he was exempt from the law was, according to Mariana, on the road to becoming a tyrant (the difference between a monarch and a tyrant is explained in I, 5):

> [M]y view is this: the regal authority, if it is lawful, ever has its source from the citizens; by their grant the first kings were placed in each commonwealth on the seat of supreme authority. That authority they hedged about with laws and obligations, lest it puff itself up too much, run riot, result in the ruin of the subjects, and degenerate into tyranny. . . . All these things are the proper marks of a tyrant. Finally he ruins the whole commonwealth; he considers it as his spoil in his wretched methods with no respect for the laws, from which he thinks himself exempt; and though he professes to be planning for the public safety, he carries on in such a way that the citizens are crushed by every kind of evil and lead a most unhappy

existence. Individually and en masse he drives them wrongfully from their paternal possessions, so that he is the sole ruler in all the estates. The common people are deprived of all their benefits, and no evil can possibly be imagined which is not a part of the misfortunes of the citizens. (1948: 141, 156 [translation slightly revised])

The tyrant was led to this puffed-up opinion of himself by the flatterers who presented the ruler with a fraudulent picture of monarchical government in an effort to gain wealth and influence (I, 2: 26–27; I, 6: 61; I, 9: 81–82). Mariana had only criticism of the usual run of courtiers (*genus hominum pestilentissimum;* I, 5: 47), and he was especially emphatic in his insistence that the prince must avoid governing through favorites (I, 5: 47; II, 9: 162–63; II, 10: 169; II, 11; III, 1: 213; III, 7: 267; III, 15: 328–29).[24] As if to echo the claims Toledo made in the Belalcázar case about the circumstances of the Puebla de Alcocer grant to Gutierre de Sotomayor, Mariana offered the reign of John II as one of his principal examples of the evils that accompanied rule through a favorite:

> Not long ago in Castile Alvaro de Luna was so powerful in the palace that the king did not change even his fare, nor his habit, nor his servants, except in accordance with the former's wish. A wretched state of affairs for the king, or the realm, or both! This evil was wiped out at last with the life of Alvaro. (1948: 228)

Mariana felt that it was the mark of a tyrant to bestow royal favor only on the wealthy few who typically surrounded him (on rewards, see III, 4). The tyrant thinks only of his own pleasure rather than the good of the community, and because his behavior provokes the hatred of his subjects (III, 15: 332), the tyrant prohibits meetings (I, 5: 50), foments lawsuits and feuds to keep the citizens divided (I, 5: 49; III, 4: 243), and employs mercenary troops (I, 5: 50; III, 5: 251). Although in his belief that the tyrant who arbitrarily violated the law must be restrained he was no innovator, Mariana's most celebrated doctrine was that of tyrannicide. Mariana asserted that if the tyrant would not reform his behavior, he could legitimately be killed, for his actions were a fundamental threat to the commonwealth's very existence and a violation of the reasons why monarchical government had been established (I, 6; I,7).[25]

Mariana harbored no illusions about the chances for effective royal government:

> It is a difficult matter to keep Princes of great and distinguished authority within the bounds of moderation. It is hard to persuade them, if they are corrupted by an abundance of wealth and puffed up by the empty talk of their courtiers, not to be thinking that it is pertinent to their dignified status and to the increase of their grandeur to augment their resources and authority, or that they are considered to be subject to the supervision of

anybody. However, the fact really is otherwise. Nothing, indeed, enhances regal resources more than moderation, if it is fixed in the minds and impressed on the very innermost consciences of Princes, when they are about to adopt a manner of thought and life, that they should serve first God, whose will governs the countries of the world and at whose nod empires rise and fall; secondly that they should be modest and honest, for by these good qualities we merit divine protection, and the well-wishing of men is thus won to them in whose hands rests the governance of affairs. Also, the judgment of the citizens should be heeded, and one should often reflect as to what history will indeed say in the far distant future. As a matter of fact, it is characteristic of a noble spirit to aspire, next to heaven, to an immortal name. (1948: 164 [translation slightly revised])

Always sensitive to the conditions of royal government that would enhance the Crown's capacity for action, Mariana stressed throughout his writings "that the authority of princes is weak once reverence has departed from the minds of the subjects" (1948: 142).

Mariana's thrust was toward "a government of law instead of will."[26] While *De rege* served as an often eloquent restatement of constitutional principles that had been widely supported for several centuries within Castile's politically active elite, it also appears that Mariana was responding to the historical developments of the second half of the sixteenth century. Although it is difficult to make a case for direct references to Philip II's practices, Mariana's books attracted the attention of an educated public frustrated by aspects of royal government that were considered arbitrary and damaging, and the situation prevailing in Castile inspired him more than the religious and international struggles dominating the rest of Europe, although he did discuss in some detail the assassination of king Henry III of France (I, 6: 51–55).[27]

Despite the resonance of his ideas about monarchy among those critical of Castilian conditions, Mariana suffered no direct reprisals for his major works. He was jailed for about a year (1609–1610) by the Inquisition, but this was apparently motivated by sharp criticism of royal advisers, among whom the royal favorite recognized himself, in an essay on the debasement of currency in Mariana's *Tractatus VII* of 1609.[28] His *De rege* provoked more spectacular reactions in neighboring France after the assassination of king Henry IV in 1610. Both the Parlement of Paris and the Sorbonne condemned the book, and it was burned by the public hangman and attacked in several French treatises of 1610. Because the Society of Jesus worried about the effect of the scandal on the order's reputation, General Aquaviva condemned the doctrine of tyrannicide and forbade any Jesuit from defending Mariana,[29] but Mariana continued to enjoy wide respect in his homeland. In recognition of his influence, in 1622 Philip IV named the elderly Jesuit royal chronicler and contributed 1,000 ducats toward a new edition of his *History of Spanish Deeds*.[30]

By the time the king gave Mariana a royal post, universities may no longer have served as the primary social environment in which the most important authors worked. Although the publications of seventeenth-century jurists and theologians holding important chairs at the major universities have not received much attention from historians,[31] centers such as Salamanca and Valladolid may have ceased to play central roles in the development of political ideas. University-level legal studies drastically declined in quality and popularity during the final Habsburg century. Moreover, the ever-closer connection between the universities' faculties and a Crown administration in Madrid that was often perceived as corrupt and arbitrary may have encouraged prudence on the part of ambitious professors who desired posts in the royal councils or great *audiencias*.[32] Max Weber was surely correct when he wrote that judicial decision making by a prince acting on the basis of nonjudicial factors "has nowhere been able to provide much stimulation for formal legal thought,"[33] and the apparent ability of the influential to shape judicial administration may have been sufficient to undermine a university-based tradition of political thought that tended to be legalistic in character.

Lope de Vega and Popular Understandings of the Monarch's Defense of Justice

Yet the written exchange of political ideas continued to be lively in Castile, and throughout the era of the great royal favorites, the duke of Lerma and the count-duke of Olivares, authors printed books and circulated manuscripts without any interference from royal or ecclesiastical censors greater than had existed in sixteenth-century Castile or in other kingdoms in the seventeenth century.[34] During the past twenty years, scholars have published extensively on these authors, whose ideas are now much more familiar to historians.[35] Moreover, the conceptual language of these works was sufficiently influential to be reflected in the discussions of royal and municipal councils and in the dialogues of contemporary *comedias* (dramatic works).

The works of *arbitristas*–essayists who suggested practical reforms to enhance the kingdom's prosperity, increase royal revenue, or improve military preparedness–and other political writers of the period continued to be tied to the university tradition, as many of them held degrees, usually in law or theology. However, the social environment of the authors and their audience was dominated more by the development of urban-based discussion groups, some of which sought a more formal institutional existence as academies. This type of cultural assembly had become an increasingly common part of European intellectual life in the sixteenth century as the Latin curriculum shaped by Renaissance Humanists became a major vehicle of elite education. Despite their recognized cultural role, the Castilian groups still await their historian. Provincial groups drew heavily from the local oligarchy for their membership and financial support, and significant literary and artistic projects were frequently brought to completion with municipal funds.[36]

The works on monarchical government by writers such as Mariana were popular with urban intellectual societies because they clearly displayed and articulated the general attitudes and political values of the members of these groups. Indeed, Mariana represented a link between the canonist and Romanist constitutional tradition used by Conciliarist leaders and the theorists of the comunero rebellion, the jurists and theologians of the so-called school of Salamanca, and the often more practical writings of the arbitristas. Although the medieval and Salamanca traditions influenced book I of *De rege,* some of the chapters in book III focused on specific administrative problems such as military affairs, taxation, currency policy (added in the 1605 edition), agriculture, poor relief, and public entertainment in the manner of seventeenth-century authors. However, the prevailing attitudes and values are also evident in other activities with which the discussion groups were closely associated. Contemporaries probably most associated these academies with the promotion of theatrical productions, and the period's dominant author of works for the commercial stage was Lope de Vega (1562–1635). Although not written to provide a realistic portrayal, the era's dramatic works nonetheless offer useful evidence about the discourse and interpretive schemes of their time, because of both the literary type of play produced and the Golden Age theater's highly commercial nature, which demanded plays whose themes would resonate with the concepts and language of the audience. Lope's texts, therefore, offer an opportunity to see how historical agents themselves viewed the world.

Modern readers may have trouble grasping the political vision on which the plots of many of Lope de Vega's best-known plays are founded, and the difficulty often stems from an inadequate sense of the playwright's audience. Those who wrote for the stage concentrated on the action and left the actors and audience to imagine the personality and motivations of each character.[37] Lope's plays characteristically provided images and metaphors to clarify matters of intense contemporary discussion, and the playwright was pushed to produce works of quality by audiences who had a highly developed understanding of these issues. Because the audience was expected to provide so much of the interpretive context of the stage action, it is not possible to grasp the meaning of many of his plays, or even to understand why his audiences enjoyed them, without some knowledge of the contemporary discourse about political and social issues. And for this purpose, the internal evidence from literary works has been an insufficient base for information about how members of the audience of the typical theater (*corral*) grasped and debated the events and developments of their time.[38]

Members of municipal oligarchies frequently played a crucial role in the construction and maintenance of theaters and in attracting playwrights and dramatic groups to undertake productions for the local stage, and they were among the most important components of Golden Age theater audiences. The prominent families had control over access to the special box seats and regularly attended performances. Because production activities were organized both by the governing municipal council and by local intellectual associations dominated by members of the oligarchy, it was only natural that successful playwrights directed their political works toward the interests and interpretive schemes of this group's social and cultural environments. In productions of the plays I discuss here, dramatists and actors evoked audience response on the basis of the frequently employed language and political perspective within whose context members of the oligarchy understood their own position in relationship to the population of their municipality and the Crown.[39]

Lope dealt with more than political themes, and even in the plays discussed here, the thematic content extends beyond such issues. However, Lope consistently exploited as a primary emphasis in his dramatic works the violation, especially by those in positions of some authority, of the expectations of behavior in a network of established relationships within the community. The creditworthiness of people in authority depended on their embrace of the common interpretive schemes that defined all citizens as members of the commonwealth. What are often described as Lope's "three famous socio-political plays about peasant honour"[40] in the face of the coercive power of seignioral lords are clearly more than that. Rather than the issue of "power," that familiar mechanistic metaphor characteristic of the political vocabulary of our time, Lope directed his attention toward people who were part of a web of relationships within which they normally shaped their identities and behavior but who acted on some occasions contrary to customary expectations.

For example, in *Peribáñez y el Comendador de Ocaña* (ca. 1605–1608),[41] Peribáñez and Casilda marry, but their seignioral lord, a comendador of a military order, is so sexually attracted to Casilda that he forgets his responsibility to provide those under his jurisdiction with protection and justice and tries to rape her. The comendador uses his authority to make Peribáñez a captain in the local militia and sends him to fight in the Granada war, but before leaving, Peribáñez extracts from the comendador a promise to guard the captain's honor and his wife. With Peribáñez apparently out of the way, the comendador enters the captain's house to rape Casilda, but Peribáñez suspects foul play and returns to save his wife by killing the comendador. Although the king cannot condone the murder of a seignioral lord, he does, as the proper source of justice, recognize that the comendador has destroyed the proper pattern of relationships between lord and vassals through his abuse of his position, and Peribáñez receives, through the exercise of royal grace, confirmation of his captaincy and a pardon that justifies a vassal's resistance to tyranny.

Modern readers are more familiar with Lope's *Fuenteovejuna* (ca. 1612–1614) in which there has been a conflict between an entire village and its lord, who has clearly abused his seignioral rights and responsibilities to such an extent that he faced general rebellion. Moreover, the lord in this tale, another comendador of a military order, sided with the Portuguese ruler in his war against the Catholic Monarchs, who eventually provide justice and restore the harmony of relationships that the comendador has violated. In this play Lope was dramatizing a historical event, which may well have been a familiar story for many in the audience.[42] Drawn from a cultural environment in which rebellion was an expected consequence of abuse of authority, the political vision that explained both the rupture of the community's peace, tranquility, and concord and the justice that restored these common elements of good government was familiar to the members of Lope's audiences.

In these two plays, vassals exercise their legitimate right of resistance to tyranny. A few years later, Lope penned a play that portrayed a monarch exercising his authority properly to defend his subjects from abuse. In *El mejor alcalde, el rey* (*The Best Magistrate, the King;* ca. 1620–1623), Lope presented to his audiences the story of a seignioral lord who refuses to recognize the king's authority while at the same time violating within his network of relationships his responsibilities to those in his jurisdiction. In this story the Galician noble Don Tello has been abusing the peasants, one of whom, Sancho, requests royal justice, but Don Tello will not accept the monarch's right to adjudicate the matter. The king comes to Galicia disguised as a royal judge and reveals his identity only when Don Tello arrogantly proclaims his independence from the judge's jurisdiction. Don Tello brags, "If the King does not come to take me, no one in the world can." To which the monarch responds with one of Lope's more famous lines: "But I am the King, peasant!").[43] His identity revealed to all, the king has Don Tello marry Elvira whom he had raped, even though she was to have been Sancho's wife. Don Tello is then executed for treason, and Elvira, now a rich widow, can marry Sancho, whose behavior has convinced the king that he has noble blood. Presumably Sancho will now provide the proper territorial authority according to generally accepted norms, which Don Tello had violated. Through the resources of the law, the monarch, as the ultimate source of justice, restores good government and the proper relationships between a seignior and the peasants of his jurisdiction and between the ruler himself and his subjects.

It is worth pointing out that all of these plays were set in the "Reconquest" period, which ended only with the fall of Granada in 1492. A focus on the events and rulers of this period characterized much of late sixteenth- and early seventeenth-century Castilian political and historical writing by arbitristas and others.[44] For example, in *De rege,* Mariana drew from the Reconquest many of the historical illustrations of his theoretical principles, which is not surprising because *De rege* was written mostly while Mariana was publishing his influential *History of Spanish Deeds.* This focus was a distinctive feature of Castilian Humanist writing in comparison with that of Italy, for example. The major monarchs of the Reconquest were perceived as successful rulers, and Golden Age authors and the political kingdom wanted to understand the foundations of this success. It is important to see that Castilians still thought that the long-accepted bases of good government were vital for the kingdom's stability, prosperity, and reputation. Moreover, Lope did not neglect the consequences of abuse by the monarch, and he was not alone among Golden Age playwrights in his portrayal of royal tyranny.[45]

Although Lope's *El Duque de Viseo* (ca. 1608–1609) deals with events perhaps less dramatic than tyrannicide, the play offers much of interest in its portrayal of the tragic consequences for a monarch who acts arbitrarily outside of the normal channels of justice. The play is Lope's version of the murder of the duke of Viseu by king John II of Portugal, and many in the seventeenth-century audiences who saw the play probably knew that the duke was the older brother of king Manuel, Philip II's grandfather, and that Manuel eventually inherited the throne on John II's death. In Lope's account, the constable of Portugal, the duke of Bragança, initiates the action when in an attempt to stop her wedding, he informs Doña Inés, who is betrothed to the king's favorite Don Egas, that her future husband has Jewish ancestors. In revenge, Don Egas convinces the king that the House of Bragança, including don Alvaro de Portugal who in exile becomes president of the Council of Castile under the Catholic Monarchs, is plotting against him. Although the duke of Viseo is the queen's brother, he is eventually implicated in the alleged plot as brother-in-law of the Braganças. Motivated by fear that his own relatives plan to harm him (John is also related to the Bragança brothers), the king condemns Viseo, without a trial that might have revealed his innocence, as a traitor and stabs him to death when no one else will execute him. Acting arbitrarily on the advice of his favorite—a type of action against which Mariana repeatedly warned—king John has killed his innocent brother-in-law, and the deed will damage his relationship with his wife and other relatives. Written at a time when anti-Machiavellian works were popular, the warning about the effects of tyrannical royal behavior could not have been clearer.

Because Lope's subject was often the consequences of the failure to observe proper reciprocal political relationships, *El castigo sin venganza* (*Justice without Revenge;* 1631) does not have a single tragic protagonist. Contemporary literary theorists and many modern scholars of the era's dramatic works have expected that one character would be the driving force in tragedies. In this particular play, however, all the major characters make significant contributions, as their mutual failure to observe the norms of proper action demanded by the relationships among them stimulates the movement toward tragedy. The duke of Ferrara has had sexual relations with a number of women, one of whom bore the duke's beloved bastard son, count Federico. Although the duke would like to see Federico inherit the throne, he does not feel that will be possible. To produce a legitimate heir, he marries Casandra, the young daughter of the duke of Mantua, but after his wedding night, the duke of Ferrara is repeatedly unfaithful to his wife. Thus abandoned, Casandra and count Federico fall in love. After the duke of Ferrara returns from a military campaign, an anonymous letter informs him of his wife's adultery. Because he wishes to preserve his reputation from any public scandal, the duke devises a trick to have the young lovers killed. He places the bound and gagged Casandra in a chair and covers her with a silk cloth. The duke then tells Federico that the person under the cover is a local noble who has been plotting against the duke, and he asks his son to kill the traitor. Once Federico has killed Casandra with his sword, the duke calls his guards and others, including marquis Gonzaga, Casandra's brother. Gonzaga then stabs count Federico when the duke accuses him of having killed Casandra to protect his inheritance from the child his stepmother was carrying. Although the Duke of Ferrara tries to justify the deaths of Casandra and Federico as punishments serving justice rather than as acts of vengeance, he is left without a direct heir to his throne and without the son he loved.

Although this brief summary leaves the impression that the duke of Ferrara must be the tragic protagonist that theorists have required, he is on stage much less than Casandra or Federico. However, the primacy of theme removes the need for a single protagonist. If the theme is the terrible damage that comes from the violation of proper relationships, then the duke, Casandra, and Federico all play significant parts in shaping the final tragedy. The young people die, but the duke is left alive among those who know he has been dishonored. Moreover, a seventeenth-century Castilian audience would have recognized another aspect of the tragedy: the population of the duchy is left in danger through the lack of a clear line of royal succession, an issue Mariana treated at length (I, 3 and 4). Because deceit in high places endangered everyone, this play is best understood as an anti-Machiavellian work in an age when this was practically a genre. The audience would have understood in this sense the servant's lines that close the play: "Here ends, senate, that tragedy of justice without revenge, which, having been disconcerting in Italy, is today an example in Spain." It is no wonder that the count-duke of Olivares, favorite of Philip IV, may have limited this play to one performance while consistently denying Lope the royal favor he so much wanted.[46]

Because internal literary evidence provides an inadequate basis for evaluating Lope de Vega's plays dealing with monarchs and their officials, we can now only grasp the meanings these works had in the Golden Age if we know how the plots interacted with the interpretive schemes of the audience. The period's treatises on political topics provide one important source for understanding prevailing conceptions of authority, and the connection should be easy to make because political authors of Lope's time were often interested in the impact of political actors' psychological dispositions. On the whole, educated Castilians did not believe that the Crown's policies and actions could be detached from the concern for justice and the common good, and they did believe that a lack of justice undermined the monarchy and, therefore, the commonwealth.[47]

Evaluating the Exercise of Royal Authority

Of course, there would always be those who chose, judged by the prevailing standards, to overstate the monarch's authority, and there would be others, judged in the same way, who wished to understate the extent of such authority. Mariana argued that the former line was the product of the courtier-flatterers whose influence corrupted monarchy into tyranny, but he also warned against the latter tendency (I, 6: 61; III, 8: 270). Baltasar Alamos de Barrientos (1550–1634), who was protected by the count-duke of Olivares, was perhaps an example of the first type, while don Mateo de Lisón y Viedma, who was one of Olivares's great opponents as a Cortes representative for Granada, was placed by some in the latter group. The arbitristas did not constitute a coherent group either; they were rather individuals who were involved in an intense debate over public policy. Some served royal favorites or sought their patronage. Not surprisingly, these arbitristas often seemed to opt for government action free of many of the constraints advocated by Juan de Mariana. Others wanted a broader reform of royal government to achieve the *conservación y aumento* (preservation and growth) of the Hispanic Monarchy and felt that rectitude of action in the light of established, venerable political thought was necessary to sustain royal authority.[48]

I do not mean to suggest that the positions taken were arbitrary ones, articulated only with an eye to immediate personal benefit. On the contrary, opposed stances in any debate over the exercise of royal authority often emerged from deeply held principles learned within a particular social and cultural context and employed as a primary means by which an individual interpreted the world and formulated judgments as a basis for planning action. It is the point of the present book that the dynamism of monarchy stemmed from the presence, although this was apparent only when difficult choices were demanded, of potentially contradictory interpretive schemes within the commonwealth's cultural environment about the nature of absolute royal authority and its exercise. Although sometimes presented utilizing an enriched vocabulary, such as that of "reason of state," the resulting contradictory judgments continued in the seventeenth century to fuel opposed political positions over the proper response to the Crown's severe financial difficulties. This variation in judgments was itself part of the pattern of monarchical politics and manifested itself particularly during periods of intense conflict brought on by perceived Crown deviations from the broadly accepted standards of royal government at the core of Castilian political identity. These are the standards one finds reflected in Lope's plays as well as in a wide variety of those cultural "performances"[49] that enjoyed an ample audience in the Habsburg era. Ultimately, in order to grasp the meaning in context of both the plays and political tracts of the late sixteenth and early seventeenth century, one would have to investigate the activities and interpretive designs of the most crucial group within the audience for both types of literary work, the governing local notables of Castile's cities and major towns, and this task is beyond the scope of the present book.

However, Diego Saavedra Fajardo (1584–1648) was a particularly articulate and influential member of the patrician group with which I am most familiar. He was a career royal official from the Cortes city of Murcia who wrote in the 1630s. Reflecting an important intellectual strategy of the era, he used skepticism to undermine faith in empirical, inductive bases of approaches to politics, which were central to some arbitrista and "reason of state" writing, whether drawn from historical reflection, experience, or study. He argued that such skepticism should make rulers humble and aware how dangerous it would be to act according to their own volition. Saavedra Fajardo indicated that the community had instituted monarchy for certain ends, especially the maintenance of the rule of law, which established limits on the prince's arbitrary administration while enhancing his legitimate authority. If these limits were not observed, the prince would become a tyrant. For Saavedra Fajardo, the residual authority of the commonwealth to restrain tyranny resided in the Cortes. In other words, the "constitutionalist" tradition represented by Mariana's *De rege* and works by other prominent authors of his time remained lively down to the 1640s, when Philip IV's government faced intensified Castilian resistance to its demands for additional revenue and troops and major rebellions in Catalonia, Portugal, Naples, and Sicily. It is worth noting that much of the newer "reason of state" literature went to great pains to point out the limits of arbitrary rule, even to the point of emphasizing that it could stimulate rebellion.[50]

However extreme Mariana's views about the institutional limits to monarchical rule may have been, and many among the commonwealth's political leaders would have considered *De rege* an eloquent presentation of their own familiar interpretive schemes, it is clear that the ideal of a king obeying the law remained influential in late sixteenth- and seventeenth-century Castile. The local notables and the magistrates with a patrician background were still not in a position personally to exercise much influence within Court circles, and they resented their dependence on the magnates who could do so. Regional elites wanted their rights and interests to be defended by the predictable guarantees of the law rather than depending on the whims of a great patron. Although supporting "absolute royal authority" in theory, the local notables did not feel that the arbitrary exercise of monarchical authority was the proper road to effective royal leadership. Urban patricians united in increasingly cohesive oligarchies and used the municipal councils they controlled to frustrate such Crown actions. Although high royal justices prudently avoided comment on the matter, it would not be wise to underestimate the Council of Castile's decision in a prominent dispute such as the Puebla de Alcocer case as a stimulus to this trend. No ruler among the last Habsburgs understood how to be a truly respected and widely supported monarch, and the resulting unstable governments dominated by an influential territorial aristocracy were unable to respond effectively to the Hispanic Monarchy's seventeenth-century difficulties.

Authority's Paradox and the Cultural Environment of Political Life

The great historian of China Joseph Levenson once wrote that we cannot hear Mozart's music as his contemporaries did, because we have heard Wagner.[51] For the same reasons, we struggle to read the political works of Juan de Mariana as his contemporaries did, because we have read those of Thomas Hobbes and John Locke and their successors. It was not the "power" of the institutions of a developing "state," Hobbes's "Leviathan," that held together the Castilian commonwealth. Instead, Castilians defined themselves as the kingdom's citizens because of their shared political identity based on the use of common interpretive schemes, expressed in common terms, to recognize patterns in the world around them as a basis for making judgments that in part shaped and constrained their actions. While for an individual Castilian the cultural environment of interpretive schemes was neither hierarchically arranged nor static, on the more general level of the commonwealth, identity stemmed from the high value given to justice as an ultimate purpose of the political community and to the conviction that the sovereign possessed "absolute royal authority" to see that justice was done in the realm. Mariana's books were widely read and appreciated at the end of Philip II's reign and during that of his son, because Mariana founded his arguments about historical events and contemporary affairs on these values, while he judged, just as his readers did, the actions of rulers and their officials. By mapping the complex Belalcázar dispute, I have provided one abstraction of how Castilians understood their political community and the exercise of authority within it, and I have suggested that, because of the consequences of such judgments, the dynamic locus of the commonwealth's political life was often away from the monarch and his or her immediate advisers.

The cultural environment of Trastámara and Habsburg Castile was defined by a number of interpretive schemes, which people absorbed over the course of their lives. Such schemes permitted people to recognize patterns in the world around them and to formulate judgments, and this continuous process shaped action, whether as "interpretation," normative action to conform to the particular scheme, or as "strategization," action designed to alter the role of the actor within the social environment or the relationship among roles. Although they were not the only ones shaping political action,[52] I have focused here on two sets of interpretive schemes, both of them dealing with the nature and conduct of the monarch, and the political languages in which they were expressed. Fifteenth-century royal officials began inserting the phrase "by my absolute royal authority" in Crown documents, but the concept appeared much earlier.[53] For elite political actors, these political languages enabled discussions of royal policies and behavior that were considered essential to the maintenance by this small percentage of Castilians of their disproportionate enjoyment of the kingdom's resources, and the use of such concepts served to give royal authority an important place within the cultural environment, and, therefore, to give royal action an important place within the social environment.

One set of these interpretive schemes, expressed in the idiom of vassalage, stressed individual service to the monarch in return for protection and rewards of jurisdictions, property, revenue shares, and offices provided by royal grace and absolute authority to violate legal provisions. By extension, the emphasis on service to the great in exchange for maintenance and defense of the client's interests could involve patrons other than the monarch. In this language of vassalage, vassals sometimes refused to comply with the sovereign's commands, claiming that these commands would damage the ruler's interests or render his or her vassals incapable of further service because of consequent harm to their estates or honor.

The other scheme embodied the paradox of monarchical authority. Castilians thought the ruler possessed an absolute authority necessary to maintain the Christian commonwealth in peace, harmony, and justice through good government. This authority was absolute because its exercise was ultimately, in theory, not formally responsible to any other earthly individual or institution. Because the monarch ruled over the entire kingdom, his or her personal interests were thought to be close to those of the commonwealth, and if the monarch had an informed, rational understanding of conditions in the kingdom, he or she would act to advance Christian piety, military defense, the subjects' material well-being, and justice. While the resulting political language offered a basis for royal commands, those using it could also articulate standards for judging the rulers' conduct and justifying resistance. If the monarch was badly informed and falsely believed that the ruler could use absolute authority to do as he or she wished in violation of morality and law, royal government would become "tyranny," which would open the door to heresy and super-stition, defeat by the infidels, general misery, crime, and factionalism within the commonwealth.

From among the many interpretive schemes available to individuals, the particular ones used to recognize patterns are cued by the previous scheme employed and by a person's experience. This book has focused on two categories of individuals: on the one hand, the great aristocrats who exercised jurisdiction over often vast territories and enjoyed great wealth; on the other, lesser nobles and local notables, particularly those forming the patriciates of the kingdom's cities and major towns. Together they con-stituted the "political kingdom," in that members of these groups, although mostly the males among them, felt that they should be involved in Castile's government. In addition to the roles of the territorial aristocracy in the social environment, the political actions of its members were on bal-ance shaped by the employment of the service-rewards perspective to rec-ognize patterns and formulate judgments. Because Castile's monarchs both needed and could not eliminate the territorial aristocracy, they had to respond to some extent to the resulting magnate expectations. On the other hand, local notables more frequently interpreted and judged the monarch's actions on the provision of justice by royal institutions. How-ever, if the politically active subjects perceived that the monarch was vio-lating, by responding to the personal interests of the grandees around him or her, the ruler's responsibility to work for the common good, insecure local notables might seek from aristocratic patrons the maintenance and protection that no longer seemed to be available through royal judicial administration. In response to attempts in recent historical writing to sal-vage the royal Court as the focus of state development in its role as patron of networks of clients, this book suggests that clientage was an ineffective administrative tool.

Because the sovereign could not coerce the necessary support of such a numerous and geographically dispersed group as the local notables, the ruler could exercise authority effectively only if he or she could gain their confidence by governing according to their expectations of royal government. It is this paradox that Juan de Mariana expressed in an observation that is almost a gloss on Emperor Justinian's *Lex digna:*

> Indeed, government is kingly which restrains itself within the bounds of modesty and moderation, while by an excess of authority, which the unwise are busy at increasing daily, it is reduced and corrupted through and through. We foolishly are deceived with an appearance of greater authority and slip off into the opposite error, not giving the matter sufficient consideration, and not realizing that authority is finally safe only when it places a limit on its own exercise. In the regal principate it does not apply as it does in possessions, that the more the latter are increased, the richer we become; the opposite, indeed, is the fact. Though the prince ought to be ruling over willing subjects, to be eliciting the good will of his citizens, and to be serving their interests, if his rule becomes irritating, as King he will lose their good will and exchange authority for incapacity. (1948: 160–61 (translation slightly revised)

The exercise of royal authority depended on local notables, and particularly on the patricians who governed Castilian cities and major towns, because there was no such reified entity as the "state," characterized by its autonomy to formulate policies and goals independently of other groups and its capacity to carry these out through coercive "power" to reshape "society." Politics centered on the municipal governing council. Even within the towns of the seignioral jurisdictions of territorial aristocrats and ecclesiastical institutions, the support of town leaders would in large part be based on their judgment of the leadership of the lord as a representative of royal justice.[54]

I do not argue that aristocrats were not interested in having their economic status and institutional positions secured by legal documents, nor that local notables lacked concern for individual honor or disdained the use of personal influence and faction. The period's history did not continuously express such a stark confrontation. Instead, I employ the dichotomy as an abstraction, a heuristic device used to explain that history. These attitudes of the territorial aristocracy and local notables were expressions of each group's most prevalent perspective in a situation that both intellectually and practically defied too close a definition of the ruler's actual conduct. Members of both groups sometimes suffered apparent ideological confusion, for the periodic turbulence of political life did not permit them consistently to employ familiar interpretive schemes to recognize patterns on which judgment and action could be based.

Because of the vast geographical extension of the activities of subjects and officials of the Castilian Crown and of the Hispanic Monarchy in general, the meanings of conflicting understandings of royal authority were made subject to continuous invention by the development of an increasingly complex social environment characterized by the opportunities of a global economy and the multiplicity and expansion of political institutions. This spatial expansion of the sovereign's domains and the external challenges to Habsburg rule of them increased the need for interactive collaboration and consensus. Because providing justice was felt to be one of the ruler's most important tasks, I have concentrated on judicial institutions as arenas of political interaction in which the roles of individuals and corporate groups melded with their aspirations and understandings to shape action. In this regard as well, the Belalcázar case provides only a partial account of political life because in addition to those examined here in some detail—specially commissioned royal judges, a Chancillería's audiencia, and the Royal Council—Castilians created and adapted a broad range of other municipal, criminal, ecclesiastical, economic, fiscal, military, and conciliar institutions with judicial competencies.[55] Each of these institutions constituted a locus of politics often quite separate from the monarch and his or her immediate advisers and associates. Therefore, although the economic and political changes of the first global age offered monarchs increased revenues and administrative resources, they also heightened the sovereign's need for broad collaboration from the commonwealth's diverse leaders.

Contrary to the frequent emphasis on Crown autonomy in statist approaches to "absolutism," pushing territorial aristocrats out of crucial royal institutions did not make monarchs free from grandee influence. In such a personalist political environment, magnate clientage networks remained a potential source of security for lesser nobles and other local notables who doubted the ability of a particular monarch to provide them with justice and protection. Among those who might seek support from the great were the letrados that Castilian monarchs used ever more frequently as ecclesiastical and royal officials. These letrados' major motivations to improve the quality of royal judicial administration would be their identification with its institutions, as contexts for the interactions significant to their lives and careers, and a desire to enhance the role of these institutions by increasing support for them within the commonwealth. When monarchs and regents acted in violation of laws and procedures in virtue of a claimed autonomous, absolute royal authority, "corruption" among the royal officials directly responsible for providing justice would drain support from the Crown. Autonomy did not enhance royal capacity but undermined it; constant concern to act in ways that would produce broad-based support among the commonwealth's leaders would help monarchs become capable of action.

It is not possible to recognize such dynamic interactions as the basis of political life by examining events during a relatively short period of time. Monarchical government cannot be understood without examining royal administration over an extended period, exceeding even particularly long reigns such as those of Philip II or Louis XIV of France.[56] How members of the political kingdom acted becomes apparent only if one looks at a relatively long period and then only if one abandons the metanarrative of "absolutism" and the rise of the "state." Rather than forming part of some transition toward authoritarianism or the "modern state," these relationships among Crown officials, local notables, and aristocrats were themselves the core of the regime.

When the early use of "by my absolute royal authority" and related statements of the concept have been recognized, the tendency has been to treat them as assertions of one "model" of monarchy sharply contested by another "model" of more limited royal government. The culmination of a struggle over these models is supposed to have been the great rebellion of 1520–1521 known as the Comunidades or revolt of the comuneros, when the aspirations of those who would limit government "power," enshrined in the declaration of rebel goals often referred to as the "Constitution of Avila," were crushed at the battle of Villalar on 23 April 1521 and "absolutism" was firmly established as the "Spanish" political norm in Europe and America. This narrative fit well with other elements of typical explanations for the "weaknesses" of Habsburg "Spain," its eventual decline, and the country's subsequent stagnation and backwardness. In a variety of interpretive works, many of them written by Spaniards, "Spain" has been presented as an *essentially* stagnant, un-European country doomed to failure at every important test in the quest for "modernity" not only by its despotic political institutions made possible by a passive population unfit for liberty, but also by the irrationality of its "culture," by its people's insistence on the preservation of backward "traditions," by its ties to a bad religion, exemplified especially by the Inquisition and the Jesuits, by its intolerance of those who are somehow different and of new ideas, and by Spaniards' extraordinary propensity for irrational violence and brutality.[57]

Yet the drafters of the Avila document in fact petitioned for redress of grievances to the Habsburg monarch, Charles I of Castile, by then also crowned as emperor Charles V, whom they asked to correct the enumerated problems through the exercise of his "absolute royal authority." Furthermore, the rebellion did not emerge out of a fifteenth-century conflict over two models of government.[58] Nor did the political vision of "absolute royal authority" providing justice die easily. As parliamentary deputies in the Andalusian port of Cádiz debated their famous Constitution of 1812, some argued for the superiority of Spain's existing constitutional defense of justice and property through the exercise of the monarch's absolute authority.[59]

Research for this book originally focused on the Comunidades and the city of Toledo as an important source of rebel leadership. As piles of uncatalogued bundles of chronologically relevant documents grew on the archive floor, the biggest pile quickly became the one of materials relating to the Belalcázar lawsuit. When I read these materials, I heard echoes of Juan de Mariana's book written many decades after the rebellion; echoes of statements that had puzzled me enormously when I began my study of Spain.[60]

This fortuitous encounter with the Belalcázar-Toledo dispute provided me with the extended trouble case I have used to understand aspects of both Castilian politics and the way Castilians identified themselves as part of a commonwealth. Through a microhistory of this case, I expose significant patterns of relationships and competing understandings of monarchy among various economic, political, and professional groups interacting in the exercise of political authority. Conflicts between groups that often emphasized different interpretive perspectives as a basis for action sustained Castile's increasingly differentiated institutional organization and, therefore, defined the shifting, conflictive understandings of monarchy as a political regime that was far from "absolutist," in the sense of a government capable of or interested in imposing administrative uniformity or obedience on a subject population through a monopoly of coercive force.[61]

Monarchs found it hard to grasp a message, such as Mariana's, about "kingly" government because they were so often surrounded by territorial aristocrats and other courtiers. Attempts by rulers and their close advisers to increase the Crown's autonomy through claims of institutionally unrestrained absolute royal authority did not enhance the capacity for effective exercise of that authority but rather undermined it. Local notables wanted effective royal government as they felt it was needed for the resolution of disputes that otherwise might lead to damaging violence. Also, they considered the monarch necessary for good government, understood as the enhancement of the material and spiritual well-being of the kingdom. This royal charge became increasingly important as late sixteenth-century local notables expected the Crown to take on ever more responsibility, similar to that of municipal councils, for enhancing production and distribution, reforming the Church and religious life, and maintaining the patricians' economic and political roles. Therefore, local notables were reluctant to damage royal authority and generally upheld the symbols and gestures that expressed it, but they would react if they felt the monarch were not providing the desired leadership. Such a reaction could range all the way from a withdrawal of support to open, violent rebellion. These results of arbitrary rule did not represent a breakdown of the political institutions of the social environment but were instead expected aspects of the relationships among these institutions as the actions of individuals and groups were cued by their culturally shaped recognition of patterns in the world around them. Further, many would enhance their patron-client relationships with the often-assertive grandees around the monarch. Thus, the monarch's capacity for effective intervention in the kingdom's political life could be sapped in two ways: the ruler could lose the necessary collaboration of local notables, including many who had become Crown officials, and territorial aristocrats could increase their influence through clientage.

Because rulers did not have the sort of ability to shape events that historians have frequently attributed to them and required the active collaboration of a broad spectrum of the commonwealth's political leadership, the dynamic core of political life was often located in the major municipal corporations. During the long period of the Belalcázar lawsuit, the local notables who governed Castile's municipalities periodically became dissatisfied with royal administration, but they professed their loyalty to the only type of political organization they felt could provide the good government and justice necessary to sustain them by maintaining domestic tranquility and the defense of kingdom and religion in a violent age. Much support for the monarch stemmed from locally prominent notables' "sociological" analysis of the social environment in terms of cleavages. Notables felt that their communities were riven by cliques whose unchecked competition would eventually lead to the introduction of violent conflict into the social environment, where the principles of both royal service and good government demanded peace and harmony.[62] Thus, factionalism was not only a part of the social environment but also a component of the interpretive schemes of the cultural environment that helped Castilians identify significant patterns in the world on which to base judgment and action. Frequent recourse to the monarch to deal with perceived domestic and foreign threats gave the ruler ample opportunities for intervention. Expectations about the significance of proper royal action gave special importance to dynastic changes, royal residency, and regency governments, all of these being issues that had a major impact on the Belalcázar dispute and continued to be foci of Golden Age Castilian history.

Books and Their "Influence"

As well as in conversations and gestures, interpretive schemes are perpetuated and developed in written works, whether people experience these primarily though personal reading or listening. When the "influence" of a work is considered, its role in relation to available interpretive schemes is of central importance. Reading or hearing the work may serve to maintain a particular interpretive scheme as a viable part of the cultural environment in that for the individuals involved, the use of a particular interpretive perspective in the work would perhaps constitute for its audience the experience and previous use that would cue the employment of that scheme for pattern recognition and judgment. Or the work could clarify for an individual a particular scheme or apply it to some unfamiliar situation, thereby altering its meaning for that person. Or the work might so emotionally heighten or enhance the authority of an interpretive scheme as to make it more likely that it would be cued in the future.[63] One possible expression of interpretive schemes involving a client's service to a lord in exchange for protection and rewards was the chivalric literature so popular among Castilian readers that its "influence" on Don Quijote became the subject of one of the greatest literary works in the language.[64] However, I have concentrated on political thought and legal theory, especially because interpretive schemes from these areas were reflected in the written transcriptions of the evidence and judicial process of the Belalcázar-Toledo lawsuit.

Although they would often continue to be stated using exactly the same conceptual terms, particularly those derived from Christian and Romanist political and legal thought, the meanings of interpretive schemes would shift as the geographic scope of the huge Hispanic Monarchy reached almost global proportions, justifying the description of the period covered by this book as the first global age. Even though revenues that came to Madrid as capital of a vast, composite monarchy had allowed the Crown elite concentrated there an important degree of autonomy, especially in international affairs, that autonomy did not translate into a capacity for the effective exercise of royal authority. For example, attempts to "centralize" the control of silver imports in Madrid undermined royal officials in Cádiz and Seville, contributed to fraud, and reduced the Crown's share of American silver production.[65] A lack of confidence in judicial administration and repeated examples of royal intervention undermined investor confidence and increasingly pushed much economic activity and resolution of disputes, among those who recognized each other's creditworthiness on the basis of a common identity, beyond the purview of monarchical institutions. The monarchy extracted resources, money and troops, but without enhancing coercion and control, and its methods directly contributed to the fraud and corruption that actually undid the political, legal, and moral order an effective monarch was supposed to maintain. The increasing worry among Castilian local notables about the lack of correspondence between royal policy and their own aspirations removed the kind of willing financial support that sustained Dutch successes in the seventeenth century and British ones in the eighteenth.[66]

In part, interactions between the Crown and major municipalities had been altered because the latter's patrician leaders had by the mid seventeenth century developed cohesive regional oligarchies that could exercise considerable autonomy from the Court's officials without re-stimulating earlier fears that dangerous, excessive divisions would emerge without the direct intervention in its internal affairs of a capable royal administration. To obtain the cooperation of the patrician oligarchies in the timely collection of revenues and troops, the Crown elite had to provide means of patronage to the municipal councils, which solidified oligarchic control.[67] The Hispanic Monarchy survived, although in a diminished state, the crisis years of the seventeenth century in part because of the emergence of these cohesive municipal oligarchies as a consequence of patrician action. Rather than fatalistically accept the period's difficulties, these men and women, from the perspective of largely familiar interpretive schemes, judged the situation and acted vigorously to maintain their authority and shape the activities of Crown officials. Unfortunately, because we still know so little about the patriciates of Castile's cities and major towns, much about the Hispanic Monarchy's survival and the crisis years themselves remains a puzzle.

In putting together some pieces of that puzzle, I have insisted in this account that historians take seriously the political and moral perspectives expressed by political actors. These were not just interpretive schemes whose expression was manipulated as part of strategization to realize narrowly defined individual, family, or solidarity group interests. Nor were they just a function of some more material determinant of action. Rather these schemes, repeatedly and frequently articulated and reelaborated in works of political thought and legal theory, in public policy discussions, and in the symbols and gestures of ceremonies and daily human interaction, themselves shaped action in ways that helped determine whether and how Castile's monarchs would receive the collaboration of the commonwealth's leaders that the rulers needed for the exercise of their authority.

Thus we have the strange paradox of the theoretically absolute authority of Castile's monarchs. Arbitrary action by a sovereign according to his or her own will rather than the dictates of the law was not a source of greater capacity for political leadership but rather reduced the support for the Crown on which effective royal government was based. Often considered "tyrannical," such rule weakened the sovereign's ties to the lesser nobility and urban notables whose active collaboration was necessary for his or her authority to be respected. A ruler acting arbitrarily in violation of the law did not enhance but actually sapped his or her ability to govern, because without the security that legal guarantees of their persons and property provided, the less influential members of the political kingdom would frequently become the clients of well-placed aristocrats who would then be in a position to shape royal actions. Adherence to the rule of law as the foundation of justice made the monarch respected and more capable of guiding political affairs; "tyranny" led to ineffectual royal government, which increasingly characterized seventeenth-century Habsburg rule.[68]

A grasp of this puzzling perspective refreshes our vision of more recent Spanish history. Because the Castilian commonwealth continued until the Napoleonic period to be defined more by a common adhesion to the values of justice sustained by the exercise of absolute royal authority than by institutional coercive muscle, the nineteenth-century Liberal constitutional movement removed the commonwealth's spine and its citizens' common identity. In this sense, the Liberals were revolutionaries and had to impose their perspective by force. To justify themselves, in terms of developments elsewhere in Europe and to those who claimed the Liberals were imposing foreign doctrines, the constitutionalists sought their origins deep in a Spanish past. By defining a "nation" in terms of the Spanish historical origins of their political vision, these revolutionaries implanted an interpretive scheme, in an invertebrate country without a commonwealth, which could be used by others, for example, Basques or Catalans, to understand their place in the second global age in ways different from the constitutionalist vision.[69] The constitutionalists' need to develop military resources gave political prominence to officers and tied Spain's splendid mineral resources and commercialized agriculture to outside interests, which guaranteed the country's subordinate role in a British-dominated Atlantic world and made Spain the site of tragic conflicts that captured global attention in the twentieth century.

NOTES

CHAPTER 1

1. On the importance of the control of borders to the way in which a "nation" is conceived, see Winichakul 1994. For an innovative look at how a fixation on royal justice tied local communities to the Castilian monarchy, see Izquiero Martín 2001.

2. For example, see petition 33 from 1447, near the beginning of the dispute (in Cortes de Castilla 1866: 540–41), and the extensive discussions of the lawsuit at the Cortes sessions of 1563 and 1567, near its end (in Cortes de Castilla 1862: 20, 106–8, 132, 204–6; Cortes de Castilla 1877: 62, 77–79, 335–36, 462–63, 517, 552).

3. Levenson 1968: I, xxvii–xxxiii. My approach in this book owes a great deal to Joseph R. Levenson's classic trilogy, especially the second volume, "The Problem of Monarchical Decay."

4. The metanarrative of "early modern state development" does not serve as a useful interpretive abstraction. Social scientists often present such a "state" as a uni-fied entity, reified into a historical actor, of sufficient *autonomy* and *capacity* to shape "society" through coercive means (Barkey and Parikh 1991). In doing so, they com-mit the "fallacy of misplaced concreteness" (Whitehead 1929). Historical change takes place through an almost stochastic process in which future behavior is not fully determined by the past and present although future possibilities are more or less probable. So many prior and contemporary occurrences influence any discrete action that, although it is shaped by these contingent factors, it is not determined by them. Therefore, the significance of an action/event can be understood only in rela-tionship to other occurrences linked to it, rather than by reference to some self-perpetuating system, such as the "state," that determines action and its consequences.

5. Obviously, this translation choice neglects the Latin word *auctoritas*, which is the etymological root of the English word "authority." Fortunately, none of the char-acters in my microhistory made use of a distinction between *auctoritas* and *potentatus*, *posse*, or *potere* (or their Castilian equivalents, *autoridad* and *poder*) in his or her charac-terization of royal action. Much of the sense of Castilians' use, when talking about political office, of *poder* or *poderío* at the beginning of the first global age appears to have become attached in our time to the English word "authority." Castilians spoke of *poderío real absoluto* as an augmentation of a monarch's ability to act beyond what was permitted to other magistrates or citizens of the commonwealth.

6. Even before Max Weber's time, Burckhardt (1860) established as the Renais-sance's defining figure the despot who created a state as a work of art through which he shaped the lives of those in the territory he ruled.

7. See Frank 1993, 1998: chap. 1; Frank and Gills 1993; Lewis and Wigen 1997: chap. 3.

8. I conceive of Castile and the Hispanic Monarchy of the first global age as a complex array of intricate, overlapping, interlocal, interactive economic, political, and information networks. The loci connected by these networks were the municipalities whose jurisdictions completely covered many of the larger political regions, and many of the networks involved locations well beyond the territorial boundaries of any part of the Monarchy. These networks represent a heuristic device rather than an expression of reality as understood by contemporaries. The "network" is not an entity like the "state" that might be taken as reality and reified into a historical actor. It is rather a metaphor to describe a type of relationship. Nor is the use of the term "interactive network" anachronistic as would be the attribution to people in the 1400–1650 period of the use of the concept "state" in its modern sense. Although it might be desirable to employ contemporary words in this description, that is not possible because Castilians of the time were insufficiently aware of the importance of such *connections*. Geertz (1983b) argues that all knowledge is ultimately *local* for individuals, and even the economic and political leaders of municipalities for which connections with other localities were vital often showed a limited understanding of these networks.

9. For a brief encyclopedia article on Mariana, see Owens 1999c.

10. Although seignioral institutions retained their importance throughout the Golden Age, there was no simple relationship between elite status and absolutist regimes such as that defended in several prominent studies (Anderson 1974; Lublinskaya 1968 [1965]; Porchnev 1963 [1948]). Instead, such monarchies operated as sites of shifting conflicts and accommodations among those whose wealth, political roles, and leadership of solidarity groups allowed them to act prominently within the commonwealth.

11. I base my approach to political language in part on Quentin Skinner's recommendation that it be analyzed as "speech acts"; see Skinner 1969, 1970, 1971, 1972a, 1972b, 1974, 1975. Also see Pocock 1987; Skinner 1988. On Skinner's work, see Tully 1983.

In order to assess the meaning of such "speech acts," I try to develop a "connected history," in the way in which that concept has been defined by Sanjay Subrahmanyam (1997). In an effort to avoid Whitehead's "fallacy of misplaced concreteness" (1929) in a "historical" explanation, Joseph Levenson (1968) had earlier produced a particularly fine example of how real connections shaped the meaning of ideas that are asserted. In a number of places he makes points such as the following:

> An idea, then, is a denial of alternatives and an answer to a question. What a man really means cannot be gathered solely from what he asserts; when he asks and what other men assert invest his ideas with meaning. In no idea does meaning simply inhere, governed only by its degree of correspondence with some unchanging objective reality, without regard to the problems of its thinker. . . . Vocabulary and syntax . . . may remain the same, late and soon, but the statement changes in meaning as its world changes. (Introduction to vol. 1, xxviii–xxix, with the quotations reversed in order.)

I make use of Skinner's approach within this Levensonian context, and I have written a microhistory of the type presented here because it is an effective way to deal with the subject. Although I have frequently been tempted to point out similarities between what happened in Castile and in other monarchies during the first global age, especially those of England and France, I have resisted doing so because to raise such comparisons above a superficial level, I would have to place the non-Castilian cases within the same sort of connected history. In such a context, apparent similarities would likely turn out to be substantial differences.

12. This extended trouble case was often referred to as the Belalcázar lawsuit because during its course, the officials of the city of Toledo refused to recognize the existence of the viscounty of Puebla de Alcocer, which was an entity created by the count of Belalcázar after the property in question was taken from Toledo. The city, however, had no name for the whole territory that was the subject of litigation. I adopted Toledo's name for the lawsuit because the bulk of the surviving trial documents are those from Toledo's municipal archive.

13. I take the "extended case" method from the Manchester school of social anthropology (see Gluckman 1965) and the "trouble case" method from legal anthropology (Llewellyn and Hoebel 1941; Pospíšil 1971).

14. On the importance of legal institutions and norms, see Geertz 1983a; Kagan 1981; Roberts 1979: chap. 10; E. P. Thompson, 1975: 258–69.

15. The dispute is a familiar one to historians of the fifteenth century. See Benito Ruano 1961: 141–44; Cabrera Muñoz 1977; Haliczer 1977; 1981: 86–88 and 217; Kagan 1981: xx, 37, 42–43, 45, 119–20; Molénat 1972: 330; Molénat 1997.

16. For a recent example of a microhistory exposing the Inquisition procedures that shaped the documentary record, see Nalle 2001.

17. In a valuable review article (1989), Thomas Kuehn asserts that "the main shortcoming of the treatment of source texts in microhistories" is "a lack of appreciation of the formative role of legal rules and procedures on those texts and on the acts they purport to disclose" (516).

18. Research on the case focused on the Osuna Collection of the Archivo Histórico Nacional (AHN) and of the Belalcázar Collection (Col. Bel.) of the Archivo Histórico Municipal de Toledo (AHMT), supplemented by additional work in Córdoba, Granada, Simancas, in the collections of the Hispanic Society of America, and in the Lea Collection of the University of Pennsylvania. I have also relied on a number of published documentary collections relating to royal, seignorial, and municipal administration and on the large body of work on Castilian administration and political history and thought published during the past quarter century.

19. See Pennington 1993: esp. chap. 4. On the generalization of legal concepts throughout Latin Christian Europe, see Bellomo 1989.

20. In my discussion of the "environments of action," I utilize, although with substantial modification, the unified social theory of Jeffrey Alexander (1988). Alexander tries to explain human action, including that purposeful agency that sometimes produces innovation, by placing it within what he calls, metaphorically, its social, cultural, and personality "environments." Unfortunately, his discussion of the personality environment is almost completely useless, based as it is on a heavily Freudian psychoanalytical approach, by now discredited by biological, psychological, and medical research. For a discussion of the weaknesses of psychoanalytic theory, see Torrey 1992.

21. The phrase "network of mutual expectations" is from Bruner 1996: 182. Alexander (1988) uses the phrase "sociological citizenship" to characterize individuals who act similarly to typify the components of their experiences on the assumption that every new impression of the world fits within their understanding of it.

22. The concept of mental models or habits-of-mind is taken from Gorman 1992 and Margolis 1987, 1993. I founded my application of their approaches on the results of experimental work on pattern recognition in cognitive psychology. However, even at the relatively simple level of visual perception, there is little agreement on the exact nature of the interpretive schemes employed in pattern recognition and little data on the impact of learning and memory. See Eysenck and Keane 1990: chap. 2; Solso 1998: chap. 4. My view of the application of these interpretive schemes has been strongly influenced by Levenson 1968; Sahlins 1985, and to some extent by Churchland 1986; Churchland and Sejnowski 1992.

23. I have completed the research for this volume and an initial draft.

24. I refer explicitly to E. P. Thompson's research focus on the "moral economy," but I will show that the interactions between the small, elite minority and the large, often impoverished majority at the core of the global Hispanic Catholic Monarchy were substantially different from those in eighteenth-century England. I currently have in progress research on clandestine economic activity and organized crime and on the development of sacred sites and the devotional practices associated with them.

25. The Castilian king Peter I (reigned 1350–1369) was murdered by his bastard half-brother, Henry of Trastámara, who became king Henry II (reigned 1369–1379) and initiated the rule of the Trastámara dynasty in Castille. Isabella was the successor of this line. When the ruler of the crown of Aragón, king Martin I, died in 1410 without a direct successor, Ferdinand of Antequera (d. 1416), the uncle of the Castilian king John II (reigned 1406–1454), asserted his candidacy, and he was elected as Aragonese ruler by the Compromise of Caspe in 1412. With this election, a branch of the Trastámara dynasty ruled the multiple realms of the Crown of Aragón. Therefore, Ferdinand of Aragón and Isabella of Castile were members of the Trastámara family and cousins.

CHAPTER 2

1. Barrientos 1946: 14.

2. Major fifteenth-century Castilian political thinkers, many of them churchmen who were prominent in Court circles, disseminated a view of tyranny founded on the ideas of Aristotle. For example, in his *De optima politia* (*Of the Ideal Government*) of about 1436, Alfonso de Madrigal, often called "El Tostado," noted that monarchy becomes tyrannical when a governor does not follow just laws, when he fails to pursue the public utility, or when he rules contrary to his subjects' will. See Madrigal 2003: par. 119.

3. For the general Cortes petition, see Cortes de Castilla 1866: 540–41 (petition #33). Normally, municipalities presented petitions about their particular concerns to the monarch outside of the Cortes' general session, but the Puebla de Alcocer grant so alarmed leaders of other cities and major towns that they included the matter in their general petition. Because he did not see how this issue related in the delegates' minds to their overall concern with the reduction of the municipalities' ability to be

of service to the monarch, Olivera Serrano (1986: 33 and note 12) found it strange that the issue was added to the register of the meeting's general petitions. Apparently, Toledo's pressure on the Crown to do something about the loss of Puebla de Alcocer was constant during the frequent Cortes meetings of the period. Although now lost, a sixteenth-century archival survey included a record of a petition presented to John II in Madrigal on 27 November 1448, when the Cortes was in session there (Col. Bel.: Leg. 1, f. 744). When a folio number is given without indication of which side is cited, it is the *recto* (front, upright, right-hand) side. When the letter "v" is added to the number, it is the *verso* (reverse, left-hand) side that is cited.

4. It is important to recognize that this account is based heavily on documents preserved precisely because of their relationship to the interests of the parties in the so-called Belalcázar case and similar disputes. Therefore, there is a potential for distortion insufficiently recognized by others using some of these documents (e.g., Cabrera Muñoz 1977).

5. Netanyahu (2001) provides an account of these attacks and the sources on which our knowledge of them is based. His discussion of the reign of John II in bk. 2 is especially detailed.

6. They were the sons of his dead uncle, Fernando de Antequera, who was the first Trastámara ruler of the Crown of Aragón.

7. This act was the origin of Córdoba's dispute with Gutierre de Sotomayor and his heirs. Gahete was granted on 6 November 1444 (confirmed 30 August 1445) while Hinojosa was given by a separate grant on the same day. The description of these grants may be found in Osuna: Leg. 323, 2/8. See Cabrera Muñoz 1977: 120–22, 388–89, doc. 9 (grant of Gahete).

8. Osuna: Carpeta (portfolio) 11–14: ff. 39–43v. The 1445 grant, now lost, was drafted by John II's secretary, Dr. Fernando Díaz de Toledo, and cited verbatim in the confirmation of 30 May 1447 (for the original, see Osuna: Carpeta 11–11).

9. AHMT: Caj. 12, Leg. 4, #12; Pedraza Ruiz 1985: 143. Toledo's fourteenth-century difficulties with Puebla de Alcocer are summarized by Cabrera Muñoz 1977: 40–51. Henry II's general restoration of Toledo's jurisdiction is in AHMT: Caj. 7, Leg. 2, #2; Pedraza Ruiz 1985: 92.

10. Torrijos, 10 January 1441, for which see Benito Ruano 1961: 167–68 (*sic* 2 January).

11. Col. Bel.: Leg. 4, ff. 37v–39; Osuna: Carpeta 55–18.

12. See Col. Bel.: Leg. 39, #22 for business conducted with Puebla de Alcocer in 1444. Some of the witnesses giving evidence during testimony taken in 1496 gave the impression that Gutierre's forces had taken the town, abandoned it, and then returned again to take the entire viscounty (see Col. Bel.: Leg. 5, ff. 224–224v, 274v–275, and 294–294v). This testimony indicates that there was one invasion of the territory in 1441–1442 and a second in 1445–1446.

13. Col. Bel.: Leg. 1, ff. 1077–1079.

14. Col. Bel.: Leg. 5, f. 343v.

15. Round 1986: 13, 16, 20, 198–200.

16. Col. Bel.: Leg. 39, #24.

17. Cabrera Muñoz 1977: 145. Much of the castle's impressive structure is still intact. See Cooper 1991: I.1, 236, 239, 245–46; III, 1323–1326; Molénat 1997: 192. For the royal order, see Osuna: Carpeta 55–20.

18. Osuna: Carpeta 11–11. Secretary: Dr. Fernando Díaz de Toledo.

19. For Piedrahita's commission, see Col. Bel.: Leg. 28, #3, ff. 10–11; original document prepared by Dr. Fernando Díaz de Toledo. On the confirmation of the earlier survey, see Cabrera Muñoz 1974: 27, note 40.

20. Aznar Vallejo, ed., 1990. This edition contains the complete text of the investigator's report.

21. Osuna: Leg. 324, 1/2 and 1/3; Cabrera Muñoz 1977: 132–34 and 149. See in Molénat (1977: 210–12 and 666) the excellent, detailed analysis of Piedrahita's Puebla de Alcocer survey and the map of the territory delineated by Piedrahita after subsequently disputed areas were returned to their rightful lords.

22. Col. Bel.: Leg. 1, ff. 1046–1131; Leg. 28, #3, ff. 11–12; Leg. 43, #13, ff. 26v–29v.

23. Col. Bel.: Leg. 28, #3, f. 18; Martínez et al. 1958: 453.

24. Osuna: Leg. 394, 2 and 7/9; AMTal: XI, Leg. 1, 6a; Col. Bel.: Leg. 5, ff. 272 and 291; Gómez-Menor 1965: 41; Suárez Fernández 1964: 5.

25. Col. Bel.: Leg. 28, #3, ff. 13–19v.

26. Osuna: Leg. 324, 8/1, doc. d; Cabrera Muñoz 1977: 152–53; Col. Bel.: Leg. 5, f. 347. In an age when the protection of one's personal and family interests might demand the aid of a powerful patron who might then enter into leagues with other magnates whose clients could include those with whom one's municipality had grievances, urban government was easily and frequently compromised. For example, in February 1448, a confederation of Alvaro de Luna's supporters was formed, including the duke of Medina Sidonia, the adelantado mayor of Andalucía, and the alcalde mayor of Seville. Among the friends to whom the duke extended the confederation's protection was Gutierre de Sotomayor, while among those of both the adelantado and the alcalde mayor was Juan de Silva, an important member of a major Toledan patrician lineage (Pastor Bodmer 1992: II, 216–18).

27. The account that follows of the aristocratic political conflicts of John II's reign owes much to the seminal works of Luis Suárez Fernández, esp. 1959, 1964, 1972. Porras Arboledas (1995) provides a useful summary of the published chronicle accounts. Of the chronicle accounts, I have used Barrientos 1946; Carrillo de Huete 1946; Crónica de Juan II 1953, 1982; Crónica de Luna 1946; Díez de Games 1940; Hinojosa 1893; Pérez de Guzmán (1953). Of works in English, see esp. Hillgarth 1976–1978: II, 300–317; A. MacKay 1977: 135–40; Nader 1979: pt. 1; O'Callaghan 1975: 541–72; W. Phillips 1978: 33–43; Round 1986. On the impressive collection of domains, offices, and other sources of wealth amassed by Alvaro de Luna, see Calderón Ortega 1998.

28. Hinojosa 1893: 121.

29. For clear, detailed accounts and interpretations of Luna's fall, see Calderón Ortega 1998: pt. 1, chaps. 5 and 6; Pastor Bodmer 1992: I, chaps. 8 and 9; Round 1986.

30. On the importance of the order of Alcántara as a financial and military base, see M. F. Ladero Quesada 1982. The order's archive has disappeared.

31. On Juan de Sotomayor, see Barrientos 1946: lxiv–lxv, 51, 73, 79, 83–84, 88, 133–37; Carrillo de Huete 1946: 8, 12, 36, 40, 42, 46–48, 50, 52, 132–35, 146; Crónica de Juan II 1953: 370, 434, 440, 443, 446, 454, 456, 464, 466, 478, 487–89, 491–92, 505–11; Crónica de Juan II 1982: 266–67; Crónica de Luna 1946: 54, 64, 92.

32. On Gutierre de Sotomayor's rise, see Barrientos 1946: 134–37, 140–41, 174–76, 194–96, 205; Cabrera Muñoz 1977: 80–110; Carrillo de Huete 1946: 131–33, 135, 138–41, 197–99, 218–19, 234, 259, 287, 352–54, 392, 411–12, 414, 417–18, 462–65, 468; Crónica de Juan II 1953: II, 505–11, 519–20, 526, 554, 586, 602, 608–9, 627–30, 633, 637–38; Crónica de Luna 1946: 153–54, 168, 450–51; Hinojosa 1893: 123, 125, 128, 132–33; Porras Arboledas 1995: 238–41, 245, 247–48, 253; Suárez Fernández 1964: 47, 100, 109–10, 125–26, 133–35, 147, 164, 168–70.

33. Carrillo de Huete 1946: 519. On 28 August 1449, John II granted to Gutierre Córdoba's town of Bélmez, along with Milagro in the jurisdiction of Toledo. Although this was followed by puzzling negotiations, the master of Alcántara finally got Bélmez on 8 March 1450, the same day on which his seizure of a large piece of Fuenteovejuna's territory was confirmed (Cabrera Muñoz 1974: 29 and note 49).

Gutierre may have been absent from Court because he was overwhelmed by problems elsewhere. For example, at the beginning of 1453, he faced first a rebellion in Fuenteovejuna and then a full-scale invasion by a Cordoban force that occupied not only that town, which had requested help, but also Gahete, Hinojosa, and Bélmez. He had not lost the king's support, however, because on 18 September 1453, John II ordered Córdoba's *corregidor* (royal high commissioner) to restore to Gutierre de Sotomayor all he had lost in the invasion (Cabrera Muñoz 1974: 36).

34. Cabrera Muñoz 1977: 163; for the marriage agreement, see Osuna: Leg. 324, 8/17. For an example of an aristocratic confederation agreement listing the master of Alcántara, see that of 21 May 1452 between the counts of Benavente and Santa Marta (Pastor Bodmer 1992: II, 333–34).

35. Bonachía Hernando 1988, 1990; Estepa Díez 1990; Martínez Moro 1985. On the relative scholarly neglect of municipalities within noble lordships, see García Hernán 1996.

36. The major defenses of this view of the significance of the period for the shaping of the Castilian social environment are Mitre Fernández 1968; Moxó 1969, 1970–1971. On the development of the territorial aristocracy in particular regions, see Quintanilla Raso 1979, 1982a, 1982b. For overviews of recent work, see Quintanilla Raso 1984, 1990a. A useful corrective stressing the degree of elite continuity throughout the fourteenth century is Biñayán Carmona 1986.

37. On the nature of these Trastámara lordships, see Beceiro Pita 1988; Grassotti 1985. Of major significance for this book is Cabrera Muñoz 1977. On the seignorial income of the Zúñigas, another family of the territorial aristocracy important for this book, see Martínez Moro 1977. On ecclesiastical lordships, see López García 1990; Pérez-Embid Wamba 1982; Suárez Alvarez 1982. On municipal lordships, see Bonachía Hernando 1988, 1990; Estepa Díez 1990; Martínez Moro 1985. Of course, the monarchs' challenge was to insert these seignorial jurisdictions into the royal judicial administration, a fundamental process in the development of the Castilian monarchy that began at least as early as the 1348 *Ordenamiento de Alcalá* (law code) of Alfonso XI. See Torres Sanz 1982: 16 and note 18.

38. For an indication of the great variety of sources of magnate wealth, see Franco Silva 1996. Also see Calderón Ortega 1998: pt. 4; Franco Silva 1994: 107–14; M. A. Ladero Quesada 1973; Mitre Fernández 1968; Moxó 1958, 1963, 1969; Quintanilla Raso 1982c; Villalobos y Martínez-Pontremuli 1975.

The classic work on entails is Clavero 1989 (1974). Also see Bermejo Cabrero 1985; Molénat 1986; 1997: pt. 3, chap. 3. Henry II initiated an important pattern by granting certain families the right to consolidate their seignioral holdings into these entailed estates. However, on frequency of internal discord in noble families, see Montero Tejada 1996: 120–22.

39. Bermejo Cabrero 1975a; Moxó 1973.

40. On the fundamental importance of the municipality within Castile's monarchy, see Nader 1996.

There were three types of community: city, town (*villa*), and unincorporated community (*lugar*). In contrast to the way we might use the terms now, the distinction among these types was legal rather than based on size, diversity of population and economic activity, or other characteristics. Indeed, on the basis of size and economic activity, all of the lugares and many of the villas would be labeled "villages" I reserve the term "village" as a translation of lugar.

41. M. F. Ladero Quesada 1996; Marcos Martín 1999; Nader 1990. On Toledo's ordinances, see Martín Gamero, ed., 1858. See also Corral García 1988; González Arce 2000; Hijano Pérez 1992; M. A. Ladero Quesada 1998; M. A. Ladero Quesada and Galán Parra 1982; Merchán Fernández 1988. For a related perspective on the issue of autonomy in the conduct of municipal business, see Marcos Martín 1991. Much recent research has made it clear that at least from the early fourteenth century, even the largest Castilian municipalities were neither economically nor politically autonomous. See Coria Colino 1995; M. A. Ladero Quesada 1993; Menjot 2002; Ruiz 1994.

42. González Alonso 1988; Valdeón Baruque 1975. On the development of these patrician municipal regimes, see Cerdá Ruiz-Funes 1970; A. MacKay 1986; Molénat 1991a; Monsalvo Antón 1990; Moxó 1981; Tomás y Valiente 1970, 1975; Val Valdivieso 1994; Valdeón Baruque 1990. A number of useful works on particular cities have appeared. For bibliographies, see M. F. Ladero Quesada 1996; Marcos Martín 1999; Passola i Tejedor 1997. On the regidores' broad authority, see M. F. Ladero Quesada 1996: 56–58. On the purposes of patrician political activity, see the astute comments of Menjot 1988: esp. 123–24.

On municipal insurrectionary currents, see Monsalvo Antón 1985: chap. 11; Sánchez León 1998: chap. 3. Commoners frequently claimed rights to a formal municipal political role, and sometimes officials were present at council meetings to defend citizen interests. In Murcia and Toledo, these officials, who represented their parishes, were called *jurados*, but these positions also often came to be controlled by particular families who increasingly merged with the patricians (see Cerdá Ruiz-Funes 1970).

43. Bonachía Hernando 1978; Casado Alonso 1988; González García 1973, 1982; M. A. Ladero Quesada 1988b; M. F. Ladero Quesada 1991; López Benito 1983; Rucquoi 1987; Ruiz 1994. There are other cities and major towns whose documentary record suggests the polarization of elite politics around two hostile lineages, but sources on such binary conflict between lineage groups reflect an interpretive scheme of contemporaries' cultural environment much more than they reflect the ways political conflicts really developed.

44. Collantes de Terán 1977; Martínez Carrillo 1980, 1985.

45. See Benito Ruano 1961: 19–23; Carrillo de Huete 1946: chap. 285; Suárez Fernández 1964: 160–65.

46. *Crónica de Juan II* 1953: 456. For a critique of the clientage model based on the French warrior noble's sense of political autonomy, see Neuschel 1989.

47. I derive this technique from the general preface of Levenson 1968: xi.

48. Carretero Zamora 1988; González Alonso 1988; Olivera Serrano 1986, 1987, 1988; Valdeón Baruque 1988. On the earlier use of the institution for counsel, consent, and support, see O'Callaghan 1988, 1989.

On the way in which the Cortes was brought under greater Crown supervision for tax approval and collection, see Dios 1988a. M. A. Ladero Quesada (1973) argued on the basis of his examination of Crown documents that royal revenue collection was relatively free of municipal intervention. However, Menjot (1978, 1979) has shown that these sources are deceptive because urban councils were significantly involved, and chronicle accounts of Cortes approval of the all-important servicios suggest that the dynamics of that part of the process have not been well understood either. Also see M. A. Ladero Quesada 1976, 1988a; Piqueras García 1988; Veas Arteseros 1991.

49. As was the case with the Cortes of Valladolid of 1447 (see Pastor Bodmer 1992: I, 104–5). Nor did the capacity of Cortes procuradores to offer vigorous opposition disappear after the fifteenth century (see, e.g., I. A. A. Thompson 1997a).

50. Garcia-Gallo 1967: II, 889 (my translation).

51. Cortes de Castilla 1866: 394–01; NR bk. 5, title 10, laws 3 and 5; García-Gallo 1967: II, 888–91. The delegates may not have gotten the binding assurances that they and their political descendants felt they had: see the comments of González Alonso 1988: 245–46.

52. Nieto Soria (1988, 1998) has argued that theories of absolute royal authority came from the monarchs and their immediate circle. There certainly were letrados, such as Diego Enríquez del Castillo, who came to work at Court in a principled effort to enhance royal authority. However, a much broader spectrum of the commonwealth's leadership supported the transition Nieto Soria describes from personalist conceptions of a monarch with individual relationships with his subjects to visions of royal authority in the context of "transpersonal" concepts such as the Crown and the "common good." On Enríquez del Castillo, see Sánchez Martín 1994: 34–42. See the suggestive comments of Mitre Fernández 1980 about the relationship of greater royal intervention in municipal affairs and the development of Crown administration.

53. Beceiro Pita 1988: 323. King Alfonso X's thirteenth-century law code, the *Siete Partidas,* often served as a source of wisdom for Castilian political writers, especially after its place among the kingdom's legal sources was defined in royal ordinances issued at the Cortes of Alcalá in 1348. In this way, it was used to clarify interpretive schemes and their application in the political turmoil of the age and to provide language in which perspectives could be articulated. On the distinction between a legitimate monarch and a tyrant, see *Partida* 2, title 1, law 10. On the fourteenth century, see Gimeno Casalduero 1972.

54. For lists and quotations from the major legal and theoretical texts clarifying this perspective, although often with little attention to the specific context that occasioned them, see Bermejo Cabrero 1975b; Nieto Soria 1988; Torres Sanz 1985.

55. Cortes de Castilla 1866: 483–91. As an interpretive gloss on earlier Castilian laws suggesting that subjects were traitors if they failed to prevent the king from damaging his "soul, honor, and the public good of his Kingdoms" (*Partida* 2, title 15, law 5), the document is complex and subject to multiple understandings, then and now.

See Nieto Soria 1998. Despite its subordinate position in Castilian law, the *Siete Partidas* retained, some two centuries after its creation, its status as a major source of wisdom, and its role throughout the Habsburg era as a source of commonplaces continued to cement in political thought understandings of monarchy and rulers' responsibilities in relation to the commonwealth.

56. Round 1986: 201–4 and 224–26.

57. Calderón Ortega 1998.

58. In his influential interpretive study of the rapacious fifteenth-century Castilian aristocracy, Suárez Fernández (1959) argued that the only viable solution was the creation of the institution of the *privado* (royal favorite). Because the *privanza* (position of favorite) was such a crucial factor in establishing effective royal government, John II and his son Henry IV were not the failures so often portrayed in histories of the century, and their respective favorites, Alvaro de Luna and Juan Pacheco, were progressive Spanish leaders. However, Suárez Fernández never really explains why, in achieving an adequate military position, it would not have been effective for the monarch himself to play this leadership role.

59. *Crónica de Juan II* 1953: 586–87; Mena 1984: 127–28 (verses CLV and CLVI); Pérez de Guzmán 1953: 718. I am grateful to Jeremy Lawrance of the University of Manchester for providing this example (8 September 1995 message to Espora-L, the History of the Iberian Peninsula Internet discussion list). On the special bases of royal authority, see Nieto Soria 1993; Ruiz 1984, 1985, 1988.

60. From Alvar García de Santa María, "Crónica de Juan II de Castilla," as quoted in Porras Arboledas 1995: 16 (my translation).

61. On the growing importance of legal studies in the fifteenth-century administrative cultural environment, see Beceiro Pita 1999.

62. On support for the audiencia, see Dios 1988b: 303–04. On royal officials, see García Marín 1987; Nieto Soria 1988: 160; Sánchez-Arcilla Bernal 1980: 46, note 115; Torres Sanz 1982: 33–34 and note 20. Regidores with legal training played a prominent role in John II's government. A major example is Toledan regidor Dr. Fernando Díaz de Toledo. Although he had been associated with the inner circle of the secret Royal Council since 1429, after he had undertaken a major reform of the audiencia, he apparently cooperated not so much as a client of Alvaro de Luna but more in hope of developing a working government in which the king's subjects would have sufficient confidence to offer their necessary collaboration (see Porras Arboledas 1995: 21; Round 1986: 13, 16, 20, 198–200). On a Murcian regidor, Alfonso Fernández de Cascales, with a similar role at Court, see Torres Fontes 1962; Menjot 1988: 126. Although better known for his prominent role in the reign of the Catholic Monarchs, Dr. Alonso Díaz de Montalvo, who was posted to Murcia as corregidor in 1444 during a particularly difficult period (Torres Fontes 1964–1965), was also part of this group.

63. Dios 1988b; González Alonso 1988. For lists of royal edicts denying validity to actions contrary to law, see Suárez Fernández 1964: 13, note 47; Round 1986: 16–17 and note 21. On Luna's fall and execution, see Calderón Ortega 1998: 90–102; Pastor Bodmer 1992: I, chaps. 8 and 9; Round 1986.

64. On a legal tactic that could be used to frustrate and delay a royal initiative considered improper by a corporate group, see González Alonso 1980. For *Partida* II, title 13, law 25, as quoted at Olmedo, see Cortes de Castilla 1866: 458–60. On the

1445 Cortes, at which Toledo's representatives were Juan de Silva and Dr. Fernando Díaz de Toledo, see Olivera Serrano 1986: 17–24; Olivera Serrano 1988.

65. I am not aware of a comparative study of fifteenth-century rebellions. Although their works are not particularly useful on Iberian polities, Bercé (1987) and Zagorin (1982) have attempted such a comparison for sixteenth- and seventeenth-century Europe. For attacks on corrupt officials believed to have deceived a just monarch, see Bercé 1987: 28–33.

66. For examples of fifteenth-century popular responses to the norms of just rule, see Barros 1990; Cabrera Muñoz and Moros Guerrero 1991.

67. For much of my treatment of rebellion, I am indebted to James 1970. In Toledo and some other Castilian cities, the prominence of conversos in positions of municipal leadership could become an excuse for deadly factional conflict. See Netanyahu 2001: 296–449, 768–813; Roth 1995.

68. At the same time that Gutierre de Sotomayor was receiving Puebla de Alcocer, John II attempted to buy Ayala's loyalty with a grant of other towns within Toledo's jurisdiction (Gómez-Menor 1965: 23, note 33; Molénat 1988; Molénat 1997: 399–404).

69. Cortes de Castilla 1866: 496–503.

70. On the revolt and the pardon of 21 March 1451, see Benito Ruano 1961: chap. 2 and 185–220; Calderón Ortega 1998: 79–84; Monsalvo Antón 1985: chap. 11; Netanyahu 2001: 662–80; Round 1966; Suárez Fernández 1964: 188–202; AHMT: Caj. 5, Leg. 6, #1; Col. Bel.: Leg. 39, #28; Osuna: Carpeta 11–14, ff. 35v–37v. Although the specific application of this pardon to the events of 1441 was not clear, at the Cortes of Valladolid in 1442, the monarch had already granted amnesty and restoration of property to all participants in the recent disturbances.

71. For John II's explanation, see Pastor Bodmer 1992: II, 348–50. In reporting to the king the decision of the twelve jurists who examined the case, Dr. Fernando Díaz de Toledo specifically accused Luna of tyrannical behavior: *ha tiranizado* (Crónica de Juan II 1953: 682).

72. W. Phillips 1978: 64–65. On Henry IV's reforms, see Viña Brito 1990: esp. 280.

73. AHMT: Caj. 7: Leg. 1, #1; Leg. 2, #6. Pérez-Bustamante 1986: xiv.

74. Col. Bel.: Leg. 40, ff. 3–14v; Osuna: Carpeta 11–14, ff. 26–32v.

75. Osuna: Leg. 324, 8/1, docs. b and h; AMC: sec. 2a, ser. 30, Caja (box) 71, doc. 38; AGS: Registro de Sello, March 1518; Cabrera Muñoz 1977: 182, 201, 207 and note 118. Because Cabrera Muñoz is more familiar with the surviving sources on the Córdoba-Belalcázar disputes, I follow his dating, taken from the copy of the *sobrecarta* (second decree, which repeated the earlier order) in the Registro de Sello, even though the version of the order in the Archivo Municipal de Córdoba, which appears to be the original of the Council of Castile's sobrecarta of 1518 (there were also several copies), gives the date of the revocation as 11 May 1465.

For the conflicting accounts of Alonso de Sotomayor's murder, see Cabrera Muñoz 1977: 182; Crónica Castellana 1991: II, pt. 1, chap. 58, p. 139. Although it has often been claimed that Gutierre's son Alonso or Alfonso de Sotomayor received from Henry IV the title of count of Belalcázar, the elevation of Gahete to the jurisdictional seat of a county and its renaming as Belalcázar did not occur until the

Sotomayor jurisdictions were under the administration of Alonso's widow, Elvira de Zúñiga [Stúñiga] (see Cabrera Muñoz 1977: 207–9).

76. Col. Bel.: Leg. 40, f. 12; AGS: Diversos de Castilla, Leg. 41, f. 19, #179; AMC: sec. 2a, ser. 30, Caja 71, #38; Osuna: Carpeta 11–14, ff. 32v–33; Leg. 324, 8/1, doc. b.; Benito Ruano 1961: 89–90 and docs. 35 and 36; Cabrera Muñoz 1977: 206–7; Enríquez del Castillo 1994: chap. 75; Pedraza Ruiz 1985: 10–11; Torres Fontes 1985: 106–08, 148–49. The fifteenth-century chronicler Palencia (1973–1975: I, 461) stated that Toledo's condition for joining Alfonso's cause was that Puebla de Alcocer and Herrera be returned and the heirs of Gutierre de Sotomayor be satisfied in some way not prejudicial to Toledo. See the useful table of Henry's grants in W. Phillips 1978: 130. Alfonso's grants are listed in detail by Torres Fontes 1985: 100–167.

77. Col. Bel.: Leg. 19, f. 47–47v. Part of the story was confirmed by an Arroba resident; f. 44–44v. On antiseignioral resistance, see Esteban Recio 1985: 71–78; Val Valdivieso 1974. On Herrera castle, see Cooper 1991: I.1, 237; III, 1327.

78. The quotation is from Cortes de Castilla 1866: 768. On the importance of this Cortes, see Nieto Soria 1998: 188–91 and 207–8; Olivera Serrano 1986: chap. 13. On the audiencia and Royal Council reforms, see Cortes de Castilla 1866: 768–69; Dios 1982: 136–39; Dios, ed., 1986: doc. 11. On factionalism, see Benito Ruano 1961: 83–102; Morales Muñiz 1988; Val Valdivieso 1975, 1991. The 1468 royal pardon is in Real Academia de la Historia 1835–1913: II, doc. 146.

CHAPTER 3

1. The quotation is from the 1469 "Capítulos de Cervera"; see the text in García-Gallo 1967: II, 683–88. At the Cortes of Aragón in 1481, Ferdinand established a similar place in the various monarchies and domains of the Crown of Aragón by declaring her "co-regent, governor, general administrator, and another us" [*otro nos*, using the royal plural]. See García-Gallo 1967: II, 691–95; Villapalos Salas 1997: 30. On the forceful way Isabella asserted her right to the crown on the death of her brother and the way she subsequently worked out an agreement for just rule with Ferdinand, see Liss 1992: 96–108. For the texts of the initial agreement of 15 January 1475 between Ferdinand and Isabella and Isabella's subsequent (28 April 1475) clarification of Ferdinand's ability to act as monarch on his own if the two of them were in different parts of the realm, see García-Gallo 1967: II, 882–91.

2. Alfonso X 1491: I, f. 1v. On Díaz de Montalvo's earlier career, see Torres Fontes 1964–1965. To complement its reform of judicial administration, the Crown called upon Díaz de Montalvo in 1480 to compile a corpus of royal ordinances, statutes, and customary laws that would serve as a standard by which royal justice could be dispensed. Urban procuradores had been calling for such a compilation at least since the Cortes of Toledo of 1462. Montalvo completed the eight books of these *Ordenanzas* on 11 November 1484, and the new printing press soon made this work widely available, thereby increasing the pressure on judges to follow standard procedures and render decisions based on properly approved law. See Díaz de Montalvo 1484; Tomás y Valiente 1995: 267–68; Van Kleffens 1968: 230. On the growing

importance of letrados' ideas in the formation of ideological positions among the commonwealth's leaders, see García Marín 1998: chap. 4.

3. Whether educated in canon or civil law, letrados had mastered a type of reasoning useful for clarifying and debating opposing viewpoints, and this training recommended them, at least from the twelfth century onward, as judges and advisory officials. Self-interest and exposure to Romanist political theory made letrados active proponents of monarchical authority, and their influence in Crown affairs opened numerous opportunities for them in urban, aristocratic, and ecclesiastical administration.

Despite the importance of these *sabidores del Derecho,* as letrados were often called in thirteenth-century Castilian legal texts, as codifiers, judges, political theorists, prelates, and administrators, and a number of fine studies of law and judicial institutions, there is no systematic work on medieval men of the law as a group in any Iberian polity. On law as a public service profession, see *Siete Partidas, Partida* 3, title 6. Among the most familiar works cited on letrados are García Marín 1987 (1974); Maravall 1953, 1973b; Moxó 1975a, 1975b, 1976. Also see W. Phillips 1986. A useful caution is Garriga 1994: 269–75. On letrados and the judicial environment of the Habsburg era, see Kagan 1974, 1981; Navas 1996; Pelorson 1980. On royal justices, see Roldán Verdejo 1989. For a general overview of the legal profession, see Fernández Serrano 1955.

4. For a comprehensive treatment of royal justice, see Sánchez-Arcilla Bernal 1980.

However, the tightly organized procedures that emerge from royal ordinances and other sources give an illusion of uniformity that was not really present. At any given time, interactive patterns involving any particular municipality fit in different ways within the procedures of any particular institution of judicial administration. Those employing statist approaches to institutions often miss this variety and continuous change because they believe that common procedures demanded by the ordinances and reflected in the official documents represent a "rational discipline" imposed through coercive power. Such a view overrates what coercion can accomplish, misses much of the fluidity and dynamism of human interaction within the context of political institutions, and frequently leads to serious misunderstandings of both the motivations and the consequences of action.

5. The standard work on the Cortes of Ferdinand and Isabella's era is Carretero Zamora 1988. Villapalos Salas (1997) provides a solid survey of the Catholic Monarchs' legal codification and reorganization of judicial institutions. A clear overview of the Catholic Monarchs' institutional reforms is provided by Azcona 1964: chap. 5. On the hermandad, see Beneyto Pérez 1954: 97; Lunenfeld 1970.

6. For the legislation, see Cortes de Castilla 1882: 154–57; NR bk. 5, title 10, law 15 (also law 17 on Henry IV's grants). Moreover, earlier provisions against improper royal grants remained law (see, e.g., NR bk. 7, title 5, law 2). See Cárdenas 1873: II, 184.

Syntheses of research on initiatives relating to ecclesiastical affairs, fiscal administration, and the Granada war can be found in M. A. Ladero Quesada 1989: I; Pérez 1988. For examples of earlier claims of the Toledo meeting's importance, see Danvila Collado 1885: I, 527; Pastor Gómez 1955. On the influence of Henry IV's reforms, see W. Phillips 1978. On the driving initiatives of municipal representatives, see González Alonso 1988.

7. For a concise history of this Council, emphasizing the growth of its technical-administrative character after the reforms of 1385–1387, see Torres Sanz 1982: chap. 7. The central role of the Royal Council in the Trastámara Court is demonstrated by Dios 1982. Also useful on the Royal Council's role in judicial administration is Sánchez-Arcilla Bernal 1980: chap. 5. For the relevant ordinances from John II's reign, see Dios, ed., 1986: docs. 6–8.

8. The 1459 ordinances are Dios, ed., 1986: doc. 9. On the Toledo provisions, see Carretero Zamora 1988: 160–65; Cortes de Castilla 1882: 111–20; Dios, ed., 1986: doc. 12; and Dios 1982: 148–52. Confusion about the Council presidency after the Cortes of 1480 is in part explained by Sánchez-Arcilla Bernal (1980: 653 and notes 380–81).

9. On the pre-Trastámara origins of the audiencia, see Díaz Martín 1997. On its Trastámara beginnings, see Garriga 1994: chaps. 1–2; Sánchez-Arcilla Bernal 1980: 381–504; Torres Sanz 1982: 154–-70. On the Briviesca reforms, see Cortes de Castilla 1863: 381–90. On John II's attempts to divert lawsuits to the audiencia, see Crónica de Juan II 1953: II, 445 and 530–31; Garriga 1994: 102–28. In terms of patrician expectations for these law courts, Torres Sanz (1982: 162, note 166) notes a clear tendency in Cortes sessions from 1371 to 1465 to allow the audiencia an autonomous existence apart from the monarch's person, with a supreme responsibility to defend justice even against the actions of the ruler or the Royal Council.

10. The major work on the Chancillería of Valladolid in this reign is Varona García 1981. The 1480 legislation is in Cortes de Castilla 1882: 121–28. On royal efforts to enhance the prestige of the second Chancillería and on the foundation of regional audiencias in Galicia and Seville to help handle the load of important cases, see Bullón Fernández 1927: 54–55; Coronas González 1981; García Fitz and Kirschberg Schenck 1991; Garriga 1994: 146–49; Sánchez-Arcilla Bernal 1980: 526–29.

11. Col. Bel.: Leg. 39, #34. On the count's presence at the Cortes, see Cabrera Muñoz 1977: 215; Izquierdo Benito 1990: doc. 167, esp. p. 282.

12. Col. Bel.: Leg. 39, #35.

13. Alonso's maternal uncle, *almirante* (admiral; honorary aristocratic Court official) Fadrique Enríquez, was an influential grandee and king Ferdinand's cousin. The count's guardian until his death in June 1491 was his uncle Fadrique de Zúñiga. His father's older brother, the former count Gutierre I, had become a famous Franciscan reformer, friar Juan de La Puebla, who returned from Rome in the mid 1480s to oversee his little nephew's education. In 1489, friar Juan enhanced his reputation for piety when he secured papal authorization to found the strict ascetic community of Los Angeles near Hornachuelos, and it has been claimed that he was Isabella's first choice in 1495 as the new archbishop of Toledo.

14. Cabrera Muñoz 1977: 184–90. Some additional details are from Cooper 1991: I.1, 268; Galíndez de Carvajal 1851a: 457–60; 1851b: 278, note 4. A supportive connection between some of these aristocratic houses and the Catholic Monarchs predated Ortiz's 1480 presentation. As a payoff for early support of Isabella in the civil war after Henry IV's death, Elvira de Zúñiga, as administrator of the estate of her son (a minor) after the murder of Alonso de Sotomayor, obtained in June 1476 a twenty-day fair in August for Belalcázar (formerly Gahete), which greatly enhanced

the town's regional economic importance and the House of Sotomayor's revenues (Cabrera Muñoz 1977: 214 and doc. 37).

15. Among the more useful works on the territorial aristocracy in this period are Atienza Hernández 1987; Nader 1979; Yun Casalilla 1987c.

16. Nieto Soria 1998: 225.

17. See Lunenfeld 1970.

18. Col. Bel.: Leg. 5, ff. 14–15v.; Leg. 30, #8.

19. For a discussion of this type of investigation, see Cabrillana Cieza 1969.

20. Col. Bel.: Leg. 19, ff. 4–6v; Leg. 28, #3, ff. 1v–2.

21. Col. Bel.: Leg. 19, ff. 6v–14v.

22. Col. Bel.: Leg. 5, ff. 9–10; Leg. 39, #36.

23. Although the *dehesa* (pasture) of Cijara lay between Herrera and Helechosa, it is hard to know what Acijara might have meant as a populated place in the fifteenth century. See the interesting discussion of this toponym in Molénat 1997: 222–23.

24. Col. Bel.: Leg. 5, ff. 6–15v.

25. Col. Bel.: Leg. 19, ff. 14v–21v and 92–93.

26. Col. Bel.: Leg. 5, ff. 15v–16 and 18v–26v.

27. Col. Bel.: Leg. 19, ff. 21v–30v.

28. Col. Bel.: Leg. 5, ff. 27–60. All of the witness responses discussed in the following paragraphs are found in Col. Bel.: Legs. 5 and 19.

29. If it is true that Gutierre de Sotomayor was asserting the territory's status as the viscounty of Puebla de Alcocer as early as the late 1440s, this assertion preceded any royal grant of the title.

30. For the relationship, see the genealogical table in Cooper 1991: I.l, 241.

31. Col. Bel.: Leg. 28, #3, f. 1v.

32. Col. Bel.: Leg. 2, ff. 2–46; Leg. 39, #39; Leg. 40, ff. 164–190v. Molénat (1997: 255) includes a good photograph of this bridge on the important *Cañada segoviana*, one of the major routes of transhumance (*trashumancia*) or seasonal migratory herding over which the Mesta moved a huge number of sheep every year (on transhumance, see Phillips and Phillips 1997). The photograph was taken when the waters of the reservoir that now covers the bridge had dropped enough to expose much of it. The medieval bridge can also sometimes be seen when one looks into the water from the modern highway bridge that was built to replace it.

33. See Cooper 1991: I.l, 234–36 and 240–45; III, 1328–1330. The castle was substantially modified in the 1540s.

34. Friar Juan had become count Gutierre I after the death of don Alonso in 1464. Because he was only ten or eleven when his father died, his mother, Elvira de Zúñiga (d. 1483), served as his guardian until the late 1470s.

35. By a Royal Council decree, prompted by a direct royal order from the Catholic Monarchs then besieging Granada, María de Velasco obtained the guardianship of Alonso de Sotomayor in the summer of 1491 after the death, in June 1491, of the boy's great-uncle Fadrique de Zúñiga, archdeacon of Talavera, brother of his grandmother Elvira de Zúñiga (d. 1483). Apparently the other guardians named for him on his mother's death, Friar Juan de la Puebla (d. 1495) and Leonor de Sotomayor, the boy's uncle and aunt (Friar Juan was himself a former count of Belalcázar), were unable or unwilling to assume the responsibility as they had both embraced particularly ascetic forms of monasticism. Friar Juan had played a role

from 1486 to 1489 in the education of his nephew. See Cabrera Muñoz 1977: 183–85 and 216–17; Col. Bel.: Leg. 2, f. 17–17v; Cooper 1991: I.2, 444. On the Velascos, see Sánchez Domingo 1999: 126–29.

36. This is the opinion of Merriman (1962: II, 119).

37. Consuelo Gutiérrez del Arroyo de Vázquez de Parga, long an archivist of the Osuna collection of the AHN, kindly provided me with her personal genealogy of the counts of Belalcázar and dukes of Béjar, for which I express my gratitude. Also see Cabrera Muñoz 1977: 175–94 and 216–17; Cooper 1991: I.1, 241; I.2, 444; Galíndez de Carvajal 1851a: 457–60; 1851b: 278–81, 288–89, 292, 308, 328, 428–29, 441; Redondo 1967: 150–51; Sanceau 1959: ix–x and 43–44.

The details of the conspiracies against John II can be found in Nowell 1952: 449–52; Sanceau 1959: chaps. 9–13. The story about Alvaro de Portugal's abuse of his position as president of the Council of Castile is told in Galíndez de Carvajal 1851b: 257. Another hint of Alvaro's potential influence at the Castilian Court can be found in W. Phillips and C. Phillips 1992: 125.

38. Three surveys provide my general orientation to the period between the deaths of Isabella and Ferdinand (Chaunu 1973: I, chap. 3; Fernández Alvarez 1969; Solano Costa 1981). I also rely heavily on the magisterial study of Pérez (1970), who correctly stresses that the dynastic problems of Castile were fundamental to the difficulties of this era and to the comunero rebellion, and on the relevant chapters of Haliczer 1981.

39. On Isabella's dissatisfaction, see Batista i Roca 1957: 329; Bullón Fernández 1927: 202–3; Díaz-Plaja, ed., 1958: 29–32; Gutiérrez Nieto 1973: 277; Isabella I of Castile 1956: esp. 21–22, 28–29, 41; Isabella I of Castile 1974: 66–67; Merriman 1962: II, 126. Haliczer (1981: chap. 5) documents the development of conflicts in earlier reigns, as well as after Isabella's death, that led to the various demands submitted to Charles V by the rebel leadership in 1520.

40. Mexía 1945: 37. On the Laws of Toro, see García-Gallo 1967: I, 394; II, 220–22; Van Kleffens 1968: 232–35; Villapalos Salas 1997: 92–103.

41. Osuna: Leg. 326, 4.

42. Gan Giménez 1988a: 219–20, 222, 223–24, 228–30, 239, 240–41, 253–55, 262, 264, 269–70, 274–75. On the role of Carvajal, Vargas, and Zapata as trusted Castilian advisers of Ferdinand, see Keniston 1960: 20. On Carvajal's ability and role as a spokesperson for Cisneros, see Brandi 1965: 72; Bullón Fernández 1927: 99. On Ayala, see Mattingly 1940: 29–30. On don Garcilaso de la Vega, see Seaver 1966: 30.

43. Cooper 1991: I.1, 133 and 138.

44. Martz (1988) has indicated that it is frustrating to try to sort out the links between individuals, families, and interests in Toledo at this time because of the sparse documentation for the period before 1540, although several fine scholars are working on related problems and we will continue to learn more about the family connections that held together some of the major factions in the city. See esp. Aranda Pérez 1992; Martz 1987, 1988, 1994, 1995, 2003; Molénat 1972, 1988, 1991a, 1991b, 1993, 1997: 348–81 and 568–92. Aranda Pérez (1999) and Montemayor (1996) have provided a massive amount of information on the later period. However, as yet we lack a systematic study of the development before the mid sixteenth century of Toledo's oligarchy, its marriage patterns and office holding, and its policy disputes and relations with royal officials such as the corregidor; therefore, the view presented

here of this patrician group is impressionistic and based on bits of evidence often isolated from context.

For Toledo, the chronicles of Alonso de Santa Cruz and Pedro de Alcocer are not particularly good sources. With regard to discovering the actual internal relations within Toledo's patriciate, Santa Cruz had too little contact with the city, and Alcocer was too immature and inexperienced in the first two decades of the sixteenth century to evaluate events (for biographies of both, see Seaver 1966: 367–68 and 370–72). Pérez (1977: 687) expresses more faith in Alcocer, who had served regidor Pedro López de Padilla, the father of comunero military commander and martyr Juan de Padilla, and witnessed some of the period's events. However, Alcocer had a number of reasons to distort his account, aside from his personal ties to rebel leaders. Toledo showed a special interest in retaining its venerable title of "loyal city" after the rebellion, and blaming the revolt on conflicts between lineage-based cliques was a useful rhetorical device to excuse the city as a corporation in an account written almost two decades after the events described. For an analysis of how even the narration of anecdotes can be coded to express an ideology, see E. P. Thompson 1997.

45. On this patrician split, see Martínez Gil 1993.

46. Gutiérrez Nieto 1973: 95–96.

47. On the involvement of Cifuentes's followers, see Haliczer 1981: 125. Much the same sort of factional fighting broke out in Cuenca. See Crews 1991: 236.

48. This explanation of the origin of independence from unreflective obedience to authority is fundamental to Jean Piaget's theory of cognitive development. This theory has been applied skillfully to historical questions by Radding 1985, 1988.

49. They had common great-grandparents. The sister of the first count of Cifuentes, don Juan de Silva (d. 1464), married the first count of Fuensalida, don Pedro López de Ayala (d. 1486). Moreover, Juan Pacheco (1419–1476), first marquis of Villena and father of don Diego López Pacheco, was the grandfather of the younger half brothers of don Juan de Silva, third count of Cifuentes, through an illegitimate daughter. See Cooper 1991: I.2, 923.

50. On the Ayala-Silva conflict of 1506, see Alcocer 1872: 20–21; Pérez 1970: 89. For information on the count of Cifuentes's presidency of the Council of Castile, see Dios 1982: 245–53; Gan Giménez 1988a: 53–56. On the attempt to retake Toledo's fortress, see Lunenfeld 1987: 31–32. The 1506 settlement can be found in Martín Gamero 1862: 1069–1073, and it is reproduced in Benito Ruano 1961: 305–10. The 1507 agreement is also in Benito Ruano 1961: 311–12.

51. Haliczer 1981: 124–27. A great deal remains to be worked out about the hostilities of this period. It was claimed in 1514 that the marquis of Villena was aiding his nephew Luis Pacheco in a lawsuit against his nephew, the fourth count of Cifuentes, whose father was Luis Pacheco's half brother, only to damage Cifuentes (Cooper 1991: I.1, 144, note 517). It should come as no surprise that conflict among close relatives could be every bit as bitter as those between unrelated rivals.

52. Lunenfeld 1987: 168; Seaver 1966: 29; Pérez 1970: 425–26. One of the best known family splits provoked by the revolt involved one of Castile's major poets, Garcilaso de la Vega (son of don Garcilaso de la Vega), who fought in the royal army. His beloved older brother, don Pedro Laso de la Vega, was one of Toledo's representatives to Charles in the spring of 1520 and one of its procuradores to the rebel Junta. They were brothers-in-law of the corregidor during the period when Toledo

was trying to form an independent assembly of Cortes cities while Charles was in Barcelona. After the death of his father in 1512, young Garcilaso's legal guardian was the later comunero leader, Juan Gaitán (Gicovate 1975: 28–29 and 31–34; Navarro Tomás 1966: viii–x).

53. Cooper 1991: II, 1106–1107.

54. On Córdoba, see Edwards 1991; Quintanilla Raso 1990b, 1991; Yun Casalilla 1980: esp. chap. 9. On Murcia, see Owens 1980. For similar considerations in other municipalities, see Casado Alonso 1985 and Pardos Martínez 1985 (on Burgos); Pretel Marín 1989 (on Chinchilla).

55. The ability of many Toledan leaders to suppress factional divisions in order to pursue general political goals is underlined well in the contemporary account of jurado Diego Hernández Ortiz 1945–1946: esp. CXVI, 462–63, and CXVII, 419. Although clearly exaggerating his own role in a memorial probably drawn up to request a reward from the Crown, Hernández Ortiz provides a valuable perspective on the rebellion because he recognized, as did cardinal Adrian, the reasonableness of Toledo's initial demands, but he was closely associated with the viceregal administration, especially with condestable Velasco, was the son of jurado Francisco Ortiz, an anti-comunero who had to flee Toledo in the spring of 1520, was involved in a patrician coup attempt against Toledo's *comunidad* (the corporation of the municipality's citizens) as members of the elite were increasingly forced into exile, and served as a secret intermediary in attempts to negotiate with rebel leaders. Although the Conde de Atarés was able to find only part of the manuscript in the 1940s, Prudencio de Sandoval made extensive use of the complete document, often to the point of plagiarism, in his version of the rebellion, published in 1604. Hernández Ortiz is not to be confused with jurado Alonso Ortiz, who was part of the four-man embassy sent to negotiate with Charles prior to his departure from Galicia in 1520, as the more violent stage of the rebellion was beginning.

The patrician cliques that emerged in León and Segovia after Isabella's death were also brought together sufficiently so that all groups were represented in the municipal councils that carried these cities to leadership in the comunero rebellion, despite continued tensions (Alvarez de Frutos 1988: 24–26; Díaz-Jiménez y Molleda 1916; Haliczer 1981: 123).

56. Col. Bel.: Leg. 28, #3, f. 2–2v. For the context, see Bullón Fernández 1927: 80–96; Dios 1988b: 311; Villapalos Salas 1997: 92–103. Once they arrive at the era of Columbus, historians of the Catholic Monarchs have shown much less interest in Castilian royal administration. Important things happened (e.g., the creation of a second Chancillería), and we need to know much more about Crown institutions and their interactions with the commonwealth during the period from Ferdinand and Isabella's extended residence in Aragón in 1493 and Isabella's death.

57. Col. Bel.: Leg. 6, f. 709–709v; Leg. 28, #3, ff. 9–9v and 20v–21; Leg. 40, ff. 193v–197v.

58. Col. Bel.: Leg. 28, #3, ff. 3–9 and 20–21; Leg. 40, ff. 197v–198. In Zomeño's official report on the business he had conducted, he indicated that the El Hornillo case had been suspended (AGS: Diversos de Castilla, Leg. 47, #24, ff. 1 and 5 [doc. dated Toledo, 27 March, but with no year given; presumably 1505]). On the fourteenth-century exchange of towns with the viscount of Cabrera, see Cabrera Muñoz 1977: 44–49 and doc. 3.

59. On Alvaro de Portugal, see Bullón Fernández 1927: 192; Merriman 1962: II, 119.

60. Col. Bel.: Leg. 40, ff. 1–2; Cabrera Muñoz 1977: 159. Earlier in the seventeenth century, a dishonest minor municipal official named Jerónimo Lozano sold over two hundred of Toledo's yearly records of city council sessions (extending back into the fourteenth century) plus an unknown number of loose documents to a bookseller and various fireworks makers. Although some of the material was recovered, the majority of the bound annuals were not. Their folio pages were formed into the casings of sky rockets, which were shot off at the great festival of the Traslación de Nuestra Señora del Sagrario in 1628. Afterwards, the municipal documents were kept under lock and key, but the damage, not only to the city but also to its future historians, had been done (AHMT: Caj. 12, Leg. 4s, ff. 88v–90).

61. Col. Bel.: Leg. 1, ff. 47v–49; Leg. 2, ff. 46–48; Leg. 39, #14; Leg. 40, ff. 192–92v and 198v–200; Osuna: Leg. 394, 1/17, f. 3. It seems that Ferdinand's order was dated 28 June. Toledo's documentary record for this period is fragmented and incomplete because the king ordered the original transcript sent to him.

62. Osuna: Leg. 324, 5 (secs. a, b, and f), 6, and 8/1 (sec. g); AMC: Sección XVI, Asuntos Judiciales, Leg. 10, Pleitos Civiles, doc. 6.

CHAPTER 4

1. I first developed this innovative interpretation of the Comunidades and of the revolt's impact on the two decades that followed in Owens 1972. That work was particularly influenced by Major 1960: chap. 1. My general interpretation of the rebellion and its impact was subsequently utilized by Haliczer 1981. Also see Haliczer 1977. For more on the lineage of my interpretation, see Fernández Albaladejo 1984: note 12; 1992b [1982]: note 54.

2. The best account of the course of the rebellion remains Pérez 1970, and he has more recently (1989) provided a readable condensed treatment. The best study of the judicial concerns of patrician leaders is Haliczer 1981. On events in the city and kingdom of Murcia, see Montojo Montojo and Jiménez Alcázar 2002; Owens 1980: chaps. 2 and 3. On the ability of the territorial aristocracy to exploit poorly supported or divided Crown governments, see Gutiérrez Nieto 1973; Haliczer 1981. I also base my account of the rebellion and the events that triggered it on information on two narratives written within the following century: Sandoval 1955–1956; Santa Cruz 1920–1925. For Toledo's circular letter of June 1520, see Belmonte Díaz 1986: 141–42. For a brief narrative, see Owens 1999a.

3. On the moderate treatment of rebels, see the detailed discussion in Pérez 1970: pt. 3, chap. 1.

4. Chancillería de Granada 1601: f. 183 (letter from Valladolid, 13 August 1513). The low quality of public administration, including the administration of justice, is clearly reflected in the letters of cardinal-archbishop Cisneros to his Brussels representative, don Diego López de Ayala, a prominent Toledan who was canon of its cathedral and had been Cisneros's vicar general. See Gayangos Arce and de la Fuente, eds., 1867. For example, see the letters in which Cisneros told Ayala to plead with the king not to suspend cases before the Chancillería of Valladolid or other high courts because of the damage done to proper judicial administration by such direct royal intervention

(letters of 12 August, 22 September, and 14 October of 1516: 135, 153–54, 169–73). On the particular problems caused by the appointment of oidores by the Royal Council in Brussels, see the letters to Ayala from Cisneros's secretary Jorge Varacaldo (Fuente, ed., 1876: esp. 89–94 [letters of 20 and 27 December 1516]). As the editor points out (xvi–xvii), the damage done to royal administration by the behavior of the territorial aristocracy is even more evident in the letters of the cardinal's secretaries than in his own. I thank Helmut Koenigsberger for directing me to these valuable sources.

5. Osuna: Leg. 324, 5, sec. c. On the effects of divided conciliar administration, see Dios 1982: 183–89; 1993: 171–81. The city of Cuenca was also disturbed by the Crown's failure to adjudicate disputes with territorial aristocrats over the seizure of places within its jurisdiction (Crews 1991). In fact, many major cities and towns had since Isabella's death suffered the loss to influential territorial aristocrats of control of municipalities and lands within traditional jurisdictions, and a disorganized and poorly supervised judiciary appeared slow to provide redress (Haliczer 1981: 69–73).

6. See Cortes de Castilla 1882: IV, 260–61; Pérez 1970: 125–28; Sandoval 1955–1956: LXXX, 123–25 and 127–28.

7. Elliott 1964: 141–43; Keniston 1960: 63–64; Klein 1920: 279–80; Koenigsberger 1971a: 8; Seaver 1966: 32 and 45.

8. AMC: Sección 2a, Serie 30, Caja 71, doc. 41. This reference to the other southern cities shows that, like the Toledo-Belalcázar dispute, the dispute between the House of Belalcázar and Córdoba was an important factor in how patricians in other municipalities evaluated monarchical administration.

9. The archbishop of Granada, Ldo. de Santiago, Ldo. Polanco, Dr. Cabrera, and Dr. Beltrán; see AMC: Sección 2a, Serie 30, Caja 71, doc. 38; AGS: Registro de Sello, March 1518.

10. Letter of 31 March 1517 in Gayangos Arce and de la Fuente, eds., 1867: 209–10; on the Toledan embassy, see also the letter of 18 October 1517: 236.

11. Col. Bel.: Leg. 1, ff. 54–72v; Leg. 44, pts. 3 and 4; AHMT: Cortes-1542: f. 2. On the Zumel bribe, see Seaver 1966: 42.

12. Madoz 1845–1850: IX, 184; Redondo 1967: 151–52.

13. Col. Bel.: Leg. 1, ff. 72v–114.

14. Col. Bel.: Leg. 1, ff. 115v–116v; Osuna: Leg. 324, 5, sec. d, and 8/3.

15. Col. Bel.: Leg. 1, ff. 116v–20; Leg. 44, part 1. The account of the proceedings was sent on 26 January 1519.

16. AHMT: Cortes-1542, f. 1–1v. This draft is undated but refers to a letter presented to the king during the Cortes of Valladolid in 1518, and the other chapters indicate that it was written prior to the king's departure from the kingdom to receive the imperial crown.

17. See Pérez 1977: 139.

18. Redondo 1967: 152–53; Keniston 1960: 50.

19. One of the other cities that would take a leadership role in the comunero movement of 1520–1521, Segovia, was also pursuing a major lawsuit to recover jurisdictions alienated by the Crown to the count of Chinchón, a grant later revoked, without effect, by queen Isabella in her will (Alvarez de Frutos 1988: 14–17; Grau 1954; Isabella I of Castile 1956: 22–25; Martínez Moro 1985: 35–37). At the beginning of the rebellion, the return of the lost places was one of Segovia's most explicit demands (Alvarez de Frutos 1984, 1988: 31–32; Gutiérrez Nieto 1973: 183–87).

20. This suggests that from the beginning, rebels in some areas were more hostile to the territorial aristocracy than some historians (e.g., Cooper 1991; 2002) would allow. In a comparison of Guadalajara and Segovia, Sánchez León (1998) has shown that a key variable in anti-magnate sentiment was the degree to which the lesser nobility had established independence from service relationships with prominent grandees.

21. Pérez 1977: 145; Seaver 1966: 49–57.

22. Bennassar 1967: 389 and 533; Brandi 1965: 87–88 and 93; Cortes de Castilla 1882: 334 (petition 59); Gutiérrez Nieto 1964: 251–54; Hernández Ortiz 1945–1946: CXVII, 420–27; Keniston 1960: 45 and 59–60; Koenigsberger 1971a: 34; Merriman 1962: III, 173–83; Pérez 1965a: 9 and 18; 1977: 147; Seaver 1966: 61–65, 67–70, 76–79. In an act viewed as one more manifestation of arbitrary royal government, Charles naturalized all of the Flemish courtiers to whom he gave royal and ecclesiastical offices, in order to circumvent Castilian laws requiring that such posts go to natives (Pérez 1970: 129).

23. Elliott 1964: 147 and 151; Koenigsberger 1971a: 34; Pérez 1965b: 155; Seaver 1966: 149.

24. For a useful reminder of the complexity of the motives of some elite participants in the rebellion, see Cooper 1996; 2002.

25. On this type of interpretation, see Pérez 1989: 168. Some scholars still feel that nationalist conceptions were fundamental to the rebellion. See, e.g., Pietschmann 1992.

26. Pérez (1970) emphasizes these themes.

27. For clear explanations, with valuable documentation, of struggles between municipal governments and the transhumant interests represented by the Mesta that fed the comunero rebellion, see Cooper 1991: I.1, 131–46; C. Phillips and W. Phillips 1997: 199–200, 252.

28. Even an anti-comunero tract such as Trinitarian friar Alonso de Castrillo's *Tractado de República* of 1521 emphasizes the ruler's fundamental mission to provide justice (Castrillo 1958; Fernández-Santamaría 1977: chap. 1; 1997: 57–105).

29. For an early, incomplete formulation of my views on this uprising by some of Talavera's towns, see Owens 1978.

30. The original of this letter is photographically reproduced in the back of Palencia Flores 1959. See also Danvila Collado 1897–1899: XXXVIII, 89. Talavera's continued loyalty benefited its corregidor, Juan Suárez de Carvajal, who later had a splendid career in royal service (Espinosa 2003: 206).

31. Danvila Collado 1897–1899: XXXVII, 159–60.

32. Ibid., 159 and 330–31. On the hermandad, see Suárez Alvarez 1982. On the role of parish assemblies, see Martínez Gil 2002: 358–59 and note 185. The position of Talavera's regidores was probably made more difficult by the fact that Toledo's cathedral canons' assembly was dominated by radical comuneros (see Haliczer 1981: 134).

33. On Acuña, see Guilarte 1979.

34. Danvila Collado 1897–1899: XXXVII, 521–22, 654–58, 665–66. On Toledo, see Haliczer 1981: 197–99; Pérez 1970: 341–47.

35. See Capella and Matilla Tascón 1957: 10; Maravall 1963: 40–41; Pérez 1963: 270–71.

36. Because the original order cannot be found, one can only deduce its contents from references in council debates and correspondence.

37. In a clear attempt to revitalize Talavera's collective lordship over its villages, its town council, with the coerced participation of some village representatives, produced a new draft of its ordinances that included in all areas the most extensive authority granted to it by earlier archbishops. Significantly, the first nine of the document's eighty-three sections dealt with wine production and sale. No archbishop would sanction these until 1539, and then only after the introduction of modifications demanded by village representatives. See Sánchez González 1992, esp. 83, 88–89, 91–92, 94–98.

38. This information on the regidores' conduct of business and the information on Talavera that follows is from AMTal: Libro de Acuerdos, 1519–1520.

39. Seaver 1966: bk. II, chap. II.

40. For details of this rural rebellion, see Owens 1978: 56–59. For an excellent study of Fuenteovejuna, Castilblanco's neighbor, and fifteenth-century antiseignioral violence, see Cabrera Muñoz and Moros Guerrero 1991. On Talavera's lands, see Gómez-Menor 1965. Many of Talavera's villages found it difficult to cope with their lord's restrictions on vine planting and the exploitation of common lands (Suárez Alvarez 1982: 107–8), and Castilblanco was among those that purchased independent town status during Philip II's reign (Sánchez González 1992: 80).

41. AMTal: Provisiones 1433–1819, Leg. 1, O-137. The actual permission referred to in the letter is not in this bundle but is perhaps no. 33 of the section on Privilegios in Palencia Flores 1959: 37.

42. On the use of rebellion by these latter municipalities, see Gutiérrez Nieto 1964: 245–46; Pérez 1970: 389 and 395; Porras Arboledas 1993: chap. 3.2 and 3.3.

43. This attitude was widely reflected by the chroniclers of the rebellion. See Martínez Gil 2002: 310–17.

44. On the continued attempts to accommodate or negotiate major rebel demands, see Pérez 1970: 205–29, 257, 272–73, 287–89.

45. Gutiérrez Nieto 1973.

46. Fernández Martín 1979; Pérez 1970: 405 and 459–66; Porras Arboledas 1993: chap. 3, pts. 1 and 2; Yun Casalilla 1980: 155–57, 163, 167–71; 1987a: 82–95. For a summary of what is known about Andalucía during the rebellion, see Porras Arboledas 2002. For the text of the La Rambla declaration, see Rodríguez Villa 1915. The meeting in La Rambla, a town near Córdoba, of delegates of eleven Andalusian cities and towns, including the Cortes cities of Córdoba, Jaén, and Seville, as well as representatives of the military order of Calatrava, itself echoed the old hermandad (municipal league) tradition of municipal confederations in support of the monarch and had no more legitimacy from the Crown's point of view than the assemblies called by Burgos in 1517 or by Toledo in 1519 and 1520. Indeed, in its inclusion of non-Cortes cities and towns, the La Rambla assembly was more radical than the comunero Cortes.

47. García García 1983: 6–7; Pérez 1989: 31 and 99. As a contemporary observer, Maldonado (1991: 150–77 and following) provides a detailed account of Osorio's dealings with this mob violence.

48. Yun Casalilla 1980.

49. Gutiérrez Nieto 1977.

50. Pardos Martínez 1985.

51. On Burgos, see Casado Alonso 1985; Gutiérrez Nieto 1964: 245; Mathers 1973: chap. 5; Salvá 1895; Sánchez Domingo 1999: 129–42. On Chinchilla, see Pretel Marín 1989. See also the suggestive documents from the mid fifteenth century mentioning "diputados" of the "comunidad" of Palencia, another important comunero city, in Fuente Pérez 1989: 567–69 and 593–96. Haliczer (1981: 263, note 74) provides an intriguing miscellaneous list of sources of dispute between plebeian groups and patrician regimes in Medina del Campo, Soria, and Toledo.

52. On the variety of experiences with parish assemblies and their representatives, see Martínez Gil 2002: 352–61. Also see Maldonado 1975: 92–99, 108–10, 123–24; 1991: 151–71 and 185–87. On Juan Maldonado, see Owens 1999b. On Murcia, see Owens 1980: chap. 2. On these representatives, see Aranda Pérez 1999: 63–65; Pérez 1970: 516–23. Also see Alvarez de Frutos 1988: 48–50. In defense of his thesis that the Comunidades was a revolution, Pérez (1989) has reemphasized that the comunero movement was fundamentally political and that its originality consisted in substituting diputados representing the vecinos of the community for corregidores and regidores in the council. Sánchez León (1998: 231–35) offers an interesting but too sanguine assessment of the possible effects of a comunero victory, which ignores important factors.

53. Pérez 1970: 301–2, 457–59, 530–31. Sánchez León (1998) shows, through a comparison of Guadalajara and Segovia, how the ability of commoner groups, especially artisans, to organize and participate in municipal government was a decisive factor in the Comunidades. On the situation in Córdoba, see Yun Casalilla 1980: especially chap. 8. On Toledo, see Martínez Gil 1981; 1993.

54. On the Junta's proclaimed *alianza y hermandad jurada,* see Fernández-Santamaría 1977: 18. On the hermandad (confederation) concept as the core of comunero ideology, see Gutiérrez Nieto 1977.

55. Haliczer 1981: 136–37 and 166; Lunenfeld 1970; Mínguez Fernández 1990.

56. For a magisterial discussion of the way that the comunero Cortes differed institutionally from those of the Catholic Monarchs, see Carretero Zamora 2002.

57. Pérez 1970: 111–15. For an indication of the magnitude of the problems involved, see Cisneros's letters to his representative in Brussels: Gayangos Arce and de la Fuente, eds., 1867.

58. Pérez 1970: 81 and note 6, 143–45, 528. Apparently Joanna had shown signs of recovery by 1516 (Haliczer 1981: 155–56). For the theoretical basis of the Junta's assumption of governing authority, see Danvila Collado 1897–1899: XXXVI, 82–85 (26 September, Junta to Valladolid).

59. On the regency of Henry III, see Dios 1988b: 316. On the 1507 Cortes, see Mexía 1945: 41–43.

60. Joseph Pérez (1970: esp. 564–68) clearly recognized the degree to which a claim for the supremacy of a representative assembly gave a revolutionary potential to the Comunidades, but he did not see that the rebel position may have been anchored in fully formulated ideological statements drawn from conciliar thought. He, therefore, couched his analysis of the Junta's ideology in distinctly anachronistic terms, while underestimating the degree to which the Comunidades' better informed opponents were shaken by the assembly's assertions of supremacy.

61. The following are useful treatments of the conciliarist tradition and its theoretical basis: Alberigo 1981; Alvarez Palenzuela 1992; Bäumer 1999; Black 1988;

Blythe 1992: chap. 13; Fasolt 1991; Helmrath 1996; 1999; Jedin 1957; 1964; Morrall 1960; Oakley 1969a, 1979: chap. 1; 1984; Ozment 1980: chap. 4; Skinner 1978: II, 114–22. On the general context, see Tierney 1982. The outstanding work on the origins of conciliar ideas in canon law is Tierney 1955. For a fine bibliography of conciliarism, see Stieber 1978. On Marsilius of Padua, see Gewirth 1951–1956. On Ockham, see Tierney 1971.

One of the ways authority could become defective was through tyranny, and Haliczer (1981: 139–44) and Pérez (1970: 565–66) have demonstrated the easy availability to Castilian intellectuals at the time of the Comunidades of the major theories about the tyrant. Although they see the doctrine as revolutionary, it is significant that while royal officials were sometimes criticized for tyrannical acts, as one would expect in a typical rebellion, Charles himself was not declared a tyrant who should be overthrown in any of the major comunero theoretical statements (see, e.g., Toledo's call for a junta in the summer of 1520, in Pérez 1970: 173). Indeed, in a 30 January 1521 letter to cardinal Adrian and almirante Enríquez, the radical diputados of Valladolid explicitly proclaimed their desire to liberate the monarch from the self-serving great nobles and the corrupt Royal Council. They eloquently argued from historical examples, echoing the older hermandades concept, that the Comunidades had defended John II, Henry IV, and the Catholic Monarchs from the disobedient territorial aristocracy. Now, while the magnates were exploiting Castile for their own gain, the *pueblos* (communities) were fighting, not for their own interests, but for the common good of their king and kingdom. Indeed, they wanted the monarch "to be Rich and Lord." On these grounds the diputados proclaimed theirs a just war, thereby making use of another major component of existing political thought. For the letter's text, see Danvila Collado 1897–1899: XXXVII, 91–94.

62. The important place of conciliarism in the development of "constitutional" ideas is emphasized by Black 1979; Oakley 1996a; Tierney 1982. For my orientation to the way conciliarists provided a more generalized political theory of the relationship between a ruler and an assembly representative of the community, I am deeply indebted to the work of Francis Oakley. In particular, see Oakley 1962, 1969b, 1977, 1994. Also see Alberigo 1978; Burns 1992: esp. chaps. 6 and 7; Rueger 1964. Almost all of the work on the "constitutionalist" impact of conciliar thought has concentrated on Protestant writers. This tendency appears to come directly from the observation by John Neville Figgis, offered in one of his Birkbeck lectures at Trinity College, Cambridge, in 1900, that there was a connection between conciliar thought and the "constitutionalism" of the English "Glorious Revolution." Because of Figgis's stereotypic ideas about French "absolutism," he assumed that the victory of papal supremacy prevented such conciliar influence in those countries that remained Roman Catholic during the Reformation era (Figgis 1916: Lecture II). Nederman (1990) challenged the idea of a link between conciliar thought and "constitutionalism," but Oakley (1995) effectively sustained his position.

63. Danvila Collado 1897–1899: XXXVI, 109.

64. Danvila Collado 1897–1899: XXXVI, 101 (letter of 1 September to Valladolid), 107–8 (20 September, Junta to Burgos), 108–9 (Burgos's representatives to their city; the quotation is p. 109), 113–15 (acceptance of the oath), 88–89 and 109–11 (two versions: 27 September, Burgos's parish assemblies to Valladolid), 245 (6 October to Adrian), 386–87 (8 October to Salamanca; the quotation is p. 386), 324–25 (18 October to the Junta).

65. Danvila Collado 1897–1899: XXXVI, 369–75 and 566–72; Sandoval 1955–1956: LXXX, 327–31. I do not wish to argue that these ideological differences were the only or even the principal reason that Burgos separated itself from the Junta. Divisions within the city and the active role of the condestable played major roles. See Maldonado 1975; 1991; Mathers 1973: chap. 5.

66. On the development of the concept of the "mystical body," see Kantorowicz 1957: chap. 5 ("Polity-Centered Kingship: Corpus Mysticum"), esp. 207–32, on the *Corpus Reipublicae mysticum* ("mystical body of the commonweal").

67. Danvila Collado 1897–1899: XXXVI, 366–67 (30 October, Junta to Burgos).

68. The complete document can be found in Belmonte Díaz 1986: 143–70; Sandoval 1955–1956: LXXX, 300–38. For a description of the Junta's claims to represent the commonwealth, see Fernández-Santamaría 1977: 17–23.

69. Belmonte Díaz 1986: 46. For the complete text, see Belmonte Díaz 1986: 171–78; Pérez 1989: 200–6.

70. Sandoval 1955–1956: LXXX, 324–25.

71. Benito Ruano 1972.

72. Black 1979: 199–203; Oakley 1981.

73. Danvila Collado 1897–1899: XXXVI, 534–41 (the quotation is p. 539).

74. Helmrath 1999.

75. On this idea of a contract, see Nieto Soria 1998: 188–91.

76. Black 1979: 202–4.

77. Danvila Collado 1897–1899: XXXVI, 272–74 (the quotation is on p. 273).

78. On Pablo de León, see Getino 1935.

79. Danvila Collado 1897–1899: XXXVI, 373.

80. Danvila Collado 1897–1899: XXXVI, 374–75. This letter can also be found in Sandoval 1955–1956: LXXX, 330–31.

81. Danvila Collado 1897–1899: XXXVI, 375.

82. Danvila Collado 1897–1899: XXXVI, 539 (letter of 22 November).

83. On the significant role of churchmen, see Haliczer 1981: 132–36; Pérez 1965a; 1970: 503–5; 1989: 23, 26, 29, 33, 133–34, 150, 152, and esp. 197–200 (the February 1520 circular letter of the Salamancan friars). On the university officials, professors, and students who were actually involved in the Comunidades, see Möller Recondo 2001; 2004.

84. On Castilians and the conciliar movement, see Goñi Gaztambide 1980; Suárez Fernández 1960. Black 1970 is a careful study of the clash of ideas in the writings of Segovia and Torquemada. The clearest idea about the importance of these men comes from reading Stieber 1978. On Torquemada, see Izbicki 1981. Pulgar (1971: 57–59) dedicated a chapter to Torquemada. On Alfonso de Santa María, see Suárez Fernández 1964: 138–42. Because some of the Basel conciliarists, particularly Juan de Segovia, carefully sought to confine their views about conciliar supremacy to an ecclesiastical context, in order to avoid losing the support of secular monarchs, Oakley (1981: 799–806) has argued that their writings were not relevant to the later development of "constitutionalism." However, because later political thinkers familiar with Segovia's history of the council and other conciliar tracts would have no reason to respect his disclaimer, they might well have been influenced by some of his formulations of the role of a representative assembly. On Juan de Segovia's library donation, see Hernández Montes 1984. It is not clear that all of these works

remained in Salamanca. However, printers began publishing Juan de Segovia's works from the conciliar era as early as 1472, and because Basel served as a major center of manuscript exchange and distribution during the conciliar years, even manuscript versions enjoyed a wide circulation. See Helmrath 1996; 1999; Hernández Montes 1977; Mann 1996: 73–74.

The works of Goñi Gaztambide 1980 and Ourliac 1979 on these men and on conciliarism must be used with care as these authors are clearly defenders of papal authority working in an intellectual environment in which disputes over the role of pope and council are far from dead issues, as the controversies that have swirled around authors such as Paul de Vooght and Hans Küng demonstrate. See Izbicki 1986; Oakley 1969a, 1996b: 20–28. Often motivated by a concern to recognize heretical doctrine, some scholars have sought to establish a distinction between "conciliar" ideas that emerged from canonist works and "conciliarist" ideas that emerged from the more innovative path founded by Marsilius and Ockham (see. e.g., Franzen 1965).

85. González Alonso 1981a; Pérez 1970: 536.

86. Pérez (1970) follows Maravall (1963) in this anachronistic approach despite his earlier critical review of the book (see Pérez 1965b on Maravall). There has been much recent work on the major eighteenth-century transformations of political and social discourse and symbolism. For the concept of "speech acts" underlying the argument in this paragraph, see Skinner 1970, 1971, 1972a, 1972b, 1974. For my discussion of why the meaning of such "speech acts" must be assessed by a "connected" history, see chap. 1, note 11, in this book.

87. Maravall 1963; Pérez 1970; Gutiérrez Nieto 1973; Haliczer 1981.

88. González Alonso 1981a; also see Chaunu 1973: I, chap. 3. The accounts of Gutiérrez Nieto and Haliczer are informed by theories of revolution developed with an eye to explaining twentieth-century conflicts, and these completely miss the role of political violence in the context of a monarchy endowed with absolute royal authority. More recently, Sánchez León (1998) has presented the Comunidades as a political rebellion, but he employs a theoretical perspective on state-building and absolutism that I reject.

89. The complete text has been republished; see Belmonte Díaz 1986: 149–70 (the version from Sandoval 1955–1956); Maldonado 1991: 450–83 (the Santa Cruz 1920–1925 version).

90. See I. A. A. Thompson 1981; Vassberg 1984; Weisser 1976.

91. See Nader 1990.

92. See Alba 1975; Contreras Contreras 2002.

93. Crane Brinton (1938) made central to his theory of revolution the idea that divisions among elite leaders provide opportunities for popular assaults on such leadership. I thank the late Robert E. Neil of Oberlin College for drawing my attention to Brinton's work and for the discussions that initially stimulated my interest in rebellion and revolution.

CHAPTER 5

1. For a valuable analysis of the importance of judicial reform, especially that of the Chancillería of Granada, to the efforts of Charles and his close advisers, particularly

Juan Tavera, president of the Council of Castile, to restore urban leaders' confidence, see Espinosa 2003: 172–79, 192–222, 240–45.

2. Brandi 1965: 91, 112–13, 214–15. Gattinara was particularly aware of the importance of quality judicial administration in Charles's lands. See Crews 1991: 246; Fernández Albaladejo 1989: 88–93; Headley 1983; Koenigsberger 1969: 12–13; 1971a: 10–11 and 14–16.

3. Brandi 1965: 93; Espinosa 2003: esp. 168–245; Fernández Albaladejo 1989: 93–97; Keniston 1960: 67 and 74.

4. Brandi 1965: 197; Elliott 1964: 111. Soria Mesa (2001) has presented a solid initial case for his assertion that in discussions of the development of the major grandee houses in relation to the Crown, the year 1520 has no significance whatsoever and represents a seventeenth-century myth. We await the final results of his interesting research.

5. Some of the count's powerful close relatives had helped bankroll the royal army (Pérez 1970: 236 and 676–78). On the pardon's context, see Pérez 1970: pt. 3, chap. 1.2.

6. Atienza Hernández 1987; Atienza Hernández and Simón López 1987; Elliott 1964: 167; Gutiérrez Nieto 1973: 293 and 313–14; Pérez 1970: pt. 3, chap. 3.2; Yun Casalilla 1987a.

7. Hendricks 1976. On Charles's responsiveness to the Cortes of Valladolid in 1523, see the letter to the infante Ferdinand, the emperor's brother, from his representative at Court, 4 October 1523, in Rodríguez Villa 1903: 132. See also the opening speech to that meeting and the formal response of the procuradores, for analyses of the causes of the rebellion and a determination to remove them, in Cortes de Castilla 1882: 334–51 and 354–57. For a summary discussion of judicial reform driven by Cortes petitions, see Alonso-Guillaume 1989.

8. On the end of the Cortes, see I. A. A. Thompson 1984a.

9. See the Junta petition in Danvila Collado 1897–1899: XXXVII, 262–77; for the royal responses to the 1523 Cortes petitions, see Cortes de Castilla 1882: 363–402. On the cities' advantageous position at this meeting in their negotiations with the Crown, see Espinosa 2003: 111–18. For an insider's look at the impact of personnel changes in the Royal Council, see the letter of 8 January 1523 from the infante Ferdinand's representative to royal treasurer Salamanca, in Rodríguez Villa 1903: 84–85. On how the Cortes prodded Charles to improve judicial administration and monitored the results, see Espinosa 2003; Puente 1958. Also see Brandi 1965: 170–71, 198, 206–7, 215; Elliott 1964: 167–68; Gounon-Loubens 1860: 120, 123–25, 175, 231; Haliczer 1981: 212–27; Kagan 1981: 153–55; Merriman 1962: III, 185–86; Tomás y Valiente 1962.

10. Atienza Hernández 1987; Kagan 1981; Nader 1990. One necessary type of supervision was enhanced, as Cortes procuradores demanded. There would be regular *visitas,* investigations of the audiencias, to ensure that these tribunals operated effectively and that individual officials remained free of corruption and retained a reputation for knowledge and decorum. On these visitas, see Espinosa 2003: chap. 4.

11. AHMT: Caj. 8, Leg. 1, #42 and #46 (Cortes of 1523 and 1528); Cortes de Castilla 1882: 387–88 (petition 80 of 1523) and 450–51 (petition 5 of 1528); Espinosa 2003: 168–87; Polaino Ortega 1964: 164, note 13.

12. Garriga 1994: chap. 3, pts. 3 and 4, and chap. 4, pt. 1; Pérez 1970: 500–501.

13. Chancillería de Granada 1601; the various ordinances for 1523 can be found throughout the text and are discussed in detail by Garriga (1994: chap. 4, pt. 3, and doc. 12 [469–82]). On the new building, see Chancillería de Granada 1601: ff. 4v–5v. On later efforts to enhance the institution's authority, see Gómez González 1998.

14. López de Ayala 1901: 100, note 5. Despite the fact that Charles's advisers favored Guevara's election as a Cortes procurador in 1520, Guevara was at that time a strident opponent of Crown policy; see Pérez 1977: 141 and note 109, 146 and note 124.

15. The two lists of negotiation points that Toledo sent to Zúñiga are in Danvila Collado 1897–1899: XXXVIII, 566–85. Pérez (1970: 373 and note 180) indicates that these same points may have been submitted to the viceroys the previous May. Almirante Enríquez apparently felt that Toledo's claims were well founded because he asked, in July and August 1521, that Charles grant him as confiscated property the rights that Toledo claimed to estates of the count of Belalcázar (Danvila Collado 1897–1899: XXXVIII, 278 and 346). Arguing that it was unmerited, Enríquez also recommended against royal approval of Córdoba's petition that the suspension of its lawsuit with the count of Belalcázar, granted to the latter, be revoked (357).

16. Col. Bel.: Leg. 1, ff. 125–129v, 131–132v, 150–154v; Leg. 44, pt. 9; Osuna: Carpeta 11–14, ff. 7v–8v; Haliczer 1981: 217.

17. Osuna: Leg. 324, 8/1 (pt. f); AMC: Sección XVI, Leg. 10, doc. 13.

18. Cortes de Castilla 1882: 383 (petition 62). On the various honors, see Elliott 1964: 170; Keniston 1960: 126–27; Merriman 1962: III, 143; Mexía 1945: 370 and 414–15; Redondo 1967: 153 and note 4.

19. For example, see Ballesteros 1946; Cunningham 1919; García-Gallo 1975; Parry 1948; Pelsmaeker Ivánez 1925; Phelan 1967; Vigil 1987.

20. Pérez 1970: 682, note 56.

21. This thesis is well argued by Shennan (1986). Although in discussing such concentration here and in an earlier book (1974), he perhaps excessively merges administrative reality with the theory of dynastic monarchy, Shennan has discovered an aspect of government frequently missed by those who like a neater narrative. However, other works on France published at about the same time or during the next few years suggest that Shennan over-drew the line between English and French political life; see, e.g., Beik 1985, 1990, 1991; Benedict 1989; Collins 1988; Hamscher 1987; Haney 1997; Kettering 1986; Mettam 1988, 1990; D. Parker 1987, 1989, 1990; Root 1987; Schneider 1989.

22. Braddick 1996; Brewer 1989; Hart 1993. I owe this perspective on public finance and war to Geoffrey Parker's lecture on 29 June 1995 at the world history institute of the University of California, Santa Cruz, and to an expansion of these ideas during a subsequent conversation.

23. Most of the *Libros de Autos* for the years of the trial were illegally sold in the seventeenth century to fireworks makers. The Archivo Histórico Municipal de Toledo now holds only the books for 1545, 1561, 1566, 1568, and 1569. During these five years, discussion of the case was the first item of annual business.

24. Cabrera Muñoz 1977: 191–94; Klein 1920: 333; Redondo 1967.

25. Klein 1920: 19, 50, 59; Molénat 1997: 667 (map); C. Phillips and W. Phillips 1997: 22, 45, 102 (map).

26. Beneyto Pérez 1958: 393; Gounon-Loubens 1860: 133–34; Valdeavellano 1968: 557. For the story about the Mexican *conquistador,* see Brandi 1965: 173; Keniston 1960: 110. Also see the comments about the attitude of the second count of Tendilla in Nader 1979: 156, 166–68, 175–76, 186, 188, 193–94, 201.

27. Kagan 1970: 49 and 61; 1974: chaps. 5, 6, and 8, esp. 182–86; 1981: 99–104 and 112–14. The quotation is from Bredemeier 1962: 82.

28. For the same argument about the Parlement of Paris, see Shennan 1968: 49, 109–10, 138, 145.

29. Braudel 1966: II, 30; Bullón Fernández 1927: 1; Gan Giménez 1988b: 223.

30. NR bk. 2, title 5, law 7.

31. For a list, see Kagan 1970: 61, note 55.

32. For a discussion of the same problem in France, see Shennan 1968: 57, 61, 66. Toledo's representatives did try on at least one occasion, in 1531, to argue the uselessness of some of the testimony the opposing barrister wanted to be taken, but the court paid no attention (Col. Bel.: Leg. 1, ff. 838–40). The monarchy was aware of the delays caused by oral testimony and had tried in 1511 to speed proceedings by ordering that only thirty witnesses be allowed to answer any one question (Chancillería de Granada 1601: ff. 155–156v).

33. Martín Postigo 1964: 533, note 138; Merriman 1962: III, 173–74; Shennan 1968: 52; Vance 1943: 121–22.

34. Gounon-Loubens 1860: 205; López Gómez 1996; Merriman 1962: III, 182–84.

35. For numerous examples of this, especially early in the trial, see Col. Bel.: Leg. 1, ff. 209v–210v, 474v, 879v–880v, 922–922v; Leg. 3, ff. 312v–313v, 332v–333, and 372v.

36. Ruiz Rodríguez 1987: 195–207.

37. For examples, see Col. Bel.: Leg. 1, ff. 187v–206, 495–531, 532–538v, and 849v–871v.

38. Col. Bel.: Leg. 1, ff. 206–12, 221v–285v, 289–329, 392v–412v, 419v–420v, and 422–59.

39. Col. Bel.: Leg. 1, ff. 547–49 and 552–552v.

40. Col. Bel.: Leg. 1, ff. 965v–958, 964–66, 972, 973v, 975v, 987–987v, 1021v–1023, 1025–1026, and 1138–1140; Leg. 3, ff. 5–21, 31–51, 63–190, 211v, 214v, 216–19, 233–235v, 248v–280, 312–14, 318v–319, and 320v–322.

41. Col. Bel.: Leg. 3, ff. 2v–3v and 4v.

42. As an example of such correspondence, when the Chancillería's president, a bishop, was preparing to return to his episcopal see for Easter, Toledo's council was afraid that he would not finish the case until his return. Therefore, letters were written, on 20 February 1555, to princess Juana, the Council of Castile, and the president of the Council asking that the bishop be ordered to stay in Granada until the work was done (AHMT: Cartas 1547–1600). See also AHMT: Caj. 8, Leg. 1, #59 and #63; AHMT: Cortes-1542, ff. 30–34, 35–38, 53, 59–62, 63–67, 84–93, 98–101, and 106–7; Col. Bel.: Leg. 4, f. 181–181v [1555]; Leg. 41, #5 and #7; Leg. 44, pts. 14 and 22.

43. Col. Bel.: Leg. 1, ff. 984v–985; Leg. 3, ff. 366v–370v and 504–505v.

44. Col. Bel.: Leg. 4, ff. 144–45 and 189v–190. For the royal edicts, see Chancillería de Granada 1601: ff. 259v–263.

45. Col. Bel.: Leg. 3, ff. 512–13 and 516–516v; Leg. 4, ff. 80–81, 87–133, and 153v–157.
46. An impression reinforced by Kagan 1981: esp. chap. 2.
47. On the original order for the refund, see Col. Bel.: Leg. 1, ff. 211–12, 1145–1147, and 1304–1311; Leg. 3, ff. 2–5, 25v–31, and 53–54. On the duke's attempt to get his money, see Col. Bel.: Leg. 3, ff. 162–68, 190–231, and 281–82. On Toledo's attempt to get more expense money, see Col. Bel.: Leg. 3, ff. 153–54 and 232v–250v. On the final settlement of the problem, see Col. Bel.: Leg. 3, ff. 299v–312.
48. Col. Bel.: Leg. 3, ff. 556–590v, 604–604v, 614–615v, 61–619v, and 655–655v.
49. Brandi 1965: 329, 397–98, 486–91, 576; Fernández Alvarez, ed., 1973–1981: II, docs. 251 and 252, esp. p. 109; Keniston 1960: 174–75. In 1530, Charles asked Juan Tavera, the president of the Council of Castile, to urge the oidores of Granada to speed up the consideration of a lawsuit involving the marquis of Zenete (see Espinosa 2003: 217 and note 119), but in doing so, the emperor simply acted as he did when the Council responded to similar petitions from Cortes cities with orders to deliberate with greater celerity on their lawsuits.
50. Col. Bel.: Leg. 3, ff. 348–351v. For the grant, see Osuna: Leg. 324, 8/1, pt. a. For an investigation of the 1518 document by Dr. Luis de Torres, oidor of the Chancillería of Valladolid, see Osuna: Leg. 324, 8/8. On the Council of Castile's summons to Córdoba, see AGS: Reg. del Sello, March 1538, f. 170; Osuna: Leg. 342, 7.
51. Col. Bel.: Leg. 3, ff. 352v–353v. AHMT: Cartas 1537–1541, letter to jurado Alonso Martínez de Mora, Toledo's representative in Granada, 15 May 1538. The Council's hearing was held in Toledo in 1539, and some of Córdoba's petitions were prepared by one of Toledo's main lawyers. For the verdict, see Osuna: Leg. 324, 7 and 8/10.
52. These were Dr. Gálvez, Dr. Peñaranda, Ldo. Melchor de León, Ldo. Fernán Bello de Puga, Ldo. don Juan Sarmiento (abbot of Santa Fé), Ldo. Lope de León, Ldo. don Diego de Córdoba, and Ldo. Rodrigo Huarte, although there was some question about the last mentioned. This left Dr. Ribera, Dr. Diego de Deza, Ldo. Andrés Ramírez de Alarcón, Ldo. Antonio de Frías, Ldo. Gómez Tello Girón, Ldo. Juan de Araña, Ldo. Hernando de Salas, and Ldo. Pedrosa. Col. Bel.: Leg. 4, ff. 27–28v.
53. Col. Bel.: Leg. 3, ff. 497v–498, 507v–508, 554v, 556v–557v, 560v–561v, 573–75, and 577; Leg. 4, ff. 16v–18, 24–26, and 29v–30v. On Hernando Niño's relatives, see AHMT: Cartas 1537–1541, letter to Martínez de Mora, 20 November 1539. On the alcaldes' role, see Chancillería de Granada 1601: f. 265.
54. On the 1503 ordinance, see BN: R-65, f. 21. Col. Bel.: Leg. 1, f. 971v; Leg. 3, ff. 353v–355v, 361v–362, 365–66, and 538v–539.
55. Col. Bel.: Leg. 3, ff. 445–65. On the wedding, see Osuna: Leg. 280, 3. On the relator, see Ruiz Rodríguez 1987: 162–66. This type of clash produced many of the charges made against Chancillería officials during the next formal investigation, including those against Dr. Gálvez himself. See AGS: Cámara de Castilla, Leg. 2739, 2740, and 2748. The charges against Gálvez are in Leg. 2739. He was also the focus of some attention in an earlier investigation, in 1539–1540 (see Leg. 2734). Without a detailed discussion of all the charges and countercharges in the surviving investigation records, which would lead us far from our subject, it would be difficult to do justice to this extensive material in a large collection, which constitutes Serie 10 of

Visitas, legajos 2710–2812, covering the years 1512–1679. At least eleven bundles contain material about officials during the period when the Belalcázar case was being heard in Granada, and a dissertation currently underway at the Universidad de Valladolid will deal with this huge body of material.

56. Col. Bel.: Leg. 3, ff. 470–478v and 482–83.

57. Col. Bel.: Leg. 1, ff. 1153v–1155v, 1157v–1203v, 1208–1260, 1263–1264v, 1267–1270v, 1273–1282v, 1290v–1300, and 1302v–1303v.

58. Osuna: Leg. 394, 1/1.

59. Chancillería de Granada 1601: ff. 398–432v. The whole matter of official rectitude in the judicial administration could use a great deal more attention. Unfortunately, archive materials in Granada will not throw much light on the subject because, although well run now and located in splendid facilities, the collection has been decimated in the past. Even the *Libros de Acuerdos* (records of decisions) are gone (Núñez Alonso 1984: 28, 31). There appears to have been some improvement in standards between 1536 and 1549, but the report of 1563 reveals an obvious deterioration. This deterioration could reflect the harm done by a few poor officials such as Luis Maza, the chief constable, and there does seem to be much more business conducted through personal connection than during the time the Toledo-Belalcázar case was being heard in Granada. For example, see the visita of 1563, chaps. 16, 18, 27, 53, 56, 57, 60, and 62. The 1567 report is somewhat better. The original documents relating to these visitas can be found in AGS, Cámara de Castilla, Serie 10, *Visitas,* Legs. 2710–2812 (Años 1512–1679), particularly Legs. 2714, 2728, 2729, 2731, 2732, 2733, 2734, 2739, 2740, and 2748.

60. Cortes de Castilla 1903: esp. 46–95. Also see Brandi 1965: 464; Elliott 1964: 201–2; Keniston 1960: 219–21; Merriman 1962: III, 166–67; Sánchez Montes 1958. On the 1532 campaign, see Bataillon 1966: 428–29, note 9; Redondo 1967: 154. On family connections, see Keniston 1960: 233; Osuna: Leg. 225, 2, and Leg. 280, 3. A second son, don Francisco, marquis of Ayamonte (and later duke of Béjar), married the daughter of another of Charles's supporters in the 1538–1539 Cortes, the duke of Infantado.

61. Redondo 1967: 156–57.

62. Osuna: Leg. 394, 1/10. For other aristocratic pressure on the Crown, see López Serrano 1997–1998.

63. AHMT: Libro de Acuerdos 1452–1682, 8 January 1539.

64. AHMT: Cartas 1537–1542, letters to Martínez de Mora, 10 January 1539 and 7 and 14 January 1541; letters of 20 December 1540 to the marquis of Elche (don Bernardino de Cárdenas, son of the duke of Maqueda), the marquis of Montemayor (don Juan de Silva y Ribera), Lope de Guzmán, and Hernando de Ayala. Elche and Montemayor are identified in the Cortes list of 1538. See Cortes de Castilla 1903: 27–32. For the carta ejecutoria in the El Hornillo case, see Col. Bel.: Leg. 28, #3. On the jurados' resolution, see AHMT: Libro de Acuerdos 1452–1682, 17 January 1541.

CHAPTER 6

1. On the need to expose the legal rules and procedures that shaped the documentary record used to develop a microhistory, see Kuehn 1989. On the development

of the general European "constitutional" perspective that stressed the importance of due process for the proper exercise of absolute royal authority, see Pennington 1993: chap. 4 and epilogue.

2. Col. Bel.: Leg. 41, #16 is an inventory, in a copy of 1564, of the documents delivered by portero Arriola of the Chancillería to Royal Council secretary Domingo de Zavala in Valladolid on 28 December 1555. The Belalcázar Collection of the Archivo Histórico Municipal de Toledo contains virtually all of this material, certainly all of the important documents. The Osuna Collection of the Archivo Histórico Nacional in Madrid holds additional material. Zavala's set of documents apparently disappeared sometime after 1609.

3. The type of context Toledo wished to show was that used by the procuradores to petition Henry IV at the Cortes of Ocaña in 1469 and the Catholic Monarchs at the Cortes of Toledo in 1480 to revoke all grants made after 15 September 1464: "because they were made during said wars and rebellions [which began on that date] and [the monarchs involved] were obligated by the inevitable necessities to make them at the time, for they run counter to the agreement and oath that your highness made when you were elevated and obeyed as king and against the laws of your kingdoms and in reduction of your patrimony and royal crown and because they anger and prejudice the commonwealth." Translated from the petitions as quoted in Villapalos Salas 1997: 195, note 313.

4. *Era de* 1284; until the late fourteenth century, Castilians added thirty-eight years to dates in the Julian calendar. The phrase *"era de"* (era of) stands for *"era espanola"* (that is, the Caesarian era that began in 38 B.C.E.).

5. Molénat (1997: 190–207) provides an excellent discussion of these documents.

6. Col. Bel.: The documents presented in 1526 and 1530 are in *legajos* (bundles) 26 and 39. The 1536 material is in Leg. 1, ff. 1026v–1138. For the material on the Mesta-Belalcázar dispute, see AHMT: Caj. 5, Leg. 1, #6. Col. Bel.: Leg. 1, ff. 1023v–1025; Leg. 27 (the case itself); Leg. 39, #37 and #38; Leg. 40, ff. 164–190v. On Puebla's charter of 1288, see Sáez Sánchez 1948.

7. Col. Bel.: Leg. 6 and 7.

8. Col. Bel.: Leg. 8; Leg. 9, pts. 1 and 2. We cannot tell how the duke's lawyers used some of this evidence because we have only some of their briefs. In October 1597, to help prepare arguments in the Córdoba case, ducal officials sent nine signed and twelve unsigned briefs about Toledo's case, all handwritten and in poor condition, from Puebla de Alcocer to Granada, and there are no surviving copies of some of these. They also sent materials about the Córdoba case. At least one of the briefs about Toledo was prepared in 1565 for presentation before the Council of Castile (another copy exists), but several of the others were definitely prepared by lawyers who worked on the case only when it was still being heard by the Chancillería of Granada. Some of these are lost. However, it seems likely that Toledo produced more than the few remaining briefs that argue its side of the case. For the itemized receipt, see Osuna: Leg. 394, 1/5.

9. Col. Bel.: Leg. 1, ff. 884–86; Leg. 4, ff. 36–37v; Leg. 11 (Carrillo), questions 53 and 54; Leg. 12 (Gadillo), pt. 1, questions 54 and 55; Leg. 22. Osuna: Carpeta 11–14, ff. 55v–56v.

10. Col. Bel.: Leg. 3, ff. 546v–547v; Leg. 17 (a portion of the documentation submitted in 1546).

11. Col. Bel.: Leg. 4, f. 16–16v; Leg. 17, ff. 227v–228. On the guide's date, see López Serrano 1969.

12. Col. Bel.: Leg. 3, ff. 589v–594 and 628–641v; Leg. 4, ff. 35–35v and 72. Leg. 37 is the Gálvez survey done in 1543.

13. For the argument of all these points, see Col. Bel.: Leg. 43, #11, ff. 44–48, 63v–64v, and 112–16.

14. I offer these observations based on my attempt, during a visit to the area, to locate such geographic features using 1:50,000 maps published originally in 1953 by Spain's Dirección general del Instituto Geográfico y Catastral, before the rising river water obscured so many aspects of the Guadiana's historic course.

15. Col. Bel.: Leg. 14, pt. 3, ff. 180–187v; Leg. 30, #2, ff. 21v–22.

16. Col. Bel.: Leg. 30, #2.

17. Col. Bel.: Leg. 3, ff. 343v–353v and 365–390v; Leg. 43, #11, ff. 1–3v.

18. Col. Bel.: Leg. 17, ff. 187–227; Leg. 43, #11, f. 44.

19. Col. Bel.: Leg. 3, ff. 526v–527; Leg. 17; Leg. 41, #4; Leg. 43, #11, ff. 46–47. On reconstructing the *Partidas* text, see García-Gallo 1967: I, 394–98.

20. Col. Bel.: Leg. 3, ff. 420v–425v and 435–40; Leg. 25.

21. Col. Bel.: Leg. 1, ff. 658v–673v and 804–809v.

22. Col. Bel.: Leg. 1, ff. 813v–816.

23. Col. Bel.: Leg. 1, ff. 874v–878; Leg. 9, ff. 76–87v.

24. Col. Bel.: Leg. 14, ff. 170–179v.

25. Col. Bel.: Leg. 1, ff. 342–377v; Leg. 3, ff. 327v–330v; Leg. 10; Leg. 18. The most interesting material involved attempts to impugn witnesses who had participated in the rising against Talavera by residents of the town of Castilblanco during the Comunidades rebellion. For a detailed analysis of this material, see chap. 4 of this book and Owens 1978.

26. Col. Bel.: Leg. 13, witness #32; Leg. 14, ff. 180–87v.

27. Col. Bel.: Leg. 11; Leg. 12.

28. These chapters are not part of the surviving trial record, but Toledo's were from the chronicle written by Fernán Pérez de Guzmán, which had been corrected by the famous royal councillor Dr. Galíndez de Carvajal. This work had been available in print since 1517. See Pérez de Guzmán 1517 and Rosell, ed., 1877, 1953: II. The source of the marquis' additions was never indicated but appears to have been the same.

29. Col. Bel.: Leg. 21; Leg. 22, pt. 1; Leg. 43, #11, ff. 68v–83; Pérez de Guzmán 1517: Año xxxii, chaps. 229, 232, and 233; Año xli, chaps. 25 and 28; Año xlv, chap. 70. A major motivation for printing these chronicles was to provide a record of royal actions and the careers of territorial aristocrats and bishops, which could be used as a basis for administrative and judicial decisions.

30. Col. Bel.: Leg. 1, ff. 1151–1152; Leg. 30, #2, ff. 13–14v.

31. Col. Bel.: Leg. 43, #11, ff. 64v–68v.

32. Col. Bel.: Legs. 11, 12, and 13; Leg. 16, ff. 110v–151; Leg. 43, #11, ff. 84v–104v.

33. Pérez de Guzmán 1517: Año xli and Año xlix. Col. Bel.: Leg. 3, ff. 392–418.

34. Col. Bel.: Leg. 4, ff. 16–16v and 37v–39; Leg. 17; Leg. 43, #11, ff. 49v–51v and 63v.

35. Col. Bel.: Leg. 4, ff. 193–95.

36. Because Benito Ruano (1961: 141–45) has already examined this defense, I touch on only the main points here. The *Información de Derecho* (the brief prepared by Ortiz) that Benito Ruano cites is now Leg. 30, #4 of the Belalcázar Collection. There are several manuscript copies: Leg. 43, #3, #6, #12. The #6 version seems to be a rough draft; #12 is perhaps the version presented prior to the 1555 decision; #3 is the version that was printed. Some version of the document was obviously presented to the audiencia before 1555 because the Béjar lawyers clearly argue against it in their 1555 protest over the verdict.

37. See Col. Bel.: Leg. 43, #11, ff. 68v–83.

38. Col. Bel.: Leg. 43, #11, ff. 84–118.

39. See Col. Bel.: Leg. 30, #2, esp. ff. 7v and 12–26; Leg. 4, ff. 256v–292v. For a list of what Toledo submitted, see Col. Bel.: Leg. 43, #11, ff. 37–43.

40. Benito Ruano 1961: 216–20; AHMT: Caj. 5, Leg. 6, #1; Col. Bel.: Leg. 26; Leg. 39, #2, pt. 3, and #28; Leg. 43, #13, ff. 29v–32v.

41. Other issues were raised: for example, whether Toledo had paid too little for the land or whether Gutierre de Sotomayor had received more than his services warranted. But responses to such questions were poorly developed, and these matters were not pursued seriously.

42. Cárdenas 1873: II, 183–85. Van Kleffens even feels that the *Partidas,* which for a number of reasons formed a kind of norm in Castilian law, precluded lawful expropriation (Van Kleffens 1968: 197). This reading is, however, convincingly disputed by Cárdenas (1873: II, 202–3), García-Gallo (1967: I, 734–35), and Valdeavellano (1968: 425). On the role of the *Partidas* in legal thought and education, see García-Gallo 1967: I, 90–91.

43. According to Cárdenas (1873: II, 202–3), the Crown could take property for a crime that merited confiscation under the law, but the legislation tried to be scrupulous in its respect for property rights. One of the basic rights of subjects was that there would be no condemnation without a hearing. This protection was the law of the kingdom of León from 1188 and of all Castile from the Cortes of Valladolid in 1307 (confirmed a few years later). See Beneyto Pérez 1940: 333.

44. Col. Bel.: Leg. 4, ff. 256v–292v; Leg. 30, #2, esp. ff. 19v–20 and 24v–25v; Leg. 30, #4, esp. ff. 7v–9 and 11–13v; Leg. 43, #11, ff. 53v–60 (for counterclaims) and 86v–87.

45. Col. Bel.: Leg. 1, f. 1088; Leg. 4, ff. 229–53; Leg. 30, #2, ff. 16–17v; Leg. 43, #13, ff. 26v–29v and 58–63.

46. Col. Bel.: Leg. 30, #4, f. 14–14v; Leg. 43, #11, ff. 53v–60. Osuna: Leg. 394, 1/10, pt. 3. Cárdenas 1873: II, 202–4; García-Gallo 1967: I, 734–35; Valdeavellano 1968: 425.

47. Cárdenas 1873: II, 204–5. On earlier formulations of these ideas by Castilian authors, see Madden 1930: 46–49, 72, 88. See Alfonso X 1491. On the impact of the works of medieval jurists on Castilian legal studies, see García y García 2000; Pérez Martín 2000.

48. In 534 C.E., the emperor Justinian (reigned 527–65) promulgated a law code that became the basis of medieval university legal education after the eleventh century. Because the emperor and his principal legal advisers, especially Tribonian, realized that many justices had received inadequate preparation for their roles, the new code was designed to do more than present the laws that were to be enforced; it was

designed to instruct. The code has three parts. The Code (*Codex Justiniani;* abbreviated C.) presents the imperial legislation or "constitutions" that were still in force. The massive Digest (*Digesta Justiniani;* abbreviated D.) contains selections from the works of past Roman jurists, such as Ulpian (murdered 223 C.E.), whose writings constitute roughly a third of the Digest. The Digest is twice the length of the Code, and justices could find in these selections the principles and rules that were to form the context within which they enforced the law. After the completion of the Digest in 333, Tribonian, the head of the drafting commission, and a few colleagues wrote a brief, elementary textbook, the Institutes (*Institutiones Justiniani;* abbreviated Inst.), which is the third part of the code. After the code was promulgated, the emperor continued to legislate, and these laws are known as Novels (*Novellae,* from *novae leges*). Several unofficial collections of these were made. On Justinian's law code, see Honoré 1978; Ullman 1975: chap. 2. On the legacy of this work, see Stein and Shand 1974: esp. chaps. 3 and 4; Watson 1981. Because it contains all of the associated material utilized by fifteenth- and sixteenth-century jurists, as well as the *glossa ordinaria* of Accursius (d. 1263), I have used a facsimile of a late fifteenth-century edition of Justinian's code (Venice: De Tortis, 1487–1489); see Justinian 1968–1969.

49. Carlyle and Carlyle 1909–1936: II, 96–101; David 1954; Esmein 1913; Fernández Albaladejo 1989: 72–85; Nieto 1980; Ullmann 1946: 40. For a particularly good discussion of this paradox of a prince with absolute authority whose conduct must nonetheless be in accordance with the law, see Kantorowicz 1957, esp. chap. 4.

50. These ideas were widely held. For a particularly good summary of the matter, which I have followed here, see Franklin 1973: 12–13 and notes 31–33. The citations from Bartolus and Baldus were commonly used by later jurists (on these authors, see Canning 1987; Woolf 1913). See esp. Baldus on C., 1, 14, 4, 1 and C., 3, 34, 2, 45. The former passage is quoted in the notes of Carlyle and Carlyle 1909–1936: VI, 20–21 and 83–84.

51. The definitive work on this subject is Nicolini 1952.

52. Particularly good on this matter is Ullmann 1946: esp. 102–3 and 185–88. Also see Franklin 1973: 84. On the position of the Glossators, see Gilmore 1941: 15–18; McIlwain 1932: 190, note 1.

53. Bartolus 1986. For an example of this view in the work of another Postglossator, see Ullmann 1946: 188–89. Other views are discussed in Carlyle and Carlyle 1909–1936: VI, 84–88. See esp. the quotation from Baldus in p. 85, note 4, where he indicates that reason is conduct according to natural law. An older statement of the general rules with full and valuable citations is Gierke 1900: 79–81 and notes 270–80. On the idea that a king who treated all property as his was uncivilized and illegitimate and that such was an "oriental" system, see Franklin 1973: 84–85.

54. For the 1442 text, see Cortes de Castilla 1866: 394–401. On the 1480 provision, see Cárdenas 1873: II, 184–85.

55. Col. Bel.: Leg. 43, #11, f. 57.

56. Osuna: Leg. 394, 1/10, pt. 3.

57. Carlyle and Carlyle 1909–1936: VI, chap. 3; Church 1941: 10–11 and 261; Franklin 1973: vii and chap. 3, esp. 41 and 50; Keohane 1980: chap. 2; Salmon 1973; Skinner 1980. On the massacres and their aftermath, see Diefendorf 1991; Kingdon 1988.

58. Later editions were printed in 1554, 1573, and 1593. Although no context is provided, a good idea of Núñez de Avendaño's views on royal authority can be gained from García Marín 1976: esp. chap. 1.B.

59. Osuna: Leg. 394, 1/10. On Avendaño, see García López 1889: 71; Malagón-Barceló 1959: 116; Owens 1977a and 1977b. Avendaño died before 1567, when his son received a royal license for the publication of his father's works. See AGS: Reg. de Sello: February 1567 (2), f. 256.

60. Osuna: Leg. 394, 1/10, pt. 3, f. 1.

61. His approach shows clearly how little observed were the various royal attempts to control the use of arguments from medieval commentators (Madden 1930: 71 and 95; Van Kleffens 1968: 19 and 226).

62. *Partida* 2, title 1, law 2 and *Partida* 3, title 18, law 31. The former deals with imperial authority and the latter with the invalidity of documents granted contrary to natural law. He also cited commentaries on C., 7, 37, 2, which actually have less to do with the problem.

63. Carlyle and Carlyle 1909–1936: VI, 445–48; Salmon 1991: 235.

64. On this concept, see especially Kantorowicz 1957: 127–42.

65. Gloss of *Partida* 5, title 5, law 53, no. 8; in Códigos Españoles 1872–1873: III, 620–22.

66. Avendaño's citations were: Joannes Andreae on *Extra,* 1, 2, 1 and *Extra,* 5, 31, 1; Baldus on C., 1, 19, 2; C., 6, 42, 14; C., 7, 37, 2; Bartolus and *doctores* on C., 1, 22, 6. The abbreviation *Extra* refers to the *Liber Extra* (a collection of new laws issued since Gratian compiled the *Concordia discordantium canonum,* later called the *Decretum,* in 1139–1140), which was prepared by a commission headed by Raymond de Pennafort and promulgated in 1234 by Pope Gregory IX. On these compilations of canon law and their influence, see Ullman 1975: chaps. 4 and 5. Johannes Andreae (d. 1348), Baldus de Ubaldis (d. 1400), Bartolus de Sassoferrato (d. 1357) were all frequently cited commentators. On abbreviations and citations in legal works, see Bryson 1975.

67. It is interesting that Avendaño felt comfortable using the word "authority" interchangeably with the Castilian and Latin words usually translated as "power." Clearly no significant theoretical distinction between *auctoritas* and *potentatus, posse,* or *potere* occupied his thought. See my comments in chapter 1 on my translation of *poderío real absoluto* as "absolute royal authority."

68. Avendaño must have felt some anxiety over how these arguments would be received by the justices because later in the brief he slipped in a mention of the territory having been seized because of Toledo's crimes of rebellion, thus introducing material his own statement of purpose suggested was irrelevant to his task.

69. On Gregorio López's professional and scholarly career, see Gibert 2000; Martínez Cardós 1960; Tomás y Valiente 1995: 311–12. López's role in the case was mentioned, for example, in the same Osuna legajo where the Avendaño brief is now located; see Osuna: Leg. 394, 1/10, pt. 1. For a good, brief discussion of López's views on expropriation, see Cárdenas 1873: II, 205. Also see López's gloss of *Partida* 2, title 1, law 2, no. 23 and *Partida* 3, title 18, law 31 in Códigos Españoles 1872–1873: II, 322–23, and III, 200–201.

70. For example, see Mariana 1969 (1599): bk. I, chaps. 2 and 9. On the more general nature of the reaction, especially among Jesuit theorists, see Monod 1999: 51–53.

71. Col. Bel.: Leg. 4, ff. 265–266v.

72. Beneyto Pérez 1940: 221, 284, 333; Dios 1993: pt. 1, chap. 2; García-Gallo 1967: I, 635–36, 696, 736–38, 742, 757, 795–96; Nieto Soria 1988: 242; 1998: 203–8; Rodríguez Flores 1971; Valdeavellano 1968: 424–28, 432, 443.

73. Cortes de Castilla 1863: 371–72; 1866: 406–7. García-Gallo 1967: I, 204 and 795; González Alonso 1995.

74. García-Gallo 1967: I, 636, 744, 830–33; Valdeavellano 1968: 425. On the responsibility to provide counsel, see Sánchez 1993. The procuradores intended the 1445 declaration of the Cortes of Olmedo to be an affirmation of this lack of institutional checks rather than a statement of a royal right to act without reference to the laws, as García-Gallo, Nieto Soria, Pastor Bodmer, and Valdeavellano have suggested. See Cortes de Castilla 1866: 483–89; García-Gallo 1967: I, 757; Nieto Soria 1998; Pastor Bodmer 1992: I, chap. 2; Valdeavellano 1968: 427.

75. Fernández-Santamaría 1997: 171–212; García-Gallo 1967: 832–33; Lewy 1960: 17; MacLachlan 1988: chap. 1; Stoetzer 1979: chap. 2.

76. Alonso-Guillaume 1989.

77. Hamilton 1963: 163.

78. Bullón Fernández 1936: 36–37, 40, 47–48, 53, 152–62, 181–82; Fernández Albaladejo 1989: 72–85; García-Gallo 1967: I, 743–44, 757, 789–91; Hamilton 1963: chaps. 1–3. Covarrubias did not hear the Toledo case in Granada, however, and he was not Council president until after the final verdict had been handed down by that body. As a Toledan, he would have been rightly challenged if he had ever been assigned to hear the case.

79. Quoted by Kagan 1970: 60. On letrado views, see Gounon-Loubens 1860: 215.

80. Quoted by Elliott 1964: 246.

CHAPTER 7

1. On the ill-kept records, see Chancillería de Granada 1601: ff. 407, 414, and 418. On the Botello challenge, see Col. Bel.: Leg. 4, ff. 151–52. Toledo's lawyers should not have known how he voted, suggesting that such secrets were not well kept. Because the Béjar title was retained by his mother after his father's death in 1544, the count's major title in 1555 was marquis of Gibraleón.

2. Col. Bel.: Leg. 4, f. 181–181v.

3. Rodríguez-Salgado (1988), who has studied the matter in great detail, argues that throughout this period, royal officials everywhere were reluctant to act decisively.

4. In 1541, cardinal Tavera as regent had ordered the case heard in final review by three of the four chambers (*salas*) into which the oidores were divided, because of its great importance (Col. Bel.: Leg. 3, ff. 483v–484), and the number of challenges, along with transfers, retirements, and deaths, meant that the court had to wait until enough justices were available. Such problems meant that the case had in fact to be remitted to four different chambers in succession so that enough oidores could judge the case to comply with the royal order, and this complicated procedure exhausted the supply of oidores who could participate before the Chancillería reached a total of twelve who represented three full salas.

5. An order of 13 May 1556 from princess Juana as regent to the Chancillería of Valladolid specifically indicated that other judges besides those of the Royal Council could be commissioned to hear such cases (Chancillería de Granada 1601: ff. 189v–190), but the legislation is ambiguous. This general order followed the specific approval on 4 August 1555 by the regent and a portion of the Council of the necessary bond for the royal prosecutor in Granada to become a party in the Belalcázar case before the audiencia at the stage of second supplication (Col. Bel.: Leg. 4, ff. 301–4).

There is no systematic scholarly work on the development of trials of second supplication, although Garriga (1994: 97 and 355–58) has provided a brief but solid legislative history of this type of appeal. For relevant legislation, see Cortes de Castilla 1863: 476–79; Díaz de Montalvo 1484: bk 2, title 4; NR bk. 4, title 20, law 1. Also see Dios 1982: 412–13; Sánchez-Arcilla Bernal 1980: 108–9, 121–22, 131–32.

6. For the two orders, see AGS: Reg. del Sello, August 1555, ff. 35 and 307. For the Granada proceedings, see Col. Bel.: Leg. 4: ff. 157–75, 203–57, and 298–304. In his instructions of 12 July 1554 to his sister Juana as regent, prince Philip had directed that when she needed the advice of a letrado, she should consult Dr. Martín de Velasco and that any time Castilian business was discussed, Velasco and Ldo. Lope de Otálora should be present. For Philip's instructions, see Fernández Alvarez, ed., 1973–1981: IV, 105–9. Also see Carlos Morales 1989; Martínez Millán 1992a: 140, 142, and notes 11 and 20.

7. For the relevant orders and related material, see AGS: Reg. del Sello, August 1555, f. 301; September 1555, f. 195, 9 September; October 1555, f. 104; Col. Bel.: Leg. 4, ff. 304–309v; Leg. 41, #16; Leg. 43, #2, ff. 30v–31. For the legislation on the tribunal's composition, see BN: R-12094; Cortes de Castilla 1882: 529.

8. The increased judicial responsibility that the Council of Castile assumed in the mid-1550s produced considerable delays. This situation prompted the Cortes to petition the Crown to establish separate Council tribunals (salas) to deal with trials on second supplication, evaluations of royal officials based on investigations of their conduct (residencias), and issues of government. Once Philip returned to Castile, the Cortes of 1560 renewed the request for a Council tribunal to handle second supplication and residencia hearings. See Ezquerra Revilla 2000: 52–53 and 80.

9. On the legislation, see Chancillería de Granada 1601: ff. 187v–188v and 190v; BN: R-65, ff. 14v–15 and 130v–131; BN: R-14090; BN: R-12094; Gil Ayuso 1935: #106 and #207; Gounon-Loubens 1860: 177; NR: bk. 4, title 2, law 15. The tightening of procedures during Charles V's reign appears to have had the desired effect, making the granting of such appeals fairly rare. By 1555, however, the princess-regent of Castile and her Council were allowing at least one or two such appeals a month. Moreover, the cases taken on appeal were not always over matters of great value or between parties of great importance. These observations are based on a review of AGS: Reg. del Sello, 1538, 1539, and 1555.

10. Rodríguez-Salgado (1988) entitles her chap. 7 "Rebellion in the Spanish Realms." On Charles V's doubts about Juana's ability, at age nineteen, to serve effectively as regent, see his instructions in Fernández Alvarez, ed., 1973–1981: IV, 40; Martínez Millán 1992a: 141, note 18. A generally favorable view of Philip's role is Kamen 1997: 12–53. On the councillors, see Elliott 1964: 205–6; Gan Giménez 1988a: 241; Keniston 1960: 303 and 306. On the regency of María and Maximilian,

see Brandi 1965: 494 and 590; Rodríguez Raso, ed., 1963: introduction; Schäfer 1935–1947: I, 75 and 79.

11. On the conflicting Habsburg courts, see Rodríguez-Salgado 1988. On the Valladolid divisions, see the articles collected in Martínez Millán, ed., 1992, 1994; and Martínez Millán 1988, 1989. On the Alba-Ruy Gómez rivalry, see Boyden 1995; Maltby 1983.

12. Rodríguez-Salgado 1988: 209–13. On the degree of insecurity among Council of Castile members, see Ezquerra Revilla 2000: chap. 2. On the growing irregularity in the dispensation of offices and grants, see Schäfer 1935–1947: I, 109–10.

13. On the fiscal problems, see Carande 1943–1967: II, especially chap. 3, and III, chaps. 3 and 4; Kellenbenz 1967; Ulloa 1977. On problems with the territorial aristocracy, see Braudel 1966: II, 55 and 271–72; Carande 1943–1967: III, 287; Keniston 1960: 265; Rodríguez Raso, ed., 1963: 4. Ldo. Palomares' memo to Philip II is described by Gelabert González 1998: 97–99. For the comments on the grandees made by royal secretary Gonzalo Pérez to Philip in 1556, see Marañón 1969: II, 897. On urban economic difficulties, see Bennassar 1967: esp. 12, chaps. 7, 8, and conclusion; Braudel 1966: II, 57; Elliott 1964: 185–97; García Sanz 1985; Gelabert González 1994; Marcos Martín 1994.

14. Cuartas Rivero 1984; Nader 1990; I. A. A. Thompson 1979.

15. Col. Bel.: Leg. 43, #8, doc. a; AHMT: Libro de Autos, 1 March 1561.

16. Gounon-Loubens 1860: 178 and 188.

17. For an overview of some of this activity, see Guillaume-Alonso 1999.

18. Chancillería de Granada 1601: ff. 99–100 and 268v–270.

19. Merriman 1962: IV, 455. On the Belluga de Moncada report, see Col. Bel.: Leg. 43, #8, doc. ii. For the order, see AGS: Reg. del Sello, February 1565, f. 121 (signed by Juan de Figueroa, Dr. Diego Gasca, Ldo. Espinosa, Ldo. Atienza, and Ldo. Gómez de Montalvo); BN: R-14090, *Pragmáticas Nuevas*. Also see the provision of 7 September 1565 about appeals in BN: R-14090, *Nuevas Provisiones*.

20. For a splendid discussion of Castilian conditions on Philip's arrival, see Rodríguez-Salgado 1988: 339–47.

21. Danvila y Burguero 1900; Ezquerra Revilla 2000: chap. 3; Martínez Millán 1994a: 214, 227; Martínez Millán and Carlos Morales 1992: 41–42, 44–45, and note 104.

22. Gounon-Loubens 1860: 179; Merriman 1962: IV, 417. On the widespread nature of this attitude, see Elliott 1963: 72–73 and note 1; Koenigsberger 1969: 70, 187.

23. On the intensified campaign against heresy, see Blázquez Miguel 1986; Elliott 1964: 213, 217, 223–24; Fernández Alvarez 1995: 74–75; Kamen 1985; Márquez 1980; Martínez Millán 1980, 1994a; Pizarro Llorente 1994; Tellechea Idígoras 1968. On the Muslim threat, see Cardaillac 1979; Chejne 1983; Domínguez Ortiz and Vincent 1979; Rodríguez-Salgado 1988: 253–78.

24. See the summary in Israel 1995: chaps. 7 and 8.

25. Bouza Alvarez (1994b: esp. 58–72) provides a valuable examination of Philip's tendency to demand personal oversight and of the difficulties and complaints generated by his administrative habits. Philip showed little ability to delegate authority and maintain royal supervision on the basis of briefings from competent ministers with well-defined responsibilities.

26. This picture of Philip's behavior during the first dozen years after his return to Castile is taken from the accounts of Elliott 1964; Koenigsberger 1969, 1971a, 1971b; Maltby 1983; Marañón 1969: I, 46–51; Mattingly 1959: 70–75; G. Parker 1978: chap. 6; G. Parker 1998: chap. 1; Pierson 1975; Schäfer 1935–1947: I, 101–2. On surveillance, see Fernández Alvarez 1995: 74–75; Merriman 1962: IV, 411 and 454. On Court ceremony, see Nader 1988; Rodríguez-Salgado 1991. For the claim that Philip made less use of the Escorial than many historians have claimed, see Boyden 1995: 64; Lynch 1964: 173. For a defense of the view that Philip II was outgoing and adept at human interaction, see Kamen 1997.

27. This interpretation is pieced together from Griffiths 1968: 3–6; Jago 1981, 1985, 1989; Koenigsberger 1971a: 79–80; Lynch 1964: 195; Merriman 1962: IV, 422–25; Rodríguez-Salgado 1988. The 1555 decree likely stemmed from Philip's distrust of his sister Juana's handling, as Castilian regent, of the Cortes of that year, for which see Rodríguez-Salgado 1988: 121–24. For the relevant earlier legislation, which remained valid, see NR bk. 6, title 7.

28. On this latter institution, see Perrone 1998.

29. Col. Bel.: Leg. 43, #8, doc. b; AHMT: Libro de Autos, 1 July and 16 December 1566. Because Philip was considering leaving Castile for the Netherlands, he may have hoped to get the Belalcázar dispute out of the way before the Court's transfer. Toledo's patriciate apparently caused concern to the dynasty, as is demonstrated by the fact that the appointment of the city's corregidor was one Charles V reserved for himself when he established prince Philip's regency government in 1543 (Martínez Millán and Carlos Morales 1992: 30, note 21; also see Fernández Alvarez, ed., 1973–1981: II, doc. 252).

Toledo had prepared as best it could for the hearing before the Council. In 1565, the city contracted with Dr. Maneanedo, a prominent lawyer representing clients at the Chancillería of Valladolid, to come to Court to assist Toledo's other representatives. See AGS: Reg. del Sello: October 1565, f. 536.

30. Cortes de Castilla 1862: 20, 106–8, 132, 204–6; Cortes de Castilla 1877: 62, 77–79, 335–36, 462–63, 517, 552.

31. AHMT: Libro de Autos, 11 February 1567; Osuna: Leg. 395, 1 (Madrid, 18 December 1564). Don Francisco had entered the case in a secondary role in the 1550s, when he was only marquis of Ayamonte, because his elder brother Alonso de Zúñiga y Sotomayor, marquis de Gibraleón, had no heirs. Don Alonso had become the principal representative of the House of Béjar in the Puebla de Alcocer and other Belalcázar disputes on the death of his father in 1544, for he directly inherited the county of Belalcázar and viscounty of Puebla de Alcocer. However, because it was his mother rather than his father who had inherited the duchy of Béjar and she outlived don Alonso, he never became duke of Béjar. On his mother's death in 1565, don Francisco added the duchy of Béjar to his vast holdings.

32. AHMT: Libro de Autos, 11 February 1567; Col. Bel.: Leg. 30, #5, f. 14v (sic f. 15v). In addition to the briefs already cited, see Col. Bel.: Leg. 30, #5; Osuna: Leg. 395, 11. These are merely Latin summaries of the points already made, which may have been published more to influence opinion through distribution and discussion than for presentation to the tribunal of the Council of Castile hearing the appeal.

No documentation about the lawsuit remains in the holdings of the AHN of Council of Castile materials; see Consejo de Castilla 1927.

33. Osuna: Carpeta 11–14, f. 64v.

34. BN: Ms. 9.175, f. 268v; López de Ayala y Alvarez de Toledo 1906: 54 (a slightly different version).

35. Asensio Toledo 1867: 5–10; López de Ayala y Alvarez de Toledo 1906: 5.

36. Horozco does not mention these debates, but López de Ayala does (1901: 117, note 65). As in other parts of his history of Toledo, López de Ayala appears to have had some other source than Horozco for his information about the case.

37. AHMT: Libro de Autos, 23 March 1568.

38. Domínguez Ortiz and Vincent 1979: chap. 1; García Oro 1980: chap. 5; García-Villoslada 1980: chap. 2.

39. There is a large and growing literature on these expedients. See, e.g., Fortea Pérez 1990; García Sanz 1980; Marcos Martín 1997, 1998, 2003b; Nader 1990; I. A. A. Thompson 1979; Ulloa 1977: chap. 22; Vassberg 1984; Zabala Aguirre 2000: chap. 7. I thank Alberto Marcos Martín for sharing with me his unpublished work on the vast extent of this royal "auction" of public resources.

40. Atienza Hernández and Simón López 1987; Yun Casalilla 1987a; 1987c: 219–44.

41. Fernández Albaladejo 1992a: pt. II; Fortea Pérez 1990; Gelabert González 1997b, 1998; Jago 1981, 1985, 1989, 1995; I. A. A. Thompson 1997a.

42. Cabrera de Córdoba 1876–1877: II, 125. Boyden (1995) stresses the personal, oral nature of the relationship between Ruy Gómez de Silva and Philip II.

43. Martínez Millán 1992a: 173, note 185. Philip eventually named the marquis of Mondéjar, Luis Hurtado de Mendoza, as Council president, and this led to a series of verdicts in favor of the marquis' relatives. See Ezquerra Revilla 2000: 70.

44. The surviving patronage book of cardinal Espinosa was significant to others after his death not only for the list of individuals proposed for royal service but also for the comprehensive list of the jobs that were available. For the text, see Martínez Millán 1993.

Although the so-called Cámara de Castilla was an important committee for the distribution of royal "grace" (*gracia*), its formal administrative position and predominance in this role was not well defined. It was only in 1588 that the Cámara would become a formalized body with its own ordinances, and by then, its members really only carried out orders given by Philip's noble-dominated junta rather than serving as patrons themselves (Martínez Millán and Carlos Morales 1992: 42 and 45).

I oppose the teleological view that patronage networks accounted for the increasing "power" of rulers and their Court officials and that such patronage activity in the Hispanic Monarchy and other major monarchical regimes constituted a necessary stage in state development. On this view, see Martínez Millán 1992b; 1994c.

45. On these men, see Carlos Morales 1994b; Pizarro Llorente 1994.

46. Often for the reasons Neuschel (1989) has given in her study of French noble clientage.

47. Simancas 1905: 153.

48. Boyden 1995: chaps. 3 and 4.

49. Ezquerra Revilla (2000: 67–68) feels that the *ebolista* clique had a distinctively aristocratic cast.

50. Martínez Millán 1992a, 1994b; Pizarro Llorente 1994: 159–60; Simancas 1905; Tellechea Idígoras 1968.

51. Boyden 1995: chap. 2.
52. For a defense of this thesis, see Boyden 1995: pt. 2. In addition to Martínez Millán 1989, 1992a, and 1994a, see Martínez Millán and Carlos Morales 1992; Pizarro Llorente 1994: 173.
53. Details taken from Boyden 1995; Pierson 1989.
54. Carlos Morales 1992: 134. At the time, the count of Olivares served Philip II as his *mayordomo* and *contador mayor de cuentas* (principal bookkeeper for accounts or chief accountant). Despite Eraso's legal problems, the count retained his good relationship with the king, and in October 1567, Philip authorized the count's oldest son, Enrique de Guzmán, to assume the position of *contador mayor* (see AGS: Reg. del Sello: October (1) 1567, f. 119). Of course, the House of Olivares provided another strong point of Court influence for the House of Béjar. The count's mother, Leonor de Zúñiga, was the aunt of Teresa de Zúñiga y Guzmán, daughter of the marquis of Ayamonte and heir to her uncle, the duke of Béjar, whose marriage in 1518 to the young count of Belalcázar, Francisco de Sotomayor, raised don Francisco to a much higher status among Castile's territorial aristocrats. For this connection, see the genealogy in Elliott 1986: between 18 and 19.
55. AGS: Reg. del Sello: June 1566, ff. 77–78 (both Madrid, 19 June 1566). On the Crown's involvement with the serious and growing indebtedness of the territorial aristocracy during the reign of Philip II, see Yun Casalilla 2002: chap. 5. On the great value for the study of such relationships between the Crown and the aristocracy of the generally underutilized *Registro General del Sello* collection, see Yun's comments in 141, note 9.
56. Boyden 1995: 143–45.
57. On Herrera, see Carlos Morales 1994a.
58. Osuna: Leg. 225, 3 and 23; Leg. 280, 3. The duke of Béjar went to considerable trouble to arrange the Guzmán marriage for his son with his niece. King Philip II helped arrange the illegal financial settlement necessary and probably helped to get the necessary dispensation. The relationship is clearly displayed in the genealogical tables in Pierson 1989: 8 and 230. Other details are in Martínez Millán 1992a: 152, note 66, and 153, note 75.
59. See Col. Bel.: Leg. 3, f. 447v; Keniston 1960: 191, 233, 335, 379.
60. Cabrera de Córdoba 1876–1877: II, 125; Elliott 1964: 235–36 and 258; Gounon-Loubens 1860: 181–82; Koenigsberger 1971a: 77–78 and 80; Pierson 1975: 92 and 120. On tribunal selection, see NR bk. 2, title 4, law 35.
61. See note 44.
62. Martínez Millán 1992a: 181 and note 240, and 190; and esp. 1993, 1994a.
63. Carlos Morales 1994b: 140–45; 1996: chap. 2, esp. 94–99; Martínez Millán 1992a: 186, note 261, 190; Martínez Millán and Carlos Morales 1992: 41–42 and note 104.
64. Martínez Millán and Carlos Morales 1991: 925.
65. Martínez Millán 1992a: 163, note 124; Martínez Millán and Carlos Morales 1991: 925 and note 74; 1992: 34, note 53; Pizarro Llorente 1994.
66. Martínez Millán 1992a: 165–66 and 174. See also Gan Giménez 1988b: 262.
67. Gan Giménez 1988a: 237; 1988b: 231, 234, 256, 287, 291, 306; Martínez Millán 1992a: 129. Dr. Gasca may not have been greatly influenced by the views of Ldo. Galarza because the latter was apparently part of the group that supported the Court

leadership of inquisitor-general Fernando de Valdés (Carlos Morales 1994b: 119–20), and Gasca does not seem to have had such a connection to Valdés. His brother, Pedro de la Gasca, was one of the letrados associated with Cardinal Tavera whom Valdés removed from Court by giving them posts elsewhere. Pedro de la Gasca went to Peru, where his mission to restore royal authority after the Pizarro revolt was a spectacular success (Martínez Millán 1992a: 140, note 13; 147–48, and note 42; 163, note 129).

68. Gan Giménez 1988a: 223; 1988b: 191, 281, 336; Martínez Millán 1992a: 161, 165, notes 138 and 141, 174, note 192; Martínez Millán and Carlos Morales 1992: 37.

There were other letrados at Court at the time who were familiar with the case. One was Ldo. Hernando de Salas (Fernando Salas, d.1571) who in 1565 was elevated to the Council of the Indies (Gan Giménez 1988b: 330). He was one of the signatories of the June 1555 verdict in Toledo's favor. However, as a Granada oidor in the early 1550s, Salas was considered to be close to inquisitor-general Fernando de Valdés (Pizarro Llorente 1992: 232–33), and therefore was not identified as someone with Eboli ties.

69. Marañón 1969: II, 775–76. On Hoyo, see Carlos Morales 1994b: 137–38; Martínez Millán and Carlos Morales 1992: 39–40, and note 89. On Pérez, see Koenigsberger 1971a: 78. In 1586, a certain Domingo de Zavala became secretary of the Council of War, but I do not know if this was the same man as the secretary who bore witness (see Fernández Conti 1998: 209).

70. Martínez Millán 1992a: 174–75.

71. Pizarro Llorente 1994: 171–72.

72. Braudel 1966: II, 54–55; Elliott 1964: 176.

73. See esp. Martínez Millán 1994a. Those officials in a position to influence the trial's outcome may also have had particular interpretive schemes cued for them by their direct involvement in bodies struggling with critical policy matters. The fact that Espinosa, Menchaca, and Velasco were all part of the junta that decided Morisco policy in 1565 may have influenced their views about some of the issues involved in the Belalcázar dispute, and this could have been important even though only Espinosa actually sat on the deciding tribunal. Velasco had also since 1562 been a member of the junta overseeing the reform of religious orders, to which there was considerable resistance, and with the royal confessor, Fresneda, he was its most important member because Fernando de Valdés and Francisco de Eraso so soon lost real political influence. Espinosa and Menchaca were both part of the reform junta of 1566 and later, and the crucial Court figure overseeing the conflictive process by which the decrees of the Council of Trent were instituted was Velasco, aided by Gonzalo Pérez, Antonio Pérez's father (Martínez Millán 1994a: 201, 205, 208). Royal authority was a central matter in all of these deliberations and administrative activities.

74. Koenigsberger (1969: 107 and 111) feels that the king had a "Christian conception of equal justice for all" as well as a "legalistic mind"; also, on Philip's interest in "the impartial administration of justice," see Koenigsberger 1969: 173. Also see Cabrera de Córdoba 1876–1877: II, 169; Elliott 1964: 245–47; Merriman 1962: IV, 26–27 and 453; Pierson 1975: 42–45; Zarco Cuevas 1927: esp. 485–94. Many of these stories can be read in Porreño 1942 [1628]: especially chap. 10, "Su justicia y rectitud," 158–72. González de Echavarri y Vivanco (1917) supports his thesis about Philip II's pursuit of justice on the basis of only seventeen carefully selected documents from the Council of Castile. See Elliott 1964: 387.

75. To quote Pierson (1975: 37), "From Philip's smile to his dagger, contemporaries remarked, was a very short distance." Also see Elliott 1964: 248–49; Fernández Alvarez 1998: 589–604; Israel 1995; Kamen 1997: 162–67; Koenigsberger 1969: 53, 83, 155; 1971a: 134; Lovett 1986, 1988; Lynch 1964: 173–74, 178, 278; Marañón 1969: I, 111; Merriman 1962: IV, 36–37, 444; Pierson 1975: 46–48; Rodríguez-Salgado 1988.

76. Gounon-Loubens 1860: 183; Tomás y Valiente 1995: 309–10. For a diary entry, see Andrés, ed., 1965: 57. On constructing Philip's legend, see Eire 1995: bk. 2.

77. Osuna: Leg. 259, 31. On aristocratic debt and the Crown, see Jago 1973, 1979; Yun Casalilla 1987a, 1987b, 1990b.
A first verdict in the Belalcázar-Córdoba trial, given by the audiencia of Granada in March 1561, was favorable to the House of Béjar. Four of the five justices who decided this case were ones involved in the 1555 decision in favor of Toledo: Ldo. Ramírez de Alarcón, Ldo. Bezerra, Ldo. Salas, and Ldo. Diego de Deza. The fifth was Dr. Diego de Covarrubias who, as a Toledan, would not have been allowed to hear Toledo's dispute with the House of Béjar. As I have suggested, the legal issues in the two cases were substantially different. See Osuna: Leg. 324, 8/6: this memorial discusses the course of the dispute until at least 1566. The trial was still before the Chancillería of Granada in 1597.

78. AHMT: Cartas 1537–1541. Letters about the execution of the sentence dominate the city council's business at this time. Col. Bel.: Leg. 28, #3; Leg. 31.

79. Merriman 1962: IV, 455–56. Also see Guillaume-Alonso 1999.

80. Cárdenas 1873: II, 204–7; Martínez Cardós 1960: 113–22; Tomás y Valiente 1995: 311–12. This edition of the *Partidas* was published by the Council of Castile. The tendency to grant the monarch absolute authority to expropriate property in violation of the law should not be exaggerated. It was a doctrine foreign to Castilian intellectual life, with few followers, and even those few scholars who argued for a supreme royal authority above the law made it clear that they did not mean it could be used unjustly in violation of natural law rights, such as those of property.

81. See Merriman 1962: IV, 454. Although concentrating on foreign and military policy, and the financial administration necessary to sustain initiatives in these areas, several recent studies support my contention that, to understand why the Council of Castile decided for the duke of Béjar and overturned two earlier verdicts of the audiencia of Granada in Toledo's favor, one must consider both the personal interactions at Court and the interpretive schemes, the ideological positions, that the king and many of his principal advisers held in common. See Carlos Morales 1996: esp. chap. 2; Fernández Conti 1998: esp. 80–123; Rivero Rodríguez 1998: chaps. 3 and 4. For a detailed, cogent defense of the thesis that the actions of Philip II and his advisers were frequently shaped by a consistent policy outlook in foreign and military affairs, see G. Parker 1998.

82. Koenigsberger 1969: 71; 1971a: 77.

83. Pizarro Llorente 1994: 173–74.

84. Blanco-González 1970; Cardaillac 1979; Chejne 1983; Domínguez Ortiz and Vincent 1979.

85. AHMT: Libro de Autos, 22 November 1568; Osuna: Leg. 398, 1/1. This change distorted the carta ejecutoria to make it appear that Toledo had not bought the land from Ferdinand III and that John II had disposed of it to reward a loyal vassal. Such distortions were common in these final summaries of cases and make them

unreliable guides to legal developments, a point not made clear by García-Gallo in his discussion of sources (1967: II, v).

86. Col. Bel.: Leg. 43, #8, docs. cc, n, and s. Other letters from officials and lawyers indicate the same level of anxiety.

87. Osuna: Leg. 398, 1/5.

88. AHMT: Libro de Autos, 13 July 1569.

89. Col. Bel.: Leg. 43, #8, doc. ee. Emphasis added.

90. Toledo may not have gained much of value with El Hornillo's recovery. Cut off from their natural pasture lands by the 1574 boundary, its residents were unable to maintain themselves in the difficult seventeenth century. The city rent book of 1682 listed the village as depopulated, having last paid rent in 1649, but the rent book for 1650 indicated that rent was only promised that year and had last been paid in 1643.

91. Toledo's efforts were obviously unproductive, but no document indicates why. See Col. Bel.: Leg. 43, #8, docs. gg, hh, ii, jj, kk, and ll (letters from jurado Juan Belluga de Moncada in Madrid).

92. Toledo's lawyers in the late 1560s were worried about the future implications of the Council of Castile's verdict for the city's jurisdiction over the Montes. Although on the basis of its attack on the letter of sale of Ferdinand III, the Mesta's case against Toledo's lordship was quite strong and the Council rejected the city's request to present more evidence in defense of its jurisdiction, the councillors, serving an elderly king whose heir was a sickly infant, lacked the confidence even to coerce a municipality badly damaged by Castile's prolonged economic and demographic crisis. Instead of taking Toledo's claimed jurisdiction, the justices issued a narrow ruling that gave the Mesta's officials more flexibility for negotiation, and Toledo's council simply ignored this decision of the kingdom's highest judicial tribunal, just as its patrician leaders of that period appear to have ignored most of what came from Madrid that was contrary to their wishes (AHMT: Caj. 12, Leg. 4s, and the *Adición al memorial;* AHN, *Consejos,* Leg. 25821 and 25822).

93. Osuna: Leg. 227, 8; Leg. 255, 6; Leg. 287, 6; Leg. 3759, 45, pts. 1 and 2. There are a number of other letters in both Leg. 255 and Leg. 3759 relating to various services requested from the House of Béjar. Also see Borromeo 1988: 99–100; Braudel 1953: II, 27–28; Lynch 1964: 309; Villamanrique 1976.

Although these men would respond to opportunities for personal service to their king, they might otherwise disobey royal laws. For example, Antonio de Guzmán y de Zúñiga, marquis of Ayamonte, who was later governor of Milan, apparently ran a lucrative smuggling operation from the sea and Portugal through his towns of Lepe, Ayamonte, and La Redondela. On this, see AGS: Reg. del Sello: May (1) 1567, ff. 953, 954, 999, 1001, 1002, 1005, and 1006; May (2) 1567, ff. 94 and 95; June (1) 1567, f. 782.

94. See the opinions compiled in Col. Bel.: Leg. 43, #8, especially doc. 1 (Martínez Muñoz's contribution).

95. Elliott 1985: 154; Kagan 1981: 155–60. Philip II's concern to portray himself as a just ruler reveals his recognition of the importance of this factor among the commonwealth's leaders toward which much of the royal propaganda was directed. On the general importance of law and judicial administration to the monarch's reputation, see Kagan 1981: 211; I. A. A. Thompson 1984b.

96. Elliott 1991; 1992.

97. Nader 1990.

CHAPTER 8

1. In his book on the prophetic dreams of Lucrecia de León, a young woman living in Madrid who came to the attention of the Inquisition, Kagan (1990) has been able to show in some detail the resonances within elite circles of "popular" complaints about royal fiscal measures and the conduct of public affairs. On the satires, see Domínguez Ortiz 1986; Egido 1973; Elliott 1964: 277; Pierson 1975: 109.

2. Fernández Albaladejo 1984; Fortea Pérez 1990; Gelabert González 1997b; Jago 1981, 1985; Lovett 1977: chap. 5, 1980, 1982, 1987; Ruiz Martín 1992; I. A. A. Thompson 1982, 1984a, 1994, 1997a.

3. Feros 1997, 2000; Jago 1995. Of course, some of this stress on personal service could have been motivated by more than a response to other political perspectives. In the case of the duke of Lerma, for example, the "favorite" of Philip III, some of the endorsement of the perspective of personal service could well have involved strategies to justify actions to increase personal wealth that others saw as manifestations of corruption. See Marcos Martín 2003a: 53–59.

4. Stradling 1979: 184–86. For Crown dependence on municipalities, see R. Mackay 1999; Nader 1990; Ruiz Ibáñez 1995; I. A. A. Thompson 1976.

5. Abellán 1980–1991: II, pt. C; III, pt. A, chap. 3; Iñurritegui Rodríguez 1998; Monod 1999: 51–53. In their discussion of the impact of the political ideas of the Second Scholasticism in Portugal, Barreto Xavier and Hespanha (1993: 127–33) offer some suggestive comments about the role of the concept of a tacit pact or contract, whose validity was guaranteed by natural law, between the monarch and his commonwealth that required the former to govern with justice and for the common good. In a way that shows how events could shape the meaning of an interpretive scheme, claims that particular monarchs had failed to rule as they should played roles in justifications for the anti-Habsburg Portuguese revolution of 1640 and the establishment of the infante Pedro's regency in the Portuguese political crisis of 1667. Given the often close intellectual connections between faculty members at the universities of Coimbra and Salamanca, which often involved men from the same religious orders, it would be interesting to know what, if anything, those at the latter university wrote about these events. Of course, the status of a contract in natural law, which a monarch could not abrogate, lay behind the desire of the Castilian Cortes to negotiate contractual agreements about Crown administration when the "kingdom" agreed to the various millones grants of tribute to the king.

6. Although it is no longer possible to assert the existence of an unvarying confluence of interests between the Crown and the Mesta, Castile's famous sheep grazers' organization, and although the absence of a systematic study of litigation involving the Mesta makes firm conclusions impossible, Klein's (1920) portrayal of the chancillerías, especially the Granadan one, as defenders of law and custom against arbitrary rule by the Crown remains plausible on the basis of the evidence he presented. On the ways in which more recent research makes it impossible to sustain a hypothesis presenting effective royal authority as the principal variable with which to explain changes in Mesta influence, income, and herd size, see Bishko 1982; Le Flem 1975; López-Salazar Pérez 1987; C. Phillips and W. Phillips 1997.

7. Domínguez Ortiz 1960; Elliott 1986. On the concerns of Lucrecia's patrons, see Kagan 1990: chap. 4.

8. For the context of some of Mariana's work, see Truman 1999. On Mariana's contemporary and fellow Jesuit, Francisco Suárez, see Lloyd 1991: 292–97.

9. *Historiae de rebus Hispaniae:* Latin, 1592a, 1592b, 1605b; Castilian, 1601, 1623.

10. *De rege et regis institutione libri III* (hereafter, *De rege*): Toledo, 1599; rev. ed., Mainz, 1605, 1611.

11. Citations within my text refer largely to the 1611 edition, indicating the book and chapter as well as the page. The English translations taken from Mariana 1948 are cited by page numbers only. Readers consulting the 1599 edition (or Mariana 1969) or Moore's translation should be aware that beginning with the 1605 edition, Mariana included a new chapter on currency policy, which was inserted as chap. 8 of book III, thereby changing the numbering of the subsequent chapters.

12. See, for example, Bullón Fernández 1936; Fernández Albaladejo 1992a; Hamilton 1963; Jago 1995. Lewy (1960) placed the book in a constitutionalist tradition, but because he did so without familiarizing himself with municipal opposition to Crown policies in the late sixteenth century, he argued that Mariana was reviving displaced medieval positions. For an indication of the continued application by European theorists of "constitutionalist" positions, see Gierke 1950. This theoretical position on the nature of royal authority formed the basis of opposition, at the Cortes of Cádiz, 1810–1813, to the drafting of a written constitution (see, e.g., García-Gallo 1967: II: 1067–1070).

13. Mariana (book III, chap. 12: 304) indicated that the manuscript was nearly complete when he became ill in 1590.

14. In fact, Mariana's *De rege* clearly reveals the Jesuit educational ideal that scholars find so obscured in the Society's various practical plans of study, including the *Ratio studiorum* of 1599 and its preliminary versions of 1586 and 1591. In concentrating on the *Ratio studiorum* of 1599, historians of Jesuit schools have shown signs of frustration because the work is mostly an organizational plan without much explanation of why things were to be done in a particular manner. See, e.g., Anselmi 1981; Donohue 1963; Farrell 1938; Fitzpatrick 1933: chap. 4; Herman 1914; McGovern 1988; Rivera Vázquez 1989. Because he concentrated specifically on the philosophical and theological aspects of the *Ratio* and its developmental tradition, Bartlett (1984) has done the best job of defining the nature of the Jesuit framework and the essentially deductive, expository form within which the Arts curriculum was to be organized. At least in terms of the Castilian schools, Olmedo (1939) has shown that one must read works by Jesuit educators to get a sense of how the *Ratio* was understood and utilized. For example, the works by Juan Bonifacio, Mariana's contemporary, were especially influential among Jesuit teachers. With the sanction of their superiors, the Society's instructors learned from Bonifacio's *Christiani pueri institutio* (Salamanca 1575; Burgos 1586, 1588) and *De sapiente fructuoso* (Burgos 1589) the framing principles that provided the context within which the specific content of the official curriculum should be taught. Apparently, these books enjoyed an especially wide circulation during the intense debates within the Society and with the Dominicans and Inquisition over the draft *Ratio* of 1586 and would, therefore, have been familiar to Mariana when he was writing *De rege*.

15. Skinner 1978: II, 172–73, 345–48; Tuck 1993: 79–80.

16. The section in question occurs within Mariana's discussion of the prince's study of Latin. It is worth quoting:

Among the authors who write history, I believe that one should select for the prince Caesar, Sallust, and Titus Livy, who are discreet in the narration of events and usually illustrate with many enlightening sentences the elegance of its style. When he has acquired a greater fluency, one should add Tacitus, whose writing is unrefined and crabbed but full of insight. His work contains a treasury of decisions and counsels on the gravest problems and reveals the evil customs and frauds of the court [a favorite theme of Mariana's]. In these remote evils and dangers that he describes, we can contemplate, almost as though in a mirror, the image of our own problems. He is truly an author that neither princes nor courtiers should leave out of their possession, and they should be going over his work day and night. (Mariana 1611: II, 6: 137; my translation)

On the study of the place of the study of history in the Latin curriculum, see Grendler 1989: 255–63.

17. Moore 1948: 87.

18. Burke 1991; Fernández-Santamaría 1980, 1983. On Cicero and Tacitus in France, see Salmon 1980. Mariana's recommendation that the prince should read Tacitus was not an innovation. For example, cardinal Juan Tavera, president of the Council of Castile for much of Charles V's reign, featured Tacitus among the Latin authors he read (Espinosa 2003: 194).

19. There are now a number of works on the attempts of the major cities to control Crown activities through the Cortes. Among the most important of these are Fernández Albaladejo 1984, 1992b; Fortea Pérez 1990, 1997a; Gelabert González 1997; Jago 1981, 1985; Lovett 1982, 1987; Ruiz Martín 1992; I. A. A. Thompson 1982, 1984a, 1994, 1997a.

20. *Estatuto Real* (1834), Art. 1 and Art. 34. The citation is to NR bk. 6, title 7, law 1 (citing legislation from the reigns of Alfonso XI, Henry III, John II, and Charles V).

21. The are other recommendations in *De rege* that remind one of the long Belalcázar trial before the audiencia of Granada:

Some means should be thought out to bring litigation to an end so that it does not go on forever. Judges selected for this purpose should finish these minor controversies after a brief hearing, and there should be no machinery for appeal. For the more important cases a time should be prescribed beyond which they may not go. This will be effected, among other means, by taking away the expectation of calling witnesses from far away places, which is fraudulent tactics. They should be considered dead if they are not able to be present within a short time. And how much perversity is there with these delays, collusive acts, postponements, as if on the misery of others an infinite number of men should live, such as lawyers, agents and clerks! (Mariana 1948: 269).

22. For John of Salisbury's commentary, see his *Policraticus* bk. IV, chaps. 1, 2, and 4. The *Lex digna* is quoted at the end of bk. IV, chap. 1.

23. It was for this reason that Mariana began book III, on the monarch's practical obligations, with a chapter on magistrates.

24. Mariana quotes, as though it was a common saying, the following:
Indicium non magni Princeps est (quod saepe repeta~.) magnos habere aulicos (III, 15: 329; emphasis in the original: "The mark of a Prince who is not great (which I will repeat often) is to have great courtiers" (1948: 344; quotation marks in the original).
This is an interesting remark to find in a treatise whose argument was apparently well known among the commonwealth's leaders throughout the seventeenth-century regimes of the royal favorites Lerma and Olivares.

25. In his arguments, Mariana was firmly within the European theoretical tradition of tyrannicide (see Lauer 1987: pt. I).

26. Lewy 1960: 62. For Mariana's concise definition of the rule of law, see III, 11: 295.

27. Lewy (1960: 68) claims that some of Mariana's descriptions of tyrannical actions were allusions to practices of Philip II. On manifestations of discontent in the 1590s, see Domínguez Ortiz 1986; Kagan 1990; Merino Alvarez 1926: 98–102.

28. For the Latin text, with German translation, of the treatise published in Cologne, see Mariana 1996. The author translated the work into Castilian, and although it was not printed until the nineteenth century, manuscript copies apparently circulated; see Mariana 1987 and the introduction by Lucas Beltrán. On Mariana's trial, see Fernández de la Mora 1993. When he became aware of the circulation within Castile of the printed Latin edition of this work, Ldo. Fernando de Acevedo, president of the Council of Castile, sent a memorandum to Philip III's favorite, the duke of Lerma, to warn him about its content (see the text in Alvarado 2000: 383–85). Acevedo particularly noted Mariana's charges of corruption, which Mariana attributed to what was said both publicly and secretly in the plazas and discussion groups, and warned that the book announced a coming Castilian translation. Although it was not usual, Philip II had already introduced the use of the Inquisition as a political tool, for which see Dedieu 1999.

29. Lewy 1960: 28–32; Mousnier 1964; Soons 1982: 66–69. See Aquaviva's decrees in Lewy 1960: 167–68.

30. Kagan 1995: 79. Mariana's *History* remained the most frequently republished and widely distributed history of Spain until the mid nineteenth century (Martínez Martín 1991). For useful biographical information, see Abellán 1980–1991: II, 583–86; Lewy 1960: chap. 2; Sánchez Agesta 1981: ix–xiii; Soons 1982: chap. 1. There are significant errors in Guy 1985: 145–52.

31. This is evident in their neglect by Abellán 1980–1991: III; Guy 1985.

32. Kagan 1974: chap. 9. On the connection between universities and royal administration, see chap. 6.

33. 1967: 281.

34. On some of the motives for censorship in the Habsburg era, see Alvarado 2000. Compare with Clegg 1997, 2001.

35. On late sixteenth- and early seventeenth-century political thought, the following are especially useful: Fernández-Santamaría 1979a, 1979b, 1980, 1983, 1985; Gordon 1974a, 1974b, 1978, 1982, 1984, 1985; Segura Ortega 1984; Vilar 1973.

36. For confusion about the arbitristas, see Gordon 1974a; for an overview emphasizing their economic ideas, see Abellán 1980–1991: III, pt. b, chap. 3. For a discussion group in Toledo in Mariana's time, see Bouza Alvarez 1994a; for a literary

evocation of one such group, see Polo de Medina 1948a. On municipal funding, see Kagan 1995.

37. A. Parker 1957; 1970.

38. I do not offer my comments as an original contribution to research on Lope de Vega. I merely use five of his best-known plays to argue for the continued resonance within the commonwealth of perspectives about royal authority that are central to my microhistory. Although with an inadequate grasp of the context, Young (1979) has discussed views about the monarch expressed by characters in twenty-six of Lope's plays, including four of the five with which I deal. Herrero García (1935) had earlier teased out of Lope's work a series of principles about the exercise of royal authority that clearly illustrate the way in which potentially contradictory ideas could be present in the same cultural environment. These principles are conveniently summarized in Young 1979: 20–21. On the resonance in Lope's plays of another of Mariana's themes–resistance to tyranny–see Gómez-Moriana 1968.

39. Díez Borque 1978: esp. 91–113 and 150–59. Particularly useful on Golden Age theater is Barceló Jiménez 1980. The surviving *corral* (theater) of 1628 in the town of Almagro, south of Toledo in Ciudad Real Province, provides a wonderful sense of the physical environment within which these plays were performed. See García de León Alvarez 2001. A brief, clear discussion of the Golden Age literary controversies that surrounded Lope de Vega's work is provided by McKendrick (1978: 109–14). However, she does not tie this literary debate to other themes of interest to members of the intellectual discussion groups involved or to the larger politically active group of which they were a part. Maravall, who tried to establish such a link (1972b), took too simplistic an approach.

40. McKendrick 1989: 86.

41. The dates of Lope's plays are those given by Morley and Bruerton 1968. The texts of *Peribáñez, Fuenteovejuna,* and *El mejor alcalde* are Vega Carpio 1972; that of *El Duque de Viseo* is Vega Carpio 1950; that of *El castigo sin venganza* is Vega Carpio 1946.

42. On the original rebellion, see Cabrera Muñoz and Moros Guerrero 1991.

43. Act III, lines 641–43 (my translation).

44. Gordon 1974b: 390, note 27; Gordon 1978: 14–15.

45. Indeed, Lauer has shown that, contrary to the opinion of many literary historians, authors of dramatic works even dealt with tyrannicide (1983, 1987: esp, chap. 7, 1988).

46. A. Parker (1957, 1970) and McKendrick (1989: 105–7 and note 29) are correct in stressing the importance of the duke's actions to the development of the plot, but McKendrick at least presents too mechanistic a view of Lope's thought. The great value of Parker's essay is that he points out the centrality of theme rather than action in Golden Age drama, but he fails to appreciate that the primacy of theme removes the need for a single protagonist. C. A. Jones (1966: 16–17) also doubts the necessity of a single tragic hero. On anti-Machiavellian writing, see Bireley 1990; Bleznick 1958.

47. Lope may have adhered to a general vision of Castilian history that saw the fourteenth and fifteenth centuries as a period of disorder, which was subsequently rectified by the restoration of good government by the Catholic Monarchs. According to this view, the first two Habsburgs continued this pattern of improvement. See Elliott 1986: 180, citing an article by Renato I. Rosaldo, Jr., which I have not seen. If

Lope embraced a propaganda line that praised the Habsburg contribution in general and that of Philip II in particular, he did not receive royal rewards. He failed to obtain an appointment as royal chronicler from Philip III's government, and despite repeated dedications of his work to the count and countess of Olivares, he was ignored by the government of Philip IV. Lope's friend in his last years and his biographer, Juan Pérez de Montalván, claimed that Lope received an annual Crown pension of 250 *ducados,* but this payment apparently is not mentioned in any other sources. See Rennert 1968: 280, 314–15, 392–93.

48. On Alamos de Barrientos, see Elliott and de la Peña 1978–1981: I, 4041; Fernández-Santamaría 1979a, 1983: chap. 5. For a rich account of the development in the reign of Philip III of such courtier views, see Feros 2000. On Lisón y Biedma, see Vilar 1971. In many cases, there was evident suspicion about some of the proposals aired at Court, and it was against the authors of these that some people used the word "arbitrista" as a derogatory term. On the moral tone of much of the reformist writing of the early seventeenth century, see Fernández-Santamaría 1979a: 299 and 1980: 355; Gordon 1978.

49. By this term, I mean any cultural expression prepared for the public, regardless of whether it was meant to be heard, seen, or read or involved a degree of public participation, such as a religious procession. It was possible for any of these to express on occasion standards of royal governments.

50. Fernández-Santamaría 1979b, 1983: chap. 6. On restraining tyranny, see Segura Ortega 1984: esp. 263–70. On the religious basis of Saavedra Fajardo's conception of politics, see Bireley 1990: chap. 8. Murillo Ferrol (1957) places the *Defensio fidei* (1613) by the Jesuit scholar Francisco Suárez in the same constitutionalist camp as Mariana.

51. Levenson 1968: I, xxviii.

52. For examples of other possibilities, see Atienza Hernández 1990, 1991; Fernández Albaladejo 1997; Hespanha 1993a.

53. Although the specific phrase "by my absolute royal authority" does not appear in surviving Castilian documents dated before the late fourteenth century, drafters invested the conception of the monarch with such authority as was necessary for justice and good government in the commonwealth in the second of the *Siete Partidas,* the great thirteenth-century Castilian law code compiled by king Alfonso X, "the Learned," and the administrative reforms late in the reign of Alfonso XI (1325–1350). See Craddock 1990; Sánchez-Arcilla Bernal 1995.

54. On such responsibilities, see esp. Atienza Hernández 1987, 1990.

55. For revealing windows on this institutional complexity, see Artola 1999: chaps. 5–7; Baltar Rodríguez 1998; Heras Santos 1991; Lorenzo Cadarso 1999; Roldán Verdejo 1989; Sánchez 1995. Tamar Herzog provides perhaps the richest discussion of the complex processes through which members of the political kingdom were able to govern in the face of general poverty, ineffective institutions, and an inability to coerce compliance (1995, 2001, 2004).

56. Historians have considered Louis XIV's reign to be the culmination of a governmental revolution that formed an important stage in the development of the so-called modern state. Recent research has overthrown the older bureaucratic-command and class-based models of "absolutism" in favor of models concentrating on how the Crown enhanced its authority through personal relationships with territorial aristocrats,

patrimonial officeholders, and local notables and through administrative reforms popular with elite groups whose support was necessary for effective monarchical government. On the place of the French experience in the historiography of "absolutism," see J. Burns 1990: 21. For a synthesis of revisionist work burying the concept of French "absolutism," see Henshall 1992. For a review of this scholarship by a defender of the thesis that royal authoritarian power was exercised through networks of patron-client relationships, see Beik 1991.

57. The post-Franco era assault on the view of Spain as a dismal case of failed modernization is transforming our understanding of the country since 1808 (Juliá 1996). There is an urgent need to consider the implications of this new vision of Spanish national history for an understanding of the much earlier Trastámara-Habsburg era.

Similar attempts have been made to crush stereotypic views of "Golden Age" Spaniards. Yet despite the persuasive effort of Caro Baroja (1978) to repair the damage done to Spaniards by the stereotypic imagination of scholars, one still encounters attempts to fashion the *español típico* of Habsburg era as an example of the failings of a national character corrupted by an irrational, repressive religion and absurd hidalgo moral codes (reflected to some extent in Eire 1995). Unable to make the transition from "feudalism" to a work-oriented, entrepreneurial "capitalism," this Spain ended up backward, weak, and poor.

It appears that, to some extent, the analysis of Spaniards and their history has become subject to an established reductionist "discourse," in the sense used by Said (1978), that has often served to justify authoritarian control of a people whose "culture" is supposed to have left them unprepared to govern themselves. It goes well beyond scholarly error to perpetuate degrading stereotypes about Spaniards' capacities as human beings, especially because their attempts to build workable democratic institutions have become exemplary for many other countries whose citizens are trying to create or recreate such institutions on the basis of a written constitution.

58. Although he still wants to hold onto the familiar two-models thesis, Nieto Soria (1998) offers an impressive, devastating demonstration of the breadth of support by the mid fifteenth century for the "constitutional" idea of a monarchy whose ruler possessed absolute royal authority.

59. See, e.g., Cárceles de Gea 1999; García-Gallo 1967: II, 1067–1070; Gibert 2000: 457 and 460 (on an article, which I have not been able to consult, by Salustiano de Dios on the variety of sixteenth-century jurists' views of absolute royal authority).

60. I wish to express my gratitude to the late John D. Lewis of Oberlin College, who introduced me to Mariana when he divined my geographic and thematic interests in political thought.

61. For a discussion of a prevailing group of interpretive schemes that permitted seventeenth-century Castilians to retain obedience to their king while refusing to respond to his commands, see Cárceles de Gea 1997.

62. Phelan (1967) showed how the commonwealth's leaders in the Quito region remained loyal to a distant Crown because of their need for outside resolution of divisive conflicts. Such divisions would not only undermine the commonwealth's internal order and prosperity, and perhaps lead to threats to elite predominance (see Owens 1980), but it would make the community vulnerable to outside attack, as

many Castilians felt the story of the eighth-century Muslim conquest of the Visigoths demonstrated. In the face of a constant factional threat, royal authority was sought in the name of justice, understood both as the adjudication of disputes and as the granting of resources for service, to control divisive conflict and provide the cohesion sufficient for defense against Castile's enemies. Although at times there were violent confrontations between bandos defined by economic or institutional roles, by solidarity groups, or by aristocratic clientage networks, when one is able to study the course of such conflict, it becomes apparent that contemporaries' understandings of it through reference, for example, to opposing lineages within a particular municipality were little more than attempts to explain highly complex situations with a convenient sociological simplicity.

63. See Oakley (1996) for a cogent response to Quentin Skinner's rejection, particularly in his earlier publications, of "influence" as a valid issue when considering why someone wrote a particular work. I do not wish to argue that the language somehow determined the thought (see Pinker 1995: chap. 3). Because language and thought are different, expressing an interpretive scheme in words does not create the scheme. The expression only has the *potential* to cue the scheme. Whether the expression really cues the interpretive scheme to the point where someone employs it to recognize patterns depends in part on how it is expressed in relation to hearers and readers and on other shaping parameters, especially within the social environment. Also, the context of the expression might lead to a scheme's rejection and the consequent cuing of alternatives.

64. For a fascinating study of the bibliographic context of Quijote's "library," see Baker 1997.

65. See Alvarez Nogal 1997.

66. On corruption, see Bernardo Ares 1993; Cárceles de Gea 1994, 1995; López Belinchón 2001; Moutoukias 1988. On the impact of low investor confidence, see Espina Montero 2001a, 2001b. Kagan (1974: 222–23 and 1981: 220–35) speculates that administrative irregularities became so great in the seventeenth century that lack of confidence in Crown institutions contributed to a decline in litigation and consequent increase in out-of-court settlements. On Dutch and English public finance, see Braddick 1996; Brewer 1989; Hart 1993, 1995; Riley 1980. The advantages to a ruler of close collaboration with the commonwealth's leaders, gained through the effective use of representative institutions, are evident even in much less economically favored polities, such as early seventeenth-century Bavaria (see Dollinger 1968).

67. On this subject, see the suggestive work of Bernardo Ares 1994, 1996; Fortea Pérez 1997b; Gelabert González 1997; Mackay 1999; Yun Casalilla 1990a, 1991. For a useful cautionary note, see I. A. A. Thompson 1997b. For a broad perspective on the importance of these families, see Dedieu and Windler 1998.

68. On the situation during the reign of the final Habsburg, Charles II, see Carrasco Martínez 1999.

69. On the development in the nineteenth and twentieth centuries of different visions of Spanish history to support alternative views of the country's political organization, see Juliá 2004.

WORKS CITED

Abellán, J. L.
1980–1991 *Historia crítica del pensamiento español.* 5 vols. Madrid: Espasa-Calpe.
ADMYTE
1995 *Archivo Digital de Manuscritos y Textos Españoles.* 2 CD-ROM disks. Madrid: Micronet.
Alba, R.
1975 *Acerca de algunas particularidades de las Comunidades de Castilla tal vez relacionadas con el supuesto acaecer terreno del Milenio Igualitario.* Madrid: Editora Nacional.
Alberigo, G.
1978 "Il movimento conciliare (XIV–XV sec.) nella ricerca storica recente." *Studi Medievali* 19: 213–50.
1981 *Chiesa conciliare: Identità e significato del conciliarismo.* Brescia: Paideia.
Alcocer, Pedro de [ca. 1490–after 1551]
1872 *Relación de algunas cosas que pasaron en estos reinos desde que murió la reina doña Isabel hasta que se acabaron las Comunidades en la ciudad de Toledo* [1554, but perhaps written before 1539]. Ed. A. Martín Gamero. Sevilla: Sociedad de Bibliófilos Andaluces.
Alexander, J. C.
1988 *Action and Its Environments: Toward a New Synthesis.* New York: Columbia University Press.
Alfonso X
1491 *Siete Partidas* [Sevilla: Pablo de Colonia, Juan Pegnitzer, y compañeros alemanes]. 2 vols. Transcr. C. Wasick. In ADMYTE (1995): disk 1.
Alonso-Guillaume, A.
1989 "Justice royale et oligarchies urbaines en Castille à travers les pétitions des *Cortes* (1518–1538)." *Mélanges de la Casa de Velázquez* 25: 103–20.
Alvarado, J.
2000 "Juristas turbadores: La censura inquisitorial a la literatura jurídica y política (siglos XVI–XVII)." In Alvarado, ed. (2000): 331–85.
Alvarado, J. (ed.)
2000 *Historia de la literatura jurídica de la España del Antiguo Régimen.* Madrid and Barcelona: Marcial Pons.
Alvarez de Frutos, P.
1984 "Segovia y la guerra de las Comunidades: Análisis social." *Hispania* 44,158: 469–94.
1988 *La revolución comunera en tierras de Segovia.* Segovia: Taller Imagen.
Alvarez Nogal, C.
1997 *El crédito de la Monarquía hispánica en el reinado de Felipe IV.* Avila: Junta de Castilla y León, Consejería de Educación y Cultura.

Alvarez Palenzuela, V. A.

1992 *La situación europea en la época del Concilio de Basilea: Informe de la delegación del Reino de Castilla*. León: Centro de Estudios e Investigación "San Isidoro" (CECEL), Archivo Histórico Diocesano.

Anderson, P.

1974 *Lineages of the Absolute State*. London: N. L. B.

Andreae, Joannes [d. 1348]

1963 *In quinque decretalium libros novella commentaria* [1581]. Turin: Bottega d'Erasmo.

Andrés, G. de (ed.)

1965 *Documentos para la historia del Monasterio de San Lorenzo el Real de El Escorial*. Vol. 8. El Escorial: Imprenta del Real Monasterio.

Anselmi, G.-M.

1981 "Per un'archeologia della *Ratio:* Dalla 'pedagogia' al 'governo.'" In Brizzi, ed. (1981): 11–42.

Aranda Pérez, F. J.

1992 *Poder municipal y cabildo de jurados en Toledo en la edad moderna (siglos XV–XVIII)*. Toledo: Ayuntamiento de Toledo.

1999 *Poder y poderes en la ciudad de Toledo: Gobierno, Sociedad y Oligarquías urbanas en la Edad Moderna*. Cuenca: Universidad de Castilla-La Mancha.

Artola, M.

1999 *La Monarquía de España*. Madrid: Alianza Editorial.

Asch, R. G., and A. M. Birke (eds.)

1991 *Princes, Patronage, and the Nobility: The Court at the Beginning of the Modern Age, c. 1450–1650*. Oxford: Oxford University Press for The German Historical Institute of London.

Asensio Toledo, J. M.

1867 *Sebastián de Horozco: Noticias y obras inéditas de este autor dramático desconocido*. Sevilla: Geofrín.

Atienza Hernández, I.

1987 *Aristocracia, poder y riqueza en la España moderna: La Casa de Osuna, siglos XV–XIX*. Madrid: Siglo XXI de España.

1990 "Paterfamilias, señor y patrón: Oeconómica, clientelismo y patronato en el Antiguo Régimen." In R. Pastor, ed. (1990): 411–58.

1991 "El señor avisado: Programas paternalistas y control social en la Castilla del siglo XVII." *Manuscrits* 9: 155–204.

Atienza Hernández, I., and M. Simón López

1987 "Patronazgo real, rentas, patrimonio y nobleza en los siglos XVI y XVII: Algunas notas para un análisis político y socioeconómico." *Revista Internacional de Sociología* 45,1: 25–75.

Azcona, T. de

1964 *Isabel la Católica: Estudio crítico de su vida y su reinado*. Madrid: Biblioteca de Autores Cristianos.

Aznar Vallejo, E. (ed.)

1990 *Pesquisa de Cabitos*. Las Palmas de Gran Canaria: Cabildo Insular de Gran Canaria.

Baker, E.

1997 *La biblioteca de Don Quijote*. Madrid: Marcial Pons.

Baldus de Ubaldus, Bartolo [ca. 1327–ca. 1400]

1616 *Commentaria in Digestum vetus, Infortiatum, Digestum novum, Codicem.* Venice.

Ballesteros, P.

1946 "La función política de las Reales Chancillerías Coloniales." *Revista de Estudios Políticos* 15: 47–110.

Baltar Rodríguez, J. F.

1998 *Las Juntas de Gobierno en la Monarquía Hispánica (siglos XVI–XVII).* Madrid: Centro de Estudios Políticos y Constitucionales.

Bandos y querellas

1991 *Bandos y querellas dinásticas en España al final de la Edad Media.* Paris: Biblioteca Española; Madrid: Ministerio de Asuntos Exteriores.

Barceló Jiménez, J.

1980 *Historia del teatro en Murcia.* 2nd ed. Murcia: Academia Alfonso X el Sabio.

Barkey, K., and S. Parikh

1991 "Comparative Perspectives on the State." *Annual Review of Sociology* 17: 523–49.

Barreto Xavier, A., and A. M. Hespanha

1993 "A representação da sociedade e do Poder." In Hespanha, ed. (1993): 121–55.

Barrientos, Lope de [d. 1469]

1946 *Refundición de la crónica del halconero.* Ed. J. de M. Carriazo. Madrid: Espasa-Calpe.

Barrios, F.

1984 *El Consejo de Estado de la Monarquía Española, 1.521–1.812.* Madrid: Consejo de Estado.

Barros, C.

1990 *Mentalidad justiciera de los irmandiños, siglo XV.* Madrid: Siglo XXI de España.

Bartlett, D. A.

1984 "The Evolution of the Philosophical and Theological Elements of the Jesuit Ratio Studiorum: An Historical Study, 1540–1599." Ed.D. diss. University of San Francisco.

Bartolus de Saxoferrato [1314–1357]

1577 *Commentaria in Digestum vetus, Infortiatum, Digestum novum, Codicem.* Turin.

1986 "On the Tyrant." In Cochrane and Kirshner, eds. (1986): 7–30.

Bataillon, M.

1966 *Erasmo y España: Estudios sobre la historia espiritual del siglo XVI.* 2nd ed. Trans. A. Alatorre. Mexico City: Fondo de Cultura Económica [1937, 1950].

Batista i Roca, J. M.

1957 "The Hispanic Kingdoms and the Catholic Kings." In Potter, ed. (1957): I, 316–42.

Bäumer, R.

1999 "Conciliarism." In Grendler, ed. (1999): II, 62–64.

Beceiro Pita, I.

1988 "Los estados señoriales como estructura de poder en la Castilla del siglo XV." In Rucquoi, ed. (1988): 293–323.

1999 "La importancia de la cultura en las relaciones peninsulares (siglo XV)." *Anuario de Estudios Medievales* 29: 79–104.

Beik, W.
1985 *Absolutism and Society in Seventeenth-Century France: State Power and Provincial Aristocracy in Languedoc.* Cambridge: Cambridge University Press.
1990 Review of Mettam (1988). *Journal of Modern History* 62: 861–63.
1991 "Celebrating Andrew Lossky: The Reign of Louis XIV Revisited" [review article]. *French Historical Studies* 17,2: 526–41.
Belenguer Cebrià, E. (ed.)
1999 *Felipe II y el Mediterráneo:* Vol. II: *Los grupos sociales.* Madrid: Sociedad Estatal para la Conmemoración de los Centenarios de Felipe II y Carlos V.
Bellomo, M.
1989 *L'Europa del diritto comune.* Rome: Il Cigno Galileo Galilei.
Belmonte Díaz, J.
1986 *Los comuneros de la Santa Junta: La "Constitución de Avila."* Avila: Caja de Ahorros de Avila.
Benedict, P.
1989 "French Cities from the Sixteenth Century to the Revolution: An Overview." In Benedict, ed. (1989): 7–68.
Benedict, P. (ed.)
1989 *Cities and Social Change in Early Modern France.* London: Unwin Hyman.
Beneyto Pérez, J.
1940 *Manual de historia del derecho.* Zaragoza: Librería General.
1954 "La política jurisdiccional y de orden público de los Reyes Católicos." *La Revista de Estudios Políticos* 52: 89–104.
1958 *Historia de la administración española e hispanoamericana.* Madrid: Aguilar.
Benito Ruano, E.
1961 *Toledo en el siglo XV: Vida política.* Madrid: Consejo Superior de Investigaciones Científicas.
1972 *La prelación ciudadana: Las disputas por la precedencia entre las ciudades de la Corona de Castilla.* Toledo: Centro Universitario.
Bennassar, B.
1967 *Valladolid au siècle d'or: Une ville de Castille et sa campagne au XVIe siècle.* Paris: Mouton.
Bentley, E. (ed.)
1970 *The Great Playwrights.* Vol. I. Garden City, New York: Doubleday.
Bercé, Y.-M.
1987 *Revolt and Revolution in Early Modern Europe: An Essay on the History of Political Violence.* Trans. J. Bergin. New York: St. Martin's Press [1980].
Bermejo Cabrero, J. L.
1975a "Mayoría de justicia del rey y jurisdicciones señoriales en la Baja Edad Media castellana." In Metodología Aplicada (1975): II, 191–206.
1975b "Principios y apotegmas sobre la ley y el rey en la Baja Edad Media castellana." *Hispania* 35,129: 3–47.
1985 "Sobre nobleza, señoríos y mayorazgos." *Anuario de Historia del Derecho Español* 55: 283–305.
Bernardo Ares, J. M. de
1993 *Corrupción política y centralización administrativa: La Hacienda de Propios en la Córdoba de Carlos II.* Córdoba: Universidad de Córdoba, Monografías, No. 196.

1994 "Fiscal Pressure and the City of Cordoba's Communal Assets in the Early Seventeenth Century" [1981]. In Thompson and Yun Casalilla, eds. (1994): 206–19.

1996 "Poder local y Estado absoluto: La importancia política de la administración municipal de la Corona de Castilla en la segunda mitad del siglo XVII." In Bernardo Ares and Martínez Ruiz, eds. (1996): 111–55.

Bernardo Ares, J. M. de, and E. Martínez Ruiz (eds.)
1996 *El municipio en la España moderna.* Córdoba: Universidad de Córdoba.

Biñayán Carmona, N.
1986 "De la nobleza vieja . . . a la nobleza vieja." In Carlé, Grassotti, and Orduna, eds. (1983–1990): IV, 103–38.

Bireley, R.
1990 *The Counter-Reformation Prince: Anti-Machiavellianism or Catholic Statecraft in Early Modern Europe.* Chapel Hill: University of North Carolina Press.

Bishko, C. J.
1982 "Sesenta años después: La Mesta de Julius Klein a la luz de la investigación subsiguiente." *Historia. Instituciones. Documentos* 8: 9–57.

Black, A. J.
1970 *Monarchy and Community: Political Ideas in the Later Conciliar Controversy, 1430–1450.* Cambridge: Cambridge University Press.

1979 *Council and Commune: The Conciliar Movement and the Fifteenth-Century Heritage.* London: Burns and Oates; Shepherdston, Maryland: Patmos Press.

1988 "The Conciliar Movement." In J. H. Burns, ed. (1988): 573–87.

Blanco-González, B.
1970 "Itinerarios de las campañas." In Hurtado de Mendoza (1970): 441–48.

Blázquez Miguel, J.
1986 *El tribunal de la Inquisición en Murcia.* Murcia: Alfonso X el Sabio.

Bleznick, D. W.
1958 "Spanish Reaction to Machiavelli in the Sixteenth and Seventeenth Centuries." *Journal of the History of Ideas* 19: 542–50.

Blickle, P. (ed.)
1996 *Theorien kommunaler Ordnung in Europa.* Munich: R. Oldenbourg.

Blythe, J. M.
1992 *Ideal Government and the Mixed Constitution in the Middle Ages.* Princeton, New Jersey: Princeton University Press.

Bonachía Hernando, J. A.
1978 *El concejo de Burgos en la Baja Edad Media (1345–1426).* Valladolid: Universidad de Valladolid.

1988 *El señorío de Burgos durante la Baja Edad Media (1255–1508).* Valladolid: Universidad de Valladolid.

1990 "El concejo como señorío (Castilla, siglos XIII–XV)." In Concejos y Ciudades (1990): 429–63.

Bonney, R. J. (ed.)
1995 *Economic Systems and State Finance.* Oxford and New York: Oxford University Press.

Borromeo, A.
1988 "Archbishop Carlo Borromeo and the Ecclesiastical Policy of Philip II in the State of Milan." In Headley and Tomaro, eds. (1988): 85–111.

Botero, Giovanni [1544–1617]

1948 *Della Region di Stato. Con tre libri "Delle cause della grandezza delle città," due "Aggiunte" e un "Discorso" sulla popolazione di Roma.* Ed. L. Firpo. Turin.

1956 *The Reason of State* [1589]. Trans. P. J. and D. P. Waley. New Haven, Connecticut: Yale Univesity Press, 1–224.

Bouza Alvarez, F.

1994a "Corte es decepción: Don Juan de Silva, conde de Portalegre." In Martínez Millán, ed. (1994): 451–502.

1994b "La majestad de Felipe II: Construcción del mito real." In Martínez Millán, ed. (1994): 37–72.

Boyden, J. M.

1995 *The Courtier and the King: Ruy Gómez de Silva, Philip II, and the Court of Spain.* Berkeley, Los Angeles, and London: University of California Press.

Braddick, M. J.

1996 *The Nerves of State: Taxation and the Financing of the English State, 1558–1714.* Manchester: Manchester University Press.

Brandi, K.

1965 *The Emperor Charles V: The Growth and Destiny of a Man and of a World-Empire.* Trans. C. V. Wedgwood. London: Jonathan Cape [1939].

Brandt, F.

1928 *Thomas Hobbes' Mechanical Conception of Nature.* Copenhagen: Levin and Munksgaard; London: Librairie Hachette.

Braudel, F.

1953 *El Mediterráneo y el mundo mediterráneo en la época de Felipe II.* Trans. M. Monteforte Toledo and W. Roces. 2 vols. Mexico: Fondo de Cultura Económica [1949].

1966 *La Méditerranée et le monde méditerranéen a l'époque de Philippe II.* 2nd ed. 2 vols. Paris: A. Colin [1949].

Bredemeier, H. C.

1962 "Law as an Integrative Mechanism." In Evan, ed. (1962): 73–90.

Breteau, C. H., and N. Zagnoli (eds.)

1993 *Production, pouvoir et parenté dans le monde méditerranéen.* Paris: Geuthner.

Brewer, J.

1989 *The Sinews of Power: War, Money, and the English State, 1688–1783.* New York: Knopf.

Brinton, C.

1938 *The Anatomy of Revolution.* New York: W. W. Norton.

Brizzi, G. P. (ed.)

1981 *La "Ratio studiorum": Modelli culturali e pratiche educative dei Gesuiti in Italia tra Cinque e Seicento.* Rome: Bulzoni.

Bruner, J.

1996 *The Culture of Education.* Cambridge, Massachusetts, and London: Harvard University Press.

Bryson, W. H.

1975 *Dictionary of Sigla and Abbreviations to and in Law Books before 1607.* Charlottesville: University Press of Virginia.

Bullón Fernández, E.

1927 *Un colaborador de los Reyes Católicos: El Doctor Palacios Rubios y sus obras.* Madrid: Ramona Velasco for Victoriano Suárez.

1936 *El concepto de la soberanía en la escuela jurídica española del siglo XVI.* 2nd ed. Madrid: Rivadeneyra for Victoriano Suárez.

Burckhardt, J.

1860 *Die Kultur der Renaissance in Italien.* Basel: Schweighauserschen Verlagsbuchhandlung.

Burke, P.

1991 "Tacitism, Scepticism, and Reason of State." In Burns and Goldie, eds. (1991): 479–98.

Burns, J. H.

1990 "The Idea of Absolutism." In Miller, ed. (1990): 21–42.

1992 *Lordship, Kingship, and Empire: The Idea of Monarchy, 1400–1525.* Oxford: Clarendon Press.

Burns, J. H. (ed.)

1988 *The Cambridge History of Medieval Political Thought, c.350–c.1450.* Cambridge: Cambridge University Press.

Burns, J. H., and M. Goldie (eds.)

1991 *The Cambridge History of Political Thought, 1450–1700.* Cambridge: Cambridge University Press.

Burns, R. I. (ed.)

1990 *Emperor of Culture: Alfonso X the Learned of Castile and His Thirteenth-Century Renaissance.* Philadelphia: University of Pennsylvania Press.

Cabrera de Córdoba, L.

1876–1877 *Filipe Segundo, Rey de España.* 4 vols. Madrid: Aribau.

Cabrera Muñoz, E.

1974 "La oposición de las ciudades al régimen señorial: El caso de Córdoba frente a los Sotomayor de Belalcázar." *Historia. Instituciones. Documentos* 1: 11–39.

1977 *El condado de Belalcázar (1444–1518): Aportación al estudio del régimen señorial en la Baja Edad Media.* Córdoba: Monte de Piedad y Caja de Ahorros de Córdoba.

Cabrera Muñoz, E., and A. Moros Guerrero

1991 *Fuenteovejuna: La violencia antiseñorial en el siglo XV.* Barcelona: Editorial Crítica.

Cabrillana Cieza, N.

1969 "Salamanca en el siglo XV: Nobles y campesinos." In Moxó, ed. (1969): 255–95.

Calderón Ortega, J. M.

1998 *Alvaro de Luna: Riqueza y poder en la Castilla del siglo XV.* Madrid: Editorial Dykinson.

Canning, J. P.

1987 *The Political Thought of Baldus de Ubaldis.* Cambridge: Cambridge University Press.

Capella, M., and A. Matilla Tascón

1957 *Los cinco gremios mayores de Madrid: Estudio crítico-histórico.* Madrid: Sáez.

Carande, R.
1943–1967 *Carlos V y sus banqueros.* 3 vols. Madrid: Sociedad de Estudios y Publicaciones.
1965 *Carlos V y sus banqueros:* Vol. 1: *La vida económica en Castilla (1516–1556).* 2nd ed., revised. Madrid: Sociedad de Estudios y Publicaciones [1943].

Cárceles de Gea, B.
1994 *Fraude y administración fiscal en Castilla. La Comisión de Millones (1632–1658): Poder fiscal y privilegio jurídico-político.* Madrid: Banco de España, Servicios de Historia Económica, No. 28.
1995 *Reforma y fraude fiscal en el reinado de Carlos II: La Sala de Millones (1658–1700).* Madrid: Banco de España, Servicios de Historia Económica, No. 31.
1997 "'Voluntase iurisdictio': Obediencia, ejecución y cumplimiento de la voluntad real en la Corona de Castilla en el siglo XVII." In Fernández Albaladejo, ed. (1997): 663–77.
1999 "Reforma/abolición del Tribunal de la Inquisición (1812–1823): La constitución de la *autoridad absoluta.*" *Manuscrits* 17: 177–99.

Cardaillac, L.
1979 *Moriscos y cristianos: Un enfrentamiento polémico (1492–1640).* Trans. M. García Arenal. Madrid: Fondo de Cultura Económica, España [1977].

Cárdenas, F. de
1873 *Ensayo sobre la historia de la propiedad territorial en España.* 2 vols. Madrid: J. Noguera.

Carlé, M. del C., H. Grassotti, and G. Orduna (eds.)
1983–1990 *Estudios en homenaje a Don Claudio Sánchez Albornoz en sus 90 años.* 6 vols. Buenos Aires: Instituto de Historia de España.

Carlos Morales, C. J. de
1989 "El Consejo de Hacienda de Castilla en el reinado de Carlos V (1523–1556)." *Anuario de Historia del Derecho Español* 59: 49–159.
1992 "Grupos de poder en el Consejo de Hacienda de Castilla: 1551–1556." In Martínez Millán, ed. (1992): 107–36.
1994a "Ambiciones y comportamiento de los hombres de negocios: El asentista Melchor de Herrera." In Martínez Millán, ed. (1994): 379–415.
1994b "El poder de los secretarios reales: Francisco de Eraso." In Martínez Millán, ed. (1994): 107–48.
1996 *El Consejo de Hacienda de Castilla, 1523–1602: Patronazgo y clientelismo en el gobierno de las finanzas reales durante el siglo XVI.* Avila: Junta de Castilla y León, Consejería de Educación y Cultura.

Carlyle, R. W., and A. J. Carlyle
1909–1936 *A History of Mediaeval Political Theory in the West.* 6 vols. New York: Barnes and Noble.

Caro Baroja, J.
1978 *Las formas complejas de la vida religiosa: Religión, sociedad y carácter en la España de los siglos XVI y XVII.* Madrid: Akal.

Carrasco Martínez, A.
1991a *Control y responsabilidad en la administración señorial: Los juicios de residencia en las tierras de Infantado (1650–1788).* Valladolid: Universidad de Valladolid.

1991b *El régimen señorial en la Castilla moderna: Las tierras de la Casa del Infantado en los siglos XVII y XVIII.* Madrid: Universidad Complutense.

1999 "Los Grandes, el poder y la cultura política de la nobleza en el reinado de Carlos II." *Stvdia Historica: Historia Moderna* 20: 77–136.

Carretero Zamora, J. M.

1988 *Cortes, monarquía, ciudades: Las Cortes de Castilla a comienzos de la época moderna (1476–1515).* Madrid: Siglo XXI de España.

2002 "Las Cortes en el programa comunero: ¿Reforma institucional o propuesta revolucionaria?" In Martínez Gil, ed. (2002): 233–78.

Carrillo de Huete, Pedro [15th century]

1946 *Crónica del halconero de Juan II.* Ed. J. de M. Carriazo. Madrid: Espasa-Calpe.

Casa de Velázquez

1991 *Tolède et l'expansion urbaine en Espagne (1450–1650).* Madrid: Collection de la Casa de Velázquez, 32.

Casado Alonso, H.

1985 "Nuevos documentos sobre la guerra de las comunidades de Burgos." In Congreso de Historia de Burgos (1985): 247–60.

1988 "Oligarquía urbana, comercio internacional y poder real: Burgos a fines de la Edad Media." In Rucquoi, ed. (1988): 325–47.

Castellano Castellano, J. L., and F. Sánchez-Montes González (eds.)

2001 *Carlos V: Europeísmo y universalidad: Congreso internacional, Granada, mayo de 2000.* 5 vols. Madrid: Sociedad Estatal para la Conmemoración de los Centenarios de Felipe II y Carlos V; Universidad de Granada.

Castrillo, Alonso de [early 16th century]

1958 *Tractado de República* [Burgos, 1521]. Madrid: Instituto de Estudios Políticos.

Caxa de Leruela, M.

1975 *Restauración de la abundancia de España* [1631]. Ed. J.-P. Le Flem. Madrid: Instituto de Estudios Fiscales, Ministerio de Hacienda.

Centre "Pierre Vilar"

1992 *1640: La monarquía hispánica en crisis.* Barcelona: Centre D'Estudis D'Història Moderna "Pierre Vilar," Editorial Crítica.

Cerdá Ruiz-Funes, J.

1970 "Hombres buenos, jurados y regidores en los municipios castellanos de la Baja Edad Media." In Cerdá Ruiz-Funes (1987): 307–65.

1987 *Estudios sobre instituciones jurídicas medievales de Murcia y su Reino.* Murcia: Academia Alfonso X el Sabio.

Chacón, Gonzalo [15th century]

1946 See Crónica de Luna 1946.

Chancillería de Granada

1601 *Ordenanças de la Real Audiencia y Chancillería de Granada.* Granada: Sebastián de Mena.

Chaunu, P.

1973 *L'Espagne de Charles Quint.* 2 vols. Paris: Société d'Edition d'Enseignement Supérieur.

Chejne, A. G.

1983 *Islam and the West: The Moriscos, A Cultural and Social History.* Albany: State University of New York Press.

Christianson, G., and T. M. Izbicki, eds.
1996 *Nicholas of Cusa on Christ and the Church*. Leiden: E. J. Brill.

Church, W. F.
1941 *Constitutional Thought in Sixteenth-Century France: A Study in the Evolution of Ideas*. Cambridge, Massachusetts: Harvard University Press.

Churchland. P. S.
1986 *Neurophilosophy: Toward a Unified Science of the Mind-Brain*. Cambridge, Massachusetts: MIT Press.

Churchland, P. S., and T. J. Sejnowski
1992 *The Computational Brain*. Cambridge, Massachusetts: MIT Press.

Clavero, B.
1989 *Mayorazgo: Propiedad feudal en Castilla, 1369–1836*. 2nd ed. Madrid: Siglo XXI de España [1974].

Clegg, C. S.
1997 *Press Censorship in Elizabethan England*. Cambridge and New York: Cambridge University Press.
2001 *Press Censorship in Jacobean England*. Cambridge and New York: Cambridge University Press.

Cochrane, E., and J. Kirshner (eds.)
1986 *The Renaissance* [Vol. 5 of the *University of Chicago Readings in Western Civilization*]. Chicago and London: University of Chicago Press.

Códigos Españoles
1872–1873 *Los códigos españoles concordados y anotados*. 2nd ed. 12 vols. Madrid: Antonio de San Martín.

CODOIN
1893 *Colección de documentos inéditos para la historia de España*. Vol. 106. Madrid: José Perales y Martínez.

Collantes de Terán, A.
1977 *Sevilla en la Baja Edad Media: La ciudad y sus hombres*. Sevilla: Ayuntamiento de Sevilla.

Collins, J. B.
1988 *Fiscal Limits of Absolutism: Direct Taxation in Early Seventeenth-Century France*. Berkeley and Los Angeles: University of California Press.

Coloquio de La Rábida
1985 *La ciudad hispánica durante los siglos XIII y XVI: Actas del coloquio en La Rábida y Sevilla del 14 al 19 de septiembre de 1981*. 2 vols. Madrid: Universidad Complutense.

Coloquio Historia de Andalucía
1982 *Andalucía Medieval: Actas I Coloquio Historia de Andalucía, Córdoba, Noviembre 1979*. Córdoba: Monte de Piedad y Caja de Ahorros de Córdoba.

Concejos y Ciudades
1990 *Concejos y ciudades en la Edad Media hispánica. II Congreso de Estudios Medievales* [León, 1989]. Avila: Fundación Sánchez-Albornoz.

Congreso de Historia de Burgos [1984]
1985 *La ciudad de Burgos: Actas del Congreso de Historia de Burgos. MC Aniversario de la Fundación de la Ciudad, 884–1984*. León: Junta de Castilla y León, Consejería de Educación y Cultura.

Consejo de Castilla
1927 *Indice de pleitos sobre mayorazgos, estados y señoríos.* Ed. A. Gonzáles Palencia. Madrid: Archive Histórico Nacional.
Contreras Contreras, J.
2002 "Profetismo y apocalipsismo: Conflicto ideológico y tensión social en las Comunidades de Castilla." In Martínez Gil, ed. (2002): 517–38.
Cooper, E.
1991 *Castillos señoriales en la Corona de Castilla.* 3 vols. in 4. Salamanca: Junta de Castilla y León, Consejería de Cultura y Turismo.
1996 "La revuelta de las Comunidades: Una visión desde la sacristía." *Hispania* 56,193: 467–95.
2002 "La iglesia y los comuneros: Una interpretación anti-antiseñorial." In Martínez Gil, ed. (2002): 279–306.
Corbett, T. G.
1975 "The Cult of Lipsius: A Leading Source of Early Modern Statecraft." *Journal of the History of Ideas* 36,1: 139–52.
Coria Colino, J. I.
1995 *Intervención regia en el ámbito municipal: El Concejo de Murcia (1252–1369).* Murcia: Real Academia Alfonso X El Sabio.
Coronas González, S. M.
1981 "La Audiencia y Chancillería de Ciudad Real (1494–1505)." *Cuadernos de Estudios Manchegos* ll: 47–139.
Corral García, E.
1988 *Ordenanzas de los concejos castellanos: Formación, contenido y manifestaciones (s. XIII–XVIII).* Burgos: Gráficos Diario de Burgos.
Cortes de Castilla
1862 *Actas de las Cortes de Castilla* [1566]. Vol. 2. Madrid: Imprenta Nacional.
1863 Real Academia de la Historia. *Cortes de los antiguos reinos de León y de Castilla* [1351–1405]. Vol. 2. Madrid: Rivadeneyra.
1866 Real Academia de la Historia. *Cortes de los antiguos reinos de León y de Castilla* [1407–1473]. Vol. 3. Madrid: Rivadeneyra.
1877 *Actas de las Cortes de Castilla* [1563]. Vol. 1. Madrid: Viuda e hijos de J. A. García.
1882 Real Academia de la Historia. *Cortes de los antiguos reinos de León y de Castilla* [1476–1537]. Vol. 4. Madrid: Sucesores de Rivadeneyra.
1903 Real Academia de la Historia. *Cortes de los antiguos reinos de León y de Castilla* [1538–1559]. Vol. 5. Madrid: Sucesores de Rivadeneyra.
Cortes de Castilla y León
1989 *Las Cortes de Castilla y León en la Edad Moderna.* Valladolid: Cortes de Castilla y León.
Covarrubias y Orozco, Sebastián de [1539–1613]
1979 *Tesoro de la lengua castellana o española* [1611]. Madrid: Ediciones Turner.
Craddock, J. R.
1990 "The Legislative Works of Alfonso el Sabio." In R. I. Burns, ed. (1990): 182–97.
Crews, D. A.
1991 "Juan de Valdés and the Comunero Revolt: An Essay on Spanish Civic Humanism." *Sixteenth Century Journal* 20,2: 233–52.

Crónica castellana
1991 *Crónica anónima de Enrique IV de Castilla, 1454–1474 (Crónica Castellana)*. Ed. M. P. Sánchez-Parra. 2 vols. Madrid: Ediciones de la Torre.

Crónica de Juan II
1517 *Comiença la Cronica del serenissimo rey don Juan el segundo deste nõbre* . . . Ed. Dr. Lorenzo Galíndez de Carvajal [d. 1532]. Logroño: Arnão Guillén de Brocar.
1953 "Crónica del Rey Don Juan, segundo deste nombre en Castilla y en León." In Rosell, ed. (1953): II, 273–695.
1982 *Crónica de Juan II de Castilla* [attributed to Alvar García de Santa María]. Ed. J. de M. Carriazo y Arroquía. Madrid: Real Academia de la Historia.

Crónica de Luna
1946 *Crónica de don Alvaro de Luna, Condestable de Castilla, Maestre de Santiago* [attributed to Gonzalo Chacón]. Ed. J. de M. Carriazo. Madrid: Espasa-Calpe.

Cuartas Rivero, M.
1984 "La venta de oficios públicos en Castilla-León en el siglo XVI." *Hispania* 44,158: 495–516.

Cunningham, C. H.
1919 *The Audiencia in the Spanish Colonies as Illustrated by the Audiencia of Manila (1583–1800)*. Berkeley: University of California Press.

Danvila Collado, M.
1885 *El Poder civil en España*. 6 vols. Madrid: Manuel Tello.
1897–1899 *Historia crítica y documentada de las Comunidades de Castilla*. 6 vols. [constitutes vols. 35–40 of Real Academia de la Historia. *Memorial histórico español.*] Madrid: Viuda e hijos de M. Tello.

Danvila y Burguero, A.
1900 *Don Cristóbal de Moura: Primer Marqués de Castel Rodrigo (1538–1613)*. Madrid: Fortanet.

David, M.
1954 *La souveraineté et les limites juridiques du pouvoir monarchique du IXe au XVe siècle*. Paris: Librairie Dalloz.

Dedieu, J.-P.
1999 "La Inquisición en el reinado de Felipe II." *Chronica Nova* 26: 79–110.

Dedieu, J.-P., and C. Windler
1998 "La familia: ¿Una clave para entender la historia política? El ejemplo de la España moderna." *Stvdia Historica: Historia Moderna* 18: 201–33.

Díaz de Montalvo, Alfonso [1405–ca. 1499]
1484 *Ordenanzas reales* [or *Copilación de las leyes del reino*]. Huete: Alvaro de Castro. Transcr.: I A. Corfus. In ADMYTE (1995): disk 1.

Díaz-Jiménez Y Molleda, E.
1916 *Historia de los comuneros de León y de su influencia en el movimiento general de Castilla*. Madrid: V. Suárez.

Díaz Martín, L. V.
1997 *Los orígenes de la Audiencia real castellana*. Sevilla: Universidad de Sevilla.

Díaz-Plaja, F. (ed.)
1958 *La historia de España en sus documentos: El siglo XVI*. Madrid: Instituto de Estudios Políticos.

Diefendorf, B. B.
1991 *Beneath the Cross: Catholics and Huguenots in Sixteenth-Century Paris.* New York and Oxford: Oxford University Press.

Díez Borque, J. M.
1978 *Sociedad y teatro en la España de Lope de Vega.* Barcelona: Antoni Bosch.

Díez de Games, Gutierre [15th century]
1940 *El Victorial: Crónica de don Pero Niño, conde de Buelna, por su alférez Gutierre Díez de Games.* Ed. J. de M. Carriazo. Madrid: Espasa-Calpe.

Dios, S. de
1982 *El Consejo Real de Castilla, 1385–1522.* Madrid: Centro de Estudios Constitucionales.
1988a "La evolución de las Cortes de Castilla durante el siglo XV." In Rucquoi, ed. (1988): 137–69.
1988b "Las Cortes de Castilla y León y la administración central." In Valdeón Baruque, ed. (1988): II, 255–317.
1993 *Gracia, merced y patronazgo real: La Cámara de Castilla entre 1474–1530.* Madrid: Centro de Estudios Constitucionales.

Dios, S. de (ed.)
1986 *Fuentes para el estudio del Consejo Real de Castilla.* Salamanca: Ediciones de la Diputación de Salamanca.

Dollinger, H.
1968 *Studien zur Finanzreform Maximilians I. von Bayern in den Jahren 1598–1618: Ein Beitrag zur Geschichte des Frühabsolutismus.* Göttingen: Vandenhoeck u. Ruprecht.

Domínguez Ortiz, A.
1960 *Política y hacienda de Felipe IV.* Madrid: Editorial de Derecho Financiero.
1986 "Un testimonio de protesta social a fines del reinado de Felipe II." In Santiago Otero et al., eds. (1986): 219–26.

Domínguez Ortiz, A., and B. Vincent
1979 *Historia de los moriscos: Vida y tragedia de una minoría.* 2nd ed. Madrid: Revista de Occidente [1978].

Donohue, J. W.
1963 *Jesuit Education: An Essay on the Foundations of Its Idea.* New York: Fordham University Press.

Edwards, J.
1982 *Christian Cordoba: The City and its Region in the Late Middle Ages.* Cambridge: University Press.
1991 "La noblesse de Cordoue et la révolte des 'Comunidades' de Castille." In *Bandos y querellas* (1991): 135–55.

Egido López, T. (ed.)
1973 *Sátiras políticas en la España moderna.* Madrid: Alianza.

Eire, C.
1995 *From Madrid to Purgatory: The Art and Craft of Dying in Sixteenth-Century Spain.* Cambridge: Cambridge University Press.

Elliott, J. H.
1963 *The Revolt of the Catalans: A Study in the Decline of Spain (1598–1640).* Cambridge: University Press.

1964 *Imperial Spain, 1469–1716.* New York: St. Martin's.

1985 "Power and Propaganda in the Spain of Philip IV." In Wilentz, ed. (1985): 145–73.

1986 *The Count-Duke of Olivares: The Statesman in an Age of Decline.* New Haven, Connecticut, and London: Yale University Press.

1991 "The Spanish Monarchy and the Kingdom of Portugal." In Greengrass, ed. (1991): 48–67.

1992 "Una sociedad no revolucionaria: Castilla en la década de 1640." In Centre "Pierre Vilar" (1992): 102–22.

Elliott, J. H., and A. García Sanz (eds.)

1990 *La España del Conde-Duque de Olivares.* Valladolid: Universidad de Valladolid.

Elliott, J. H., and J. F. de la Peña (eds.)

1978–1981 *Memoriales y cartas del Conde Duque de Olivares.* 2 vols. Madrid: Ediciones Alfaguara.

Enríquez del Castillo, Diego [15th century]

1994 *Crónica de Enrique IV.* Ed. A. Sánchez Martín. Valladolid: Universidad de Valladolid.

Esmein, A.

1913 "Le maxime *Princeps legibus solutus est* dans l'ancien Droit public français." In Vinogradoff, ed. (1913): 201–14.

Espina Montero, A.

2001a "Deuda pública y confianza en el gobierno de España bajo los Austrias." *Hacienda Pública Española* 156,1.

2001b "Oro, plata y mercurio, nervios de la monarquía de España." *Revista de Historia Económica* 19,3: 507–38.

Espinosa, A.

2002 "President Tavera's Policy of Equity, 1524–1537." Paper presented at the annual meeting of the Society for Spanish and Portuguese Historical Studies, Athens, Georgia, April.

2003 "The Formation of Habsburg Rule in Spain, 1517–1528." Ph.D. diss. University of Arizona.

Estatuto Real

1975 "Estatuto Real" [1834]. In Farias (1975): 209–16.

Esteban Recio, A.

1985 *Las ciudades castellanas en tiempos de Enrique IV: Estructura social y conflictos.* Valladolid: Universidad de Valladolid.

Estepa Díez, C.

1990 "Realengo y el señorío jurisdiccional concejil en Castilla y León (Siglos XII–XV)." In Concejos y Ciudades (1990): 465–506.

Evan, W. M. (ed.)

1962 *Law and Sociology: Exploratory Essays.* Glencoe, Illinois: Free Press.

Eysenck, M. W., and M. T. Keane

1990 *Cognitive Psychology: A Student's Handbook.* Hove and London, UK; Hillsdale, New Jersey: Lawrence Erlbaum Associates.

Ezquerra Revilla, I. J.

2000 *El consejo real de Castilla bajo Felipe II: Grupos de poder y luchas faccionales.* Madrid: Sociedad Estatal para la Conmemoración de los Centenarios de Felipe II y Carlos V.

Farias, P.
1975 *Breve historia constitucional de España (seguido de los textos constitucionales desde la Carta de Bayona a la Ley Orgánica)*. Madrid: Doncel.
Farrell, A. P.
1938 *The Jesuit Code of Liberal Education: Development and Scope of the Ratio Studiorum*. Milwaukee: Brice.
Fasolt, C.
1991 *Council and Hierarchy: The Political Thought of William Durant the Younger*. Cambridge and New York: Cambridge University Press.
Fernández Albaladejo, P.
1984 "Monarquía, Cortes y 'cuestión constitucional' en Castilla durante la Edad Moderna." *Revista de las Cortes Generales* 1: 11–34.
1989 "Los Austrias Mayores." In Fernández Albaladejo (1992a): chap 1.
1992a *Fragmentos de Monarquía: Trabajos de historia política*. Madrid: Alianza Universidad.
1992b "Monarquía y Reino en Castilla: 1538–1623." In Fernández Albadalejo (1992a): 241–83.
1997 "Católicos antes que ciudadanos: Gestación de una 'Política Española' en los comienzos de la Edad Moderna." In Fortea Pérez, ed. (1997): 103–27.
Fernández Albaladejo, P. (ed.)
1997 *Monarquía, imperio y pueblos en la España Moderna*. Vol. I. Alicante: Caja de Ahorros del Mediterráneo; Universidad de Alicante.
Fernández Alvarez, M.
1969 "La crisis del nuevo estado (1504–1516)." In Suárez Fernández and Fernández Alvarez, eds. (1969): II, 643–729.
1995 *Poder y sociedad en la España del Quinientos*. Madrid: Alianza.
1998 *Felipe II y su tiempo*. Madrid: Espasa Calpe.
Fernández Alvarez, M. (ed.)
1973–1981 *Corpus documental de Carlos V.* 5 vols. Salamanca: Consejo Superior de Investigaciones Científicas; Universidad de Salamanca; Fundación Juan March.
Fernández Conti, S.
1998 *Los Consejos de Estado y Guerra de la Monarquía Hispana en tiempos de Felipe II (1548–1598)*. Valladolid: Junta de Castilla y León, Consejería de Educación y Cultura.
Fernández de la Mora, G.
1993 "El proceso contra el padre Mariana." *Revista de Estudios Políticos* 79: 47–99.
Fernández Martín, L.
1979 *El movimiento comunero en los pueblos de Tierra de Campos*. León: Centro de Estudios e Investigación "San Isidro"; Caja de Ahorros y Monte de Piedad; Archivo Histórico Diocesano.
Fernández Navarrete, Pedro [ca. 1580–after 1632]
1982 *Conservación de monarquías y discursos políticos* [1626]. Ed. M. D. Gordon. Madrid: Instituto de Estudios Fiscales.
Fernández-Santamaría, J. A.
1977 *The State, War and Peace: Spanish Political Thought in the Renaissance, 1516–1559.* Cambridge: University Press.

1979a "Baltasar Alamos de Barrientos' *ciencia de contingentes:* A Spanish View of Statecraft as Science during the Baroque." *Bibliothèque d'Humanisme et Renaissance* 41: 293–304.

1979b "Diego Saavedra Fajardo: Reason of State in the Spanish Baroque." *Il Pensiero Politico* 12,1: 19–37.

1980 "Reason of State and Statecraft in Spain (1595–1640)." *Journal of the History of Ideas* 41,3: 355–79.

1983 *Reason of State and Statecraft in Spanish Political Thought, 1595–1640.* Lanham, Maryland: University Press of America.

1985 Reply to M. D. Gordon. *American Historical Review* 90: 272.

1997 *La formación de la sociedad y el origen del Estado: Ensayos sobre el pensamiento político del Siglo de Oro.* Madrid: Centro de Estudios Constitucionales.

Fernández Serrano, A.

1955 *La abogacia en España y en el mundo.* 2nd ed. 3 vols. Madrid: Librería Internacional de Derecho.

Feros, A.

1997 "El viejo monarca y los nuevos favoritos: Los discursos sobre la privanza en el reinado de Felipe II." *Stvdia Historica: Historia Moderna* 17: 11–36.

2000 *Kingship and Favoritism in the Spain of Philip III, 1598–1621.* Cambridge: Cambridge University Press.

Figgis, J. N.

1916 *Studies of Political Thought from Gerson to Grotius, 1414–1625.* 2nd ed. Cambridge: Cambridge University Press [1907].

Firpo, L.

1948 "Introduzione." In Botero (1948): 9–48.

Fitzpatrick, E. A.

1933 "St. Ignatius and Education." In Fitzpatrick, ed. (1933): 3–43.

Fitzpatrick, E. A. (ed.)

1933 *St. Ignatius and the Ratio Studiorum.* New York and London: McGraw-Hill.

Fortea Pérez, J. I.

1990 *Monarquía y Cortes en la Corona de Castilla: Las ciudades ante la política fiscal de Felipe II.* Salamanca: Cortes de Castilla y León.

1997a "Entre dos servicios: La crisis de la Hacienda Real a fines del siglo XVI. Las alternativas fiscales de una opción política (1590–1601)." *Stvdia Historica: Historia Moderna* 17: 63–90.

1997b "Las ciudades, las Cortes y el problema de la representación política en la Castilla Moderna." In Fortea Pérez, ed. (1997): 421–45.

Fortea Pérez, J. I. (ed.)

1997 *Imágenes de la diversidad: El mundo urbano en la Corona de Castilla (S. XVI–XVIII).* Santander: Universidad de Cantabria; Asamblea Regional de Cantabria.

Franco Silva, A.

1994 *El condado de Fuensalida en la baja Edad Media.* Cádiz: Universidad de Cádiz.

1996 *La fortuna y el poder: Estudios sobre las bases económicas de la aristocracia castellana (s. XIV–XV).* Cádiz: Universidad de Cádiz.

Frank, A. G.

1993 "Transitional Ideological Modes: Feudalism, Capitalism, Socialism." In Frank and Gills, eds. (1993): 200–217.

1998 *ReORIENT: Global Economy in the Asian Age.* Berkeley: University of California Press.

Frank, A. G., and B. K. Gills

1993 "The Cumulation of Accumulation." In Frank and Gills, eds. (1993): 81–114.

Frank, A. G., and B. K. Gills (eds.)

1993 *The World System: Five Hundred Years or Five Thousand?* London and New York: Routledge.

Franklin, J. H.

1973 *Jean Bodin and the Rise of Absolutist Theory.* Cambridge: University Press.

Franzen, A.

1965 "The Council of Constance: Present State of the Problem." *Concilium* 5: 29–68.

Friedman, J.

1993 *The Battle of the Frogs and Fairford's Flies: Miracles and the Pulp Press during the English Revolution.* New York: St. Martin's Press.

Fuente, V. de la (ed.)

1876 *Cartas de los secretarios del cardenal D. Fr. Francisco Jiménez de Cisneros durante su regencia en los años de 1516 y 1517.* Madrid: Viuda e hijo de D. E. Aguado.

Fuente Pérez, M. J.

1989 *La ciudad de Palencia en el siglo XV: Aportación al estudio de las ciudades castellanas en la Baja Edad Media.* Madrid: Universidad Complutense de Madrid.

Galíndez de Carvajal, Lorenzo [1472–1528]

1851a "Adiciones genealógicas a los claros varones de Castilla de Fernán Pérez de Guzmán Señor de Batres . . ." Ed. R. Floranes Robles y Encinas. In Salvá Munar and Sainz de Baranda, eds. (1851): 423–536.

1851b "Anales breves del reinado de los Reyes Católicos Don Fernando y Doña Isabel, que dejó manuscritos el Dr. D. Lorenzo Galíndez de Carbajal, y una continuación de la crónica de aquellos Reyes que hasta ahora no se ha publicado." Ed. R. Floranes Robles y Encinas. In Salvá Munar and Sainz de Baranda, eds. (1851): 227–422.

Gan Giménez, P.

1988a *El Consejo Real de Carlos V.* Granada: Universidad de Granada.

1988b *La Real Chancillería de Granada (1505–1834).* Granada: Centro de Estudios Históricos de Granada y su Reino.

García de León Alvarez, C.

2001 "El corral de comedias de Almagro: Construcción, propiedad y arrendamiento." *Boletín de la Real Academia de la Historia* 198,3: 507–55.

García de Santa María, Alvar [15th century]

1982 See Crónica de Juan II 1982.

García Fitz, F., and D. Kirschberg Schenck

1991 "Las Ordenanzas del concejo de Sevilla de 1492." *Historia. Instituciones. Documentos* 18: 183–207.

García-Gallo, A.

1967 *Manual de historia del derecho español.* 3rd ed. 2 vols. Madrid: Artes Gráficas y Ediciones.

1975 *Las Audiencias en Indias.* Caracas: Academia Nacional de Historia.

García García, H.

1983 *El pensamiento comunero y erasmista de Juan Maldonado.* Madrid: Gráficas Marsiega.

García Hernán, D.
1996 "El Gobierno Municipal en las villas de señorío: Siglo XVI." In Bernardo Ares and Martínez Ruiz, eds. (1996): 191–215.

García López, J. C.
1889 *Ensayo de una tipografía complutense.* Madrid: M. Tello.

García Marín, J. M.
1976 *La burocracia castellana bajo los Austrias.* Jerez de la Frontera: Gráficas del Exportador for the Instituto García Oviedo of the Universidad de Sevilla.
1987 *El oficio público en Castilla durante la Baja Edad Media.* 2nd ed. Alcalá de Henares, Madrid: Instituto Nacional de Administración Pública [1974].
1998 *Teoría política y gobierno en la Monarquía Hispánica.* Madrid: Centro de Estudios Políticos y Constitucionales.

García Oro, J.
1980 "Conventualismo y observancia: La reforma de las órdenes religiosas en los siglos XV y XVI." In González Novalín, ed. (1980): III-1, pt. 4, 211-349.

García Sanz, A.
1980 "Bienes y derechos comunales y el proceso de su privatización en Castilla durante los siglos XVI y XVII: El caso de tierras de Segovia." *Hispania* 40,144: 95-127.
1985 "Auge y decadencia en España en los siglos XVI y XVII: economía y sociedad en Castilla." *Revista de Historia Económica* 3,1: 11-27.

García-Villoslada, R.
1980 "Felipe II y la Contrarreforma católica." In González Novalín, ed. (1980): III-2, pt. 7, 3-106.

García y García, A.
2000 "Derecho Romano-Canónico medieval en la Península Ibérica." In Alvarado, ed. (2000): 79-132.

Garriga, C.
1994 *La Audiencia y las Chancillerías castellanas (1371-1525): Historia política, régimen jurídico y práctica institucional.* Madrid: Centro de Estudios Constitucionales.

Gayangos Arce, P. de, and V. de la Fuente (eds.)
1867 *Cartas del cardenal don fray Francisco Jiménez de Cisneros, dirigidas a don Diego López de Ayala.* Madrid: Colegio de Sordo-Mudos y de Ciegos.

Geertz, C.
1983a "Local Knowledge: Fact and Law in Comparative Perspective." In Geertz (1983b): 167-234.
1983b *Local Knowledge: Further Essays in Interpretive Anthropology.* New York: Basic Books.

Gelabert González, J. E.
1994 "Urbanisation and Deurbanisation in Castile, 1500-1800." In Thompson and Yun Casalilla, eds. (1994): 182-205.
1997a "Ciudades en crisis: Castilla, 1632-1650." In Fortea Pérez, ed. (1997): 447-73.
1997b *La bolsa del rey: Rey, reino y fisco en Castilla (1598-1648).* Barcelona: Crítica.
1998 "El sistema español en la época de los Austrias: El modelo político e institucional (1516-1659)." *Obradoiro de Historia Moderna* 7: 89-126.

Getino, L. G. A.

1935 *Vida e ideario del maestro fray Pablo de León, verbo de las comunidades.* Salamanca: Establecimiento Tipográfico de Calatrava.

Gewirth, A.

1951–1956 *Marsilius of Padua: The Defender of Peace.* 2 vols. New York: Columbia University Press.

Gibert, R.

2000 "La glosa de Gregorio López." In Alvarado, ed. (2000): 423–72.

Gicovate, B.

1975 *Garcilaso de la Vega.* Boston: Twayne.

Gierke, O. F. von

1900 *Political Theories of the Middle Ages.* Trans. F. W. Maitland. Cambridge: Cambridge University Press [1881].

1950 *Natural Law and the Theory of Society, 1500 to 1800.* Trans. E. Barker. Cambridge: Cambridge University Press [1913].

Gil Ayuso, F.

1935 *Noticia Bibliográfica de textos y disposiciones legales de los Reinos de Castilla impresos en los siglos XVI y XVII.* Madrid: Patronato de la Biblioteca Nacional.

Gilmore, M. P.

1941 *Argument from Roman Law in Political Thought, 1200–1600.* Cambridge, Massachusetts: Harvard University Press.

Gimeno Casalduero, J.

1972 *La imagen del monarca en la Castilla del siglo XIV: Pedro el Cruel, Enrique II y Juan I.* Madrid: Revista de Occidente.

Gluckman, M.

1965 *Politics, Law and Ritual in Tribal Society.* Chicago: Aldine.

Gómez González, I.

1998 "La visualización de la justicia en el Antiguo Régimen: El ejemplo de la Chancillería de Granada." *Hispania* 58,199: 559–74.

Gómez-Menor, J.

1965 *La antigua tierra de Talavera: Bosquejo histórico y aportación documental.* Toledo: Diputación Provincial.

Gómez-Moriana, A.

1968 *Derecho de resistencia y tiranicidio: Estudio de una temática en las comedias de Lope de Vega.* Santiago de Compostela: Porto.

González Alonso, B.

1980 "La fórmula 'obedézcase, pero no se cumpla' en el Derecho castellano de la baja Edad Media." *Anuario de Historia del Derecho Español* 50: 469–87.

1981a "Las Comunidades de Castilla y la formación del Estado absoluto." In González Alonso (1981b): 7–56.

1981b *Sobre el Estado y la Administración de la Corona de Castilla en el Antiguo Régimen: Las Comunidades de Castilla y otros estudios.* Madrid: Siglo XXI de España.

1988 "Poder regio, Cortes y régimen político en la Castilla bajomedieval (1252–1474)." In Valdeón Baruque, ed. (1988): II, 201–54.

1995 "De Briviesca a Olmedo (algunas reflexiones sobre el ejercicio de la potestad legislativa en la Castilla bajomedieval)." In Iglesia Ferreirós, ed. (1995): 43–74.

González Arce, J. D. (ed.)
2000 *Ordenanzas de la Ciudad de Murcia (1536)*. Murcia: Universidad de Murcia.

González de Echávarri y Vivanco, J. M.
1917 *La Justicia y Felipe II: Estudio histórico-crítico en vista de diez y siete Real Cédulas y cartas del Consejo inéditas*. Valladolid: E. Zapatero.

González García, M.
1973 *Salamanca: La repoblación y la ciudad en la baja Edad Media*. Salamanca: Centro de Estudios Salmantinas.
1982 *Salamanca en la Baja Edad Media*. Salamanca: Universidad de Salamanca.

González Novalín, J. L. (ed.)
1980 *Historia de la Iglesia en España:* Vol. 3: *La Iglesia en la España de los siglos XV y XVI*. 2 vols. Madrid: Biblioteca de Autores Cristianos.

Goñi Gaztambide, J.
1980 "Presencia en España de los concilios generales del siglo XV." In González Novalín, ed. (1980): I, 25–114.

Gordon, M. D.
1974a "The Arbitristas: An Historiographical and Bibliographical Survey." *Newsletter of the Society for Spanish and Portuguese Historical Studies* 2, 7 & 8 (May): 7–23.
1974b "The Science of Politics in Seventeenth-Century Spanish Thought." *Il Pensiero Politico* 7: 379–94.
1977 Review of Maravall (1972). *Hispanic American Historical Review* 57: 113–14.
1978 "Morality, Reform, and Politics in Seventeenth-Century Spain." *Il Pensiero Politico* 11: 3–19.
1982 "Moralidad y política en la España del siglo XVII: El pensamiento de Pedro Fernández Navarrete." In Fernández Navarrete (1982): vii–xlii.
1984 Review of Fernández-Santamaría (1983). *American Historical Review* 89: 457–58.
1985 Reply to Fernández-Santamaría. *American Historical Review* 90: 273.

Gorman, M. E.
1992 *Simulating Science: Heuristics, Mental Models, and Technoscientific Thinking*. Bloomington: Indiana University Press.

Gounon-Loubens, M. J.
1860 *Essais sur l'administration de la Castille au XVIe siècle*. Paris: Guillaumin.

Gouron, A., and A. Rigaudiere (eds.)
1988 *Renaissance du pouvoir législatif et genèse de l'Etat*. Montpellier: Société d'Histoire du Droit; Institutions des Anciens Pays de Droit Ecrit (for the Centre National de la Recherche Scientifique).

Grassotti, H.
1985 "Hacia las concesiones del señorío 'con mero y mixto imperio.'" In Carlé, Grassotti, and Orduna, eds. (1983–1990): III, 113–50.

Grau, M.
1954 "Un pleito secular de la Comunidad y Tierra de Segovia." *Estudios Segovianos* 6: 243–76.

Greengrass, M. (ed.)
1991 *Conquest and Coalescence: The Shaping of the State in Early Modern Europe*. London: Edward Arnold.

Grendler, P. F.

1989 *Schooling in Renaissance Italy: Literacy and Learning, 1300–1600*. Baltimore, Maryland: Johns Hopkins University Press.

Grendler, P. F. (ed.)

1999 *Encyclopedia of the Renaissance*. 6 vols. New York: Scribner's.

Griffiths, G.

1968 *Representative Government in Western Europe in the Sixteenth Century: Commentary and Documents for a Study of Comparative Constitutional History*. Oxford: Clarendon Press.

Guilarte, A. M.

1979 *El obispo Acuña: Historia de un comunero*. Valladolid: Editorial Miñón.

Guillaume-Alonso, A.

1999 "La politique judiciaire de Philippe II: Une affaire de pouvoir." In Moliné-Bertrand and Duviols, eds. (1999): 97–107.

Gutiérrez Nieto, J. I.

1964 "Los conversos y el movimiento comunero." *Hispania* 24: 237–61.

1973 *Las comunidades como movimiento antiseñorial: La formación del bando realista en la guerra civil castellana de 1520–1521*. Barcelona: Planeta.

1977 "Semántica del término 'comunidad' antes de 1520: Las asociaciones juramentadas de defensa." *Hispania* 37,136: 319–67.

Guy, A.

1985 *Historia de la filosofía española*. Trans. A. Sánchez. Barcelona: Anthropos Editorial de Hombre [1983].

Haliczer, S. H.

1977 "Construcción del estado, decadencia política y revolución en la Corona de Castilla (1475–1520)." In Homenaje Gómez Orbaneja (1977): 301–23.

1981 *The Comuneros of Castile: The Forging of a Revolution, 1475–1521*. Madison: University of Wisconsin Press.

Hamilton, B.

1963 *Political Thought in Sixteenth-Century Spain: A Study of the Political Ideas of Vitoria, De Soto, Suárez, and Molina*. Oxford: Clarendon Press.

Hamscher, A. N.

1987 *The Conseil Privé and the Parlements in the Age of Louis XIV: A Study in French Absolutism*. Philadelphia: American Philosophical Society [*Transactions*, vol. 77, pt. 2].

Haney, S.

1997 "Social Sites of Political Practice in France: Lawsuits, Civil Rights, and the Separation of Powers in Domestic and State Government, 1500–1800." *American Historical Review* 102,1 (February): 27–52.

Hanke, L., and C. Rodríguez (eds.)

1976 *Los virreyes españoles en América durante el gobierno de la Casa de Austria: México*. Vol. 1. Madrid: Biblioteca de Autores Españoles.

Hart, M. C. 't

1993 *The Making of a Bourgeois State: War, Politics, and Finance during the Dutch Revolt*. Manchester: Manchester University Press.

1995 "The Emergence and Consolidation of the 'Tax State': II. The Seventeenth Century." In Bonney, ed. (1995): 281–93.

Headley, J. M.

1983 *The Emperor and His Chancellor: A Study of the Imperial Chancellery under Gatti-nara.* Cambridge: Cambridge University Press.

Headley, J. M., and J. B. Tomaro (eds.)

1988 *San Carlo Borromeo: Catholic Reform and Ecclesiastical Politics in the Second Half of the Sixteenth Century.* Washington, DC: Folger Shakespeare Library; London and Toronto: Associated University Presses.

Helmrath, J.

1996 "Basel, The Permanent Synod? Observations on Duration and Continuity at the Council of Basel (1431–1449)." In Christianson and Izbicki, eds. (1996): 35–56.

1999 "Basel, Council of." In Grendler, ed. (1999): I, 187–88.

Hendricks, C. D.

1976 "Charles V and the Cortes of Castile: Politics in Renaissance Spain." Ph.D. diss. Cornell University.

Henshall, N.

1992 *The Myth of Absolutism: Change and Continuity in Early Modern European Monar-chy.* London and New York: Longman.

Heras Santos, J. L. de las

1991 *La justicia penal de los Austrias en la Corona de Castilla.* Salamanca: Universi-dad de Salamanca.

Herman, J.-B.

1914 *La Pédagogie des Jésuites au XVIe siècle: Ses sources. Ses caractéristiques.* Louvain: Bureaux.

Hernández Montes, B.

1977 "Obras de Juan de Segovia." In Repertorio (1977): Vol. VI, 267–347.

1984 *Biblioteca de Juan de Segovia: Edición y comentario de su escritura de donación.* Madrid: C.S.I.C., Instituto Francisco Suárez.

Hernández Ortiz, D. [early sixteenth century]

1945–1946 "Memoria de las que obo en el reyno llamadas comunidades . . ." Ed. Conde de Atarés. *Boletín de la Real Academia de la Historia* 116: 417–67; 117: 417–48; 118: 479–545; 119: 341–52.

Herrero García, M.

1935 "La monarquía teorética de Lope de Vega." *Fén* 1: 179–224 and 303–62.

Herzog, T.

1995 *La administración como un fenómeno social: La justicia penal de Quito, 1650–1750.* Madrid: Centro de Estudios Constitucionales.

2001 *Rendre la justice à Quito (1650–1750).* Paris: Harmattan.

2003 *Defining Nations: Immigrants and Citizens in Early Modern Spain and Spanish America.* New Haven, Connecticut, and London: Yale University Press.

2004 *Upholding Justice: Society, State, and the Penal System in Quito (1650–1750).* Ann Arbor: University of Michigan Press.

Hespanha, A. M.

1993a "La economía de la gracia." In Hespanha (1993b): 151–76.

1993b *La gracia del derecho: Economía de la cultura en la Edad Moderna.* Trans. A. Cañellas Haurie. Madrid: Centro de Estudios Constitucionales.

1994 *As vésperas do Leviathan: Instituições e poder político, Portugal–Séc. XVII.* Coimbra: Livraria Almedina [1989].

Hespanha, A. M. (ed.)
1993 *O Antigo Regime (1620–1807):* Vol. IV: *História de Portugal.* Lisbon: Editorial Estampa.

Hexter, J. H.
1957 "*Il principe* and *lo stato.*" *Studies in the Renaissance* 4: 113–38.
1973 *The Vision of Politics on the Eve of the Reformation: More, Machiavelli, and Seyssel.* New York: Basic Books.

Highfield, R. (ed.)
1972 *Spain in the Fifteenth Century, 1369–1516: Essays and Extracts by Historians of Spain.* London: Macmillan.

Hijano Pérez, A.
1992 *El pequeño poder: El municipio en la Corona de Castilla: Siglos xv al xix.* Madrid: Editorial Fundamentos.

Hillgarth, J. N.
1976–1978 *The Spanish Kingdoms, 1250–1516.* 2 vols. Oxford: Clarendon Press.

Hinojosa, Gonzalo de la [15th century]
1893 "Continuación de la Crónica de España del arzobispo don Rodrigo Jiménez de Rada, por el obispo don . . ." In CODOIN (1893): Vol. CVI, 1–141.

Historia de la Hacienda Española
1982 *Historia de la Hacienda española (Épocas Antigua y Medieval): Homenaje al profesor García de Valdeavellano.* Madrid: Instituto de Estudios Fiscales.

Hoffman, P. T., and K. Norberg (eds.)
1994 *Fiscal Crises, Liberty, and Representative Government, 1450–1789.* Stanford, California: Stanford University Press.

Homenaje Gómez Orbaneja
1977 *Homenaje a Emilio Gómez Orbaneja.* Madrid: Moneda y Crédito.

Honore, T.
1978 *Tribonian.* Ithaca, New York: Cornell University Press.

Hurtado de Mendoza, Diego [1503–1575]
1970 *Guerra de Granada* [1627]. Ed. B. Blanco-González. Madrid: Castalia.

Iglesia Ferreirós, A. (ed.)
1995 *El Dret Comú: Catalunya.* Barcelona: Fundació Noguera.

Iñurritegui Rodríguez, J. M.
1998 *La gracia y la república: El lenguaje política de la teología católica y "El príncipe cristiano" de Pedro de Rybadeneyra.* Madrid: Universidad Nacional de Educación a Distancia.

Isabella I of Castile [1451–1504]
1956 *Testamento y codicilo de Isabel la Católica* [1504]. Madrid: Artes Gráficas "Arges" for the Ministerio de Asuntos Exteriores.
1974 *Testamentaria de Isabel La Católica.* Ed. A. de la Torre and E. Alsina. Barcelona: Viuda de Fidel Rodríguez Ferrán.

Israel, J. I.
1995 *The Dutch Republic: Its Rise, Greatness, and Fall, 1477–1806.* Oxford: Clarendon Press.

Izbicki, T. M.
   1981 *Protector of the Faith: Cardinal Johannes de Turrecremata and the Defense of the Institutional Church.* Washington, DC: The Catholic University of America Press.
   1986 "Papalist Reaction to the Council of Constance: Juan de Torquemada to the Present." *Church History* 55: 7–20.
Izquierdo Benito, R.
   1990 *Privilegios reales otorgados a Toledo durante la Edad Media (1101–1494).* Toledo: Instituto Provincial de Investigaciones y Estudios Toledanos, Diputación Provincial.
Izquierdo Martín, J.
   2001 *El rostro de la comunidad: La identidad del campesino en la Castilla del Antiguo Régimen.* Madrid: Consejo Económico y Social, Comunidad de Madrid.
Jago, C. J.
   1973 "The Influence of Debt on the Relations between Crown and Aristocracy in Seventeenth-Century Castile." *Economic History Review* 2nd ser, 26: 218–36.
   1979 "The 'Crisis of the Aristocracy' in Seventeenth-Century Castile." *Past and Present* No. 84: 60–90.
   1981 "Habsburg Absolutism and the Cortes of Castile." *American Historical Review* 86: 307–26.
   1985 "Philip II and the Cortes of Castile: The Case of the Cortes of 1576." *Past and Present* No. 109: 24–43.
   1989 "Crisis sociales y oposición política: Cortes y Monarquía durante el reinado de Felipe II." In Cortes de Castilla y León 1989: 315–40.
   1995 "Taxation and Political Culture in Castile, 1590–1640." In Kagan and Parker, eds. (1995): 48–72.
James, M. E.
   1970 "Obedience and Dissent in Henrician England: The Lincolnshire Rebellion, 1536." *Past and Present* No. 48: 3–78.
Jedin, H.
   1957 *A History of the Council of Trent:* Vol. I: *The Struggle for the Council.* Trans. E. Graf. Edinburgh: Nelson [1949].
John of Salisbury, Bishop of Chartres [d. 1180]
   1909 *Policratici sive De nugis curialium et vestigiis [Policraticus].* Ed. C. C. J. Webb. 2 vols. Oxford: Clarendon Press.
   1990 *Policraticus: Of the Frivolities of Courtiers and the Footprints of Philosophers.* Ed. and trans. C. J. Nederman. Cambridge: Cambridge University Press.
Jones, C. A.
   1966 "Introduction." In Vega Carpio (1966): 1–23.
Jones, M. (ed.)
   1986 *Gentry and Lesser Nobility in Late Medieval Europe.* New York: St. Martin's Press.
Juliá, S.
   1996 "Anomalía, dolor y fracaso de España: Notas sobre la representación desdichada de nuestro pasado y su reciente abandono." *Society for Spanish and Portuguese Historical Studies: Bulletin* 21,2 (Spring): 6–27.
   2004 *Historias de las dos Españas.* Madrid: Taurus.
Kagan, R. L.
   1970 "Universities in Castile, 1500–1700." *Past and Present* No. 49: 44–71.

1974 *Students and Society in Early Modern Spain*. Baltimore, Maryland: Johns Hopkins University Press.

1981 *Lawsuits and Litigants in Castile, 1500–1700*. Chapel Hill: University of North Carolina Press.

1990 *Lucrecia's Dreams: Politics and Prophecy in Sixteenth-Century Spain*. Berkeley: University of California Press.

1995 "Clio and the Crown: Writing History in Habsburg Spain." In Kagan and Parker, eds. (1995): 73–99.

Kagan, R.[L.], and G. Parker (eds.)

1995 *Spain, Europe, and the Atlantic World: Essays in Honour of John H. Elliott*. Cambridge: Cambridge University Press.

Kamen, H.

1985 *Inquisition and Society in Spain in the Sixteenth and Seventeenth Centuries*. Bloomington: Indiana University Press.

1997 *Philip of Spain*. New Haven, Connecticut: Yale University Press.

Kantorowicz, E. H.

1957 *The King's Two Bodies: A Study in Medieval Political Theology*. Princeton, New Jersey: Princeton University Press.

Kellenbenz, H.

1967 "The Impact of Growth on Government: The Example of Spain." *Journal of Economic History* 27: 340–62.

Keniston, H.

1960 *Francisco de los Cobos: Secretary of the Emperor Charles V*. Pittsburgh, Pennsylvania: University of Pittsburgh Press.

Keohane, N. O.

1980 *Philosophy and the State in France: The Renaissance to the Enlightenment*. Princeton, New Jersey: Princeton University Press.

Kettering, S.

1986 *Patrons, Brokers, and Clients in Seventeenth-Century France*. New York: Oxford University Press.

Kingdon, R. M.

1988 *Myths about the St. Bartholomew's Day Massacres, 1572–1576*. Cambridge, Massachusetts, and London: Harvard University Press.

Klein, J.

1920 *The Mesta: A Study in Spanish Economic History, 1273–1836*. Cambridge, Massachusetts: Harvard University Press.

Koenigsberger, H. G.

1969 *The Practice of Empire*. 2nd ed. Ithaca, New York: Cornell University Press [1951].

1971a *The Habsburgs and Europe, 1516–1660*. Ithaca, New York: Cornell University Press.

1971b "The Statecraft of Philip II." *European Studies Review* 1: 1–21.

Kuehn, T.

1989 "Reading Microhistory: The Example of *Giovanni and Lusanna*." *Journal of Modern History* 61 (September): 512–34.

Ladero Quesada, M. A.

1973 *La Hacienda Real de Castilla en el siglo XV*. Sevilla: Universidad de La Laguna.

1976 "Instituciones fiscales y realidad social en el siglo XV castellano." In M. A. Ladero Quesada (1982): 58–87.

1982 *El siglo XV en Castilla: Fuentes de renta y política fiscal.* Barcelona: Ariel.

1988a "Economía y poder en la Castilla del siglo XV." In Rucquoi, ed. (1988): 371–88.

1988b "Linajes, bandos, y parcialidades en la vida política de las ciudades castellanas (siglos XIV y XV)." *Society of Spanish and Portuguese Historical Studies: Bulletin* 13,2: 20–22.

1989 *Los Reyes Católicos: La Corona y la unidad de España.* Valencia: Asociación Francisco López de Gómara.

1993 *Fiscalidad y poder real en Castilla (1252–1369).* Madrid: Departamento de Historia Medieval, Editorial Complutense.

1998 "Las ordenanzas locales: Siglos XIII a XVIII." *En la España Medieval* 21: 293–337.

Ladero Quesada, M. A. (ed.)

1980 *En la España Medieval I. Estudios dedicados al profesor D. Julio González González.* Madrid: Universidad Complutense.

1982 *En la España Medieval II. Estudios en memoria del profesor D. Salvador de Moxó.* 2 vols. Madrid: Universidad Complutense.

Ladero Quesada, M. A., and I. Galán Parra

1982 "Las ordenanzas locales en la Corona de Castilla como fuente histórica y tema de investigación (siglos XIII al XVIII)." *Anales de la Universidad de Alicante: Historia Medieval* 1: 221–43.

Ladero Quesada, M. F.

1982 "La Orden de Alcántara en el siglo XV: Datos sobre su potencial militar, territorial, económico y demográfico." In M. A. Ladero Quesada, ed. (1982): I, 499–541.

1991 "Consideraciones metodológicas sobre el estudio de los núcleos urbanos de la Castilla bajomedieval." *Espacio, Tiempo y Forma* ser. III, 4: 353–66.

1996 *Las ciudades de la Corona de Castilla en la Baja Edad Media (siglos XIII al XV).* Madrid: Arco Libros.

Laslett, P., W. G. Runciman, and Q. Skinner (eds.)

1972 *Philosophy, Politics and Society.* 4th ser. New York: Barnes and Noble.

Lauer, A. R.

1983 "The Killing of the Tyrannical King in the Spanish Theater of the Golden Age (1582–1671)." Ph.D. diss. University of Michigan.

1987 *Tyrannicide and Drama.* Stuttgart: Franz Steiner Verlag Wiesbaden [*Archivum Calderonianum:* Vol. 4].

1988 "The Use and Abuse of History in the Theater of the Golden Age: The Regicide of Sancho II as Treated by Juan de la Cueva, Guillén de Castro, and Lope de Vega." *Hispanic Review* 56: 17–37.

Le Flem, J.-P.

1975 "¿Miguel Caxa de Leruela, defensor de la Mesta? Un testimonio sobre la ruptura ecológica del siglo XVII." In Caxa de Leruela (1975): xv–lii.

Levenson, J. R.

1968 *Confucian China and Its Modern Fate: A Trilogy.* Berkeley: University of California Press.

Lewis, M. W., and K. E. Wigen
1997 *The Myth of Continents: A Critique of Metageography.* Berkeley, Los Angeles, and London: University of California Press.

Lewy, G.
1960 *Constitutionalism and Statecraft during the Golden Age of Spain: A Study of the Political Philosophy of Juan de Mariana, S.J.* Geneva: Droz.

Lieberman, V. (ed.)
1997 *Beyond Binary Histories: Re-imaging Eurasia to c. 1830.* Ann Arbor: University of Michigan Press.

Liss, P. K.
1992 *Isabel the Queen: Life and Times.* New York and Oxford: Oxford University Press.

Llewellyn, K. N., and E. A. Hoebel
1941 *The Cheyenne Way: Conflict and Case Law in Primitive Jurisprudence.* Norman: University of Oklahoma Press.

Lloyd, H. A.
1991 "Constitutionalism." In Burns and Goldie, eds. (1991): 254–97.

López Belinchón, B. J.
2001 "'Sacar la sustancia al reino': Comercio, contrabando y conversos portugueses, 1621–1640." *Hispania* 59,209: 1017–1050.

López Benito, C. I.
1983 *Bandos nobiliarios en Salamanca al iniciarse la Edad Moderna.* Salamanca: Centro de Estudios Salmantinos.

López de Ayala y Alvarez de Toledo, J. (Conde de Cedillo)
1901 *Toledo en el siglo XVI después del vencimiento de las Comunidades.* Madrid: Hijos de M. G. Hernández.
1906 *Algunas relaciones y noticias toledanas que en el siglo XVI escribía el Licenciado Sebastián de Horozco.* Madrid: San Francisco de Sales.

López García, J. M.
1990 *La transición del feudalismo al capitalismo en un señorío monástico castellano: El abadengo de la Santa Espina (1147–1835).* Valladolid: Consejería de Cultura y Bienestar Social, Junta de Castilla y León.

López Gómez, P.
1996 *La Real Audiencia de Galicia y el Archivo del Reino.* 2 vols. Santiago de Compostela: Xunta de Galicia.

López López, R. J., and D. L. González Lopo (eds.)
2003 *Balance de la Historiografía modernista, 1973–2001: Actas del VI Coloquio de Metodología Histórica Aplicada.* Santiago de Compostela: Xunta de Galicia.

López-Salazar Pérez, J.
1987 *Mesta, pastos y conflictos en el Campo de Calatrava (s. XVI).* Madrid: Consejo Superior de Investigaciones Científicas.

López Serrano, A.
1997–1998 "En torno a los problemas y confusión jurídica en la posesión del señorío de Villena (s. XV y XVI)." *Miscelánea Medieval Murciana* 21–22: 171–214.

López Serrano, M.
1969 *Libro de la Montería del Rey de Castilla Alfonso XI: Estudio preliminar.* Madrid: Patrimonio Nacional.

Lorenzo Cadarso, P. L.

1999 *La documentación judicial en la época de los Austrias: Estudio archivístico y diplomático*. Cáceres: Caja Duero; Universidad de Extremadura.

Lovett, A. W.

1977 *Philip II and Mateo Vázquez de Leca*. Geneva: Droz.

1980 "The Castilian Bankruptcy of 1575." *Historical Journal* 23: 899–911.

1982 "The General Settlement of 1577: An Aspect of Spanish Finance in the Early Modern Period." *Historical Journal* 25: 1–22.

1986 *Early Habsburg Spain, 1517–1598*. Oxford and New York: Oxford University Press.

1987 "The Vote of the *Millones* (1590)." *Historical Journal* 30: 1–20.

1988 "Philip II, Antonio Pérez and the Kingdom of Aragon." *European History Quarterly* 18,2: 131–53.

Lublinskaya, A. D.

1968 *French Absolutism: The Crucial Phase, 1620–1629*. Trans. B. Pearce. Cambridge: Cambridge University Press [1965].

Lunenfeld, M.

1970 *The Council of the Santa Hermandad: A Study of the Pacification Forces of Ferdinand and Isabella*. Coral Gables, Florida: University of Miami Press.

1987 *Keepers of the City: The Corregidores of Isabella I of Castile (1474–1504)*. Cambridge: Cambridge University Press.

Lynch, J.

1964 *Spain under the Habsburgs*. Vol. 1. New York: Oxford University Press.

MacKay, A.

1977 *Spain in the Middle Ages: From Frontier to Empire, 1000–1500*. New York: St. Martin's.

1986 "The Lesser Nobility in the Kingdom of Castile." In Jones, ed. (1986): 159–80.

Mackay, R.

1999 *The Limits of Royal Authority: Resistance and Obedience in Seventeenth-Century Castile*. Cambridge: Cambridge University Press.

MacLachlan, C. M.

1988 *Spain's Empire in the New World: The Role of Ideas in Institutional and Social Change*. Berkeley and Los Angeles: University of California Press.

Madden, M. R.

1930 *Political Theory and Law in Medieval Spain*. New York: Fordham University Press.

Madoz, P.

1845–1850 *Diccionario geográfico-estadístico-histórico de España y sus posesiones de ultramar*. 16 vols. Madrid: Imprenta del Diccionario.

Madrigal, Alfonso de ["El Tostado"; ca. 1410–1455]

2003 *El gobierno ideal* [*De optima politia;* ca. 1436]. Bilingual ed. Ed. and trans. N. Belloso Martín. Pamplona: Universidad de Navarra (EUNSA).

Major, J. R.

1960 *Representative Institutions in Renaissance France, 1421–1559*. Madison: University of Wisconsin Press.

Malagón-Barceló, J.

1959 *La literatura jurídica española del siglo de oro en la Nueva España: Notas para su estudio*. Mexico: Biblioteca Nacional de México, Instituto Bibliográfico Mexicano, Universidad Nacional Autónoma de México.

Malament, B. C. (ed.)

1980 *After the Reformation: Essays in Honor of J. H. Hexter*. Philadelphia: University of Pennsylvania Press.

Maldonado, Juan [ca. 1485–1554]

1975 *La revolución comunera: El movimiento de España, o sea historia de la revolución conocida con el nombre de las Comunidades de Castilla* [1540]. Trans. J. Quevedo. Madrid: Ediciones del Centro [1840].

1991 *De motu hispaniae: El levantamiento de España*. Bilingual ed. Ed. and trans. M. A. Durán Ramas. Madrid: Centro de Estudios Constitucionales.

Maltby, W. S.

1983 *Alba: A Biography of Fernando Alvarez de Toledo, Third Duke of Alba, 1507–1582*. Berkeley: University of California Press.

Mann, J. D.

1996 "Juan de Segovia's *Super materia contractuum de censibus annuis:* Text and Context." In Christianson and Izbicki, eds. (1996): 71–85.

Marañón, G.

1969 *Antonio Pérez: El hombre, el drama, la época*. 8th ed. 2 vols. Madrid: Espasa-Calpe [1947; 3rd ed., revised and enlarged, 1951].

Maravall, J. A.

1953 "La formación de la conciencia estamental de los letrados." *Revista de Estudios Políticos* 48: 53–82.

1960 *Carlos V y el pensamiento político del Renacimiento*. Madrid: Instituto de Estudios Políticos.

1961 "The Origins of the Modern State." *Cahiers d'Histoire Mondiale/Journal of World History* 6,4: 789–808.

1963 *Las Comunidades de Castilla: Una primera revolución moderna*. Madrid: Revista de Occidente.

1972a *Estado moderno y mentalidad social: Siglos XV a XVII*. 2 vols. Madrid: Revista de Occidente.

1972b *Teatro y literatura en la sociedad barroca*. Madrid: Seminarios y Ediciones.

1973a *Estudios de historia del pensamiento español*. 2nd ed. Madrid: Ediciones Cultura Hispánica [1967].

1973b "Los 'hombres de saber' o letrados y la formación de su conciencia estamental." In Maravall (1973a): 355–89 [republication of Maravall (1953)].

Marcos Martín, A.

1991 "¿Que es una ciudad en la época moderna? Reflexión histórica sobre el fenómeno de lo urbano." In Casa de Velázquez (1991): 273–88.

1994 "Medina del Campo 1500–1800: An Historical Account of Its Decline" [1986]. In Thompson and Yun Casalilla, eds. (1994): 220–48.

1997 "Evolución de la propiedad pública municipal en Castilla la Vieja durante la Epoca Moderna." *Stvdia Historica. Historia Moderna* 16: 57–100.

1998 "España en almoneda: Enajenaciones por precio de alcabalas y tercias en el siglo XVI." In Ribot and Belenguer, eds. (1998): 25–65.

1999 "Oligarquías urbanas y gobiernos ciudadanos en la España del siglo XVI." In Belenguer Cebrià, ed. (1999): 265–93.

2003a *"Desde la hoja del monte hasta la piedra del río . . .": La venta al duque de Lerma de las once villas de Behetría de Castilla la Vieja*. Palencia: Institución Tello Téllez de Meneses.

2003b "Enajenaciones por precio del patrimonio regio en los siglos XVI y XVII: Balance historiográfico y perspectivas de análisis." In López López and González Lopo 2003: 419–43.

Margolis, H.

1987 *Patterns, Thinking, and Cognition: A Theory of Judgment*. Chicago: University of Chicago Press.

1993 *Paradigms and Barriers: How Habits of Mind Govern Scientific Beliefs*. Chicago and London: University of Chicago Press.

Mariana, Juan de [1535/1536–1624]

1592a *Historiae de rebus Hispaniae. Libri XX*. Toledo: Typis Petri Roderici.

1592b *Historiae de rebus Hispaniae. Libri XXV*. Toledo: Typis Petri Roderici.

1599 *De rege et regis institutione libri III*. Toledo: Apud Petrum Rodericum.

1601 *Historia general de España. Compvesta primero en latin, despues buelta en catellano por Iuan de Mariana, D. theologo, de la Compañia de Iesus*. 2 vols. [Vol. 1, books 1–15; vol. 2, books 16–30] Toledo: Pedro Rodriguez.

1605a *De rege et regis institutione libri III*. Mainz: Typis Balthasaris Lippii.

1605b *Historiae de rebus Hispaniae libri XXX*. Mainz: Typis Balthasaris Lippii.

1611 *De rege et regis institutione libri III. Eiusdem de ponderibus & mensuris*. Mainz: Typis Wechelianis, apud haeredes Ioannis Aubrii.

1623 *Historia General de España. Compvesta, emendada y añadida por el Padre Ivan de Mariana de la Compañia de Iesvs. Con el Svmario y Tablas*. 2 vols. Toledo: Diego Rodriguez.

1948 *The King and the Education of the King* [1599]. Ed. and trans. G. A. Moore. Chevy Chase, Maryland: The Country Dollar Press.

1950 *Obras del Padre Juan de Mariana*. Ed. F. Pi y Margall. 2 vols. Madrid: Ediciones Atlas [Biblioteca de Autores Españoles, vols. 30–31 (1854, 1872)].

1969 *De rege et regis institutione libri III* [Toledo: Typis Petri Roderici, 1599]. Aalen: Scientia Verlag.

1981 *La dignidad real y la educación del rey (De rege et regis institutione)* [1605]. Ed. and trans. L. Sánchez Agesta. Madrid: Centro de Estudios Constitucionales.

1987 *Tratado y discurso sobre la moneda de vellón*. Ed. L. Beltrán. Madrid: Ministerio de Economía y Hacienda, Instituto de Estudios Fiscales.

1996 *De monetae mutatione/Über die Münzveränderung* [Cologne, 1609]. Ed. and trans. J. Falzberger. Heidelberg: Manutius Verlag.

Márquez, A.

1980 *Literatura e Inquisición en España, 1478–1834*. Madrid: Taurus.

Marsilius of Padua [d. ca. 1348]

1956 *Defensor pacis*. Trans. A. Gewirth. In Gewirth (1951–1956): II.

Martín Gamero, A.

1862 *Historia de la ciudad de Toledo, sus claros varones y monumentos*. Toledo: Severiano López Fando.

Martín Gamero, A. (ed.)
1858 *Ordenanzas para el buen régimen y gobierno de la ciudad de Toledo*. Toledo: José de Cea.

Martín Postigo, M. de la S.
1964 "La Cancillería castellana en la primera mitad del siglo XVI." *Hispania* 24: 348–67 and 509–51.

Martínez, J. M. et al.
1958 *Aristocracia: Anuario genealógico y heráldico*. Madrid: Gráficas Madrid.

Martínez Cardós, J.
1960 *Gregorio López, Consejero de Indias, glosador de las Partidas (1496–1560)*. Madrid: Instituto Gonzalo Fernández de Oviedo.

Martínez Carrillo, M. de los L.
1980 *Revolución urbana y autoridad monárquica en Murcia durante la Baja Edad Media (1395–1420)*. Murcia: Universidad de Murcia, Academia Alfonso X El Sabio.
1985 *Manueles y Fajardos: La crisis bajomedieval en Murcia*. Murcia: Academia Alfonso X El Sabio.

Martínez Gil, F.
1981 *Toledo en las Comunidades de Castilla*. Toledo: Diputación Provincial.
1993 *La ciudad inquieta: Toledo comunera, 1520–1522*. Toledo: Instituto Provincial de Investigaciones y Estudios Toledanos.
2002 "Furia popular: La participación de las multitudes urbanas en las Comunidades de Castilla." In Martínez Gil, ed. (2002): 309–64.

Martínez Gil, F. (ed.)
2002 *En torno a las Comunidades de Castilla: Actas del Congreso Internacional "Poder, conflicto y revueta en la España de Carlos I" (Toledo, 16 al 20 de octubre de 2000)*. Cuenca: Universidad de Castilla-La Mancha.

Martínez Martín, J.
1991 *Lectura y lectores en el Madrid del siglo XIX*. Madrid: Consejo Superior de Investigaciones Científicas.

Martínez Millán, J.
1980 "Aportaciones a la formación del Estado moderno y a la política española a través de la censura inquisitorial durante el período 1480–1559." In Pérez Villanueva, ed. (1980): 537–78.
1988 "Elites de poder en tiempos de Carlos V a través de los miembros del Consejo de Inquisición." *Hispania* 48,168: 103–67.
1989 "Elites de poder en tiempos de Felipe II (1539–1572)." *Hispania* 49,171: 111–49.
1992a "Grupos de poder en la Corte durante el reinado de Felipe II: La facción ebolista, 1554–1573." In Martínez Millán, ed. (1992): 137–97.
1992b "Introducción: La investigación sobre las élites del poder." In Martínez Millán, ed. (1992): 11–24.
1993 "Un curioso manuscrito: El libro de gobierno del Cardenal Diego de Espinosa (1512?-1572)." *Hispania* 53,183: 299–344.
1994a "En busca de la ortodoxia: El Inquisidor General Diego de Espinosa." In Martínez Millán, ed. (1994): 189–228.
1994b "Familia real y grupos políticos: La princesa doña Juana de Austria (1535–1573)." In Martínez Millán, ed. (1994): 73–105.

1994c "Introducción: Los estudios sobre la corte. Interpretación de la corte de Felipe II." In Martínez Millán, ed. (1994): 13–35.

Martínez Millán, J. (ed.)
1992 *Instituciones y élites de poder en la Monarquía Hispana durante el siglo XVI.* Madrid: Ediciones de la Universidad Autónoma de Madrid.
1994 *La corte de Felipe II.* Madrid: Alianza Editorial.

Martínez Millán, J., and C. J. de Carlos Morales
1991 "Los orígenes del Consejo de Cruzada (Siglo XVI)." *Hispania* 41,179: 901–32.
1992 "La administración de la Gracia real: Los miembros de la Cámara de Castilla (1543–1575)." In Martínez Millán, ed. (1992): 25–45.

Martínez Moro, J.
1977 *La renta feudal de la Castilla del siglo XV: Los Stúñiga. Consideraciones metodológicas y otras.* Valladolid: Universidad de Valladolid.
1985 *La tierra en la comunidad de Segovia: Un proyecto señorial urbano (1088–1500).* Valladolid: Universidad de Valladolid.

Martz, L.
1987 "La familia y hacienda del Doctor Sancho de Moncada." *Anales Toledanos* 24: 51–90.
1988 "Converso Families in Fifteenth and Sixteenth Century Toledo: The Significance of Lineage." *Sefarad* 58: 117–96.
1994 "Pure Blood Statutes in Sixteenth-Century Toledo: Implementation as Opposed to Adoption." *Sefarad* 54,1: 83–107.
1995 "*Toledanos* and the Kingdom of Granada, 1492–1560s." In Kagan and Parker, eds. (1995): 103–24.
2003 *A Network of Converso Families in Early Modern Toledo: Assimilating a Minority.* Ann Arbor: University of Michigan Press.

Mathers, C. J.
1973 "Relations between the City of Burgos and the Crown, 1506–1556." Ph.D. diss. Columbia University.

Mattingly, G.
1940 "The Reputation of Doctor De Puebla." *English Historical Review* 55: 27–46.
1959 *The Armada.* Boston: Houghton Mifflin.

McGovern, A. F.
1988 "Jesuit Education and Jesuit Spirituality." *Studies in the Spirituality of Jesuits* 20,4 (September): 1–39.

McIlwain, C. H.
1932 *The Growth of Political Thought in the West: From the Greeks to the End of the Middle Ages.* New York: Macmillan.

McKendrick, M.
1989 *Theatre in Spain, 1490–1700.* Cambridge: Cambridge University Press.

Memorias de Enrique IV
1913 See Real Academia de la Historia.

Mena, Juan de [1411–1456]
1984 *Laberinto de Fortuna.* Ed. J. G. Cummins. 3rd ed. Madrid: Cátedra.

Menéndez Pidal, R. (ed.)
1964 *Historia de Espana:* Vol. 15, *Los Trastámaras de Castilla y Aragón en el siglo XV.* Madrid: Espasa-Calpe.

Menjot, D.

1978 "La incidencia social de la fiscalidad directa de los Trastámaras de Castilla en el siglo XV." In Menjot (1986): 205–45.

1979 "La instauración de la fiscalidad directa de los primeros Trastámaras en Murcia en el último cuarto del siglo XIV." In Menjot (1986): 181–204.

1986 *Fiscalidad y sociedad: Los murcianos y el impuesto en la Baja Edad Media*. Murcia: Academia Alfonso X el Sabio.

1988 "La ville et l'Etat moderne naissant: La monarchie et le Concejo de Murcie dans la Castille des Trastamares d'Henri II à Henri IV." In Rucquoi, ed. (1988): 115–35.

2002 *Murcie castillane: Une ville au temps de la frontière (1243–milieu du XVe s.)*. 2 vols. Madrid: Casa de Velázquez.

Merchán Fernández, A. C.

1988 *Gobierno municipal y administración local en la España del Antiguo Régimen*. Madrid: Editorial Tecnos.

Merino Alvarez, A.

1926 *La sociedad abulense durante el siglo XVI: La nobleza*. Madrid: Patronato de Huérfanos de los Cuerpos de Intendencia.

Merriman, R. B.

1962 *The Rise of the Spanish Empire in the Old World and in the New*. 2nd ed. 4 vols. New York: Cooper Square [1918–1934].

Metodología Aplicada

1975 *Actas de las I Jornadas de Metodología Aplicada de las Ciencias Históricas*. 2 vols. Santiago: Universidad de Santiago de Compostela.

Mettam, R.

1988 *Power and Faction in Louis XIV's France*. Oxford and New York: Basil Blackwell.

1990 "France." In Miller, ed. (1990): 43–67.

Mexía, Pedro [1497–1551]

1945 *Historia del Emperador Carlos V*. Ed. J. de Mata Carriazo. Madrid: Espasa-Calpe.

Miller, J. (ed.)

1990 *Absolutism in Seventeenth-Century Europe*. New York: St. Martin's Press.

Mínguez Fernández, J. M.

1990 "Las Hermandades Generales de los Concejos en la Corona de Castilla (Objetivos, estructura interna y contradicciones en sus manifestaciones iniciales)." In Concejos y Ciudades (1990): 537–67.

Mitre Fernández, E.

1968 *Evolución de la nobleza en Castilla bajo Enrique III (1396–1406)*. Valladolid: Andrés Martín.

1980 "Mecanismos institucionales y poder real en la Castilla de Enrique III." In Ladero Quesada, ed. (1980): 317–28.

Molénat, J.-P.

1972 "Tolède et ses finages au temps des Rois Catholiques: Contribution à l'histoire sociale et économique de la cité avant la révolte des Comunidades." *Mélanges de la Casa de Velázquez* 8: 327–77.

1986 "La volonté de durer: Majorats et chapellanies dans la pratique tolédane des XIII–XV siècles." *En la España Medieval* 9: 683–96.

1988 "Formation des seigneuries tolédanes aux XIVème et XVème siècles." In Rucquoi, ed. (1988): 349–70.

1991a "L'oligarchie municipale de Tolède au XVe siècle." In Casa de Velázquez (1991): 159–77.

1991b "Réflexions sur les origines agraires de la révolte des Comunidades à Tolède." In Rucquoi, ed. (1991): 193–208.

1993 "Pouvoir municipal et parenté à Tolède au XVe siècle." In Breteau and Zagnoli, eds. (1993): 217–29.

1997 *Campagnes et monts de Tolède du XIIe au XVe siècle.* Madrid: Casa de Velázquez.

Moliné-Bertrand, A., and J.-P. Duviols (eds.)

1999 *Philippe II et l'Espagne.* Paris: Université de Paris-Sorbonne.

Möller Recondo, C.

2001 "Carlos V y la Universidad de Salamanca." In Castellano Castellano and Sánchez-Montes González, eds. (2001): 429–60.

2004 *Comuneros y universitarios: Hacia la construcción del monopolio del saber.* Buenos Aires and Madrid: Miño y Dávila.

Moncada, Sancho de

1974 *Restauración política de España* [1619]. Ed. J. Vilar. Madrid: Instituto de Estudios Fiscales, Ministerio de Hacienda.

Monod, P. K.

1999 *The Power of Kings: Monarchy and Religion in Europe, 1589–1715.* New Haven, Connecticut, and London: Yale University Press.

Monsalvo Antón, J. M.

1985 *Teoría y evolución de un conflicto social: El antisemitismo en la Corona de Castilla en la Baja Edad Media.* Madrid: Siglo XXI de España.

1990 "La sociedad política en los concejos castellanos de la Meseta durante la época del regimiento medieval: La distribución social del poder." In Concejos y Ciudades (1990): 357–413.

Montemayor, J.

1996 *Tolède entre fortune et déclin (1530–1640).* Panazol: Presses Universitaires de Limoges.

Montero Tejada, R. M.

1996 *Nobleza y sociedad en Castilla: El linaje Manrique (siglos XIV–XVI).* Madrid: Caja de Madrid.

Montojo Montojo, V., and J. F. Jiménez Alcázar

2002 "Conflictos internos en la época de Carlos V: Las Comunidades en la región de Murcia." In Martínez Gil, ed. (2002): 431–59.

Moore, G. A.

1948 "Introduction." In Mariana (1948): 1–93.

Morales Muñiz, M. D.-C.

1988 *Alfonso de Avila, Rey de Castilla.* Avila: Instituto "Gran Duque de Alba," Diputación Provincial.

Morley, S. G., and C. Bruerton

1968 *Cronología de las comedias de Lope de Vega: Con un examen de las atribuciones dudosas, basado todo ello en un estudio de su versificación estrófica.* Trans. M. R. Cartes. Madrid: Editorial Gredos.

Morral, J. B.
1960 *Gerson and the Great Schism*. Manchester: Manchester University Press.

Mousnier, R.
1964 *L'assassinat de Henri IV, 14 Mai 1610: Le problème du tyrannicide et l'affermisse-ment de la monarchie absolue*. Paris: Gallimard.

Moutoukias, Z.
1988 *Contrabando y control colonial en el siglo XVII: Buenos Aires, el Atlántico y el espa-cio peruano*. Buenos Aires: Centro Editor de América Latina.

Moxó, S. de
1958 "Los orígenes de la percepción de alcabalas por particulares." *Hispania* 18: 307–39.

1963 *La Alcabala: Sobre sus orígenes, concepto y naturaleza*. Madrid: Consejo Superior de Investigaciones Científicas, Instituto "Balmes" de Sociología.

1969 "De la nobleza vieja a la nobleza nueva: La transformación nobiliaria caste-llana en la baja Edad Media." In Moxó, ed. (1969): 1–210.

1970–1971 "La nobleza castellana en el siglo XIV." *Anuario de Estudios Medievales* 7: 493–511.

1973 "Los señoríos: Cuestiones metodológicas que plantea su estudio." *Anuario de Historia del Derecho Español* 43: 271–309.

1975a "La promoción política y social de los 'letrados' en la corte de Alfonso XI." *Hispania* 35: 5–30.

1975b "La sociedad política castellana en la época de Alfonso XI." *Cuadernos de Historia* 6: 187–326.

1976 "La elevación de los 'letrados' en la sociedad estamental del siglo XIV." In Semana de Estudios Medievales (1976): 183–215.

1981 "El auge de la nobleza urbana de Castilla y su proyección en el ámbito administrativo y rural a comienzos de la Baja Edad Media (1270–1370)." *Boletín de la Real Academia de la Historia* 178: 407–510.

Moxó, S. de (ed.)
1969 *Estudios sobre la sociedad castellana en la Baja Edad Media*. Madrid: Consejo Superior de Investigaciones Científicas [*Cuadernos de Historia* Vol. 3].

Murillo Ferrol, F.
1957 *Saavedra Fajardo y la política del Barroco*. Madrid: Instituto de Estudios Políti-cos.

Nader, H.
1979 *The Mendoza Family in the Spanish Renaissance, 1350–1550*. New Brunswick, New Jersey: Rutgers University Press.

1988 "Habsburg Ceremony in Spain: The Reality of the Myth." *Historical Reflec-tions/Réflexions Historiques* 15,1: 293–309.

1990 *Liberty in Absolutist Spain: The Habsburg Sale of Towns, 1516–1700*. Baltimore, Maryland: Johns Hopkins University Press.

1996 "'The More Communes, the Greater the King': Hidden Communes in Absolutist Theory." In Blickle, ed. (1996): 215–23.

Nalle, S. T.
2001 *Mad for God: Bartolomé Sánchez, the Secret Messiah of Cardenete*. Charlottesville, Virginia: University Press of Virginia.

Navarro Tomás, T.
1966 "Introduction." In Navarro Tomás, ed. (1966 [1935]).

Navarro Tomás, T. (ed.)
1966 *Garcilaso: Obras.* Madrid: Espasa-Calpe.

Navas, J. M.
1996 *La abogacia en el siglo de oro.* Madrid: Colegio de Abogados.

Nederman, C. J.
1990 "Conciliarism and Constitutionalism: Jean Gerson and Medieval Political Thought." *History of European Ideas* 12: 189–209.

Netanyahu, B.
2001 *The Origins of the Inquisition in Fifteenth Century Spain.* 2nd ed. New York: New York Review of Books [1995].

Neuschel, K. B.
1989 *Word of Honor: Interpreting Noble Culture in Sixteenth-Century France.* Ithaca, New York: Cornell University Press.

Nicolini, U.
1952 *La proprietà, il principe e l'espropriazione per pubblica utilità: Studi sulla dottrina giuridica intermedia.* 2nd ed. Milan: Dott. A. Giuffrè [1940].

Nieto, A.
1980 "El derecho como límite del poder en la Edad Media." *Revista de Administración Pública* 91: 7–73.

Nieto Soria, J. M.
1988 *Fundamentos ideológicos del poder real en Castilla (siglos XIII–XVI).* Madrid: EUDEMA.
1993 *Ceremonias de la realeza: Propaganda y legitimación en la Castilla Trastámara.* Madrid: Editorial Nerea.
1998 "El 'poderío real absoluto' de Olmedo (1445) a Ocaña (1469): La monarquía como conflicto." *En la España Medieval* 21: 159–228.

Nowell, C. E.
1952 *A History of Portugal.* New York: D. Van Nostrand.

Nueva Recopilación [abbreviated as NR. This law code is always cited in this form. Here I provide the reference to the edition I have consulted.]
1982 *Recopilación de las leyes destos reynos hecha por mandado de la Magestad Católica Rey don Felipe Segundo . . .* [1640]. 3 vols. Valladolid: Editorial Lex Nova [facsimile reprint].

Núñez Alonso, M. P.
1984 *Archivo de la Real Chancillería de Granada: Guía del investigador.* Madrid: Ministerio de Cultura.

Núñez de Avendaño, Pedro [mid 16th century]
1543 *De exequendis mandatis regum hispaniae.* Alcalá de Henares: Juan de Brocar.

Oakley, F.
1962 "From Constance to 1688: The Political Thought of John Major and George Buchanan." *Journal of British Studies* 1: 1–31.
1964 *The Political Thought of Pierre d'Ailly: The Voluntarist Tradition.* New Haven, Connecticut: Yale University Press.
1969a *Council over Pope? Toward a Provisional Ecclesiology.* New York: Herder and Herder.

1969b "Figgis, Constance, and the Divines of Paris." *American Historical Review* 75,2: 368–86.

1979 *The Western Church in the Later Middle Ages*. Ithaca, New York: Cornell University Press.

1981 "Natural Law, the *Corpus Mysticum,* and Consent in Conciliar Thought from John of Paris to Matthias Ugonius." *Speculum* 56,4: 786–810.

1984 *Natural Law, Conciliarism and Consent in the Late Middle Ages: Studies in Ecclesiastical and Intellectual History*. London: Variorum Reprints.

1994 "Constance, Basel, and the Two Pisas: The Conciliarist Legacy in Sixteenth- and Seventeenth-Century England." *Annuarium Historiae Conciliorum* 26: 87–118.

1995 "Nederman, Gerson, Conciliar Theory and Constitutionalism: *sed contra*." *History of Political Thought* 16: 1–19.

1996a "'Anxieties of Influence': Skinner, Figgis, Conciliarism and Early Modern Constitutionalism." *Past and Present* No. 151 (May): 60–110.

1996b *"Verius est licet difficilius:* Tierney's *Foundations of the Conciliar Theory* after Forty Years." In Christianson and Izbicki, eds. (1996): 15–34.

O'Callaghan, J. F.

1975 *A History of Medieval Spain*. Ithaca, New York: Cornell University Press.

1988 "Las Cortes de Castilla y León (1230–1350)." In Valdeón Baruque, ed. (1988): I, 153–81.

1989 *The Cortes of Castile-Leon, 1188–1350*. Philadelphia: University of Pennsylvania Press.

Oestreich, G.

1982 *Neostoicism and the Early Modern State*. Ed. B. Oestrich and H. G. Koenigsberger. Trans. D. McLintock. Cambridge: Cambridge University Press.

Olivera Serrano, C.

1986 *Las Cortes de Castilla y León y la crisis del reino (1445–1474): El registro de Cortes*. Burgos: Congreso Internacional sobre la Historia de las Cortes de Castilla y León.

1987 "Las Cortes de Castilla en el primer tercio del siglo XV." *Hispania* 47: 405–36.

1988 "Las Cortes de Castilla y el poder real (1431–1454)." *En la España Medieval* 11: 223–60.

Olmedo, F. G.

1939 *Juan Bonifacio (1538–1606) y la cultura literaria del Siglo de Oro*. Santander: Sociedad de Menéndez Pelayo.

Ourliac, P.

1979 *Études d'histoire du droit médiéval*. Paris: Éditions A. et J. Picard.

Owens, J. B.

1972 "Despotism, Absolutism, and the Law in Renaissance Spain: Toledo versus the Counts of Belalcázar (1445–1574)." Ph.D. diss. University of Wisconsin-Madison.

1977a "Diana at the Bar: Hunting, Aristocrats and the Law in Renaissance Castile." *Sixteenth Century Journal* 8: 17–36.

1977b "The Conception of Absolute Royal Power in Sixteenth Century Castile." *Il Pensiero Politico* 10: 349–61.

1978 "A City for the King: The Impact of Rural Revolt on Talavera during the *Comunidades* of Castile." *Societas: A Review of Social History* 8: 53–64.

1980 *Rebelión, monarquía y oligarquía murciana en la época de Carlos V.* Murcia: Universidad de Murcia.

1999a "Comuneros, Revolt of the." In Grendler, ed. (1999): II, 60–62.

1999b "Maldonado, Juan." In Grendler, ed. (1999): IV, 27.

1999c "Mariana, Juan de." In Grendler, ed. (1999): IV, 39–40.

Ozment, S.

1980 *The Age of Reform, 1250–1550: An Intellectual and Religious History of Late Medieval and Reformation Europe.* New Haven, Connecticut: Yale University Press.

Palencia, Alonso F. de [1423–1492]

1973–1975 *Crónica de Enrique IV.* 2 vols. Trans. A. Paz y Melia [Biblioteca de Autores Españoles: Vols. 207–8]. Madrid: Ediciones Atlas.

Palencia Flores, C.

1959 *El Archivo Municipal de Talavera de la Reina: Relación de sus más importantes documentos.* Talavera: Ayuntamiento de Talavera.

Pardos Martínez, J. A.

1985 "Constitución política y Comunidad en Burgos a finales del siglo XV (Reflexiones en torno a un documento de 1475)." In Coloquio de La Rábida (1985): I, 545–80.

Parker, A. A.

1957 *The Approach to the Spanish Drama of the Golden Age.* London: Hispanic and Luso-Brazilian Councils [*Diamante*, Vol. VI].

1970 "The Spanish Drama of the Golden Age: A Method of Analysis and Interpretation." In Bentley, ed. (1970): 679–707 [revised and expanded version of A. A. Parker's 1957 essay].

Parker, D.

1987 "Class, Clientage and Personal Rule in Absolutist France." *Seventeenth Century French Studies* 9: 192–213.

1989 "Sovereignty, Absolutism and the Function of the Law in Seventeenth-Century France." *Past and Present* No. 122: 36–74.

1990 "French Absolutism, the English State and the Utility of the Base-Superstructure Model." *Social History* 15,3: 287–301.

Parker, G.

1978 *Philip II.* Boston: Little, Brown.

1998 *The Grand Strategy of Philip II.* New Haven, Connecticut, and London: Yale University Press.

Parry, J. H.

1948 *The Audiencia of New Galicia in the Sixteenth Century: A Study in Spanish Colonial Government.* Cambridge: Cambridge University Press.

Passola i Tejedor, A.

1997 *La historiografía sobre el municipio en la España Moderna.* Lleida: Universitat de Lleida [*Espai/Temps*, No. 30].

Pastor, R. (ed.)

1990 *Relaciones de poder, de producción y parentesco en la Edad Media y Moderna: Aproximación a su estudio.* Madrid: Consejo Superior de Investigaciones Científicas.

Pastor Bodmer, I.

1992 *Grandeza y tragedia de un valido: La muerte de don Alvaro de Luna.* 2 vols. Madrid: Caja de Madrid.

Pastor Gómez, J.
1955 "Las Cortes de Toledo de 1480." *Toletum: Boletín de la Real Academia de Bellas Artes y Ciéncias Históricas de Toledo* 66–68: 55–89.
Pedraza Ruiz, E.
1985 *Catálogo: Archivo Secreto, Excmo. Ayuntamiento de Toledo.* Toledo: Gómez-Menor.
Pelorson, J.-M.
1980 *Les "Letrados," juristes castillans sous Philippe III: Recherches sur leur place dans la société, la culture et l'état.* Le Puy-en-Velay (Poitiers): L'Eveil de la Haute Loire.
Pelsmaeker Iváñez, F. de
1925 *La Audiencia en las colonias españolas de América.* Madrid: Revista de Archivos.
Pennington, K.
1993 *The Prince and the Law, 1200–1600: Sovereignty and Rights in the Western Legal Tradition.* Berkeley: University of California Press.
Pérez, J.
1963 "Pour une nouvelle interprétation des *Comunidades* de Castille." *Bulletin hispanique* 65: 238–83.
1965a "Moines frondeurs et sermons subversifs en Castille pendant le premier séjour de Charles-Quint en Espagne." *Bulletin hispanique* 67: 5–24.
1965b Review of J. A. Maravall (1963). *Bulletin hispanique* 67: 152–56.
1970 *La révolution de "Comunidades" de Castille (1520–1521).* Bordeaux: Institut d'Etudes Ibériques et Ibero-Américaines de l'Université de Bordeaux.
1977 *La revolución de las Comunidades de Castilla (1520–1521).* 2nd ed. Trans. J. J. Faci Lacasta. Madrid: Siglo XXI de España.
1988 *Isabel y Fernando: Los Reyes Católicos.* Madrid: Nerea.
1989 *Los comuneros.* Madrid: Historia 16.
Pérez-Bustamante y González de la Vega, R.
1986 "Cortes de Castilla en el siglo XV: Hacia una nueva dimensión institucional." In Olivera Serrano (1986): ix–xxxi.
Pérez de Guzmán, Fernán [d. 1460?] (see Crónica de Juan II 1517, 1953)
1517 *Començã la Cronica del serenissimo rey don Iuan el segundo deste nõbre . . .* Ed. Dr. Lorenzo Galíndez de Carvajal [d. 1528]. Logroño: Arnao Guillén de Brocar.
1953 "Generaciones y semblanzas e obras de los excelentes Reyes de España don Enrique el Tercero e don Juan el Segundo y de las venerables perlados y notables caballeros que en los tiempos destos Reyes fueron, ordenados por el noble caballero Fernán Pérez de Guzmán." In Rosell, ed. (1953): II, 697–719.
Pérez-Embid Wamba, J.
1982 "Don Alvaro de Luna, los monjes y los campesinos: Un conflicto en la Castilla bajomedieval." In Ladero Quesada, ed. (1982): II, 231–45.
Pérez Martín, A.
1988 "El renacimiento del poder legislativo y la génesis del Estado Moderno en la Corona de Castilla." In Gouron and Rigaudiere, eds. (1988): 189–202.
2000 "La literatura jurídica castellana en la baja edad media." In Alvarado, ed. (2000): 61–78.
Pérez Royo, J.
1980 *Introducción a la teoría del Estado.* Barcelona: Editorial Blume.

Pérez Villanueva, J. (ed.)

1980 *La Inquisición española: Nueva visión, nuevos horizontes*. Madrid: Siglo XXI de España.

Perrone, S. T.

1998 "The Castilian Assembly of the Clergy in the Sixteenth Century." *Parliaments, Estates and Representation* 18: 53–70.

Phelan, J. L.

1967 *The Kingdom of Quito in the Seventeenth Century: Bureaucratic Politics in the Spanish Empire*. Madison: University of Wisconsin Press.

Phillips, C. R., and W. D. Phillips, Jr.

1997 *Spain's Golden Fleece: Wool Production and the Wool Trade from the Middle Ages to the Nineteenth Century*. Baltimore, Maryland: Johns Hopkins University Press.

Phillips, W. D., Jr.

1978 *Enrique IV and the Crisis of Fifteenth Century Castile, 1425–1480*. Cambridge, Massachesetts: Mediaeval Academy of America.

1986 "University Graduates in Castilian Royal Service in the Fifteenth Century." In Carlé, Grassotti, and Orduna, eds. (1983–1990): IV, 475–90.

Phillips, W. D., Jr., and C. R. Phillips

1992 *The Worlds of Christopher Columbus*. Cambridge: Cambridge University Press.

Pierson, P.

1975 *Philip II of Spain*. London: Thames and Hudson.

1989 *Commander of the Armada: The Seventh Duke of Medina Sidonia*. New Haven, Connecticut: Yale University Press.

Pietschmann, H.

1992 "El problema del 'nacionalismo' en España en la Edad Moderna: La resistencia de Castilla contra el emperador Carlos V." *Hispania* 52,180: 83–106.

Pinker, S.

1995 *The Language Instinct*. New York: HarperPerennial [1994].

Piqueras García, M. B.

1988 *Fiscalidad real y concejil en el reinado de Enrique IV: El ejemplo de Murcia (1462–1474)*. Cádiz: Universidad de Cádiz; Academia Alfonso X el Sabio de Murcia.

Pizarro Llorente, H.

1992 "Las relaciones de patronazgo a través de los inquisidores de Valladolid durante el siglo XVI." In Martínez Millán, ed. (1992): 223–62.

1994 "El control de la conciencia regia: El confesor real fray Bernardo de Fresneda." In Martínez Millán, ed. (1994): 149–88.

Pocock, J. G. A.

1987 "Texts as Events: Reflections on the History of Political Thought." In Sharpe and Zwicker, eds. (1987): 21–34.

Polaino Ortega, L.

1964 "Un pleito sobre el Adelantamiento de Cazorla entre la Corona y la Mitra." *Toletum: Boletín de la Real Academia de Bellas Artes y Ciéncias Históricas de Toledo* 72–74: 157–74.

Polo de Medina, Salvador Jacinto [1603–1676]

1948a "Academias del Jardín" [1630]. In Polo de Medina (1948b): 1–159.

1948b *Obras completas*. Murcia: Sucesores de Nogués.

Porchnev, B.
1963 *Les soulèvements populaires en France de 1623 à 1648.* Paris: S.E.V.P.E.N. [1948].
Porras Arboledas, P. A.
1993 *La ciudad de Jaén y la revolución de las Comunidades de Castilla (1500–1523).* Jaén: Diputación Provincial de Jaén, Instituto de Estudios Giennenses.
1995 *Juan II, 1406–1454.* Palencia: Diputación Provincial de Palencia; Editorial La Olmeda.
2002 "Las Comunidades en Andalucía." In Martínez Gil, ed. (2002): 461–77.
Porreño, Baltasar [d. 1639]
1942 *Dichos y hechos del Rey D. Felipe II* [1628]. Madrid: Saeta.
Pospíšil, L.
1971 *Anthropology of Law: A Comparative Theory.* New York: Harper and Row.
Potter, G. R. (ed.)
1957 *The New Cambridge Modern History.* Vol. 1. Cambridge: Cambridge University Press.
Pretel Marín, A.
1989 *La "Comunidad y República" de Chinchilla (1488–1520): Evolución de un modelo de organización de la oposición popular al poder patricio.* Albacete: Instituto de Estudios Albacetenses de la Excma. Diputación de Albacete; C.S.I.C., Confederación Española de Centros de Estudios Locales.
Puente, E. de la
1958 "Carlos V y la administración de justicia." *Revista de Indias* 18: 397–461.
Pulgar, Fernando del [late 15th century]
1971 *Claros varones de Castilla* [Toledo, 1486]. Ed. R. B. Tate. Oxford: Clarendon Press.
Quintanilla Raso, M. C.
1979 *Nobleza y señoríos en el reino de Córdoba: La Casa de Aguilar (siglos XIV y XV).* Córdoba: Monte de Piedad y Caja de Ahorros de Córdoba.
1982a "Estructuras sociales y familiares y papel político de la nobleza cordobesa (siglos XIV y XV)." In Ladero Quesada, ed. (1982): II, 331–52.
1982b "Estructuras sociales y papel político de la nobleza cordobesa (siglos XIV y XV)." In Coloquio Historia de Andalucía (1982): 245–58.
1982c "Haciendas señoriales nobiliarias en el reino de Castilla a finales de la Edad Media." In Historia de la Hacienda Española (1982): 767–98.
1984 "Nobleza y señoríos en Castilla durante la Baja Edad Media: Aportaciones de la historiografía reciente." *Anuario de Estudios Medievales* 14: 613–39.
1990a "Historiografía de una élite de poder: La nobleza castellana bajomedieval." *Hispania* 50,175: 719–36.
1990b "Les confédérations de nobles et les bandos dans le royaume de Castille au bas Moyen Age: L'exemple de Cordoue." *Journal of Medieval History* 16: 165–79.
1991 "Estructura y función de los bandos nobiliarios en Córdoba a fines de la Edad Media." In Bandos y querellas (1991): 157–83.
Radding, C. M.
1985 *A World Made by Men: Cognition and Society, 400–1200.* Chapel Hill: University of North Carolina Press.
1988 *The Origins of Medieval Jurisprudence: Pavia and Bologna, 850–1150.* New Haven, Connecticut: Yale University Press.

Real Academia de la Historia
1835–1913 *Memorias de Don Enrique IV de Castilla:* Vol. 2: *Colección Diplomática.* Madrid: Fortanet.

Redondo, A.
1967 "La Bibliothèque de Don Francisco de Zúñiga, Guzmán y Sotomayor, troisième Duc de Béjar (1500?–1544)." *Melanges de la Casa de Velázquez* 3: 147–96.

Rennert, H. A.
1968 *The Life of Lope de Vega (1562–1635).* New York: Benjamin Blom [1904].

Repertorio
1977 *Repertorio de historia de las ciencias eclesiásticas en España.* 7 vols. Salamanca: Pontificia Universidad Eclesiástica de Salamanca, Instituto de Historia de la Teología.

Revueltas y alzamientos
1992 *Revueltas y alzamientos en la España de Felipe II.* Valladolid: Universidad de Valladolid.

Ribot, L., and E. Belenguer, eds.
1998 *Las sociedades ibéricas y el mar a finales del siglo XVI:* Vol. 4: *La Corona de Castilla.* Madrid: Los Centenarios de Felipe II y Carlos V; Pabellón de España, Expo 98.

Riley, J. C.
1980 *International Government Finance and the Amsterdam Capital Market, 1740–1815.* Cambridge and New York: Cambridge University Press.

Rivera Vázquez, E.
1989 *Galicia y los Jesuitas: Sus colegios y enseñanza en los siglos XVI al XVIII.* La Coruña: Fundación Barrie de la Maza, Instituto "P. Sarmiento" de Estudios Gallegos.

Rivero Rodríguez, M.
1998 *Felipe II y el gobierno de Italia.* Madrid: Sociedad Estatal para la Conmemoración de los Centenarios de Felipe II y Carlos V.

Roberts, S.
1979 *Order and Dispute: An Introduction to Legal Anthropology.* New York: St. Martin's Press.

Rodríguez Flores, M. I.
1971 *El perdón real en Castilla (Siglos XIII–XVIII).* Salamanca: Universidad de Salamanca, "Acta Salmanticensia" Derecho, 26.

Rodríguez Raso, R. (ed.)
1963 *Maximiliano de Austria, Gobernador de Carlos V en España: Cartas al Emperador.* Madrid: Consejo Superior de Investigaciones Científicas.

Rodríguez-Salgado, M. J.
1988 *The Changing Face of Empire: Charles V, Philip II, and Habsburg Authority, 1551–1559.* Cambridge: Cambridge University Press.
1991 "The Court of Philip II of Spain." In Asch and Birke, eds. (1991): 205–44.

Rodríguez Villa, A.
1903 "El emperador Carlos V y su Corte." *Boletín de la Real Academia de la Historia* 47: 468–81; 48: 5–240.
1915 "Córdoba y la guerra de las Comunidades." *Revista Europa* 53: 553–62.

Roldán Verdejo, R.

1989 *Los jueces de la monarquía absoluta: Su estatuto y actividad judicial. Corona de Castilla, siglos XIV-XVIII.* Santa Cruz de Tenerife: Universidad de La Laguna.

Root, H. L.

1987 *Peasants and King in Burgundy: Agrarian Foundations of French Absolutism.* Berkeley and Los Angeles: University of California Press.

Rosell, C. (ed.)

1877 *Crónicas de los Reyes de Castilla.* Vol. 2. Madrid: Biblioteca de Autores Españoles, vol. 68.

1953 *Crónicas de los Reyes de Castilla desde Don Alfonso el Sabio, hasta los Católicos Don Fernando y Doña Isabel.* 3 vols. Madrid: Real Academia Española [Biblioteca de Autores Españoles, vols. 66, 68, and 70].

Roth, N.

1995 *Conversos, Inquisition, and the Expulsion of the Jews from Spain.* Madison: University of Wisconsin Press.

Round, N. B.

1966 "La rebelión toledana de 1449." *Archivium* 16: 385–446.

1986 *The Greatest Man Uncrowned: A Study of the Fall of Don Alvaro de Luna.* London: Tamesis Books.

Rucquoi, A.

1987 *Valladolid en la Edad Media.* 2 vols. Valladolid: Junta de Castilla y León, Consejería de Educación y Cultura.

Rucquoi, A. (ed.)

1988 *Realidad e imágenes del poder: España a fines de la Edad Media.* Valladolid: AMBITO Ediciones.

1991 *Genèse médiévale de l'Espagne Moderne. Du refus à la révolte: Les résistances.* Nice: Université de Nice.

Rueger, Z.

1964 "Gerson, the Conciliar Movement and the Right of Resistance (1642–1644)." *Journal of the History of Ideas* 25: 467–86.

Ruiz, T. F.

1984 "Une royauté sans sacre: La monarchie castillane du Bas Moyen Age." *Annales: Economies, Sociétés, Civilisations* 39,3: 429–53.

1985 "Unsacred Monarchy: The Kings of Castile in the Late Middle Ages." In Wilentz, ed. (1985): 109–44.

1988 "Fiestas, torneos y símbolos de realeza en la Castilla del siglo XV: Las fiestas de Valladolid de 1.428." In Rucquoi, ed. (1988): 249–65.

1994 *Crisis and Continuity: Land and Town in Late Medieval Castile.* Philadelphia: University of Pennsylvania Press.

Ruiz de Celada, J.

1990 *Estado de la bolsa de Valladolid. Examen de sus tributos, cargas y medios de su extinction. De su gobierno y reforma* [Valladolid, 1775]. Ed. B. Yun Casalilla. Valladolid: Universidad de Valladolid.

Ruiz Ibáñez, J. J.

1995 *Las dos caras de Jano: Monarquía, ciudad e individuo: Murcia, 1588–1648.* Murcia: Ayuntamiento de Murcia; Universidad de Murcia.

Ruiz Martín, F.
1992 "Las oligarquías urbanas de Castilla y Felipe II." In Revueltas y alzamientos (1992): 117–37.

Ruiz Rodríguez, A. A.
1987 *La Real Chancillería de Granada en el siglo XVI.* Granada: Diputación Provincial de Granada.

Sáez Sánchez, E.
1948 "Fueros de Puebla de Alcocer y Yébenes." *Revista de Archivos, Bibliotecas y Museos* 54: 109–16.

Sahlins, M.
1985 *Islands of History.* Chicago: University of Chicago Press.

Said, F. W.
1978 *Orientalism.* New York: Pantheon.

Salmon, J. H. M.
1973 "Bodin and the Monarchomachs." In Salmon (1987): 119–35 [originally published in H. Danzer, ed., *Verhandlungen der internationalen Bodin Tagung.* Munich: C. H. Beck].
1980 "Cicero and Tacitus in Sixteenth-Century France." In Salmon (1987): 27–53 [originally published in *American Historical Review* 85].
1987 *Renaissance and Revolt: Essays in the Intellectual and Social History of Early Modern France.* Cambridge: Cambridge University Press.
1991 "Catholic Resistance Theory, Ultramontanism, and the Royalist Response, 1580–1620." In Burns and Goldie, eds. (1991): 219–53.

Salvá, A.
1895 *Burgos en las Comunidades de Castilla.* Burgos: Hijos de Santiago Rodríguez.

Salvá Munar, M., and P. Sainz de Baranda (eds.)
1849 *Colección de documentos inéditos para la historia de España.* Vol. 14. Madrid: Viuda de Calero.
1851 *Colección de documentos inéditos para la historia de España.* Vol. 18. Madrid: Viuda de Calero.

Sanceau, E.
1959 *The Perfect Prince: A Biography of the King Dom João II, Who Continued the Work of Henry the Navigator.* Porto: Livraria Civilazação.

Sánchez, D. M.
1993 *El deber de consejo en el estado moderno: Las Juntas "ad hoc" en España (1474–1665).* Madrid: Ediciones Polifemo.
1995 *Las juntas ordinarias: Tribunales permanentes en la corte de los Austrias.* Madrid: Universidad Nacional de Educación a Distancia.

Sánchez Agesta, L.
1981 "El Padre Juan de Mariana: Un humanista precursor del constitucionalismo." In Mariana (1981): ix–lxv.

Sánchez-Arcilla Bernal, J.
1980 *La administración de justicia real en León y Castilla (1252–1504).* Madrid: Universidad Complutense.
1995 *Alfonso XI, 1312–1350.* Palencia: Diputación Provincial de Palencia; Editorial La Olmeda.

Sánchez Domingo, R.
1999 *El régimen señorial en Castilla Vieja: La Casa de los Velasco.* Burgos: Universidad de Burgos.

Sánchez González, R.
1992 "Ordenanzas de la Comunidad de villa y tierra de Talavera de la Reina, 1519." *Anales Toledanos* 19: 77–132.

Sánchez León, P.
1998 *Absolutismo y comunidad: Los orígenes sociales de la guerra de los comuneros de Castilla.* Madrid: Siglo XXI de España.

Sánchez Martín, A.
1994 "Introducción." In Enríquez del Castillo (1994): 7–128.

Sánchez Montes, J.
1958 "Sobre las Cortes de Toledo de 1538–1539: Un procurador del Imperio en un momento difícil." In Universidad de Granada (1958): 595–641.

Sandoval, Prudencio de [ca. 1560–1621]
1955–1956 *Historia de la vida y hechos del Emperador Carlos V* [1604–1606]. Ed. C. Seco Serrano. Madrid: Biblioteca de Autores Españoles, vols. 80–82.

Santa Cruz, Alonso de [ca. 1500–1567/1572]
1920–1925 *Crónica del Emperador Carlos V.* Ed. R. Beltrán Rozpide and A. Blázquez Delgado-Aguilera. 5 vols. Madrid: Patronato de Huérfanos de Intendencia é Intervención Militares.

Santiago Otero, H., et al. (eds.)
1986 *Homenaje a Pedro Sáinz Rodríguez: III, Estudios históricos.* Madrid: Fundación Universitaria Española, Monografías, No. 44.

Schäfer, E.
1935–1947 *El Consejo real y supremo de las Indias: Su historia, organización y labor administrativa hasta la terminación de la Casa de Austria.* 2 vols. Sevilla: Carmona [1935], Gráficas Sevillanas [1947].

Schneider, R. A.
1989 *Public Life in Toulouse, 1463–1789: From Municipal Republic to Cosmopolitan City.* Ithaca, New York: Cornell University Press.

Seaver, H. L.
1966 *The Great Revolt in Castile: A Study of the Comunero Movement of 1520–1521.* New York: Octagon [1928].

Segura Ortega, M.
1984 *La filosofía jurídica y política en las "Empresas" de Saavedra Fajardo.* Murcia: Academia Alfonso X El Sabio; Caja de Ahorros de Murcia.

Semana de Estudios Medievales
1976 *XII Semana de Estudios Medievales, 1974.* Pamplona: Diputación Foral de Navarra; Institución Príncipe de Viana; Amigos del Camino de Santiago; Consejo Superior de Investigaciones Científicas.

Serrano y Sanz, M. (ed.)
1905 *Autobiografías y Memorias.* Madrid: Bailly-Bailliére [Nueva Biblioteca de Autores Españoles, vol. 2].

Shapin, S., and S. Schaffer
1985 *Leviathan and the Air-Pump: Hobbes, Boyle, and the Experimental Life.* Princeton, New Jersey: Princeton University Press.

Sharpe, K., and S. N. Zwicker (eds.)

1987 *Politics of Discourse: The Literature and History of Seventeenth-Century England.* Berkeley: University of California Press.

Shennan, J. H.

1968 *The Parlement of Paris.* London: Eyre and Spottiswoode.

1974 *The Origins of the Modern European State, 1450–1725.* London: Hutchinson.

1986 *Liberty and Order in Early Modern Europe: The Subject and the State, 1650–1800.* London and New York: Longman.

Simancas, Diego de [16th century]

1905 "La vida y cosas notables del señor Obispo de Zamora Don Diego de Simancas, natural de Córdoba, colegial del Colegio de Santa Cruz de Valladolid." In Serrano y Sanz, ed. (1905): 151–210.

Skinner, Q.

1969 "Meaning and Understanding in the History of Ideas." *History and Theory* 8: 3–53.

1970 "Conventions and the Understanding of Speech Acts." *Philosophical Quarterly* 20: 118–38.

1971 "On Performing and Explaining Linguistic Actions." *Philosophical Quarterly* 21: 1–21.

1972a "Motives, Intentions, and the Interpretation of Texts." *New Literary History* 3: 393–408.

1972b "'Social Meaning' and the Explanation of Social Action." In Laslett, Runciman, and Skinner, eds. (1972): 136–57.

1974 "Some Problems in the Analysis of Political Thought and Action." *Political Theory* 2: 277–303.

1975 "Hermeneutics and the Role of History." *New Literary History* 7: 209–32.

1978 *The Foundations of Modern Political Thought.* 2 vols. Cambridge: Cambridge University Press.

1980 "The Origins of the Calvinist Theory of Revolution." In Malament, ed. (1980): 309–30.

1988 "A Reply to my Critics." In Tully, ed. (1988): 231–88.

Solano Costa, F.

1981 "La regencia de Fernando el Católico." In Suárez Fernández, ed. (1981): 615–68.

Solso, R. L.

1998 *Cognitive Psychology.* 5th ed. Boston: Allyn and Bacon.

Soons, A.

1982 *Juan de Mariana.* Boston: Twayne Publishers.

Soria Mesa, E.

2001 "La grandeza de España en la Edad Moderna: Revisión de un mito historiográfico." In Castellano Castellano and Sánchez-Montes González, eds. (2001): IV, 619–36.

Stein, P., and J. Shand

1974 *Legal Values in Western Society.* Edinburgh: Edinburgh University Press.

Stieber, J. W.

1978 *Pope Eugenius IV, the Council of Basel, and the Secular and Ecclesiastical Authorities in the Empire: The Conflict over Supreme Authority and Power in the Church.* Leiden: E. J. Brill.

Stoetzer, O. C.
1979 *The Scholastic Roots of the Spanish American Revolution.* New York: Fordham University Press.
Stradling, R. A.
1979 "Seventeenth Century Spain: Decline or Survival?" *European Studies Review* 9: 157–94.
Suárez Alvarez, M. J.
1982 *La villa de Talavera y su tierra en la Edad Media (1369–1504).* Oviedo: Universidad de Oviedo.
Suárez Fernández, L.
1959 *Nobleza y monarquía: Puntos de vista sobre la historia castellana del siglo XV.* Valladolid: Andrés Martín [2nd, corrected ed. Universidad de Valladolid, 1975].
1960 *Castilla, el cisma y la crisis conciliar (1378–1440).* Madrid: Concejo Superior de Investigaciones Científicas.
1964 "Los Trastámaras de Castilla y Aragón en el siglo XV (1407–74)." In Menéndez Pidal, ed. (1964): 3–327.
1972 "The Kingdom of Castile in the Fifteenth Century." In R. Highfield, ed. (1972): 80–113.
Suárez Fernández, L. (ed.)
1981 *Historia general de España y América:* Vol. 5: *Los Trastámara y la unidad española (1369–1517).* Madrid: Rialp.
Suárez Fernández, L., and M. Fernández Alvarez (eds.)
1969 *La España de los Reyes Católicos (1474–1516).* Vol. 2 [Vol. 17 of R. Menéndez Pidal (ed.). *Historia de España*]. Madrid: Espasa-Calpe.
Subrahmanyam, S.
1997 "Connected Histories: Notes towards a Reconfiguration of Early Modern Eurasia." In Lieberman, ed. (1997): 289–316.
Symposium Historia de la Administración
1970 *Actas del I Symposium de Historia de la Administración.* Madrid: Instituto de Estudios de la Administración.
Tellechea Idígoras, J. I.
1968 *El Arzobispo Carranza y su tiempo.* 2 vols. Madrid: Ediciones Guadarrama.
Thompson, E. P.
1975 *Whigs and Hunters: The Origin of the Black Act.* New York: Pantheon.
1997 *Beyond the Frontier: The Politics of a Failed Mission; Bulgaria 1944* [Camp Lectures, 1981]. Stanford, California: Stanford University Press.
Thompson, I. A. A.
1976 *War and Government in Habsburg Spain, 1560–1620.* London: Athlone Press, University of London.
1979 "The Purchase of Nobility in Castile, 1552–1700." *Journal of European Economic History* 8: 313–60.
1981 "El concejo abierto de Alfaro en 1602: La lucha por la democracia municipal en la Castilla seiscientista." *Berceo* 100: 307––31.
1982 "Crown and Cortes in Castile, 1590–1665." *Parliaments, Estates and Representation* 2: 29–45.
1984a "The End of the Cortes of Castile." *Parliaments, Estates and Representation* 4: 125–33.

1984b "The Rule of the Law in Early Modern Castile." *European History Quarterly* 14: 221–34.

1990 "Castile." In Miller, ed. (1990): 69–98.

1994 "Castile: Absolutism, Constitutionalism, and Liberty." In Hoffman and Norberg, eds. (1994): 181–225.

1997a "Oposición política y juicio del gobierno en las Cortes de 1592–98." *Stvdia Historica: Historia Moderna* 17: 37–62.

1997b "Patronato real e integración política en las ciudades castellanas bajo los Austrias." In Fortea Pérez, ed. (1997): 475–96.

Thompson, I. A. A., and B. Yun Casalilla (eds.)

1994 *The Castilian Crisis of the Seventeenth Century: New Perspectives on the Economic and Social History of Seventeenth-Century Spain.* Cambridge, New York, and Melbourne: Cambridge University Press, in association with the Instituto de Estudios Fiscales, Madrid.

Tierney, B.

1955 *Foundations of the Conciliar Theory: The Contribution of the Medieval Canonists from Gratian to the Great Schism.* Cambridge: Cambridge University Press.

1971 *Ockham, the Conciliar Theory, and the Canonists.* Philadelphia: Fortress Press [republication of an article in the *Journal of the History of Ideas* 15 (1954): 40–70, with a new introduction by H. A. Oberman].

1982 *Religion, Law, and the Growth of Constitutional Thought, 1150–1650.* Cambridge: Cambridge University Press.

Tomás y Valiente, F.

1962 "La Diputación de las Cortes de Castilla, 1525–1601." In Tomás y Valiente (1982): 37–150 [orig. *Anuario de Historia del Derecho Español* 32: 347–469].

1970 "Origen bajomedieval de la patrimonialización y enajenación de oficios públicos en Castilla." In Symposium Historia de la Administración (1970): 125–59.

1982 *Gobierno e instituciones en la España del Antiguo Régimen.* Madrid: Alianza Editorial.

1995 *Manual de historia del derecho español.* 4th ed. Madrid: Tecnos [1979].

Torres Fontes, J.

1962 "El Señorío de Puebla de Soto." *Miscelánea de Estudios Arabes y Hebráicos* ll: 75–105.

1964–1965 "Alfonso Díaz de Montalvo, corregidor de Murcia (1444–1445)." *Anales de la Universidad de Murcia: Filosofía y Letras* 23: 31–73.

1985 *El príncipe don Alfonso y su itinerario: La Contratación de Guisando, 1465–1468.* 2nd ed. Murcia: Departamento de Historia Medieval, Universidad de Murcia [1971].

Torres Sanz, D.

1982 *La administración central castellana en la Baja Edad Media.* Valladolid: Departamento de Historia del Derecho, Universidad de Valladolid.

1985 "Teoría y práctica de la acción de gobierno en el mundo medieval castellano-leonés." *Historia. Instituciones. Documentos* 12: 9–87.

Torrey, E. F.

1992 *Freudian Fraud: The Malignant Effect of Freud's Theory on American Thought and Culture.* New York: HarperCollins.

Truman, R. W.

1999 *Spanish Treatises on Government, Society and Religion in the Time of Philip II: The "De Regimene Principum" and Other Associated Traditions.* Leiden: Brill.

Tuck, R.
1989 *Hobbes.* Oxford and New York: Oxford University Press.
1993 *Philosophy and Government, 1572–1651.* Cambridge: Cambridge University Press.
Tully, J.
1983 "The Pen is a Mighty Sword: Quentin Skinner's Analysis." In Tully, ed. (1988): 7–25 [orig. *British Journal of Political Science* 13].
Tully, J. (ed.)
1988 *Meaning and Context: Quentin Skinner and his Critics.* Princeton, New Jersey: Princeton University Press.
Ullmann, W.
1946 *The Medieval Idea of Law as Represented by Lucas de Penna: A Study in Fourteenth-Century Legal Scholarship.* London: Methuen.
1975 *Law and Politics in the Middle Ages: An Introduction to the Sources of Medieval Political Ideas.* Ithaca, New York: Cornell University Press.
Ulloa, M.
1977 *La Hacienda Real de Castilla en el Reinado de Felipe II.* 2nd ed. Madrid: Fundación Universitaria Española, Seminario Cisneros [1963].
Universidad de Granada
1958 *Carlos V (1500–1558): Homenaje de la Universidad de Granada.* Granada: Universidad de Granada.
Val Valdivieso, M. I. del
1974 "Resistencia al dominio señorial durante los últimos años del reinado de Enrique IV." *Hispania* 34: 53–104.
1975 "Los bandos nobiliarios durante el reinado de Enrique IV." *Hispania* 35: 249–93.
1991 "La sucesión de Enrique IV." *Espacio, Tiempo y Forma* ser. III, 4: 43–78.
1994 "Ascenso social y lucha por el poder en las ciudades castellanas del siglo XV." *En la España Medieval* 17: 157–84.
Valdeavellano, L. G. de
1968 *Curso de historia de las instituciones españolas de los orígenes al final de la Edad Media.* Madrid: Revista de Occidente.
Valdeón Baruque, J.
1975 *Los conflictos sociales en el Reino de Castilla en los siglos XIV y XV.* Madrid: Siglo XXI de España.
1988 "Las Cortes de Castilla y León en tiempos de Pedro I y de los primeros Trastámaras (1350–1406)." In Valdeón Baruque, ed. (1988): I, 183–217.
1990 "Las oligarquías urbanas." In Concejos y Ciudades (1990): 507–21.
Valdeón Baruque, J. (ed.)
1988 *Las Cortes de Castilla y León en la Edad Media.* 2 vols. Valladolid: Cortes de Castilla y León.
Vance, J. T.
1943 *The Background of Hispanic-American Law: Legal Sources and Juridical Literature of Spain.* New York: Central Book.
Van Kleffens, E. N.
1968 *Hispanic Law until the End of the Middle Ages.* Edinburgh: Edinburgh University Press.
Varona García, M. A.
1981 *La Chancillería de Valladolid en el Reinado de los Reyes Católicos.* Valladolid: Universidad de Valladolid, Departamento de Paleografía.

Vassberg, D. E.
1984 *Land and Society in Golden Age Castile.* Cambridge: Cambridge University Press.

Veas Arteseros, M. del C.
1991 *Fiscalidad concejil en la Murcia de fines del medievo.* Murcia: Universidad de Murcia.

Vega Carpio, Lope Félix de [1562–1635]
1946 *Comedias escogidas.* Vol. 1. Ed. J. E. Hartzenbusch. Madrid: Biblioteca de Autores Españoles [vol. 24].
1950 *Comedias escogidas.* Vol. 3. Ed. J. E. Hartzenbusch. Madrid: Biblioteca de Autores Españoles [vol. 41].
1966 *El castigo sin venganza.* Ed. C. A. Jones. Oxford: Pergamon Press.
1972 *Fuente Ovejuna. Peribáñez y el Comendador de Ocaña. El mejor Alcalde, el Rey. El Caballero de Olmedo.* Ed. J. M. Lope Blanch. 7th ed. México: Editorial Porrúa [1962, 1967].

Vigil, R. H.
1987 *Alonso de Zorita: Royal Judge and Christian Humanist, 1512–1585.* Norman: University of Oklahoma Press.

Vilar, J.
1971 "Formes et tendances de l'opposition sous Olivares: Lisón y Viedma, defensor de la Patria." *Melanges de la Casa de Velázquez* 7: 263–94.
1973 *Literatura y economía: La figura satírica del arbitrista en el Siglo de Oro.* Trans. F. Bustelo G. del Real. Madrid: Revista de Occidente.
1974 "Conciencia nacional y conciencia económica." In Moncada (1974): 1–81.

Villalobos y Martínez-Pontremuli, M. L.
1975 "Los Estúñiga: La penetración en Castilla de un linaje de la Nobleza Nueva." *Cuadernos de Historia* 6: 327–42.

Villamanrique, marqués de [d. 1590]
1976 Documents: "Alvaro Manrique de Zúñiga, marqués de Villamanrique (1585–1590)." In Hanke and Rodríguez, eds. (1976): 251–329.

Villapalos Salas, G.
1997 *Justicia y monarquía: Puntos de vista sobre su evolución en el reinado de los Reyes Católicos.* Madrid: Marcial Pons.

Vinogradoff, P. (ed.)
1913 *Essays in Legal History.* London: Oxford University Press.

Viña Brito, A.
1990 "Don Pedro Girón y los orígenes del señorío de Osuna." *Historia. Instituciones. Documentos* 17: 267–85.

Viroli, M.
1992 *From Politics to Reason of State: The Acquisition and Transformation of the Language of Politics, 1250–1600.* Cambridge: Cambridge University Press.

Waley, D. P.
1956 "Introduction." In Botero (1956): vii–xi.

Watson, A.
1981 *The Making of the Civil Law.* Cambridge, Massachusetts, and London: Harvard University Press.

Weber, M.
1967 *On Law in Economy and Society.* Ed. M. Rheinstein. Trans. E. Shils and M. Rheinstein. 2nd ed. New York: Simon and Schuster [1954].

Weisser, M. R.
1976 *The Peasants of the Montes: The Roots of Rural Rebellion in Spain.* Chicago: University of Chicago Press.

Whitehead, A. N.
1929 *Process and Reality: An Essay in Cosmology.* London and New York: Macmillan [reprinted by The Humanities Press, New York, 1957].

Wilentz, S. (ed.)
1985 *Rites of Power: Symbolism, Ritual, and Politics since the Middle Ages.* Philadelphia: University of Pennsylvania Press.

Winichakul, T.
1994 *Siam Mapped: A History of the Geo-body of a Nation.* Honolulu: University of Hawai'i Press.

Woolf, C. N. S.
1913 *Bartolus of Sassoferrato: His Position in the History of Medieval Political Thought.* Cambridge: Cambridge University Press.

Young, R. A.
1979 *La figura del rey y la institución real en la comedia Lopesca.* Madrid: Ediciones J. Porrúa Turanzas.

Yun Casalilla, B.
1980 *Crisis de subsistencias y conflictividad social en Córdoba a principios del siglo XVI: Una ciudad andaluza en los comienzos de la modernidad.* Córdoba: Diputación Provincial.
1987a "Carlos V y la aristocracia: Poder, crédito y economía en Castilla." *Hacienda Pública Española* 108–9: 81–100.
1987b "La aristocracia castellana en el seiscientos: ¿Crisis, refeudalización u ofensiva política?" *Revista Internacional de Sociología* 45, 1: 77–104.
1987c *Sobre la transición al capitalismo en Castilla: Economía y sociedad en la Tierra de Campos (1500–1830).* Salamanca: Junta de Castilla y León.
1990a "Introducción." In Ruiz de Celada (1990): 7–41.
1990b "La situación económica de la aristocracia castellana durante los reinados de Felipe III y Felipe IV." In Elliott and García Sanz, eds. (1990): 519–51.
1991 "Aristocracia, Corona y oligarquías urbanas en Castilla ante el problema fiscal, 1450–1600 (Una reflexión en el largo plazo)." *Hacienda Pública Española* 2nd ser., 1: 25–41.
2002 *La gestión del poder: Corona y economías aristocráticas en Castilla (siglos XVI–XVIII).* Madrid: Akal.

Zabala Aguirre, P.
2000 *Las alcabalas y la hacienda real en Castilla: Siglo XVI.* Santander: Universidad de Cantabria.

Zagorin, P.
1982 *Rebels and Rulers, 1500–1660.* 2 vols. Cambridge: Cambridge University Press.

Zarco Cuevas, J.
1927 "Ideales y normas de gobierno de Felipe II." *Boletín de la Real Academia de la Historia* 90: 445–97.

INDEX

Aachen, 80

absolute royal authority, concept of, 1–3, 10, 17–18, 47, 143, 162–64, 238, 242, 276n1, 279n49, 295n53; different interpretations of, 15, 31–37, 164–72, 190, 215, 232, 234–35, 253n52, 288n80, 296n58. *See also lex digna; lex regia;* López, Gregorio; monarchy, nature of; Núñez de Avendaño, Dr. Pedro; *poderío real absoluto; Siete Partidas*

Accursius (d. 1263 C.E.), jurist, 279n48

Acevedo, Ldo. Fernando de, president of the Council of Castile, 293n28

Acijara, 56, 259n23

Acuña, Antonio de, bishop of Zamora, 92–93, 97, 99

adelantado mayor of Andalucía, 250n26

Adrian of Utrecht, cardinal and Castilian regent, 81, 90–91, 97–98, 101–2, 104, 268n61

Alamos de Barrientos (1550–1634), 231

Alarcón, Ldo., Granada *oidor,* 136

Alba, count of, 33

Alba, duke of, 88, 120. *See also* Alvarez de Toledo, Fernando

Alburquerque, duke of, 191

Alburquerque, 27–28

alcalde (criminal magistrate of an *audiencia*), 49, 135

alcalde of the Court (criminal magistrate), 198

alcalde mayor (appellate magistrate), 21, 30

alcalde mayor of Seville, 250n26

Alcántara, order of, 19–28, 86, 145, 150–51

Alcántara, town of, 24, 27

Alciatus, Andreas, jurist, 166

Alcocer, 146, 148–51

Alcocer, Pedro de, chronicler, 69, 261n44

Alconchel, 27–28

Alderete, Ldo., royal councillor, 203

Alexander, Jeffrey, 247n20

Alfonso (1453–68), half-brother of Henry IV and pretender, 43–44, 152–53

Alfonso V, Portuguese king (reigned 1438–81), 65

Alfonso X, Castilian king (reigned 1252–84), 145–46, 152, 155, 253n53, 295n53

Alfonso XI, Castilian king (reigned 1312–50), 21, 74, 145–46, 148, 150, 295n53; and judicial administration, 251n37. *See also Ordenamiento de Alcalá*

alfoz, 30

Algarve, 208

Alía, 59

Almagro, 294n39

Alvarez, Juan, *vecino* of Toledo, 136

Alvarez, Ldo. Antonio, *jurado* of Toledo, 137

Alvarez de Toledo, Fernando, duke of Alba (1507–82), 181, 197; and Court factions, 180, 193–94, 200–201; and the Netherlands, 185, 197, 200, 204

Alvarez de Villareal, Alonso, barrister of Toledo, 75–76, 86–87, 136

Anaya, Dr., royal councillor, 178

Andalucía, 28, 85, 202, 208; and the Comunidades, 81, 98–100, 266n46

Andreae, Johannes, jurist (d. 1348), 280n66

Anne of Austria (d. 1580), fourth wife of Philip II, 208

Aquaviva, Claudio, general of the Society of Jesus, 224

Aragón, 12, 19, 113, 193

Aragón y Mendoza, Guiomar de, marquise of Ayamonte, daughter of the duke of Infántado, 165, 196. *See also* Infantado, duke of

Araña, Ldo. Juan de, Granada *oidor*, 130, 274n52

arbitristas, 225–26, 231–32, 295n48

Arcos, duke of, 153–55, 196, 205

Arévalo, 28, 33

Armada of 1588, 194, 215

Arriola, *portero* of the Chancillería of Granada, 276n2

Arroba, 44, 59–61, 149

Arroyomolinos, battle of, 27

Atienza, Ldo. Bartolomé, royal councillor, 188, 200

auctoritas, Latin, 245n5, 280n67

audiencia (high royal appellate tribunal), 22, 38, 49, 115, 177, 209, 254n62, 258n9. *See also* Audiencia of Santiago; Audiencia of Seville; Chancillería of Ciudad Real; Chancillería of Granada; Chancillería of Valladolid; *visitas*

Audiencia of Santiago, 126

Audiencia of Seville, 126

Augustine, order of St., 108

Augustinian order. *See* Augustine, order of, St.

Austria, 140

autonomy of the Chancillería of Granada, 133–35

Avendaño, Dr. Pedro Núñez de. *See* Núñez de Avendaño, Dr. Pedro

Avignon, 102–3

Avila, 33, 43, 69

Avila, Alfonso de, royal secretary, 50

Avila, bishop of, president of the Chancillería of Granada, 130

Aviz, order of, 66

Ayala, Hernando de, *regidor* of Toledo, 275n64

Ayala, Juan de, *regidor* of Talavera, 96

Ayala, Juan de, *regidor* of Toledo, 136

Ayala, Martín de, *regidor* of Toledo, 188, 205

Ayala, Pedro de, *procurador* of Toledo to the Santa Junta, 72

Ayamonte, marquis of, 87–88, 119, 202, 208

Azebedo, Br. Martín de, *juez de términos,* 139

Azpilcueta Navarro, Martín de (1491–1586), theologian, 172

Badajoz, Alfonso de, royal secretary, 153

Badajoz, city of, 27, 97

Badajoz, Hernando de, royal secretary, 153

Badajoz, province of, 18

Baeza, Ldo. Juan Rodríguez de. *See* Rodríguez de Baeza, Ldo. Juan

Baldus de Ubaldus, Bartolo (ca. 1327–ca. 1400), jurist, 279n50, 279n53, 280n66

bandos, 31. *See also* factional conflict

Barclay, William, jurist, 167

Barrientos, bishop Lope, fifteenth-century chronicler, 17, 37–38

Bartolus de Saxoferrato (1314–57), jurist, 279n50, 280n66

Basel, Council of (1431–49), 103, 107, 109–10, 269n84

Bavaria, 297n66

Béjar, duke of, 67–68, 84, 122, 136, 207; and the petition to Charles V, 140–41, 181

Béjar, House of, 8, 14–15, 181–82, 187, 190, 195, 202–5; and absolute royal authority, 164–65, 167–70; and its legal briefs, 276n8; and Córdoba, 169, 288n77; evidence presented, 147–57, 215; and Philip II, 202, 208, 215, 289n93. *See also* Ayamonte, marquis of; Béjar, duke of; Belalcázar, count of; Gibraleón, marquis of; Puebla de Alcocer, viscount of

Belalcázar, castle of, 57, 63

Belalcázar, count of, 8, 14, 51–52, 67, 146, 272n15; and early sixteenth-century hearings, 72–77; and hearings of 1495 and 1496, 54–63; and hearings of 1516–20, 83–88; and trial before the Chancillería of Granada, 119–42

Belalcázar, county of, 122, 202, 255n75

Belalcázar, town of, 20, 59–60, 63, 120, 169, 255n75, 258n14. *See also* Gahete

Belalcázar Collection, 10, 207, 238–39, 247n12, 247n18, 249n4, 276n2, 278n36

Bello de Puga, Ldo. Fernán, Granada *oidor,* 274n52

Belluga de Moncada, Juan, *jurado* of Toledo, 183

Bélmez, 43, 85, 251n33

Beltrán, Dr., royal councillor, 264n9

Benavente, count of, 67, 251n34

Berenguela, Castilian queen, wife of Ferdinand III, 151

Bernaldín, viscount of Cabrera, 60, 74, 146, 151

Bezerra, Ldo. Diego, Granada *oidor,* 130, 288n77

Bilbao, friar Juan de, Franciscan *comunero* ideologue, 108

Bisigniano, princess of, 133–34

Bodonales, Los (modern name: Bohonal), 56, 73

Bohemia, 103

Bonifacio, Juan, Jesuit educational writer, 291n14

Borja, Francisco de, Jesuit leader elected general in 1565, 191

Botello, Ldo., Granada *oidor,* 176

boundary judge. *See juez de términos*

Briviesca de Muñatones, Gracián, royal councillor, 199

Burckhardt, Jacob, 245n6

Burgos, 32, 85; and the assembly of 1517, 80, 83, 101, 266n46; and the Comunidades rebellion, 82, 98–100, 102, 104–9, 269n65

Buzarabajo *heredamiento,* 72

Cabrera, Bernaldín de. *See* Bernaldín, viscount of Cabrera

Cabrera, Dr., royal councillor, 264n9

Cabrera de Córdoba, Luis, royal chronicler, 201

Cáceres, 27

Calatrava, order of, 19–20, 26, 42–43, 155, 266n46; and the boundary of the Montes de Toledo, 146

Calderón de la Barca, Pedro, dramatist, 172

Cámara of Castile, 197–98, 285n44

Canary Islands, 23

Cano, Dr., royal councillor, 178

canon law, 103, 110, 166. *See also Corpus Iuris Canonici; Decretum;* Gratian; *Liber Extra*

Capilla, 149

capitalism, concept of, 3–4, 296n57

Cárdenas, Bernardino de, marquis of Elche and *regidor* of Toledo, 275n64

Cárdenas, Francisco de, *receptor,* 128

Cárdenas, García de, *receptor,* 128–30, 132

Caribbean, 127

Carlos (1545–1568), prince, son of Philip II, 201, 204

Carolina, Imperial law code, 134

Carranza, Bartolomé de (d. 1576), cardinal-archbishop of Toledo, 184, 193

Carrillo, Alfonso (d. 1482), archbishop of Toledo, 94–96

Carrillo, Juan, *regidor* of Toledo, 70

Carrillo family, Toledo, 70

carta ejecutoria (sealed royal writ announcing a verdict), 139, 288n85

Casa de Contratación. See House of Trade

Casas de Don Pedro, 56, 74, 139, 146, 150–51

Castilblanco, 57–59, 96–97, 277n25

Castile, Council of, 64–66, 68, 81, 83, 89, 91, 105, 124, 135, 154, 172, 207, 209–10, 289n92; and judicial administration, 14, 49, 118, 120, 123, 126, 133, 139–40, 177, 209, 274n49, 282n8, 285n43, 287n74; and the trial of the Belalcázar lawsuit, 14–15, 52, 54, 61–62, 64, 73–74, 83, 85, 87, 119–20, 136, 138, 141–42, 149, 151,

Castile, Council of *(continued)*
175–82, 187–201, 202–3, 205–6, 210,
273n42, 284n29, 284n32, 287n73,
288n81. *See also* Córdoba, and the
lawsuit to recover the county of
Belalcázar; El Hornillo; Royal
Council
Castilla, Alonso de (d. 1541), royal
councillor, 68
Castilla, Ldo. Alonso de, Granada *oidor,*
130
Castilla, Pedro de, *corregidor* of Toledo,
70–71
Castillo Portocarrero, Antonio del,
Cortes *procurador* of Salamanca, 187
Castrillo, friar Alonso de, Trinitarian
anti-*comunero* writer, 265n28
Castro, Alfonso de, theologian, 172
Castro, Isabel de, daughter of don
Alvaro de Portugal and countess of
Belalcázar, 64
Catalonia, 12, 113, 146, 193
Catherine (Catalina) of Habsburg
(1507–1578), Castilian princess, Por-
tuguese queen, 120
Catherine (Catalina) Micaela
(1567–1597), daughter of Philip II,
204
Catholic Monarchs, 63–64, 66–67, 95,
164; and the aristocracy, 13, 46–48,
53, 63–64, 66, 69, 202; and the
Cortes, 117, 276n3; and judicial
administration, 45–50, 118, 123, 177;
and Toledo, 50–55, 73, 75, 146–47.
See also Ferdinand II of Aragón
(1479–1516), V of Castile
(1474–1504), the Catholic; Isabella I,
the Catholic, Castilian queen
(1474–1504)
Cayzedo, Gastón de, barrister of the
House of Béjar, 128, 130, 132,
134–35, 137, 151–54
Cedillo, 41
Cerezuela, Juan de, archbishop of
Toledo, 27, 38, 155
certa scientia, Latin, 163. *See also cierta
ciencia*

chancillería, 35, 49, 126, 130, 178, 183,
216–17, 290n6. *See also audiencia,*
Chancillería of Ciudad Real;
Chancillería of Granada;
Chancillería of Valladolid
Chancillería of Ciudad Real, 49, 74, 76,
124, 136
Chancillería of Granada, 9, 49, 83,
118–19, 172, 188–90, 198–99, 281n1;
and the Belalcázar trials, 14, 61, 76,
85–88, 115–16, 120–42, 165–66,
169–73, 176–78, 281n4, 282n5,
288n77; and reform, 270n1. *See also*
autonomy of the Chancillería of
Granada; corruption in court proceedings; delays of trials; prestige of
the Chancillería of Granada, protecting; second supplication
Chancillería of Valladolid, 49, 83,
95–96, 118–19, 124, 126, 178, 192,
199, 263n4
Charles I, Castilian king. *See* Charles V
Charles II, Castilian king (reigned
1665–1700), 216
Charles V, Holy Roman Emperor
(reigned 1519–58), King of Castile (as
Charles I, reigned 1516–56), 14,
68–69, 156, 176–77, 181–82, 201–3,
209, 274n49; and the Comunidades
rebellion, 80–82, 92, 94, 98–113,
238; and the *corregidor* of Toledo,
284n29; and the Cortes of 1520,
88–91; and Flemish courtiers,
265n22; and the hearings of 1516–20,
83–88; and his reform program,
115–19, 140, 271n7, 271n9, 282n9;
and suspension of trials, 263n4
Chávez, Luis de, barrister of the count
of Belalcázar, 61, 73
Chinchilla, 100
Chinchón, count of, 264n19
Church, 20
Cicero, M. Tullius (106–43 B.C.E.),
Roman politician and author, 219
cierta ciencia (reasoned consideration),
Castilian, 20, 31, 164, 168. *See also
certa scientia*

Cifuentes, House of, 206
Cijara, 73, 146, 151, 259n23
Cisneros. *See* Jiménez de Cisneros, friar
Francisco
Cisneros, Alonso de, *jurado* of Toledo,
189
Cisneros, Juan de, *jurado* of Toledo,
205–6
Ciudad Real, 124. *See also* Chancillería
of Ciudad Real
civil law, 110, 166–67. *See also Corpus
Iuris Civilis*
clausula non obstante, 163
clientage, 6–7, 18, 32–34, 66–69, 181,
191–92, 209, 285n44; in France,
253n46, 285n46, 295n56; and its
impact on municipal government,
69–72, 250n26
Cobos, Francisco de los (d. 1547), royal
councillor, 116, 140, 179, 181, 196,
203
codification of laws, 126, 171, 221, 256n2
Coimbra, University of, 290n5
Colegio de Oviedo, 124
comendador, 26
Compromise of Caspe, 248n25
común, 31
comuneros, revolt of. *See* Comunidades
rebellion
Comunidades rebellion, 7, 66–67,
69–72, 77, 79–82, 88–113, 117–18,
120, 143–44, 221, 226, 238; and
commoner participation, 98–101,
267n53; and ideology, 101–2, 104–8,
110–11, 268n61; and interpretations
of it, 13–14, 111–13, 263n1, 265n25,
267n52, 267n60, 270n88; and rebel
attitudes toward Charles V, 268n61;
and the Santa Junta, 266n46. *See
also* Conciliar thought; rebellion;
Talavera, and the Comunidades
rebellion
Conciliar thought, 102–4, 221, 226,
267n60, 268n62, 269n84
condestable, 25, 141. *See also* Fernández
de Velasco, Iñigo; Fernández de
Velasco, Pedro

Congregation of the Clergy, 186; Luna,
Alvaro de; Fernández de Velasco,
Bernardino
Constance, Council of (1414–17), 103,
107, 109–10
Constitution of Cádiz (1812), 238
Conversos, 20, 41, 255n67
Córdoba, 23–24, 28, 31, 89, 145, 148,
151, 155, 202; and its attempt to
reconquer its towns from Gutierre de
Sotomayor, 67–68, 251n33; and the
Comunidades rebellion, 72, 81,
98–99, 110, 266n46; and the grants
to Gutierre de Sotomayor, 20, 28, 63,
159, 249n7; and the lawsuit to
recover the county of Belalcázar, 76,
84–85, 87, 120, 129–30, 135, 169,
264n8, 272n15, 288n77; and the ordinance about the Belalcázar case, 75;
and revocation of Henry IV, 43–44,
85, 154, 255n75, 274n50, 274n51
Córdoba, Antonio de, *corregidor* of
Toledo, 89
Córdoba, Francisca de, countess of
Belalcázar, marquise of Gibraleón,
136, 140, 195
Córdoba, Ldo. Diego de, Granada *oidor,*
274n52
Coronel, Ldo. 133, 137–38
Coronel de Guzmán, Andrea, countess
of Belalcázar, 196, 202, 286n58
Corpus Iuris Canonici, 162. *See also* canon
law
Corpus Iuris Civilis, 162–64, 167–68,
278n48
corregimiento, 71
corruption in court proceedings,
135–39, 274n55, 275n59
Cortés, Hernán (d. 1547), marquis of El
Valle de Oaxaca, 123
Cortes of Aragón, 256n1
Cortes of Cádiz (1810–13), 291n12
Cortes of Castile, 12, 72, 101–2, 143,
209, 232; and the Belalcázar-Toledo
conflict, 2, 18–19, 87, 129, 160,
248n3; of Briviesca (1387), 49, 171;
and Charles V, 117–20, 126, 186; and

Cortes of Castile *(continued)*
judicial administration, 178, 182, 209,
258n9, 282n8; and the law, 20,
34–35, 38, 89, 126, 160, 164, 171–72,
221; of Madrid (1329), 160; of
Madrid (1510), 68; of Madrigal
(1476), 48; and the *millones,* 190–91,
209, 214–15, 221, 290n5, 292n19; of
Niebla (1473), 152; of Ocaña (1422),
35; of Ocaña (1469), 44, 107, 276n3;
of Olmedo (1445), 37, 39, 253n55,
281n74; and fifteenth-century opposition to Crown policies, 34–35,
253n49; and Philip II, 186–87,
190–91, 193, 214–15; and the Santa
Junta, 104–11; of Santiago-La
Coruña (1520), 79–81, 87–91, 108; of
Segovia (1390), 177; and *servicios,*
253n48; of Toledo (1462), 256n2; of
Toledo (1480), 48–50, 276n3; of
Toledo (1502), 73; of Toledo
(1538–39), 139–40, 275n60, 275n64;
of Tordesillas-Valladolid (1446–47),
18, 22, 56, 253n49; of Toro (1371),
49; of Toro (1505), 67; of Valladolid
(1307), 278n43; of Valladolid (1442),
35–36, 50, 84, 164, 171, 255n70; of
Valladolid (1518), 80, 83–85, 88; of
Valladolid (1523), 118–20, 271n7; of
Valladolid-Tordesillas-Madrigal
(1448), 41
Cortes of Catalonia, 89
Cortes of León (1188), 278n43
Council of Basel. *See* Basel, Council of
Council of Castile. *See* Castile, Council
of
Council of Constance. *See* Constance,
Council of
Council of Finance. *See* Finance, Coun-
cil of
Council of Pisa. *See* Pisa, Council of
Council of State. *See* State, Council of
Council of the Indies. *See* Indies, Coun-
cil of the
Council of the Mesta. *See* Mesta, Coun-
cil of the
Council of Trent. *See* Trent, Council of

Covarrubias, Alfonso de, *vecino* of
Toledo, 189
Covarrubias, Marcos de, *vecino* of
Toledo, 189
Covarrubias de Leyva, Antonio de,
jurist, 189
Covarrubias de Leyva, Dr. Diego de,
jurist, bishop, president of the Coun-
cil of Castile, 124, 172, 189, 202,
281n78, 288n77
Crasso, Antonio de, royal secretary, 207
Crónica general de España, 156
Croy, Guillaume de (d. 1521), arch-
bishop of Toledo, 84, 92, 94, 97
Croy, Guillaume de (1458–1521), lord of
Chièves, Grand Chamberlain of
Charles V, 84, 89, 94
Cruz, friar Alonso de la, 86. *See also*
Sotomayor, Alonso de
Cuadrilla de Herrera, 148–49
Cuenca, 90, 100, 110, 124, 261n47,
264n5
cultural environment, concept of, 10–11,
247n20, 294n38. *See also* interpretive
schemes, concept of
Curia, 123

Danvila Collado, Manuel, 109
Dávalos, Alonso, Toledo's representative at Court (1568), 189
Decius, Philippus, jurist, 166
Decretum, twelfth-century compilation of
canon law, 280n66
delays of trials, 125–31, 273n32, 273n42,
274n49, 281n4, 292n21
Denia, marquis of, 80
Deza, Dr. Diego de, Granada *oidor,*
274n52, 288n77
Díaz de Montalvo, Dr. Alonso, jurist
and royal councillor, 46–47, 162,
254n62, 256n2
Díaz de Rivadeneira, *mariscal* Hernán,
regidor of Toledo, 72
Díaz de Toledo, Dr. Fernando, *regidor*
of Toledo and royal secretary, 22,
33, 158, 249n8, 254n62, 255n64,
255n71

Díez, Juan, secretary of Francisco de Mendoza, 95. *See also* Mendoza, Francisco de

Digest. *See Corpus Iuris Civilis*

diputados (parish representatives), 94–97, 99–101

Dôle, 116

Dominic, order of St., 20, 108, 291n14

Dominicans. *See* Dominic, order of St.

Durango, Dr. Gaspar, royal councillor, 188, 198–99

Eboli, prince of. *See* Gómez de Silva, Ruy

Ebolistas, 189–203, 205–6, 285n49, 287n68

El Hornillo, 24, 54, 56, 148–49; and the boundary trial before the Chancillería of Granada, 136–37, 148–49, 203, 207, 277n12; and the hearing before Ldo. Zomeño, 73–74, 262n58; and Toledo, 289n90; and the trial before the Council of Castile, 61–62, 87, 120, 141–42, 202–3, 288n78

Elizabeth of Valois (d. 1568), third wife of Philip II, 204–5

England, 4, 103–4, 268n62; comparisons with, 121, 213, 246n11, 268n62, 272n21

Enrique de Trastámara (d. 1445), *infante*, 26–28, 32–33, 40, 155–59, 161

Enríquez, aristocratic lineage, 75

Enríquez, Alonso (d. 1485), *almirante*, 64

Enríquez, Fadrique, *almirante*, 258n13

Enríquez, Teresa de (d. 1489), countess of Belalcázar, 52, 64

Enríquez de Cabrera, Fadrique, *almirante*, duke of Medina del Rioseco, 64, 67, 81–82, 91, 97–98, 102, 109, 117, 268n61; and attempts to aid the count of Belalcázar, 272n15

Enríquez del Castillo, Diego, jurist, 253n52

Era de, calendar system, 276n4

Eraso, Francisco de (d. 1570), royal secretary and chief accountant, 192, 195, 197, 200, 286n54, 287n73

Escalona, 33

Escobedo, Francisco de, notary of the Chancillería of Granada, 178

Escobedo, Juan de (d. 1578), secretary of the governor of the Netherlands, 201

Escorial, 185–86

Espinosa, Ldo. Diego de (1502–72), president of the Council of Castile, 182, 184, 188–93, 195–98, 202–4, 285n44, 287n73

Estatuto Real (1834), 221

Estena, 73–74, 146, 149

Eugenius IV, pope (reigned 1431–1447), 103, 110

expropriation of property, 160–70, 288n80. *See also* property rights

extended case method, 8, 247n13

Extra, abbreviation for the *Liber Extra,* 280n66

Extremadura, 9, 21, 27

factional conflict, 13, 38, 66–69, 179–81, 185, 192, 197; in municipalities, 32, 40, 69–72, 252n43, 255n67, 261n44, 297n62; and royal authority, 5–6, 208–9, 240, 296n62

Fajardo, Juan, *comunero* leader, 100

favorite, 24, 37–38, 254n58. *See also* Gómez de Sandoval, Francisco; Gómez de Silva, Ruy; Guzmán, Gaspar de; Luna, Alvaro de; Manuel, Juan; Pacheco, Juan

Felix V, schismatic pope (reigned 1439–47), 103

Ferdinand I, Aragonese king (reigned 1412–16), 248n25

Ferdinand II of Aragón (reigned 1479–1516), V of Castile (reigned 1474–1504), the Catholic, 13, 23, 46, 66–68, 70–71, 80, 82–83; and the Belalcázar lawsuits, 52, 64, 73–74, 76, 86, 141; and the Trastámara dynasty, 45, 248n25. *See also* Catholic Monarchs

Ferdinand III, Castilian king (reigned 1217/1230–52), and the sale of the Montes de Toledo, 21, 58, 74,

Ferdinand III *(continued)*
134–35, 145–52, 207, 278n41,
288n85, 289n92
Ferdinand of Antequera. *See* Ferdinand I
Ferdinand of Habsburg, Castilian prince
(later king of Bohemia and Hungary
and Holy Roman Emperor), 82,
271n7
Feria, count (later duke) of. *See* Suárez
de Figueroa, Gómez
Fernández, Martín, *vecino* of Siruela, 60
Fernández de Angulo (d. 1516), Dr.
Martín, royal councillor, 68
Fernández de Cascales, Alfonso, *regidor*
of Murcia, 254n62
Fernández de Córdoba, Francisco,
count of Cabra, 67
Fernández de Córdoba, Gonzalo
(1524–1578), duke of Sessa, 195
Fernández de Velasco, Bernardino (d.
1512), *condestable,* 64
Fernández de Velasco, Iñigo, *condestable*
(Comunidades era), duke of Frías,
81–82, 91, 97–98, 105, 269n65
Fernández de Velasco, Pedro
(1414–1492), *condestable,* 52, 64
feudalism, concept of, 3–4, 296n57
Figgis, John Neville, 268n62
Finance *(Hacienda),* Council of, 118, 190,
194–95, 197–99
fiscal (prosecutor), 49
Fontanarejo, 44
France, 11–12, 19, 103, 116, 211; com-
parison with, 121, 246n11, 268n62,
272n21
Franche-Comté, 116
Francis, order of St., 20, 108
Franciscans. *See* Francis, order of St.
French Revolution, 110–12
French Wars of Religion, 165, 167, 215
Frequens (1417), 103, 107, 110
Fresneda, friar Bernardo de, Franciscan,
bishop of Cuenca, confessor of
Philip II, 192–93, 198, 200, 204,
287n73
Frías, Ldo. Antonio de, Granada *oidor,*
136, 274n52

Fuenlabrada, 44, 56, 59–60, 73, 75, 85,
146, 149, 151, 202
Fuenteovejuna, 24, 43, 85, 251n33

Gadillo, Fernando del, *receptor,* 136
Gadillo, Hernando del, *receptor,* 133
Gahete, 20, 23–24, 28, 43, 63, 84–85,
249n7, 251n33, 255n75. *See also*
Belalcázar, town of
Gaitán, Gonzalo, *regidor* of Toledo, 72,
89
Gaitán, Juan, *regidor* of Toledo, 71–72,
262n52
Galarza, Ldo. Beltrán de (d. 1557),
Granada *oidor* and royal councillor,
178, 199, 286n67
Galicia, 81, 90
Galíndez de Carvajal, Dr. Lorenzo (d.
1527), royal councillor, 65, 68,
277n28
Gálvez, Dr., Granada *oidor,* 136–37,
149–50, 274n52, 274n55, 277n12
Ganivet, Angel, 90
García de Cisneros, Diego, *regidor* of
Toledo, 51–52, 55–56
García de Santa María, Alvar, fifteenth-
century chronicler, 38
García de Toledo, Diego, *alguacil mayor*
of Toledo, 145–46, 148, 150
Gasca, Dr. Diego de la, royal councillor,
178, 188, 199, 286n67
Gasca, Ldo. Pedro de la (1485–1567),
president of the *audiencia* of Lima,
287n67
Gasco, Ldo. Pedro, royal councillor,
188, 200
Gattinara, Mercurino Arborio di
(1465–1530), jurist and Grand Chan-
cellor, 116, 118, 133, 271n2
Generation of 1898, 90
Germanía, 113
Gibraleón, marquis of, 122, 136, 202,
281n1. *See also* Béjar, duke of; Belal-
cázar, count of
Giro, Diego, *regidor* of Talavera, 95
Girón, Ldo., Granada *oidor,* 130–31
Girón, Pedro, *comunero* leader, 83

Girón, Pedro, grandmaster of Calatrava, 26, 28, 42–43, 85

Glossators, 163, 280n61

Golden Age, 1, 8, 12, 19, 112

Gómez, Alvar, royal secretary, 153

Gómez, Pascual, *vecino* of Villarta, 59–61

Gómez de Sandoval, Francisco (1553–1625), duke of Lerma, 225, 290n3, 293n24, 293n28

Gómez de Silva, Juan, *regidor* of Toledo, 189, 205

Gómez de Silva, Ruy (1516–1573), prince of Eboli, duke of Pastrana, 180, 192–95, 202, 204

González de Polanco, Ldo. Luis (d. 1542), royal councillor, 68

González de Segovia, Juan Alfonso. *See* Segovia, Juan de

Gracián, Antonio, royal secretary, 202

Granada, 81

Granada, archbishop of, royal councillor, 264n9

Granada, region; and under Muslim rule (Nasrid dynasty), 19, 36, 48, 51–54, 101, 157

grandeza, 116–17

Gratian, twelfth-century canon lawyer, 280n66

Great Britain, 121

Great Schism (1378–1418), 102–3

Gregory IX, thirteenth-century pope, 280n66

Guadalajara, 100, 265n20, 267n53

Guadalajara, Ordinances of (1436), 49

Guadalemar River, 151

Guadalupe, 23, 122

Guadamur, 41

Guadiana River, 9, 18, 24, 61, 120

Guedeja, Br., *relator,* 137

Guerrero, Ldo. Miguel, royal councillor, 68

Guevara, Gutierre de, *regidor* of Toledo and Cortes *procurador* (1523), 119, 272n14

Guevara, Gutierre de, Toledo's representative at Court (1568), 189

Gutiérrez, Ldo. Francisco, attorney of Toledo, 137–38

Gutiérrez de Madrid, Alonso, *regidor* of Toledo, 75–76

Gutiérrez Egea, María, wife of Alfonso Covarrubias, 189

Guzmán, Enrique de (1540–1607), *contador mayor* and second count of Olivares (in 1569), 286n54

Guzmán, Gaspar de (1587–1645), count-duke of Olivares, favorite of Philip IV, 195, 209, 225, 231, 293n24, 295n47

Guzmán, Juan de, *regidor* of Toledo, 42

Guzmán, Lope de, *regidor* of Toledo, 275n64

Guzmán, Pedro de, *regidor* of Toledo, 205–6

Guzmán family, Toledo, 70

Guzmán y Sotomayor, Francisco, marquis of Ayamonte, 131

Guzmán y Zúñiga, Antonio de (d. 1580), marquis of Ayamonte, governor of Milan, 194–95, 208, 289n93

Guzmán y Zúñiga, Pedro de (d. 1569), first count of Olivares, 195, 286n54

Habsburg dynasty, 121

Haec sancta (1415), 103, 110

Heiligerlee, battle of, 185

Helechosa, 54, 56, 73, 146, 151

Henao, Juan de, Cortes *procurador* of Avila, 187

Henry, Castilian prince, 25–26, 28, 41–42, 155. *See also* Henry IV

Henry II, Castilian king (reigned 1369–79), 21, 29, 45, 49, 146, 156; and the aristocracy, 252n38; and the murder of Peter I, 248n25

Henry III, Castilian king (reigned 1390–1406), 17, 24, 102

Henry III, French king (reigned 1574–1589), 215, 224

Henry IV, Castilian king (reigned 1454–74), 29, 42–45, 48, 50–51, 59, 67, 70, 72, 99–101, 107, 117, 156; and the Cortes, 276n3; and Juan Pacheco,

Henry IV *(continued)*
254n58; and revocations of grants of
John II, 43–44, 74, 85, 135, 145–46,
152–54, 160, 255n75. *See also* Henry,
Castilian prince
Henry IV, French king (reigned
1589–1610), 224
hermandades, 101, 266n46, 268n61
Hernández, Ldo. Alonso, *relator,* 137
Hernández de Córdoba, Catalina, mar-
quise of Priego, 196
Hernández de Liévana, Ldo. Francisco,
royal councillor, 198–99
Hernández Ortiz, Diego, *jurado* of
Toledo, 89, 262n55
Herrera, 21, 44, 56, 59–60, 73–75,
85–86, 146, 148–51, 157, 202, 256n76
Herrera, Ldo. Francisco de, archbishop
of Granada, president of the
Chancillería of Granada, 119
Herrera, Melchor de, marquis of
Auñón, 195
Herreruela, 148–49
hidalgo, 182, 190
Hidalgo, Juan, bribed chronicler,
137–38
Hinojosa, 20, 23–24, 28, 43, 63, 84–85,
120, 169, 249n7, 251n33
Hita, Miguel de, *jurado* of Toledo, 89
Hobbes, Thomas (1588–1678), political
philosopher, 3, 233
Holland. *See* Netherlands; United
Provinces of the Netherlands
Holy Roman Empire, 80, 134
Horcajo, 58, 149
Hornillo. *See* El Hornillo
Horozco, Sebastián de, jurist, 188–89
Hospitalers, order of. *See* John, order of
St.
Hoyo, Pedro de, royal secretary, 200
House of Trade (*Casa de Contratación*),
181
hoz of the Guadiana, 149–51, 277n14
Huarte, Ldo. Rodrigo, Granada *oidor,*
274n52
Huecas, 41
Humanes, 41

Hurtado de Mendoza, Luis, marquis of
Mondéjar, 284n43
Hus, John (1369–1415), Bohemian reli-
gious reformer, 103

Ibáñez de Aguirre (d. 1547), Ldo.
Fortún, royal councillor, 68
imperial authority, 280n62
Indies, Council of the, 118, 193, 198–99
Infantado, duke of, 71, 122, 165, 169,
196, 207, 275n60
infantes of Aragón, 20, 25–27, 33, 37,
155, 166, 204; identity of, 249n6
Inquisition, 9, 82, 116, 180, 184–85, 196,
224, 238, 291n14, 293n28; and
microhistory, 247n16
institutions, importance of, 47–48,
295n55
interpretive schemes, concept of, 2, 4–5,
7–8, 10–11, 15, 34, 37, 143–44,
213–14, 217, 234–35, 290n5, 294n38,
297n63; and cognitive psychology,
248n22; and reading, 240–42,
297n63; and the *Siete Partidas,*
253n53. *See also* cultural environment, concept of
Isabella I, the Catholic, Castilian queen
(reigned 1474–1504), 13, 23, 28–29,
45–46, 48, 52, 62, 65–68, 70, 72–75,
77, 84, 88, 91, 118; testament of,
264n19; and the Trastámara dynasty,
248n25. *See also* Catholic Monarchs
Isabella Clara Eugenia (1566–1633),
daughter of Philip II, 204
Isabella of Castile (1470–98), Portuguese
queen, 64–65
Isabella of Portugal (1503–39), Castilian
queen, 120, 179
Islam, 12. *See also* Granada, under Muslim rule
Italy, 11. *See also* Naples, kingdom of;
Sicily, kingdom of

Jaén, 81, 97, 99, 151–52, 266n46
Jarava, Ldo. Gaspar de, Granada *oidor*
and royal councillor, 130, 197–98
Jemminghen, battle of, 185

Jerez de la Frontera, 71
Jesuits. *See* Society of Jesus
Jews, 20, 41
Jiménez de Ariel, Pedro, *receptor,* 153
Jiménez de Cisneros, friar Francisco
 (1436–1517), cardinal-archbishop of
 Toledo, 68, 71, 80, 82, 85, 88, 94–96,
 101, 263n4
Joanna I (d. 1555), Castilian queen,
 67–68, 76, 80–82, 84–85, 102, 104–5,
 112, 186
John I, Castilian king (reigned 1379–90),
 49
John I, Portuguese king (reigned
 1384–1433), 64
John II, Aragonese king (reigned
 1458–79), 45
John II, Castilian king (reigned
 1406–54), 6, 8–9, 17–20, 24–28,
 31–37, 45, 48–50, 70, 171, 214–16;
 and Alvaro de Luna, 15, 28–29,
 37–38, 40–41, 223, 254n58; and Ferdinand of Antequera, 248n25; and
 grants to Gutierre de Sotomayor,
 20–24, 51, 59–60, 74, 84–87, 135,
 145–47, 153, 155–61, 164–70, 190,
 203–4, 223, 288n85; and pardon of
 1451, 41, 160. *See also* Luna, Alvaro
 de
John II, Portuguese king (reigned
 1481–95), 65–66, 229
John III, Portuguese king (reigned
 1521–57), 120
John, order of St., 19–20, 86, 88
John of Salisbury (d. 1180), bishop of
 Chartres, 222, 292n22
Jorge, *comendador* of the order of Alcántara, 60
Juan (1478–97), Castilian prince, 64
Juan de Trastámara, *infante,* king of
 Navarra, 156–57, 166. *See also* John
 II, Aragonese king
Juana de Austria (1535–73), Castilian
 princess and regent, 176–82, 198,
 201, 204, 273n42, 282n5, 282n6,
 282n9, 284n27
juez de residencia, 132

juez de términos, 23
Junta. *See* Santa Junta
jurados, 252n42
juros (government bonds), 190
just war, 169, 268n61
Justinian, Roman emperor (reigned
 527–65), 278n48
Justinian's Code. *See* Corpus Iuris Civilis

Kuehn, Thomas, 247n17
Küng, Hans, 270n84

La Rambla meeting, 266n46
Lanzarote, 23
Laso de la Vega, Pedro, *regidor* of
 Toledo, 68, 89, 261n52
League of Compromise, organization of
 Netherlands' nobles, 184–85
League of La Rambla (1521), 99
León, 262n55
León, *adelantado* of, 25
León, Ciprián de, attorney of the duke
 of Béjar, 136
León, Ldo. Lope de, Granada *oidor,*
 274n52
León, Lucrecia de, subject of a
 sixteenth-century Inquisition investi-
 gation, 217, 290n1
León, Ldo. Melchor de, Granada *oidor,*
 136, 274n52
León, friar Pablo de, Dominican
 comunero ideologue and *procurador* of
 León, 108
Lerma. *See* Gómez de Sandoval, Francisco
letrados, 10, 38, 47, 118, 123, 129,
 143–44, 184, 191, 201–2, 237, 257n3;
 and absolute royal authority, 10, 162,
 253n52
Levenson, Joseph R. (d. 1969), 233,
 245n3, 246n11, 253n47
lex digna, 162, 221–22, 236, 292n22. *See
 also Corpus Iuris Civilis*
lex regia, 162. *See also Corpus Iuris Civilis*
Liber Extra, 280n66
Lisón y Viedma, Mateo de, Cortes
 procurador of Granada, 231

Loaisa y Mendoza, García de (d. 1546), cardinal-archbishop of Seville, 179, 203

Locke, John (1632–1704), philosopher, 233

Lope de Vega. *See* Vega Carpio, Lope Félix de

López, Gregorio, jurist, 168–70, 203, 280n69

López de Alcocer, Pedro, Valladolid *oidor,* 126

López de Arrieta, Ldo. Pedro (d. 1563), Granada *oidor* and royal councillor, 199

López de Ayala, Diego, canon of Toledo's cathedral, 71, 85, 263n4

López de Ayala, Pedro (d. before 1454), *alcalde mayor* of Toledo, 33, 40–41, 147, 156, 158–59; and grants from John II, 255n68

López de Ayala, Pedro (d. 1486), first count of Fuensalida, 70, 261n49

López de Ayala, Pedro (d. 1537), third count of Fuensalida, 69–72

López de Ayala, Dr. don Pedro (d. 1513), royal councillor, 68

López de Padilla, Pedro, *regidor* of Toledo, 261n44

López de Palacios Rubios, Dr. Juan (d. 1524), royal councillor, 68, 123–24

López de Portillo, Diego, *receptor,* 136

López Pacheco, Diego (1443–1529), second marquis of Villena, 70–71, 261n49, 261n51. *See also* Villena, marquis of

Los Cobos. *See* Cobos, Francisco de los

Los Vélez, convent of, order of Santiago, 152

Los Vélez, marquis of, 205

Los Yébenes, 149

Louis XIV, French king (reigned 1643–1715), 4, 8, 237, 295n56

Low Countries. *See* Netherlands; United Provinces of the Netherlands

Lozano, Jerónimo, dishonest official of Toledo, 263n60, 272n23

Luna, Alvaro de (1388–1453), favorite of John II of Castile, 25–29, 31–33, 35, 37–38, 40–41, 53, 61, 155–56, 159, 214–15, 223, 254n58; and his supporters, 250n26

Machiavelli, Niccolò (1469–1527), writer, 218, 230

Madrigal, Alfonso de, political thinker, 248n1

Maldonado, Juan, sixteenth-century writer, 100, 266n47

Maneanedo, Dr., attorney of Toledo, 284n29

Manjárrez (Manjares), Ldo., lawyer of the House of Béjar, 149–52, 157, 159, 161

Manrique, Leonor, marquise of Ayamonte, 87

Manrique de Zúñiga y Sotomayor, Leonor (d. 1582), countess of Niebla, 194–96

Manuel, Juan, favorite of Philip I, 67

Manuel I, Portuguese king (reigned 1495–1521), 64–65, 229

Marañón, Francisco de, *regidor* of Toledo, 119, 137, 154

Margaret of Habsburg (1480–1530), aunt of Charles V, 116

Margaret of Parma (d. 1586), governor of the Netherlands, 184–85

María of Habsburg, Castilian princess and regent, 180

Mariana, Juan de (1535/36–1624), Jesuit writer, 15, 19, 165, 170, 211, 213–26, 231–36, 291n13, 293n25, 296n60; *History of Spanish Deeds,* 217, 224–25, 229, 293n30; *The King and the Education of the King,* 4, 217–25, 232, 238–39, 291n11, 291n12, 291n14, 291n16, 292n21, 292n23, 293n24, 293n27; *Tractatus VII,* 224, 293n28

Márquez, Juan, political writer, 172

Marsilius of Padua, fourteenth-century political philosopher, 103, 270n84

Martin I, Aragonese king (reigned 1395–1410), 248n25

Martínez, Pedro, *vecino* of Arroba, 59–60
Martínez de Mora, Alonso, *jurado* of
Toledo, 137–38, 141–42
Martínez Muñoz de Jarandilla, Br. Francisco, *letrado* of Toledo, 210
Mary I (Tudor), English queen (reigned
1553–58), 180
Maximilian of Habsburg, Austrian
prince and Castilian regent, 180
Maza, Luis, chief constable of the
Chancillería of Granada, 275n59
Medina, friar Alonso de, Dominican
comunero ideologue, 108
Medina del Campo, 267n51; and its
conquest in 1441, 27, 38, 155; and
fire of 1520, 81, 102, 104; ordinances
of (1489), 125, 177
Medina Sidonia, duchy of, 83
Medina Sidonia, duke of, 250n26
Medinaceli, duke of, 197
Medrano, Juan de, barrister of the
House of Béjar, 86–87, 127–28, 133
Mena, Juan de, poet, 38
Menchaca, Ldo. Francisco de, royal
councillor, 197–200, 287n73
mendicant orders, 20. *See also* Dominic,
order of St.; Francis, order of St.
Mendoza, Diego de, second count of
Mélito, duke of Francavila, 193–94
Mendoza, Francisco de, governor of
the archbishopric of Toledo, 92,
95–98
Mendoza, Juana de, duchess of Béjar,
207
Mendoza y de la Cerda, Ana de
(1540–1592), princess of Eboli, wife
of Ruy Gómez de Silva, 193–94
menudos, 31
Mérida, 97
Mesta, 84, 90, 122, 265n27, 290n6; and
the lawsuit with Toledo over the
Montes de Toledo, 207, 289n92; and
the Villarta bridge, 61, 146
Mesta, Council of the, 124
microhistory, concept of, 9–10, 144,
246n11, 247n16, 247n17, 275n1
Milagro, 251n33

military orders, 19–20, 26, 30. *See also*
Alcántara, order of; Calatrava, order
of; John, order of St.; Santiago, order
of
Molina, Luis (1535–1600), Jesuit theologian, 172
monarchy, nature of, 4–7, 31–32, 34–35,
37, 45–46, 52, 79, 115, 143–44,
208–9, 211, 235–37, 239–40, 246n10,
253n52, 285n44, 289n95, 290n5,
296n61, 296n62, 297n66. *See also*
absolute royal authority, concept of;
clientage; factional conflict; rebellion; state, concept of; tyranny, concept of
monastic reform, 198
Mondéjar, marquis of, 205
Montalbán, 122
Montalvo, Ldo. Gómez de, Granada
oidor and royal councillor, 130, 198
Montemor, marquis of, 65
Montigny, Florent de Montmorency
(1527–70), baron of, 201
montes, 30
Montes de Toledo, 9, 21, 58, 61, 63, 74,
145, 148–51, 203; and the Mesta,
207, 289n92
Moriscos, 12, 184, 190, 197, 205, 207–8,
287n73
Morillas, Ldo. Cristóbal, royal councillor, 198–99
municipality, 29–31, 252n41, 253n48,
264n5; types of, 252n40
Murcia, 12–13, 32, 56, 100; and the
Comunidades, 72, 82, 100
Muslims, 20, 202

Naples, kingdom of, 12, 113, 133–34,
193
natural law, 10, 280n62, 288n80, 290n5
Navahermosa, 148
Navalmoral, 148
Navalpino, 44
Navalucillos, 148
Navarra, 19, 116, 118, 192
Navarra, *mariscal* Pedro de, *corregidor* of
Toledo, 137

Netherlands, 11, 116, 184–85, 204
networks, 246n8
New Spain, 129
Niebla, count of, 155
Niño, Fernando (or Hernando), *regidor*
of Toledo, 203
Niño, Hernando, archbishop of
Granada, president of the
Chancillería of Granada, 135
Niño, Juan, *regidor* of Toledo, 135
Niño de Guevara, Fernando, Toledan in
Salamanca, 205
Niño de Guevara, Hernando, president
of the Council of Castile, 198–99
Nueva Recopilación, 168, 178–79, 199, 221
Núñez, Ldo. Bela, *juez de términos,*
54–64, 66, 73–74, 146–47. *See also*
Toledo, and the hearings of 1495 and
1496
Núñez de Avendaño, Dr. Pedro, jurist,
164–70, 280n58, 280n59, 280n66,
280n67, 280n68

Ockham (Occam), William of (d. 1349),
philosopher, 103, 270n84
oidor (justice), 22
Olivares. *See* Guzmán, Gaspar de
Oliverio, Juan Bautista, *jurado* of Toledo,
203
Olmedo, battle of (1445), 26, 28, 33, 37,
40, 60, 155–56, 159, 166
Olmedo, law of (1445), 253n55, 254n64,
281n74
Ordenamiento de Alcalá, 251n37, 253n53
Orellana, Diego de, 24
Oropesa, count of, 191
Ortega, Pedro de, *jurado* of Toledo, 73
Ortiz, Ldo., lawyer of Toledo, 157–59,
278n36
Ortiz, Br. Alonso, *jurado* of Toledo,
75–76, 89, 262n55
Ortiz, Br. Francisco, *jurado* of Toledo,
50–51, 54, 64, 146
Ortiz, Francisco, *jurado* of Toledo,
262n55
Osorio, Diego, *corregidor* of Córdoba,
99, 266n47

Osuna Collection, 247n18, 276n2
Otálora, Ldo. Lope de, royal councillor,
177–78, 198, 282n6
Ottoman Empire. *See* Turks

Pacheco, friar Francisco, Franciscan,
queen's confessor, 198
Pacheco, Juan (1419–76), favorite of
Henry IV, first marquis of Villena,
26, 28, 42, 254n58, 261n49
Pacheco, Luis, 261n51
Padilla, Juan de (1490–1521), *comunero*
leader, 82, 100, 119
Padua, Marsilius of. *See* Marsilius of
Padua
Palacios Rubios, Dr. Juan López de.
See López de Palacios Rubios,
Dr. Juan
Palencia, 267n51
Palomares, Ldo., informant of Philip II,
181
Papacy, 200
Pardo de Tavera, Juan. *See* Tavera, Juan
Pardo de
Parlement of Paris, 273n28
patronage. *See* clientage
Paz, Sancho de, royal treasury official,
196
Pedro de Trastámara, *infante,* 27, 155
Pedrosa, Ldo. Pedro de, Granada *oidor*
and royal councillor, 198, 274n52
Peloche, 56, 149
Pennafort, Raymond de, thirteenth-
century jurist, 280n66
Peña, Melchor de la, barrister of the
House of Béjar, 138, 177, 205
Peñaranda, Dr., Granada *oidor,* 136,
274n52
Peñas, Dr., Granada *oidor,* 132
Pérez, Antón, barrister of Toledo, 86–87
Pérez, Antonio (1540–1611), royal
secretary, 199–200, 203, 287n73
Pérez, Gonzalo, royal secretary, 287n73
Pérez Caro, Luis, *receptor,* 132, 137–38,
149–50, 156
Pérez de Cabitos, Esteban, *juez de
términos,* 23

Pérez de Guzmán, Fernán, fifteenth-century chronicler, 277n28
Pérez de Guzmán, Hernán, *regidor* of Toledo, 86–87, 89
Pérez de Guzmán el Bueno, Alonso, duke of Medina Sidonia, 194–95
Pérez de Montalván, Juan, biographer of Lope de Vega, 295n47
Pérez de Ubeda, Gregorio (or Gonzalo), *jurado* of Toledo, 189
Peromoro, 41
Peru, 128
Peter I, Castilian king (reigned, 1350–69), 45, 156, 248n25
Philip I, the Handsome, Castilian king (reigned 1504–6), 67–68, 70, 102
Philip II (reigned 1556–98), 2, 4, 8, 11, 14–15, 18–19, 134, 175–77, 187, 190–91, 196–97, 208–11, 214–15, 224, 237, 290n1, 293n27; and the aristocracy, 191, 285n43, 286n54, 286n58; and Juana as princess-regent, 282n6; and his leadership style, 283n25, 288n75, 289n95; and the Netherlands, 284n29; and possible intervention in the Belalcázar decision, 201–7, 213, 221, 288n81; and reform program, 182–87, 282n8; as regent, 177–82, 201, 284n27, 284n29
Philip III, Castilian king (reigned 1598–1621), 191, 218, 290n3, 295n47
Philip IV, Castilian king (reigned 1621–65), 12, 117, 191, 209, 224–25, 231, 289n92, 295n47
Piaget, Jean, 261n48
Piedrahita, Br. Diego de, *juez de términos*, 161; and his survey, 23–24, 73–74, 76, 86, 145, 147; and testimony about him, 57, 61
Pimentel, Ana, countess of Salinas, 195
Pisa, Council of (1409), 103
Pius II, pope, 103
Plasencia, 69
Plasencia, count of, 26
Plasencia, duchy of, 202
plenitudo potestatis, 163, 167. *See also Corpus Iuris Civilis*

poderío real absoluto (absolute royal authority), 20, 31, 164, 168–69; translation of, 3, 245n5, 280n67. *See also* absolute royal authority
Polanco, Ldo., royal councillor, 264n9
Ponce de León, Rodrigo, marquis of Zahara, 196
Porras, Juan de, 137–38
Portocarrero family, 187
Portugal, 11–12, 19, 27, 113, 208, 210, 290n5
Portugal, Alvaro de (d. 1503), president of the Council of Castile, 54, 61, 64–66, 74, 85
Portugal, Diogo de (d. 1484), duke of Viseu, 65
Portugal, Fernando de (d. 1483), duke of Bragança, 65
Portugal, Isabel de, Castilian queen, 28
Portugal, Jorge de, 66
Postglossators, 162–64, 166, 280n61
prestige of the Chancillería of Granada, protecting, 131–33
Priego, marquis of, 67–68
printing, 47, 66, 240–42, 277n29, 284n32
property rights, 278n43, 279n53, 288n80
propio motu (own initiative), Castilian, 20, 31, 164, 168.
proprio motu, Latin, 163.
Protestant Christianity, 12, 184–85, 193
Provincia de los Angeles, 86
Puebla, Ldo., attorney of Toledo, 141
Puebla, friar Juan de la (d. 1495), 64, 86, 258n13, 259n34. *See also* Sotomayor, Gutierre I de
Puebla de Alcocer, castle of, 22, 141, 249n17
Puebla de Alcocer, town of, 28, 31, 56–63, 85–86, 139, 256n76; and conquest by Gutierre de Sotomayor, 20–22, 58–61, 145, 147, 249n12; as a party to the lawsuit, 130, 157, 202; and Toledo's jurisdiction, 20–22, 33, 35, 60, 145–46, 148–51, 157, 159–60
Puebla de Alcocer, viscount of, 136

Puebla de Alcocer, viscounty of, 9, 18–19, 29, 41–44, 46, 50, 63, 73–77, 117, 122, 149, 164–65, 169–70, 173, 215; and the decision by the Council of Castile, 175, 179, 187–89, 202–4, 207–9; origins, 74, 145, 151, 259n29. *See also* Bernaldín, viscount of Cabrera
Puebla de Montalbán, 137
Puente del Arzobispo, 93
Puertocarrero, Luis de, count of Palma, *corregidor* of Toledo, 86, 89, 261n52
Puertocarrero (Portocarrero), Pedro de, lord of Moguer and Villanueva de Fresno, 67–68

Quintana, Ldo., royal councillor, 202–3
Quirós, Josepe de, barrister of Puebla de Alcocer, 157
Quito, 296n62

Rámaga, 25
Ramírez, Pedro, companion of Br. Martín de Azebedo, 139
Ramírez de Alarcón, Ldo. Andrés, Granada *oidor,* 274n52, 288n77
Ramírez de Lucena, *comendador* Diego, *regidor* of Toledo, 55
Ramírez de Vargas, Juan, *jurado* of Toledo, 86–87
Raudona, Gonzalo de, *comendador* of Lares of the order of Alcántara, 60
rebellion, 13–14, 39–41, 111–13, 156–61, 210, 270n88, 270n93. *See also* Comunidades rebellion; monarchy, nature of; Toledo, city of, and the rebellion of 1441; Toledo, city of, and the rebellion of 1449
receptor (receiver of evidence), 126–27, 129–30
regency, 25, 69, 176, 179–82, 281n3. *See also* Jiménez de Cisneros, friar Francisco; Juana de Austria, Castilian princess and regent; María of Habsburg, Castilian princess and regent; Maximilian of Habsburg, Austrian prince and Castilian regent; Tavera, Juan Pardo de

regidor (councilman), 22, 31, 69
Reichshofrat, 134
Reichskammergericht, 134
relator (court reporter), 125, 136
religious orders, reform of, 287n73
Renaissance Humanism, 217–18, 226
residencias, 282n8
Retuerta, La (modern name: Retuerta de Bullaque), 61
revolution, 111–13, 267n52, 270n88, 270n93. *See also* rebellion
Ribera, *adelantado* Perafán de, *regidor* of Toledo, 155, 158
Ribera, Dr., Granada *oidor,* 274n52
Ribera, Dr., royal councillor, 178
Ríos Fríos, 73–74
Rivera, Perafán de, *regidor* of Toledo, 42
Rodrigo, archbishop of Toledo (13th century), 148–51
Rodríguez, García, *vecino* of Brozas, 155, 160
Rodríguez, Gonzalo, son-in-law of *relator* Rodríguez de Baeza, 136
Rodríguez de Baeza, Ldo. Juan, *relator,* 136–37
Rol, friar Martín, *comendador,* 86
Rojas, Alonso de, *regidor* of Toledo, 189
Rojas, Diego de, *jurado* of Toledo, 120
Rojas, Francisco de, *regidor* of Toledo, 187
Royal Council, 35, 49, 177; and the Comunidades, 102, 104–5, 109; and Henry IV, 42–44; and John II, 22, 28, 33, 49. *See also* Council of Castile
Ruiz, R., Granada *oidor,* 130
Ruiz de Agreda, Martín, royal councillor, 199

Saavedra Fajardo, Diego (1584–1648), political writer, 232
St. Bartholomew's Day Massacre, 165, 217
Salamanca, 31, 89, 104, 108, 123
Salamanca, University of, 108, 124, 205, 226, 290n5; and Juan de Segovia, 110, 269n84

Salas, Ldo. Hernando de (d. 1571),
  Granada *oidor* and royal councillor,
  130, 136, 274n52, 287n68, 288n77
Salisbury, John of. *See* John of Salisbury
Sánchez, Pedro, *alcalde* of Herrera, 61
Sánchez Calderón, Dr. Fernando, royal
  councillor, 50
Sánchez de Cerro, Martín, *vecino* of
  Fontanarejo, 44
Sánchez de la Torre, Pedro, Toledo's
  barrister at Court, 205–6
Sancho IV, Castilian king (reigned
  1284–96), 156
Santa Cruz, Alonso de, sixteenth-
  century chronicler, 69, 261n44
Santa Hermandad (Holy Brotherhood),
  48, 53, 101
Santa Junta, 81–82, 92, 98–102, 104–8,
  117–18; and conciliar thought, 103–11
Santamaría, Ldo., *jurado* of Toledo, 205
Santa María, monastery of, 86
Santa María, Alfonso de, bishop of Bur-
  gos, 110
Santa Marta, count of, 251n34
Santestevan, Luis de, *receptor,* 136
Santiago, Ldo. de, royal councillor,
  264n9
Santiago, order of, 19–20, 25–26, 28, 66,
  152
Santo Domingo, 124, 127
Sarmiento, Ldo. Juan (d. 1564),
  Granada *oidor* and president of the
  Council of the Indies, 136, 199,
  274n52
Sarmiento, Pedro, *alcalde mayor* of
  Toledo, 28, 40–42, 156, 159
Sarmiento y de la Cerda, count of Sali-
  nas, 195
Savoy, duke of, 116
Scholasticism, 218
Second Scholasticism, 216, 226, 290n5
second supplication, 177–82, 198, 206,
  210, 282n5, 282n8, 282n9
Segovia, 28, 90, 110, 262n55, 264n19,
  265n20, 267n53
Segovia, Juan de, fifteenth-century the-
  ologian, 110, 269n84

Segovia, Law of (1390), 177, 206. *See also*
  second supplication
seignioral jurisdiction (lordship), 29–31,
  246n10, 251n37. *See also* Puebla de
  Alcocer, viscounty of
Sessa, duke of, 136, 140, 192, 196, 205
Seville, 31, 81, 155, 266n46
Shennan, J. H., 272n21
Sicily, kingdom of, 12, 113, 201
Sierra de Lares, 150
Siete Partidas, 39, 152, 161–62, 167–69;
  role in Castilian legal thought, 46–47,
  169, 203, 253n53, 254n55, 288n80,
  295n53
Silva, Diego de, *regidor* of Toledo, 188
Silva, Fernando de, fourth count of
  Cifuentes, 71, 261n51
Silva, Francisco de, *regidor* of Toledo,
  206
Silva, Juan de (d. 1464), first count of
  Cifuentes (in 1455), 250n26, 255n64,
  261n49
Silva, Juan de, third count of Cifuentes
  and president of the Council of
  Castile (d. 1512), 68–71, 261n49
Silva, Juan de, fifth count of Cifuentes,
  194
Silva y Ribera, Juan de, marquis of
  Montemayor and *regidor* of Toledo,
  275n64
Silva y Mendoza, Ana de, daughter of
  Ruy Gómez de Silva, duchess of
  Medina Sidonia, 194
Simancas, Dr. Diego de, jurist, bishop of
  Zamora, 192–93
Siruela, 24, 57–60, 122
Siruela River, 151
Skinner, Quentin, 218, 246n11. *See also*
  speech acts
social environment, concept of, 10–11,
  247n20, 297n63. *See also letrados*
Society of Jesus, 180, 218, 224, 238,
  291n14. *See also* Mariana, Juan de
Soranzo, Giovanni, Venetian ambassa-
  dor, 200
Soria, 23, 267n51
Sosa, Alonso de, *jurado* of Toledo, 119

Sosa, Ldo. Francisco de (d. 1508), royal
councillor, 68
Soto, friar Domingo de (1494–1560),
theologian, 172
Soto, Fernando de, nephew of Juan de
Sotomayor and lord of Alconchel, 27
Sotomayor, Alonso de (d. 1464), son of
Gutierre de Sotomayor, 20, 24, 28,
42–43, 258n14, 259n34; and the title
of count of Belalcázar, 255n75
Sotomayor, Alonso II de, count of Belalcázar (b. ca. 1481), 52, 55, 67–68,
85–86, 259n35; and his protectors,
258n13. *See also* Cruz, friar Alonso
de la
Sotomayor, Francisco de, count of Belalcázar, 86–88. *See also* Zúñiga,
Guzmán y Sotomayor, Francisco I de
Sotomayor, Gutierre de (ca. 1400–53),
19–24, 26–27, 31, 35, 42–43, 54, 56,
63, 75–76, 84–85, 155–57, 159–60,
167–70, 190, 203–4, 215, 223,
251n34, 278n41; and Alvaro de
Luna, 27–29; and the Battle of
Olmedo, 28, 155, 159; and the conquest of Puebla de Alcocer, 21, 145;
in Medina del Campo, 27, 38, 155;
testimony about, 58–61, 147; and the
viscounty of Puebla de Alcocer,
259n29. *See also* Luna, Alvaro de;
Olmedo, battle of
Sotomayor, Gutierre I de, count of
Belalcázar, 43, 86, 258n13, 259n34.
See also Puebla, friar Juan de la
Sotomayor, Gutierre II de (d. 1484),
count of Belalcázar, 52, 55, 57, 63–64
Sotomayor, House of, 18, 24, 29, 43–44,
52, 56, 63, 74, 85, 122, 164, 256n76.
See also Béjar, House of; Belalcázar,
count of; Puebla de Alcocer, viscount
of
Sotomayor, Juan de, grandmaster of the
order of Alcántara, 26–27, 29
Sotomayor, Leonor de, sister of Gutierre
I de Sotomayor, count of Belalcázar,
259n35
speech acts, 246n11, 270n86

state, concept of, 1–4, 7, 142, 175,
213–14, 245n4, 245n6, 246n8, 257n4,
285n44, 295n56
State, Council of, 120, 184, 204
stereotypes and Spanish historiography,
296n57
Suárez, Francisco, jurist and theologian,
165, 172, 295n50
Suárez, Vasco, *vecino* of Toledo, 70–71
Suárez de Carvajal, Juan, *corregidor* of
Talavera, 265n30
Suárez de Figueroa, Cristóbal, writer, 172
Suárez de Figueroa, Gómez, count of
Feria, first duke of Feria, 196, 204
Suárez de Figueroa, Lorenzo, count of
Feria, 196
Suárez de Toledo, Alonso, *regidor* of
Toledo, 89
Suárez family, Toledo, 70
Suárez Valtodano, Alonso, president of
the Council of Castile, 68
Subrahmanyam, Sanjay, 246n11
sumiller de corps (gentleman of the bed-
chamber), 194

Tacitus, Publius Cornelius (55–118 C.E.),
Roman author, 218–20, 292n16,
292n18
Tajo River
Talarrubias, 56
Talavera, 24, 60, 73, 122, 137, 145,
266n37; and the Comunidades rebel-
lion, 79–80, 91–99, 265n32, 277n25
Tavera, Juan Pardo de (1472–1545),
archbishop of Granada and president
of the Council of Castile, 116, 179,
203, 270n1, 274n49, 281n4, 287n67,
292n18
Tello, Gregorio, *jurado* of Toledo, 130
Tello Girón, Ldo. Gómez, Granada
oidor, 274n52
términos, 30–31
Thompson, E. P., 248n24
Tierra del Campos, 99
Tiraquellus, Andreas, jurist, 166
Toledo, archbishop of, 24, 27, 38, 60;
and Talavera, 91–98

Toledo, Baltasar de, *jurado* of Toledo, 187

Toledo, city of, 8–9, 12–15, 18, 20–24, 31, 33–34, 183, 215, 267n51, 289n91; and its legal briefs, 276n8, 284n32; and the call for an assembly in 1519, 80, 87, 101, 107, 266n46; and the Comunidades rebellion, 82, 110, 117, 262n55, 266n46, 272n15; and the Cortes of 1520, 89–91; and damage to its archive, 55, 263n60, 272n23; and the evidence presented, 145–47, 154–55; and factions, 69–72, 261n44; and the hearings of 1495 and 1496, 54–63, 66, 147; and the early sixteenth-century hearings, 72–77, 147; and the hearings of 1516–20, 83–88; and Henry IV, 42–44; and the Mesta, 207, 289n92; and the ordinance of 1509, 75, 122, 272n23; and the pardon of 1451, 41, 160, 255n70; and the petition of 1480, 50–51; and the petition of 1490, 51–52, 64; and the petition of 1493, 54, 64; and prince Alfonso, 256n76; and the protest of the final verdict, 205–7, 210, 289n86; and the rebellion of 1441, 21, 32–33, 156–57, 161, 204–5; and the rebellion of 1449, 28, 40–41, 156, 205; and second supplication, 177–78; and Talavera, 91–98; and the trial before the Chancillería de Granada, 119–42, 176–77; and the trial before the Council of Castile, 182–83, 187–89, 202–4, 284n29. *See also* El Hornillo; Mariana, Juan de

Toledo, Diego de, son of the duke of Alba, 88

Toledo, Juan de, barrister of Toledo, 55

Toledo, Law of (1480), 48, 54–55, 57, 61, 164

Toledo y de Figueroa, María de (d. 1565), duchess of Arcos, 196

Tordesillas, 80–82, 100–101, 104

Toro, Laws of (1505), 67, 73

Torquemada, friar Juan de, fifteenth-century theologian, 109–10

Torres, Dr. Luis de, 274n50

Trastámara dynasty, 13, 18, 24, 45, 66–72, 112, 171

Trent, Council of (1545–63), 124, 189–90

Tribonian, sixth-century C.E. Roman jurist, 278n48

trouble case method, 8, 247n13

Trujillo, 27, 139

Tuck, Richard, 218–19

Turks, 12, 140, 184, 201, 205, 210

Turrecremata, Johannes de. *See* Torquemada, friar Juan de

tyrannicide, 223–24, 293n25, 294n45

tyranny, concept of, 18, 36–37, 39, 159, 163–64, 171–72, 215, 230, 294n38; in Alfonso de Madrigal, 248n1; and Alvaro de Luna, 41, 159, 255n71; and the Comunidades rebellion, 268n61; in Juan de Mariana, 223–25; in the *Siete Partidas,* 39, 253n53, 253n55. *See also* John of Salisbury

Ulpian (d. 223 C.E.), Roman jurist, 279n48

United Provinces of the Netherlands, 121, 213

Urena, count of, 83

Valdecaballeros, 59

Valdés, Fernando de (d. 1568), archbishop of Seville, inquisitor-general, 180, 193, 287n67, 287n68, 287n73

Valero y Covarrubias, María, wife of Sebastián de Horozco, 189

Valladolid, 24, 31, 89, 101, 104, 268n61

Valladolid, law of (1442), 23, 35–36, 50, 164, 171, 253n51; in revocation of Henry IV, 43, 146. *See also* Henry IV, and revocations of grants of John II

Vargas, Ldo. Francisco de (d. 1524), royal councillor, 68

Vázquez, Francisco, *regidor* of Talavera, 95

Vázquez Menchaca, Francisco de, jurist, 172

Vázquez de Rojas, Martín, *regidor* of
  Toledo, 54, 62, 75–76
vecinos (citizens), 31
Vega, Garcilaso de la (d. 1512), royal
  councillor, 68, 261n52
Vega, Garcilaso de la, poet, 68, 261n52
Vega Carpio, Lope Félix de
  (1562–1635), dramatist, 19, 214,
  225–31, 294n38, 294n39, 294n46,
  294n47; *El castigo sin venganza,*
  230–31, 294n46; *El Duque de Viseo,*
  229; *Fuenteovejuna,* 228; *El mejor
  alcalde, el rey,* 228–29; *Peribáñez y el
  Comendador de Ocaña,* 227–28
veinticuatro, 31
Velasco, Hernando de, lord of Siruela,
  60
Velasco, María de (d. 1506), widow of
  the *almirante,* 52, 55, 57–58, 61, 64,
  259n35
Velasco, Dr. Martín de, royal councillor,
  177–78, 197–98, 200–201, 282n6,
  287n73
Villamanrique, marquis of (d. 1590),
  viceroy of New Spain, 208
Villa Real, Lope de, *jurado* of Toledo,
  51–52
Villareal, Alonso Alvarez de. *See*
  Alvarez de Villareal, Alonso
Villalar, battle of (1521), 82, 92, 119, 238
Villarta, 44, 54, 56, 59, 73, 146, 151
Villarta bridge over the Guadiana River,
  54, 56, 58, 62, 146, 259n32
Villena, marquis of, 42, 67. *See also* López
  Pacheco, Diego; Pacheco, Juan
Viseu, duke of, 229. *See also* Portugal,
  Diogo de
visitas (investigations), 139; and *audien-
  cias,* 271n10, 274n55, 275n59. *See also*
  corruption in court proceedings
Vitoria, Francisco de (d. 1546), Domini-
  can theologian, 172
Vooght, Paul de, 270n84

Weber, Max, 225, 245n6
Whitehead, Alfred North, 246n11
world history, concept of, 4, 142

Ximenes. *See* Jiménez de Cisneros,
  Francisco

Yáñez, Alonso, accountant and lawyer
  of Talavera, 96
Yucatán, 127

Zamora, 31
Zapata, Ldo. Luis de (d. 1522), royal
  councillor, 68
Zavala, Domingo de, royal secretary,
  178, 199–200, 207, 276n2, 287n69
Zayas, Gabriel de, royal secretary, 198
Zenete, marquis of, 274n49
Zomeño, Ldo., *juez de términos,* 62–63,
  73–74, 147, 262n58
Zorita (Zocorita), Francisco de, grantee
  of king John II, 156
Zújar River, 150
Zumel, Dr., Cortes *procurador* of Burgos,
  83–85
Zúñiga, Alvaro de, chief royal justice,
  26, 28–29, 42
Zúñiga, Alvaro de (d. 1531), second
  duke of Béjar, 87–88, 120
Zúñiga, Antonio de, prior of the order
  of St. John, 88, 119, 272n15
Zúñiga, aristocratic lineage, 43, 69, 75
Zúñiga, Elvira de (d. 1483), countess of
  Belalcázar, 28, 64, 256n75, 258n14,
  259n34, 259n35
Zúñiga, Fadrique de (d. 1491),
  archdeacon of Talavera, 64,
  258n13, 259n35
Zúñiga, Guzmán y Sotomayor, Francisco I de (d. 1544), count of Belalcázar, marquis of Ayamonte, duke of
  Béjar, 87–88, 117, 119–20, 122–23,
  148–49, 188, 284n31, 286n54. *See
  also* Sotomayor, Francisco de, count
  of Belalcázar
Zúñiga, Juan de (d. 1546), Philip II's
  tutor, 179
Zúñiga, Leonor de, duchess of Medina
  Sidonia, 286n54
Zúñiga, Teresa de, marquise of Zahara,
  196

Zúñiga y Guzmán, Teresa de (d. 1565), duchess of Béjar, marquise of Ayamonte, 87–88, 140, 284n31, 286n54

Zúñiga y Sotomayor, Alonso, count of Belalcázar, marquis of Gibraleón, 148, 165, 176–80, 195, 202–3, 284n31. *See also* Gibraleón, marquis of

Zúñiga y Sotomayor, Alonso Diego (d. 1619), duke of Béjar, 207

Zúñiga y Sotomayor, Francisco II de (d. 1591), marquis of Ayamonte (later count of Belalcázar and duke of Béjar), 165, 202, 205–8, 275n60, 284n31, 286n58; and influence at Court, 189–96, 286n54; and trial before the Council of Castile, 187–89, 284n32. *See also* Ayamonte, marquis of

Zúñiga y Sotomayor, Francisco III de (d. 1601), count of Belalcázar, duke of Béjar, 194, 196, 202, 286n58